Public Finance and Public Choice

Second Edition

John Cullis and Philip Jones

OXFORD UNIVERSITY PRESS

Oxford University Press, Great Clarendon Street, Oxford OX2 6DP
Oxford New York
Athens Auckland Bangkok Bogota Buenos Aires Calcutta
Cape Town Chennai Dar es Salaam Delhi Florence Hong Kong Istanbul
Karachi Kuala Lumpur Madrid Melbourne Mexico City Mumbai
Nairobi Paris São Paolo Singapore Taipei Tokyo Toronto Warsaw
and associated companies in
Berlin Ibadan

Oxford is a registered trade mark of Oxford University Press

Published in the United States by
Oxford University Press Inc., New York

© John Cullis and Philip Jones, 1998

First published 1998

British Library Cataloguing in Publication Data
Data available

Library of Congress Cataloging in Publication Data
Public finance and public choice/John Cullis and Philip Jones.-2nd ed.
Includes bibliographical references and index.
1. Finance, Public. 2. Social choice. I. Jones, Philip R., 1948-   . II. Title.
HJ141.C84 1997   336-dc21   97-14439
ISBN 0-19-877580-6
ISBN 0-19-877579-2 (pbk.)

10 9 8 7 6 5 4 3 2

Printed in Great Britain
Bookcraft (Bath) Ltd,
Midsomer Norton, Somerset

Preface and acknowledgements to the Second Edition

Reviewers, users (and rejecters) of the first edition of this book all share an interest in what is new about the second edition in so far as they can update their opinions about a text which David Collard calls 'death by diagrams'. The theme of the revisions have been to lend greater emphasis to the microeconomic aspects and also to introduce more material on the European Community. Substantive sections have been added on:

- the private provision of public goods
- privatization and the 'internal' market
- the European Community budget
- tax harmonization
- tax evasion
- taxation and the theory of the firm
- QALYs (Quality Adjusted Life Years)
- public debt
- public sector size and economic growth
- social security spending

We have rewritten some sections, e.g. on the welfare costs of taxation and elsewhere we have amended the text in the interests of clarity. The introductory macroeconomic sections of Chapter 10 and the whole of Chapters 15 and 18 of the first edition have been omitted to create space. Those interested in the contents of Chapter 18 are directed to our paper in *Public Choice* (Jones and Cullis 1993). Also it is now the case that, when dealing with 'macroeconomic issues', we have re-ordered some material; so now readers will first consider the fiscal instruments usually controlled by central government (Chapter 10 of this edition) before proceeding to review a public choice analysis of macroeconomic policy.

A number of users of the text have taken the time to help us with detecting errors, omissions and other limitations of the first edition. We are grateful for this help. Simon Vicary of Hull University kindly loaned us his annotated copy of our text which has been very valuable in the revision process. Professor Neville Norman of the University of Melbourne kindly provided positive comments on the whole of the text and many, if not all, of his points are incorporated in this new edition. David Collard, Chris Heady and Hermoine Parker have been especially helpful on specific issues, for which we are grateful. Tracy Mawson at OUP provided encouragement and enthusiasm for this second edition and again we are very grateful. Students at the University of Limberg proved conscientious critics (too conscientious!) and provided us with a list of helpful suggestions. In this connection we would particularly like to thank Thomas Dohmer, Svante-Carlos Glöckner, Matthij Rozema and Roger Verstrheten. (Students at Bath University tell us they 'loved the book'!) Gill Chapman at Bath University diligently word-processed countless 'inserts' which was a great help in preparing this edition. According to two anonymous referees the first edition was either 'an example of academic writing at its worst' or 'written in a clear and concise manner which students find easy to work with'—*caveat emptor*!

The first volume of the journal *International Tax and Public Finance* has a symposium on the future of public economics (public finance or fiscal economics depending on the author) built around a survey by Pestieau (1994) of the opinions of public finance economists essentially on the issue of 'whither public choice after the golden decade of the 1970s'. The short contributions were interesting in a number of ways. Some of the responses echoed themes (luckily?) already part of the first edition others, such as a greater emphasis on international issues, are reflected in this edition. All of the respondents were noted public sector economists (Musgrave, Brennan, Slemrod and Besley) and either explicitly or implicitly offered very different judgements and perspectives which confirmed, to us at least, that the premise of the first edition, that there is sharp contrast of serious opinion and analysis, remains. Whilst some authors seemed to hanker after a consensus view, this edition continues in the vein of the first edition in suggesting that it is the lack of consensus that is interesting and the conflict of ideas and analysis that cannot be 'amalgamed' by academic mercury that is the continuing *status quo*.

References

Jones, P. R. and Cullis J. G. (1993) 'Public Choice and Public Policy: The Vulnerability of Economic Advice to the Interpretation of Politicians', *Public Choice*, 75, 1, pp. 63–77.
Pestieau, P. (1994) 'The Current State and Future Directions of Public Finance', *International Tax and Public Finance*, 1, 2, pp. 169–74.

Preface and acknowledgements to the First Edition

At the risk of 'signalling' ourselves among the people who can't do, teach or carry out research (see Blaug 1970, p. xv), we have written a textbook. This book is partly the result of accident and partly the result of design. The accident was the amicable collapse of plans to produce an Anglicized version of R. A. Musgrave and P. B. Musgrave, *Public Finance in Theory and Practice*, now in a fifth edition. The design was the feeling that insufficient attempt is generally made in existing texts fully to recognize and incorporate alternative views or perspectives in public finance (see Gravelle 1989). Buchanan (1989), Nobel Laureate for his work on public choice, clearly feels this, writing of 'the insider Harvard–Musgrave vision' and 'the outsider Chicago–Virginia . . . vision' (p. 291) in his review of Musgrave's collected writings. With this in mind, we have attempted to write a book that does capture the picture of 'big names' saying very different things about the same topic or finding different topics more or less important. In short, we have tried to highlight intellectual friction rather than consensus in the field of public finance by, so far as we found possible, introducing in each chapter the traditional 'social optimality' perspective alongside alternatives, the majority of which are drawn from the public choice school. Some of these alternatives are drawn from other social science disciplines.

We have outlined our own position more fully elsewhere (see Cullis and Jones 1987), which, to summarize drastically, finds the framework of the public choice school an attractive one. However, given its almost blanket anti-public-sector criticism in what has become known as the Leviathan debate/hypothesis, we would argue that its critique of government needs to be more firmly set against the failings of the market. In sentiment, this puts us closer to the Musgrave position that 'a Democratic society is more likely to flourish in a mixed economy, one where a public sector is needed to supplement the market' (Musgrave 1989, p. 7). Against this background of inevitable personal bias, we have tried to outline the positions of authors we review and to use (rather than critically assess) their contributions. The objective has been to create a 'cut, thrust and parry' approach as opposed to a 'cut and dried' one. The emphasis is everywhere on the analytical principles involved in the various arguments at the expense of both institutional detail and current statistical material. Those looking for a 'stat. attack' on the public sector will not find it here. However, this is not to imply that empirical results and some relevant statistics are completely ignored, rather, they have not been our primary focus.

If we have been at all successful in meeting our objective, this reflects the help of a number of our colleagues and friends as well as the cited authors. Simon Vicary of Hull University worked his way through the whole text, and, although we cannot claim to have followed all his suggestions, a large number of improvements are due to his very considerable effort and insight. Oliver Morrissey of Nottingham University carefully and usefully commented on chapter 11, while other colleagues, all at Bath University, read and offered criticisms on chapters as follows: David Collard (chapters 7 and 16); Chris Heady (chapter 16); Edward Horesh (chapters 1 and 18); John Hudson (chapter 10); Stephen Jenkins (chapter 9); Alan Lewis (chapter 8); Adrian Winnett (chapters 2 and 3). Chapter 18 draws on our article published in *Public Choice* (1993) and we would like to thank the publishers, Kluwer, for permission to use copyright material. The copy editing was done very skilfully by Sue Hughes. Hilary Strickland did a first rate job on the art work, Lavinia Porter on production and Kathrine Wallis-King on word processing. Despite all this help, errors of style and content surely remain and (anticipating some American sales) the buck for these stops with the authors!

While we like to view this book as an integrated whole (hence our reluctance to formally divide it into parts), there are a number of ways in which it can be used. Chapters 1–6 deal essentially with expenditure analysis which might form the basis of a course on social policy. Chapters 7–13 deal in part with taxation but also with distribution and stabilization, completing an account of Musgrave's (1959, 1989) three branches of the public household. As such, chapters 1–13 can be used as the basis of a traditional public finance course (although each of the chapters presented here contains sections offering alternative, especially public choice, perspectives). What might be termed the third part of the text deals with topics that use the earlier chapters as the essential building blocks. It includes a treatment of the current and recent major themes in public finance and could be used in isolation for a course that gives full weight to the public choice perspective. Students would, however, need to have an understanding of basic public finance/public sector economics if this option is pursued. The contents of the book follow recent trends in public sector courses (see Hewett 1987), with expenditure being afforded as much room as finance and micro-economics being emphasized at the expense of macroeconomics.

As regards the degree of difficulty, the book is designed for those with a good grounding in microeconomic theory, which suggests that students at or beyond second-year UK university-level economics should be able to cope with most, if not all, of the text. We have tried to give enough of the arguments presented to establish for the readers the point at hand in a reasonably 'tight' but often not formally rigorous way. However, as Hewett (1987) points out, technical complexity is but one aspect of difficulty. Given our focus on analysis, it is hoped that we have avoided difficulties arising from trying to be encyclopaedic. For undergraduates, and indeed for some more sophisticated readers, it may be that the 'open' nature of the results of the various discussions is a source of 'angst'. Those looking for 'hard', irrefutable, always-and-everywhere type conclusions about any aspect of the public sector will not find them here. The absence of such conclusions is, in good part, our conclusion, and the reasons for this absence are the book's content.

References

Blaug, M. (1970) *An Introduction to the Economics of Education*. Harmondsworth: Penguin.

Buchanan, J. M. (1989) 'Richard Musgrave: Public Finance and Public Choice', *Public Choice*, 61, 3, pp. 289–91.

Cullis, J. G. and Jones, P. R. (1987) *Microeconomics and the Public Economy: A Defence of Leviathan*. Oxford: Basil Blackwell.

Gravelle, H. (1989) Review of Starrett [1989], *The Manchester School*, 57, 3, pp. 312–13.

Hewett, R. S. (1987) 'Public Finance, Public Economics and Public Choice: A Survey of Undergraduate Textbooks', *Journal of Economic Education*, 18, 4, pp. 425–35.

Musgrave, R. A. (1959) *The Theory of Public Finance*. New York: McGraw-Hill.

Musgrave, R. A. (1989) 'The Three Branches Revisited', *Atlantic Economic Journal*, 17, 1, pp. 1–7.

Musgrave, R. A. and Musgrave, P. B. (1989) *Public Finance in Theory and Practice*. Fifth edition. New York: McGraw-Hill.

Starrett, D. A. (1989) *Foundations of Public Economics*, Cambridge: Cambridge University Press.

Contents

Contents

Detailed Contents

List of Figures

List of Tables

1 Market possibilities and prescriptions

1.1 Introduction

The perfectly competitive industry is the theoretical benchmark against which economic arrangements are judged or evaluated. Indeed, government intervention is conventionally justified only by reference to market outcomes that fail by so much to meet this ideal that there is the prospect of improvement from policy intervention. The 'top of the bill act' in microeconomic theory is generally to demonstrate the optimality of perfect competition. Depending on the sophistication of the course, this is demonstrated in either a partial equilibrium or a general equilibrium context. Both approaches will be briefly revised and geometrically illustrated below, while some of the associated mathematics is reserved for the Appendix. (Students who are already familiar with general equilibrium analysis and Pareto optimality may wish to begin at section 1.7.) However, in order to say that something is 'optimal' it is first necessary to have a set of evaluative criteria against which outcomes do or do not conform. This is the immediate task of the next section and section 1.5 below.

However, even with a set of evaluative criteria that embrace what Ng (1987a) calls the social optimality approach (and can be viewed as the standard or traditional approach), there is still scope for discussion. The main argument muddying the water at the technical level is the problem of second best, which is introduced not only as a topic of interest in itself but also as a way of setting up the first of many contrasts between the social optimality approach and the public choice approach. It is contrasts and conflicts that are the interest in any (sub)discipline. In the chapters that follow the object is to keep that interest by offering different interpretations of mainstream topics.

1.2 The notion of Pareto optimality

The value judgements that mainstream economists implicitly or explicitly accept are the so-called Paretian ones (derived from the work of an Italian social scientist, Vilfredo Pareto). Although often presented in an uncontroversial, matter-of-fact way, each represents a strong position to hold. These value judgements can be listed as follows.

1. Each individual is taken to be the best judge of his or her own welfare or utility.
2. Society is, or adequately can be, captured in a non-organic way as simply the sum of the individuals that make it up—i.e. individuals alone comprise society.
3. If it is possible on a reallocation of resources to increase the utility of one individual without decreasing the utility of any other individual, then the welfare of society is raised.

Value judgement 3 is vital in that it defines what economists understand by the term 'inefficiency'.[1] Indeed, an efficient economy is one in which the existing allocation of inputs and outputs is such that it is impossible to make one person better off without making someone else worse off by a reallocation. Although this seems an innocuous statement, it can have a strong cutting edge when applied to different economic arrangements, as it is hoped will be illustrated amply in the remainder of this text. However, before considering the notion of efficiency in more detail, some further discussion of the Paretian value judgements is warranted.

All the value judgements are strong ones to accept. Mishan (1981) points out that the first one can be adopted either as essentially a belief, *or* as a moral judgement (we ought to act as if this is the case), *or* as a political tenet. (In Western democracies, if political decisions are referred to individuals, should not economic ones be also?) But what of individuals themselves? They may not accept that in all situations they are the best judges of their own welfare. For

---

[1] It must be noted that this term has different meanings in different disciplines and is much abused in casual conversation. Economists when using it have a precise interpretation in mind.

example, (a) Tthey may believe that 'expert' knowledge is available and/or desirable; (b) they may not wish to make a judgement of their own welfare because of lack of experience, ill health, irrationality, etc.; (c) they may not want to take the responsibility for making their own judgements and may prefer to delegate to others. The issues involved are clearly complex and controversial and are further discussed in connection with the merit wants concept in chapter 3. A reason for accepting this value judgement for the purpose of this text is simply that public sector economic analysis, for the most part, is conducted in this strongly anti-paternalistic way. Some notable exceptions are discussed below.

As for conceiving of society in a non-organic way, this is obviously at odds with the practice of other disciplines. So, for example, sociology takes as its unit of analysis not individuals but society itself: society is the organism, not the individual. One way of classifying different disciplines is by their unit of analysis, ranging from physicists' sub-particles and biologists' cells, through subjects that are individually based like economics and psychology, to sociology. What seems natural to someone trained as an economist may appear as a very strange set-up to individuals from another discipline. While some may explain this as a methodological distinction, it is based on the value judgement that there are no superior interests to those of the individual.

With regard to the third value judgement, which is sometimes known as 'the' Pareto criterion, this too is a far from obvious view to accept. It avoids making interpersonal comparisons of welfare. However, by so doing it can sanction the wealthiest person in the world being made better off as long as no one is made worse off. It is also evident that Paretianism is 'end-state'-orientated, in that it is the utility levels *achieved* by the individuals comprising society that alone count, and that Paretian efficiency is an outcome such that no individual can improve his or her own utility level without worsening those of others. It is the conflict between efficiency conceived of in this way and other considerations, especially equity, that are at the very heart of much economic discussion and are central to many of the chapters below.

This short discussion of the Paretian value judgements serves to introduce the notion that in economics, as in any other discipline, we are imposing a restrictive framework on the world around us to give it order and meaning. This order and meaning is one of many, and the adoption of a different set of value judgements would make us view the world very differently.

1.3 Achieving efficiency: partial equilibrium

Assuming that the Paretian value judgements are adopted, what forms of economic organization allow the achievement of a 'top-level' efficient economy and why? One form of arrangement noted below that produces this result is universal perfect competition, and there is a theorem in economics which states that, subject to a number of assumptions,[2] *each and every* competitive equilibrium is a Pareto optimum. In Fig. 1.1 the simplest of microeconomic tools is employed to give a partial equilibrium account of this result. D in part (b) is the market demand curve for good X, and because the good is assumed to be rival (i.e. each consumer has to have his or her own quantity allocation to enjoy the consumption benefits of X) it represents the horizontal sum of individual demand curves. S is the market supply curve, derived as the horizontal sum of the individual firms' marginal cost curves (above average variable cost). The intersection of market supply and demand yields the market-clearing price for X, which each individual producer and consumer must take as given.

The consequences for a 'representative' producer or supplier are summarized in part (a) of the figure, where freedom of entry and exit mean that the profit-maximizing output choice is Oq, conforming to the rule that marginal cost is equated with marginal revenue (when the former is rising). At this price—quantity outcome the revenue from sales, OP_e1q, is just sufficient to cover the total costs of production (average cost times quantity) including normal profit. Price is as low as it can be to maintain these survival conditions for the firm. An implication of this is that each producer must be getting maximum physical outputs per unit of inputs employed and is choosing combinations of inputs that give least cost output. That is, the firms producing X are technically or X-efficient: it is impossible to increase the output of X (thereby making one person better off) except by decreasing output elsewhere.

But what of allocation (the quantity of X produced)? Part (c) of the figure illustrates the position of a representative consumer or demander with individual demand curve d. With the market price P_e she chooses quantity Oq_d. For her to choose less than this quantity, say Oq^1, would leave her in a position where her valuation of the good at the margin q^12 (a measure of her marginal benefit from purchasing

[2] The strong qualifications are introduced below.

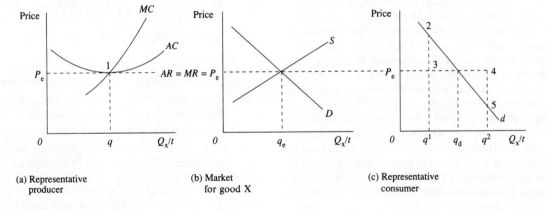

Figure 1.1 Efficiency in partial equilibrium.

that unit) exceeds price; i.e. she could compensate the suppliers for the costs they have incurred and improve her welfare by the vertical distance 23. To buy more than Oq_d, say Oq^2, would reverse the situation and make the individual worse off to the extent of vertical distance 45. The outcome being described at Oq_d is one in which it is impossible for the individual to make herself better off unless somehow she can induce suppliers to make themselves worse off—an unlikely event! In short, Oq_d is the efficient quantity for the representative consumer, and analogously Oq_e, is the efficient quantity for the market for good X. The outcome is allocatively efficient. Once an individual equates her marginal benefit of units of X per unit of time (as represented by d) with the lowest achievable marginal cost of producing the good, both X-efficiency and allocative efficiency obtain. It is impossible to make a change that will not reduce output elsewhere or make a producer or consumer worse off.

1.4 Achieving efficiency: general equilibrium

Above, the competitive market for X was viewed in isolation. A more satisfactory account of the results described can be developed in a general equilibrium context[3] using Edgeworth-Bowley trading boxes. The model illustrated in Fig. 1.2 is a two-sector one

[3] Important because some results that are not obvious in a partial equilibrium context become explicit in a general equilibrium. What matters then is to choose the appropriate level of analysis for the issue or problem at hand.

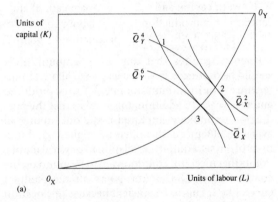

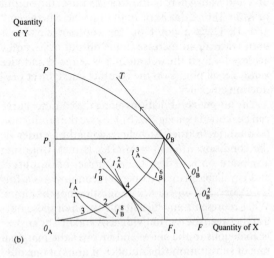

Figure 1.2 Efficiency in general equilibrium.

involving two individuals (unimaginatively labelled A and B); two goods (X and Y); and two inputs, capital (K) and labour (L). The length of the Edgeworth-Bowley trading box defines the quantity of inputs available. The isoquants in the interior of the 'box' relevant to each origin indicate the outputs of X and Y that are attainable from different allocations of the two inputs to the two outputs. The question is where efficient input allocations are to be found. The answer involves the marginal rate of technical substitution (the number of units of one input that can be given up in a production process and replaced by one additional unit of the other input while keeping output at a constant level) and can be summarized as

$$(1.1) \qquad MRTS_{kl}^{X} = MRTS_{kl}^{Y}$$

[Marginal rate of technical substitution between capital and labour in the production of good X] = [Marginal rate of technical substitution between capital and labour in the production of good Y]

Efficiency requires that any given amount of X should be produced in such a way as to allow, simultaneously, the maximum amount of Y to be produced and vice versa. In addition, this implies that the production technology employed is the one among all available 'blueprints' that offers the highest combinations of physical outputs in relation to physical inputs. Points that meet this condition are to be found on the contract curve $O_X O_Y$. Any point off the contract curve, like 1, fails to be efficient because reallocation of K and L anywhere in the area 123 raises the output of X (at 2) or Y (at 3) or both (anywhere between 2 and 3). Once a point on the contract curve has been reached, an increase in the output of X can be achieved only if the output of Y is reduced and vice versa, i.e. all points on the contract curve meet production efficiency.

The output combinations along the contract curve can be plotted (see Fig. 1.2(b)) to give the production possibilities frontier. Anywhere along the frontier PF the condition $MRTS_{kl}^{X} = MRTS_{kl}^{Y}$ is met. Choosing any point on it defines the quantities of outputs X and Y available in this two-person economy. At O_B this is OP_1 of Y and OF_1 of X. The question now becomes, What represents an efficient allocation of these outputs between the two individuals A and B? The answer is analogous to the above and involves the marginal rate of substitution (the number of units of one output that can be sacrificed in order to obtain one additional unit of another output while keeping utility at a

constant level, i.e. the slope of the indifference curve); it can be stated as

$$(1.2) \qquad MRS_{xy}^{A} = MRS_{xy}^{B}$$

[Marginal rate of substitution between good X and good Y for individual A] = [Marginal rate of substitution between good X and Y for individual B]

The marginal rate of substitution in consumption between goods X and Y must be the same for the two consumers A and B. When this condition obtains, the rate at which A and B will be willing to trade the last unit of X for additional units of Y will be identical. If A is willing to give 1 unit of X for 4 units of Y, while B will give 5 units of Y for 1 unit of X, it will be to the advantage of both to exchange, with A increasing her consumption of Y and B consuming more of X. Such trades are attractive until equality of the marginal rates of substitution is established.

Output allocations on the contract curve meet this condition. To establish this, consider the Edgeworth-Bowley trading box in Fig. 1.2(b). Beginning at O_A as the origin, I_A^1 to I_A^3 are consumer A's indifferences curves, showing A's preferences over X and Y. The curves have the usual property that while moving down any one curve A remains equally well off, with more of X being consumed and less of Y. At the same time, A will be better off when moving from a lower to a higher indifference curve, say from I_A^2 to I_A^3. Curves I_B^6 to I_B^8 are a similar pattern of indifference curves for B, but now O_B is the relevant origin. That is, B's quantity of X is measured by moving left along $O_B P_1(F_1 O_A)$ and B's quantity of Y is measured by moving down along $O_B F_1(P_1 O_A)$. Various successively higher indifference curves for B are shown as I_B^6, I_B^7 and so on. It can be shown that the efficient allocations all lie along the 'contract curve' or conflict curve joining O_A and O_B which traces out the tangency points of the two sets of indifference curves. If the initial position is at 1, movement to 2 will improve A's utility without decreasing B's, just as movement to 3 will improve B's utility without decreasing A's. By moving to a point somewhere between 2 and 3, both A and B gain. By following the third Paretian value judgement, a gain to A without a loss to B (and vice versa) is an improvement, and the efficient solutions must lie along $O_A O_B$. Since all these points are points at which the two sets of indifference curves are tangent, and since the slope of the indifference curves equals the MRS_{xy} (marginal rate of substitution in consumption between X and Y), it also follows that at each point on $O_A O_B$ the MRS_{xy} for A and B are equal. This corresponds to the consumption efficiency condition above.

There is, however, one step further to go on narrowing down efficient allocations, i.e. a third condition to be met, which is that

(1.3) $MRS^A_{xy} = MRS^B_{xy} = MRT_{xy}$

[The common marginal rate of substitution between the two goods X and Y for the individuals A and B]	=	[The marginal rate of transformation between X and Y]

The marginal rate of substitution of X for Y in consumption should be the same as the marginal rate of transformation in production. The latter is defined as the number of additional units of X that can be produced if production of Y is reduced by 1 unit, which turns out to be the ratio of the marginal cost of X to that of Y. (See Appendix for a derivation.) Thus, if the marginal rate of substitution in consumption is 3 X and 1 Y, while the marginal rate of transformation in production is 4 X for 1 Y, it will be efficient to increase the output of X and reduce that of Y. Utility stays the same if 3 units of X are substituted for 1 unit of Y, and the change in the pattern of production would leave 1 unit of X to to make 'someone better off and no one worse off'.

Having the marginal rate of substitution equal the marginal rate of transformation indicates that not all points on $O_A O_B$ can be part of the final efficient configuration of the economy. The marginal rate of transformation at O_B is measured by the slope of tangent T to the production possibilities frontier at that point. By considering the marginal rates of substitution along $O_A O_B$ in turn, it is possible to isolate a point such as 4 where the common tangencies of the indifference curves (I^2_A and I^7_B) share the same slope and hence the same value of the marginal rate of transformation. While it is tempting to breathe a sigh of relief and say 'well, that's efficiency dealt with', matters are not that easy.

Point 4 is not the only point that meets all three efficiency conditions. A moment's reflection suggests that the chosen point to construct the Edgeworth-Bowley trading box, O_B (in Fig. 1.2(b)), might well have been O^1_B, O^2_B or any other points along PF yielding their equivalents of point 4 along $O_A O_B$. Point 4 identifies an ordinal utility level for A and for B recorded as point 1 on Fig. 1.3. The equivalent exercise for O^1_B and O^2_B can be visualized as points $1'$ and $1''$ in the figure. Choosing all conceivable starting-points along PF in Fig. 1.2 will generate a continuous frontier labelled UF in Fig. 1.3 and known as the Grand Utility

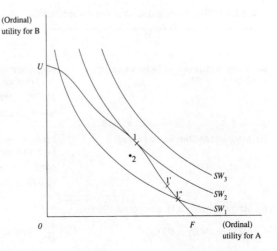

Figure 1.3 Utility possibilities.

Possibility Frontier. In terms of the three efficiency conditions set out above, there is nothing to choose between any point on UF. The frontier shows the maximum (ordinal) utility obtainable by individual B given a level for individual A and vice versa. The 'wavy' nature of UF is a reminder of ordinality, and the negative slope everywhere conforms to Paretian value judgement 3, that efficient situations are ones where it is impossible to make one person (A) better off without making someone else (B) worse off.[4]

It can now be noted that perfect competition guarantees the achievement of so-called 'top-level' efficiency (the first fundamental theorem of welfare economics). This amounts to saying that it automatically achieves a point on UF, the Grand Utility Possibility Frontier. Reconsider the three conditions introduced above, which are relisted as (a)-(c) in column A of Table 1.1. The contents of column B are a summary of the arguments which ensure that every competitive equilibrium is a Pareto optimum. For the factor substitution condition to be met, all producers must respond to a common price ratio, $(-)w/r$, for the two inputs capital (K) and labour (L). The price of labour (the wage) is w and the rental (price) of capital is r. The outcome of competitive factor markets will be market-clearing prices for capital and labour, at which producers can purchase as much or as little of the

---

[4] Positive slopes can arise where utility functions are interdependent, i.e. where, say, the utility level of A is positively related to the utility level of B. In these circumstances, if B is made better off A's utility can also rise simultaneously because of his 'concern' for the fate of B. The efficient section of the utility frontier remains the negatively sloping part (see chapter 9).

Table 1.1 Perfect competition and Pareto optimality

A	B
(a) Marginal condition for factor substitution: $MRTS^X_{kl} = MRTS^Y_{kl}$	For production to be at *minimum* cost, $MRTS_{kl} = (-)w/r$. The latter will be the same for both producers of X and Y, and therefore $MRTS^X_{kl} = MRTS^Y_{kl} = (-)w/r$ (see Fig. 1.4(a))
(b) Marginal condition for exchange: $MRS^A_{xy} = MRS^B_{xy}$	For consumers to *maximize* utility, $MRS_{xy} = (-)p_x/p_y$ and the latter will be the same for both A and B, so that $MRS^A_{xy} = MRS^B_{xy} = (-)p_x/p_y$ (see Fig. 1.4(b))
(c) Marginal condition for product substitution: $MRS^A_{xy} = MRS^B_{xy} = MRT_{xy}$	Profit *maximization* occurs where $P = MC$ (i.e., $P_x = MC_x$ and $P_y = MC_y$), or $\dfrac{MU_x}{MU_y} = MRS_{xy} = \dfrac{P_x}{P_y} = \dfrac{MC_x}{MC_y} = MRT_{xy}$

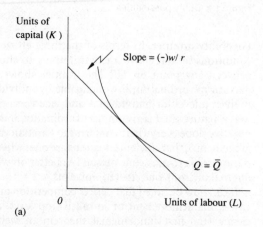 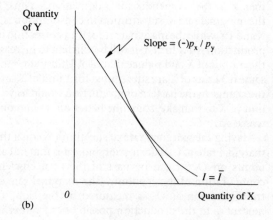

Figure 1.4 Competition and efficiency.

input as they wish (see Fig. 1.4(a)). The marginal condition for exchange is similarly met when all consumers are responding to market-clearing prices for goods Y and X; i.e. they face a common price ratio $(-)p_x/p_y$ where p_x is the price of good X and p_y is the price of good Y. This is illustrated in Fig. 1.4(b)). The final condition (see Appendix on p. 18 for a derivation) for a top-level efficient outcome is met when it is recognized that

$$(1.4) \qquad MRT_{xy} = MC_x/MC_y$$

and that, in perfect competition,

$$(1.5) \qquad P_x = MC_x$$

$$(1.6) \qquad P_y = MC_y$$

yielding the series of efficiency equalities recorded as part (a) under column B in the table. This allows us to state the first of the so-called fundamental theorems of welfare economics, which, abstracting from the various 'market failure' difficulties discussed below, indicates that a perfectly competitive equilibrium is a Pareto optimum. (For a rigorous treatment of the fundamental theorems of welfare economics and other microeconomic analysis in this book see Mas-Colell, Whinston and Green (1995).)

It should be noted, however, that universal perfect competition is a sufficient but not a necessary condition for a 'top-level' efficient economy. Perfect central planning could also secure this outcome.[5] The importance of the market-clearing condition can be illustrated by reference to Fig. 1.5, where $MRS^A_{xy} = MRS^B_{xy}$, but this is not an efficient outcome. The

---

[5] See Buck (1982) for a discussion of this and related issues.

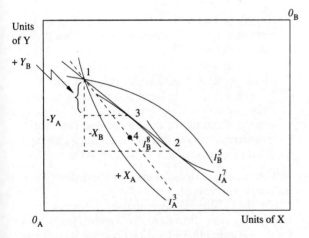

Figure 1.5 The importance of the price ratio.

consumers are effectively responding to the 'wrong' price ratio. At points 2 and 3 on I_A^7 and I_B^8 respectively, the consumers are responding to the price ratio $(-p_x/p_y)$ through their original allocations at point 1, yielding an outcome where A is willing to give up Y_A to secure $+X_A$ while B is prepared to give up X_B for $+Y_B$. It is evident that individual A wishes to give up more Y at price ratio $(-p_x/p_y)$ than B is prepared to demand. A revision of the relative price of X upwards until the $+Y$ and $-Y$ cancel establishes the market-clearing relative price ratio which would be represented as a more steeply sloped price ratio, e.g. the 'dashed' price ratio in Fig. 1.5 and the establishment of a point on the contract curve, say at a point such as 4, where A's and B's indifference curves (not drawn) are assumed to be tangential. This observation leads to the second of the fundamental theorems of welfare economics, that any Pareto-efficient allocation can be achieved as the result of a competitive equilibrium with a suitable redistribution of initial resource endowments.

To illustrate, given point 4 on the contract curve and the price ratio that secures it from the initial endowment position at 1, the second theorem effectively reverses the first theorem above and establishes that any Pareto-optimal allocation, like point 4, can be achieved by establishing a competitive market and an appropriate initial endowment of goods (in this exchange economy example). With the 'competitive' price ratio implied by the dashed line, an initial endowment like 1 would, as we have already noted, serve to result in the final allocation given by 4. Indeed, it is worth noting that any initial endowment on the dashed line would achieve point 4.

However, this attractive result that any technically feasible outcome is achievable is not the signal that all problems are over. While in principle it is possible to use lump-sum transfers to set the initial endowment of goods (or factors, if the picture embraces a production economy) so that perfect competition will establish both an equitable and an efficient outcome, this begs a large number of questions that are the 'stuff' of this book. If lump-sum adjustments are not available, so that fiscal measures will distort the price ratio, resulting in inefficiencies (see chapter 7); the types of market failure central to chapters 2 and 3 have been assumed away; the government does not begin in an 'original' position with a clean slate, nor does it have the kind of knowledge encapsulated in the various illustrations presented so far in this chapter; even if it did possess the knowledge, the public choice theorists would argue that it has no incentive to act like a benevolent despot—to establish the desired 'equity' point—it has its own maximand (see chapter 16); the analysis presupposes that what equity comprises is uncontroversial (see chapter 9) or that it would be easy to find out in a democratic way (see chapter 4). For the moment, it is the equity point that is pursued.

While the value judgements embodied in 'efficiency' are seldom given emphasis, the additional value judgement necessary to identify an 'equitable' outcome is very much the subject of a large and more complex literature. The appropriate form of the equity-deciding social welfare function within economics, unlike the general desirability of efficiency, is a controversial area. Some illustrative social welfare curves are labelled SW_1 to SW_3 in Fig. 1.3. It is easy to illustrate that some inefficient outcomes are preferred to efficient but less equitable ones. Inefficient point 2 in the figure would be on a higher social indifference curve (not drawn) than efficient point $1''$ on SW_1. An introduction to the form and role of the social welfare function is the task of the next section, whereas the actual distribution of income that arises in a market economy is discussed in chapter 9.

1.5 Equity and a social welfare function

The literature on social welfare functions is both large and complex. The basic problem is to compare different economic configurations. Given the individualistic nature of neoclassical economic theory, it is not surprising that economists have shied away from reference to an imposed choice in search of a ranking dependent on individual utilities. This so-called 'welfaristic' (from 'welfarism') view has been criticized because it ignores other information, such as the identity and personal characteristics of any individual (see Sen 1977). Even if it is agreed that it is individual utilities only that are to matter, there is the question of utilities over what? In the broader Arrow-type formulation (see chapter 4) it is individual utility views over a complete description of all individuals' allocations of each good and service and inputs (X); in the narrower Bergson–Samuelson formulation it is the individuals' utility view of his or her own consumption bundle x_i that comprises the basic data. Next, there is the question of how to sum and weight them. For the purposes here, it is convenient to introduce a mathematical form that has the ability under different assumptions to offer many different shapes for 'social indifference curves'. This constant elasticity function is given by

$$(1.7) \qquad W = \frac{\sum_{i=1}^{n} a_i (U_i)^{1-e}}{1 - e}$$

where W = social welfare
a = parameter
U = utility
$1/e$ = constant elasticity of substitution of a social indifference curve

Boadway and Bruce (1984) indicate what happens as different assumptions are made.[6]

1. If $e = 0$ and $a_i = 1$, then $W = \sum_{i=1}^{n} U_i$, which is the so-called Benthamite or utilitarian social welfare function that maximizes the sum of utilities of the individuals and, in the two-person case, gives the social indifference curves like those depicted in Fig. 1.6(a).

2. If $e = 0$ and $a_i \neq 1$, the so-called generalized utilitarian social welfare function arises, which is a weighted sum of the utilities of the individuals and in the two-person case gives a constant slope of other than minus unity to the social indifference curves (see Fig. 1.6(b)). As $a_i \to 0$ for one of the individuals, this amounts to maximizing the utility of the other (see Figs. 1.6(c) and (d)).

3. If $e \to 1$ and $a_i = 1$, a social welfare function associated with Nash is derived as $W = \Pi_{i=1}^{n} U_i$, which maximizes the product of individual utilities and in the two-person case yields social indifference curves that are rectangular hyperbolas, as illu-

strated in Fig. 1.6(e). (For a discussion of the form equation [1.7] takes when $e = 1$, see p. 220 also see chapter 15.)

4. If $e \to \infty$ and $a_i = 1$, the well-known Rawlsian social welfare function is obtained, so that $W = \min(u_1, \ldots, u_n)$ and the choice is to maximize the utility of the least well off individual in society, dictating, in the two-person case, social indifference curves that are right angles along a 45° ray from the origin, illustrated as Fig. 1.6(f).

N.B. As e rises so does concern with equality ($e = 0$ indicates no concern).

For these 'shapes' illustrated by reference to X (complete)-type allocations see Varian (1987), and for the x_i (individual allocation) case see Russell and Wilkinson (1979). Further discussion of these issues is postponed until chapters 4 and 9. In chapter 4 the use of majority voting to aggregate individual preferences over X-type allocations is discussed in the context of Arrow's Impossibility theorem. In chapter 9 the ethical appeal or otherwise of some forms of social welfare function are discussed, especially the Rawlsian form. The point here is that, once a social welfare function has been adopted and imposed on the Grand Utility Possibility Frontier, an equitable and efficient configuration of the economy is established.

1.6 Equity and 'ability to pay'

This wider discussion of equity leads into the narrower question of the principle that drives much tax assignment in Western democracies, that is the principle that determines 'fair' tax payments. The determination of fair tax contributions is both one of the oldest and one of the most central problems in public finance and it remains, in some measure, unresolved (see chapters 7 and 15). The issues raised are similar to those involved in the social welfare function literature. The principle labelled 'ability to pay' raises the question of the utility enjoyed by different individuals. The underlying rationale of the 'ability to pay' approach is that individual taxpayers should make an equal sacrifice when they pay their tax. Whether this means an equal absolute loss of utility, an equal proportional loss of utility or an equal marginal loss of utility is less clear.

Income is used as the measure of ability to pay, and the question is, What form of tax system—proportional, regressive or progressive—is consistent with ability to pay, and to what extent should unequals be

---

[6] The mathematics of this are not easily summarized. Interested readers should consult Varian (1978, chapter 1) and Heathfield and Wibe (1987, chapter 5).

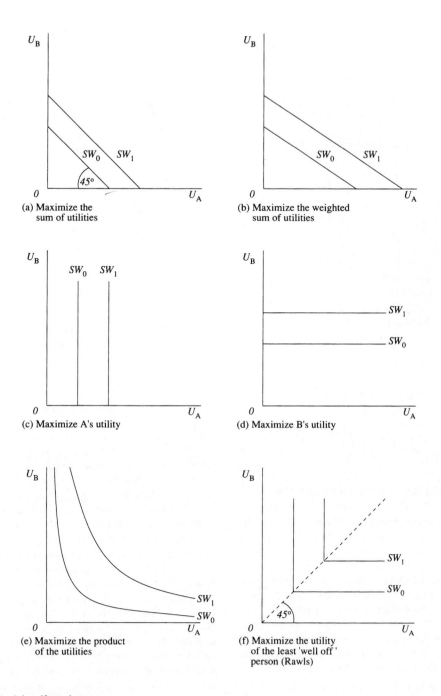

Figure 1.6 Social welfare shapes.

treated unequally (so-called vertical equity)? The equal treatment of equals is known as horizontal equity. Figure 1.7 illustrates the basic concepts. It is assumed that the utility secured from income for individuals A and B is measurable in cardinal terms

and that A and B have the same marginal utility of income schedules. Individual A is assumed to be rich and B poor, so that A's income Y_A is greater than B's, Y_B. Horizontal equity is met when those with the same income pay the same tax. But what of A's and B's

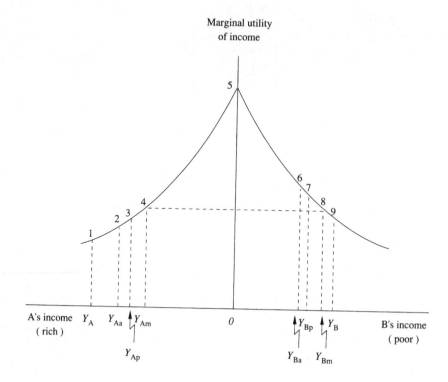

Figure 1.7 Ability to pay and vertical equity.

situation? The recipe for vertical equity generally depends both on the form that the marginal utility of income schedule takes and on the so-called 'equal sacrifice' rule.

Equal absolute sacrifice involves A and B losing the same amount of utility, so that after-tax income Y_{Aa} and Y_{Bb} for A and B respectively involve their losing utility areas Y_A12Y_{Aa}, equal to Y_B96Y_{Ba}. The amount of tax paid equals $(Y_A - Y_{Aa}) + (Y_B - Y_{Ba})$. With diminishing marginal utility of income, tax liability increases with income; however, proportionality, progression or regression depends on whether the elasticity of the marginal utility of income schedule with respect to income is equal to, less than or greater than unity (see Musgrave 1959). Equal proportional sacrifice requires the proportion of total utility lost by A and B to be the same for A and B, so that

$$(1.8) \qquad \frac{Y_A13Y_{Ap}}{Y_A150} = \frac{Y_B97Y_{Bp}}{Y_B950}$$

The tax paid is $(Y_A - Y_{Ap}) + (Y_B - Y_{Bp})$. A decreasing but straight-line marginal utility of income schedule is sufficient but not necessary to call for progression. Finally, equal marginal sacrifice involves A paying $Y_A - Y_{Am}$ and B paying $Y_B - Y_{Bm}$ so that the marginal

utility associated with their post-tax incomes is $Y_{Am}4 = Y_{Bm}8$. In this case any decreasing marginal utility of income schedule implies a progressive income tax schedule. While this rule minimizes the total loss of utility, it levels down to equality post-tax incomes and can be expected to have disincentive effects!

While 'rules' summarized in Table 1.2 help in determining the requirements for different tax schedules, it is recognized that the utilities of individuals are not cardinally measurable and comparable and that their utility functions are likely to differ. After all, it was explicitly to avoid interpersonal comparisons of welfare that the concept of Pareto optimality was so readily adopted. Even accepting interpersonal comparison of welfare, there is no obvious need to link the 'ability to pay' argument with progressive taxation. First, it depends on which concept of equal sacrifice is thought desirable. Secondly, it may depend on the slope of the marginal utility schedule. How can marginal utility be estimated? Is there any necessity to think that the marginal utility of income for a rich man is lower than that for a poor man? (The rich man may be a miser, the poor man a monk!) Estimating marginal utility is then difficult and, unless equal marginal sacrifice is required, we need to know not

Table 1.2 'Ability to pay' and 'progression'

Sacrifice rule	Meaning[a]	Requirement for progression
Equal absolute sacrifice	$U(Y) - U(Y-T)$ same for all	$\dfrac{YU'(Y)}{(Y-T)U'(Y-T)} < 1$ Elasticity of the marginal utility of income schedule less than unity
Equal proportional sacrifice	$\dfrac{U(Y) - U(Y-T)}{U(Y)}$ same for all	Decreasing but straight-line marginal utility of income schedule sufficient but not necessary
Equal marginal sacrifice	$\dfrac{dU(Y-T)}{d(Y-T)}$ same for all	Any decreasing marginal utility of income schedule

[a] Y = income
T = tax paid
U = utility

only that the marginal utility of income declines but also the rate at which it declines.

Finally, even if all these matters could be resolved, there is still the point that the tax structure may be set with respect to the pursuit of other objectives. Progressive taxes may be required for the 'ability to pay' approach, but with strong disincentive effects they may reduce the rate of economic growth. Other objectives (e.g. economic growth, stabilization policy) need to be taken into account. It is then possible to agree with Blum and Kalven (1953) that, even starting with an 'ability to pay' approach, the case for progressive taxation is 'uneasy'.

1.7 Contestable markets versus perfect competition

Despite the caveat in the opening sentence to this chapter, the contestable markets notion has purchase on a number of points made subsequently, so that its main points are salient in this text.

The contestable markets approach dates most recently from Baumol (1982) and Baumol, Panzer and Willig (1982) and is seen as a less restrictive ideal form against which other economic arrangements can be appraised. Additionally, while it is different demand conditions meeting common neoclassical U-shaped cost structures that drives the traditional market forms, the emphasis in contestability is on the cost side. The crucial assumption is that of freedom of entry to and exit from a market. Not only must a

potential entrant be able to compete fully on entry, but also, there must be no penalty for exit. A particular issue relating to exit is the existence of sunk costs that are not recoverable (see chapter 5). For the moment, let us assume that this entry/exit condition is met and see how, almost unaided, it can generate the same results as perfect competition. If 'hit and run' entry and exit are viable, then existing firms in an industry can only make normal profits or return, as any surplus will be removed by such entry and exit even in the short run. Similarly, if a firm adjusts to other than the base of its short-run average cost (at the lowest point of long-run average cost), it can expect its sales to be displaced by lower-cost entrants.

But what of price equalling marginal cost, the very essence of a competitive equilibrium? Consider Fig. 1.8, which depicts the marginal cost curve of a firm in a contestable market. If output is q_e then marginal cost pricing demands that price OP_e be charged, but what happens if you deviate on the high and the low side in a 'contestable' context? If 'too high' a price OP_h is charged for Oq_e, an entrant can come in and charge a price very slightly below OP_h, equating with MC at point 3, and sell Oq_h, displacing the sales of the greater-than-marginal-cost-pricer. The entrant raises profits over the incumbent by the difference between additional revenue ($q_e 2 3 q_h$) and additional costs ($q_e 1 3 q_h$), which equals triangle 123. Hence anyone pricing above MC can expect to be displaced. But what about producing Oq_e and selling at a price below MC at, say, OP_1? Now an entrant can produce Oq_1 at a marginal cost equal to OP_1 and make more profit than the initial low-cost producer enjoyed by slightly lowering the price. This is because saved costs

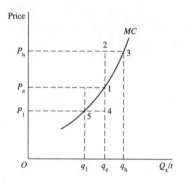

Figure 1.8 Marginal cost pricing and 'contestability'.

are $q_1 5 1 q_e$ and lost revenue is only $q_1 5 4 q_e$ so that additional profit compared with that earned by the initial firm is triangle 145. In short, anyone pricing either above or below MC can expect entry to take place so that they are 'punished' for such actions by losing their sales. The important point is that this outcome is dependent only on whether existing firms producing X (which can be very few in number) are open to the threat of entry and exit by potential competitors. In this respect, it is a prime aim of policy to maintain such conditions by preventing the existence of barriers to entry and exit.

1.8 'Second-best' theory

The analysis so far represents 'first-best' theory, in that either it is assumed that other markets are in equilibrium (the partial case), or the concern is expressly with equilibrium in all markets (the general case). A question arises of what to do if for any reason you are sure that one of the equilibrium conditions is not met in one sector of the economy. Intuition might suggest that the best way forward is to achieve as many efficiency conditions in as many markets as is possible. The surprising conclusion of second-best theory is that, once one efficiency condition is violated, a preferable outcome is attained by violating other efficiency conditions even if they are attainable (Lipsey and Lancaster 1956).

Winch (1971) illustrates this result with respect to a three-good world in which good Z is added to the (ubiquitous) goods X and Y. The analysis employs the properties of an equilateral triangle (see Fig. 1.9). The sum of the distances from any point (e.g. 1 in the figure) within the triangle to the respective sides along a perpendicular to each side sum to a constant

that is the height of the triangle measured by dropping a perpendicular from its apex to its base. The numbers in Fig. 1.9 have this property. Winch assumes linear transformation curves and further adjusts quantities so that they are equal (hence the equilateral triangle).

A circular indifference map for a representative individual shows combinations of goods X, Y and Z yielding equal utility, with point 2 in Fig. 1.9 being the top of an (ordinal) utility mountain. Conditions for a first best optimum are that the marginal rates of substitution between each pair of goods is equal to the marginal rate of transformation, so that

(1.9) $$MRS_{xy} = MRT_{xy}$$

(1.10) $$MRS_{zy} = MRT_{zy}$$

(1.11) $$MRS_{xz} = MRT_{xz}$$

A locus of points meeting these three separate conditions in isolation can be derived from the equivalent of an income consumption path, with the changes in income corresponding to successive levels of provision of the first good and, hence, the remaining possible 'budget' to be allocated between the second and third goods. Figure 1.10 illustrates the derivation process with provision of X as the first good and the choice being between Y and Z. If 20 units of X are provided, then there are a remaining 50 units to be allocated to either X or Y (60 with 10 units of X, 40 with 30 units of X, and so on).

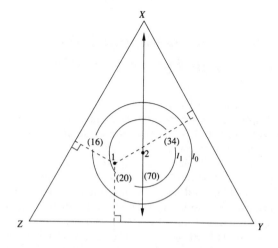

Figure 1.9 The equilateral triangle.

Source: adapted from Winch, D. M. (1971) *Analytical Welfare Eco- nomics*. Reproduced by permission of Penguin Books Ltd., Middlesex.

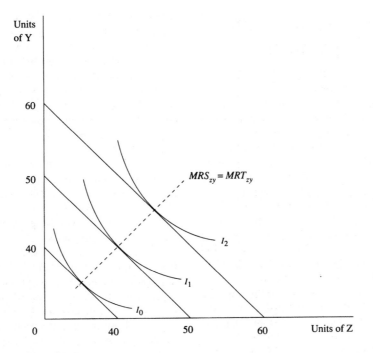

Figure 1.10 Forming the 'equilibrium' paths.

These assumptions make the slope, the marginal rate of transformation between Z and Y, equal to -1. Equilibrium points are picked up in the conventional way with tangency to the preference map indicating $MRS_{zy} = MRT_{zy}$. If this process is repeated with Y and

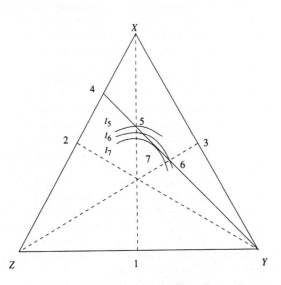

Figure 1.11 Illustrating 'second best'.

Z taking the place of the first good, the three paths in Fig. 1.11 can be derived with $Z3$ conforming to condition (1.9), $X1$ to (1.10) and $Y2$ to (1.11). Now if condition (1.11) cannot be met, the possible adjustments that the individual can make are confined to the line Y4. The options involve: meeting condition (1.10) at point 5 and being on I_5; meeting condition (1.9) at point 6 and being on I_6, and missing all conditions at point 7 and being on I_7. Hence the highest attainable utility for the representative individual occurs where none of the three conditions is met. The second best principle, that once one of the necessary conditions for a Pareto optimum cannot be fulfilled it is generally no longer attractive to pursue the others, is thus illustrated.

The relevance of this apparently very damaging result for normative analysis has been the subject of much debate. One major controversy centres around the existence of possible 'optimal' adjustments in second best contexts. Another, more recent one, questions whether the context in which much public policy takes place can be considered to be first best or second best. These two debates are introduced in Section 1.10 as a way of illustrating the differences between a 'traditional' and a 'public choice' approach to a particular issue.

1.9 Adjusting the focus: the public choice approach

Broadly speaking, there are two ways in which it might be useful to delineate a discipline or sub-discipline within economics. First, the topics studied, and second, the dominant methodology and hence approach taken to each topic. As regards topics, Buchanan (1975) indicates four areas that were key to the development of the public choice sub-discipline: the demand for public goods (see chapter 3); voting theory (see chapter 4); the theory of constitutions (see chapters 14 and 16) and the theory of supply of public goods (see chapter 5). These developments brought both public expenditure and the nature and structure of collective decisions to the attention of what was 'tax with everything' traditional public finance. Important though these topics are, it is a methodological difference that they reflect, and this separates out the alternative views explored in the subsequent chapters of this book.

The conditions for a Pareto optimum or top-level efficient economy have been elaborated. In short, they demonstrate what is required if the allocation of resources is to reflect individual preferences and also ensure that each good or service is priced at its marginal cost (in terms of the other goods or services those resources might have produced). Wiseman (1980) describes the starting-point of a public choice perspective as the recognition of the weakness of the above marginal equivalences in drawing attention away from the equally important efficiency of 'allocative systems or techniques' (p. 250). The role of government is the correction of 'market failure', with this role viewed as being outside the analysis and largely unproblematic. While the earlier sections of this chapter deal with what Wiseman calls *outcome* efficiency, the inclusion of non-market decision mechanisms within the boundary of the analysis serves to highlight *process* efficiency. In an uncertain world, Wiseman (1985) emphasizes the notion that efficient choice behaviour must relate to the procedures of decision-making and not to the outcomes. Outcomes in the presence of uncertainty will often be ones unanticipated by the decision-maker, but this is not where inefficiency is located. It is a question of whether 'other *decision-processes* could imaginably have produced a "superior" outcome . . .' (p. 36; emphasis is ours). Wiseman observes that this 'test' can only be a matter of *ex post* judgement.

As regards the application of a systematic analytical stance, the (now) more traditional 'outcome' approach as exemplified by Musgrave (1959) and Musgrave and Musgrave (1989) is normative in orientation in that it attempts to show how economically 'correct' decisions can be analysed and described in a public sector context. In contrast, the more 'process'-orientated public choice school, while carrying very significant normative overtones, is at the proximate level more 'positive' in outlook, indicating what self-interested actors will find attractive in different public sector contexts. In doing this, 'public choice' extends the boundaries of the more traditional analysis and raises questions about political entrepreneurs, elected representatives, bureaucrats, etc., that fail to surface if government is not viewed as comprising maximizing individuals who are integral to the analysis. In the more traditional view, the literature is answering the question, What *should* a public sector actor, mindful of economic efficiency (and equity) criteria, do in a given context? whereas in the 'public choice' school the question is more, How do or will utility-maximizing individuals in government *behave* in a given context to offend economic efficiency (and equity), and how can they be constrained? Wiseman points out that, 'to get away with' the traditional approach, the simplifying assumption is that a given set of individual rights and preferences is accepted. In contrast, the wider public choice approach, of necessity, involves the incorporation of individual preferences over property rights (what individual rights in general are and, indeed, the rules that allow the amendment of those rights). It is not just individual preferences within a given system of economic arrangements that matters: these pertain to the rights of property, etc., and the rules for changing those rights are part of what is to be specified in a full efficiency analysis. This ties in with Buchanan's concern with constitutional economics (see Congleton 1988), introduced below and in chapters 14 and 16.

While it is evident that both the 'traditional' approach and the public choice approach take so-called 'methodological individualism' as the starting-point (individuals are the units of analysis; individuals are the best judges of their own welfare; individual valuations of arrangements are what matter), there may be more willingness to recognize its limitations in the traditional approach. Two not unrelated works bring this out as a possibility: one relates to social welfare functions, discussed briefly here, and the other to merit wants, discussed in chapter 3.

Congleton (1988) suggests that the traditional perspective presumes that an 'intuitively persuasive social welfare function' (p. 132) exists which will allow the comparison of different tax and expenditure policies. In section 1.5 the shapes of different possible social welfare functions were introduced, but their justification and relative merits remain open to debate. In the public choice approach, no appeal is made to a social welfare function as an evaluative device because of a lack of agreement about the method to aggregate individual utilities. Note that it is the aggregation of individual utilities that is being considered. The notion of a social welfare function based on a view of social welfare that is above and beyond the utility of individuals as judged by themselves falls into a view of society that is 'organic' and admits the possibility that those selected/elected (?) to articulate this necessarily wider concept of 'social welfare' will not always respect individuals' own perceptions of their utility as the only relevant information. In such circumstances there is an incommensurability because, having begun with methodological individualism, it is difficult to 'tack on' other value judgements to 'close' or make the system determinate, however attractive this may seem.

How then do the public choice theorists assess whether one policy or programme option is better than the other? The answer is by reference to unanimity. If everyone agrees to the superiority of a new proposal over existing arrangements, then the change is a 'good' one. In this context it is possible to save the notion of a social welfare function if all individuals agree on the one that is to be used to evaluate different economic arrangements—unanimity is the only fundamental or constitutional test of relevance. Following the lead of Wicksell (1896), Buchanan and Tullock (1962) fully recognize the limitations of the unanimity principle and assess optimal decisions at the day-to-day level that minimize the total costs arising from both the efficiency loss of a less than unanimous decision and the delay and decision costs of establishing unanimity (see chapter 4). Such deviations are optimal because all are prepared to accept them at the fundamental or constitutional level. If this complete consensus breaks up in the face of the demonstrated unattractiveness of the outcomes, then it is a change of rules based on unanimous agreement that is the way forward. The relative merits of different institutional arrangements in the public sector are the stuff of public choice analysis, but at the end of the day it is for all citizens to agree to any change.

It is worth re-emphasizing that, in outcome efficiency, government is essentially an agent outside the analysis. It will enact welfare maximizing prescriptions and, given this, might be expected to be viewed with less concern and hostility than is found in a process efficiency context, where individuals in government have their own interests to pursue. These interests are, in the public choice account, invariably reducible to actions consistent with income/wealth maximization. Indeed, part of their stock in trade is to offer 'self-interested' accounts of events that have been explained elsewhere by appeal to higher motives. As an example of the latter, the public choice explanation of the 1833 English Factory Acts is couched not in terms of the moral outrage felt by society in general at the treatment of children, but rather in terms of rent-seeking by either a section of employers (Marvel 1977) or by skilled male textile workers (Anderson and Tollison 1984). An example of the former is an explanation of South African apartheid laws in terms of income gains to white landowners and white unskilled workers as opposed to an inherent dislike of 'blacks' (see Lowenberg 1989 and Roback 1989). Kelman (1988) criticizes the almost exclusive use of this single motivational account as part of a swingeing attack on the public choice school, protesting that no one-dimensional model of human motivation is adequate.

Closely connected to the points made above is the general antipathy towards government, in virtually all its guises, that runs through what has become 'mainstream' public choice. Even when government attempts to help, it appears to make matters worse. Paradoxically, in Roback's (1989) model of racism it is government ability to solve the 'free rider' problem (a market imperfection) that makes race a politicized issue and the subject of segregationist legislation. The stereotypical public choice account of legislation is that it favours some producers by offering them a source of competitive advantage, e.g. by excluding foreign competition or new entrants while hurting consumers via higher prices. Even safety legislation designed to protect consumers is claimed to be nullified by offsetting 'risk compensation' behaviour by consumers resulting in no overall changes. Concern with the inefficiencies and inequalities caused by government broadly defined are the material of many subsequent sections of this book and require no further elaboration here.

In this section it has been argued that, while the traditional social optimality approach to public finance and the public choice approach share similar basic tenets, the latter lays greater emphasis on:

1. Non-taxation topics;
2. The analysis of non-market (process) efficiency as opposed to non-market (outcome) efficiency;

3. Methodological individualism to the complete exclusion of even hints of non-individualistic perspectives (this, of course, is consistent with the observation that the major public choice economists are political 'libertarians or right-wingers', depending on your choice of language);

4. Economic actors driven by their own 'narrow' self-interest;

5. Arguments that tend to minimize the scope for government intervention to improve on market allocations.

At the risk of reading more into the distinction than is there, the view of human nature varies in different perspectives. The typical public choice economist has an assumptive world, in which people can be expected quickly and effectively to find their own narrow self-interest in any institutional setting and take a narrowly self-interested view of the institutional setting to be chosen. However it would be wrong to take the view that there are no divisions within the public choice approach itself. A cue can be taken from the words 'outsider Chicago–Virginia ... vision' quoted above. (Preface, p. vii). Rowley and Vachris (1995) distinguish Chicago public choice from Virginia public choice. In the Chicago approach efficient results are viewed as likely in both economic and democratic political markets because self-interest drives individuals in both market places. The Virginian perspective takes great issue with the claimed efficiency potential of political markets because of their institutional and other defects. In the absence of constitutional reform Virginia public choice analysis finds political and economic inefficiencies in the political sector. Most, but not all, of the public choice literature discussed in this text is in this less optimistic vein.

1.10 Second-best theory once more

A convenient issue to illustrate differences of approach with respect to material introduced in this chapter is as regards the 'second best'. As stated in section 1.8, the theorem is very damaging to public policy recommendations based on the efficiency considerations outlined earlier. Once an irremovable distortion is located in one sector of the economy, the implication is that meeting marginal conditions in the other sectors is no longer desirable, and, at first blush, this suggests that the economic policy advocate stays

largely silent. This raises two questions. First, how is it that the one thing advocates of economic policy are not is silent? Secondly, and relatedly, why is it relatively rare that specific 'second-best' policies are discussed?

Regarding the first question, it is clear that the incentive for economists is to try and limit the threat posed by second best. Such a damage limitation exercise has been mounted on essentially two fronts: one we label 'traditional', the other we associate with a more 'public choice' approach. In the traditional approach a number of arguments have been advanced.

1.10.1 Separability conditions

In the example developed in section 1.8, goods X, Y and Z are unavoidably related and this in a sense causes a problem. However, in circumstances where the price and output connections between X, Y and Z can be treated as 'negligibly' interrelated, first-best policies can safely be followed. This is essentially the separability argument developed in detail by Davis and Whinston (1965). It is worth noting that utility functions that take the extreme additively separable form can be written in the three-good case:

$$(1.12) \qquad U(X, Y, Z) = U(X) + U(Y) + U(Z)$$

Such a function has some attractive properties. One of which is that the marginal utility of each of the goods depends only on the quantity of that good and is independent of the quantities of any of the other goods. A second, useful to the discussion of optimal taxation in chapter 15, notes that, given the marginal rate of substitution between any pair of goods is simply the ratio of their marginal utilities, it also is independent of the quantity of any other good.

1.10.2 Specific second-best policies

One way to respond to the second-best theorem is to design policies that deliberately respond to the existence of an immutable non-optimal constraint. A typical example is the presence of monopoly pricing in one sector of the economy. Suppose industry X is monopolized while Y is produced under competitive conditions so that $P_x > MC_x$ but $P_y = MC_y$. For a Pareto optimum,

$$(1.13) \qquad MRS_{xy} = MRT_{xy}$$

but, given the above,

$$(1.14) \qquad MRS_{xy} = \frac{P_x}{P_y} > \frac{MC_x}{MC_y} = MRT_{xy}$$

The correction is to raise the competitive price (P_y) above MC_y by the same proportion as P_x exceeds MC_x (Mishan 1962), so that for perfect substitutes

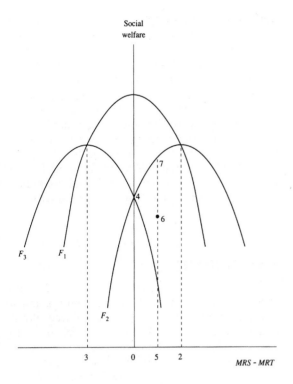

Figure 1.12 What's best?

Source: based on Ng, Y. K. (1977).

$$(1.15) \qquad \frac{P_x - MC_x}{MC_x} = \frac{P_y - MC_y}{MC_y}$$

In raising the price of Y, the slope of the budget constraint between the two goods to which consumers adjust is being corrected. A more complex case is explored below in chapter 5.

Designing second-best policies raises the responses categorized by Ng (1977). His position can be illustrated by reference to Fig. 1.12, where levels of social welfare are related to the deviation between the marginal rate of substitution and the marginal rate of transformation. In the early sections of the chapter, F_1 implicitly applies, with social welfare globally maximized and $MRS = MRT$. The functions F_2 and F_3 relate to second-best situations, where only optimal deviations from $MRS = MRT$ maximize social welfare albeit at a lower level than in the first-best world. Ng explicitly incorporates the information and implementation costs of devising and applying specific second-best policies and dubs the context 'third-best'.[7]

'Information' refers to knowledge of the relevant distortion and production functions and comes at three levels.

1. *Information abundance* describes costless information situations, in which it is appropriate to follow the second-best prescriptions in the third-best context. In Fig. 1.12 the deviation appropriate to F_2 and F_3 would be $O2$ and $O3$ respectively.

2. *Information poverty* involves uncertainty in that there is no knowledge of the direction and extent of the distortion. Under such circumstances the application of first-best rules in the non-distorted sectors is recommended as a way of increasing expected social welfare in the third-best context. Under information poverty either F_2 or F_3 may obtain—you are in a second-best situation—but by following first-best prescriptions the expected result is where F_2 and F_3 cross where $MRS - MRT = 0$; i.e., social welfare level is $O4$. The expected result from adopting a second-best policy like deviation $O5$ will be half-way between the values of F_2 and F_3 at 5, which is the distance 56. As a consequence, the expected outcome from second-best policies is less than for first-best policies (distance $O4$).

3. *Information scarcity* is the in-between case of limited information on the extent and direction of any distortion and this is the cutting edge of the third best. In this scenario whether F_2 or F_3 is relevant can be judged, as well as the shape and skewness of the F curves. The response generally involves some but not perfect 'corrective' policy in the correct direction. In Fig. 1.12, if F_2 applies, the deviation $O5$ yields a rise in social welfare level as measured by the vertical distance 47.

McKee and West (1981, 1984) are authors who 'get around' the problem of the second best in an opposing fashion. They suggest that the second best is a solution that is in search of a real problem to solve. The basic insight is that the offending immutable distortion that triggers the second-best argument is in fact the result of and not the impediment to public policy action; that is, observed distorted contexts are first-best ones and the economy is always on F_1 in Fig. 1.12. An example they cite concerns information. If it is accepted that the non-excludability of information reduces the incentive to seek inventions, a policy response to this aspect of market failure may be the introduction of patent rights that offer (at least temporary) monopoly power. It is then inappropriate to view this monopoly as a distortion in need of a *second-best* correction.

---

[7] The list of distortions calling for second- and third-best policies include uncorrected externalities, natural monopolies not created by political decisions, and the use of non-lump-sum taxes in revenue-raising.

In their more favoured account of this proposition, it is actors in the political market-place that are the origin of the supposed second-best distortions. Hence their connection to the public choice is, in part, the degree of emphasis being placed on processes. They view these distortions 'as part of the Paretian solution and their existence constitutes part of the first best allocation' (McKee and West 1984, p. 250). Politicians weild power as defined by political constitutions. These powers involve the ability to redistribute income and to reassign property rights in the economy. Such redistribution and reassignment that arises will be a reflection of the incentives the political actors face. It is the fact that distortions are the outcome of a 'market' process that confers their efficiency property. The politicians' incentive for action is a share of the benefits (economic rents) obtainable from policy action. The policy-makers' objective function is the relevant maximand because, as just noted, the constitution grants them this role, which includes the ability to alter property rights structures. It is costs and benefits interpreted in the light of the policy-makers' objective functions that are argued to count, and any decision rule that maximizes *this* objective function is described as an automatic Pareto optimum. Considering the incentives facing political actors. McKee and West point out that it would not be in their interest to impose second-best policies to offset the impact of the property rights structures they have, in fact, created. The observed result is the outcome of the incentive structure, and the absence of second-best policies at the practical level of government intervention is the proof of the pudding. At one stroke, the argument rescues first-best policy analysis and explains the historical lack of real policy interest in the second best without recourse to Ng's first- and third-best arguments. To further add to Ng's discomfort, McKee and West suggest that his informational costs should more properly be seen as part of the production function constraint in an economy rather than an added issue or constraint.

In a subsequent response and interchange, the issue was left unresolved but some, if not all, of the issues were clarified. Ng (1987a, 1987b) recognizes that some (but by no means all—see note 7) distortions are the product of the existing political policy incentives and that it is an uphill task to try and alter these outcomes. However, he notes that the role of the economist is to articulate the social optimality approach outlined in sections 1.2 to 1.5, including second- and third-best propositions. In short, economic analysis is about referring to all individuals and not just the policy-maker. Secondly, Ng argues that

the type of distortions McKee and West describe are distribution-motivated, and their adverse efficiency consequences may still suggest other than first-best policies as an offsetting response that need not neutralize the distribution effects as they 'correct' the efficiency effects. Thirdly, even for the patent induced monopoly example posed above, the efficiency of the whole system may still be raised by considering price marginal cost ratios in, say, pricing policy in the public sector, i.e. along the lines of section 1.10.2. For Ng, second- and third-best policies remain central to the welfare economics of public policies, while for McKee and West they remain at best a peripheral curiosity that can be safely ignored.

1.11 Summary

In this chapter the basic theory that informs much of the later discussion has been introduced. While none of it is novel, an attempt has been made to place it in a less than cut-and-dried context. Different economists say different things about the same problem areas, and this is the 'stuff' of economics in general. A particular issue—second best—has been explored as a first example of the divide between what are labelled here as traditional social optimality public finance economists and the more recent arrivals, the public choice school. Here it is appropriate to echo the words of Ng (1987b, p. 154) to the effect that 'both the traditional social-optimality approach... [sections 1.2.1.5]... and the public choice approach... [sections 1.8 and 1.9]... are useful in their respective roles'. Establishing their respective roles and estimating how useful they are is the task of the reader of this book.

Appendix: Deriving some of the rules

In this section a more precise formulation of the statements in sections 1.2 to 1.4 is offered as revision and help in understanding the logic of the underlying arguments and results employed in subsequent chapters.

The three conditions for a top-level efficient economy can be derived more formally using the Lagrangean multipliers method.

Efficiency condition (1.1) states that

(A1) $$MRTS_{kl}^{Y} = MRTS_{kl}^{X}$$

The production frontier shows the maximum amount of X that can be produced given the level of output of Y, say $\bar{Y}$, and the endowment of capital and labour (K and L) respectively. Lower-case x and y indicate factor allocations to those activities.

Given the resource constraint

(A2) $$\bar{L} = L_x + L_y$$

(A3) $$K = K_x + K_y$$

and the production functions

(A4) $$X = X(K_x, L_x)$$

(A5) $$Y = Y(K_y, L_y)$$

the object is to maximize $X = X(K_x, L_x)$ subject to

(A6) $$\bar{Y} = Y(\bar{L} - L_x, \bar{K} - K_x)$$

Forming the Lagrangean,

(A7) $$Z = X(K_x, L_x) + \lambda[\bar{Y} - Y(\bar{L} - L_x, \bar{K} - K_x)]$$

Differentiating with respect to K_x and L_x and setting equal to zero,

(A8) $$\frac{\partial Z}{\partial K_x} = \frac{\partial X}{\partial K_x} + \lambda \frac{\partial Y}{\partial K_x} = 0$$

(A9) $$\frac{\partial Z}{\partial L_x} = \frac{\partial X}{\partial L_x} + \lambda \frac{\partial Y}{\partial L_x} = 0$$

so that

(A10) $$\frac{\partial X/\partial K_x}{\partial Y/\partial K_x} = -\lambda = \frac{\partial X/\partial L_x}{\partial Y/\partial L_x}$$

and

(A11) $$MRTS_{kl}^{Y} = \frac{MP_l^Y}{MP_k^Y} = \frac{\partial Y/\partial L_x}{\partial Y/\partial K_x} = \frac{\partial X/\partial L_x}{\partial X/\partial K_y}$$
$$= \frac{MP_l^X}{MP_k^X} = MRTS_{kl}^{X}$$

where MP is marginal product.
Efficiency condition (1.2) states that

(A12) $$MRS_{xy}^{A} = MRS_{xy}^{B}$$

Here the structure of the problem is similar in that the objective is to maximize the utility of one individual, say A, while holding the level of utility achieved by B constant at, say, $\bar{U}^B$.

The individual utility functions are given by

(A13) $$U^A = U^A(X, Y)$$

(A14) $$U^B = U^B(X, Y)$$

where X and Y are, as before, the outputs in the two-good world. Forming the Lagrangean,

(A15) $$L = U^A(X^A, Y^A) + \lambda[\bar{U}^B - U^B(X^B, Y^B)]$$

Differentiating L with respect to X and Y and setting equal to zero yields

(A16) $$\frac{\partial L}{\partial X} = \frac{\partial U^A}{\partial X^A} - \lambda \frac{\partial U^B}{\partial X^B} = 0$$

(A17) $$\frac{\partial L}{\partial Y} = \frac{\partial U^A}{\partial Y^A} - \lambda \frac{\partial U^B}{\partial Y^B} = 0$$

(A18) $$\frac{MU_x^A}{MU_x^B} = \frac{\partial U^A/\partial X^A}{\partial U^B/\partial X^B} = \lambda = \frac{\partial U^A/\partial Y^A}{\partial U^B/\partial Y^B}$$
$$= \frac{MU_y^A}{MU_y^B}$$

and

(A19) $$MRS_{xy}^{A} = \frac{MU_x^A}{MU_y^A} = \frac{\partial U^A/\partial X^A}{\partial U^A/\partial Y^A}$$
$$= \lambda = \frac{\partial U^B/\partial X^B}{\partial U^B/\partial Y^B} = \frac{MU_x^B}{MU_y^B} = MRS_{xy}^{B}$$

where MU is marginal utility.
Efficiency condition (1.3) states that

(A20) $$MRS_{xy}^{A} = MRS_{xy}^{B} = MRT_{xy}$$

This involves adding to efficiency condition (1.2) the production possibilities frontier or production transformation function (in implicit form)

(A21) $$T = T(X, Y)$$

to be on the frontier

(A22) $$T(X, Y) = T(X^A + X^B, Y^A + Y^B) = 0$$

so that

(A23) $$\frac{\partial T}{\partial X} dX + \frac{\partial T}{\partial Y} dY = 0$$

and

(A24) $$\frac{dY}{dX} = (-)\frac{\partial T/\partial X}{\partial T/\partial Y} = MRT_{xy}$$

Adding the transformation function constraint to the Lagrangean (A15) yields

(A25) $$L = U^A(X^A, Y^A) + \lambda[\bar{U}^B - U^B(X^B, Y^B)]$$
$$+ u[0 - T(X, Y)]$$

Differentiating with respect to X^A, Y^A, X^B and Y^B and setting equal to zero,

(A26) $$\frac{\partial L}{\partial X^A} = \frac{\partial U^A}{\partial X^A} - u\frac{\partial T}{\partial X} = 0$$

(A27) $$\frac{\partial L}{\partial Y^A} = \frac{\partial U^A}{\partial Y^A} - u\frac{\partial T}{\partial Y} = 0$$

(A28) $$\frac{\partial L}{\partial X^B} = -\lambda\frac{\partial U^B}{\partial X^B} - u\frac{\partial T}{\partial X} = 0$$

(A29) $$\frac{\partial L}{\partial Y^B} = -\lambda\frac{\partial U^B}{\partial Y^B} - u\frac{\partial T}{\partial Y} = 0$$

Rearranging and dividing each of the pairs of equations yields

(A30) $$MRS^A_{xy} = \frac{\partial U^A/\partial X^A}{\partial U^A/\partial Y^A} = \frac{\partial T/\partial X}{\partial T/\partial Y}$$

and

(A31) $$MRS^B_{xy} = \frac{\partial U^B/\partial X^B}{\partial U^B/\partial Y^B} = \frac{\partial T/\partial X}{\partial T/\partial Y}$$

Given that the right-hand term in these equations is the marginal rate of transformation and is common, the outcome is the condition that

(A32) $$MRS^A_{xy} = MRS^B_{xy} = MRT_{xy}$$

As regards perfect competition achieving these three conditions, this result relies on the utility-maximizing behaviour of consumers and cost-minimizing behaviour of profit-maximizing producers.

Individual consumers A and B wish to maximize their utility from the consumption of goods X and Y subject to their income I and the prices of the two goods p_x and p_y respectively. Forming the Lagrangean,

(A33) $$L = U(X, Y) + \lambda(I - p_x X - p_y Y)$$

Differentiating with respect to X and Y and setting equal to zero,

(A34) $$\frac{\partial L}{\partial X} = \frac{\partial U}{\partial X} - \lambda p_x = 0$$

(A35) $$\frac{\partial L}{\partial Y} = \frac{\partial U}{\partial Y} - \lambda p_y = 0$$

so that both A and B will conform to the condition

(A36) $$\frac{MU_x}{p_x} = \frac{\partial U/\partial X}{p_x} = \lambda = \frac{\partial U/\partial Y}{p_y} = \frac{MU_y}{p_y}$$

and

(A37) $$MRS_{xy} = \frac{MU_x}{MU_y} = \frac{\partial U/\partial X}{\partial U/\partial Y} = (-)\frac{p_x}{p_y}$$

i.e. so long as both consumers face the same output price ratio, as is the case in perfect competition,

(A38) $$MRS^A_{xy} = MRS^B_{xy} \quad [\text{condition (1.2)}]$$

Individual producers of good X and Y must, if they are to profit-maximize, minimize the total cost C of production of, say, good X, subject to the price of the inputs labour and capital, w and r respectively. That is, the problem can be represented as

(A39) $$R = wL + rK + \lambda[\bar{X} - X(L, K)]$$

Again, differentiating with respect to L and K and setting equal to zero yields

(A40) $$\frac{\partial R}{\partial L} = w - \lambda\frac{\partial X}{\partial L} = 0$$

(A41) $$\frac{\partial R}{\partial K} = r - \lambda\frac{\partial X}{\partial K} = 0$$

so that

(A42) $$\frac{w}{\partial X/\partial L} = \lambda = \frac{r}{\partial X/\partial K}$$

or

(A43) $$\frac{MP^X_l}{w} = \frac{\partial X/\partial L}{w} = \lambda = \frac{\partial X/\partial K}{r} = \frac{MP^X_k}{r}$$

or

(A44) $$MRTS^X_{kl} = \frac{MP^X_l}{MP^X_k} = \frac{\partial X/\partial L}{\partial X/\partial K} = (-)\frac{w}{r}$$

i.e. as long as the producers of X and Y respond to the same input price ratio, as they will with perfectly competitive factor markets, they will automatically have

(A45) $$MRTS^X_{kl} = MRTS^Y_{kl} \quad [\text{condition (1.1)}]$$

Now each producer, say of X, wishing to maximize profits π as the difference between total costs C and total revenue R must ensure that

(A46) $$MR_x = MC_x$$

because with

(A47) $$\pi = R_x - C_x$$

a maximum is found where a change in the level of output will not momentarily increase or decrease profit; i.e. $d\pi/dX = 0$ (or, for the producer of Y, $d\pi/dY = 0$). This means that for X

(A48) $$\frac{d\pi}{dX} = \frac{dR}{dX} - \frac{dC}{dX} = 0$$

(A49) $$MR_x = \frac{dR}{dX} \quad \frac{dC}{dX} = MC_x$$

Now MC_x is the change in cost, say w the wage, of employing one more unit of input, say labour, in the production of, say, X divided by the output secured; i.e.

$$(A50) \quad MC_x = \frac{w}{\partial X/\partial L} = \frac{w}{MP_x}$$

Noting that in perfect competition for each firm $P_x = MR_x$, profit maximization dictates that

$$(A51) \quad MC_x = \frac{w}{\partial X/\partial L} = MR_x = P_x$$

and similarly for Y:

$$(A52) \quad MC_y = \frac{w}{\partial Y/\partial L} = MR_y = P_y$$

(Note that $r/\partial X/\partial K)$ and $r/(\partial Y/\partial K)$ could be added to these equalities.)

If it can be established that the marginal rate of transformation introduced above (the slope of the production possibilities frontier) is equal to the ratio of the marginal costs of X and Y, this will enable the closing of the argument. It is the case that

$$(A53) \quad MRT_{xy} = (-)\frac{dY}{dX} = \frac{dC_x/dX}{dC_y/dY} = \frac{MC_x}{MC_y}$$

$$(A54) \quad C_x = wL_x + rK_x$$

$$(A55) \quad C_y = wL_y + rK_y$$

$$(A56) \quad dC_x = wdL_x + rdK_y$$

$$(A57) \quad dC_y = wdL_y + rdK_y$$

$$(A58) \quad \bar{L} = L_x + L_y$$

$$(A59) \quad \bar{K} = K_x + K_y$$

Hence

$$(A60) \quad dL_x = -dL_y$$

$$(A61) \quad dK_x = -dK_y$$

yielding by substitution

$$(A62) \quad dC_x = -wdL_y - rdK_y$$

$$(A63) \quad dC_x = -dC_y$$

$$(A64) \quad \frac{dC_x}{dC_y} = -1$$

and

$$(A65) \quad (-)\frac{dY}{dX} = \frac{MC_x}{MC_y}$$

Hence utility-maximizing consumers and profit-maximizing producers in conditions of perfect competition will conform to

$$(A66) \quad \frac{MU_x}{MU_y} = MRS_{xy} = \frac{p_x}{p_y} = \frac{MC_x}{MC_y} = MRT_{xy}$$

Utility-maximizing Profit-maximizing [condition (1.3)]

References

Anderson, G. M. and Tollison, R. D. (1984) 'A Rent-Seeking Explanation of the British Factory Acts', pp. 187–201 in D. Colander (ed.), *Neo-classical Political Economy*. Cambridge, Mass.: Ballinger.

Bator, F. M. (1957) 'The Simple Analytics of Welfare Maximisation', *American Economic Review*, 47, 1, pp. 22–59.

Baumol, W. J. (1982) 'Contestable Markets: An Uprising in the Theory of Industry Structure', *American Economic Review*, 72, 1, pp. 1–15.

Baumol, W. J., Panzer, J. C. and Willig, R. D. (1982) *Contestable Markets and the Theory of Industrial Structure*. San Diego: Harcourt Brace Jovanovich.

Blum, W. J. and Kalven, H. (1953) *The Uneasy Case for Progressive Taxation*. Chicago: University of Chicago Press.

Boadway, R. W. and Bruce, N. (1984) *Welfare Economics*. Oxford and New York: Basil Blackwell.

Buchanan, J. M. (1975) 'Public Finance and Public Choice', *National Tax Journal*, 28, 4, pp. 383–94.

Buchanan, J. M. and Tullock, G. (1962) *The Calculus of Consent*. Ann Arbor: University of Michigan Press.

Buck, T. (1982) *Comparative Industrial Systems*. London: Macmillan.

Congleton, R. D. (1988) 'An Overview of the Contractarian Public Finance of James Buchanan', *Public Finance Quarterly*, 16, 2, pp. 131–57.

Davis, O. A. and Whinston, A. B. (1965) 'Welfare Economics and the Theory of Second Best', *Review of Economic Studies*, 32, 1, pp. 1–14.

Heathfield, D. F. and Wibe, S. (1987) *An Introduction to Cost and Production Functions*. London: Macmillan.

Kelman, M. (1988) 'On Democracy Bashing: A Sceptical Look at Theoretical and "Empirical" Practice of the Public Choice Movement', *Virginia Law Review*, 74, 2, pp. 199–273.

Lipsey, R. G. and Lancaster, K. (1956) 'The General Theory of the Second Best', *Review of Economic Studies*, 24, 1, pp. 11–32.

Lowenberg, A. D. (1989) 'An Economic Theory of Apartheid', *Economic Inquiry*, 27, 1, pp. 57–74.

Marvel, H. P. (1977) 'Factory Regulation: A Reinterpretation of Early English Experience', *Journal of Law and Economics*, 20, 2, pp. 379–402.

Mas-Colell, A. Whinston, M. D. and Green, J. R. (1995) *Microeconomic Theory*, Oxford: Oxford University Press.

McKee, M. and West, E. G. (1981) 'The Theory of Second Best: A Solution in Search of a Problem', *Economic Inquiry*, 19, 3, pp. 436–48.

McKee, M. and West, E. G. (1984) 'Do Second-Best Considerations Affect Policy Decisions', *Public Finance/Finances Publiques*, **39**, 2, pp. 246–60.

McKee, M. and West, E. G. (1987) 'Further Perspectives on the Theory of Second Best', *Public Finance/Finances Publiques*, **42**, 1, pp. 146–51.

Mishan, E. J. (1962) 'Second Thoughts on Second Best', *Oxford Economic Papers*, **14**, 3, pp. 205–17.

Mishan, E. J. (1981) *Introduction to Normative Economics*. Oxford: Oxford University Press.

Musgrave, R. A. (1959) *The Theory of Public Finance*. New York: McGraw-Hill.

Musgrave, R. A. and Musgrave, P. B. (1989) *Public Finance in Theory and Practice*. New York: McGraw-Hill.

Ng, Y. K. (1977) 'Towards a Theory of Third Best', *Public Finance/Finances Publiques*, **32**, 1, pp. 1–15.

Ng, Y. K. (1979) *Welfare Economics: Introduction and Development of Basic Concepts*. London: Macmillan.

Ng, Y. K. (1987a) ' "Political Distortions" and the Relevance of Second- and Third-best Theories', *Public Finance/Finances Publiques*, **42**, 1, pp. 137–45.

Ng, Y. K. (1987b) 'The Role of Economists and Third-Best Policies', *Public Finance/Finances Publiques*, **42**, 1, pp. 152–5.

Roback, J. (1989) 'Racism as Rent Seeking', *Economic Inquiry*, **27**, 4, pp. 661–81.

Rowley, C. K. and Vachris, M. A. (1995) 'Why Democracy does not Necessarily Produce Efficient Results', *Economica delle Scelte Pubbliche*, 2–3, pp. 95–111.

Russell, R. R. and Wilkinson, M. (1979) *Microeconomics: A Synthesis of Modern and Neoclassical Theory*. New York: Wiley.

Sen, A. (1977) 'On Weights and Measures: Informational Constraints in Social Welfare Analysis', *Econometrica*, **45**, 7, pp. 1539–72.

Varian, H. R. (1978) *Microeconomic Analysis*. New York: W. W. Norton.

Varian, H. R. (1987) *Intermediate Microeconomics*. New York: W. W. Norton.

Wicksell, K. (1896) 'A New Principle of Just Taxation', reprinted as pp. 92–118 in R. A. Musgrave and A. T. Peacock (eds.), *Classics in the Theory of Public Finance*. New York: St Martin's Press, 1967.

Winch, D. M. (1971) *Analytical Welfare Economics*. Harmondsworth: Penguin.

Wiseman, J. (1980) 'The Choice of Optimal Social Expenditures', pp. 249–61 in K. Roskamp (ed.), *Public Choice and Public Finance*. Paris: Editions Cujas.

Wiseman, J. (1985) 'Economic Efficiency and Efficient Public Policy', pp. 33–44 in H. Hanusch, K. W. Roskamp and J. Wiseman (eds.), *Public Sector and Political Economy Today*. Stuttgart: Gustav Fischer Verlag.

2 Evaluating public finance policy: consumer surplus, welfare criteria and market failure

2.1 Introduction

The Pareto optimality conditions discussed in chapter 1 provide an important benchmark for public finance decisions. In many cases, however, analysts have regarded them as 'too restrictive' for policy appraisal and have considered ways of amending the framework.

First, an estimate of welfare may be required to enable policy-makers to consider how 'well off' any individual will be under alternative tax regimes and different public expenditure programmes. Secondly, it is very likely that policy-makers will be unable to avoid interpersonal comparisons. While Pareto optimality provides the marginal equivalence conditions for optimality, these conditions do not enable the estimation of welfare for any individual. Indeed, a motivation for establishing the Pareto framework was to avoid the necessity of making interpersonal comparisons of welfare. Despite this, there are very few government policy proposals that will not make at least one person worse off and hence violate a Paretian value judgement.

Although there are difficulties in estimating and comparing welfare, it is sometimes necessary to attempt the exercise—at least as a first step in the process of public sector decision-making. Here the intention is to provide a critique of some concepts that may prove useful. The first concept for consideration is what is referred to as 'consumer surplus'. After examining the usefulness of this estimate, it will be possible to consider the difficulties that arise in comparing such estimates between different individuals. While it is difficult to make interpersonal comparisons, specific welfare criteria have been designed to indicate whether or not to accept particular policy proposals.

Later in the chapter we shall illustrate how these concepts can be applied to public policy issues. The example used in this chapter is the response of public policy to the topical problem of environmental pollution. The costs and benefits associated with different policies inevitably fall on different individuals in the community. How can we answer the question of where the government-imposed limits on pollution should be set? How can we select the most appropriate public finance instrument for dealing with those who create a pollution problem? To answer these questions, we are thrown back on the analysis of consumer surplus and welfare criteria. However, one of the consistent themes in this text is that those policies that would be advocated by reference to the principles of 'traditional' welfare criteria are often not the policies that are adopted by government. For example, welfare criteria may indicate that public policy should utilize taxes in order to deal with a problem of pollution (or congestion), and yet regulation may be resorted to more often. Why should this be so? One of the strengths of the public choice school is that, by an economic analysis of the political process, contributors are able to offer an explanation for such decisions. They focus on the decision-making process and therefore highlight why particular public finance policies are selected to tackle particular problems. Here we take the opportunity to contrast a public choice analysis of government policies with that premised on the 'traditional' principles of welfare criteria. It may be that the political process explains why those recommendations that spring from welfare criteria are rejected, but it is for readers to question whether the account offered by public choice theorists is reasonable.

Inevitably, we must begin by acquiring information on some basic welfare principles, and it is to these foundations that attention is now turned.

2.2 Consumer surplus: estimating the welfare effects associated with price changes

Throughout this text there will be discussion of government policies that affect prices in the economy. Taxes and subsidies are obvious examples. But how costly are taxes to individuals? How valuable are subsidies? If government provides services, how much are these services worth? All government decisions will affect the welfare of different groups: how can this welfare change be estimated? A most important starting-point for dealing with these questions is the concept of consumer surplus. Alfred Marshall (1920) defined an individual's consumer surplus as 'the excess of the price which he would be willing to pay rather than go without the thing over that which he actually does pay' (p. 103). What does this mean?

An individual's demand curve for any good X records the quantities per unit of time that would be chosen at different prices. Alternatively, the demand curve indicates the price that individuals are 'willing to pay' for successive increases in the quantity of that particular good per period, i.e. an estimate of the value of that good to the individual. In Fig. 2.1 we illustrate an individual's demand curve D for good X. Framing our analysis around the above interpretations, it is clear that, in the first instance, the demand curve tells us that at price P_1 the individual would be willing to buy Oq^1; at price P_2 she would choose to purchase Oq^2, and so on. Yet, in so far as this information provides a basis upon which we can estimate the value of the good to the individual, we can read the diagram another way. We can argue that the first unit Oq^1 is worth P_1; the second unit Oq^2 is worth P_2 and so on. The first three units, therefore, are worth the area under the demand curve between O and Oq^3, i.e. $O12q^3$. By interpreting the individual's demand curve in this way, we can explain why the difference between what an individual is 'willing to pay' and the market price she actually does pay can be used as an estimate of consumer surplus.

Assume that the market price is P_3. In Fig. 2.1, the individual is willing to pay P_1 for unit q^1 and the difference on this unit of $P_1 - P_3$ is a measure of consumer surplus, as defined by Marshall. It measures the amount that the individual would be prepared to pay over the price P_3 she has to pay. For the number of units that the individual chooses to purchase at price P_3, i.e. Oq^3, she would be willing to pay the sum $O12q^3$ (i.e. P_1 for the first unit, P_2 for the second unit and so

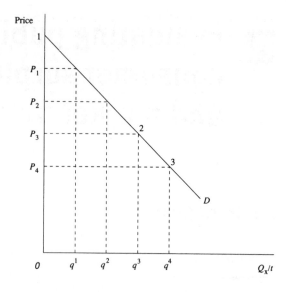

Figure 2.1 Marshallian consumer surplus.

on). However, for Oq^3 she actually pays OP_32q^3, i.e. P_3 per unit. Hence, triangle $12P_3$ equals Marshall's description of consumer surplus. It is clear also that, as the price of the good falls in the market-place, the consumer surplus enjoyed increases. For example, if the price of the good were to fall to P_4, consumer surplus would increase by area P_323P_4. Another way of looking at this would be to argue that the individual would be 'willing' to give up P_323P_4 for this price change. If government reduced the price of this good by a subsidy of $P_3 - P_4$, this would be worth P_323P_4 to the individual. Generally speaking, it appears possible to estimate the effect of any price change as the change in consumer surplus associated with it—the amount that individuals would pay to see the change occur. As many of the decisions of government lead to changes in prices in the economy, this formulation is a basis for evaluating the welfare effect of these government measures.

An important objection to the use of this area under the demand curve as an estimate of consumer surplus is that, as the price of goods changes, the real income of the consumer changes. If the question is 'how much will an individual pay for a price fall when the initial price is P?' then this reference point determines a particular level of *real* income (defined by reference to a particular utility level for an individual) which necessarily affects the amount of money that will be offered. Holding that level of real income constant and asking how much the individual would pay for a change will clearly limit the amount that she would pay for such a change. A fall in price increases the real income of the individual. It enables her to purchase more of all goods. She buys more of a good because, as the price falls, there is a substitution effect in favour of the cheaper good. However, for normal goods, she also buys more because, as real income has increased, there is an income effect. The Marshallian demand curve is an ambiguous concept (Culyer 1971). One interpretation would be that it is drawn under the assumption that *money income* is held constant but not *real income*.[1] Our objective is not to determine what Marshall was holding constant, but to show that there is a difference in the estimate of consumer surplus according to which variable is held constant. For this purpose it may be helpful to think of the demand curve as a Marshallian uncompensated demand function (Deaton and Muellbauer 1980, p. 25). When the price falls money income may be constant, as that money will now buy more goods and services, real income has increased. If consumers are able to enjoy the increase in real income, they will obviously offer more for the price change. Our question however is, How much would they offer at a given real income?

If government were considering the introduction of a change that improved conditions for taxpayers, it is reasonable to ask how much the taxpayers would pay for such a change. What is the maximum sum they would be prepared to give up for it? The point is that, if they paid the maximum they were prepared to pay for the change in question, there could, by definition, be no positive income effect associated with the price fall, as real income would be maintained.

Friedman (1949) draws attention to the difference in the amounts that individuals are prepared to pay when money income is held constant and when real income is held constant. In Fig. 2.2 the Marshallian demand curve (money income held constant) for an individual consumer of a normal good is shown as D. Assume that initially the price is set so high that the individual can afford to buy nothing. If we ask how much (holding money income constant) this individual will be prepared to buy at prices like P_1, we can trace out the Marshallian demand curve. If we ask how much an individual will pay for the first unit (and take this sum away from her); how much the individual will pay for the second unit (and take this sum away from her); how much the individual will pay for the third unit (and take this sum away from her) and so

[1] Blaug (1968, p. 361) notes: 'real income increases along a Marshallian demand curve as the price falls'.

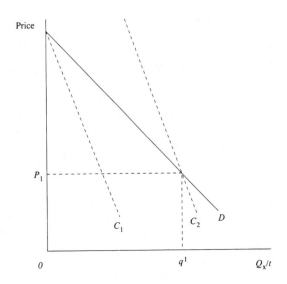

Figure 2.2 Marshallian and compensated demand.

on, we trace out the real income (or income-compensated) demand curve C_1. The compensated demand curve will lie inside the Marshallian demand curve as long as the good is 'normal', i.e. has a positive income elasticity. On each occasion, the individual is forced to give up the maximum she would pay in the case of the compensated demand curve. All along the Marshallian demand curve the real income of the individual is increasing, but along the compensated demand curve real income is, by definition, kept constant.

As the real income of the individual is increasing along the Marshallian demand curve, it follows that there are different compensated demand curves (relating to each constant level of income) at each point along D. In Fig. 2.2, C_1 and C_2 are two income-compensated curves. The income-compensated demand curve C_2 (by contrast with that at C_1) begins with the real income of an individual set at a point where she is entitled to buy Oq^1 units of the good at a price of OP_1. We then discover the curve C_2 by asking what is the maximum sum that she would pay for an additional unit of the good holding her real income constant (or, alternatively, what is the maximum quantity she would demand when price rises but real income is held constant). If the individual's real income increases as we move down D, it is not surprising that C_2 is to the right of C_1.

In part (a) of Fig. 2.3, it is possible to compare the estimates of consumer surplus associated with a price fall from P_1 to P_2 when we use the Marshallian demand curve and when we use the compensated

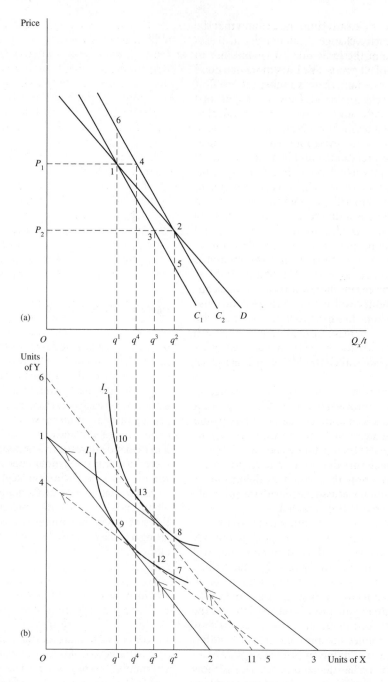

Figure 2.3 Consumer surplus.

demand curve. At P_1 the amount that an individual would pay, according to the Marshallian demand curve, is $P_1 12 P_2$. However, holding constant the real level of income, the amount that an individual will pay for such a price fall is $P_1 13 P_2$, i.e. a smaller sum than

the Marshallian estimate, because the real income of the individual has not been allowed to increase. The smaller sum $P_1 13 P_2$ is referred to as the *price-compensating variation*, i.e. the maximum sum an individual would be prepared to give up for a favourable change (or receive for an unfavourable change) and yet keep constant her real income.

Hicks (1943) drew attention to more estimates of consumer surplus. His analysis can be explained by reference to indifference curves, and in part (b) of Fig. 2.3 it is possible to show more clearly how the price-compensating variation is determined. Initially, when the price of good X is P_1, the budget line is 12 and the individual is maximizing welfare at 9 on I_1. If the price should fall to P_2 the budget line would shift to 13 and the individual would now maximize welfare at 8 on I_2. How much better off is the individual as a result of the price change? How much can we take from the individual to leave her as well off as she was before the price change? If we shift the budget line backwards, parallel to 13, we maintain relative prices but reduce the real income of the individual. If we locate the parallel budget line 45 at a point of tangency to indifference curve I_1, the individual is left at 12 choosing q^3 enjoying exactly the same level of real income (defined in terms of the same utility level) as in the initial situation. The amount of income we have taken from her can be measured on the y axis and is equivalent (in units of Y) to 14. The sum 14 is, therefore, the price-compensating variation and is equal to $P_1 13 P_2$ in part (a) of the figure.

However, within this analysis there is yet another concept of consumer surplus. Suppose we ask the question, How much would an individual require to make her as well off as if she experienced a particularly favourable change? Suppose we ask not, How much would an individual pay for a price fall from P_1 to P_2? but rather, How much would we have to give her to make her as well off as if a price fall did occur? If a price fall was proposed and did not in fact take place, how much would we have to give the individual to her as well off *as if* the price fall had taken place? In Fig. 2.3, it is clear that, if the price had fallen, the individual would be on a higher level of real income. The relevant income-compensated demand curve would be C_2 and the relevant starting-point would be point 8 and q^2 (i.e. on indifference curve I_2). In part (b) of the diagram, the amount of money that would have to be given to make the individual as well off as if the price had fallen is 16. The budget line 6–11 (drawn parallel to 12) has been shifted until it is tangential to I_2 at 13 determining q^4; the real income of the individual is now equal to that which can be achieved when the budget line is 13 (again defined in utility terms), even though relative prices are still those shown by 12. In part (a) of the diagram, the amount of money that would have to be given to the individual to make her as well off is now determined by reference to the line C_2.

The sum of money in question is $P_1 42 P_2$. This measure of consumer surplus (16 in (b) or $P_1 42 P_2$ in (a)) is referred to as the *price-equivalent variation*. The price-compensating variation is not equal to the price-equivalent variation in this example. The maximum sum of money that an individual would give up (holding her real income constant) to experience a fall in the price of good X is typically less than the amount of money that she would require to make her as well off as if the price of a normal good X had fallen by the same amount. In Fig. 2.3, $14 < 16$ in (b) and $P_1 13 P_2 < P_1 42 P_2$ in (a). The reason is clear. The reference position has altered. The price-compensating variation refers to the amount of money the individual would give up when her starting-point is indifference curve I_1; the price-equivalent variation starts on the assumption that the individual is at indifference curve I_2, i.e. that she is entitled to the price fall.[2]

Hicks also drew attention to another interpretation of consumer surplus. This assumes that the individual is constrained to consume the quantity of the good chosen by reference to the Marshallian demand curve. If there was this additional constraint, the amount that she would be willing to pay for the price change would alter. In Fig. 2.3(a), it is clear that, if the individual had to pay as much as she was prepared to pay, then she would stop consuming the good at quantity q^3. With reference to the Marshallian demand curve, she purchases q^2 as she has experienced a positive income effect. If she had to consume q^2, i.e. beyond the level she would choose when paying the maximum for the price change, the estimate of consumer surplus would need to be adjusted accordingly. It would be $P_1 13 P_2$ minus 325 (or vertical distance 87 in part (b) of the diagram). This is the *quantity-compensating variation*. Similarly, the *quantity-equivalent*

---

[2] The circumstances in which the income-compensated demand curve and the Marshallian demand curve coincide have been the cause of confusion. Figure 2.1n illustrates the condition that, if the income effect of a price change is zero, then Marshall's measure of consumer surplus will equal that of a compensated demand curve. Suppose the budget constraint is such that, with price P_{x1}, the utility-maximizing individual achieves point 1 on I_0. Then this picks out point 4 on the demand curve in part (b) of the figure. If P_{x1} falls to P_{x2}, then point 2 on I_1 is achieved and a demand curve incorporating a substitution and income effect (i.e. the whole of the price effect) would pick up point 5 on D in part (b). Now consider making a compensating variation in income, allowing the individual to attain her initial utility level I_0 at the new price ratio. Point 3 represents this exercise and also picks up point 5 on the demand curve D. That is, there is no difference between the Marshallian and the income-compensated demand curve and associated consumer surplus measures in these circumstances. In short, the worry about differences between which demand curve to use arises when income effects are thought to be significant.

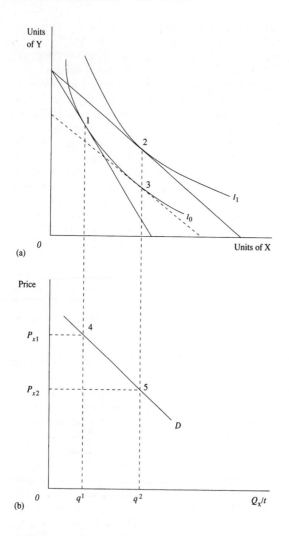

Figure 2.1n The equivalence of the Marshallian and income-compensated demand curve.

variation is the amount that the individual requires to make her as well off as if the price were P_2 and she were constrained to consume that quantity which she would consume if the price were P_1 (i.e. Oq^1). The quantity-equivalent variation in Fig. 2.3(a) is $P_1 42 P_2$ plus triangle 164 (i.e. vertical distance 9 10 in part (b)). These quantity constraints are artificial, and in this text it will prove sufficient to focus on the price-compensating variation and the price-equivalent variation (often simply referred to as 'compensating variation' and 'equivalent variation' hereafter).

The concept of consumer surplus is applied in public finance analysis—in both traditional public finance theory and public choice theory. However,

I.M.D. Little (1957) has referred to it as no more than 'a totally useless theoretical toy' (p. 180) and certainly there are problems when using the concept.

1. The analysis as described in Fig. 2.3(a) is a partial equilibrium analysis; it supposes that, when the price of good X changes, all other prices in the economy remain constant.

2. The implicit objective that consumer surplus 'should' be maximized presupposes that price is set equal to marginal cost everywhere else in the economy. In the absence of this condition the second-best theory may be relevant. The simple fact is that, in one market, setting price equal to marginal cost does not mean that welfare has been increased, even if consumer surplus has increased in that market because the second-best theorem requires optimum deviations from marginal cost pricing (see chapter 1).

3. Consumer surplus is not visible, and it is argued that there is no way of knowing, after any economic change, whether it has actually been increased, let alone maximized (see also Littlechild 1978).

These reservations (particularly the first two) must be borne in mind when considering the use of consumer surplus to assess changes in welfare. In the case of the third reservation, there is little recourse but to have confidence that, if estimated correctly, consumer surplus measures are relevant. They are as useful as the procedure by which they are estimated. With all these qualifications in mind, therefore, consumer surplus can prove of value for the following reasons.

1. It enables us to test for the *total* conditions of welfare maximization (i.e. to maximize consumer surplus) and, thereby, adds another dimension to the Pareto-*marginal* equivalences (discussed in chapter 1).

2. For goods that are indivisible in consumption, the rule enables us to determine whether or not the good should be provided. In this case there may be no possibility to adjust at the margin, and the conditions that focus on total welfare may be more relevant in assessing whether the good should be provided or not.

3. In certain cases, consumer surplus may underline the possibilities that the benefits that arise from provision of the good are worthwhile even though, following the marginal equivalence conditions, there appears to be a loss in actually providing the good. For example, when there are economies of scale in production, marginal cost may be lower

than average cost, so that a rule that led to prices equalling marginal cost would result in losses. (See the example discussed in chapter 5.)

4. Although described as 'a theoretical toy', consumer surplus is a vital ingredient in estimating the benefits of government expenditure in cost–benefit analysis (see chapter 6). Moreover, in chapter 7 consumer surplus is seen to be at the heart of estimates of the welfare costs of taxation.

5. In so far as consumer surplus measures the amount people would give up either to have or not to have a proposed change, it proves a basis for a (qualified) interpersonal comparison of welfare, which can become necessary when deciding whether public policies 'should' be accepted. Of course, in this respect all the value judgements outlined in chapter 1 are relevant. Attention is now focused on the topic of welfare criteria.

2.3 Welfare criteria: Pareto improvement and potential Pareto improvement as a guide to the acceptability of policy

While consumer surplus is a means by which welfare can be estimated, it will be obvious that, up to this point, we have focused on one 'representative' individual. Can the concept be employed to compare the welfare effects of particular changes between individuals? It is this comparison that the Pareto criterion explicitly avoids. A Pareto improvement occurs when at least one individual is made better off and no individual is made worse off. If the enactment of a policy achieves such an outcome, then there is no need to estimate just how much better off the change has made the individual.

The problem with the Pareto criterion is that, at any moment of time, there are few policies on a government's agenda which would make no one individual worse off. Awareness of this limitation led economists to propose alternative welfare criteria, and these explicitly employ consumer surplus and the notion of 'willingness to pay'. In this section we outline alternative welfare criteria and consider their deficiencies. Following Baumol (1977), we assume that there are two individuals in a community, A and B, and ask what economic changes would be permissible under alternative welfare criteria.

2.3.1 The Pareto criterion

In Fig. 2.4 use is made of utility possibility or feasibility curves (already discussed in chapter 1). The axes of this figure show the utility of individual A and individual B respectively. A policy is proposed which will lead to changes in resource allocation. The present situation is that depicted by point 1. How would individuals A and B fare by comparison with the initial position? If the proposed change were to lead to a new outcome on the utility feasibility curve UF in Fig. 2.4(a), it would be acceptable by reference to the Pareto criterion, provided it led to a position such as 2, 3 or 4. Any new position in the north-east quadrant of point 1 would pass the Pareto criterion, because it makes one individual better off without making any other individual worse off. However, movement to a new point such as 5 or 6 would not pass the Pareto criterion: while such a move would make one of the two individuals better off, it would leave the other person worse off than at the initial position.

2.3.2 The potential Pareto improvement criterion

The strong constraint of the Pareto criterion (that no one be made worse off) led Hicks (1940) and Kaldor (1939) to suggest a broader criterion. It was suggested that, in Fig. 2.4(b), a move from 1 to 5 might be acceptable because with costless redistribution it is always possible for redistribution to occur, so as to move the individual from 5 to 3—and point 3 would pass the Pareto criterion. Point 1 is on an initial utility feasibility curve UF, and the reallocation of resources shifts the community to another utility feasibility curve U^1F^1. Costless redistribution implies that there could be a movement along the utility feasibility curve, e.g. from 5 to 3. The ability to make this redistribution means that the amount by which the gainers' gain exceeds the amount by which the losers lose, and it is on this basis that the policy proposal should be accepted. As such, it is possible *conceptually* for the gainers to compensate the losers and still benefit from the change. It is in this context then that 'willingness to pay' for some economic change (or the compensating variation of the gainers) is compared with 'willingness to accept' to have the change (or the compensating variation of the losers). Note that *actual* compensation is not required—gainers will remain gainers and losers will remain losers. If there was actual compensation then this proposal would satisfy the Pareto criterion.

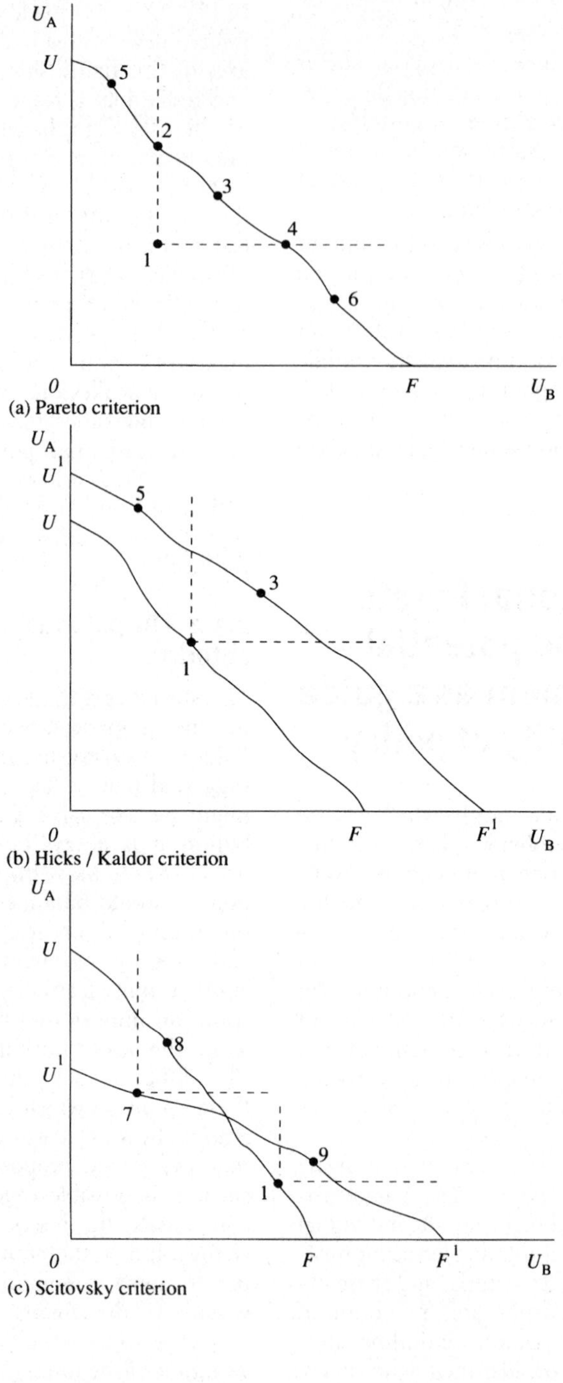

Figure 2.4 Welfare criteria.

2.3.3 The Scitovsky criterion

One of the problems with the Hicks/Kaldor criterion arises when the utility feasibility curves intersect. Scitovsky (1941) pointed out that, while in Fig. 2.4(c) the move from 1 to 7 passes the Hicks/Kaldor test (because with costless redistribution it is possible to move from 7 to a point such as 9—and 9 is a Pareto improvement by comparison with 1), it is also the case that the move back from 7 to 1 passes the same criterion, because at 1, if there were costless redistribution, it would be possible to move to a position such as 8—and 8 is a Pareto improvement by reference to 7. In response to this problem, he proposed the 'doubled-edged criterion', i.e. that any move from a position should pass the Hicks/Kaldor test, but that any move back from the new position to the initial point should fail the Hicks/Kaldor criterion. In Fig. 2.4(b) the move from 1 to 5 would pass the double-edged criterion, whereas in Fig. 2.4(c) the move from 1 to 7 would fail this criterion.

This discussion by no means exhausts the alternatives that have emerged in the literature on welfare criteria. (For a more comprehensive treatment, see Nath 1969.) In this text reference will generally be made to the potential Pareto improvement criterion, though it will be made in recognition of the Scitovsky criticism (e.g. see chapter 6).

2.4 Externalities: why are they a problem?

An externality is said to be present when the utility of an individual depends not only on the goods and services the individual purchases and consumes but also on the activity of some other individual. Therefore, in the following utility function, individual A's welfare depends upon a range of goods and services which she consumes $(x_1, x_2, x_3, \ldots, x_n)$, as well as on some activity, y^1, carried out by another individual B. This activity could be anything; individual B may be smoking cigarettes, creating litter, playing his radio too loudly. The activity may increase the welfare of individual A (an external economy or positive externality) or may reduce the welfare of individual A (an external diseconomy or negative externality):

$$(2.1) \qquad U^A = U^A(x_1, x_2, x_3, \ldots, x_n, y^1)$$

A distinguishing feature of an externality, therefore, is that it is an *interdependence* between one individual and another. Also, however, and most important, *it is an interdependency that occurs outside of the price mechanism*; i.e. it has not been compensated for, or, in the jargon, it is 'uninternalized'. Within the economy anything that one individual does may at the margin have some effect on others (Mishan 1988). For example, if individuals switched from consumption of butter to consumption of margarine they would, other things equal, increase the price of margarine and potentially reduce the welfare of existing consumers of margarine. The important factor here is that all of this operates via the price mechanism. If, in the above example, individual A suffers from the smoking of cigarettes by individual B, this is an interdependency that does not work through the price mechanism. If individual A has no control over the decision of individual B, as far as smoking is concerned, she then suffers an external diseconomy. If individual A persuades (by negotiation, or bribes or the offer of payment) individual B to alter his consumption of cigarettes, then this activity will be brought into the price mechanism. The externality would be 'internalized'.

While an externality has been described as an interdependence between the consumption of one individual and that of another, there is no reason to suppose that it occurs only between consumers. Externalities exist in the economy between consumer and consumer, producer and producer, producer and employee, producer and neighbour. They may be reciprocal or unidirectional. They may be marginal $(\partial U^A / \partial y^1 \neq 0)$ or infra-marginal $(\partial U^A / \partial y^1 = 0)$. For example, if there were pollution in a lake, individuals would find that they could not swim in the lake—the externality is marginal. However, the lake could still be polluted up to a certain higher level before boating was affected—the externality to this level is infra-marginal. A taxonomy of externalities is explored in chapter 6.

Here, we select an example based on the externality that emerges from producer to consumer in order to illustrate the problems that arise. One such problem is that markets, even perfectly competitive ones, no longer guarantee that a Pareto-optimal solution emerges. Other problems follow in terms of the question of how best to deal with this form of market failure.

Assume that, in the production of a unit of steel, a producer incurs private costs (such as wages and interest payments paid for factors of production). In the production process, however, the producer also creates costs to nearby individuals in terms of noise and air pollution of the environment. The producer

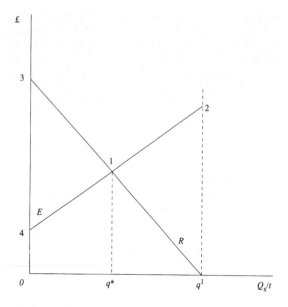

Figure 2.5 Internalizing an external diseconomy.

sells a unit of steel and receives revenue as a consequence. In Fig. 2.5, the line R represents the incremental net revenue (i.e. marginal profit) that is earned by the producer as a result of producing and selling additional units of steel. It is clear that a profit-maximizing producer would continue to engage in this activity up to the point at which there is no further additional profit, i.e. output q^1 where $R = 0$. However, in the production process, the external costs (noise, etc.) of the activity are such that neighbours would offer compensation to the producer to reduce her production. The line E in Fig. 2.5 measures the maximum sum that neighbours would pay in order to induce the producer to reduce successively, by one additional unit, her production of steel. (Note that, even when there is no output, the existence of the plant that produces the steel still creates negative spill-over effects distance $O4$; e.g. it depreciates the scenic value of the environment.)

These sums are the maximum the neighbours can pay without reducing their welfare. They are, of course, a measure of the compensating variation—the maximum sum that individuals would pay to achieve a particular welfare-enhancing change. If the producer produces Oq^1 and the externality continues, it is clear that the market will not produce an outcome that is Pareto-optimal. At q^1, the amount that some individuals in the economy would offer to reduce the output by one unit outweighs the value of that marginal unit of output to the rest of the economy.

If neighbouring individuals were to offer the maximum sum (q^*12q^1) to the producer to reduce her output to q^*, the producer would gain triangle $12q^1$. If she were offered only q^*1q^1 then her neighbours would gain triangle $12q^1$. Certainly, it is fair to say that, as long as the externality exists, there are gains from trade equal to triangle $12q^1$ which can be divided between both parties. In this way, following Buchanan and Stubblebine (1962), we can refer to the externality as being 'Pareto-relevant'. If the externality is 'internalized', at least one person could be made better off without the other person being made worse off.

While the externality exists, it is obvious that markets will not maximize welfare. Following Coase (1960), however, is it reasonable to think that this problem will persist? If the amount that losers suffer exceeds the net gains of the producer, is it not likely that the producer will accept some compensation from the neighbours to reduce the activity in question? In the diagram this looks possible everywhere up to output q^*. At this point, the losers could not offer sufficient to the producer to make her reduce output by one further unit.

But why *should* those who suffer have to pay the person who creates the diseconomy? This is a normative question. Moreover, is there a danger that this will set up 'blackmail' incentives? Perhaps we should start from a set of property rights, whereby the producer has to compensate her neighbours in order to get their permission for her to set up operations. It is evident that they could be persuaded to accept an output level as high as q^*, because up to this point the producer can offer more to increase output by one successive unit than the losers require in order to put up with the external costs. The producer would offer, at most, area $O31q^*$ and the neighbours would require, at least, $O41q^*$. Again, such compensation can prove successful and again, if bargaining occurs over the marginal unit, output will be q^*. Either way, it would appear that the parties involved can rectify the problem, and, as far as resource allocation (efficiency) is concerned, it does not seem to matter who compensates whom. It matters, of course, as far as the distribution of income is concerned, but in this example the allocation of resources is uniquely determined irrespective of who is legally entitled to compensation.[3] If bargaining takes place, the externality will be 'internalized' and this will satisfy the criterion of Pareto improvement. But will such a process occur? Moreover, if such a

---

[3] It is quite easy to demonstrate that the allocation of resources is unique only if there are no income effects associated with the allocation of property rights (see Mishan 1981).

process does occur, will it prove sufficient to meet the problem of externalities?

The bargaining response to the problem of externalities is, of course, quite general. Where there is an external diseconomy, the output of the producer is 'too large' and those affected would attempt to offer compensation to secure a reduction of the activity in question. Where there is an external economy, output of the good would be 'too small' and compensation would be offered to increase the activity. Surely, if all parties perceive gains from trade, such transactions will take place on a voluntary basis—but do they? Take the following example as a case in point.

In the theoretical literature on externalities, Meade (1952) uses an example of the spillover that exists between apple growers and honey-producing bee-keepers. Meade refers to the 'case of an unpaid factor, because the situation is due simply and solely to the fact that the apple farmer cannot charge the beekeeper for the bees' food,...' (p. 57). The beekeepers, in this way, provide a positive external effect for apple growers. However, there is clearly another way of telling the story; i.e. the externality need not be unidirectional. Bees also create a positive external effect for apple growers in pollinating apples. If bees pollinate apple blossoms and this externality does not figure in the calculations of beekeepers, there is likely to be under-investment in beekeeping. Which of these effects is most relevant is an empirical issue, but the interesting question is whether, in a market situation, side-payments would emerge between these sets of producers to internalize the spillover.

Cheung (1973) decided to undertake a quite detailed study of this example. In the state of Washington it appeared that there was indeed a long history of both explicit and implicit contractual arrangements, which provided for beekeepers to be compensated for the beneficial contribution made by their bees to the apple crop. As Cheung (1978, p. 61) notes, 'Contrary to what most of us have thought, apple blossoms yield little or no honey.' In the light of this contractual arrangement, we can illustrate this example by assuming that the direction of the external effect is from beekeepers to apple growers (reversing Due and Friedlaender 1973). What outcome would have arisen if the spillover had not been internalized?

Apple and honey production is viewed as dependent on the labour allocation L_a and L_h respectively from the total labour supply constraint $\bar{L} = L_a + L_h$, so that the production functions are

(2.2) $$H = H(L_h)$$

(2.3) $$A = A[L_a, H(L_h)]$$

where the term $H(L_h)$ in the apple production function captures the externality relationship. Constant returns to scale are assumed and the object is to maximize the value of output $(P_a A + P_h H)$, where P_a and P_h are the (constant) price of apples and honey respectively, subject to the production functions and the labour supply constraint. The wage rate is w and the relevant Lagrangean is

(2.4) $$L = P_h[H(L_h)] + P_a A[L_a, H(L_h)] + w(\bar{L} - L_a - L_h)$$

Differentiating the function with respect to the labour inputs and setting equal to zero provides the first-order conditions

(2.5) $$\frac{\partial L}{\partial L_h} = P_h \frac{\partial H}{\partial L_h} + P_a \frac{\partial A}{\partial H} \frac{\partial H}{\partial L_h} - w = 0$$

(2.6) $$\frac{\partial L}{\partial L_a} = P_a \frac{\partial A}{\partial L_a} - w = 0$$

implying that labour should be employed in apple production until

(2.7) $$P_a \frac{\partial A}{\partial L_a} = w$$

(i.e. the value of the marginal product of labour in apple production = the wage rate) and in honey production until

(2.8) $$P_h \frac{\partial H}{\partial L_h} + P_a \frac{\partial A}{\partial H} \frac{\partial H}{\partial L_h} = w$$

The honey producer left alone will equate the value of the marginal product of labour in honey with the market wage, rationally ignoring the positive production externality in the second term of the LHS of (2.8) because she cannot reap the gain the honey production provided elsewhere in apple production. The policy problem then is the mechanism to internalize the externality. However, provided that voluntary negotiation will internalize the externality, there is no public policy issue.

The example provided by Cheung illustrates Coase's theorem in action. Other case studies would obviously prove of value. However, while such a study is supportive for those who look to markets for a solution to externalities, even if such a solution were discovered, this does not mean that private arrangements are necessarily the 'best' means of tackling the externality problem.

Problems with the Coase solution, therefore, remain. For example:

(a) The first problem to note is that inevitably there are *transactions costs* involved. Pigou (1932) points correctly to costs in terms of time and effort required for bargaining. Let T = transactions costs, B = gains from the bargain, G = the 'transactions' costs of a government solution. If $T < B$ a bargain might take place voluntarily. If $T > B$ a bargain would not occur. However, if $T > G < B$ government regulation would be efficient even though a voluntary solution would not occur.

Looking simply at the transactions costs T, the presence of large lump-sum transaction costs means that a discrete decision (either allowing or banning) the activity may be the answer, with the relevant question being whether welfare is higher with or without the activity. This depends, in Fig. 2.6, on whether triangle 431 exceeds $12q_1$ (see Mishan 1981).

(b) A second problem is that bargaining will never proceed if a *large number of individuals* is involved. If the pollution problem were experienced by a large number of neighbours then each may prefer to sit quietly and hope that the others will offer enough compensation to produce a less polluted atmosphere. In this way, each may seek to 'free-ride' (a problem of which we say more in chapter 3). Clearly, if all behave in this way, the process of negotiation will not get off the ground. ('Class' legal actions may help on this point.)

(c) Bargaining between producers and those affected by the externality may not lead to an optimum outcome if there is *imperfect competition*. For bargaining to lead to a social optimum (as described) it is necessary that there is a *perfectly competitive market*. In Fig. 2.5 bargaining between the two parties meant that marginal external costs E were made equal to R, the marginal profit (incremental net revenue of the producer). In perfect competition marginal profit (or marginal net revenue), i.e. R, is the difference between marginal private cost and the price received. Therefore, in Fig. 2.5 when R is to set equal to E this is the same as saying that $P - MPC$ is set equal to E or, as $MPC + E$ is marginal social cost, that P is equal to MSC.

In Fig. 2.6 the demand for a product is shown by D and marginal cost by MPC. If there is an external diseconomy and the marginal external cost is E, the output in a perfectly competitive market will be Oq_c i.e. where price (P_1) equals marginal cost at point 1. The optimum output is Oq^*, i.e. where price (P_2) equals marginal social cost ($MPC + E$) at point 2. If, by negotiation, those who suffered the cost are able to internalize the costs into the decision calculus of the producer, the producer is prepared to reduce output from Oq_c (at point 1). If the compensation offered is E per unit for a reduction in output then at Oq_c this is

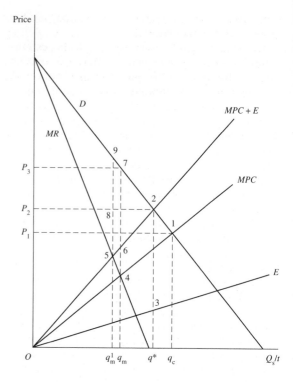

Figure 2.6 Coasian solutions.

greater than $P - MPC$ (The incremental net revenue received). As $P - MPC$ is zero at q_c it is clear that output will be reduced until point 2 is reached. At point 3, E is $q^*3(= P_2)$ minus MPC. In other words P_2 is equal to $MPC + E$, i.e. P_2 is equal to MSC and the social optimum is at output Oq^*.

Now relax the assumption of perfect competition output. Assume the good is produced by a monopoly so that output is where marginal revenue (MR) is set equal to marginal private costs (MPC) at point 4. Now Coasian negotiation appears to make things worse (Buchanan 1969; Pearce and Turner 1990). If the good were produced by a monopolist there is already under-provision at output Oq_m. Negotiation between the producer and those affected by the externality reduces output further. After negotiation, output would be at Oq_m^1 which is even further from the optimum output Oq^*. At point 5 $MR - MPC$ is set equal to E, i.e. marginal profit (or net marginal revenue) is set equal to the external costs as the Coasian solution would suggest. However, the output (Oq_m^1) is one which reduces welfare (the so-called dead-weight loss has increased from triangle 267 to triangle 259). Coasian negotiation only worsens the problem of 'under production'.

Whether such a criticism is fair is questionable, Buchanan (1969) suggests that the 'Coasian' solution requires that consumers of the good that is produced are also involved in negotiations. Their interests have not been fully incorporated. Buchanan (1969, pp. 176–7) notes that 'ignoring the costs of organization, the buyers of the monopolist's product could bribe the monopolist to increase output'. Unless some allowance is made for market imperfection the Coasian solution will not achieve the social optimum. However, if Buchanan's solution were introduced, the transactions costs associated with mobilizing consumers and increasing negotiations from two-way to three-way discussion can not be ignored.

(d) Following on from this, it is important that there are 'well behaved' marginal external cost and marginal profit functions if bargaining between the producer and those affected by the external cost is to achieve a social optimum. If, in Fig. 2.5, the externality was such that external costs fell as output increased and the marginal externality cost curve (E) cut the incremental marginal profit curve (R) from above (rather than from below) the outcome would be unstable. It would

now be the case that, to the right of the intersection point producers can compensate those affected to accept increases in output and to the left of E sufferers can compensate polluters back to a zero output. (For further discussion on non-convexity, see Baumol and Oates 1988 and Pearce and Turner 1990.)

(e) It is not necessarily the case that negotiation will produce a Pareto improvement if both parties do not have *access to all the available knowledge*. As Davis and Kamien (1971) point out, there may be situations of asymmetric information so that one side may have rather more information than the other. This may lead to cheating or blackmail. For example, in the above case, if the neighbours did not know the producer's profit function, the producer may threaten to produce a greater output level than q_1 unless the neighbours offer him a larger sum in compensation. In Fig. 2.7 for example, it is possible that the producer may threaten to produce an output level of Oq_2 and be in a position to ask for as much as area $q_1 25 q_2$ extra to reduce his output to Oq^*. If individuals in the neighbourhood knew his cost and revenue functions, they would realize that the producer would make losses on

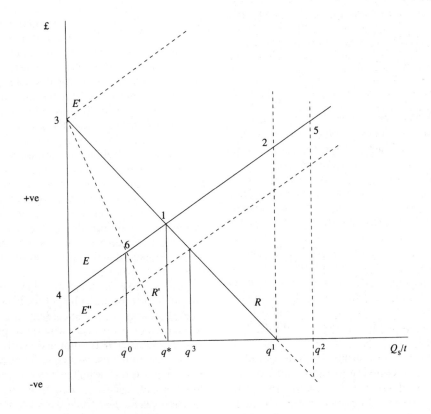

Figure 2.7 Public sector responses to externalities.

the additional output $q_2 - q_1$ (i.e. the net incremental profit line has moved into the negative section of the diagram). In the absence of this information, individuals in the neighbourhood may be blackmailed into offering the additional compensation to the producer. Wellisz (1964) offers another example of this problem of cheating which emerges as bargaining occurs over more than the marginal unit.

(f) In the example above, in order to attempt to offset the free rider problem, property rights would have to be granted to each individual neighbour as to a quantum of noise-free, pollution free air. As Mishan (1988) points out, it is difficult, if not impossible, to do this. Even if it could be done, there would be no market perfectly functioning in pollution-free air as each individual would have property rights to a specific defined quantum. Each individual would then have a monopoly position.

(g) It is also necessary that bargaining parties can be identified. For example, set the Coase theorem in an inter-temporal context. Many pollutants are long lived. They stay in the environment and the people who will be affected may not yet be born. How then can negotiation occur? As another example, consider the difficulties of identifying responsibility. Suppose farmers use chemicals which ultimately pollute streams. Who is culpable? The manufacturers of chemicals, the farmers who use the chemicals or the government which permits this? If the law is such that it accords with the 'pollutor pays principle' (i.e. that those creating the external diseconomy are liable), who, in this example, is liable?

(h) The Coase theorem may operate with respect to one externality provided that there is not an additional externality in operation. Aivazian and Callen (1981) provide an example of firms A and B which produce smoke that affects a nearby laundry. They attempt to demonstrate that the solution from negotiation will not be efficient but Mueller (1979, p. 33) shows that this is because of the presence of another externality (between firms A and B). Mueller generalizes the Coase theorem to state: 'the elimination of each externality is independent of the assignment of property right so long as there is separate liability for each externality, bargaining on one externality is independent of bargaining on all others and the zero transactions cost assumption holds.'

All of these problems indicate that a market solution may not be readily forthcoming and that if one occurred it would involve transaction costs. The list of transaction problems (by no means exhaustive) casts some doubt on the proposition that the market can adequately resolve the problem of externalities. However, if government takes a direct interventionist role (beyond simply determining property rights and which party should expect compensation), it becomes clear that transaction costs of a different nature arise.

2.5 Solutions to problems of externality: the role of the public sector and the importance of transactions costs

In principle, a solution to the externality as illustrated in Fig. 2.7 can be achieved as a result of government intervention. Several examples can be given here.

One mechanism would be the use of a *tax* arrangement which is designed to bring the external costs to the attention of the decision-maker. In Fig. 2.7, a tax on output could be devised which reduced the incremental net revenue of the producer, thereby drawing R inward to R'. The producer would now respond by producing the socially correct output q^*. It should be noted, however, that Buchanan and Stubblebine (1962) question whether such a tax, imposed only on the producer, is a satisfactory solution. If the tax were placed only on the producer, the outcome would be not q^* but q^0, because those affected by the externality are able to offer area $16q^0q^*$ to reduce output to q^0 and the producer requires only triangle q^06q^*. Buchanan and Stubblebine argue that both parties should be taxed, in order to ensure that the output level is not pushed lower than q^*. Mishan (1988) disputes this argument, claiming that a tax solution is required in the first place only to the extent that such voluntary transactions do not take place. If they do not take place before the government intervenes, then it is hardly likely that they will do so after a tax has been levied on the producer.

An alternative public sector policy is to *regulate* the output of the producer. Output could be regulated to q^*, or standards of noise or effluent emission could be set such that the producer would not produce more than q^*. Note that this is not necessarily a charter for the ecologist and a 'blank cheque' for an all-out 'Green Party'. There is no reason to strive for a pollution-free environment. Such an outcome would require that the producer be *prohibited* from production. Yet, as described, with marginal adjustment possible, there is no cause to stop the activity in question altogether. It is necessary simply to bring it under control. Individuals value the output of the producer. (We may not wish to live without motorcars, even though we may wish to regulate their use.) There is, therefore, an 'optimal' level of pollution and this may well exceed zero. Only if the E curve is as high as E' in Fig. 2.7 will prohibition be the desired response.

Another public sector approach might be to focus more closely on the external costs E. For example, *subsidies* could be offered to people living nearby to help them to move further away from the area. In this way, the social costs E would be reduced. This would reduce the curve E in Fig. 2.7 (to E'') and thereby would increase the output of the good that is regarded as 'optimal' (to Oq^3). Alternatively, subsidies could be offered to the producer to introduce devices that would reduce the output of pollution or muffle the discharge of noise. This would affect the slope of the E curve.

Finally, *unitization* may also provide a solution if the producer and neighbours can somehow be combined into one decision-making unit. The external costs E will be internalized with the net profit curve R to produce a community net profit or 'benefit' curve. Such a 'benefit' curve will be equal to zero at q^*, where R equals E by construction.

Against the potential Pareto improvement criterion, all of these options may be considered. They will be acceptable to the extent that the gainers' gains (the most they would pay for a change) outweigh the losses to the losers (the most that they would require to accept the change). That is the same as saying that the compensating variation of the gainers must exceed the compensating variation of the losers. If this occurs, then the change will be a potential Pareto improvement. However, in any of these public sector responses, it is not impossible that some may be made worse off. For example, in the tax case illustrated, the producer is unlikely to be better off—her profit is reduced by taxes (the area under R is reduced). The important point is that the gainers (her neighbours) are made better off by more than the producer loses and the change passes the Hicks/Kaldor test; i.e. it is a potential Pareto improvement.

It is clear that, just as there are transaction costs in the Coasian solution, there are also significant transaction costs involved in a public sector response. These must also be taken into account. First, if the net gains to gainers do not exceed these transaction costs, then any intervention by government will be called into question. Secondly, if the government does intervene, it should attempt to choose that form of intervention which rectifies the misallocation of resources at minimum transaction costs. For example, if regulation is difficult to monitor and to police, it may prove a more expensive option than taxation and be rejected accordingly.

The transaction costs of government are of a different nature to those of the market solution. They are based on two major types of problem.

First, there is the question of *information*. How does the government know the correct level of output to aim at? One attractive feature of a perfectly functioning market is that it presents considerable information in terms of the prices that it creates. However, if market prices are unacceptable, because of the problem of externalities, how are social costs and social benefits to be estimated? (This question is considered more formally in chapter 6.)

Secondly, there is the problem of *agreement*. How are the various groups involved to reach agreement? In principle, the gainers may outweigh the losers in terms of their impact, but if there is a majority of losers these policies may not be readily enacted, although they pass the potential Pareto improvement criterion. (The costs of coming to agreement and of the political process will be considered further in chapter 4.)

It is very often the nature of the transaction costs that dominates the question as to whether there should be a public sector response and, therefore, how large the public sector should be (see Arrow 1971). The public choice school has highlighted the costs and failings of the political process, and it is hardly surprising that members of this school are generally more disposed to a Coasian solution than to a public sector solution. They emphasize the problems of information and of agreement in the political process. In so doing, readers are warned to think long and hard before advocating a public sector response to market failures such as externalities. After all, it is evident that externalities may be inframarginal, marginal but Pareto-irrelevant, already internalized, and/or may involve prohibitive transaction costs in a government remedy. Pigou (1932) has been associated with a form of analysis that suggests that the identification of market failures generates a case for a public sector role. The public choice school points to failings in the political process which make such an 'automatic' Pigovian response inappropriate.

2.6 Taxes versus regulation

The above discussion has outlined alternative public sector arrangements for dealing with externalities.

Focusing on the problem of external diseconomies, it demonstrated that, if there is to be a public sector solution, then, broadly speaking, there are two candidates: (1) a tax/subsidy mechanism and (2) regulation by quota. In considering this choice, Buchanan and Tullock (1975, p. 139) state that: 'Economists of different political persuasion agree on the superior efficiency of penalty taxes as instruments for controlling external economies....' In this section we examine why such an argument is made and why, if it is true, regulation is used to deal with the problem of external economies.

2.6.1 Taxes versus regulation: an efficiency comparison

If information were costless, and if it were possible to tailor-make taxes and/or regulations, there would still be an alleged advantage to using a tax arrangement rather than a quota. Buchanan and Tullock (1975, p. 141) state quite emphatically: 'Regulation is less desirable on efficiency grounds even in the presence of full information...'. The reason is that the quota would need to be monitored and enforced. However, information is not costless, and governments are seldom able to tailor policies to meet the requirements of the situation in quite the way described above. In

general, therefore, the case against regulation and for penalty taxes appears persuasive.

In the example already discussed it has been demonstrated, with reference to Fig. 2.7, that either a tax (which moved the R curve inward) or regulation of output (at q^*) would resolve the problem of an external diseconomy. However, inasmuch as firms have a different impact on the pollution level, or in so far as the value of the goods they produce are different, the R and E schedules in Fig. 2.7 would differ between firms. The implication of this difference is that there would need to be as many taxes, or regulations, as there were firms creating externalities. When information is costly, there will then be a case for adopting the public policy instrument that reduces information costs and permits firms themselves to respond to a given tax or a given regulation standard.

If either a tax or a regulatory standard is to be applied 'across the board', economists have tended to favour price adjustments rather than regulation. This choice is based on the argument that there is greater leeway for the affected parties to respond in an optimizing manner to the tax constraints. The following two examples are designed to illustrate this proposition.

In the first example (based on Rosen 1988) there are two firms M and N. In Fig. 2.8, MPC refers to the

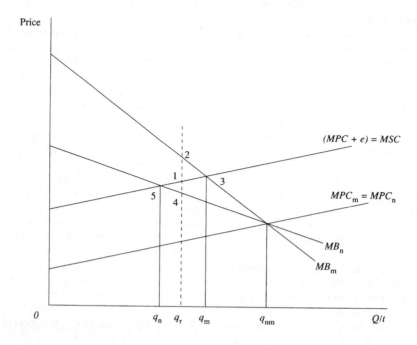

Figure 2.8 Taxes versus regulation.

Source: based on Rosen (1988) *Public Finance*, 2nd edn., Richard Irwin Inc., Homewood, Illinois.

marginal private cost of production (those costs incurred by the producer) and MSC is marginal social cost of production. Marginal social cost is equal to marginal private cost plus the marginal cost of the external diseconomy e (assumed constant) which is created in the production of output by the two goods. The curves MB_m and MB_n are incremental benefit curves of consumers of the two goods, showing the marginal benefit that consumers enjoy as a consequence of additional output of each firm. They are the demand curves for the product of the firms, reflecting the amounts that individuals would be willing to pay for additional units of output. Initially, if both firms are constrained only by their private costs, they will each produce at an output level of q_{nm}. (For the purposes of exposition, this is the same output for each firm, i.e. where $MB = MPC$.)

If a penalty tax (set equal to the value of the external cost created by additional production) is applied, optimal production levels will be achieved by both firms. That is to say, firm M will produce at q_m and firm N will produce at q_n. It is clear that efficiency will not require both firms to reduce output identically. However, if both firms were regulated (so that they complied to an identical production constraint q_r $(= \frac{1}{2}[q_m + q_n])$, it is evident that neither firm would be at an optimum. Firm M would be at an output level at which $MSC < MB$, and firm N would be producing at an output level at which $MSC > MB$. (The welfare loss from the production of firm M at Oq_r is triangle 123 and for firm N it is triangle 145.)

In this simple example, the general problem that has been highlighted is that a given identical regulation standard will affect each producer equally irrespective of any other consideration. Firms are unable to adjust their behaviour in order to optimize within the parameters of their specific cost and demand conditions. The marginal benefit functions for the two producers are not identical, and therefore to cut them equally below a quantity of q_{nm} (to q_r) would be a mistake. (For a demonstration of this principle in the context of a general equilibrium model context, see Jones and Cullis 1988.)

To emphasize this conclusion, a second example (based on Shone 1981) is described in Fig. 2.9. It illustrates the same principle, although here the difference between the two firms is in their capacity to introduce pollution-reducing technology. Here we compare the marginal costs of *reducing* pollution for two firms M and N. One firm (N) may be using equipment that is much older than the other firm. This makes it more costly for N to reduce pollution. Assume that it is desirable to reduce pollution

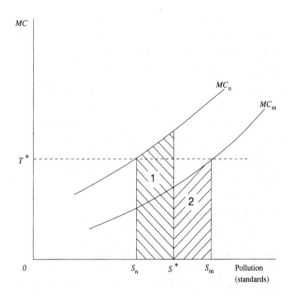

Figure 2.9 Public policy and regulation.

Source: adapted from Shone, R. (1981) *Applications in Intermediate Micro Economics*. Basil Blackwell, Oxford.

by an amount equal, in the Figure, to twice OS^*. Then

either:

A tax of OT^* (reflecting the cost of the spillover) can be set which achieves this reduction in such a way that firms will adjust their own pollution levels. In the example shown, the reduction by firm N (S_n) is less than the reduction by firm M. However, $S_m + S_n = 2(OS^*)$ and the desired overall reduction in pollution has been achieved.

or:

Regulation may be set, by which each firm must reduce pollution by OS^* in order to achieve the total overall reduction in pollution of $2(OS^*)$.

The costs of regulation are obviously higher than the price adjustment option (via a tax solution). With regulation, firm N must reduce pollution by a greater amount than it would had a tax been applied. This implies that additional costs (equal to the shaded area 1) are incurred. As far as M is concerned, there would be no need to reduce pollution to more than S^*, and therefore there is a cost saving of area 2. The additional cost of using the quota is the difference between areas 1 and 2 which is positive. Once again, the additional freedom of response to the price adjustment makes uniform taxation a more efficient fiscal instrument than uniform regulation.

While the above argument appears quite persuasive, it should be noted that it is not being claimed here that tax adjustments are always preferred to regulation in every circumstance. As usual, everything depends on the nature of the problem, and it is quite possible to think of specific circumstances in which regulation would be the better instrument. (For a useful discussion see Hartwick and Olewiler 1986.)[4] However, having made this qualification, it is by no means surprising that Buchanan and Tullock (1975) should indicate that price adjustments are typically more acceptable to economists as an instrument of government policy.

Why, then, in spite of the prescriptions that stem from economic theory, is regulation preferred by pressure groups, politicians, voters and others who are influential in policy-making? Here the comparison between traditional public finance theory (as devised to assist benevolent governments) and public choice theory (as applied to explain political processes) stands proud.

2.6.2 Taxes versus regulation: a public choice rationale

Buchanan and Tullock (1975) deal with this question of why regulation is chosen when externalities are created by producers.

Regulation and producer groups

Assume that an external diseconomy (noise, environmental pollution) is created in the production of a particular product. A regulatory response might be to assign production quotas to firms in the industry concerned. In Fig. 2.10 we illustrate the cost and revenue considerations that are usually presented in any microeconomics text (see chapter 1), in order to consider the decision of firms in a perfectly competitive market. It will come as no surprise to readers to note that, for long-run equilibrium, the firm produces that output at which price P is equal to marginal cost and to average cost. As firms are price-takers, this means that output is set at minimum average cost. In the figure each firm produces Oq^0 units.

How would a firm be affected if regulation were introduced to deal with the problem of external diseconomies? Assume that the firm is constrained by regulation to produce no more than Oq^1 units of the good. If each existing firm is regulated to keep output within this production level, then:

1. At an output of Oq^1, with an unchanged number of firms, price is above marginal cost (in the figure, price is P_1) and each firm has the possibility of earning economic rent.[5]

2. Given that each existing firm enjoys a pecuniary economic rent from the constraint on total output, there is an incentive for firms to enter the industry. With regulation, there is always the temptation for other firms to enter the industry. Irrespective of the condition of perfect competition, there is therefore a presumption that regulation will be more inefficient than price adjustments, because there will be the need for the state to act as a monitoring policeman to stop new firms entering the industry.

3. As the regulation solution means that the administrator faces a policing task, the administrator must ensure that individual firms do not violate the quotas assigned and he or she must somehow

---

[4] There are circumstances that favour regulation, though how likely these may be is a matter for debate. For example, in Fig. 2.2n, it is assumed that the demand for (and therefore the marginal benefit of) providing a particular good (X) is not known with certainty. The policy-makers' best guess is that the net marginal benefit curve (i.e. the difference between marginal benefit and the private costs of producing additional units of the good) is NMB, but in the event this proves an underestimate. (Note that the line NMB is the relevant function for policy-makers wishing to maximize social welfare, but that, in effect, *for our analysis* it is the counterpart to R in the text.) The marginal damage caused by the externality is estimated by the line E. In comparing the suitability of the two instruments (tax policy and regulation), it is necessary to consider the costs that occur if policy-makers underestimate.

Assume that a tax solution is to be applied. Then, if the government expected the net marginal benefit curve to be NMB, a tax of rate Ot would be introduced. If the relevant net marginal benefit function is NMB′, the tax rate was not set high enough. When it is clear that the actual net marginal benefit curve is NMB′, the optimal quantity is Oq^*. The quantity produced with a tax solution of Ot is Oq^1, which exceeds the optimum. Hence if the marginal benefit function turns out to be NMB′, the deadweight losses associated with this *incorrect* tax rate t are estimated as triangle 123.

By comparison, if the government relied upon regulation of Oq^0, then, irrespective of the change in the net marginal benefit function, the output of the firm could not increase. It would stay at the regulated level of Oq^0, which is too little by comparison with the optimum output Oq^*. The welfare losses in this instance comprise the area of triangle 145.

It is clear that, under uncertainty, the government may not be indifferent as to the choice between taxes and regulation. Where the NMB curve is flatter than curve E, the regulation solution would minimize losses and vice versa (see e.g. Hartwick and Olewiler 1986). There is no presumption therefore that, in circumstances when the government is faced with uncertainty as to the position of the NMB curve, regulation is not best. There is moreover no doubt that, in specific cases, regulation may be advised, but these are quite specific cases and quite different from the problem in hand. The more general problem set for consideration in this chapter is that arising from the variation in circumstances of those parties likely to be affected by the tax.

---

[5] Each firm is not in short-run equilibrium and would (if it could) expand output. However, the regulation proscribes this and changes what was a competitive situation into an arrangement more like a cartel.

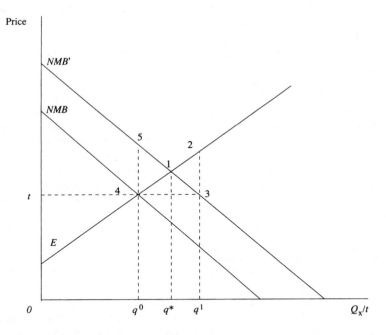

Figure 2.2n Taxes versus regulation in conditions of uncertainty.

Source: based on Hartwick and Olewiler (1986).

prevent new entrants. It may be the case therefore that within the public sector there will be a preference for this solution, as it implies a greater role for administrators and bureaux.

4. As far as the firms are concerned, the administrator enables them to behave as a cartelized industry.

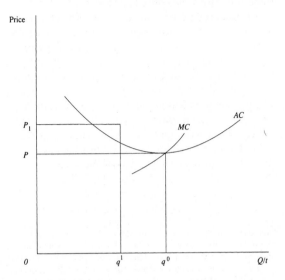

Figure 2.10 A regulated firm.

These costs of cartelization are offloaded to the public sector. The government must prevent new entrants in order to achieve its goal.

By comparison, under the tax solution, producers will find that their costs have increased. As a consequence, it is inevitable that short-run losses will be experienced by firms and, indeed, some existing firms will leave the industry. This exit must continue up to the point where the total supply of the industry has fallen sufficiently so that the price of the good rises. This will then enable remaining firms once again to make a normal profit. Firms will produce at the minimum point of their average cost curve, but this will be augmented by the effect of the tax. Note that, with the tax alternative:

1. There is no economic rent for firms.
2. In the short run firms actually make losses, while in the long run some of the firms will be forced out of business.
3. In the long run remaining firms make only normal profits (i.e. as noted under item 1—no economic rent). The final outcome is one where remaining firms retain normal returns only after a sufficient number of their competitors have shifted to other industries.

4. There is no administrative role created for the bureau. There is, therefore, no reason to expect a preference on the part of bureaux for the tax option.

There is little doubt then that, if external diseconomies are to be dealt with, producer groups and bureaux (administrators) will have a preference for regulation rather than taxation.

Having established that producer groups and bureaux will be more disposed to a regulatory solution, it is important to set this conclusion into a literature that ascribes influence to producer groups. Producer groups are generally more easy to mobilize than consumer groups (Olson 1971). They are smaller in number than consumer groups and they have more clear-cut common vested interests. Indeed, considerable evidence indicates that, when regulation applies, producer groups can generally influence regulatory bodies and 'work the system' to their own advantage (e.g. Stigler 1975). At the same time, empirical evidence suggests that, within regulatory schemes, bureaux in the USA are inclined to increase the extent of their work so as to increase their own importance (Eckert 1973). As is usual in this literature, the consumer is left with very little influence. If the consumer/taxpayer were aware of the efficiency difference between tax and regulation, it might be expected that she would have a preference for taxation; the tax revenue raised by this fiscal instrument could be spent on government programmes to the advantage of all in the community. A lack of such awareness, and a general difficulty of mobilization on the part of consumers, leaves producers and bureaux to influence policy, and their interests lie with regulation. Buchanan and Tullock stress the lack of awareness on the part of the average voter as to the advantage that can be enjoyed from any tax revenue that arises when producers are constrained by tax, rather than regulatory, schemes. As they note,

Those who anticipate benefits from the utilisation of tax revenues, whether from the provision of publicly supplied goods or from the reduction in other tax levies, should prefer the tax alternatives and they should make this preference known in the political process. The political choice setting is one, however, where an intensely interested small pressure group may be more effective than a much larger majority of persons each of whom might expect to secure benefits in the second order of smalls. (Buchanan and Tullock 1975, p. 142)

Tax versus regulation: the distortion by the political process

It is clear that, on the traditional analysis of public finance theory where 'efficiency' (in terms of reference to the potential Pareto improvement criteria) determines the choice of policy, taxes are preferred to regulation. For example, Kay (1990, p. 40) notes that 'it has long been argued that taxation is a more appropriate mechanism for dealing with the consequences of external effects', but adds that, 'whatever the conclusions of economic analysis, policy makers have tended to prefer regulation to the use of fiscal policy'.[6] By an analysis of the political process where the role of interest groups and the consent of voters are crucial, regulation may be preferred to taxation. Taxpayers' awareness of policies plays an important part in this reversal of ranking of the policy instruments. In chapter 4 the implications of voter ignorance are further considered.

2.7 Summary

In this chapter the objective was to provide the concepts and techniques that are utilized in evaluating public finance policy. In both an analysis of government 'efficient' intervention and a critique of the political process (which determines the nature of such intervention), concepts such as consumer surplus have been employed. However, while traditionally the potential Pareto improvement criterion has played an important role in the selection of policies and fiscal instruments, the more recent public choice analysis illustrates the difference between selection based on this criterion and the choice that emerges frequently from the political process.

A number of points can be noted within this chapter. For example, with respect to consumer surplus, some terms need to be carefully defined. The price-compensating variation (CV) is the *maximum* sum that someone will give up to have (and the *minimum* sum she will accept to tolerate) a particular change. The price-equivalent variation (EV) is the *maximum* sum an individual will accept (pay) to make her as well off *as if* the change in question did (did not) occur.

With respect to welfare criteria, the potential Pareto improvement criterion (Hicks/Kaldor test) states that a particular change is acceptable if the amount

---

[6] Kay (1990, p. 40) notes, however, that 'there are clear indications of a change in trend. It is now common to levy charges for industrial pollution, especially of water. The use of tax policy to encourage the introduction of unleaded petrol in several European countries is a striking example of the extension of the principle that the pollutor pays...'. Pearce (1991) considers the advantages and disadvantages of using carbon taxes in responding to the problem of global warming.

that the gainers gain exceeds the amount that the losers lose, i.e. if the CV of the gainers exceeds the CV of the losers. It makes an explicit interpersonal comparison, and it can fall foul of the Scitovsky doubled-edged criterion.

An externality is not simply an interdependence (e.g. between consumer and consumer): it is an interdependence that operates outside the price mechanism. In resolving market failure one approach would be to reduce (increase) those activities that create external diseconomies (economies), as long as the gains of the gainers exceed the losses of the losers. It has been argued that the market mechanism should deal with the problem of externalities, but this is really effective only if property rights are clearly defined and if transaction costs are not prohibitive, i.e. in 'small number' cases. When bargaining resolves the problem of externalities, resource allocation will be unique as long as there are no welfare effects associated with the allocation of property rights.

Government intervention can deal with the problem of externalities by way of a tax/subsidy or a regulatory policy. The case for government intervention, however, depends upon the transaction costs associated with such activity and the costs in leaving the problem to the market mechanism. The choice of fiscal instrument can be made on the basis of an 'efficiency' comparison. Typically, a tax arrangement will prove superior to a regulatory arrangement when dealing with external diseconomies because it facilitates individual marginal adjustment. By contrast, the actual selection of fiscal policies is more readily explained by an analysis of the political process.

References

Aivazian, V. A. and Callen, J. L. (1981) 'The Coase Theorem and the Empty Core,' *Journal of Law and Economics*, **24**, 1, pp. 211–21.

Arrow, K. J. (1971) 'The Organisation of Economic Activity: Issues Pertinent to the Choice of Market versus Nonmarket Allocation', pp. 59–73 in R. H. Haveman and J. Margolis (eds.), *Public Expenditure and Policy Analysis*. Chicago: Markham.

Baumol, W. J. (1977) *Economic Theory and Operations Analysis*, 4th edn. Hemel Hempstead: Prentice-Hall International.

Baumol, W. J. and Oates, W. E. (1988) *The Theory of Environmental Policy* 2nd edn. Cambridge: Cambridge University Press.

Blaug, M. (1968) *Economic Theory in Retrospect*, 2nd edn. London: Heinemann.

Buchanan, J. M. (1969) 'External Diseconomies, Corrective Taxes and Market Structure,' *American Economic Review*, **59**, pp. 174–7.

Buchanan, J. M. and Stubblebine, W. C. (1962) 'Externality', *Economica*, **29**, 116, pp. 371–84.

Buchanan, J. M. and Tullock, G. (1975) 'Polluters' Profits and Political Response: Direct Controls versus Taxes', *American Economic Review*, **65**, 1, pp. 139–47.

Cheung, S. N. S. (1973) 'The Fable of the Bees: An Economic Investigation', *Journal of Law and Economics*, **16**, pp. 11–34.

Cheung, S. N. S. (1978) *The Myth of Social Cost*, Hobart Paper No. 82. London: Institute of Economic Affairs.

Coase, R. H. (1960) 'The Problem of Social Cost', *Journal of Law and Economics*, **3**, pp. 1–44.

Culyer, A. J. (1971) 'A Taxonomy of Demand Curves', *Bulletin of Economic Research*, **23**, 1, pp. 3–23.

Davis, O. A. and Kamien, M. I. (1971) 'Externalities, Information and Alternative Collective Action', pp. 74–95 in R. H. Haveman and J. Margolis (eds.), *Public Expenditure and Policy Analysis*. Chicago: Markham.

Deaton, A. and Muellbauer, J. (1980) *Economics and Consumer Behavior*. Cambridge: Cambridge University Press.

Due, J. F. and Friedlaender, A. F. (1973) *Government Finance*, 5th edn. Homewood, Ill.: Irwin.

Eckert, R. D. (1973) 'On the Incentives of Regulators: The Case of Taxicabs', *Public Choice*, **14**, pp. 90–100.

Friedman, M. (1949). 'The Marshallian Demand Curve', *Journal of Political Economy*, **57**, 6, pp. 463–74.

Hartwick, J. M. and Olewiler, N. D. (1986) *The Economics of Natural Resource Use*. New York: Harper and Row.

Hicks, J. R. (1940) 'The Valuation of Social Income', *Economica*, **7**, 195, pp. 105–24.

Hicks, J. R. (1943) 'The Four Consumer Surpluses', *Review of Economic Studies*, **XI**, 1, pp. 31–41.

Jones, P. R. and Cullis, J. G. (1988) 'Employment of the Disabled: A Rationale for Legislation in the United Kingdom', *International Review of Law and Economics*, **8**, 1, pp. 37–49.

Kaldor, N. (1939) 'Welfare Propositions and Interpersonal Comparisons of Utility', *Economic Journal*, **49**, 195, pp. 549–52.

Kay, J. A. (1990) 'Tax Policy: A Survey', *Economic Journal*, **100**, 399, pp. 18–75.

Little, I. M. D. (1957) *A Critique of Welfare Economics*. Oxford: Oxford University Press. First published in 1950.

Littlechild, S. (1978) 'The Use of Cost–Benefit Analysis: A Reappraisal', pp. 390–409 in M. J. Artis and A. R. Nobay (eds.), *Contemporary Economic Analysis*. London: Croom Helm.

Marshall, A. (1920) *Principles of Economics*, 8th edn. London: Macmillan.

Meade, J. E. (1952) 'External Economies and Diseconomies in a Competitive Situation', *Economic Journal*, **62**, 245, pp. 54–67.

Mishan, E. J. (1981) *Introduction to Normative Economics*. Oxford: Oxford University Press.

Mishan, E. J. (1988) *Cost–Benefit Analysis*, 4th edn. London: George Allen & Unwin.

Mueller, D. C. (1989) *Public Choice II*, Cambridge: Cambridge University Press.

Nath, S. K. (1969) *The Reappraisal of Welfare Economics*. London: Routledge & Kegan Paul.

Olson, M. Jr, (1971) *The Logic of Collective Action*. Cambridge, Mass.: Harvard University Press.

Pearce, D. (1991) 'The Role of Carbon Taxes in Adjusting to Global Warming', *Economic Journal*, **101**, 407, pp. 938–47.

Pearce, D. W. and Turner, R. K. (1990) *Economics of Natural Resources and the Environment*, London: Harvester Wheatsheaf.

Pigou, A. C. (1932) *The Economics of Welfare*, 4th edn. London: Macmillan.

Rosen, H. S. (1988) *Public Finance*, 2nd edn. Homewood, Ill.: Irwin.

Scitovsky, T. (1941) 'A Note on Welfare Propositions in Economics', *Review of Economic Studies*, **9**, pp. 77–88.

Shone, R. (1981) *Applications in Intermediate Microeconomics*. Oxford: Martin Robertson.

Stigler, G. J. (1975) *The Citizen and the State*. Chicago: University of Chicago Press.

Wellisz, S. (1964) 'On External Diseconomies and the Government-assisted Invisible Hand', *Economica*, **31**, 123, pp. 345–62.

3 Public goods

3.1 Introduction

The main objectives of this chapter are threefold. First, the intention is to define the concept of public goods and discuss the conditions necessary for Pareto-optimal provision of public goods. To do this it will be necessary to explain the characteristics of a public good. A second objective is to consider those goods which, though not *pure* public goods, nevertheless bear some of the characteristics of pure public goods. An attempt is made to outline ways of providing a taxonomy of goods according to the degree of publicness that they possess. Finally, the question is raised of the provision of such goods in the market or by government finance and/or production. Will individuals reveal their preferences for such goods so that governments may provide them in a Pareto-optimal way?

These objectives are quite narrowly defined, but throughout the chapter it is our intention to use the analysis of public goods as another illustration of the difference in approach between the 'traditional' public finance scholar and the public choice scholar. In traditional public finance theory the conclusions that arise with respect to the conditions that are required to produce an 'optimal' quantity of the good are virtually identical to those developed by the public choice school. It should be noted that in this chapter the difference between the two stands proud in terms of their respective methodologies. The standard methodology of traditional public finance is in terms of the maximization of a function (e.g. utility function, social welfare function) subject to constraints (e.g. a given state of technology and a fixed supply of factors of production). By this methodology, the conditions for 'efficient' resource allocation are established. In chapter 1 the technique was outlined with respect to an economy that produces private goods, and in section 3.3 below the same

approach is demonstrated with respect to an economy that produces a public good.

Buchanan (1986) is critical of this almost mechanistic approach to economics; by comparison, he stresses a methodology that looks at the process of interaction between individuals in the economy. He focuses upon the processes of exchange, which affect how resources are allocated. Such analysis is described as the study of political economy. 'Efficiency' is determined not so much by those mathematical conditions that emerge from the maxima of a constrained social welfare function, but by the consent of individuals to proposals for the reallocation of resources. Buchanan's approach to the optimal provision of public goods would be that of a *contractarian* solution, whereby individuals are prepared to accept the attendant 'tax' or, rather, 'exchange' arrangements associated with public good provision.

Buchanan's position has been consistent. In 1986 he wrote:

What should economists do? My 1962 as well as my 1982 response to this question was to urge that we excise the maximising paradigm from its dominant place in our tool kit, that we quit defining our discipline, our 'science', in terms of the scarcity constraint, that we change the very definition, indeed the very name of our 'science', that we stop worrying so much about the allocation of resources and efficiency thereof, and, in place of this whole set of ideas, that we commence concentrating on the origins, properties and institutions of *exchange*, broadly considered.... The approach to economics that I have long urged and am urging here was called 'catallactics', the science of exchanges, by some nineteenth century proponents.... This approach to economics, as the subject matter for inquiry, draws, our attention directly to the *process* of exchange, trade and agreement, or contract. (Buchanan 1986, p. 20)

As this chapter proceeds it will become clear that we switch our approach from one that asks; 'what conditions will be required to achieve Pareto optimality?' to one that asks: 'will people voluntarily consent to share the costs of providing a public or collective good?' In this way both traditional and public choice approaches are employed in dealing with the questions outlined. Readers may note this change in approach as the discussion unfolds. However, to emphasize the distinction, a comparison of sections 3.2 (and 3.3) with section 3.5.2 should prove useful.

While our main purpose is to tackle the questions outlined above, once again, a comparison of alternative approaches is possible.

3.2 What are public goods?

A public good (sometimes referred to as a 'collective good' or a 'social good') was defined by Samuelson (1954, p. 387) as one 'which all enjoy in common in the sense that each individual's consumption of such a good leads to no subtraction from any other individual's consumption of that good'. It was emphasized that public goods differ markedly from private goods, which 'can be parcelled out among different individuals' (Samuelson 1954, p. 387). In the case then of a private good, it is possible to refer to total consumption as the sum of each individual's consumption. If X is, as before, a private good (e.g. apples, loaves of bread), and if there are two individuals A and B, then total consumption X_c is the sum of each individual's consumption:

$$(3.1) \qquad X_c = X_a + X_b$$

By contrast, from Samuelson's definition it follows that, for public goods, each individual may consume all of the good. In the case of a public good (G), the total amount consumed is the same for each individual, so that

$$(3.2) \qquad G_c = G_a = G_b$$

An example of such a good is said to be national defence, in the specific sense that, if defence expenditure deters attack on a nation, then each individual resident may enjoy fully the additional security created by such expenditure. It will be possible to say more about examples of public goods when the characteristics they bear have been analysed more thoroughly.

3.2.1 Non-rival consumption

One characteristic implied, or, rather, described, by the definition of public goods is that they are non-rival in consumption; i.e. the consumption of one individual does not reduce the benefits derived by all other individuals. One implication of this characteristic is that, when considering aggregate demand for the good, individuals' demand curves must be added vertically rather than horizontally. Compare the familiar demand and supply diagram for private goods with that for public goods in Fig. 3.1 (where we assume there are no problems with the revelation of demand curves).

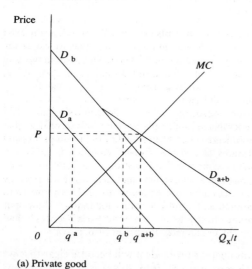

(a) Private good

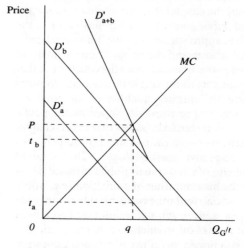

(b) Public good

Figure 3.1 Aggregate demand: public choice and private goods.

In part (a) of the figure D_a and D_b are the demand curves of individuals A and B for a private good X. In order to find the aggregate demand curve D_{a+b} the usual procedure is to add the quantities that each individual demands at each price. For example, at price OP A demands q^a and B demands q^b. The market demand is q^{a+b}. The addition is clearly horizontal, *over* quantity *at* any price. The marginal cost of production is shown by MC. It is therefore possible to detect, in this partial equilibrium context, the Pareto-optimal quantity of the good. If producers price at marginal cost, then, as each individual will consume the good when the marginal benefit from so doing exceeds the price, the 'optimal' quantity to be produced of the private good is q^{a+b}. At this position individuals are willing either to more than cover or (at the margin) just to cover the resource costs of producing an extra unit of this good. From the diagram, it is clear that the condition for optimal provision is

(3.3) $$MC_x = P_x = MB_a = MB_b$$

It has been shown in chapter 1 that, provided there are no other distortions in the economy, this condition is Pareto-optimal (i.e. the quantity provided is an efficient one).

In Fig. 3.1(b), D'_a and D'_b are the demand curves of individuals A and B for a public good G. In order to find the aggregate demand D_{a+b} it is not sensible to talk about the quantity A consumes as distinct from the quantity that B consumes. By definition, each individual can consume the same quantity of the public good. In this case it becomes more appropriate to ask how much individual A would pay for a given quantity of the good and how much individual B would pay for a given quantity of the good, and to add these sums together. At q individual A would pay t_a and individual B would pay t_b for this quantity. The aggregate demand curve is therefore D'_{a+b}; it is established by repeating this addition at every quantity level. It should be clear that addition is now vertical, i.e. addition *over* price *at* any quantity.

In this case, if again the marginal cost curve is shown as MC, the Pareto-optimal conditions can be shown to be satisfied when the sum of the marginal benefits or demands of the two individuals equals the marginal cost. As such, by the *Benefit Principle of Taxation*, individual A would pay a tax of Ot_a and individual B would pay a tax of Ot_b; i.e. each individual would pay a tax equal to the marginal benefit to them of the good financed via the public sector. By comparison with the case above, it is now optimal that

(3.4) $$MC_g = MB_a + MB_b$$

The Benefit Principle of Taxation, therefore, tells us (a) that the total optimal quantity to produce is that amount where the appropriate sum of the marginal benefits of individuals equals the marginal costs of production, and (b) that each individual should be taxed according to the marginal benefit that each derives from the public (or private) good.[1]

The characteristic of non-rivalness in consumption in this way plays an important part in altering the specification of the Pareto-optimal conditions in the case of public goods. However, in order to demonstrate this, it is necessary to draw the demand curves for the individuals. The second characteristic of a public good, non-excludability, throws doubt on the likelihood that it is possible to know anything reliable about the demand curves of the individuals. This characteristic suggests that, if anything, preferences for public (or private) goods are likely to be under-revealed.

3.2.2 Non-excludability

The second characteristic is that consumers cannot (at less than prohibitive cost) be excluded from consumption benefits. If the good is provided, one individual cannot deny another individual consumption of the good. In the case of private goods, markets may operate such that consumption of the good may be contingent upon payment of a 'price' for it. An individual may be denied consumption of the good unless he is able to establish property rights to the good. However, with public goods, if the good has been provided by one individual he has no sanction to prohibit or restrict consumption of the good. Even if the individual has the sanction, there is no ready mechanism by which it can be enforced. The absence of such excludability almost inevitably appears to cause a problem of preference revelation for such goods. If individuals may consume a good without having to pay for it, there may be an incentive to 'keep quiet', in the hope that others will bear the cost of provision; for if they do, and the good is provided, it

---

[1] It is also worth bearing in mind that conditions which emerge from economic theory are sensitive to the assumptions on which the theory is based. It is not the case that a certain set of equilibrium conditions will hold in *all* cases. For example, suppose that there are two individuals A and B consuming a private good X: the change in the marginal costs of production is dMC_x and arises when A and B each demand one more extra unit. Then, even for a private good, $MB_x^a + MB_x^b = dMC_x$. Moreover, suppose that, for a public good, the marginal benefit for individual A and individual B is equal to zero: then it must, by definition, be true that $MB_g^a = MB_g^b = MC_g = 0$ (see Mishan 1981a).

can be enjoyed at no personal cost. This is the strategy of a 'free rider'. Yet it will obviously fail when each individual plays the same strategy. If everyone attempts to free-ride nothing will be provided, and a free ride for anyone becomes impossible.

Buchanan (1968) illustrates the problem by way of a pay-off matrix similar to Table 3.1. Assume that an individual is one of many who would benefit to the extent of £10 if a public good were provided. She is asked to contribute only £5 to its provision. Therefore, if she contributes (and others also contribute), the good may be provided such that in the pay-off matrix her net return is £5. Of course, if others attempt to free-ride and hence do not contribute she will have lost her £5 contribution (as no refund is possible). By contrast, if she attempts to free-ride (refuses to contribute) and others cover the costs of provision, she cannot be excluded and her pay-off is £10. Moreover, if she does not contribute and others also free-ride, she cannot lose anything. Therefore each individual faced with the decision to contribute voluntarily to a public good chooses the best 'pay-off' and attempts to free-ride even though all would gain £5 if everyone contributed. Here is a *rationale for government intervention*. It is arguable that it is in everyone's interests to pay taxes to finance the production of the good—provided, of course, that the taxes are determined appropriately (e.g. as illustrated in Fig. 3.1 (b)). The problem is that the information used in part (b) of the figure, i.e. individuals' demand curves, is not likely to be readily revealed.

Table 3.1 Pay-offs from public goods: voluntary contribution versus free riding

	Outcomes	
Strategies	Others contribute (good provided)	Others free-ride (good not provided)
Individual contributes	(£10 − £5) = £5	−£5
Individual free-rides	£10	£0

The optimal provision of public goods was established in Fig. 3.1 given that the demand curves of individuals could be determined. The issue of free riding is one to which we will return, but, continuing with the assumption that preferences for public goods are known, we now turn to a general equilibrium analysis of the optimum provision of public goods.

3.3 The general model for public goods

The preceding discussion of taxation and the provision of public goods has been presented in a partial equilibrium framework. It is also possible to determine, within a general equilibrium analysis, the conditions that must exist for Pareto optimality to be attained when an economy provides private and public goods. The efficiency conditions emerge within an approach first developed by Samuelson (1955). The discussion and the solution should be compared with the Pareto-optimal conditions for economies that provide only private goods (presented in chapter 1).

In Fig. 3.2 the transformation curve is shown for a particular economy as TT in part (a). This shows the production possibilities of the economy. If the economy operates efficiently, it will be on the boundary of this production frontier. The boundary shows the combinations of the two goods (X—a private good—and G—a public good) that can be produced. It has a slope of MRT_{gx}. The question is, How should resources be allocated? What combination of private and public goods should be produced?

It is inevitable that, when a question is posed in this manner, a normative decision must be reached. In Samuelson's analysis a strong normative decision is made explicitly. Pareto optimality requires that the economy operates at a point at which it is impossible to make one individual better off without making another individual worse off. Samuelson's approach is to decide just how well off one individual is going to be and then to search for that combination of private and public goods which makes the other individuals as well off as possible. In this way, he is interpreting the requirements of Pareto optimality as making any individual as well off as possible, provided that the other individual is made no worse off than some reference level of welfare.

In Fig. 3.2(b) and (c) the indifference curve maps for two individuals A and B are shown. In (b) the indifference curves are shown for individual A and the initial decision is made explicitly to hold A on the indifference curve I_A^2, in this way fixing her level of welfare. Now, by definition, each individual must consume the same amount of the public good. The indifference curve I_A^2 shows the alternative quantities of good X and good G that keep A on the fixed level of welfare. Therefore, when individual A consumes Og of good G, she will also consume $g1$ (in both (a)

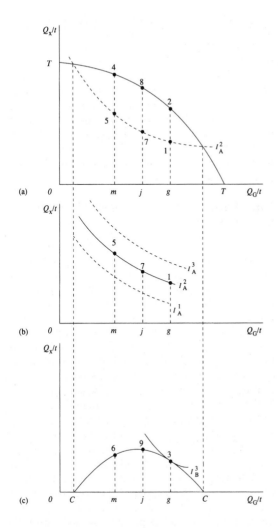

Figure 3.2 Public goods in a general equilibrium model.

and (b)) of the private good in order to remain on the indifference curve I_A^2. However, if this were so, individual B would similarly be able to consume Og of the public good, and the amount of the private good that would be available for him if the economy operated efficiently would be $(g2 - g1)$, which is equal to $g3$ in part (c) of the diagram. Repeating this line of argument makes clear that when, for example, the total amount of the public good is equal to Om, the total amount of the private good produced by an efficient economy would be $m4$. Of this total of private goods, $m5$ (in both (a) and (b)) must be consumed by A if her welfare level is to be kept constant. This, of course, would leave $m6(= m4 - m5)$ available for B.

Repeating this process for every possible output of the public good (e.g. Oj) produces, in part (c), a curve equal to CC. This curve is, in effect, the set of consumption possibilities available to individual B assuming that A is kept on I_A^2. It has been derived by deducting I_A^2 from TT, bearing in mind that, when units of the public good are provided for one individual, they are also provided for the other. The remaining problem is now simply to find that output level for private and public goods which maximizes the welfare of individual B. This, of course, will be shown by the tangency point between I_B^3 and the curve CC. In the example shown, the Pareto-efficient allocation of resources for the economy would be that Og public goods were provided and g2 private goods.

With reference to the tangency at point 3, it is clear that the tangency has been found by deducting (at Og) the MRS_{gx} for individual A from MRT_{gx} and then equating the MRS_{gx} of individual B to the slope of CC (in part (c))—which by definition is ($MRT_{gx} - MRS_{gx}^a$). Obviously, instead of stating the condition as

(3.5) $$MRS_{gx}^b = [MRT_{gx} - MRS_{gx}^a]$$

we can write this more easily as

(3.6) $$\sum_{i=1}^{n} MRS_{gx}^i = MRT_{gx}$$

This condition becomes the 'top-level' condition (see chapter 1) for Pareto optimality in an economy that produces public and private goods.

The approach by Samuelson was highly significant in the development of the theory of public goods. It was not without criticism, however. For example, the approach is obviously *individualistic*, focusing as it does on the marginal rates of substitution of the individuals. However, would individuals' preferences be the same (in terms of the way in which they treated provision in the public sector) as their preferences revealed in choices between goods in the private sector? Colm (1956) offers this criticism as a consideration in determining the optimal provision of public goods. Musgrave and Musgrave (1989) argue that the approach of Samuelson (1955) would be improved if the decision on the correct income distribution could be separated further from the efficiency conditions in the analysis. However this is, in general, not an easy option.

In this connection, it is worth noting that the whole process described above can be notionally repeated for each indifference curve for individual A, so that a utility possibility frontier similar to that in Fig. 1.6 in chapter 1 can be derived in the presence of the public good. All points on such a frontier would meet (by construction) condition (3.6), leaving the vexed question of a social welfare function to solve the equity–income distribution issue.

Even if the equity matter were solved via the establishment of a fair income distribution, the 'free rider' problem remains. Why would preferences of individuals be revealed? Also, at this juncture, it is worth considering that the efficiency conditions involve *different* MRS_{gx} (or MB) for individuals suggesting that no single common price ratio (tax price) is appropriate for all. This increases the problem of preference revelation, for it suggests that discriminatory pricing is appropriate for public goods. (Students may reflect that, for private goods and services, such price discrimination is a feature of monopoly and not competitive markets. However, the distinction between the two scenarios is that with monopoly provision the profit-maximizing output would be $MR_a + MR_b = MC_g$ (not $MB_a + MB_b = MC_g$); i.e. the monopolist would act by reference to marginal *revenues* and not marginal *benefits*.)

These are all points to consider, but at this juncture, having recognized the important contribution of Samuelson, we turn to a very fundamental criticism of the whole theory: i.e. do public goods really exist, or are they just a theoretical construct?

3.4 Pure and impure public goods

One of the criticisms of the concept of public goods was that such goods were not obvious in the real world (Margolis 1954). Where is it possible to perceive goods that perfectly satisfy the non-rivalness definition of Samuelson (1954)? In the provision of law and order (or medical care), the use by individual A of the law courts (or hospitals) subtracts from consumption by individual B if they must now wait. Even defence, in so far as it is associated with protection, may not completely satisfy the description of a public good in the purest sense (Sandler 1977). If armies are employed in the north, will this not detract from protection for communities in the south? Indeed, in the case of another example of public goods quoted by Samuelson (1954)—lighthouses—subsequent research confirmed that these were traditionally associated with provision within the private sector (Coase 1974; Peacock 1979). Market failure was clearly not

such as to preclude lighthouse provision, even if they may have been provided sub-optimally. These observations tend to confine pure public goods to benefits that are of an intangible kind, such as the feeling of security felt by many as a result of deterrence-type defence. Samuelson's position with respect to the question of observability was to emphasize a distinction between *pure* public goods and *pure* private goods (Samuelson 1969); between the extremes there will exist *impure* public goods which may be readily observable, but how can a taxonomy of such goods be established?

3.4.1 Excludability and non-rivalness in consumption

One approach to this question was to focus on the characteristics of public goods, i.e. on non-rivalness in consumption and non-excludability (Head 1962; Peston 1972). In Table 3.2, four categories of goods are identified. Goods in category D are non-rival in consumption and non-excludable: they are pure public goods. Those in category A are rival in consumption and excludable: they are pure private goods. Goods that fall in category B are rival but non-excludable. Common resources may prove an example. Let us assume, in the spirit of the case discussed in chapter 2, that bees from the hives of different beekeepers collect the nectar from a nearby orchard of apples. The blossom is rival: nectar collected for one hive is unavailable to another. Even so, it may be inconceivable to try to deny any particular honeybee access; i.e. the situation is non-excludable (Meade 1952). By contrast, goods in category C are non-rival in consumption but excludable. A toll booth may exclude traffic from roads unless payment is made, yet if the road is not congested one car may utilize it with no loss of benefit even though other cars are also consuming the road service. Similarly, admission to a theatre (circus, swimming pool) has the potential of exclusion, but (below capacity limits) each individual admitted may consume services without subtracting from the benefit of others. Here the market could be applied, but the existence of at least limited non-rivalness indicates that exclusion would cause ineffi-

Table 3.2 A taxonomy of goods

	Excludable	Non-excludable
Rival	A	B
Non-rival	C	D

ciency. (One person could be made better off by the consumption of the good without fully denying consumption to another.)

The usefulness of this technique may be questioned in so far as 'the same "good" may fall into one category on one set of circumstances and into another category on other sets' (Peston 1972, p. 14). Even so, within the different categories it is possible to develop the requirements for efficiency in provision. Perhaps the best example here relates to category C. Buchanan (1965) developed a theory of clubs and established the conditions for optimum output and membership. Clubs are consumption-sharing arrangements providing goods from which consumption can be excluded but for which consumption by one member may be non-rival with consumption by another member (below capacity limits). The theory of clubs will be developed and applied below.

3.4.2 Mixed goods/quasi-public goods

A second approach to the classification of impure public goods focuses on the mix of services that stem from the provision of the good. Suppose for instance that A derives benefits from being inoculated against polio; she creates not only a private benefit but also an external effect in so far as she reduces the chance of infection for all other individuals with whom she comes into contact. The concept of externalities was examined in chapter 2. Here it is clear that the external effect associated with consumption of a private good may itself bear the characteristics of a public good. For example, education may improve an individual's earning potential, but at the same time it may facilitate basic research, creating non-rival and non-excludable knowledge or information which benefits others in the community. Such development, in terms of culture or technology, may then bear public good characteristics. Recognition of the private–public mix means that goods can be viewed as having private benefits as well as external effects which bear the characteristics of public goods. (For a clear distinction between public goods and externalities, see Evans 1970.)

Take for example education. In Fig. 3.3 the demand curve for education is shown as D_p. This is the demand that would be forthcoming, at different prices, in the market for education. It reflects the private benefits that students believe they will enjoy as a result of education. These may be viewed as the 'private return' on education and they depend in part on the income differential that students expect to

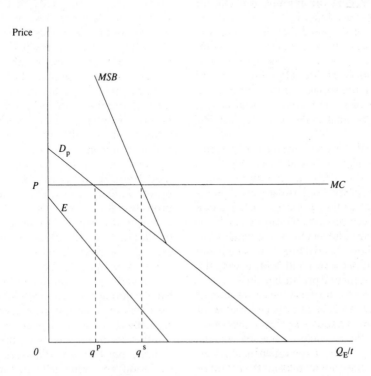

Figure 3.3 Mixed goods: the demand for education.

receive during their working life as a result of education. If, however, there are other benefits (external benefits) contingent upon education, the social benefits from education will differ from the private benefits. The value of external benefits to others in the community is indicated by the line E. This shows what the rest of the community would pay for the various levels of education shown on the x axis. Adding vertically the values of E to the private demand gives the line MSB. This shows that there are positive social benefits from education over and above the private benefits. The external gains that arise from education may include the benefits to others of: (a) the research undertaken at educational establishments; (b) the more cultural environment and the heritage for future generations; (c) the screening device which education provides for the labour market to determine the quality of labour; (d) the improved decision-making of voters and the behaviour of educated citizens. Blaug (1965) has a comprehensive list of factors (many of which he questions) to distinguish the social rate of return on education from the private rate of return. Some of these factors (e.g. cultural environment and heritage) have the characteristic of a public good; that is, they can be consumed by one individual in society without reducing the amount available for consumption by others. Indeed, it is for this very reason that it is often supposed that the market will not properly internalize such factors in the decision-making calculus of individuals. In Fig. 3.3 it is clear that the private demand at price OP is only Oq^p and that this is less than the socially optimal output Oq^s (i.e. the point at which the marginal social benefit MSB of education is equal to the marginal cost MC of education).

This approach to dealing with the blend of privateness and publicness in goods is dealt with by Musgrave (1969). Obviously, it provides an important framework for policy purposes. We have already demonstrated in chapter 2 just how pervasive such external effects can be. To operationalize this approach, however, may prove more difficult. One attempt may be to take the ratio of spillover benefit to private benefit and think of a taxonomy between 1 and 0. Measuring the effect of spillover benefit and private benefit is a problem to be considered in chapter 6, when we look at cost–benefit analysis. It will be clear that estimation of social benefit is not without significant problems. However, in principle, it would be possible to take the ratio of external benefits to private benefits as an indicator of the private–public mix and the extent of publicness.

In a similar vein, Weisbrod (1988) tries to use the manner in which goods are financed as an indication of the public–private split. The more public good effects there are, the less may organizations finance themselves by sales, as there are no direct property rights to goods that can be enjoyed on a non-excludable basis. The more, instead, the organization will rely upon donations, gifts or grants to finance provision. This split may be thought symptomatic of the mix between public good output and private good output, and, in this way, the more that an organization relies upon gifts, grants and donations, the more eligible it may be to subsidy. Weisbrod (1988) argues along these lines in defending the subsidy given to non-profit organizations.

3.4.3 Consumption sharing

Yet another approach to the question of taxonomy was developed by Buchanan (1968). In Fig. 3.4 (drawn on the assumption of a given population and given property rights) a relationship is depicted between the degree of indivisibility and the number of people P consuming the good. At one extreme are purely private goods (category (1)), which are fully divisible between single persons (or single households); at the other extreme are goods that remain fully indivisible over large groups, in the sense that each member of the group may consume the same good. An example offered is mosquito-spraying; the benefits from this service are probably indivisible between individuals in one specific suburb. In essence, the key is the extent to which sharing is possible. Category (2) may refer to fire extinguishers that are shared (indivisible) between a small number of neighbours. Category (4) could represent swimming pools, which are uncongested when used by small numbers. By contrast, item (3) may refer to services such as inoculation against disease, which when experienced by any individual provides an additional degree of protection for everyone else with whom that person comes into contact. Of course, item (5) is a pure public good, an example of which is national defence expenditure which deters aggression.

It may be argued that goods such as (1) 'should' be left to market provision. Goods in category (2) may be left to voluntary arrangements between the individual members of small groups concerned. Category (4) arguably contains goods that are provided by clubs. 'Clubs' are arrangements in the private sector by which goods that are, to a degree, non-rival in consumption are voluntarily provided. Typically, the good is excludable (i.e. there is a membership fee)

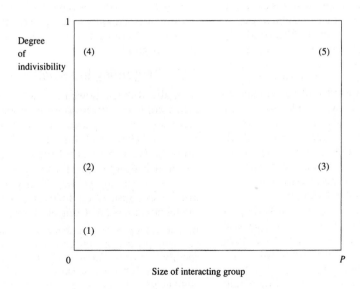

Figure 3.4 Consumption sharing.

Source: Buchanan (1968).

but it is by no means private (i.e. below capacity limits consumption is non-rival). Buchanan (1965) has made an important contribution in the analysis of such goods: he has established efficiency conditions for the provision of such goods via clubs. These will be discussed again in chapter 12, where the analysis is applied to local government expenditure.

In this way discussion of impure public goods enables consideration of the appropriate provision of a range of goods bearing both 'public' and 'private' characteristics. In some instances this has called into question the 'appropriate' role of the public sector. Such goods which are not perfectly public may be better supplied within the market. We turn in the later chapters to consider the 'appropriate' role of the state.

3.5 Free riding and public good provision

It has been argued that public goods will not be optimally provided because individuals will not honestly reveal their preferences. There are at least two issues here. First, will any of the public good be voluntarily provided? Secondly, are there mechanisms that can be applied to bring about an honest revelation of preferences?

In considering the first of these questions, we are dealing very much with the public choice approach to collective good provision, which places far more emphasis on exchange and agreement. It has already been argued in chapter 2 that the Coasian approach to resolving the problem of externalities places greater emphasis on voluntary exchange. Will individuals engage in voluntary exchange to provide a public good?

3.5.1 Voluntary provision of public goods

Johansen (1977, p. 147) notes: 'I do not know of many historical records or other empirical evidence which show convincingly that the problem of correct revelation of preferences has been of any practical significance.' The problem of free riding is one that has been illustrated in the most extreme context in section 3.2, but how reliable is this prediction?

Bohm (1971, 1972) reports that, in an experiment wherein individuals were made to feel that they were members of a large group, they honestly revealed their preferences for which (non-excludable) television programme to watch. Perhaps this was because individuals generally behave honestly, and, perhaps out of a sense of duty, make their preferences known with respect to contributing to a public good. This is so-called 'free revelation'. There is also the 'joint contract hypothesis', which notes that *ex ante* the provision of a public good can be made excludable. If it is clear that unless the cost of provision of the public good is covered *ex ante* there will be no public good, the individual placed in this 'joint contract' context may reveal a preference.

Marwell and Ames (1981), on the basis of game-theoretical experiments, suggest that individuals do not attempt to free-ride. Kim and Walker (1984) are critical of such studies in that the experiments are contaminated by invalidating factors (e.g. in their experiments the public good is not pure; public goods are not discrete; there are misunderstandings and vagueness; the group is sometimes a small group; etc.). When the experimental setting is 'purified', so as to address the free rider issue more clearly, there is more evidence of free riding. However, McCaleb and Wagner (1985) are sceptical. After a review of such studies, they conclude (p. 489): 'we would have expected that choice settings could be designed in which something very close to full free riding would emerge', but 'results from experiments conducted in "purified" settings...still leave us a long way from understanding the social processes through which real world choices are made'.

It may be, then, that economists have placed too great an emphasis on the free rider and that individuals consider broader issues when deciding whether or not to reveal a preference. Here, however, we retain the usual '*Homo economicus*' assumption and continue with the view that individuals are motivated by selfish goals. Even so, Buchanan (1968) has

shown that, in the case both of small groups and impure public goods, some agreement may be forthcoming with respect to the voluntary provision of collective goods.

3.5.2 Bargaining in a small group

It has already been shown in section 3.3 that in general equilibrium the Pareto-optimal conditions for the provision of a public good are that $\sum_{i=1}^{n} MRS_{gx}^i = MRT_{gx}$, and equivalently in partial equilibrium the (vertical) sum of the marginal benefits of individuals should equal the marginal cost.

A somewhat different way of deriving this same rule can be established by following the approach of Buchanan (1968). As Congleton notes,

Buchanan's approach to the analysis of public goods reaches the same conclusion about the optimal level of a public good, but via a different route. As usual, his line of reasoning emphasises the private exchange analogy. To Buchanan, the optimal level of a public good is simply the amount that exhausts all potential gains to trade, given initial endowments and some specification of property rights. (Congleton 1988, p. 144).

It is well worth studying this particular derivation because (a) it confirms the conditions for optimal provision of public goods and (b) it shows that, where bargaining is possible, there are cases in which individuals may agree to the 'tax' conditions required for the provision of public goods.

In Fig. 3.5 the demand curves for a public good for two individuals A and B are shown as D_a and D_b

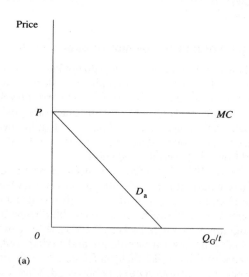

(a)

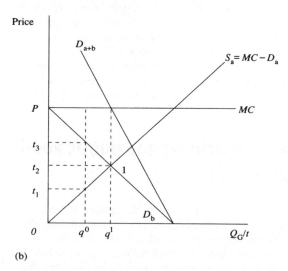

(b)

Figure 3.5 Providing a public good by voluntary co-operation.

(assumed identical for expositional simplicity). To help the exposition, the marginal costs MC of providing a public good are assumed constant. In part (a) the demand curve of individual A represents the most that she would be prepared to pay towards the provision of a public good. As it never covers the marginal costs of providing the good, individual A alone would not consume any of the good. In part (b) the same is seen to be true of individual B; i.e. alone he cannot cover the marginal costs of providing the good.

In part (b) the curve S_a represents the minimum that individual A would require to supply the good; i.e., it is the vertical difference between the demand for the good on the part of individual A and the marginal cost of the good as shown in part (a). In part (b), individual B would be willing to pay Ot_3 per unit of Oq^0 units of the public good, but, at minimum, individual A would require only that B pays Ot_1 per unit in an agreement to provide Oq^0 of the good. There are then clear gains to both from bargaining, and this form of bargaining is possible up to an output of Oq^1. For quantities up to Oq^1 the amounts that both individuals are prepared to pay per unit will cover the total costs involved in providing the good. At this point individual A and individual B will each pay Ot_2 and each will enjoy a consumer surplus as shown by triangle t_2P1.

Since voluntary co-operation is possible up to, but not beyond, output Oq^1, this output level would be one that is optimal against the criterion that individuals must consent to such an arrangement. Bargaining over the question of whether output should be increased by one more unit can lead individuals to output Oq^1 but certainly no further. This output level, it should be noted, is one at which the consumer surplus enjoyed by both individuals is maximized. It is also the point at which, by definition, the sum of the marginal benefits (i.e. the vertical addition of D_a and D_b) is equal to marginal costs.

The quantity of the good Oq^1 accords with the output at which the *sum* of the marginal benefits is equal to the marginal cost. Since it is always possible, up to this point, to find a basis for agreement between individuals by which one individual can be made better off without another being made worse off, increasing the output of the public good to Oq^1 would be a Pareto improvement. It is also a move to which each person would agree. The approach to determining the output and cost-share of a public good is similar, though not identical, in nature to that presented by Erik Lindahl (1919).

3.5.3 The Lindahl–Johansen solution

As long as there are some gains from trade in the provision of public goods, it can be expected that some mechanism might arise to secure some of the gains. In an early contribution, Lindahl (1919) discussed the question of the determination of the optimal provision of public goods and the assignment of tax shares. This approach was revised by Johansen (1963) and is interesting, in that it tackles the question in a bargaining-type context. Two individuals A and B gain utility from a private good X and a public good G whose tax share is h for A and $(1 - h)$ for B. With given total revenue Y divided between A and B as Y_a and Y_b, the budget constraints of the individuals will be

$$(3.7) \qquad Y_a = X_a + hG$$

$$(3.8) \qquad Y_b = X_b + (1 - h)G$$

so that

$$(3.9) \qquad Y = Y_a + Y_b = X_a + X_b + G$$

The conventional price consumption curve can be illustrated as in Fig. 3.6. The price consumption curve for A is derived by varying h from zero to one. As h falls, the equilibrium points (1, 2, 3) suggest the conventional outcome, i.e. that more public good is demanded at a lower tax share. Whereas the original utility function for A and B (illustrated below for A) takes the form

$$(3.10) \qquad U_a = U_a(X_a, G)$$

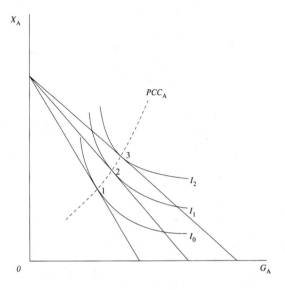

Figure 3.6 The price consumption curve for the private and public good.

$$(3.11) \qquad U_b = U_b(X_b, G)$$

it is convenient in the analysis to express them in terms of h and G, which can be done by rewriting (3.7) and (3.8) as

$$(3.12) \qquad X_a = Y_a - hG$$

$$(3.13) \qquad X_b = Y_b - (1 - h)G$$

so that the utility functions become

$$(3.14) \qquad U_a = U_a(Y_a - hG, G)$$

$$(3.15) \qquad U_b = U_b[Y_b - (1 - h)G, G]$$

This enables a counterpart of Fig. 3.6 to be constructed, with the axes labelled for tax shares h and the public good G (see Fig. 3.7). The slope of A's indifference curve between G and h is the ratio of the marginal utility of G to the marginal utility of h, which can be derived in two steps as follows:

$$(3.16) \qquad MU_a G = \frac{\partial U_a}{\partial G} = -h\frac{\partial U_a}{\partial X_a} + \frac{\partial U_a}{\partial G}$$

$$(3.17) \qquad MU_a h = \frac{\partial U_a}{\partial h} = -G\frac{\partial U_a}{\partial X_a}$$

with

$$\frac{MU_a G}{MU_a h} = MRS_{gh}^A = \frac{\partial U_a/\partial G}{\partial U_a/\partial h} = \frac{h}{G} - \frac{1}{G}\frac{\partial U_a/\partial G}{\partial U_a/\partial X_a}$$

$$(3.18)$$

and equivalently for B:

$$(3.19) \qquad \frac{MU_b G}{MU_b h} = MRS_{gh}^B = \frac{\partial U_b \partial G}{\partial U_b/\partial h}$$
$$= \frac{(1 - h)}{G} - \frac{1}{G}\frac{\partial U_b/\partial G}{\partial U_b/\partial X_b}$$

The tax prices are represented as horizontal lines in Fig. 3.7 because, at each tax share h and $1 - h$, A and B respectively can choose as much of G as maximizes their utility. Again, the shape of the price consumption curves PCC_A and PCC_B reflect that more G is chosen at lower tax shares. Figure 3.7 gives the overall picture. PCC_A and PCC_B are forms of demand curves for G at the different values of h. With h set at h' in Fig. 3.8, A wants G_A and B wants G_B, which are inconsistent quantities. For efficiency and stability, in the sense of being on the contract curve (i.e. C) and both wanting the same quantity, h^* and G^* must be achieved at point 1. That is for an equilibrium point on the contract curve:

$$(3.20) \qquad MRS_{gh}^A = MRS_{gh}^B = 0$$

$$\frac{h}{G} - \frac{1}{G}\frac{\partial U_a/\partial G}{\partial U_a/\partial X_a} = \frac{(1 - h)}{G} - \frac{1}{G}\frac{\partial U_b/\partial G}{\partial U_b/\partial X_b} = 0$$
$$(3.21)$$

which is reduced to

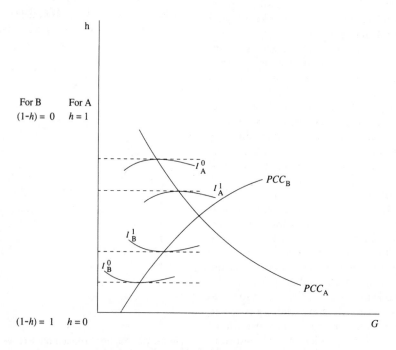

Figure 3.7 Price consumption curve between tax shares and the public good.

(3.22) $$MRS_{gx}^A = h$$

(3.23) $$MRS_{gx}^B = 1 - h$$

and the public goods efficiency condition that[2]

(3.24) $$MRS_{gx}^A + MRS_{gx}^B = 1$$

However, there is no obvious mechanism to effect this. Johansen suggests that it might be possible to agree 'somewhat unsatisfactorily' (p. 350) that B, who desires more G, could offer to increase his own tax share and reduce that of A, resulting in a convergence at point 1. Indeed, in the bargaining context, A and B will bargain to maximize their utility subject to the price consumption curves of each other. In Fig. 3.8 it is clearly advantageous for B to achieve point 2 on I_B^1 rather than 1 on I_B^0. Point 3 is the equivalent of point 2 for individual A. This illustrates the unsatisfactory element. In the bilateral monopoly-type context, Lindahl thought that in the case of dispute the lower of the values preferred by the individuals would dominate, limiting the outcomes to 213 with point 1 being approached only when bargaining was approximately equal. (NB: 52 and 43 are irrelevant because both A and B gain by moving from 5 to 2 and 4 to 3.) However, this itself makes most sense if h is determined before the decision about G, since with both h and G on the bargaining table a point on the contract curve will always be preferable. While the 'gains from trade'

---

[2] This particular result arises because Lindahl employs a linear transformation frontier between G and X.

aspect of public goods provision is well illustrated, Johansen notes that the location of point 1 depends, not surprisingly, on the initial distribution of income between A and B and hence the need for a social welfare function. More critically, the problem of preference revelation is not really solved. A and B have an incentive to minimize their tax shares for each level of provision of the public good and to bias their preferences towards understatement.

3.5.4 The theory of clubs

Goods that are non-rival in consumption but excludable may be provided in the market by consumption-sharing arrangements. As noted above, Buchanan (1965) has introduced a theory of clubs to explain the conditions for efficiency in the provisions of such goods. Sports clubs (swimming associations) or social clubs (e.g. providing theatrical entertainment) provide goods that, below congestion levels, are non-rival in consumption. To determine the optimal quantity of the good to provide and the optimal number of members of the club, it is helpful to adopt the analysis in Fig. 3.9. It should be emphasized that the objective is to consider optimal provision in terms of the welfare of club members.

In part (a) of the figure the curve C_1 shows how the average cost per member of the club falls. The average cost of producing a given quantity of the good will fall as more people join the club and share the costs. Thus, if a swimming pool is provided, the average cost to

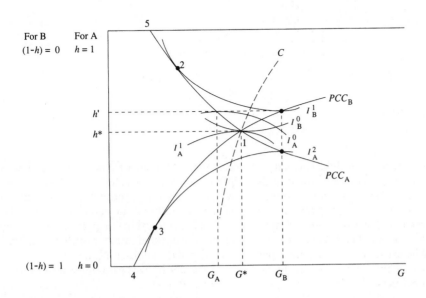

Figure 3.8 The Lindahl-Johansen approach.

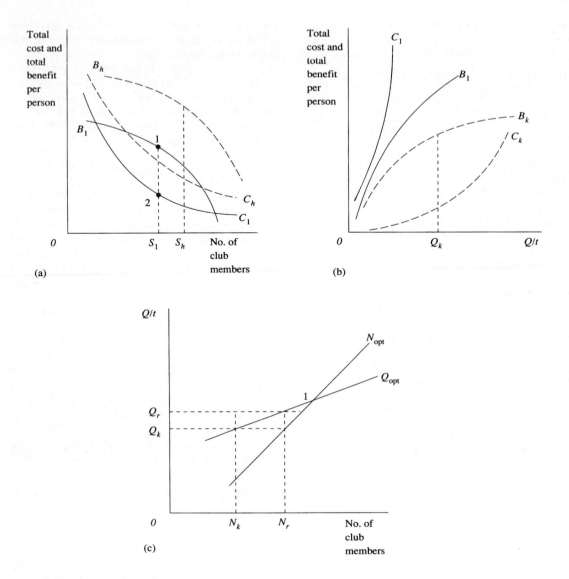

Figure 3.9 Optimum size of clubs.
Source: based on Buchanan (1965).

each member falls as more join the club. The benefit per person for a swimming pool of this dimension is shown to vary as the number of club members increases. Initially it may rise (e.g. the prospect for team sports such as water polo may increase benefits); however, after a particular number have joined the club, congestion will be experienced and benefit per person will fall. When membership is S_1, the difference between benefit per person S_1 and cost per person C_1 is at a maximum, i.e. distance 12. If the size of the swimming pool were larger then the benefits per

person might be greater (B_h) and, though the cost per person might rise (e.g. to C_h), the increase in quantity would increase the optimal membership size to S_h. For any quantity of the good in question there is an optimal membership. In part (c) of the figure, we record the optimal number of club members for any quantity of the goods as N_{opt}.

In Fig. 3.9(b), we begin by assuming a given number of club members. At the extreme, a swimming pool may be consumed privately by one individual. The costs to that individual of increasing the size of the pool increase as C_1. If the benefits enjoyed by the individual varied as B_1, then it is clear that she would not purchase any quantity of the good. However, if a group of individuals formed a club, the costs per person would be reduced to C_k while the benefits, given non-rivalness in consumption, would not fall as much (i.e. only to B_k). From this cost and benefit function relating to a club size of k, the optimal quantity is Q_k (i.e., net benefit per club member is maximized at Q_k). For any given club size, then, there is an optimal quantity (optimal-sized swimming pool). This information is recorded as Q_{opt} in Fig. 3.9(c).

In so far as it is possible to record the optimal membership size *for any given quantity* and the optimal quantity *for any given membership size*, it is possible to solve for the optimal quantity and optimal membership simultaneously. In part (c), if the membership is N_k it is clear that the optimal quantity is Q_k, but at quantity Q_k the optimal number of members is N_r. With a membership of N_r the optimal quantity is Q_r, and so on. Eventually, at point 1, there is the solution for the optimal quantity and the optimal membership size.

It should be emphasized that the above solution maximizes the welfare of members, and in the case of one club this may not maximize the welfare of society. (For those conditions necessary to maximize welfare of society when only one club is established, see Ng 1973.) Nevertheless, the point is made that goods which bear the characteristic of non-rivalness in consumption can be provided voluntarily in markets via clubs. There is no necessity for government intervention to ensure that the good will be provided. The existence of the possibility of exclusion means that the incentive to reveal preferences is present.

3.5.5 Private provision of pure public goods

Section 1.8 introduced the properties of a (Winch) equilaterial triangle in the context of second-best problems. Those same properties are revised here closely following the work of Ley (1996) to illustrate various results concerning public goods. There are two goods; a private good X and a public good G and again two individuals A and B who are not identical. Reinterpreting point 1 from Fig. 1.9 in the setting of Fig. 3.10, in what Ley terms a Kolm triangle, would now indicate A enjoys 16 units of the private good (X_A), B enjoys 34 units of the private good (X_B) and they both enjoy 20 units of the public good ($G_A^c = G_B^c = G$; G_A, G_B without the 'c' superscript is the amount of public good each individual pays for whereas G is the quantity they consume). (Along

$O_A - O_B$, $G = 0$, along $O - O_B$, $X_B = 0$ and along $O - O_A$, $X_A = 0$.) Further because of the properties of the equilaterial triangle

$$X_A + X_B + G = W_A + W_B = W$$
$$(16 + 34 + 20 = 70)$$

Where W_A and W_B are A's and B's initial (wealth) endowments and it is a '70 unit' society (All the arithmetic in this section is based on this 70 unit equilateral triangle and is rounded to give whole units. Given this all the illustrated triangles are replica's of each other with consistent notation.) The prices of the private and public good are adjusted to both equal unity by a suitable choice of units. Illustrative indifference curves (for X and G as normal goods) for A and B are depicted in Fig. 3.10 and from point 1 preferred allocations for A lie within the hatched area as they involve more X_A and more G than point 1. The shaded area to the north-west of point 1 has an identical interpretation for individual B.

Ley (1996) now uses this framework to illustrate four results from the literature on public goods.

(i) *Nash equilibrium*

A Nash equilibrium arises when the pair of strategies (an allocation between A and B) is such that each of the players (persons A and B) choice is optimal *given* the opponent's strategies. In Fig. 3.11 the initial wealth allocation is that associated with point 1 involving $W_A = X_A = 26$ units and $W_B = X_B = 44$ units, i.e. zero units of G. As illustrated the *share* of wealth going to A is the ratio of distances $O_A - 1/O_A - O_B = 3/8$ and to B is $O_B - 1/O_A - O_B = 5/8$. If B enjoys 44 units of X and makes no contribution to G then A must adjust individually along the line 1–2. If A enjoys 26 units of X and makes no contribution to G then B must adjust along 1–3. If B moves first and maximizes utility on I_B^0 at point 4 along the line 1–3 providing 26 units of G then A's adjustment path, because of the non-rivalness of G becomes the line 4–5. A now maximizes utility at point 6 on indifference curve I_A^3. Such a point cannot be a resting place because B's adjustment line now becomes 7–8 and point 9 is duly chosen as the utility maximizing position on indifference curve I_B^2. This zig-zag adjustment process has a limit at point 10 where a Nash equilibrium is achieved, i.e. given the allocation decision of B(A) then A(B) has no incentive to alter his or her allocation. Point 10 is the cross over point of A's reaction curve r_A and B's reaction curve r_B. Inspection makes it clear that point 10 would also be achieved if the process of adjustment began with A at point 11. At the Nash equilibrium $X_A = 10$ units, $X_B = 30$ units and $G = 30$ units with $G_A = 16$ units and $G_B = 14$

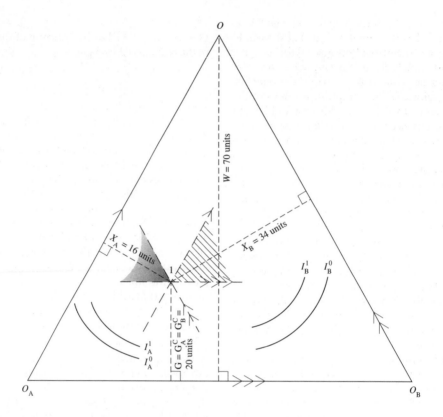

Figure 3.10 The Winch/Kolm triangle.

units. Quantities X_A, X_B and G are found using the perpendiculars to the sides of the triangle as with Fig. 3.10. The amount of public good provided by A and B individually is found by putting in the perpendiculars to the $O_A - O_B$ axis from the bases (point 12 for A point 14 for B) of the Nash equilibrium adjustment lines for A 14–15, for B 12–13.

The triangle contains much information. While point 10 is a Nash equilibrium it is not a Pareto optimum. At point 10 the indifference curves I_A^1 and I_B^3 cross and therefore the contract curve cannot run through point 10. It can be seen that a tangency between A's and B's indifference map must be in the hatched area to the north of point 10. In the hatched area both A and B would be on higher indifference curves but Nash adjustment will not put them in that region. It is also clear that the 'northness' of a Pareto optimum means a greater amount of public good would be provided, i.e. Nash equilibrium involves a less than optimal amount of the public good.

(ii) Redistribution of income
Ley illustrates Warr's (1983) neutrality theorem that indicates within limits the Nash equilibrium at 10 is independent of the income distribution. Figure 3.12 reproduces the key features of the Fig. 3.11 initial allocation between A and B. Moving point 1 to the left in Fig. 3.12 raises the share of income going to B. The effect of this would be to attenuate B's reaction curve r_B and extend A's along the dashed segment of r_A. However, until the share indicated by extending 12–13 to the axis $O_A - O_B$ is reached the $r_A - r_B$ crossover point is unaffected. The same is true if the share going to A is increased and point 1 moves to the right. Within A_{min}, B_{max}, A_{max}, B_{min} the shares to A and B will not affect the crossover point so that the Nash equilibrium is independent of the income distribution within that range.

(iii) Stackelberg equilibrium
A common alternative equilibrium to Nash is the Stackelberg equilibrium which assigns dominance to one of the individuals (players). The dominance takes the form of making the first move. As the rich are almost invariably at an economic advantage individual B is assumed to be dominant. Using Fig. 3.13 the best B can do is to maximize his position given the reaction curve of A, r_A. Points on r_A to the right of 10

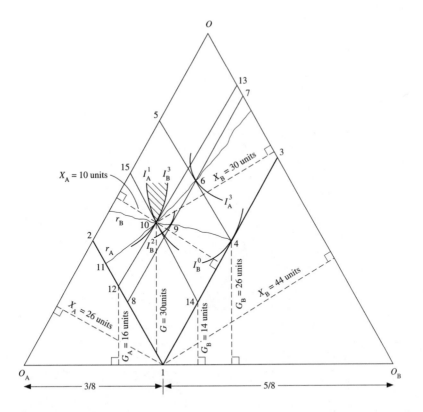

Figure 3.11 Nash equilibrium with a public good.

clearly offer B lower levels of utility. To the left of point 10 the best B can do is to choose point 5 allowing the utility level associated with I_B^4 to be achieved. Concentrating on the public goods effects alone, it can be seen that compared to the Nash equilibrium the level of G is reduced from 30 to 25 units. Powerful B's contribution is reduced from $G_B = 14$ units to $G_B = 6$ units. Conversely A's contribution increases from $G_A = 16$ units to $G_A = 19$ units. Moving to a Stackelberg equilibrium lowers A's utility (I_A^1 to I_A^0), increases B's (I_B^3 to I_B^4) and reduces the amount of the public good by 5 units.

(iv) Subsidizing contributions

Individual A perhaps aggrieved at the Stackelberg equilibrium might say to B 'let me subsidize your purchase of public good G'. Using Fig. 3.14 the wisdom of this apparently generous offer can be assessed. Offering to subsidize the price of the public good to individual B has the effect of swivelling his initial individual adjustment line from 1–3 to 1–16. This 'price line' in turn moves B's reaction curve from r_B to one involving more of the subsidized good, i.e. $r_{B'}$. The new Nash equilibrium is at point L with 42 units

of the public good. More fully:

Allocation at point 10		Allocation at point L	
Individual A	Individual B	Individual A	Individual B
$X_A=10$	$X_B=30$	$X_A=14$	$X_B=14$
$G_A=16$	$G_B=14$	$G_A=7+5=12$	$G_B=30$
$W_A=26$	$W_B=44$	$W_A=26$	$W_B=44$
$X=40$		$X=28$	
$G=30$		$G=42$	
$W=70$		$W=70$	

It is evident that A does better both in terms of G and X and must be on a higher indifference curve I_A^4 as compared to I_A^1. A 'spends' 14 units of his endowment on X and 12 units on G. Of the 12 units expended on G he pays 7 units directly found by dropping a perpendicular from the subsidized price line through the L-equilibrium) and 5 units in subsidy to B ($G_A^s = 5$ units). As indicated by Fig. 3.14 this is found by calculating in the subsidy slice 1-16-3 the vertical distance between B's contribution to the public good ($G_B = 30$ units) at his initial price line 1–3 and the contribution he is induced to make with the subsidy ($G_B + G_A^s = 35$ units).

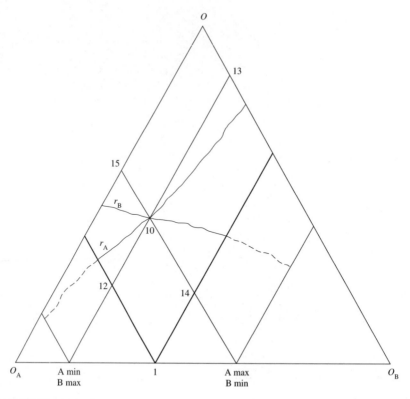

Figure 3.12 The neutrality theorem.

Whilst B enjoys more of the public good at point L compared to point 10 he contributes more (30 units as opposed to 14 units) and has a reduced amount of private good X ($X_B = 14$ rather than $X_B = 30$). Not surprisingly this reduces B's utility level from I_B^3 to I_B^1. (This is guaranteed by the slope of I_B^3 at point 10.) A's offer of a subsidy is a Greek gift of a wooden horse: it benefits A and costs B.

The theorem that with non-identical individuals who both view X and G as normal goods the one individual will always want to subsidize the other individual even if the individual has to pay all of the subsidy himself is surprising and fairly general.

3.5.6 Public provision of pure public goods: the Clarke tax

The extreme example of the problems of free riding exists when a pure public good is provided and the number of individuals is large. By 'large' we mean that no one individual feels that her own decision to contribute (reveal her preference) will have any impact on the behaviour of others. Even in this scenario, however, there is a mechanism by which individuals can be

led to reveal their preferences. The essence of this mechanism is to convert the 'large'-number situation into a 'small'-number. The mechanism is to employ the Clarke tax to induce honesty (Clarke 1971). Here we follow an exposition of this mechanism outlined by Tideman and Tullock (1976). (Further discussion is provided by Groves and Ledyard 1977.)

By converting a 'large'-number situation into a 'small'-number situation, the individual is made to feel that there is some significance associated with *her* action. For this to occur, the individual must be liable directly for the consequences of her revealing (or not revealing) her preference. Assume that a large group of individuals is considering the collective provision of a pure public good. The marginal costs of providing the good are constant and are shown as *MC* in Fig. 3.15. The aggregate demand function (added vertically) is *AD*. The problem is to produce an incentive mechanism that will reveal this information. For any representative individual *i*, we proceed by apportioning the share of *MC* to be paid by individual *i* (this is P_i); the remainder of the share ($MC - P_i$) is paid by the rest of the group. In order to make *i* reveal her true preference, she must be made conscious of the effect

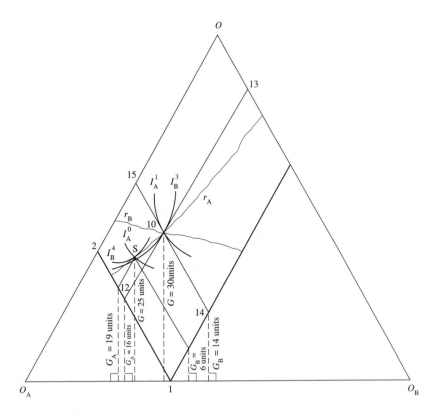

Figure 3.13 Stackelberg equilibrium with a public good.

of her vote on the remainder of the group. The Clarke tax operates in this way. In Fig. 3.15 the group would produce Oq^1 of the public good if i paid her share (P_i), but individual i played no role in the decision-making; i.e. $(AD - D_i)$ is equated with $(MC - P_i)$ at output Oq^1. If i votes to increase output of the good beyond this, then her preferences are playing a role. Clearly, output will increase from Oq^1 to Oq^2 if her demand is added to the rest of the community demand. If this happens then individual i imposes costs on the rest of the community equal to triangle 123. This is the excess burden the rest of the community carries as a consequence of increasing output from Oq^1 to Oq^2. The additional costs to the other individuals is area $12q^2q^1$ but the additional benefits are $13q^2q^1$. The Clarke tax that is applied is an estimate of these costs. Individual i is charged according to the additional costs she imposes on the rest of the community. The line $MC - P_i$ is the marginal costs she imposes on others as she influences output. The line S_i, however, reflects the net marginal costs i imposed on others being constructed as $(MC - P_i) - (AD - D_i)$. It is, in effect, the supply curve of the public good to i. In the diagram, and in the context of this example, the Clarke tax = triangle 456. (It is the mirror image of triangle 123.) It is clearly worthwhile for individual i to record her preference. The additional benefit to her (net of her share of costs of production) for $Oq^1 - Oq^2$ units of the public good is 6745, whereas the Clarke tax is only triangle 456. However, if she dishonestly overestimates her demand as D_i^1 then, on the additional units q^2q^3, she pays more in tax than the additional net benefits she actually receives, the net loss being triangle 489. It is, therefore, wise to neither underestimate nor overestimate her preference, but rather to reveal her true preference.

How would such a Clarke tax be applied? The practicalities of such an arrangement are obviously questionable. In Table 3.3 we give the example of such an arrangement when the case is that of voting between two options R and S (which could relate to different levels of output of a public good). The Clarke tax is determined by the following procedure:

1. Ask voters how much they would be prepared to offer to see either option adopted.

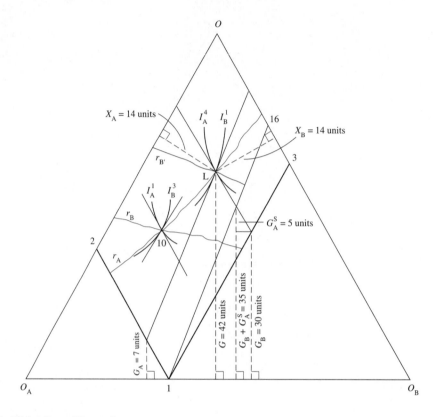

Figure 3.14 Subsidizing the public good.

2. Sum the total values recorded for each option (T_r and T_s respectively), and choose to adopt that option which records the highest value.
3. Apply a Clarke tax to each voter according to the rule that each voter must pay the absolute difference ($T_r - T_s$) between the sums (calculated without i's vote) for the two options.

In Table 3.3 it is clear that, following the above procedure, option R would be chosen ($T_r > T_s$). Individual 1 would pay a Clarke tax of 30 (i.e. she reduces net welfare of the 'others' by 30 to the extent that, if she did not vote, individual 2 would be better off by 50 and individual 3 would be worse off by 20). Voter 2 pays no

tax; her vote did not change the outcome. Voter 3 pays a tax of 10 as his vote does alter the outcome and the difference between the two sums involved without his vote is (50 – 40).

If individual 1 had overestimated her preference in order to secure the selection of R, either she would have no effect on the final outcome or she would run the risk of paying more than the true value of R to her. For example, suppose that individual 1 had claimed (falsely) that the option R was worth 80 to her in order to make sure that that option succeeded. In the event that option R wins it does not affect her Clarke tax, as the tax is based on the way in which her vote changes net welfare (and in this case it is still 50 – 20). However, suppose that the exaggeration did alter the outcome. Suppose that individual 2 had said that the option S was worth 70, and in this way ensured that option S exceeds option R and wins. Now the Clarke tax for individual 2 would be based on the change in welfare estimated as a result of her vote, which would now be equal to 60. Remember, the difference is estimated in the absence of the individual's vote. If individual 2 had not voted, 1 and 3 would have gained 60 from the

Table 3.3 The mechanics of the Clarke tax

Voter	Option R (T_r)	Option S (T_s)
1	40	0
2	0	50
3	20	0
Total	60	50

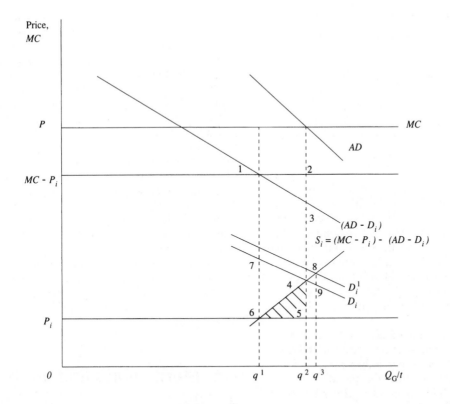

Figure 3.15 The Clarke tax.

option R and there would be no welfare loss (in the absence of 2) from not having option S. Therefore, the tax for individual 2 would be 60, and this is greater than the 'true' value of having option S instead of option R. Clearly, there is no gain in overestimating preferences—either it makes no difference or it results in losses.

Suppose instead we look at the potential outcome from under-revealing preferences. Suppose that individual 1 decided to under-reveal her preference and claim that she benefited by only 20 from option R. In this case, while she would pay no Clarke tax (because her vote does not change the outcome), she would not receive the option that is worth most to her. Alternatively, if she claimed she would offer 35, then option R would be accepted, but her under-revealing of preferences would not mean that she paid any different Clarke tax: the Clarke tax is based on the difference in sums without her vote, and this remains $50 - 20 = 30$. In this way the individual either gains nothing by under-revealing or stands to lose the option that offers her the most benefit.

Though the principle of this Clarke tax is clear-cut, it poses many practical difficulties, of which the following are examples.

First, the money raised in the tax cannot be returned to voters. To return the money would be to incur the likelihood that individuals would change their demand for the good and thereby negate the exercise. It is argued, however, that, as the number of voters increases, the tax surplus is likely to become less important (see Tideman and Tullock 1976).

Secondly, coalition voting must be prohibited or else the system can still be manipulated. The following example, based on Ng (1978), illustrates this point. In Table 3.4 there are four voters. If there is no coalition possible then it should be evident that option M is chosen rather than option N. In these circumstances voter 1 pays a Clarke tax of 35 and voter 3 pays a Clarke tax of 15. However, suppose voters 2 and 4 form a coalition. Voter 2 agrees to claim that option N is worth 100 to her and voter 4 is prepared to claim that option N is worth 90 to him. By exaggerating their demands for this option, they secure its attainment. However, when it comes to the Clarke tax, voter

Table 3.4 The effect of coalition voting

Voter	Option M (T_m)	Option N (T_n)
1	40	0
2	0	50
3	20	0
4	0	5
Total	60	55

Source: based on Ng (1978).

2 will pay $(40 + 20 - 90 = -30)$, while voter 4 will pay $(40 + 20 - 100 = -40)$. Neither voter 2 nor voter 4 has a tax liability because their votes actually appear to increase the net benefit of the remaining voters.

Thirdly, there is always the possibility that, being unbounded, the Clarke tax might lead to bankruptcy for the individual concerned. It is not clear how you deal with the preferences of those voters who have affected the outcome but who cannot subsequently pay the Clarke tax.

Fourthly, the success of the Clarke tax depends upon there being a motivation to vote on the part of individuals. The whole mechanism may run foul of what has been referred to as the 'paradox of voting' (Downs 1957). This is discussed in greater detail in the next chapter. The essence of this paradox is that, because the individual is one of many voters, she feels that her vote is of very little consequence in determining the outcome and therefore is unprepared to incur the costs of participating in the vote. (See chapter 4 for a discussion of this argument.)

3.5.6 Preference revelation in large and small groups

Before moving on from the question of free riding, it is worth highlighting one of the conclusions that emerges from the preceding discussion. From the review of the free rider literature, once again there is

another set of 'inverted' results associated with the private and public good opposites. The incentive for non-revelation can be seen to vary sensitively with the numbers involved in providing the good and the nature of the good. In Table 3.5 we outline a taxonomy which may be used to contrast the public and private good situation according to the numbers involved in consumption.

The observation that preference revelation is likely to be a function of the size of the group is important for research in this area. Indeed, with respect to the Clarke tax, one interpretation of this voting mechanism is that, for the provision of a public good, it transforms a 'large' group scenario into one in which the individual feels as though he is a member of a small group. The function of the Clarke tax mechanism that is relevant here is that it changes the game to one in which the individual is made aware of her impact on everyone else. In a sense, while the group is large in number, there are now only two players that are relevant: the individual and 'everyone else' (see Cullis and Jones 1987).

3.6 Merit wants and merit goods

Familiar in public finance and social policy texts is the concept of a merit want. Musgrave defines it in the following terms:

Such wants are met by services subject to the exclusion principle and are satisfied by the market within the limits of effective demand. They become public wants if considered so meritorious that their satisfaction is provided for through the public budget, over and above what is provided for by private buyers. (Musgrave 1959, p. 13)

A long and intermittent debate has taken place over this concept. One problem is the issue of why, and

Table 3.5 Private and public goods

Nos.	Private goods	Preference revelation	Public goods	Preference revelation
Small	Strategic behaviour or demand revelation will affect equilibrium prices; therefore quite a strong incentive to act strategically.	Less likely	Cost share is substantial—failure to reveal demand means supply reduced dramatically; therefore likely to reveal (may distort but reveal some preference).	Very likely
Large	Strategic behaviour on demand revelation will not affect equilibrium prices greatly; therefore little incentive to distort preferences.	Very likely	Cost share minimal if failure to reveal has little impact; therefore will try to 'free-ride'.	Less likely

how, an outside agency can know better than the individual what is in her own (long-term) interests. Arguments advanced to sustain this approach typically boil down to two difficult matters. One concerns information and the other, rationality. A key question for the different contributions is the extent to which the concept can be integrated consistently into the neoclassical framework and, in particular, the value judgement that each individual is the best judge of her own welfare. Information has characteristics that make it subject to 'market failure' arguments and can be introduced into the framework that way. Knowledge and information are non-rival, in that their use does not decrease the total available. Indeed, they may be supra-non-rival, in that, if learning takes place, use may actually increase the quantity available. This suggests that it is likely to be inefficient to use the market to achieve exclusion.

Furthermore, the nature of information makes exclusion difficult. It is possible to know the value of information to you only after you have it, but then you have an incentive to avoid paying for it. Furthermore, the passing of information from one individual to another makes it difficult for an originator to maintain a property right over its use. These considerations suggest under-provision in the market. In terms of consumer-type goods, it is those whose quality is difficult to inspect, and/or are seldom repeat purchases,[3] and which involve harmful consequences or side-effects, that are the most obvious candidates for policy concern. There is then a basis for information provision in some circumstances, but its appropriate production and dissemination method is likely to be open to debate. However, what if an efficient quantity of information is present and individuals still appear to do the wrong thing?

Rationality is a difficult concept. Economists have, as part of their framework, actors who act purposefully (know their preferences, ranking alternatives, etc.) to their best advantage (not necessarily defined in a narrowly self-interested way) and generally adopt the value judgement that each individual is the best judge of her own welfare. As Mishan (1981b, p. 10) points out, this may be a judgement of fact (a belief that individuals generally are the best judges of their own welfare), a judgement of morality (it is appropriate to act *as if* individuals are the best judges of their own welfare), or a judgement about political expediency (it is politically expedient, in the Western

world at least, to act on the *assumption* that individuals are the best judges of their own welfare).[4] Whatever the basis of the judgement, it is part of the economist's 'story'. How can the judgement be suspended in some parts of economic analysis, without it smacking of inconsistency and arbitrariness? Mooney (1979) has an escape route in which individuals choose (in their own best interests) to delegate their decisions to government—they choose to have what would have been their individual choice 'corrected'. If there is a lack of information, the individual may not think that she ought to make a decision on such and such. Mental and other limitations may make some people feel unable to make decisions. They may think some issues are 'too big' for them and they may not want to have the responsibility for making decisions.

Despite these 'rationalizations', commentators remain rather sceptical of the concept especially approached in this 'outcome'-orientated way. Littlechild and Wiseman (1986) concentrate on restriction of choice and the question of what is the best framework in which to approach this question. They argue that the market failure approach cannot deal adequately with the idea that somehow individual preferences may simply be wrong on the question of what is to comprise an individual's rights in society. They see the paternalist framework as being based partly on the lack of information and incompetence of individual decision-making noted above. More distinctively, in the context of this section, they discuss briefly the idea that preferences are endogenous, so that people who are the product of a 'faulty' environment or childhood experiences (etc.) will have 'faulty' preferences which need not be respected in the conventional value judgement. Their third framework is the libertarian one that is associated with extensive liberty, subject to not violating the rights of other individuals. In this context, the authors note that any restriction of choice imposed by government on an individual must flow from the social decision-making rule adopted by individuals as being acceptable to justify public policy (e.g. unanimity).

Littlechild and Wiseman recognize that the three frameworks they consider will sometimes be compatible, albeit for different reasons. However, the way forward is seen to be the analysis of the connections between decision-making/institutional settings and the policies that are selected within them, with a view to isolating those collective decision-making

---

[3] When the item is purchased frequently and takes a small part of income, consumers can be expected to 'learn' and producers, anxious to retain customers, are likely to offer helpful information.

[4] Rowley and Peacock (1975) relate the issue to solipsism, which is a philosophy in which the only knowledge an individual can possess is of him- or herself.

processes that a majority would be likely to find acceptable. The shift from outcomes to processes is characteristic of the public choice perspective. Consensus might be found between the advocating of different 'frameworks' on the basis of equal access and the social decision-making process. 'If citizens accept that the social decision-making processes from which policies emerge are fair, then they will be willing to accept the possibility that at least some policies emerge which will be contrary to their best interests, since this is the price they must pay to obtain agreement from others on the policies they themselves want' (p. 170). In this 'contractarian' approach to cases, where 'public policy aims at an allocation of resources which deviates from that reflected by consumers sovereignty' (Musgrave 1959, p. 9), the rules to change and create the law and the constitution must also be included in the larger picture.

While this account of the merit want concept is not exhaustive, it raises fundamental questions, both about the nature of the 'welfare economics' approach to evaluation in itself, and about the 'outcome' versus 'processes' approach to an issue.

3.7 Summary

Over forty years after Samuelson's original (1954) article on public goods, an assessment is due. Were the early critics too sceptical, or were they correct that the concept would yield little insight for policy purposes? Has sufficient been done to sustain the argument that the concept of a public good is a valuable input for fiscal theory? While these questions demand more analysis than we have space for here, we would suggest that the fact that public goods appear to be theoretical extremes should not blind the analyst's perception of the importance of the concept. As the polar extreme to private goods, they provide an alternative perspective to an important spectrum or taxonomy of goods. Of course, theoretical extremes are difficult to observe in practice. What student of economics has not met the criticism that perfect competition in its extreme theoretical description is seldom visible? However, in just the same way as perfect competition acts as a polar extreme to monopoly for the analysis of markets, public goods and private goods take up their positions at either end of a spectrum for an analysis of the provision of goods and services. The contrasts between pure public and pure private goods are obvious, as the following examples make clear.

1. The total provision of private goods is the *sum* of private consumption, whereas the total provision of public goods is *equal* between individuals:

   [for private goods: $X_a + X_b = X$; for public goods: $G_a = G_b = G$]

2. The consumer in general pays the *same* price and consumes *different* quantities of the good when there is efficient provision of private goods; the consumer pays *different* prices and consumes the *same* quantity of the good when there is efficient provision of public goods:

   [for private goods: $MB_{ax} = MB_{bx} = MC_x$; for public goods: $MB_{ag} + MB_{bg} = MC_g$]

3. For pure private goods *markets perform well* when there are very many buyers and very many sellers, i.e. in an atomistic market. For pure public goods market provision is possible but not Pareto optimal when there are very many consumers.

These contrasting points provide important benchmarks for the development of theoretical literature. Margolis's (1954) point, that pure public goods do not abound, may have a relevance for practical policy, but the challenge is to deal with goods that bear some characteristics of publicness.

Perhaps one of the most important implications of public good theory is the rationale that free riding offers for the existence of the state (see Schmidtz 1991). The fact that individuals are better off if they choose to be coerced to pay taxes is an important conclusion for those who would permit an active role for government. For the public choice analyst this argument has been 'overplayed', and by contrast the case is repeatedly made that the free rider problem is not as daunting as theory would allow. If individuals can create mechanisms that will provide public goods then this is important, although it is questionable why the state itself cannot more often be viewed (within a 'contractarian' approach) as a vehicle for the provision of goods and services. If individuals choose, in consensus, to see a coercive mechanism introduced so that all can prosper, then public choice concern is to limit the abuse of coercion. Even so, while coercive mechanisms are open to abuse, they may offer positive and widely accepted advantages for dealing with the free rider as far as individuals in the community are concerned.

Once it is recognized that the free rider problem may act as a spur to individuals to choose state involvement—and, indeed, state coercion—to finance taxation, it seems but a small step to argue that, when there are problems in the consumption of other goods, a consensus may also emerge for an even greater reduction in personal liberty. Individuals may recognize their limitations in terms of access to information and understanding as to the quality of some goods. To this extent, they may accept the intervention of 'experts' who do not simply advise, but sometimes enforce or preclude their consumption of goods in the name of the merit good argument. If a consensus exists that such sublimation of individual's preferences is desirable, then, again, 'coercion' appears to have been condoned. Of course, again, it would be foolish to ignore the possibility that coercion can be abused, but here we have argued that its apparent existence may be explained by the concepts of public and merit goods.

References

Blaug, M. (1965) 'The Rate of Return on Investment in Education in Great Britain', *The Manchester School*, 33, 3, pp. 205–51.

Bohm, P. (1971) 'An Approach to the Problem of Estimating the Demand for Public Goods', *Swedish Journal of Economics*, 73, pp. 55–66.

Bohm, P. (1972) 'Estimating Demand for Public Goods: An Experiment', *European Economic Review*, 3, 2, pp. 111–30.

Buchanan, J. M. (1965) 'An Economic Theory of Clubs', *Economica*, 32, 125, pp. 1–14.

Buchanan, J. M. (1968) *The Demand and Supply of Public Goods*. Chicago: Rand McNally.

Buchanan, J. M. (1986) *Liberty, Market and State: Political Economy in the 1980s*. Brighton, Sussex: Harvester Press.

Clarke, E. H. (1971) 'Multi-part Pricing of Public Goods', *Public Choice*, 11, pp. 17–33.

Coase, R. (1974) 'The Lighthouse in Economics', *Journal of Law and Economics*, 17, pp. 357–76.

Colm, G. (1956) 'Comment on Samuelson's Theory of Public Finance', *Review of Economics and Statistics*, 38, 4, pp. 408–13.

Congleton, R. D. (1988) 'An Overview of the Contractarian Public Finance of James Buchanan', *Public Finance Quarterly*, 16, 2, pp. 131–57.

Cullis, J. G. and Jones, P. R. (1987) *Microeconomics and the Public Economy: A Defence of Leviathan*. Oxford: Basil Blackwell.

Downs, A. (1957) *An Economic Theory of Democracy*. New York: Harper & Row.

Evans, A. W. (1970) 'Private Goods, Externality, Public Goods', *Scottish Journal of Political Economy*, 17, 1, pp. 79–89.

Groves, T. and Ledyard, J. (1977) 'Optimal Allocation of Public Goods: A Solution to the "Free Rider" Problem', *Econometrica*, 45, 4, pp. 783–809.

Head, J. G. (1962) 'Public Goods and Public Policy', *Public Finance/Finances Publiques*, 17, 3, pp. 197–219.

Johansen, L. (1963) 'Some Notes on the Lindahl Theory of Determination of Public Expenditures', *International Economic Review*, 4, 3, pp. 346–58.

Johansen, L. (1977) 'The Theory of Public Goods: Misplaced Emphasis?' *Journal of Public Economics*, 7, 1, pp. 147–52.

Kim, O. and Walker, M. (1984) 'The Free Rider Problem: Experimental Evidence', *Public Choice*, 43, 1, pp. 3–24.

Ley, E. (1996) 'On the Provision of Public Goods: A Diagrammatic Exposition,' *Investigaciones Económicas*, 20, 1, pp. 105–23.

Lindahl, E. (1919) 'Just Taxation—A Positive Solution', pp. 168–76 in R. A. Musgrave and A. T. Peacock (eds.), *Classics in the Theory of Public Finance*. London: Macmillan, 1967.

Littlechild, S. C. and Wiseman, J. (1986) 'The Political Economy of Restriction of Choice', *Public Choice*, 51, 2, pp. 161–72.

Margolis, J. A. (1955) 'Comment on the Pure Theory of Public Expenditure', *Review of Economics and Statistics*, 37, 4, pp. 347–9.

Marwell, G. and Ames, R. E. (1981) 'Economists Free-Ride, Does Anyone Else? Experiments on the Provision of Public Goods, IV', *Journal of Public Economics*, 15, 3, pp. 295–310.

McCaleb, T. S. and Wagner, R. E. (1985) 'The Experimental Search for Free-Riders', *Public Choice*, 47, 3, pp. 479–90.

Meade, J. E. (1952) 'External Economies and Diseconomies in a Competitive Situation', *Economic Journal*, 62, 245, pp. 54–76.

Mishan, E. J. (1981a) *Economic Efficiency and Social Welfare*. London: George Allen & Unwin.

Mishan, E. J. (1981b) *Introduction to Normative Economics*. Oxford: Oxford University Press.

Mooney, G. H. (1979) 'Values in Health Care', pp. 23–44 in K. Lee (ed.), *Economics and Planning*. London: Croom-Helm.

Musgrave, R. A. (1959) *The Theory of Public Finance*. New York: McGraw-Hill.

Musgrave, R. A. (1969) 'Provision for Social Goods', in J. Margolis and M. Guitton (eds.), *Public Economics*. New York: St Martin's Press.

Musgrave, R. A. and Musgrave P. B. (1989) *Public Finance in Theory and Practice*, 5th edn. New York: McGraw-Hill.

Ng, Y. K. (1973) 'The Economic Theory of Clubs: Pareto Optimality Conditions', *Economica*, 40, 159, pp. 291–8.

Ng, Y. K. (1978) *The Clarke–Groves Solution to the Free-Rider Problem in Public Goods: A Non-Mathematical*

Exposition and Some Practical Considerations, Seminar Paper No 71, Monash University, mimeo.

Peacock, A. (1979) *The Economic Analysis of Government and Related Themes*. Oxford: Martin Robertson.

Peston, M. (1972) *Public Goods and the Public Sector*. London: Macmillan.

Rowley, C. K. and Peacock, A. T. (1975) *Welfare Economics: A Liberal Restatement*. London: Martin Robertson.

Samuelson, P. (1954) 'The Pure Theory of Public Expenditure', *Review of Economics and Statistics*, **36**, 4, pp. 387–9.

Samuelson, P. A. (1955) 'Diagrammatic Exposition of a Theory of Public Expenditure', *Review of Economics and Statistics*, **37**, 4, pp. 350–6.

Samuelson, P. A. (1969) 'Pure Theory of Public Expenditure and Taxation', pp. 98–123, in J. Margolis and H. Guitton (eds.), *Public Economics*. New York: St Martin's Press.

Sandler, T. (1977) 'Impurity of Defense: An Application to the Economics of Alliances', *Kyklos*, **30**, 3, pp. 443–60.

Schmidtz, D. (1991) *The Limits of Government*. Boulder: Westview Press.

Tideman, T. N. and Tullock, G. (1976) 'A New and Superior Process for Making Social Choices', *Journal of Political Economy*, **84**, 6, pp. 1145–59.

Warr, P. (1983) 'The Private Provision of a Public Good is Independent of the Income Distribution', *Economics Letters*, **13**, pp. 207–11.

Weisbrod, B. A. (1988) *The Nonprofit Economy*. Cambridge, Mass.: Harvard University Press.

4 Collective decision-making: searching for the 'public interest'

4.1 Introduction

In this chapter the focus is on collective decision-making in the public sector. Collective decision-making rules are used, at some stage, to decide which goods are to be provided in the public sector and which taxes are to be levied. Such decisions affect the distribution of welfare between individuals. While in chapter 1 we were able to skirt around this problem by postulating the existence of a social welfare function, eventually if we are to make decisions we are faced with the question of what the social welfare function looks like.

The typical Bergson–Samuelson social welfare function has already been described in chapter 1. Welfare W depends upon the distribution of utilities (U_i) of individuals in the community, which in turn rests on their allocation of goods and services. (Whereas in the broader formulation the social welfare function depended on the utility of the individual associated with the allocation of goods and services across all individuals—a total specification.) Each of us will have our own view as to what constitutes the 'best' or 'most equitable' distribution of utilities. This view is premised on value judgements, and there is no obvious logical basis on which we can state that one individual's view must take precedence over another. Collective decision-making rules provide, or seek to provide, a mechanism for aggregating the social welfare functions of individuals. If such a process were successful then we would be in a position to make a *social choice*.

In traditional public finance the role of the welfare economist is to make recommendations as to which fiscal instrument will best achieve a stated goal. The final choice, however, is left to government, and ultimately government may accept or reject the advice offered. In the actual choice process the economist has no claim to greater influence on the decision than any

other individual (see e.g. Mishan 1988). It is, however, necessary that decision-makers be informed. It is also of more than passing interest to public finance theorists to know whether specific collective decision-making rules will affect collective choice. The work of social choice theorists is, in this way, of key importance for traditional public finance. Bonner (1986) provides a good introduction to that literature on social choice theory which exists outside the more specific area of public choice.

It will already be evident that the strength of the public choice approach is the analysis of the political process generally. One specific element in this approach has been the importance of the assumption of '*Homo economicus*', i.e. that individuals maximize their self-interest. Buchanan (1989) provides a useful taxonomy of the public choice literature in which this assumption is highlighted. Within such studies it soon becomes clear that the political process may itself be a source of governmental failure. Moreover, there is a clear tendency for such self-interested behaviour of actors in the political process to lead to an 'excessive' growth of government, i.e. for the public sector to grow like a 'Leviathan'.

With this introduction as a background to the literature, we are interested in this chapter in quite specific questions. For example, are the decisions that emerge from a collective decision-making process likely to be optimal? Also, does it matter which voting rule is used as a means of aggregating individuals' preferences, and are individuals expected to reveal their preferences honestly in a political decision-making process?

Market failure has been explained in previous chapters, and it has been demonstrated that it can form the basis of an argument for government intervention. But, in so far as market failure implies a rejection of outcomes generated in the market-place, how are we to make decisions with respect to such intervention? How are we to interpret signals generated in the political market? Will there be failure within political markets?

The following analysis depends quite heavily on the 'simple majority voting rule' as a means of illustrating arguments. In the early part of this chapter we shall show how social choice theorists would question the application of this rule. Later in the chapter we describe how a public choice approach would suggest that application of the simple majority voting rule will lead to an 'excessive' size of public sector budgets. Does the simple majority voting rule spawn a 'Leviathan'? To begin, however, it is useful to flaunt this general chapter plan, in order to resort to a public choice analysis of the basic question of why taxpayers vote at all. Here, premised on the assumption of self-interest, we outline Downs' (1957) 'rational voter hypothesis'.

4.2 Why taxpayers vote

One starting-point for a discussion of voting rules is the question of why individuals choose to vote. Downs (1957) presented the 'rational voter hypothesis'. The rational voter is assumed to base his decision to vote on the expected utility that may be enjoyed as a result of his participation in the political process. When deciding to vote, the individual assesses how much better off he will be if his vote leads to his preferred result. Assume that the individual prefers outcome X to an alternative that yields him no utility at all. The utility of outcome X can be referred to as $U(X)$ and measures the extent to which the individual is better off if this outcome is chosen (i.e. the individual gets no utility from the alternative). The probability that his vote will influence the outcome of the election is P. So the expected utility from voting is $P[U(X)]$. However, there are costs associated with the act of voting, and these can be denoted, in utility terms, as C. They may include the costs of gathering information as well as the costs of actually voting. The costs of voting may be in terms of time, effort and pecuniary expense. The net expected utility $E(U)$ from voting therefore becomes

(4.1) $$E(U) = P[U(X)] - C$$

However, the problem with this approach is that, since it is very unlikely that the act of one individual voter will be decisive in an election, it is unlikely that anyone will vote. If P, which is less than one, is extremely small, then $P[U(X)]$ is unlikely to exceed the certain costs C.

In Fig. 4.1 we illustrate such a decision. We assume that a collective decision is to be taken with respect to a change in the tax structure. The change in tax policy will leave this individual at a higher after-tax position. The individual's total utility function is assumed to be concave and shown as OU. Initial after-tax income is Y_1, and if the vote is successful this will increase to Y_2 and this difference comprises X. Obviously Y_2 is preferred, as it yields greater utility (U_2). Even if the individual does not vote, there is a chance that this policy change will succeed in the poll booths: a majority of other individuals may support it. If he does not vote, his expected income is therefore Y_E and his expected utility is U_E. We have arbitrarily assumed that there is a 50–50 chance that the vote will succeed even if he does not take part. (In this case $(Y_E - Y_1)/(Y_2 - Y_1) = 0.5$.)

If the individual votes there may be an increased likelihood that the preferred outcome will succeed, but there are also transaction costs of voting (equal to T). When these transaction costs are incurred, the individual's income will be $Y_2 - T$ if the best outcome occurs and $Y_1 - T$ if the worst outcome occurs. However, provided that the expected income of voting is not less than Y_E, the individual will be prepared to engage in political activity. If, by voting, he increases the chances that the policy change will be adopted, then, although costs are incurred, the expected income of voting may be the same as or greater than the expected income when not voting, i.e. Y_E. It will be obvious from the distances on the horizontal axis that, for the expected income of voting to exceed that of not voting, the probability of success when voting must be equal to or greater than

$$\frac{Y_E - (Y_1 - T)}{(Y_2 - T) - (Y_1 - T)}$$

which is greater than 0.5. The individual must increase the likelihood of success by his participation (i.e. the probability that he will influence the outcome must be positive) in order to make voting worthwhile (Jones and Cullis 1986). But how likely is it that his involvement in the vote will increase the chances of success? Can the individual assume that his vote will be of consequence?

In order to actually change the outcome of the vote, it is necessary either that (a) there is an even distribution between the votes of all other voters, or (b) the preferred outcome will lose by one vote. Mueller comments that

Several people have noted that the probability of being run over by a car going to or returning from the polls is similar to the probability of casting the decisive vote. If being run over

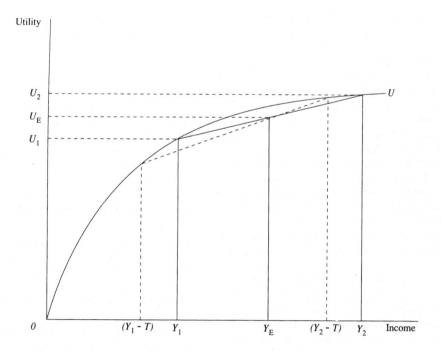

Figure 4.1 Why taxpayers vote.

Source: Jones and Cullis (1986).

is worse than having one's preferred candidate lose, then the potential cost of voting alone would exceed the potential gain, and no rational self interested individual would ever vote (Mueller 1987, p. 79)[1]

Indeed, voters may even be unwilling to incur the costs of gathering information. Hence this analysis leads to the conclusion of rational voter ignorance. It should be noted that the argument concerning the costs of information has been challenged (eg. Wittman 1989). The media may prove an inexpensive means of signalling information about politicians' policies and personalities (e.g. Jones and Hudson, 1996). However, the public choice conclusion regarding rational voter ignorance will be important later, when we discuss fiscal illusion on the part of voters.

So why do individuals turn out to vote? Mueller (1987) surveys the empirical work on turnout with this question in mind. He identifies at least three lines of argument.

[1] Mueller estimates that, even when the likelihood of each voter's voting for one of two candidates is 0.5, the probability of a single vote being decisive in a community of 100 000 000 is 0.000 06. When there are positive costs of voting, the expected utility of voting is likely to be negative unless the utility from the issue in question is extremely large.

4.2.1 Individuals derive utility from the act of voting

Voting may be seen as a duty and a civic right. The individual may feel better off exercising this right. By assuming that there are psychic benefits (measured in utility terms as D) from voting, the expected utility $E(U)$ of voting reads

(4.2) $$E(U) = P[U(X)] - C + D$$

However, if people simply do things because they like to do things, the original theory of Downs seems to lose its 'cutting edge' and become almost tautological: i.e. individuals vote because they like voting. As a consequence, the predictive element of the analysis is reduced. It may be possible to separate issues on which duty is more or less likely than economic self-interest to play a role. Lee (1988), for example, suggests that there are issues on which individuals enjoy supporting their ideological objectives, and in this way the act of voting can be seen as a consumption activity rather than an investment of resources in the hope of personal gain. But how important are psychic benefits from the act of voting?

(1) Riker and Ordeshook (1968) tested the equation $R = P[U(X)] + D - C$, where R is utility from

voting, by reference to 1952, 1956 and 1960 pre-presidential election questionnaires. They suggest that $P[U(X)]$ and D are important in explaining voter turnout but that a high sense of citizen duty (a higher value of D) has a quantitatively greater impact on voter turnout than do high values of either the probability of affecting the outcome or the benefit derived from the outcome.

(2) Ashenfelter and Kelly (1975) examine survey data on voter attitudes in an attempt to explain the large difference in turnouts in the two presidential elections of 1960 and 1972. Results suggest that the variables referred to in the rational voter hypothesis are important. Several measures of voting cost (e.g. the existence of a poll tax and literacy tests) were statistically significant in reducing the probability that an individual would vote. However, the perception of the individual as to whether the election was close run (a proxy for P) did not appear to affect the decision to vote. The importance of the issue (i.e. $U(X)$) was judged by the answer to the question, 'How do you think you will vote?' and was found to be important. If an individual appeared undecided as to how he would vote, the probability that he would vote at all was 40 per cent lower. In this study the obligation to vote was also important. Individuals who felt a strong obligation to vote did so with a 30 per cent higher probability.

Some empirical work offers some support for the view that individuals are more likely to vote when they feel an obligation to vote. Yet other studies offer support for the expected utility approach, without allowance for the psychic benefit of voting. Mueller (1987) reviews a number of other studies which regressed turnout figures on P (the expected vote of the leading candidate) and N (the size of the jurisdiction) to find support for the original Downs formulation. But can this 'opportunity cost of voting' approach, as described by Downs, explain the turnout figures as between different income groups?

Frey (1971) questions the approach of Downs (1957). Drawing on Lane (1966), he argues that voter turnout at elections is higher for high-income groups and that this is incompatible with the opportunity cost theory of voting: it is inconsistent that higher-income individuals vote in greater numbers, when the cost of giving up time to vote will be greater for them. Cavanagh (1981), for example, confirms this trend. In the USA the turnout rate in the 1976 election was 46 per cent for those with an income of less than $5000 and 60 per cent for those with an income of more than $25000. In order to reconcile

this behaviour with the expected utility theory, Frey argues that high-income individuals might be more productive in the use of their time in the political process. However, while this may be so for such activities as lobbying, it is difficult to apply the argument to the act of voting *per se*. Jones and Cullis (1986) offer an argument to reconcile the rational voter hypothesis with the evidence on turnout by income. They demonstrate that when individuals are risk-averse the lower-income individual may be less willing to gamble any certain cost of electoral participation against a given expected gain.

4.2.2 Voting and the minimax strategy

In answer to the question of why individuals vote, an alternative explanation depends on a different response to the problem of uncertainty. Ferejohn and Fiorina (1974) argue that voters utilize another decision-making strategy when dealing with uncertainty. This is the minimax-regret strategy. In Table 4.1 there are alternative outcomes (or states of nature) labelled S_1 and S_2. The matrix records how much the individual would regret if he had chosen to vote or not to vote. For example, the case of S_1 may be typical. Here the individual's vote has no impact on the electoral result. If the individual had voted, he would regret the utility loss C created by the costs involved in voting, feeling that it proved (in the end result) a waste of resources. It is worth stressing that what is in the matrix is the value of the amount the individual regrets after the event. The objective that he is assumed to be pursuing is the minimization of any such regret.

While outcomes like S_1 are quite likely, it is always possible that there is one outcome (such as S_2) where the individual's vote is important. Now, provided that the benefits from voting (which we continue to refer to as $U(X)$) exceed the costs of voting, the individual will regret nothing if he chooses to vote. However, if the individual does not vote he will have lost the value of $U(X) - C$ that could have been attained had the decision been made to participate in the vote. Therefore, against the strategy of not voting we record the regret as the difference between $U(X)$ and C.

Table 4.1 The decision to vote

	Alternative states	
	S_1	S_2
Vote	C	0
Abstain	0	$U(X) - C$

This approach appears to solve the paradox of the rational voter hypothesis, but only by assuming a very extreme assumption, i.e. that the voter adopts a cautious strategy. If we assume that the voter will always attempt to minimize the worst of the outcomes that might occur, then, provided that $U(X) - C > C$, he would vote. Is it reasonable to assume that individuals order their lives to avoid extremely unlikely outcomes, however bad such outcomes may be? Ferejohn and Fiorina (1975) use survey data to support their proposition. Under the minimax-regret argument, they propose that the value of the benefit to individuals should be related to voter turnout. The probability of the individual's vote being decisive (P) is of little consequence (because as long as P is positive—i.e. as long as there is even the remotest chance of a state of nature such as S_2—it will result in the individual choosing to vote). From this distinction they conclude that, in an analysis of pre- and post-election survey results for 1952, 1956, 1960 and 1964, the minimax-regret hypothesis was supported five times while the Downsian hypothesis (relying on Palso) was supported only once.

4.2.3 The ethical voter

Mueller's response (1987) to this literature is to suggest that, in deciding whether or not to vote, an individual i, as an ethical voter, is maximizing an objective function of the following form:

$$(4.3) \qquad O_i = U_i + \theta \sum U_j$$

where O_i = the objective of individual i
$\qquad U_i$ = the utility individual i derives from consuming goods and services
$\qquad \sum_{j \neq i} U_j$ = the sum of the utilities of other individuals in the community
$\qquad \theta$ = a parameter

When the individual is selfish, $\theta = 0$ and the individual is in the position of Downs' rational voter. However, when $\theta = 1$ the individual can be deemed altruistic; he is concerned with the utilities of others in the community.[2] The individual votes not simply because he is concerned with his own welfare, but because he is concerned with the welfare of others (Hudson and Jones 1994, explore this idea). The utility from voting is therefore likely to be much higher,

and voting is a rational response for those who look more broadly on the effect of their vote on the community at large. With $\theta > 0$, the individual has far more at stake in any vote than simply the effect on his own utility (U_i).

Plott (1987), however, points to a problem with this explanation. Suppose that you are concerned for the well-being of others. You will still vote only if the probability that you can change the outcome, multiplied by the benefit you derive from the *difference* between the outcomes with and without your vote, exceeds the costs of voting. Assume there are two issues X_1 and X_2, each affecting the public as a whole. The benefits to any individual from voting will be $B = O_i(X_1) - O_i(X_2)$, i.e. the difference that each issue may have on O_i. The expected benefit is PB, but when P is small this approaches zero, and there is still no reason for them to participate.

To explain why individuals vote is difficult in the context of the Downs hypothesis, because each individual voter is assumed to have such a small significance in the electoral process. Readers may note the obvious parallels with the literature on the provision of public goods when the individual is one of a large group. At the end of the day, however, individuals do vote, and, in just the same way as it has been claimed that the free rider hypothesis is a problem 'only for economists' (see chapter 3), the same might be said about voter turnout.

4.3 The design of voting rules

In appraising the design of voting rules, there are two approaches that might be applied. One is a strongly normative approach; a set of criteria is established and used to decide which constitutions are good. The social choice analyst must make explicit those requirements of a social decision-making rule. Different voting rules are then assessed by reference to such a criterion. This was the approach K. J. Arrow discussed in 1951. (See Arrow 1963 for the second edition of this work.)

In this section we begin by examining the work of Arrow and, in particular, his conclusion that no constitutional rule would fulfil what might be regarded as eminently reasonable conditions. The conclusion is illustrated by reference to one of the simplest and most widely used constitutional rules: a simple majority rule whereby, if 50 per cent of the electorate plus one more individual vote for a particular policy ($50\% + 1$), that policy is chosen.

---

[2] How can we predict when voters act ethically? To make such predictions it is necessary to have a theory of how ethical preferences are formed and what determines their strength. It is argued by Mueller (1987) that ethical behaviour is learned. Therefore we must look to variables such as home environment during childhood, education experience, community stability and religion.

Later in this section, following Mueller (1979), we utilize another approach to the analysis of a simple majority voting rule. This focuses on the characteristics of the rule; it analyses the impact of the rule on decisions and looks at the costs of making a decision. Thereafter, it is left to readers to decide whether or not a simple majority voting rule is more acceptable than an alternative decision-making rule.

4.3.1 Arrow's impossibility theorem

Arrow has shown that there is no constitutional rule that will simultaneously satisfy what might be considered to be a list of 'reasonable' conditions. Given the limitations of traditional welfare economics, the importance of such an analysis should be evident. In chapter 1 it was shown that, even within the Paretian framework, ultimately reference would generally need to be made to a social welfare function to provide information about the preferred income distribution within the community. But in what sense is it possible to provide this information for decision-making in the public sector? It is quite reasonable to believe that each individual has his or her own social welfare function; i.e. at the individual level preferences might be expressed as to whether one income distribution is to be preferred to another. However, the problem is aggregating these individual preferences to guide a collective choice. That there is no satisfactory constitutional rule by which individual preferences can be aggregated creates an important obstacle for decision-making in the public sector.

A constitutional rule may be regarded as a mechanism for aggregating the preferences of individuals in order to establish a collective choice between different alternatives. Arrow refers to the alternatives as different 'social states' (e.g. A, B, C), within which issues of allocation and distribution are settled in a particular way. He argues that there are five 'conditions of correspondence' which *any* constitutional rule must satisfy.

1. *Collective rationality* The preference ordering that results from collective choice must satisfy the requirements of any 'rational' individual's preference ordering. In economics, rationality is dependent on consistency in decision-making rather than on the choice of any particular outcome. A preference ordering must, therefore, possess the attributes of *connexity* (outcomes must be capable of being compared) and *transitivity*. A transitive ordering of three alternatives A, B, C is one in which, if A is preferred to B and B is preferred to C, then A must be preferred to C.

2. *The Pareto principle* This condition is quite reasonable in so far as it demands that, if all members of the community prefer A to B, then the collective choice that emerges from a constitutional rule must also indicate that A is preferred to B.

3. *The independence of irrelevant alternatives* This is one of the more controversial conditions. It says that, if a choice has to be made between two alternatives A and B, that choice should not be influenced by the ranking of either A or B with other alternatives such as C or D. These latter alternatives are irrelevant in that they are not part of the decision. The decision is a simple binary choice between A or B. If, for example, any individual changed his own ranking as between A and C, this should not alter the collective choice between A and B. More discussion of this condition can be found below.

4. *Non-dictatorship* This condition is more obvious: there should be no one individual whose preferences are automatically the preferences expressed for the community.

5. *Unrestricted domain* This is a condition that Arrow has made explicit. It stipulates that no individual should be excluded from contributing to the establishment of a collective choice, provided that the individual has a transitive ordering of preferences. There is no way that a particular 'rational' individual should be disenfranchised because of his choices.

The Arrow Impossibility Theorem demonstrates that no constitutional rule will comply with all these conditions. For example, with the simple majority voting rule (50% + 1) there is the classic problem described by the Marquis de Condorcet in the eighteenth century. In Table 4.2 three individuals (voters A, B and C) choose between three alternatives (X, Y, Z). The rankings of the individuals are shown as 3, 2, 1 (in order of preference with 3 'most preferred'). It is clear that each voter has a transitive preference ordering. (For example, A prefers X to Y, prefers Y to Z and also prefers X to Z.) If a collective decision was required as between X and Y, the majority would choose X (voters A and C); between Y and Z, a majority would opt for Y (voters A and B). As a consequence, to satisfy the condition of collective rationality, majority voting 'should' lead to a preference for X rather than Z. However, in the example voters B and C constitute a majority in favour of Z rather than X. In this way, the simple majority voting fails the Arrow test. The final winner is dependent on which vote is taken first. For example, the sequence of votes in Table 4.3 indicates alternative

Table 4.2 Majority voting: cyclical

| | Options | | |
Voters	X	Y	Z
A	3	2	1
B	1	3	2
C	2	1	3

Table 4.3 Outcome dependency on agenda setting

Vote between	Vote between	Outcome
Y $v.$ X	X $v.$ Z	Z
X $v.$ Z	Z $v.$ Y	Y
Z $v.$ Y	Y $v.$ X	X

winners, and this is clearly unattractive. This example may appear contrived. Of course, there are cases in which the preference rankings of individual voters will not lead to a 'cyclical' outcome. These are discussed later in the chapter. However, the point to emphasize here is that such a cyclical outcome cannot be ruled out because of the condition of unrestricted domain.

It should be emphasized that any voting rules also fail the Arrow test. Take for example the Borda Count. Voters give each of the n options a score (n, $n-1$, etc.) according to their ranking of the options. The option with the highest total score is selected by the community. The following example (based on Sen 1970) illustrates the vulnerability of this voting rule to the requirement of the independence of irrelevant alternatives. Assume that a community has to choose between X and Z. In this choice Y is not available; i.e. it is an irrelevant alternative. In Tables 4.4 and 4.5, under a Borda Count rule the ranks of the preferences of the three voters are now summed to find the preferred alternative for the community. It is clear that in Table 4.5 the choice between X and Z has altered as a result of a change in the ranking on the part of indi-

Table 4.4 Borda Count voting

| | Options | | |
Voters	X	Y	Z
A	3	2	1
B	2	1	3
C	2	1	3
Totals	7	4	7

Table 4.5 Borda Count voting with changed preferences

| | Options | | |
Voters	X	Y	Z
A	3	1	2
B	2	1	3
C	2	1	3
Totals	7	3	8

vidual A with respect to Y and Z. Whereas in Table 4.4 the community is indifferent as between X and Z (i.e. an equal score of 7), in Table 4.5 Z is preferred to X. The only change in the tables is with respect to a ranking between Z and, what we may regard as an irrelevant alternative Y. The Borda Count, therefore, also fails the Arrow test.

4.3.2 What is the significance of the Arrow impossibility theorem?

By now it is clear that the combination of the above 'conditions of correspondence' are not easily met. It is not surprising then that an immediate response was to call in question the need for all these conditions. Little (1952), for example, doubted that the condition of independence of irrelevant alternatives would be required because traditionally welfare economics requires that individuals' preferences are assumed constant. Buchanan (1954) questioned whether the collective choice ranking need be subject to the same restriction of transitivity that applies to the individual preference function.

Discussion will inevitably continue as to the 'desirability' of the criteria. In 1963 Arrow took issue with his critics. For example, he argued that, irrespective of the traditional assumptions of economic theory, preferences do change and it is, therefore, necessary to impose the condition of independence of irrelevant alternatives. If all the conditions of correspondence can be defended, what is the importance of the Impossibility Theorem?

The absence of a constitutional rule that 'fits the bill' means that we are left, at least in the first instance, with criteria such as the Paretian framework, rather than simply putting alternatives directly to the vote. In a sense we are obliged to 'grope' for a solution, in the absence of a clear statement from an acceptable social welfare function. The welfare criteria discussed in chapter 2 retain their importance as a first step in analysis prior to decision-taking in the public sector.

4.4 Some characteristics of the majority voting rule

While voting rules fail the Arrow criteria, it is never-theless necessary to consider the characteristics of the simple majority voting rule, if only because of its importance in the collective decision-making of Western democracies. It is important to be aware of the potential failings of such a rule. Already the pro-blem of cyclical outcomes has been introduced. Here we begin by asking, What conditions would be required to avoid such a paradox? Later the discussion is opened more generally to other features of this voting rule.

4.4.1 Majority voting and the median voter

Duncan Black (1948) has shown that a transitive social ordering of different alternatives can be pro-duced if individuals' preferences conform to a specific pattern. To illustrate this it is usual to contrast a non-cyclical outcome with the above example of a cyclical voting outcome. In Table 4.6 three individuals A, B, C choose between three alternative options X, Y, Z. With a majority voting rule, individuals A and B would prefer Y to Z; individuals B and C would prefer Z to X, and individuals B and C would prefer Y to X. Hence the ordering of the social choice is transitive: Y p Z; Z p X, and Y p X. Suppose that X, Y and Z relate to the size of a government budget. Assume that X is a small budget, Y is a moderate-sized budget and Z is a large budget. Individual B is the 'median voter': she prefers the median alternative. It is clear that the 'median voter's' preferences are those that determine the out-come of the majority vote. With the sequence of pre-ferences shown in Table 4.6, it is the preference of the 'median voter' that indicates the alternative chosen by a majority vote.

It is possible to plot in Fig. 4.2 the preferences for each voter. The pattern that emerges is significant. The characteristic that is relevant in this case is that pre-ferences are single-peaked for each voter.

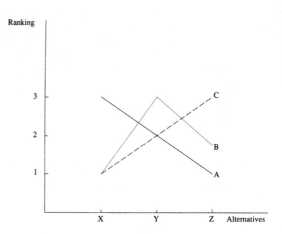

Figure 4.2 Single-peaked preferences.

Single-peaked preferences for the three individuals are also illustrated in Fig. 4.3, but this time in terms of the individuals' utility. They will be evident when each voter's most preferred outcome is such that the utility for every other alternative decreases monotonically with the distance between the most preferred out-come and the alternative. Reference to this diagram confirms that the choice of the median voter will win. If an alternative outcome to O_2 were proposed (i.e. O_3 which is greater than O_2), individuals A and B would vote for O_2 rather than O_3. Conversely, if an alternat-ive outcome less than O_2 were proposed, individuals B and C would form a majority in favour of O_2. Once again, the choice of the median voter defeats any other alternative. This is the preferred position of the med-ian voter. Looking at Fig. 4.2, readers can confirm that preferences are single-peaked in that pattern: for each voter they rise to a unique peak.

By comparison, Table 4.4 showed a configuration of preference orderings which will give a cyclical out-come (repeated for the reader's convenience as Table 4.7). The result noted above is that majority voting gives arbitrary results. Everything depends on the choice that is offered and the ability to set the agenda is crucial. In the associated Fig. 4.4 preferences are shown to be multi-peaked and this is what causes the

Table 4.6 Majority voting: non-cyclical

	X	Y	Z
A	3	2	1
B	1	3	2
C	1	2	3

Table 4.7 Majority voting: cyclical

	X	Y	Z
A	3	2	1
B	1	3	2
C	2	1	3

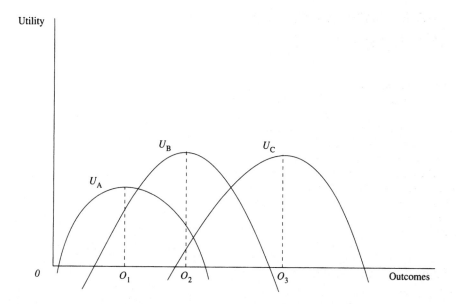

Figure 4.3 Illustrating single-peaked preferences.

problem. Individual C is seen to prefer outcome Z but, failing this, prefers outcome X to outcome Y. (As Musgrave and Musgrave (1989) note, the individual is something of an 'extremist'. However, it should be stressed that she is not irrational: C's preference order is transitive. This may have a quite reasonable interpretation in terms of an 'all or nothing' view of the world.)

Yet, as noted by Ingberman and Inman (1988), the concept of single-peaked preferences has an intuitive appeal. First, it corresponds to the notion of a con-

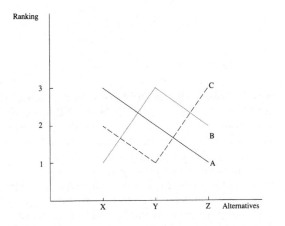

Figure 4.4 Multi-peaked preferences.

tinum of preferences which spans the divide between left-wing and right-wing politics. Secondly, single-peaked preferences can often be perceived in a quite natural way when considering consumer choice. Fig. 4.5 illustrates this. In part (a) of the figure the preferences of a voter are shown as between a public good (G) and income (Y). The budget constraint is determined by the before-tax income and the effective tax price. It is evident that g^* indicates the voter's most preferred allocation of resources. Fig. 4.5(b) maps each level of G in the form of a ranking of different quantities of the good at the tax price. This ranking is based upon the preference ordering implicit in the indifference curves of part (a). The voter's bliss or ideal point is g^*. Feasible levels of G further and further from g^* are valued less and less. Preferences for G in part (b) of the figure are therefore single-peaked.

The argument by Duncan Black (1948) that single-peaked preferences are important is, however, subject to qualification. While single-peaked preferences are important to avoid a cyclical outcome, this applies when a single issue is the focus of decision-taking (e.g. the level of G). The property of single-peak preferences loses its significance when there is more than one issue. Assume the vote is in terms of the quantities of two public goods G_1 and G_2. In Fig. 4.6 voter A's preferences are shown for the two goods by the utility curves I_A. The most preferred combination

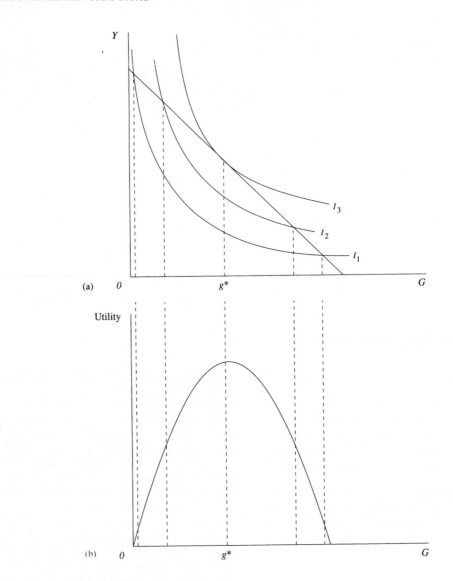

Figure 4.5 Single-peaked preferences and consumer demand.

Source: based on Ingberman and Inman (1988).

of the two goods for A is K_A and the utility curves are to be read as contour lines on a map, indicating that the further from K_A (the summit of an ordinal utility 'mountain'), the lower the level of utility. The same applies for the other two voters, B and C. It is clear that for all three individuals preferences are single-peaked (the contours moving to a single peak in each case). Assume that the community has to vote between three options I, II and III, which relate to three alternative combinations of the two public goods. Voters B and C form a majority in favour of

II rather than I, while voters A and C form a majority in favour of I rather than III. It should follow, therefore, by the property of transitivity, that II is preferred to III, and yet in Fig. 4.6 voters A and B form a majority in favour of III rather than II. The cyclical outcome from majority voting has not been removed, even though preferences are single-peaked. Single-peaked preferences are no guarantee that a cyclical outcome from majority voting will not occur when the issues are multidimensional rather than unidimensional.

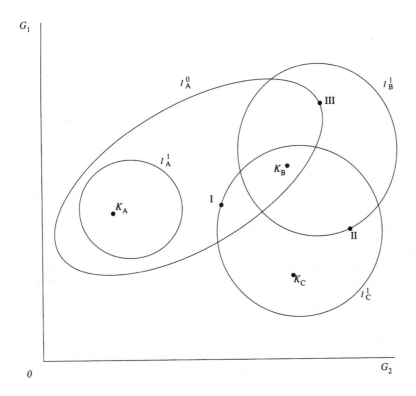

Figure 4.6 Single-peaked preferences and multi-dimensional issues.

4.4.2 Majority voting and welfare criteria

Given the reference in public economics to welfare criteria, it is important to consider whether majority voting might generate either Pareto-optimal improvements or potential Pareto improvements. Following Mueller (1979), it is easy to demonstrate that neither of these results is guaranteed. In Fig. 4.7 two groups are assumed to be active in the community. Members of group I (individuals i), who are rich, and members of group J (individuals j), who are poor, may feel that they share common interests with respect to any proposed legislation. If majority voting would guarantee a Pareto improvement, then, with respect to the utility feasibility curves U_1F_1 and U_2F_2 in Fig. 4.7, only those movements from 1 to the range between 2 and 3 would pass the majority vote. If we suppose that I are in a majority, then of course it is possible to move anywhere along $U_2 2$ of the utility feasibility curve U_2F_2. If this occurred, then a movement to the range 23 would be a potential Pareto improvement. However, the will of the majority is not limited to this range. Starting from 1, they may move anywhere in the quadrant $4U_2 21$; moving along

U_1F_1, they could accept policies that moved to outcomes such as 5. Indeed, there is nothing to preclude them from moving to a point U_1. In other words,

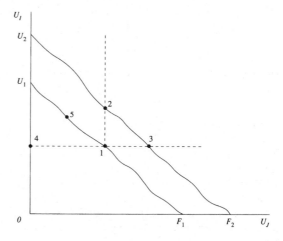

Figure 4.7 Majority voting and welfare criteria.
Source: based on Mueller (1979).

there is no reason to suppose that majority voting may not lead to pure redistribution from one section of the community to another. The will of the majority may, in this way, create costs for the minority, and this has long been recognized (de Tocqueville 1835).

The voting rule that will guarantee a Pareto improvement is not majority voting but the rule of unanimity. For unanimity to be attained, no one individual can be made worse off by the change in question, otherwise he or she would use the effective power of a veto by voting against the motion. In economics the importance of the unanimity rule has been well established in this context (e.g. Wicksell 1896).

4.4.3 The costs of the majority voting rule

While the majority rule is not perfect, could it be cost-effective? One attempt to consider the costs associated with different voting rules is presented by Buchanan and Tullock (1965) in *The Calculus of Consent*. In Fig. 4.8 the vertical axis records the costs associated with different voting rules. Assume that the total number of individuals in the community is N_{max}. The proportion N/N_{max} is one way of describing the required support necessary in a voting rule to attain acceptance of any electoral proposition. A simple majority voting rule $(50\% + 1)$ would require a proportion, as shown by a point just over half-way on the x axis. Clearly, it would similarly be possible to describe other voting rules requiring respectively greater or lesser percentage approval in an election. At the extreme, the voting rule of unanimity would require all (N_{max}) to approve.

The costs of voting are represented in Fig. 4.8 by E and D respectively. E are the *external* costs that are created by the winning majority. Individual members of the minority are subjected to the decisions of the majority, decisions with which they may well disagree and thus suffer a welfare loss. In Fig. 4.8 it is clear that, as the size of the necessary majority increases, so these external costs fall. The potentially coerced minority falls in number as we move along the x axis. At the extreme (point N_{max}) unanimity would apply and these costs would disappear. Any person disagreeing with the proposition has the right to veto this proposal.

The costs D are the costs of *decision-making*, inherent in the need to get agreement. In the case of unanimity it is unlikely that agreement will easily be achieved with respect to any issue: there is always likely to be some person who disagrees with the proposition in hand. Here, then, the costs are lower when any one person can take the decision and, as the proportion required to agree on any issue increases, it is likely that the costs of finding agreement between the winning majority is likely to increase.

The two costs are summed as $E + D$. Note that the minimum total cost situation does not necessarily occur at the intersection point of E and D: it depends

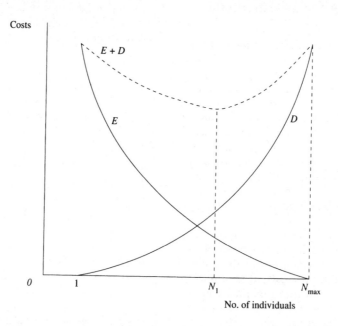

Figure 4.8 The costs of voting.

on their rate of change also. The position at which the minimum cost situation occurs N_1 is where the absolute values of the slope of E and D are equal. However, there is no necessity that it always exists at this point and may easily imply minority rule. Everything will depend on the issue. For some propositions it may be easier to achieve consensus than on others, and some decisions will involve higher or lower external costs.

4.4.4 Majority voting and intensity of preference

Does it matter which voting rule is applied? It is possible, following Musgrave and Musgrave (1989), to illustrate how the result that emerges from a collective choice will differ according to the voting rule applied. At the same time, another deficiency of the simple majority voting rule can be noted, i.e. its failure to permit intensity of preference.

In Table 4.8 the preferences of voters A, B and C are shown with respect to three alternative choices X, Y and Z. The table shows the rank that each voter gives each particular option. However, in order to consider the intensity of preference that individuals attach to each option, the assumption is made that each individual has been asked to allocate a total of 10 points between the three options. If a simple majority rule mechanism is applied, the vote between options X and Y would place Y preferred to X (a majority of B and C); Y preferred to Z (a majority of A and C); and Z preferred to X (a majority of B and C). A Borda Count would apply when the rankings awarded to each option are added. In this example a rank of 3 is given to the most preferred alternative, and therefore the outcome with the highest total rank will be the one chosen. Again, this type of decision-making would lead to Y proving successful, as the highest aggregate rank for all options applies for Y. However, with point voting the highest score is for option Z. (The score for Z is 12, for Y 11 and for X 7.)

The use of point voting allows individuals to express their intensity of preference. However, a general problem with voting mechanisms, often emphasized in this context, is the incentive to act strategically. Voters, anticipating that their true choice is not popular with others, have an incentive to distort these point allocations to try and ensure that their second choice is secured. As a rule, the more sophisticated the voting mechanism, the more open it is to strategic manipulation.

A simple majority voting rule is said to be deficient to the extent that it does not indicate preference intensity. However, logrolling might be useful in this respect. *Logrolling* refers to the trading of votes: one voter agrees with another to vote for an issue about which he may have very little interest in return for the agreement of the other voter to support an issue of interest to the first. With reference to Table 4.9, three voters A, B and C are considering two options X and Y. The importance of the two options to each voter is shown by the values of the utility increase (or decrease) that will be experienced if either electoral option is passed and adopted.

If each of these options requires the consent of the majority to be adopted, then it is clear that neither issue will be adopted. Voters A and C will form a majority against the adoption of X and voters A and B will form a majority against Y. Voter B has a particular preference for X, while voter C particularly likes Y. However, this intensity of preference has no role to play in majority voting. If logrolling were possible, B might agree with C to vote for Y provided that C agreed to vote for X.

The explicit vote trade appears to resolve the problem. In terms of the potential Pareto improvement criterion, the community is better off to the extent that the gainers in both cases could compensate the losers. In both cases the net change in utility for the community as a whole, as a result of passing the

Table 4.8 Majority voting and intensity of preference

	Options					
	X		Y		Z	
	Rank	Points	Rank	Points	Rank	Points
A	3	5	2	3	1	2
B	1	1	2	3	3	6
C	1	1	3	5	2	4
Aggregate score	5	7	7	11	6	12

Table 4.9 The process of logrolling

Voters	Issues	
	X	Y
A	−3	−3
B	6	−3
C	−2	7

proposals, is 1 util. Such a conclusion is, however, unwarranted. Readers may confirm this simply. If the util losses for A were increased from −3 to −5 in both cases, then the adoption of X and Y does not pass the potential Pareto improvement criterion. Moreover, the introduction of logrolling is no answer to the problem of the cyclical paradox of majority voting (see Mueller 1979).

4.4.5 An assessment of majority voting

After this critique of majority voting, readers may be surprised at the resilience with which majority voting is defended by Western democracies. However, it is important to remember the message of the Arrow Impossibility Theorem. No constitutional rule is satisfactory on Arrow's criteria. Similarly, with respect to the above critique it is not clear that any voting rule is unambiguously preferable. Frey (1983) considers other alternatives, including the following.

1. *Approval voting* Here voters are allowed to vote for, or approve of, as many issues (or candidates) as they wish—but not more than one vote may be cast for each issue. The option receiving the greatest number of votes is chosen.

2. *Probabilistic voting on the basis of a referendum* Here the number of votes going to each of the two alternatives is counted (as would be the case with majority rule). Then the social choice is determined by attributing probabilities to the alternatives according to the percentage shares in the vote, the final vote being based on the probabilities. An advantage is that when the majority is small, as for example in the case of 55 per cent 'yes' and 45 per cent 'no', the large minority is not necessarily suppressed; they simply have a lower chance of winning.

3. *Voting by veto* Each individual may present his own proposal. The social decision is taken by each individual's deleting from the set of alternatives that proposal to which he is most strongly opposed.

These examples are by no means exhaustive. However, they also have deficiencies. In concluding this assessment of the simple majority voting rule, Frey (1983) qualifies his assessment: 'as is the case with all other decision-making systems, majority rule is imperfect' (p. 90). Here then we stress that, while simple majority voting is not perfect, there is no automatic first preference for a rule for decision-making in the public sector.

4.5 Representative democracy: the role of politicians and political parties

Downs (1957) assumed that politicians, as well as voters, act in their own self-interest. It is assumed that the objective of a politician is to maximize political power. The attainment of such power furnishes politicians with prestige and influence. However, in order to secure political power, the politician must maximize votes. This means that politicians will not always choose policies that accord to the 'public interest'. Their first consideration may, instead, be how any policy will affect their political popularity. For example, it is possible that a long-term public sector investment may yield impressive returns to the community, and selection of such a project may be considered to be in the public interest. However, a politician may be more concerned with the timing of the 'pay-off' with respect to the date of the next election. Hence those projects that have a visible pay-off prior to and close to the election date are more likely to be acceptable. Long-term projects may be rejected, even if they yield higher social returns, if voters are unaware of the long-term project or if they are myopic. It will be important to the politician that the public investment wins him votes.

4.5.1 Logrolling and political manifestos

In selecting policies to offer the electorate, politicians and political parties engage implicitly in the process of logrolling. Vote-trading between individuals is secured by the design of the political manifesto. Politicians offer voters the opportunity to support issues on which they feel strongly, in return for voting for issues about which they may be indifferent. Assume that there are three voters (or three groups of voters), A, B and C, and that in an election there are two main issues, expenditure on defence and the country's membership of the EC. Currently A and B form a winning majority. They both support increased expenditure on national defence whereas C, in the minority, prefers a reduction of defence expenditure. A political party wishing to win majority support may do so if it can offer a platform that links reduced expenditure on defence with another policy on which either A or B feels strongly. For example, B may strongly support increased international involvement in the EC. A manifesto that coupled the proposals to increase contribution to the EC budget with reduction of defence expenditure would form an implicit arrangement between voters B and C, whereby each individual would vote for a proposal she dislikes in order to secure the outcome for which she has a particular preference.

The example outlined in Table 4.10 (based on Musgrave and Musgrave 1989) illustrates the way in which a coupling of policies can lead to electoral success. In the table the policy proposals have been paired: the electorate is asked to choose X or Y and Z or W. For purposes of exposition, information of intensity of preference is available. (For example, it might be assumed that each voter is asked to allocate a total of £100 between each alternative.) It is clear that a simple majority voting rule would lead to proposals Y and Z being successful. The temptation for any party to couple policies Y and Z would, however, ignore the intensity of feeling that voters have with respect to the policies in question. Clearly, a political entrepreneur would be advised to write a manifesto that coupled X and W. In Table 4.10 both voters A and B would vote for such a manifesto. Each is implicitly prepared to trade his vote on one issue for the other's vote for that proposal which is most valued: A votes for W because of the importance of X and B votes for X because of the importance of W. Once again, there is no safeguard that the advent of an astute political entrepreneur

Table 4.10 Intensity of preference and party manifestos

Voters	Policy proposals			
	X or Y		Z or W	
A	90	10	58	42
B	45	55	10	90
C	45	55	55	45
	Combination Y & Z		Combination X & W	
A	68		132	
B	65		135	
C	110		90	

Source: R. A. Musgrave and P. B. Musgrave, *Public Finance in Theory and Practice*, 5th edn. New York: McGraw-Hill, 1989. Reproduced with the permission of McGraw-Hill, Inc., with some amendment.

necessarily leads to the pursuit of the 'public interest'. In the event that voter C would allocate say £90 to both Y and Z, the aggregate point score for Y and Z would exceed that for X and W, though X and W would still command a majority. To the extent that pound-value interpersonal comparisons can be made, this outcome does not maximize welfare for the community. That it may open the door to another party to offer a second coupling is, of course, another possibility.

In terms of party competition, it is obvious that a political party P1, coupling Y and Z, will fail against a political party P2, coupling X and W, and that the reason for this is that P1 has not realized that, while voter B prefers Y to X, he more strongly opposes Z to W. Party P1 clearly needed information that indicated the relative importance of his position on X/Y to that of his position on Z/W. Information as to intensity of preference will clearly affect the support that any party can expect. Therefore, when selecting policy positions, it is essential to gauge how important each position is to the party's overall electoral support.

4.5.2 Vote maximizing and the median voter rule

The work of Anthony Downs (and that of Harold Hotelling) suggests that, when politicians are vote maximizers, the median voter preferences are still critical in determining the outcome of a majority vote. In Fig. 4.9, the distribution of voters from left-wing political views to right-wing political views are shown along the x axis. The distribution is assumed to be unimodal and symmetric. Two candidates are presented for election. These may be members of two different political parties, reflecting respectively left- and right-wing political ideologies. If it is assumed that every voter will vote and that each voter votes for the candidate whose views best reflect his or her political position, then it can be shown that the two candidates will adopt a position midpoint in the distribution. If L and R are the initial positions of the two candidates, then it is clear that, by moving from L to L-ish, the left-wing candidate will win the votes of those electors midway between L-ish and R without losing any of the voters to the left of L-ish. Alternatively, if the right-wing candidate moves from R to R-ish, this candidate stands to gain all the votes of those electors up to midway between R-ish and L, without losing the votes of those electors to the right of R-ish. It is clear that if each candidate adopts this strategy then, step by step, both will move side by side at the position of the median voter.

This analysis is a useful reference in explaining the growth of consensus politics in two-party politics. It

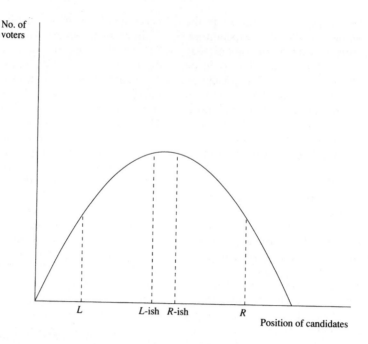

Figure 4.9 Politicians and the median voter.

is, however, very dependent on the assumptions outlined above. Tullock (1976) discusses the impact of a three-party system when platform differentiation within limits becomes the vote-maximizing strategy. Mueller (1979) surveys literature that introduces the assumption that political loyalty to candidates may be lost by shifts towards the 'centre ground'. In this way, the analysis is capable of refinement to meet the particular assumptions thought most relevant.

For political scientists, perhaps the biggest weakness of this discussion is in the direction of causality, with electoral preferences causing party platforms. Instead, perhaps the essence of good politicians and leaders is their ability to devise their own platform and cause the electorate to move their preferences to them (at least on occasions).

4.6 Voting and the Leviathan hypothesis: will majority voting provide 'excessive' public expenditure?

As we have seen in our earlier analysis of public goods and private goods, the benefits of which are largely external, there will be undersupply without public provision. Too little will be provided by reference to the Paretian optimum. This leaves open the question of whether the scope of public provision will be 'deficient' or 'excessive'. We begin by asking the question of whether or not there are circumstances in which majority voting will actually provide a Pareto optimum output of public goods.

Bowen (1943) presents an analysis of majority voting and public good provision. In Fig. 4.10 it is assumed, for simplicity, that public goods can be provided at constant marginal cost. The marginal cost is divided equally between N individuals, who constitute the community for which the public good is provided. Each individual voter assumes, therefore, that the costs to him are MC/N. The demand curves represent the marginal benefit that each individual derives from the good. Any point on the demand curve, therefore, records 'willingness to pay' for the public good (the marginal rate at which money will be substituted for an additional unit of the good). Each voter would prefer that output of the public good at which marginal benefit from additional units of output is equal to the tax price MC/N. If each voter votes for such an output, then voter A votes for q^a, voter B for q^b and so on. Given this behaviour, it is clear in Fig. 4.10 that the majority voting rule implies that the

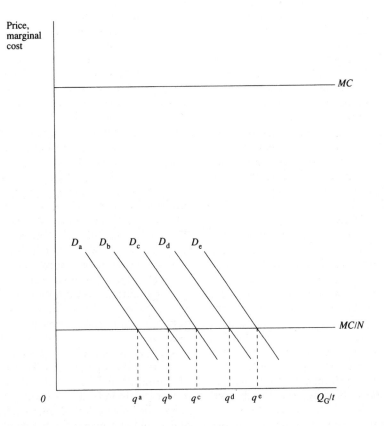

Figure 4.10 Majority voting and optimal provision of a public good.

median voter's wishes hold. Everyone would agree that output should be at least q^a; voters B, C, D, E would agree that output should be q^b; C, D, E agree that output should be q^c, but, thereafter, there is no majority in favour of an expansion of output. Output is then determined by majority voting to be q^c, and the preferred position of the median voter is that which emerges from majority voting.

In this partial equilibrium setting, if the demands of the individuals were symmetrically distributed around the median, this output is the Pareto-optimal output for the public good. If such demand curves are vertically added, then, by definition, the aggregate demand would equal marginal cost at Oq^c. The conclusion is that there are quite specific circumstances in which majority voting would generate a Pareto-optimal outcome. As Musgrave (1985) points out, the question of 'over'- or 'under'-provision appears to rest in the model on the distribution of preferences. If D_a were shifted to the left, holding other preferences constant, then the output emerging from a majority vote would be an 'excessive' output. Conversely, if the

distribution altered so that D_c shifts to the right, then output would be 'too little'. The assumption, generally, that there is a bias in majority voting in favour of 'excessive' provision may be typical within the 'Leviathan school' but is not necessarily realistic. Nevertheless, it is possible to predict 'excessive' provision if assumptions are amended. A re-examination of the assumptions that underlie the above analysis indicates how the Leviathan case can be established.

4.6.1 Tax price and majority voting

Tullock (1959) concluded that majority voting would lead to a greater provision of private goods within the public sector than would be the case in the private sector. He introduced the example of five individual farmers who use the simple majority voting rule for deciding on a public expenditure programme to maintain access roads to their farms. Of the five farmers A, B, C, D, E, a majority may be expected to vote for expenditure on *their* roads up to a point where the marginal cost involved for them is equal to the marginal value of the benefits experienced by them. Maintenance of roads for A, B and C is financed by general taxation, so that two-fifths of the tax cost is borne by D and E. The marginal cost for A, B and C in Fig. 4.10 are reduced further, because there is no expenditure on roads for D and E and the marginal cost of the road programme is still shared between the five. MC will fall as only three roads are involved, whereas N is the same. Given that the decision of the median voter is still central, A, B and C will still vote for the programme, but this time they will vote for even greater public expenditure if demand is price-elastic. In effect, the fact that the programme is shared over the whole of the economy displaces some of the costs to the minority. Given this implicit subsidy, those farmers involved will consume a greater amount of road maintenance than they would have done had this been provided and priced in the private sector.

There are questions that may be asked of this analysis. First, as Musgrave (1985) points out, why is this essentially private good provided by the public sector at all? The access roads are private to the farmers involved and there is no reason to suppose that this must be provided via the public sector. Why will the two farmers D and E not find it in their interests to induce C (possibly by some form of side-payment) to form a coalition to resist the programme (Cullis and Jones 1987)?

Nevertheless, if this price effect noted by Tullock were operative, then it would occur on other public expenditure decisions also. The majority involved may differ according to the question in hand (e.g. sometimes A, B, C, sometimes A, B, D), and therefore income effects in the long run can be expected to cancel. Yet on each occasion, the price effect would lead to greater provision than if the good were provided via the private sector.

4.6.2 Fiscal illusion

It has long been argued that voters underestimate the costs of public expenditure programmes (Puviani 1903). There are a number of reasons for believing this.

1. As the costs of programmes are spread over a large number of voters, the tax price to any one voter may appear very small. In Fig. 4.10, as N becomes very large the significance of MC/N may be lost for any programme. To the extent that MC/N appears lower than the 'true' tax price it is clear, by reference to the median voter's demand curve, that majority voting will lead to a greater level of public expenditure. Voters are not able to attach great weight to the tax

cost because it is so widely shared. Moreover, it is argued that, as the programme benefits may be more visible to small groups who wish to see the expenditure advanced (see chapter 2), the electorate is now less resistant to pressure for the programme. It is precisely this argument that has led commentators to call for tax reform which would place greater reliance on the visibility of taxes (e.g. Brennan and Buchanan 1980). There is clear evidence to suggest that some forms of taxation are more visible than others (e.g. Wagner 1976).

2. The fact that not all government revenue is raised as a result of taxation is thought to lead voters to underestimate the costs of government programmes. Government may choose to cover a deficit on the budget (i.e. the difference between taxation and government spending) by borrowing from the public. Those who lend to government do so *voluntarily*. They *choose* to adjust their portfolio of assets, possibly to forgo current consumption for future consumption (Buchanan 1958). The fact that it is done voluntarily does not make it appear the same cost as the 'sacrifice' inherent in taxation. Furthermore, as resources are not all drawn from taxation, the tax price is again apparently lower than the true cost of the programme. In Fig. 4.10, taxation would finance only a portion of MC. Thus voters would suffer illusion. The total tax bill (T) may be shared between the voters and they may make decisions on the basis of T/N, but $T/N < MC/N$.[3]

3. Tax awareness is also said to be reduced to the extent that there are forces in the economy that *automatically* boost government revenue, without the formal need to introduce a new tax or change the tax rate. Inflation raises nominal income and thereby moves taxpayers into higher income bands. With a progressive tax rate structure, this will imply that the real value of taxation has increased for taxpayers. To this extent, the tax costs of some aspects of expenditure programmes are never brought to the taxpayers' attention, and as a result greater expenditure is sanctioned than would be the case if the tax/expenditure alternatives were more explicit.

Set against this argument is the proposition that voters are underinformed as to the benefits of public expenditure programmes and that, if any bias exists, it is in terms of 'under'-provision. Downs (1960) argues that the programmes of government are often associated with benefits of an intangible nature or with benefits to be reaped a long time in the future. Expend-

---

[3] For further discussion on the tax-debt issue see section 10.3.8 below.

iture on defence or on overseas aid, for example, would fall into this category. In this case, with reference to Fig. 4.10, the demand curves of the voters would be to the left of 'fully informed' demand. Galbraith (1962) has put forward arguments in keeping with this general position. He believes that private goods are more vigorously advertised by private entrepreneurs than are publicly produced goods and services. If this is true, it again would suggest 'under'-provision.

There is little empirical evidence to suggest that the net impact of fiscal illusion is to bias the size of the public sector one way or another. Such evidence as exists would not support either *optimistic* illusion (tax price lower than actually the case) or *pessimistic* illusion (benefits lower than actually the case). (For further discussion see Cullis and Jones 1987.)

4.6.3 The tyranny of the majority

In the case described by Tullock (1959), the majority voted for 'too large' a public expenditure programme because they were able to offset the costs on the minority. This affected the tax price that they perceived. A more general argument along these lines, however, is that the majority can directly redistribute from the minority. It has long been argued (see e.g. Shehab 1953) that the development of progressive taxation and the introduction of social security arrangements can best be explained historically by the extension of suffrage to the poorer classes. Such schemes may be supported by a majority as they imply that the more wealthy minority will be taxed to assist the lower-income majority. The possibility that a majority may operate in this way has long been recognized (see e.g. de Tocqueville 1835). The result of such electoral activity may be to increase the transfers that are found in the public budget.

While this process appears explicit, it is worth noting that such redistribution via the political process may not be obvious and may not simply be between lower-income and higher-income groups. One specific example to note in passing is the transfers that may exist between those who work in the private sector and those who work in the public sector. It has been argued, for example, that the public sector grows by a 'snowball' effect (Musgrave 1981), to the extent that, as the number of public employees grows, so the public sector will grow more quickly. As more individuals in the economy are dependent for their livelihood on the public sector, so the chances increase that there will be a majority in favour of public expenditure increases.

Musgrave (1981) has questioned the 'tyranny of the majority' argument (that the majority will strive to redistribute as much as possible from the minority). First, individuals may be conscious of intertemporal considerations; that is to say, they may not choose a particularly steep progressive rate of taxation if they imagine that in the future they will rise from the low-income to the high-income ranks. Secondly, they may be conscious that such redistribution can affect the total output of the economy. High tax rates may be a disincentive to work, invest or take risks (see chapters 7 and 10). The prospect of continued redistribution may, if taken to excess, mean that there is less output to redistribute (Meltzer and Richard 1981). Thirdly, there may be a strong normative acceptance of the entitlement to earnings which limits redistribution.[4]

4.7 Summary

The main focus of this chapter is the voting rules that might be used for decision-making in the public sector. The Arrow Impossibility Theorem demonstrated that there is no voting rule that will simultaneously satisfy the 'conditions of correspondence'. That such a rule 'should' pass these requirements is, of course, a normative judgement, though they are conditions that might be regarded as attractive. In the case of the simple majority voting rule (50% + 1), it has been shown that, with multi-peaked preferences, the rule could fail the requirement of collective rationality, in so far as it produces an intransitive ordering of alternatives. Moreover, it is worth emphasizing that the simple majority voting may fail in a world in which voters are assumed to be perfectly informed and there are no imperfections created by political parties, pressure groups and politicians. In a straightforward direct majority vote, when voters are perfectly informed, this rule can create a cyclical result.

It is clear that on a number of counts the simple majority voting rule can be criticized. Even when preferences are single-peaked, it does not provide a transitive ordering of alternatives when collective choice is multi-dimensional. There is no safeguard that a simple majority vote constrains outcomes to those that are Pareto-optimal or, indeed, potentially Pareto-optimal. The simple majority voting rule is not necessarily the most cost-effective means of col-

---

[4] In addition to these constraints to the will of the majority, it should be noted that there are circumstances in which there may be a 'tyranny of the minority' (see e.g. Bowles and Jones 1990).

lective decision-making; nor will it allow for intensity of preference—unless accompanied by logrolling (or, indeed, by vote-selling). All these criticisms are cause for disquiet. However, as in the face of the indictment that stems from Arrow's Impossibility Theorem, it must be borne in mind that alternative mechanisms of collective decision are also less than perfect.

For the 'public choice' school, one important cause for concern is the proposition that majority voting has an in-built bias for 'over-expansion' of the public budget. There can be no question but that there are examples where this result occurs. An opportunity to reduce tax price for the majority, fiscal illusions as to the tax price, and the unbridled tyranny of the majority may all lead to public budgets (both exhaustive and transfer spending) that are larger than would be predicted from a traditional approach to public finance. However, it is important to note that it is such imperfections in the political process, rather than the rule itself, that lead to an 'excessive' level of public expenditure.

References

Arrow, K. J. (1963) *Social Choice and Individual Values*, 2nd edn. New Haven, Conn.: Yale University Press.

Ashenfelter, O. and Kelly, S. Jr. (1975) 'Determinants of Participation in Presidential Elections', *Journal of Law and Economics*, 18, pp. 695–733.

Black, D. (1948) 'On the Rationale of Group Decision Making', *Journal of Political Economy*, 56, 1, pp. 23–34.

Bonner, J. (1986) *Politics, Economics and Welfare*. Brighton: Wheatsheaf.

Bowen, H. R. (1943) 'The Interpretation of Voting in the Allocation of Economic Resources', *Quarterly Journal of Economics*, 58, 1, pp. 27–48.

Bowles, R. and Jones, P. (1990) 'Medical Insurance in the UK: A Public Choice Approach', *Geneva Papers on Risk and Insurance*, 14, 54, pp. 27–40.

Brennan, G. and Buchanan, J. M. (1980) *The Power to Tax: Analytical Foundations of Fiscal Constitution*. Cambridge: Cambridge University Press.

Buchanan, J. M. (1954) 'Individual Choice in Voting and the Market', *Journal of Political Economy*, 62, 4, pp. 334–43.

Buchanan, J. M. (1958) *Public Principles of Public Debt*. Homewood, Ill.: Richard Irwin.

Buchanan, J. M. (1989) *Essays on the Political Economy*. Honolulu: University of Hawaii Press.

Buchanan, J. M. and Tullock, G. (1965) *The Calculus of Consent*. Ann Arbor: University of Michigan Press.

Cavanagh, T. E. (1981) 'Changes in American Voter Turnout, 1964–1976', *Political Science Quarterly*, 96, pp. 53–65.

Cullis, J. G. and Jones, P. R. (1987) *Microeconomics and the Public Economy: A Defence of Leviathan*. Oxford: Basil Blackwell.

de Tocqueville, A. (1835) *Democracy in America*, reprint edn. Oxford: Oxford University Press.

Downs, A. (1957) *An Economic Theory of Democracy*. New York: Harper & Row.

Downs, A. (1960) 'Why the Government is Too Small in a Democracy', *World Politics*, 13, pp. 541–63.

Ferejohn, J. A. and Fiorina, M. P. (1974) 'The Paradox of Not Voting: A Decision Theoretic Analysis', *American Political Science Review*, 68, 2, pp. 525–36.

Ferejohn, J. A. and Fiorina, M. P. (1975) 'Closeness Counts Only in Horseshoes and Dancing', *American Political Science Review*, 69, pp. 678–90.

Frey, B. S. (1971) 'Why Do High Income People Participate More in Politics?', *Public Choice*, 46, 2, pp. 141–61.

Frey, B. S. (1983) *Democratic Economic Policy*. Oxford: Martin Robertson.

Galbraith, J. K. (1962) *The Affluent Society*. Harmondsworth: Penguin.

Hudson, J. and Jones, P. R. (1994) 'The Importance of the "Ethical Voter": An Estimate of "Altruism"', *European Journal of Political Economy*, 10, 3, pp. 499–509.

Ingberman, D. E. and Inman, R. P. (1988) 'The Political Economy of Fiscal Policy', pp. 105–60 in P. G. Hare, *Surveys in Public Sector Economics*. Oxford: Basil Blackwell.

Jones, P. R. and Cullis, J. G. (1986) 'Is Democracy Regressive? A Comment on Political Participation', *Public Choice*, 51, 1, pp. 101–7.

Jones, P. R. and Hudson, J. (1996) 'The Quality of Political Leadership: A Case Study of John Major', *British Journal of Political Science*, 26, 2, pp. 229–4.

Lane, R. E. (1966) 'Political Involvement Through Voting' in B. Seasholes (ed.) *Voting, Interest Groups and Parties*. Glenview, Ill.

Lee, D. R. (1988) 'Politics, Ideology, and the Power of Public Choice', *Virginia Law Review*, 74, 2, pp. 191–9.

Little, I. M. D. (1952) 'Social Choice and Individual Values', *Journal of Political Economy*, 60, 5, pp. 422–32.

Meltzer, A. H. and Richard, S. F. (1981) 'A Rational Theory of the Size of Government', *Journal of Political Economy*, 84, 5, pp. 31–7.

Mishan, E. J. (1988) *Cost Benefit Analysis*, 4th edn. London: Unwin Hyman.

Mueller, D. C. (1979) *Public Choice*. Cambridge: Cambridge University Press.

Mueller, D. C. (1987) 'The Voting Paradox', pp. 77–99 in C. K. Rowley (ed.), *Democracy and Public Choice:*

Essays in Honour of Gordon Tullock. Oxford: Basil Blackwell.

Musgrave, R. A. (1981) 'Leviathan Cometh—or Does He?', pp. 77–120 in H. Ladd and N. Tideman, *Tax and Expenditure Limitations*, Coupe Papers on Public Economics no. 5. Washington: Urban Institute.

Musgrave, R. A. (1985) 'Excess Bias and the Nature of Budget Growth', *Journal of Public Economics*, **28**, 3, pp. 287–308.

Musgrave, R. A. and Musgrave, P. B. (1989) *Public Finance in Theory and Practice*, 5th edn. New York: McGraw-Hill.

Plott, C. R. (1987) 'The Robustness of the Voting Paradox', pp. 100–2 in C. K. Rowley (ed.), *Democracy and Public Choice: Essays in Honour of Gordon Tullock.* Oxford: Basil Blackwell.

Puviani, A. (1903) *Teoria della Illusione Finanziaria.* Palermo: Sandron.

Riker, W. H. and Ordeshook, P. C. (1968) 'A Theory of the Calculus of Voting', *American Political Science Review*, **62**, 1, pp. 25–42.

Sen, A. K. (1970) *Collective Choice and Social Welfare.* Edinburgh and San Francisco: Oliver & Boyd and Holden-Day.

Shehab, F. (1953) *Progressive Taxation: A Study in the Development of the Progressive Principle in the British Income Tax.* Oxford: Clarendon Press.

Tullock, G. (1959) 'Some Problems of Majority Voting', *Journal of Political Economy*, **67**, 6, pp. 571–9.

Tullock, G. (1976) *The Vote Motive.* Hobart Paperback No. 9, London: Institute of Economic Affairs.

Wagner, R. E. (1976) 'Revenue Structure, Fiscal Illusion and Budgetary Choice', *Public Choice*, **25**, pp. 45–61.

Wicksell, K. (1896) 'A New Principle of Just Taxation', *Finanztheoretische Untersuchungen.* Jena: Gustav Fisher. Reprinted as pp. 72–118 in R. A. Musgrave and A. T. Peacock, *Classics in the Theory of Public Finance.* London: Macmillan, 1958.

Wittman, D. (1989) 'Why Democracies Produce Efficient Results', *Journal of Political Economy*, **97**, 6, pp. 1395–1424.

5 Rent-seeking, public provision and the 'return to the market'

5.1 Introduction

In this chapter a variety of approaches to economics are demonstrated in the context of the public sectors of economies. Four interrelated issues are the focus of discussion. The first deals with the motivating forces that drive the economic processes of production and the welfare loss it entails. The second outlines both positive and negative aspects of government as an 'intervener' in the market economy with respect to production (broadly defined). There is a contrast drawn between the 'public choice' view of the government as an inefficient 'intervener' in market processes and less pessimistic views. The less pessimistic views typically take the debate beyond the confines of traditional welfare economics-based analysis in at least two ways. First, acknowledgement is made of institutional schools of thought that focus on notions of exchange transactions, property rights, agency and transactions costs mentioned above. Transaction costs, property rights and agency study are complementary lines of thought, rather than being fundamentally different from one another. The differences tend to be ones of focus and emphasis. Secondly, although the unit of analysis remains the individual, the nature of that individual is modified in the light of psychological perspectives which call into question some of the standard neoclassical descriptions. The individuals that inhabit part of this chapter have characteristics that provide a richer view of individuals.

The third issue under study is the performance of so called 'nationalized industries' which draws on a number of arguments met in the chapter and in earlier chapters. The final issue is 'privatization'. The location of production in the public or private sector is a widely debated topic in all countries with policies of 'privatizing' found to be in fashion almost everywhere, including countries of the Third World. The merits of private versus public production partly turn on

arguments about the incentives created by different external and internal environments of public and private firms. The *external* environment of firms is what essentially drives the market forms discussed in every microeconomics text (ranging from perfect competition to monopoly). The *internal* environment of firms is often less than central to microeconomics texts (because the theory of the firm is essentially about price–output decisions), but nevertheless is important in any consideration of efficiency. As regards the formation of firms themselves and their internal organization, writers like Coase (1937), Alchian and Demsetz (1972), Leibenstein (1966) and more recently Rees (1985) all have made relevant observations.

Coase attributes firm foundation to the possibilities of reducing the transaction costs of taking all decisions via the market. A limit is set to firm organization by the transaction costs of internal planning and control. Alchian and Demsetz extended the work of Coase by emphasizing the gains to firm output from 'team production'. The limiting argument here is the opportunity for 'shirking' in such a system. The features of the classical firm—saleable property right, monitoring, a residual claimant, etc.—are then deduced as a response to these possibilities. Leibenstein's *X*-inefficiency writings concern the efficiency with which production activities are carried out, and, as such, are important for public organizations. Many of these themes can be captured in the 'principal–agent' context which is surveyed by Rees (1985). The main point is that the location of production—public or private economy—is largely irrelevant with respect to whether objectives are met if the internal organization is lacking. What matters is the incentive structures the principal can construct for agents (managers and employees) in a context where (a) agents have access to more information concerning production than does the principal, and (b) agents' actions are directly unobservable, so that monitoring may rely on observing actual outcomes that are the result not only of agents' actions but also of the impact of random events.

While many governments are attempting to move away from 'state' or public production to 'market' alternatives, there is much academic debate over the attraction of private market organization and the recent antipathy to public sector firms.

5.2 Rent-seeking costs and the political process

The trigger to action in the 'public choice' school of economics is rent-seeking. The amount of rent being earned by a factor owner is the difference between the supply price (the smallest amount a resource owner would accept to have it employed in the way it is) and the price he or she actually receives. Seeking monopoly profits is a key process to grasp in this context.

Neoclassical economists have long offered estimates of the deadweight losses that arise from 'inefficient' public, or indeed, private provision of goods and services. For such economists, the government is an omniscient and benign authority so that the focus of attention is the distortive impact that emerges within the price mechanism. In the private sector, for example, the efficiency costs of monopoly have been estimated by the loss in consumer surplus associated with an output that is 'too small'. In Fig. 5.1, D is the demand curve for a product X. The price of the good would be P_c and the output of the good would be q^c if the good were produced by a competitive industry (i.e. price would be set equal to marginal cost). However, a monopolist producer would equate marginal revenue with marginal cost so that the price would be P_m and the output would be q^m. In the figure it is clear that consumers are denied $q^c - q^m$ of the good in order that the monopolist can set the price higher. The monopolist gains from this because a higher price $(P_m - P_c)$ is set for the output she sells (Oq^m). The monopolist gains $P_m 13 P_c$ as monopoly profit or *economic rent*. However, society's loss is the consumer surplus that they would have enjoyed on the units $q^c - q^m$ (i.e. triangle 123).

This neoclassical estimate of the costs of monopoly turns out to be empirically quite small. Tollison (1982) notes that such low estimates raised a question mark over the importance of the role of the eco-

nomist. He observes that Mundell (1962, p. 622) commented that, 'unless there is a thorough re-examination of the validity of the tools upon which these studies are found, . . . someone will inevitably draw the conclusion that economics has ceased to be important'. In point of fact, the analysis of Fig. 5.1 was soon to be re-examined. Tullock (1967) argued that, if there were gains for the monopolist of $P_m 13 P_c$, then individuals might spend resources to acquire such rents.[1] Indeed, at maximum it was conceivable that the total $P_m 13 P_c$ would be paid to acquire monopoly status. The costs of monopoly were now equal not simply to triangle 123 but to the trapezoid $P_m 12 P_c$.[2]

While neoclassical analysis is dominated by the impact of price effects in the market on consumers and producers, public choice scholars consider the way in which political coalitions establish property rights through the political process. The state, in this analysis, is by no means benign, and decisions have more to do with the self-interest of those engaged in the political process. This different perception attracts attention to costs, which were previously ignored. Political groups may lobby government for legislative changes or for licences that would increase their future income stream. The maximum amount that they will pay in such lobbying will be equal to the expected capitalized value of the discounted future income stream. However, this expenditure reflects a use (or consumption) of resources—for advertising

[1] However, rent-seeking had been noted in Adam Smith's *Wealth of Nations*, where he writes that 'the cruellest of our revenue laws . . . are mild and gentle in comparison to some of those which the clamour of our merchants and manufacturers has extorted from the legislature, for the support of their own absurd and oppressive monopolies' (quoted in Brooks and Heijdra 1989, p. 35).

[2] The same analysis can be undertaken for situations in which marginal costs are not constant but are upward-sloping. In the case of monopoly, for example, the deadweight losses can be identified in Fig. 5.1n. The demand curve is shown as D and the marginal cost curve as MC. The output of a perfectly competitive industry would be identified as one where price was set equal to marginal cost, i.e. output q^c. A monopoly producer would restrict output to reap additional profits. If output were reduced to q^m, then consumer surplus would be reduced by $P_c P_m 12$. However, as far as producers are concerned, they would gain the price difference on all output sold (i.e. $P_c P_m 13$ on output Oq^m) less the producer surplus lost on the output no longer sold (i.e. triangle 243). The net sum will be positive and it will pay the monopolist to reduce output on the market until marginal cost (MC) is equal to marginal revenue (MR). The loss to society as a whole, however, is the loss of triangle 142. The area $P_c P_m 13$ is simply a transfer from consumers to producers. To effect this transfer, there has been a loss to society as a whole of the consumer surplus (triangle 123) and the producer surplus (triangle 243) on the output no longer made available.

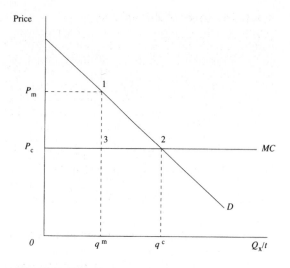

Figure 5.1 The social costs of monopoly.

their arguments, for persuading government officials—in order to effect an income transfer. The area $P_m 1 3 P_c$ is a transfer of income from the consumer to the producer, but the producer is prepared to pay as much as $P_m 1 3 P_c$ to effect this

transfer. In this way, rent-seeking has been defined as 'the expenditure of scarce resources to capture an artificially created transfer' (Tollison 1982, p. 578).

With this insight, it appeared that the lid had been taken off the estimate of monopoly costs. The political process might be awash with such expenditures. As long as a rent could be identified, there was the possibility that an equivalent expenditure would be undertaken to appropriate this transfer. Posner (1975) identified the conditions in which the costs of rent-seeking would be the entire area $P_m 1 3 P_c$. Suppose that obtaining a monopoly right is a competitive process. The monopoly right is worth £100 000 and there are ten risk-neutral bidders. If there were no collusion, each producer would spend £10 000 on attaining the monopoly right and society would dissipate the £100 000 by the attempt to capture the transfer. Following this line, we may note that Posner establishes the following conditions in order to predict that the value of the transfer be completely dissipated by rent-seeking: '(1) obtaining a monopoly is itself a competitive activity, (2) long run supply of all inputs used in rent seeking is perfectly elastic, (3) rent seeking itself creates no externalities, (4) the monopoly privilege is granted for one period only and (5)

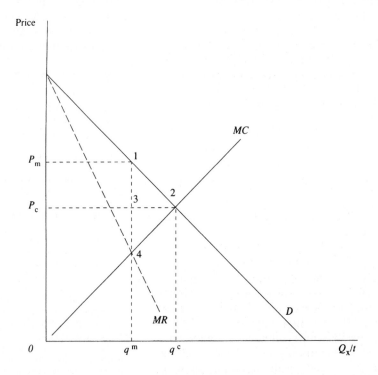

Figure 5.1n Rent-seeking and increasing marginal costs.

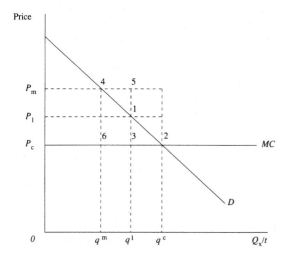

Figure 5.2 Rent-seeking: producers versus consumers.

individual rent seekers are risk neutral' (Brooks and Heijdra 1989, p. 36).[3]

Perhaps more important, however, is the implication that the identification of rent-seeking costs to *acquire* monopoly rights could be matched by lobbying costs to *resist* the acquisition of such monopoly rights. This would mean that the total expenditure on rent-seeking could *exceed* the area of the value of the transfer. In Fig. 5.2 a producer wishes to lobby a regulatory agency to allow a price increase from P_c to P_m. Consumers wish to persuade the regulatory agency to keep the price at P_c. Each party regards the expected price to be equal to $[(P_m + P_c)/2]$, i.e. P_1 in the figure. The producer, at maximum, will spend as much as P_cP_113 and the consumers will spend at maximum P_cP_112. Total expenditure will then equal P_cP_m512, which *exceeds* the value of the transfer. The value of the transfer is P_cP_113. Indeed, rent-seeking now exceeds the value of the original Tullock estimate by area 45126 (Baysinger and Tollison 1980).

In any analysis of decisions in the public sector, clearly it would be unwise to ignore rent-seeking costs, which are a characteristic of the political process; but, by the same token, it may be unwise to apportion them too great a consideration. The analysis, so far, points towards the extreme. There are, however, mitigating considerations.

5.2.1 The costs of *X*-inefficiency

In the case of monopoly, the existence of rent-seeking costs mitigates the impact of X-inefficiency. Schap (1985) notes that 'there is overlap between what are currently thought to be the X-inefficiency and rent seeking components of the welfare loss due to monopoly'. In Fig. 5.3 X-inefficiency refers to the fact that with a monopoly position the producer does not drive costs to the least-cost position. Marginal costs are then higher for a monopolist (i.e. they are MC' for an X-inefficient monopolist, rather than MC).

If we estimate the costs of X-inefficiency in the absence of rent-seeking costs, we would note the following:

1. The social cost of an X-efficient monopoly is triangle 123.
2. The social cost of an X-inefficient monopoly is area $43P_175$ (i.e. the deadweight triangle is now an underestimate because costs are higher and output correspondingly lower at q^3 than at q^2, the additional loss being $56P_17$).
3. Of the social costs attributable to monopoly $43P_175$, X-inefficiency accounts for $412P_175$.

Now, in the presence of rent-seeking, the analysis can be repeated for comparison purposes:

1. The social cost for an X-efficient monopoly is $13P_1P_2$ (i.e. including rent-seeking costs ($12P_1P_2$)).
2. The social cost for an X-inefficient monopolist is $43P_1P_3$.

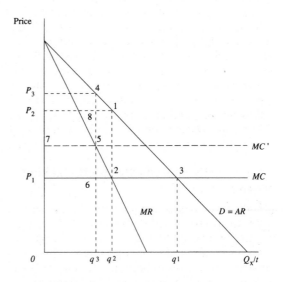

Figure 5.3 Rent-seeking and X-inefficiency.

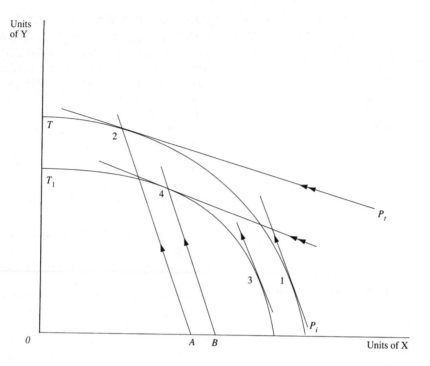

Figure 5.4 DUP activities.

3. Now the social costs attributable to monopoly $43P_1P_3$ represent a net rise of $457P_3$ that is attributable to rent-seeking.

The conclusion is that rent-seeking costs would appear to overlap with other costs of monopoly. Rent-seeking costs that would arise in the absence of X-inefficiency, P_212P_1, are hence reduced to P_3457; i.e., area $12P_1758$ of rent-seeking is converted to consumer surplus loss 4126 and resource wastage $56P_17$. The analysis thus suggests that X-inefficiency mitigates some rent-seeking behaviour because potential rent-seekers 'see' that in the monopoly position costs will rise and economic profit will correspondingly fall. Tollison and Wagner (1991) offer further insight on the question of monopoly reform.

5.2.2 Directly unproductive profit-seeking activity

Related to the rent-seeking literature is the directly unproductive profit-seeking activity (DUP) analysis in international trade. One legislative change that would increase rents for home producers is the introduction of a tax on imports (see chapter 13). An import tax would reduce the supply of imports, so that the price of the import good would increase. As a

result, home producers would receive a higher price for each unit of the good they produced. Interestingly, however, it has been shown that, in a second-best world, rent-seeking may again mitigate the costs that arise from other distortions. In Fig. 5.4, T is the transformation curve for the economy and, with free trade, production is at point 1 (where the ratio of marginal cost of the two products, which is shown by the slope of the transformation curve, is equal to the international price ratio P_i). If an import tax were introduced, the relative price of the import good Y would increase[4] (and the slope of the price line would steepen, to P_t). With the price ratio P_t the new production point would be at 2. However, if there were rent-seeking expenditures, the transformation curve would shift inwards to T_1. The initial trading position in this case would have been 3 and the tariff-protected position would be 4. Now, if we compare welfare at points 2 and 4, it is clear that national income, measured at world prices, increases from OA to OB when there are rent-seeking costs. Once again, the theory of second best calls into question intuitive analysis. If

---

[4] Assuming away the possibility of what international trade students will know as the 'Metzler paradox', where the price of the import good may become less in the domestic market even though an import tax has been placed on it.

there is a distortion (the tariff itself), then rent-seeking costs actually lead to a higher level of welfare (Bhagwati and Srinivason 1980, 1982).

5.2.3 Social costs

Even within the context of the rent-seeking literature, it should be noted that not all expenditures are without some social value. Rent-seeking may yield information to others in the economy (Quibria 1989). Moreover, like other aspects of the public choice literature (see the theory of bureaucracy in chapter 14), there is no allowance for the possibility that utility is reaped from the expenditures on rent-seeking (e.g. the utility gained from taking politicians to lunches or to pleasant receptions). While these gains may not fully compensate for the costs to society, they do reduce their importance (see Samuels and Mercuro 1984).

5.2.4 Entrepreneurial returns

One important problem with the rent-seeking literature is how to draw the line between activities that are considered rent-seeking and those that are profit-seeking. The former reduces welfare but the latter increases it. A strong case has been put by DiLorenzo (1988) that 'the problem of objectively identifying "wasteful" rent seeking is intractable, and that rent-seeking waste can only be identified by introducing one's own subjective standards of value' (p. 318). The rent that producers gain from tariff protection, for example, is an income gain to them, and only with a normative framework which includes the utility of consumers (and looks to criteria such as those underlying potential Pareto improvement—see chapters 2 and 6) will the analyst see this as simply a transfer. As DiLorenzo notes, 'since benefits and costs are subjective and interpersonal comparisons are impossible, rent seeking waste can only be identified by introducing one's own standard of value' (p. 331).

While the early literature looked at rent-seeking through the state, it has been more broadly defined to include expenditures on all kinds of activities in the private sector that would lead to monopoly returns, e.g. advertising and excessive product differentiation. But Littlechild (1981) notes that, within a dynamic setting, the gains that are labelled rents are the temporary returns that act as a reward and a stimulus for entrepreneurship. So when are such expenditures rent-seeking (to be frowned on) and when are they entrepreneurial (to be applauded)?

Ricketts (1987) attempts to tackle the problem by defining rent-seeking activities as 'the use of resources to challenge existing property rights' (p. 462). For him, entrepreneurs accept the status quo distribution of property rights, while rent-seekers attempt to change them. Such a distinction is, of course, fraught with problems. For example, lobbying to repeal a law that banned competition would be labelled rent-seeking. Although the removal of property rights would generally be regarded as welfare-enhancing, a group lobbying to alter this feature of the status quo would be regarded as rent-seeking.

Dnes (1989) attempts to approach the problem of defining rent-seeking by establishing a taxonomy of entrepreneurial and rent-seeking activities according to whether such activity was permitted within the constitution and whether or nor it led to efficiency gains or losses. However, at the heart of this problem it is difficult not to return to the position established by DiLorenzo, that at the end of the day such activities will be defined as rent-seeking according to the normative framework in which they are analysed. In this respect, DiLorenzo looks to a framework of 'classical political economy' in which voluntary co-operation is advocated but coercion is deplored. Lobbying to remove laws that banned co-operative action would be welcomed, unless there were coercive implications for others. Thus, a law that banned corporate mergers may be seen as denying the economic advantages associated with such co-operation, while a law that reduced the stagnative impact of interest groups would be valued within the classical political economy approach. By contrast, in Ricketts's approach, if expenditures were undertaken to change either of these features of the status quo, they would be deemed rent-seeking. Whether or not you would substitute another framework for that suggested by DiLorenzo, an explicitly normative approach may be, ultimately, the best way forward. Certainly, while rent-seeking may not be as persuasive as once first thought, it remains central to a 'public choice' understanding of the economy as witnessed below. (See chapter 10 for a discussion of rent-seeking applied to tax reform.)

5.2.5 Rent-seeking and the regulatory process

The 'public choice' economics of regulation is particularly associated with the University of Chicago and authors like George Stigler and Sam Peltzman (e.g. 1976). The theory it explores, at its simplest, says that regulation is about transferring wealth to gain the political support of well-defined producer groups, and that the mechanism of this transfer is *reduced* entry and competition in the regulated

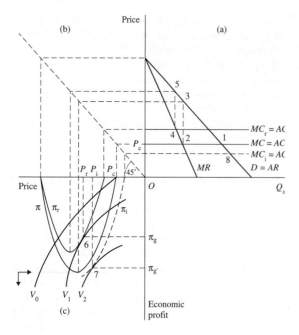

Figure 5.5 Stylized regulatory capture.

industry. Kelman (1988) dubs this the 'cartels in the closet' approach to regulation. How might this work? In Fig. 5.5 panel (a) describes a constant cost market situation for the production of good X. The initial cost structure ($MC = AC$) leads to a competitive price P_c developed from point 1. The 45° line in panel (b) allows P_c to appear on the horizontal axis at the 'top' of panel (c). A government that represented the consumer would have an indifference map that viewed economic profit as well as any price above P_c as a 'bad' so that P_c would be the outcome. If, however, the government was driven by vote maximization the picture is different. As depicted, votes depend on price and economic profit in a negative and positive way respectively. A lower price increases votes from consumers while a price above P_c allows producers economic profit and gains their votes (the direction of vote gains is indicated by the arrows in panel (c)). When P_c obtains V_o votes are achieved as this is the isovote curve that runs through P_c in panel (c) (the curvature indicates that successive increases in price beyond P_c requires greater gains in economic profit to hold overall political support constant). Now suppose that government regulation both raises costs in panel (a) $MC = AC$ to $MC_r = AC_r$ and serves to produce an entry barrier allowing an imperfectly competitive price–output combination to be chosen in panel (a). With $MC = AC$ producers would profit maximize at

point 2 and charge the price associated with point 3. The equivalent points when $MC_r - AC_r$ applies are 4 and 5 respectively, i.e. the economic profit 'valley' in panel (c) moves from π to π_r a vote maximizing government would find equilibrium on V_1 at point 6 and the equilibrium would involve price $P_r (> P_c)$ and economic profit π_g. Producers gain at the expense of the consumers of good X and the government enjoys greater political support. Of course the 'trappings' of special interest effects aids this process. Consumers are likely to be ill-informed as to the real purpose of regulation as the costs of being informed on the location of P_c are high and, even if informed, consumer groups are difficult to organize because the potential individual gains from cheaper purchases of good X are low and the 'free rider' problem looms large. Governments for their part dress the regulation up in the clothes of 'safety', preventing imports from low quality 'sweat shop' economies, etc. Furthermore, placed in a dynamic setting the process will be difficult to observe. If a technological invention facilitates a lowering of the cost structure to, say $MC_i - AC_i$ the 'profit valley' becomes π_i and the government finds equilibrium at point 7 where political support has increased to V_2, economic profit to π_g^1 and price lowered to Pi—everyone gains! The problem is, however, that the efficient outcome is the price quantity combination associated with point 8 but the regulatory process has long since obscured this.

While this may look a speculative argument it is a strand of analysis that has been empirically explored in a number of contexts. Kelman (1988) is very sceptical of this exploration. He notes that there is a common purpose to the empirical work:

1. to empirically demonstrate that regulation does not serve its straight forward public purpose (the 'naïve' hypothesis) but instead to demonstrate that its benefit–cost ratio is less than unity (the 'sophisticated' hypothesis);

2. to indicate how regulations allow the big producers to decrease competition from smaller competitors or new entrants offering private wealth gains to a well-defined producer group.

The case studies he reviews involve:

(a) Peltzman (1975) on car safety regulation where the 'naïve' hypothesis is reduced accidents etc. and the 'sophisticated' one is 'risk compensation'—to leave yourself exposed to a constant amount of risk. If the costs of a potential accident are reduced you increase the probability of an accident by taking more risks.

(b) Viscusi (1985) on product safety regulation and 'childproof' caps where the 'naïve' hypothesis is reduced accidental poisonings and the 'sophisticated' one is no impact (because either complicated caps are also difficult for adults who consequently leave medicine containers open or adults 'lulled' by the better caps do not store medicines away from children).

(c) Bartel and Thomas (1985) on occupational safety regulations where the 'naïve' hypothesis is reduced work-place accidents and the 'sophisticated' one that of ineffective legislation (because either there is little compliance reflecting poor enforcement or that the regulations are not closely connected to safety).

(d) Linneman (1980) on the 'Mattress Flammability Standard' where the 'naïve' hypothesis is reduced fires and the 'sophisticated' one is positive but little beneficial impact.

Kelman takes savage critical swipes at the underlying data, their transformation and interpretation in these studies. He tends to find in favour of the 'naïve' hypotheses casting doubt on point 1 above. In relation to point 2 above, Kelman considers cases (c) and (d) and again finds them sadly lacking. He does not doubt that there are elements of truth in the regulatory capture thesis, but at the very minimum he finds for the case that the empirical evidence is not sufficient for it to dispel a view that well-designed regulation can increase welfare. Similarly, there is no doubt the regulatory capture argument has gained considerable stature in the eyes of many economists and lay people.

5.3 Public sector provision

Having established the notion of rent-seeking behaviour and its potential costs (especially in a production context), a richer account of the nature and role of the public sector can be recounted. It would be very convenient if the two-by-two classification of goods and services in Chapter 3 on p. 50 mapped into a two-by-two taxonomy of forms of provision. Unfortunately, this convenience is missing so that many goods, for example, generally classified as quasi-public, are provided in a variety of very different ways within and between countries. Taking the word 'provision' to cover two separate components, namely finance and production, it is popular to build a two-by-two taxonomy (Table 5.1) which will help shape the discussion that follows.

Table 5.1 A taxonomy of provision

Finance	Production	
	Private	Public
Private	1	2
Public	3	4

Taking each characteristic in Table 5.1 in turn, it is possible briefly to state the case in favour of each mix before looking at specific contributions in more detail.

Private finance, through user-charges or prices, links directly with the discussion of the benefit principle in chapter 3. Where a good is excludable and rival, generating no Pareto-relevant marginal externalities, and the distribution of income is deemed fair, then such an approach is almost by definition the one to follow. Each sovereign consumer can be left to maximize his or her utility by equating price with marginal benefit and the outcome is both efficient and distributionally acceptable.

Public finance is likely to be significant where a good is non-rival and/or offering significant externalities or where the purpose of policy is redistributive. While public finance can be related to the benefit principle (with the exception of much redistribution), the use of taxation, grants, etc., links more directly with the 'ability to pay' principle. On the grounds that most tax systems are based on ability to pay, largely independent of any consumption benefits from goods and services thus provided, the suggestion would be that more often than not public finance addresses issues of equity and shared responsibility, rather than allocative efficiency as such.

Private production with competitive markets, as noted at the outset, is deemed 'ideal'. In such circumstances both X- (production) and allocative efficiency are generated by profit maximization. As long as the price signal is 'correct', concern is directed towards the external (competitive) environment of firms. In this context the traditional lack of concern in most economics texts with the internal organization of firms is justified. Property rights theorists would stress private ownership and the disposability of assets as incentives to their efficient utilization. Where managers do not own the enterprise assets, an efficient capital market may nevertheless exert some pressure upon them to act in the shareholders' interests to minimize costs at any level of output. This is because takeovers by specialized share-owners may be made when share prices are unduly depressed. In an efficient capital market this will occur whenever managers do not ensure maximum profit (through the adoption of cost-minimizing techniques of production and the adaptation of production lines to consumers' preferences). However, the mechanism may be less effective to the extent that there are principal–agent problems.

Public production, for those embracing the neoclassical framework, has predictably been more difficult to justify than the other three categories of the taxonomy. However, there is a case to be made for it. Forte (1967) outlines a number of arguments that suggest that leaving all production to private markets and using grants and other financial devices to achieve government policy aims may not be totally satisfactory. His economic arguments relate to size, market distortion and low marginal cost. Where a project is both indivisible and of very large scale, it may be that only public sector production is possible. Similarly, it is possible that private sector production of a good may confer economic power. Monopoly or monopsony power might obtain and the argument would be that these goods or services are better held in public rather than private control. Where some public production already takes place, there may exist unexploited economies of scale so that additional activities can be added at little marginal cost.

The other two arguments that Forte employs are extra-economic. Private production of a good or service may offer access to political influence or power for some private individuals beyond their constitutional rights. Finally, the production of a good may need to be clothed with the mantle of the state. There is a 'quality' aspect of some activities that is lost with private production. Titmuss (1970) made much of voluntary blood donorship in a state health care system as a way of allowing individuals to demonstrate their altruism. One argument against having some paid donors alongside voluntary ones was that the presence of the cash nexus destroyed the nature of the service provided and caused voluntary donors to cease to be donors. Few activities, at one time or other, have not been provided by the market although judicial systems might be an exception. The idea of a judge who is hired from Arthur's Judicial Services Ltd lacks the appearance of independence and the operation of *societal* rules and sanctions that individuals—especially defendants—expect.

Table 5.2 offers a more detailed view of types of goods and forms of provision. Recall that provision encompasses a location of production and a finance mechanism. The extremes are represented by categories 1 and 8. It is accepted that the list could be further stretched between the extremes of public provision and private provision, but the main options are listed. As for the types of goods, the typical named varieties are listed with a summary of characteristics that generally conforms to a majority of what economists have in mind. The problem, already outlined in the introduction, is that each type of good can be, and has been, matched with one or more (or all) forms of provision. Further complications arise if goods or services are broken down by their characteristics. So the good health care has elements that may make health conform to most if not all of A–F, depending

Table 5.2 Goods types and provision forms

Type of goods	Forms of provision
	Public provision
A Public (non-rival; non-excludable)	1 Public sector production without user charges ('free goods')
B Club/toll (non-rival to a congestion limit; excludable)	2 Public sector production with user charges
C Quasi-public (rival; excludable; significant externalities)	3 Public sector production with user charges and vouchers or grants to consumers
D Common pool (rival; exclusion possible but absent leading to congestion/exhaustion/extinction)	4 Public contracts to private producers to supply goods or services to the government for user charge or 'free' disposal
E Private (rival; excludable)	5 As 4, but 'free' disposable and grants to producers or consumers with vouchers or grants to cover charges
F Merit wants (appropriate information absent and/or assessment complex for the typical consumer)	6 Public/private mixed production and/or finance
	7 Voluntary, non-profit (charity) production with private finance and/or government grants finance
	8 Private sector production with private finance
	Private provision

Source: S. Paul (1985) 'Privatization and the Public Sector', *Finance and Development*, **22**, 4, pp. 42–5. Reproduced with permission from the International Monetary Fund.

on the element in focus. Some economists have matched up types of good with feasible modes of provision (see Paul 1985), but the argument here is that it is difficult to absolutely rule out any of 1–8, although using the brief discussion associated with Table 5.1 might help suggest which forms of finance and production are more or less appropriate. One major focus of this chapter is public production, and this dominates the next three sections of the chapter.

5.4 A positive case for public production

In this section the search is for arguments that suggest that public production has a positive advantage over other forms of production.

5.4.1 Transactions costs economics

At root, the case for public production as developed so far in the literature relates broadly to one, or a combination, of the following considerations or themes:

(a) there is something about the nature of some goods that make them good candidates for public production;

(b) there are limits within people as information processors that suggest you can improve their welfare via selective public production;

(c) the motivations of individuals are such that when (a) and or (b) arise the resulting trades are of great benefit to one party and the disadvantage of the other.

Williamson (e.g. 1985) is the author who has pioneered an approach to economics in general that involves an explicit formulation of the above. In his 'transactions costs' approach he sees the market as running into great difficulties in the relatively common situation where three conditions apply:

(i) there is asset specificity with respect to use or users;

(ii) there is bounded rationality so that individuals exhibit limited computational and information processing capacities;

(iii) there is opportunistic behaviour which is self seeking behaviour with guile.
    The market can cope with the presence of any two:

(a) if asset specificity is absent (and assets therefore easily switched in use) mistakes because of

'bounded' decisions will be easily corrected and opportunistic behaviour should not have major consequences;

(b) if bounded rationality is absent all contingencies can be imagined and 'contracted' for, so that asset specificity and opportunism can be accommodated;

(c) if opportunistic behaviour is absent problems arising from asset specificity and bounded rationality can be resolved in an honest context where actors are not seeking to take advantage of unexpected situations that arise.

In the circumstances where all three apply, contracts and the like cannot successfully deal with the situation. The underlying principle of Williamson's economics becomes the organization of transactions to minimize the effects of bounded rationality whilst safeguarding individuals from opportunism.

Dugger (1993) explains the school of thought with respect to the state and highlights its non-laissez faire implications. The role of the state is as a transactions cost minimizer and, as such, is a valid participant in the market economy (and not just an intervener to 'correct' market failures). The state, however, is defined in a wider way than is the case in traditional public finance. The state is defined as 'an agent that exercises sovereignty' (Dugger 1993, p. 190). In turn sovereignty is collective action that defines property rights, resolves disputes and monitors performance. Large corporations (especially multinationals) are seen as having the power to exercise sovereignty and are therefore part of the state. He dubs the traditional state the 'nation state' and large multinational corporations the 'corporate state'. With this as background, Dugger asks a number of questions relevant to this chapter and the theme of the book. First, what is the role of the state in the institutionalization of exchange transactions? The market mechanism can only exist with the exercise of sovereignty that provides the traders or transactors with a whole series of institutionalized services. These services include: the nature and the distribution of property rights; the provision of specific channels of information that allow traders to find out the 'P's and Qx/t' depicted throughout this text; standards of weight, measure and product; market infrastructure (roads, rail, canals, etc.) and the routines of trade (Who is allowed to be a market participant and how they are allowed to trade?). A second question concerns the role of the state in adjudicating disputed exchange transactions. Typically buyers 'move first' paying the seller and in subsequently delivering the good or service the seller has second mover advantage. Given opportunistic behaviour there are frequent disputes over the performance/quality of the good or service provided. Such disputes are resolved in complex fashions that involve the exercise of sovereignty.

A further question of importance concerns the provision of public goods. Here an illustration of direct relevance is the provision of the public good defence. Dugger notes that the USA opted to 'buy-in' (ironically what in the UK is called 'contracting-out') the production of defence equipment and argues that this was not the least transactions cost solution. The elements that cause market mechanisms to fail are present:

(i) bounded rationality which in this context takes the form of so-called 'information impactedness' on behalf of suppliers (relevant information to a decision is not freely available because it is not in the suppliers interest to divulge it);

(ii) asset specificity in that suppliers have to make large investments in long-lived equipment with only low value in their next best alternative use;

(iii) opportunistic behaviour in this area would offer very large pay-offs.

Given this, defence contractors have a very powerful incentive to corrupt and confuse the nation state buyer. In such circumstances there is evidence that subsidy-maximizing and cost-maximizing procedures of defence contracting have arisen significantly reducing the productivity of US industry. National defence on this argument should be publicly produced. The point to note is that the argument is largely independent of the non-rival–non-excludable attributes of certain types of defence that is usually associated with the case for public production.

5.4.2 Moral hazard

Baumol (1984) outlines a positive case for public production based on the concept of moral hazard familiar in the insurance literature. Fair insurance involves a premium that is the product of the probability of the event and the size of the expenditure to be covered. However, what insurance companies noticed was that, once insured, individual behaviour changed. Two effects tended to take place. First, the probability of the insured event rose as insurance altered individual behaviour in the form of taking less care, i.e. being more negligent about the insured event—those insured for fire damage may be more careless with matches! Secondly, individuals demanded greater expenditures if the event insured against occurred—the worn-out carpet becomes a

Persian rug! What was a fair premium *ex ante* turns out to be too low when compared with *ex post* behaviour. Insurance, then, alters people's behaviour. Now consider a related argument.

There are situations where private production runs into this moral hazard problem of altering incentives. Two examples that Baumol provides relate to tax farming (i.e. selling the right to collect taxes) and to private armies. It is easy to imagine the incentives for tax farmers arbitrarily to raise both the incidence and the volume of taxation. Similarly, mercenaries who potentially face unemployment may well find opportunities to make work for themselves. In short, there are situations where you may wish to reduce the incidence and volume of 'work' done. Tullock doubts the significance of these arguments: he points out that it is 'public' armies that have been the source of instability in many polities, e.g. Greece.[5] It is agreed, however, that any army pursuing private gain is to be avoided.

5.4.3 Transaction costs

Even for those not wishing to embrace 'transaction cost economics' transactions costs as such remain important. Typically, exchanges are assumed to be 'frictionless' in that all that matters is a willingness to pay an amount that matches the marginal cost of production of a unit of output. However, the existence of transaction costs may make some 'trades' unattractive or, at least, may reduce the area over which beneficial trades are mutually attractive. In general, these costs are associated with the fact that information is imperfect. The forms they take are often collected under the following headings:

Search costs: the costs of establishing the distribution and location of offers to trade.

Bargaining and negotiating costs: the costs involved in establishing what the terms of a mutually beneficial agreement to trade will be.

Contract costs: the costs involved in making the conditions of a trade clear and 'policeable' (e.g. lawyers may be involved).

Clearly, markets play a role in reducing transaction costs both informally and formally. Informally, consumer observation of markets at work offers information on goods and services, prices and the cost of time and trouble. Formally, some actors in the market specialize in reducing transaction costs by dealing in information. Middlemen of all types

---

[5] Gordon Tullock, in private correspondence. However, readers may consider historical counter-examples.

earn their living in this way. Estate agents in the housing market, collecting information on housing available, its characteristics and the prices demanded by existing owners, are a classic example in this context.

Transactions of a bilateral kind are likely to involve lower transaction costs than multilateral ones. A case for government intervention or provision of a good or service might be built around transaction costs. Arrow (1971) argues that the case for public or private provision may be expressed in terms of which sector has the lowest transaction costs. Government, by establishing the rules of the 'trading' game, may well improve the operation of the market or may provide the basis of a case for public provision.

Wiseman (1978, p. 90) has written that there are not, in his view, 'many public goods' but rather 'poor systems of property rights'. The implication is that exclusion is always possible and hence that private markets can always be made to work. However, the Achilles' heel of this form of argument is likely to be the transaction costs of organizing the market. Exclusion may always be possible but may often be very costly. One-by-one negotiation with individuals on their desired defence requirements and the erection of the necessary exclusion barriers is almost certainly likely to be rejected in favour of collective provision in terms of least-cost provision. Weisbrod (1975) argues that a case for the public provision of private goods can be built around transaction costs where there is consensus about the quality of a private good that individuals wish to consume or wish others to enjoy. If government already collects taxes to provide public goods, then adding the tax price of the accepted level of private good may be a least-cost solution. This clearly links with Forte's (1967) argument of unexploited economies of scale in government, allowing additional tasks to be accomplished at low marginal cost.

The administration costs of various provision schemes can also be considered under this heading. Take, for example, the reform currently popular with political conservatives of using vouchers for education provision. There are many well-rehearsed facets to this argument, but an important one is the role of administration costs in the enactment of a voucher scheme.

Figure 5.6 helps to capture this side of the debate. The curve labelled MC_g is the marginal cost of the provision of education services E by the government in the public sector, and MSB is the marginal social benefit of education, yielding Oq^g as the optimum level of provision. Advocates of vouchers suggest that competition between institutions would lower the

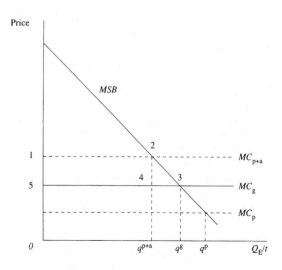

Figure 5.6 Administrative costs and vouchers for education.

marginal cost of provision and raise the quality. For simplicity, it is assumed here that these alleged beneficial effects of vouchers can be captured in a lowered marginal cost curve MC_p. The optimal level of provision would now be Oq^p. Now suppose there are constant marginal variable costs of administering the scheme which raise MC_p to MC_{p+a}, generating level of provision Oq^{p+a}. Realistic comparison, including administration costs, suggests that vouchers lower the optimal provision of education, increasing the real resource cost of provision over public (non-voucher) provision by rectangle 1245. In addition, it reduces consumer surplus by area 234. Although this is a 'constructed' example, it may not do too much injustice to events, in that trial experiments with vouchers in Kent in 1990 encountered very high administration costs, causing the Conservative-led council to reconsider the attractions of the policy. The message of this section is that there are costs in making markets work that in some cases suggest that it is attractive to settle for public production, even if it is inefficient to some extent.

To spot the difference between considering these type of costs and transactions cost economics the views of Dugger (1993) are again relevant. With bounded rationality and opportunism in education transactions, uncontained by state officials overseeing the market, problems arise. On the sellers side of the market opportunistic teachers and school administrators provide misleading information and irrelevant inducements to parents to attract their vouchers. On the buyers side of the market the bounded rationality of parents will not be a match for the sellers and the quality of education will suffer and the problems vouchers seek to address would remain.

5.4.4 Co-ordination and countervailing power

One area where the relative merits of various forms of provision have been the centre of intensive and often heated debate is health care. While not going into all the details here, Culyer (1983) argues that considerations on the supply side tip the balance towards public production because it offers possibilities that are not available with market production. The four characteristics Culyer picks out are: medical effectiveness, medical monopolies, non-profit motivation, and the agency role of doctors. There are great difficulties in establishing who is ill and determining the effectiveness of various forms of treatment. The lesson of much of the literature is to see health care production in a broader context in which education and environment are vital influences. The argument is that this broader overall policy perspective is more easily established in a unified set of public provision policies rather than in a set of uncoordinated private markets.

The medical profession of virtually all countries typically forms a well-organized professional monopoly, and the question that arises is how this may best be confronted. The answer seems to be that state monopsony power in the form of something like the National Health Service (NHS) is appropriate. The lack of non-profit motivation in the NHS is a potential weakness; however, given that insurance-based health care systems tend not to be characterized by competition for profit, this weakness is not so decisive. Finally, doctors are typically both the suppliers and demanders of their own services, acting as the agent of the consumer–patient who is generally at a large informational disadvantage compared to the doctors. This suggests that a state system does not imply any loss of consumer sovereignty. What is required is the divorce of the doctor's income from treatment provision. This consideration tends to favour salary payment systems over fee-for-service. Salary pay structures are more common in state health care systems. The first two arguments are more central to this section in that they suggest that state health care systems can, in principle at least, 'reach the parts' others cannot. The second two arguments have more in common with section 5.4 in that they say that costs commonly associated with non-market provision are largely missing in the case of health care provision; i.e. they are part of a more 'negative' case for public production.

5.4.5 Sunk capital costs and making markets contestable

In the discussion of contestable markets in chapter 1, it was the possibility of free entry and costless exit that made the market form 'work'. Hence the securing of least-cost production, no economic profit and price equal to marginal cost turns on whether the assumption is approximated in reality. One of the problems that prevents costless exit is the existence of sunk costs. These are costs that have been incurred that cannot be recovered if an enterprise wishes to leave an industry. In effect, exit costs act as a barrier to entry in the first place. If markets are to be made contestable, it may be that government must undertake the capital provision that is sunk. A good example might be railway tracks, stations, etc. A potential entrant is unlikely to invest in such a network if there is a risk that most of this sunk cost will be lost. If, however, the public sector produces the track and stations, and then offers their use at a price that reflects the user cost of capital and their depreciation, it may be able to secure contestability. The existence of large sunk costs are a main reason for the natural monopoly situation discussed below.

However, this assumes that contestable outcomes are always desirable, and this may not always be the case, so that government intervention becomes relevant. Rashid (1988) discusses a weakness inherent in truly contestable markets. If an industry is subject to hit-and-run entry, there must be no sunk costs. If such an industry comprises many producers, a large proportion of which are 'transients', there is little incentive to care about the quality of the product. Rashid takes milk sales in Dhaka as one of his examples. There, milk adulterated with water (sometimes from irrigation ditches!) is commonplace. Hundreds of peasants are suppliers and the only fixed cost—a cow—is easily bought and sold. With the transient nature of the business and the large number of producers, no single producer expects repeat sales and there is no incentive to build up a reputation for good quality. Rashid doubts the effectiveness of regulation as a replacement for reputation, questioning the likelihood of honest enforcement. To raise quality requires the presence of irrevocable fixed costs (i.e. sunk costs), which tells consumers a producer is here to stay and therefore must please customers; but this, of course, negates contestability. (Some libertarians might argue that consumers actually desired watered milk, but Rashid counters, Why not buy milk and dilute to taste with clean water!)

5.4.6 Public production and psychology

A powerful case for government involvement in making individual decisions can be put if a concept familiar in psychology is employed. Ackerlof and Dickens (1982) develop such an argument. Cognitive dissonance suggests that individuals need to feel that their words and actions are consistent or make sense, so that something has to change when the beliefs individuals hold and their actual behaviour are in contradiction. Tullock (1971) earlier employed this concept in his article entitled 'The Charity of the Uncharitable', where the paradox individuals had to resolve was that of persistently advocating redistributive policies while at the same time doing nothing that would reduce their own income by effecting an income transfer. The resolution in Tullock's view is to vote for and politically support a party whose manifesto includes redistribution in the confidence that, even if the party gets into power, it will not enact the platform. Hence the espousal of redistributive ideas can be made dissonant with no actual redistribution by the action of voting for a redistributive party. (The actions of the so-called 'champagne socialists' in the UK may fit this description.)

The essence of the Akerlof–Dickens argument is that individuals can choose what to believe but once they have chosen a belief it is unalterable. The context is a hazardous job in a two-period model with individuals initially enjoying all the relevant information. The variables are:

C_a = the cost to the individual of an accident
C_f = the cost to the individual of a unit of 'fear' of being in a hazardous job
C_s = the cost of safety equipment that becomes available in the second period
p = the probability of an accident
p^* = the individual's subjective probability of an accident
$F = p^*/p$ = the level of fear, which can be lowered by 'managing' p^* downwards (once lowered it cannot be revised).

Table 5.3 summarizes the heart of the argument. Individuals must get a compensation in a hazardous job (W_h) that equals the return (W_s) obtainable in a safe job; i.e. over the two periods they must obtain $2W_s$. That is, a compensating wage differential is required to allow for the risks in the hazardous job. At the outset individuals in a hazardous job can choose to believe their job is hazardous or not, but their choice of belief determines their subsequent actions. Workers are seen as making a 'least-cost' choice over what to believe. In the second period cost-effective safety equipment ($C_s < pC_a$) is assumed to have become available. However, only

Table 5.3 Compensation and hazardous jobs

Period	(1) Choose safe job	(2) Choose hazardous job in the absence of legislation	(3)	(4) Choose hazardous job in the presence of legislation
		Choose to believe 'safe' and do not buy equipment in period 2 ($p^* = 0$)	Choose to believe 'risky' and do buy equipment in period 2 ($p^* = pC_s/(pC_a + C_f)$)	
1	W_s	$W_h = W_s + pC_a + (pC_a - C_s)$	$W_h = W_s + pC_a + \dfrac{C_s C_f}{pC_a + C_f}$	$W_h = W_s + pC_a$
		[Work in hazardous industry and receive compensation for expected accident costs plus cost of 'wrong' decision in period 2 when will not buy safety equipment]	[Work in hazardous industry and receive compensation for expected accident costs plus cost of fear]	[Work in hazardous industry and receive compensation for expected accident costs. There is no cost of fear (p^* has been managed to zero) and prevented from wrong decision.]
2	W_s	$W_h = W_s + C_s - pC_a < W_s$ 'Perceived' as $W_s + C_s$	$W_h = W_s + C_s$	$W_h = W_s + C_s$
		[Receive safe wage plus expense of safety equipment—which will not buy—minus expected accident costs]	[Receive safe wage plus expense of safety equipment which is bought]	[Receive safe wage plus expense of safety equipment which is bought]

Source: G. A. Akerlof and W. T. Dickens, 'The Economic Consequences of Cognitive Dissonance', *American Economic Review*, **72**, 3, 1982, pp. 307–19.

those who 'believe' they are in a hazardous job will choose to buy it, i.e. those who have chosen a sufficiently high p^*. To be indifferent about buying the newly available safety equipment in period 2, the individual must equate the perceived cost of an accident plus the perceived cost of fear with the cost of the equipment, which is

(5.1) $$p^* C_a + (p^*/p) C_f = C_s$$

Multiplying by p yields

(5.2) $$p p^* C_a + p^* C_f = p C_s$$

and

(5.3) $$p^* (p C_a + C_f) = p C_s$$

So

(5.4) $$p^* = p C_s / (p C_a + C_f)$$

The choice of belief is either to maintain p^* at the sufficiently high level outlined above so that safety equipment is bought in period 2, or to 'manage' p^* to zero and therefore reduce the cost of fear to zero. If the second course of action is chosen the individual will incur the cost of the 'wrong' decision in period 2 in not buying the cost-effective safety equipment, which is $(p C_a - C_s)$. If the first course of action is chosen the individual must incur the cost of fear that triggers equipment purchase, i.e. $(p^*/p) C_f$, which, when p^* is substituted using the right-hand side of equation (5.4), becomes $p C_s / (p C_a + C_f)$ times C_f and equals $C_s C_f / (p C_a + C_f)$. The options are set up in columns (2) and (3) of Table 5.3, which state the wage paid in each period and describe what is being compensated for. The acid question in relation to both columns is how government intervention can

improve on the outcome. The response is summarized in column (4). If individuals know that in period 2 with the introduction of safety equipment the government will pass legislation enforcing its use, they then can 'manage' the risk down to zero in period 1 because they do not have to fear the wrong decision or keep fear high so as to trigger the purchase of safety equipment.

Figure 5.7 sets out the relevant wage elements where Akerlof and Dickens make suitable assumptions so that D_L 'doubles' for the demand for the product and Q_L/t for the quantity of output. In part (c) of the figure the gain from government intervention is the shaded area $(W_s + p C_a)$123. (In the figure for the sake of illustration $(p C_a - C_s)$ has been set equal to $C_s C_f / (p C_a + C_f)$, whereas in the actual model the individual is seen as choosing the option associated with the lower of these two terms.) It represents a Pareto-superior outcome. The workers in the hazardous industry are no worse off, as they get the same expected wage over the two periods; however, consumers are better off because in period 1 an element of the compensating wage differential does not have to be paid.

The authors supply a list of further possible applications, one of which is especially relevant in the public sector context. This is the provision of old age pensions or other age-related social security benefits. If individuals find it difficult or uncomfortable to contemplate old age and their own mortality, one option is to choose to manage the probability downwards. (They choose to believe they live in a 'safe' job (= world) even though they are in a hazardous job (= world).) Such 'cosy' beliefs mean that they have no

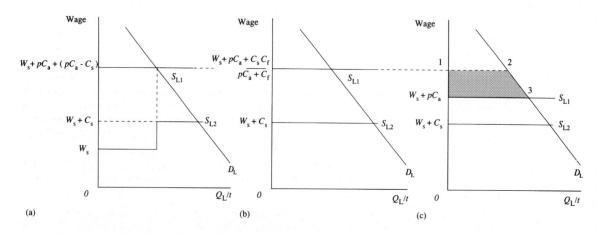

Figure 5.7 Gaining from compulsory government legislation.

Source: The American Economic Review, 72, 3, 1982, pp. 307–19.

need to prepare for retirement and old age as they have chosen not to believe these will occur. However, this implies insufficient saving and preparation for the later years of a life-span, and government mandatory pension schemes and provisions can play the same role as the enforcement of safety legislation. Two issues are important here. The first is that a positive efficiency case for government intervention has been made. The case is based on Paretian welfare analysis and not on paternalism. Second, the introduction of concepts from another discipline, namely psychology, has proved fruitful. At the time Akerlof and Dickens made this contribution intellectual economic imperialism was rampant, and an example in which economic theory 'imported' concepts was as a counterbalance to that trend.

A different case for government intervention can be made if other aspects of the psychology of preferences is explored. Frey and Eichenberger (1989 and 1994) note that economics has a large literature on individual rationality, resulting in collective irrationality as in, for example, the free rider problem, but little on the reverse configuration. They point out that there is now a significant body of evidence from economic psychology and experimental economics concerning how individuals systematically deviate from rationality in the choices they make. The authors list many types of anomaly in individual behaviour (see appendix). One is the 'sunk cost effect' where individuals take foregone costs into account in their decision—people do cry over spilt milk! Another is the 'opportunity cost effect', which indicates that out-of-pocket monetary costs are given greater weight in decisions than opportunity costs of the same size. The point that is relevant here is that individuals realize their shortcomings and 'rationally' protect themselves from them via the creation of institutions—hence the title of Frey and Eichenberger's (1989) paper, 'Anomalies and Institutions'.

In particular, government institutions and regulations can be seen as irrationality-reducing. Preventing the emergence of anomalies, reducing the cost of anomalies and redistributing the costs of anomalies can be seen as the functions of much government intervention. Compulsory car insurance, safety standards regulation and the use of public funds in 'disasters' can be seen as examples of these functions. The arguments presented provide a basis for questioning individual rationality and hence a foundation for the merit want concept introduced earlier. However, what is most significant here is the support they give to official bureaucracy. Government administrators painstakingly (slavishly) following well-established traditional decision and implementation rules are often the target of harsh criticism, but cast in this light 'bureaucratic rationality' is the individuals' chosen response to their own recognized irrationality!

A convenient link to the next section involves the authors view that the volume of anomalous behaviour observed is endogenous. By this they mean that economic incentives affect the extent of psychological anomalies. Producers/sellers wish to set commercial traps to exploit anomalous behaviour whereas consumer/buyers wish not to have their systematic weaknesses traded upon—they wish to 'spike traps'. Government policy can affect the relative costs of setting and spiking traps and hence the efficient quantity of resources devoted to such activities. The appendix to this chapter lists the main types of anomalous behaviour (ordered with respect to the past, present and future) some of which were introduced above. The process Frey and Eichenberger have in mind can be illustrated if one of the anomalies, the endowment effect (i) b), is chosen for consideration. The endowment effect says that goods in a person's endowment are valued more highly than those that are not part of their endowment. Whilst this effect has attracted considerable interest in cost–benefit analysis a simpler application is outlined here which involves the practice of book clubs sending you books that you do not have to pay for until some period in the future. The hope is that with the new books in their endowment the potential purchasers will revise their valuation of the books upwards so that they will pay for books, at a later date, they otherwise would not have purchased. The failure rate of such traps with consumer/buyers depends on their ability to spot the trap. Frey and Eichenberger note this spotting task is facilitated when (i) you can compare your behaviour with the actions of other non-anomalous individuals (ii) it results in out-of-pocket costs (iii) the individual is more educated and/or experienced. The size of the utility gain from avoiding traps is also important. If falling into a trap threatens insolvency it is more likely to be avoided. It is also noted that the marginal cost of acting 'differently' to avoid anomalous behaviour is higher the greater the complexity of the situation. In some circumstances 'rule guided' anomalous behaviour may remain the least cost course of action. But what is the positive case for government intervention in this area? Potential efficiency gains arise if fewer real resources are devoted to the setting and spiking of traps. Furthermore, equity may be served if the exploiters of anomalies lose and the exploited gain. Policy intervention on the producer/seller side could involve:

(a) increasing the marginal costs of the trap setters, e.g. making it very costly to mail unasked for advertising material back or more generally insisting that consumers be compensated for any time and trouble costs generated by unwanted solicitations by sellers;

(b) allowing monopoly power. The analogy here is 'overfishing'. (A monopoly exploiter will be careful to preserve the consumer 'shoal' and impose costs that are sufficiently low to avoid consumer resistance.)

On the consumer/buyer side government intervention might:

(a) lower the marginal cost of avoiding traps, e.g. make them more easily perceived (with 'watchdog' bodies and information provision) and corrected (cooling off periods for contracts signed in 'high-pressure' situations);

(b) raise the marginal benefit from avoiding traps by, for example, refusing to help those who repeatedly fall foul of trap situations. This might involve the eventual refusal of help via social security and the like.

Clearly this is a fascinating area of research for those wishing to depart from the assumption of 'Homo-economicus' and explore the more typical behaviour of the 'economic psychological individual'.

5.5 A negative case for public production

The above arguments about public production relied on its positive attributes. In this section some arguments are suggested that establish the case for public production by 'default', i.e. by the weakness of alternative mechanisms. We are assuming that there is a case for government intervention of some form. The alternatives considered are administrative, regulatory and fiscal (taxes and subsidies). Note that the arguments propounded, especially those concerned with regulation, fiscal devices and privatization, rely for their strength on the self-interested behaviour of those subject to these alternative forms of control. The basic point is that economic actors respond to the incentives they are set.

5.5.1 Administrative intervention

Administrative intervention would entail the introduction of something akin to the vouchers mentioned above, where individuals in effect get 'tokens' to spend at the supplier of a particular good of their choice. When this approach was reviewed in section 5.4.3 it was argued that any efficiency gains could be swamped by the administrative costs of the scheme. The real resource costs of the mechanisms to make any policy work have to be considered, and they may suggest that public production with warts is superior to private production including the cost of wart remover.

5.5.2 Regulation

Where regulation is of the 'public choice' variety, attendant welfare and other costs are almost a matter of definition. However, even where the motivation of regulation is benign it may have unintended or unanticipated consequences. The Averch–Johnson (1962) effect describes how rate-of-return regulation may result in the use of too much capital in the production of a given level of output. This over-capitalization implies higher costs and prices than would otherwise be the case. With two inputs, capital K and labour L, which have prices r and w respectively, total cost TC is given by

$$(5.5) \qquad TC = rK + wL$$

Further, suppose that with total revenue TR the regulatory agency sets the maximum 'fair rate of return' on capital R_m and calculates actual R simply so that

$$(5.6) \qquad R = \frac{TR - wL}{K} < R_m$$

Now economic profit π is conventionally measured as a surplus over all costs, so that

$$(5.7) \qquad \pi = TR - TC = TR - (rK + wL)$$

hence

$$(5.8) \qquad \pi + rK = TR - wL$$

Substituting (5.8) into (5.6),

$$(5.9) \qquad \frac{\pi + rK}{K} < R_m$$

$$\pi + rK < R_m K$$

or

$$(5.10) \qquad \pi < (R_m - r)K$$

This regulatory profit constraint is illustrated in Fig. 5.8 (a) and indicates that the profit-maximizing use of capital K^* associated with point 1 would involve a return on capital deemed excessive. The best the regulatee can do is to meet the constraint at 2 and choose labour–capital combination 2' in preference to the

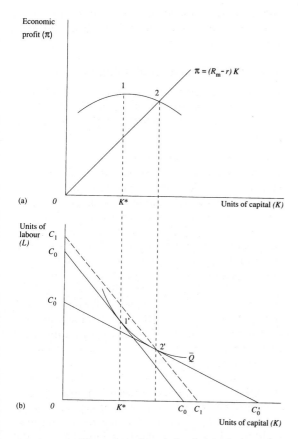

Figure 5.8 An illustration of regulation-induced overcapitalization.

actual least-cost factor combination indicated at $1'$. The difference between isocost lines $C_0 C_0$ and $C_1 C_1$ in Fig. 5.8 (b) measures the extent to which costs of production of a given output $\bar{Q}$ have been raised by the regulation which in effect causes the producer to view $C'_0 C'_0$ as the isocost curve; that is, the regulation makes capital appear to be less expensive so that its overuse in the choice of 'distorted' factor proportions seems rational.

The intuition of the effect is that the firm can purchase both labour and capital at their market prices but there is an additional consideration concerning capital. The purchase of a capital good becomes part of the base on which the approved rate of return can be earned; e.g. with a rate of return of 10 per cent and a £10 000 piece of equipment, the profit allowed rises by £1000 per annum over the equipment's life. An outlay of £10 000 on labour will raise costs and output price to maintain the existing rate of return but has no profit-facilitating property.

For our present purposes it is the general point—i.e. that individual decision-takers will respond to the regulation set in a way that may well be unanticipated and inefficient—that matters, rather than the fact that this hypothesis has received mixed empirical support.

5.5.3 Subsidies

Peacock (1980) sets out an 'analysis' in which individual producers learn that it pays to be inefficient. In such circumstances the subsidy arrangement could be more inefficient than public production.

In Peacock's scenario it is imperfections of the government decision-makers that cause an imperfect market situation to be more imperfect. In Fig. 5.9 suppose that, because of an externality argument, an output subsidy of 12 is justified, shifting $MC_1 = AC_1$ to $MC_2 = AC_2$ allowing for a normal rate of return on the efficient output level Oq^*. Now the incentives for the profit-maximizing producer are to choose output level Oq^1 where $MC_2 = MR$, receiving subsidy 12 per unit on Oq^1 units of output. However, this solution fails to secure the efficient output level Oq^*, in which case the firm suggests that costs are $MC_3 = AC_3$, so that when the subsidy is introduced it can equate $MC_4 = AC_4$ with MR, meeting the desired target and its profit maximizing objective. In the construction the distances 23 and 41 are equal, representing the subsidy being taken off the 'imagined' costs $MC_3 = AC_3$ and the actual costs $MC_1 = AC_1$ respectively.

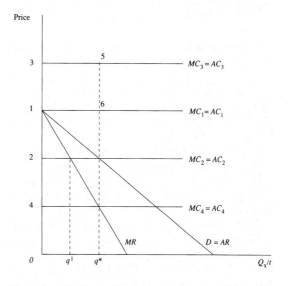

Figure 5.9 Exploiting a subsidy.

The final link in Peacock's argument is that this subsidized firm cannot be seen to be making more than normal profit and is therefore induced to allow the cost curves to rise via X-inefficiency to $MC_3 = AC_3$. The overall result of trying to subsidize the output level to correct a market failure has been to generate a further market failure in the form of X-inefficiency equal to rectangle 1356. In such circumstances public production at Oq^* might well be less costly than the subsidy option.

5.6 Prescriptions for and predictions about 'nationalized industries'

For whatever reason, the fact is that governments all over the world are responsible for the production of some goods and services. Given this, two questions naturally arise: first, What considerations should influence the price–output decisions? and secondly, How can public sector producers be expected to act and react? The former is a traditional concern, the latter the subject of more recent contributions. These differences of approach that surface elsewhere in this text can be vividly illustrated with respect to the public production of private (excludable) goods that are privately financed, case 2 in Table 5.1. Two major approaches are illustrated:

1. Efficiency (and equity) considerations in pricing and output decisions (the nationalized industry case).
2. The political economy (property rights) approach.

In section 5.6.1 the context is one of neutral and apolitical agents who work in or for government and whose job is to follow the normative prescriptions of welfare economics in the specified circumstances (i.e. actors who are followers of an economic recipe book).

In section 5.6.2 the context is one of self-interested agents who find it impossible to follow the prescriptions of welfare theory, either because it cannot be operationalized or because it conflicts with their self-interest.

The distinction can be viewed in part as one of a normative versus a positive approach, i.e. between what ought to be done and what will be done. Also, the distinction is in part between the external and internal environments of firms. In section 5.6.1 the object is essentially to set the appropriate external rules or environment via government. In section 5.6.2 the internal content of firms shows up much more strongly.

5.6.1 The 'nationalized' industry case

In advising government how to price the output of nationalized industries, there are many problems that must be confronted. The first of these is the problem of second best.

The problem of second best

In chapter 1 it was argued that, if certain marginal equivalencies held in the economy, a Pareto-optimal allocation of resources could be attained. This 'first-best' solution required that all marginal equivalencies held simultaneously. If within the economy one marginal equivalence could not be attained, the problem of 'second best' becomes relevant. For example, if one good (e.g. good Y) was produced by a monopolist (so that $P_Y > MC$), or if one externality in the production of good Y remained Pareto-relevant (so that $MSC_y \neq MSB_y$), it is not the case that the conditions for Pareto optimality could be followed automatically in other markets in the knowledge that this would lead to a welfare improvement.

As Baumol (1965) pointed out, it is tempting from the Pareto-optimal model to suppose that each marginal rate of substitution that can be brought into line with its price ratio means an improvement in welfare. But, as illustrated in chapter 1, this is not so. When one marginal equivalence cannot be attained (i.e. when a non-Paretian constraint exists), policy-makers do not necessarily follow such rules as 'set price equal to marginal cost' in other sectors of the economy nor feel that they are increasing welfare for the community. Moreover, as Lipsey and Lancaster (1956) note, there is no sense in counting the number of Paretian conditions that would hold in certain second-best economies and arguing that one is preferable to another because more marginal conditions hold. In this model it would appear it is a case of 'all or nothing'! That is to say, only when all the conditions hold (i.e. first best) can we rest easy that welfare has been maximized. If one marginal equivalence does not hold, it *may* be necessary that all others be abandoned. However, it is not clear in what direction these departures should be. It will come as no surprise to readers that many textbooks, and indeed many journal articles, avoid the issue of second best because to confront it poses formidable problems.

Though readers' disillusionment with welfare economics may increase, it is not necessary to abandon all hope. By a process of piecemeal optimization, it is possible to respond to second-best constraints, but as we will demonstrate, this may mean amending certain resource allocation rules.

To demonstrate the response to a non-Paretian constraint, it is useful to utilize the concept of consumer surplus which has been discussed in chapter 2. The particular example we will focus on is one where price is not set equal to marginal cost for one good in the economy and there is nothing that can be done directly to resolve this problem. Suppose there are two goods, X and Y. Good Y is produced by a monopolist and sold at a price above marginal cost. Good X is produced in the public sector. How should good X be priced? Is the principle of setting price equal to marginal cost helpful?

To deal with this question, it is best to eschew such pricing rules. The pricing rule to follow should be a result of the process of welfare maximization and not vice versa. In order to maximize welfare by changing price, a simple procedure is to recommend price changes as long as the net incremental effect on welfare is positive. When it is impossible to change price so as to increase net welfare, then the optimal price has been discovered (irrespective of whether or not this equals marginal cost).

Here we follow an approach outlined in Turvey (1971) and Webb (1976). In Fig. 5.10 we depict the demand curves for goods X and Y respectively. These are linear income-compensated demand curves. The value of the goods is estimated in terms of willingness to pay for the goods. Therefore the value to consumers of a small change in the price of good X (i.e. ΔP_x) is equal to the value of the additional units of X (Δq^x) that are consumed as a consequence. In part (a) the shaded area illustrates the value of these additional units of good X to consumers. The area is equal to

$$(5.11) \qquad (P_x + \Delta P_x/2)\Delta q^x$$

If goods X and Y are substitutes, a change in the price of good X will shift the demand curve for good Y. If the price of good X increases, the demand for good Y will shift to the right (and vice versa). Assume that demand for good Y shifts from D_y^1 to D_y^2 as shown in Fig. 5.10 (b). The value of the additional units of good Y is equal to the maximum sum that consumers are prepared to pay. As the demand curve shifts to the right, the dashed line maps the price paid for the marginal unit. Thus the shaded area in part (b) measures willingness to pay for these additional units. The area can be measured as

$$(5.12) \qquad (P_y + \Delta P_y/2)\Delta q^y$$

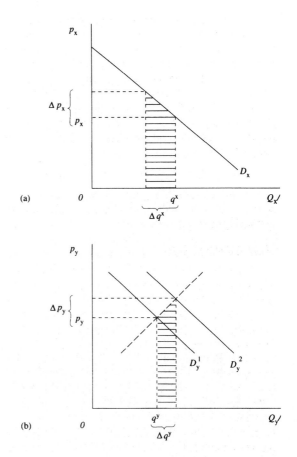

Figure 5.10 'Second-best' considerations.
Source: based on Webb (1976).

When the output of good X increases, there is obviously a change in the costs of production. This can be estimated as the marginal costs of production multiplied by the number of units of good X, i.e. $M_x\Delta q^x$. Similarly, the additional costs of producing good Y can be written as $M_y\Delta q^y$. It should be clear then that a change in the price of good X affects consumer welfare (by the value of willingness to pay for the good and for substitutes) and also the costs of production (by $M_x\Delta q^x + M_y\Delta q^y$). Yet it is reasonable to argue that a change in the price of good X should be acceptable as long as the net effect on welfare is positive.

The net effect on welfare is equal to $[(P_x + \Delta P_x/2)\Delta q^x] + [(P_y + \Delta P_y/2)\Delta q^y]$ less ($M_x\Delta q^x + M_y\Delta q^y$). Therefore the rule should be to continue to change P_x until

$$(5.13) \quad \frac{(P_x + \Delta P_x/2)\Delta q^x + (P_y + \Delta P_y/2)\Delta q^y}{- M_x \Delta q^x - M_y \Delta q^y = 0}$$

If we rearrange these terms, then at this point

$$(5.14) \quad \begin{aligned} P_x &= M_x - \Delta q^y/\Delta q^x (P_y - M_y) \\ &\quad - \frac{1}{2} \frac{(\Delta P_x \Delta q^x + \Delta P_y \Delta q^y)}{\Delta q^x} \end{aligned}$$

and as ΔP_x and ΔP_y tend to zero we can ignore the last term. Therefore P_x should be set as

$$(5.15) \quad P_x = M_x - \Delta q^y/\Delta q^x (P_y - M_y)$$

The term $\Delta q^y/\Delta q^x$ is extremely important. If $\Delta q^y/\Delta q^x$ is negative the goods are substitutes and if $\Delta q^y/\Delta q^x$ is positive the goods are complements. The last equation therefore says that the price of X should be set *above* marginal cost if the goods are substitutes (i.e. $\Delta q^y/\Delta q^x$ is negative so the effect of $-\Delta q^y/\Delta q^x$ $(P_y - M_y)$ is positive). The amount that it should be set above marginal cost is dependent on the *excess price* of good Y above marginal cost. (Note, of course, that if the goods are complements $\Delta q^y/\Delta q^x$ is positive and P_x should be below M_x when $P_y > M_y$.)

This rule can be easily generalized for many goods (see e.g. Mishan 1988). If there are many goods that are substitutes for good X, then the price of good X should be set above M_x according to a weighted average of the *excess price* of all other goods—weights to depend upon the closeness to which the other goods are substitutes to good X. The intuition behind this rule should be clear. If, in the example above, good Y is priced above marginal cost, then by Paretian standards 'too little' of good Y is being produced. Consumers of good Y would pay more than the marginal costs of producing an additional unit of that good.

The fact that good X is now priced *above* marginal cost will reduce demand for good X and increase demand for good Y. More resources will be moved into the production of good Y from the production of good X—which is what is prescribed on Paretian grounds.

While the intuition that lies behind the above pricing strategy appears logical, there can be no doubt that far more information is required in this piecemeal optimization approach. We need to know how close substitutes/complements the goods are. We need to know how far above marginal cost the other goods are priced. To economize on the informational requirements it is possible to suggest certain broad guidelines. For example, if all other goods are substitutes and are priced above marginal cost, then at least we know that the public sector good should be priced above marginal cost (see Farrel 1958). If the good is a close substitute for some goods, then we may decide to focus on this sector. For example, the public sector price for coal will be influenced mainly (solely?) by the *excess price* of electricity, oil, gas and other energy sources. None of these short-cuts should be taken to imply that the task is easy, but a piecemeal optimization approach to the pricing of public sector produce does exist.

The problem of decreasing costs

Even if everywhere in the economy 'first best' was achieved, there arise distinct problems from the fact that many nationalized industries experience decreasing costs of production. Here there are distinct difficulties in retaining the rule of price = marginal cost. The central argument is that an individual firm can achieve sufficient economies of scale that it can meet industry demand while $(LR)AC$ remains below the demand $(= AR)$ curve. This is usually associated with large sunk costs. The problem it raises is that, when marginal cost MC is equated with AR, the price per unit P_c does not cover AC per unit and a loss is made equal to area $P_c C_c 12$ in Fig. 5.11. The trick for policy is to secure the efficient quantity Oq^*. The process of loss-making is envisaged to drive out all individual firms until one only is left. This firm will have the incentive to profit-maximize and produce Oq^m at price OP_m where $MC = MR$. Even if the remaining firm could be induced to average-cost-price, producing where $AC = AR$ and covering normal profit with a price of P_a per unit, Oq^a is an inefficiently small quantity. The extent of the allocative inefficiency loss is the area 432, being the difference between AR and MC over the range of output $Oq^a Oq^*$. The stage is thus set for the entrance of public sector production of Oq^* with the loss thus generated being covered by general taxation and/or the use of multipart pricing (block tariffs). If prices of nationalized industries are to be set above MC, there is a rule (akin to the Ramsey rule discussed in chapter 15) for marking up prices (see e.g. Rees 1976). Literature inspired by this initial rationale relates to questions of peak-load pricing when there is a great variability in demand and the need to make a decision as to when a new plant or facility is to be constructed.

As a prelude to the next section and change of emphasis, the remarks of Wiseman and Littlechild (1986) are worth considering. Their brief discussion of pricing and investment policies in UK nationalized industries notes that the 1930s–1970s represent the high water-mark of interest in optimal policies such as marginal cost pricing. While not commanding universal support at any level, they note that the

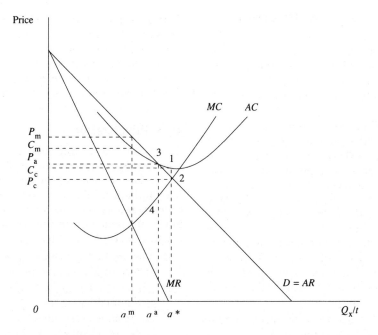

Figure 5.11 The 'decreasing cost' industry.

economic guidelines were ignored by both the nationalized industries and the government. The authors suggest the 1970s were characterized by concern with different political and administrative structures and the 1980s with privatization and competition, so that the focus has become decision processes that inhere in different institutional contexts and not normative prescriptions.

5.6.2 The political economy (property rights) approach

In this section an account of nationalized industries (public utilities) offered by Wiseman (1978) is drawn up, as his writing contrasts starkly with the subsection above. Indeed, Wiseman's comments on the prescription above is worth quoting:

> The most formal espousal of this perception of [Pareto] efficiency... required that nationalised industry products should be sold at prices equal to their long-run marginal cost. I have argued elsewhere that the practical relevance of this prescription is of the same order as would be an injunction to price according to the principle God is Love: the sentiment is difficult to deny, the practical consequences of conformity unidentifiable. (Wiseman 1978, p. 74)

As for arguments justifying public production, Wiseman accepts the sunk capital costs argument but denies the existence of any relevant public goods

(non-exclusion) arguments and the 'commanding heights' argument that some have adduced in this context. The latter is basically a macro counterpart to the co-ordination argument presented above. It suggests that public production gives government economic tools through which influence can be exerted on the economy, presumably by, for example, pricing and budgetary policy. Wiseman's approach emphasizes (a) that we must view all individuals as decision-takers and that the values relevant to decisions are those perceived by individuals; and (b) that group behaviour, in which individuals may belong to more than one group whose objectives may conflict, and property rights, the product of law and custom, determine the costs and benefits faced by individual decision-makers. In this way Wiseman focuses more on the *process* of decision-making than on outcomes and thereby paints a different economic picture to that viewed above.

With these building blocks, a number of implications about the operation of nationalized industries are derived by the author:

1. Because there are no owners (shareholders) of the assets tied up in nationalized industries, no one has a direct interest in the yield from the assets.

2. The equivalent of the private sector owner is the minister responsible for nationalized industries in Parliament, and he or she cannot exert any sanc-

tions by selling the assets as would be the case with shares in a private enterprise.

3. Because of the lack of an efficient capital market which offers a capital valuation reflecting expected future profitability of the enterprise, there is difficulty in deciding the appropriate capital requirements.

4. Management will be less constrained in nationalized industries in that poor management will not depress the capitalized value of the enterprise and therefore be visible. Indeed, profit and the possibility of sharing in it may not be part of the objectives or property rights structure within the enterprise. Furthermore, the minister, or ministers, given their degree of discretion, are more likely to act in arbitrary, unpredictable fashions. In short, divergencies in the individual decision-takers, no matter what group or groups they fall into, are likely to be larger than in the market context of private enterprise.

5. The often legislated absence of competition dulls interest in profitable (entrepreneurial) innovation and fosters bureaucracy.

6. Workers and union members realize that loss-making may not lead to bankruptcy and unemployment but rather to losses covering general taxation-financed grants from government. They have a property right on the prospect that losses will be covered.

As with the economics of bureaucracy, it is the incentives created by the form of economic structure that matter, not the fact that public production involves a different type of human being. Hence, even if Wiseman accepted that the prescriptions of welfare theory had some practical significance, he would argue that none of the actors would have any reason to employ them except in so far as they coincided with their own self-interests. However, there is some optimism in his mind to the extent that the undesirable outcomes outlined above, although serious, are not hopeless. De-nationalization (privatization) is one avenue, but improving the decision-making relationships, i.e. the internal structure of the organization, is another. It is these prescriptions of 'privatization' and 'internal markets' that are considered next.

5.7 A return to the market

Whatever the rights and wrongs of the arguments presented above, the 1980s and 1990s have seen the dominance of the anti-public sector school of thought. The practical outcrop of the dominance has been policies concerned with reintroducing and strengthening market processes. In this chapter this 'reform' process is considered under two headings: 'Privatization' and 'Quasi (or Internal) Markets'.

5.7.1 Privatization

'Privatization' is a word used to describe a host of policies all sharing the common aim of strengthening the market and reducing the role of the public sector. Looking back at Table 5.1 it is clear that the provision of goods and services might take the form of different mixes of public/private finance and public/private production. From that table:

(i) category 1 refers to goods and services that were financed and produced in the private sector;

(ii) category 2 refers to goods produced in the public sector but financed through prices in the form of 'user charges' (e.g. library services or leisure services—see chapter 12 for further discussion);

(iii) category 3 contains goods which were financed by the public sector but produced by private firms;

(iv) category 4 refers to goods which were financed and produced in the public sector.

Using these categories it is possible to classify different processes of privatization. For example:

(i) the sale of nationalized industries would represent a movement from category 2 to category 1;

(ii) the introduction of 'contracting out' would represent a movement from category 4 to category 3 (e.g. in the UK local government has 'contracted out' the provision of refuse collection, hospitals 'contract out' the provision of catering and laundry services, etc.);

(iii) a greater reliance on tax relief (i.e. subsidy) for private giving to charities (rather than provision of welfare services by the state) would represent a movement from category 4 to category 3.

As all of these changes reflect an attempt to 'strengthen' the market, there is then more than one way to 'privatize'. However, the popular perception appears to be that 'privatization' is achieved by a transferal of ownership. Industries which were once owned and operated in the public sector (i.e. nationalized) have been 'privatized' by a transferal of ownership to the private sector. In the UK, throughout the 1980s there have been a series of 'privatizations' or sales of government holdings. As examples of such sales consider the following 'privatizations': 1984 (and 1991) British Telecom; 1986 National Bus Company; 1987 British Gas; 1987 British Airways; 1989 and 1990 water companies; 1990 electricity distribution and 1991 electricity generation. The question considered here is what motivates such a process of privatization and is it likely to prove 'successful'?

5.7.1a 'Privatization' and efficiency

Perhaps the most important rationale for undertaking privatization is to increase efficiency. The argument in favour of privatization is that the incentive structure within the public sector causes inefficiency; costs of producing goods will be higher in the public sector as (for many) seems 'obvious' because state-owned companies need to rely on subsidies. There are two schools of criticism (Parker 1993). The first is the 'public choice school' which highlights the influence of bureaucrats and politicians on day-to-day management and demonstrates its inconsistency with efficient production. The incentives faced by bureaucrats and politicians leads to inefficient intervention with day-to-day management. For example, politicians may attempt to influence management of nationalized industries for electoral purposes, e.g. (i) causing industries to invest in geographical locations which bring greatest electoral support (i.e. where there are closely contested or 'marginal' seats) rather than in areas that would be cost effective; (ii) constraining management's request for price increases so as to avoid the electoral unpopularity that such increases would generate.

The second set of criticisms comes from the 'property rights school'. Here the argument is that, if companies are 'owned' by shareholders in the private sector, shareholders of private companies have an incentive to ensure that managers make efficient decisions. Such an incentive is not felt by voters as far as nationalized enterprises are concerned as voters do not recognize their ownership interests in the companies. Therefore, ownership of companies by private shareholders stimulates the pursuit of profit and the implementation of efficiency. Moreover, private ownership would also offer another source of finance. If there was concern about overall levels of public sector borrowing, companies within the public sector might find it difficult to finance new investment projects. By contrast, private ownership permits companies to issue shares to finance new investment programmes (Bishop et al. 1994).

If privatization is to be achieved by a transfer of ownership, how successful is this likely to be?

Inevitably there are transactions costs in the sale of companies and it is necessary that such a transfer of ownership increases efficiency significantly. However, there are reasons for scepticism:

(i) *If privatization reduces the requirement for state subsidy does this imply that production is more 'efficient'?* Reliance of some nationalized industries on state subsidies has often proved an easy target for critics. However, to equate profits with efficiency is spurious. Often nationalized industries are 'natural monopolies', with high fixed costs of production (e.g. provision of exchanges in the case of telecommunications; provision of pipelines in the case of water or gas; provision of track and signaling in the case of the railways). As rehearsed in section 5.6.1 if (in conditions of 'first best'—see chapter 1) prices are constrained to equal marginal cost then, when marginal cost is less than average cost, losses are inevitable even though production is undertaken efficiently. The 'efficient' level of output is by definition one in which total costs cannot be covered by total revenue (as prices are set equal to marginal cost). The point is that, if constraints are set on nationalized industries, so that prices are set lower than average cost, losses are predictable even when production is efficient. By contrast, if companies were told to maximize profit, a nationalized industry might achieve this by simply charging higher prices and restricting output to an inefficient level (if it is a natural monopoly). It follows that the creation of profits (or the absence of any requirement of subsidy) is not an 'obvious' indication of efficiency.

(ii) *Comparative studies suggest lower costs of production in the private sector than in the public sector.* If profits are not an automatic indicator of efficiency, perhaps it is better to focus on comparisons of costs of production. Evidence on the relative efficiency of private and public production is difficult to establish. In principle there is: (a) a cross-section approach (comparing production of output in a public and private context either nationally or internationally); (b) a time-series approach (assessing comparative efficiency via before-and-after studies in cases of privatization or nationalization) and (c) an *ex ante* approach. Clearly, the Achilles' heel of all approaches is comparing like with like except for the variable under dispute. Here we take the variable under dispute to be productive efficiency, so that maximum outputs should be obtained from units of inputs and the least-cost combination of inputs chosen.

(a) *Cross-section studies* have been employed where private and public enterprises are found operating side by side. Canadian railways and Australian airways are two prominent examples. The Canadian Pacific Railway is privately owned and the Canadian National Railway publicly owned; in Australia the privately owned Ansett Transport Industries competes with the publicly owned Trans Australia Airlines. The general conclusion on the comparative performance of these enterprises is that there is not all that much difference, which has led some to conclude that the observation made above, that it is competition and not ownership that matters, is valid.

(b) *Time-series studies* are possible as case studies of industries that have moved from the private to the public sector and vice versa. Here it is a question of analysing historical data. Rowley (1978), in comments on the contribution of Wiseman described above, draws attention to a study he co-authored on British Steel, which was a private sector cartel from 1953 to 1967 and was then nationalized, and suggests that the case-study approach is viable. Two limitations do, however, loom large. First, once quite long periods of time have elapsed, any *ceteris paribus* assumptions that may be part of the analysis look untenable. Secondly, in the absence of economic experimentation on a grand scale, there is the necessity of waiting for 'nature' to provide changes of enterprise context and then waiting for any differences to become apparent. One way of, to some extent, avoiding the second wait is to look to the stock market.

(c) *Ex ante approach.* Boardman, Freedman and Eckel (1986) use stock market evidence to estimate the expected cost of government ownership as compared with private ownership. In Canada in 1981 two Quebec crown corporations gained control of a private corporation, Domtar. In the following week Domtar shares made an abnormal loss of 25 per cent (a loss of market value equal to $150 million). Allowing for other influences, the authors attribute between 8 and 19 per cent of this loss to the market's view of the cost of pursuing non-profit objectives, such as reduced efficiency and the pursuit of socio-political objectives. However, it is difficult to know how to interpret this result. Reduced efficiency in most circumstances is unattractive, but socio-political objectives may not be. It may be that achieving justified socio-political objectives is costly, and the question then becomes whether this approach is the least-cost way to achieve them. The illustration of the use of the stock market as an efficient provider of an unbiased estimate of a firm's expected future profit is thus important here.

The general point is that even if it is accepted that many comparative studies of the costs of production in the private and in the public sector suggest that costs are lower in the private sector (for a review see Mueller 1989, pp. 262–5) the conclusion that 'the evidence that public provision of a service reduces efficiency of its provision seems overwhelming' (Mueller 1989, p. 266) may be difficult to sustain.

First, very often the *quality* of service provided by private firms and public sector provision are not comparable (e.g. see Knapp 1984). Second, the view that private provision is always more cost effective is not unanimous. In some cases public provision is at lower cost. The issue is not whether ownership is in the private or public sector, but rather whether there is *competition* (e.g. Millward and Parker 1983). Publicly owned firms are more efficient if they face competition. It is not transference of ownership that is likely to increase efficiency but exposure to competition.

(iii) *Private Sector Incentives—will they prove effective?* Consider more closely the argument that shareholders constrain management to act efficiently. Has any one shareholder the incentive to attend a shareholder meeting and question day-to-day management? Evidence has long suggested that management in private firms enjoy discretion (Jackson and Price 1993). Individual shareholders would find it costly to attend shareholder meetings and closely monitor managerial decisions. At the same time, management may have their own interests, e.g. their prestige and salary may be linked to turnover rather than profits.

Of course, the 'property rights school' argue that there is no reason for 'active intervention' by each shareholder. If a company does so badly that its share prices falls below the value of assets, the company may face 'take over' threats from other companies. If shareholders sell their shares the 'take over' may result in a loss of jobs for top management and the fear of this would act as the constraint on management. But this line of argument is questionable. Reviewing the evidence, Jackson (1994, p. 10) concludes 'while a theoretical case can be erected to demonstrate that the management for corporate control is an important discipline on the management of a firm...the empirical evidence to support it is weak...'. Moreover, many of the companies that are transferred from the public to the private sector are so large that takeover could not really be considered feasible. Bishop and Kay (1989, p. 650) argue that:

'Even where performance is considered weak, however, the threat of management being replaced is not strong. Size is generally a more important factor in safeguarding firms from takeover than is successful profit performance ...'. They add 'the newly privatized British Telcom and British Gas are among the largest private enterprises in the United Kingdom. Restrictions on the concentration of either shareholdings mean that hostile takeover is entirely implausible.'

5.7.1b Alternative options

All of this would suggest that simple transference of ownership (from the public to the private sector) is no guarantee of increased efficiency. To effect an improvement, greater emphasis needs to be placed upon the introduction of competition. But if a nationalized industry is a 'natural monopoly' how is this possible? Are there alternatives to transferal of ownership?

(1) *Restructuring* is one possibility. Some of the activities of the nationalized industry might be transferred into the public sector when these involve the production of private (rather than public goods) and when they are more likely to be exposed to competitive forces. For example, in the UK, British Rail undertook ferry services across the English Channel. Privatization was a way of separating rail and ferry concerns. This might increase efficiency to the extent that it removes any inefficiency arising from cross subsidization within companies (Bishop *et al.* 1994). By providing more clear information on costs, improved decisions may be possible.

Why was there less reliance on restructuring than on the transferal of ownership in the UK? One argument suggests that management did not want their empire broken up. Experience with privatization shows that the compliance of top management to the process was only secured by the promise that public sector companies would not be broken up in the process of privatization (Bishop and Kay 1989).

(2) *Franchising.* The theory of contestable markets introduced by Baumol (1982—see chapter 1) reveals that it is not the existence of competition that is important but the *potential* of competition. Even when markets are characterized by a small number of suppliers, competition may be present as long as there is ease of entry and exit of potential producers. While high fixed costs of production may preclude entry, in some cases franchising can be introduced. Private firms bid for the option of managing existing resources that remain owned by the public sector. It is

the potential of entry by new firms that is the source of competition. One simple method would be to hold an auction; the winner would be the bidder who offers the franchiser the largest monetary sum. For example, in the UK, with privatization of British Rail, the government offered private companies the chance to bid for the franchise to operate services. Private companies agree to operate a service that will satisfy minimum quality constraints and the company that wins the franchise will have to be very cost-effective to make a profit. The Railways Act of 1993 provided for the privatization of British Rail. It was decided that initially eight franchises should be put on offer, e.g. the Gatwick Express service from London to Gatwick Airport; the Great Western service from London to South Wales; the East Coast service from London to Leeds, Newcastle, Edinburgh, Aberdeen, etc.

However, while franchising appears to offer a means of introducing competition there are still problems. For example:

(i) bidding might attract only a few competitors;
(ii) when taking investment decision, there are disincentives for incumbents know they may be displaced after the period of franchise;
(iii) specification of the contract is difficult, particularly with respect to quality;
(iv) there is the problem of the 'winner's curse'. If there is a franchise up for auction that offers the same profit possibilities to all bidders, the winning bid tends to exceed the value of the franchise. Assume that each bidding firm uses its experts to assess the net value of the franchise, and, indeed, that the mean of these valuations is 'correct'. This gives the expert valuation distribution in Fig. 5.12. Suppose the firm's decision-makers are risk-averse and that each reduces the bid the experts offer. The mean bid will be somewhere below the mean valuation (and true value), say at $£(X - A)$. The winning bid, however, will be above that as long as point 2 remains to the right of $£X$.

The winner will be the one furthest away from the mean of the expected valuations in the shaded tail at point 2. Here she is cursed in the sense of making a loss on the franchise. To add insult to injury, even if somehow the mean expert valuation was below the true valuation, there is a large gap between the winning expert valuation and the winner's actual profit. This is the disappointment distance 12 in Fig. 5.12. Such a mechanism helps explain why contract holders may be quick to try and renegotiate conditions or renege on quality constraints—indeed, it could explain the

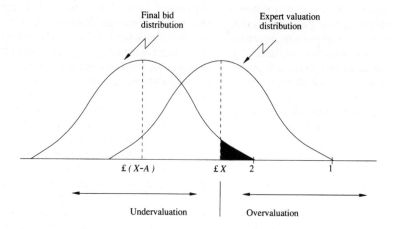

Figure 5.12 The winner's curse.

'thinness' of many auctions. The suggestion is that bidders realize that the only ones they can win without collusion will be ones they will lose on, and therefore it is best for them not to bid at all. The curse and evidence related to it are both discussed in Thaler (1988).

5.7.1c Regulating privatized companies

It is clear from the above discussion that it is difficult to rely on transfer of ownership to ensure that competition will be introduced. If companies are simply transferred from the public sector to the private sector there is a danger that privatization will simply introduce private monopoly. As a safeguard, the response in the US is to use regulatory agencies to prevent companies from exploiting monopoly power. UK privatization replaced nationalization with regulation as the mechanism for providing a safeguard against monopoly. But regulation itself poses problems. For example:

(i) *Regulatory Capture.* Here the implications of section 5.2.5 are prominent. The independence of the regulatory board may be called into question. If the regulatory agency does not have an independent source of information then it may be 'captured' by the industry (Stigler 1975; Peltzman 1976). The industry may supply data that will justify price changes, investment changes, etc. There is also the problem that the agency may be captured by producer groups and this may mean that prices are set to the advantage of producer groups relative to consumer groups ((e.g. Stigler and Friedland 1962; see also the discussion in chapter 2). In the UK, there is already the

suggestion that managers of privatized companies have 'captured' government policy for privatization. Jackson and Price (1994, p. 16) quote the assessment of Abromweit (1988) that: 'the BT managers ... succeeded—quite conspicuously—in inducing the Government to drop most of its original ideas about liberalization in the telecommunications industry.'

(ii) *Regulating Rates of Return.* One way to limit the profits of regulated companies would be to limit the rate of return that they can earn on their capital stock. The problem, analysed above, is that this can lead to inefficient production (Averch and Johnson 1962) since firms could increase their profit by having a larger capital stock. Inefficiency arises as a result of over capital intensive methods of production. (See the discussion in section 5.4.2.)

(iii) *Regulating RPI−X.* This form of regulation is used in the UK to place a ceiling on the annual increase in an enterprise's prices. Prices are permitted to increase at the same rate as the retail price index minus X percentage points. For example, for British Telecom X was initially fixed at three and for the British Airport Authority at one. In the case of some companies, e.g. those concerned with water supply, the formula was amended to RPI + X as allowance was made for the need to finance future investment, e.g. to improve water quality. This regulatory formula then remains in place for a period of five years after which it is renegotiated. The intention of setting price increases below the increases in the retail price index is to induce management to drive prices down in order to retain maximum profits. However, this regulatory formula is also open to criticism:

(a) Firms may not maximize profits. If there is managerial discretion managers may be as interested in the size of departments for which they are responsible and therefore the constraint on management intended to drive down costs will not be as great (see Helm 1987 for a discussion of the extent to which profit maximization can be enforced).

(b) This particular form of regulation appears to overcome the distortionary effects noted with respect to US regulation. The RPI minus X was intended to control prices and yet permit increased profits from lower costs. However, ultimately the determination of X depends on what the regulator thinks appropriate. Unless the assessment of the regulator is independent of the enterprise's achieved level of costs and efficiency, RPI $-$ X regulation will, in practice, become equivalent to 'rate of return regulation' with all its associated weakness. If the privatized company feels that the next time that RPI $-$ X is set it will be influenced by current profits then the incentive to drive costs down are reduced. Parker (1993, p. 190) comments: 'in practice it appears that the X factor is indeed being set with a view to what the regulatory body considers to be a "satisfactory rate of profit"...'.

(c) Bishop and Kay (1989, p. 651) argue that: 'even if an independent judgment on costs and efficiency can be reached scope still exists for a capital intensive enterprise to evade the constraints imposed by the regulatory formulae by reorganizing its investment profile to enhance short term financial performance at the expense of longer term prospects.'

5.7.1d Privatization: a multi-dimensional policy

It has been argued that a central objective of privatization is the pursuit of efficiency, but in an attempt to achieve efficiency there are other effects. For example, there are income distribution effects. When industries are nationalized citizens have a 'stake' in the industry. When these holdings are sold 'too cheaply' then those citizens unable to purchase shares lose to others who are able to purchase shares. In the UK the premium on the shares of companies on the first day of trading on the Stock Exchange stand as testimony to the under valuation of companies that were privatized.

With reference to efficiency, Jackson and Price (1994) argue that privatization policy has been focused on efficiency in a 'static' sense. They would broaden consideration to include the impact of privatization on dynamic considerations (e.g. the effectiveness of investment in new productive capacity). With risk-pooling advantages of the public sector

(Arrow and Lind 1970), 'the case for private decision making need not be as clear cut as is often supposed...' (Jackson and Price 1994, p. 8).

There are further considerations which are said to make privatization attractive. For example, Rees (1986) considers the arguments that privatization will: (a) reduce government borrowing; (b) undermine trade union power; (c) offer a wide choice of share-owning possibilities; (d) foster efficiency and innovation; (e) decrease the extent of political intervention; (f) stimulate employee co-operation. To this list, it is possible to add: (g) reduce the opportunity for cross subsidization; (h) increase political popularity. The list may look impressive but the longer the list the more scepticism that it will be possible to achieve everything; are all these objectives consistent? For example:

(i) *Private Ownership of Shares/Increased Efficiency.* Parker (1993) notes that at the beginning of the 1980s an objective of the Conservative government in the UK had been to reverse the decline in individual share ownership. By giving priority to small shareholders when selling state assets the proportion of adults owning shares trebled in the UK from around 7 per cent to 25 per cent throughout the 1980s. However, if private share ownership was to act as a constraint on management was it advisable to have broadened the ownership of shares? If each shareholder has only a very small stake in the company there is less incentive to monitor the behaviour of management. It is arguable that greater constraint on management would emerge from a more concentrated share ownership.

(ii) *Private Ownership of Shares/Reducing Government Borrowing.* In the 1980s the sale of companies in the UK reduced government borrowing but the extent of this saving has been much exaggerated. Parker (1993, p. 182) notes that 'in terms of the share of public spending in gross domestic product (GDP) they reduced the percentage by 1.5 points in 1988–9 but in other years by less'. Perhaps one reason why the impact was not greater was that the shares were sold at a low price, possibly to encourage shareholding. For example, shares sold by the government in British Telecom in 1984 were to sell at more than an 80 per cent premium on the first day's trading. In 1987 shares sold by the government in British Airways were to sell at a premium of almost 70 per cent on the first day of trading. Again there is a potential inconsistency between two of the objectives of privatization.

(iii) *Efficiency/Reducing Government Borrowing.* It has been argued that the simple transferal of ownership of companies is not enough to improve efficiency.

Privatization must also increase competition. But, when considering the sale of companies, Jackson and Price (1994, p. 16) note: 'The maintenance of a monopoly structure also made the sale of assets more attractive in terms of the share price at flotation.' If a government is more interested in revenue then it will recognize that potential monopoly profits will increase share prices and the introduction of competition or rigorous regulation may reduce share prices. In the UK Jackson and Price (1994, p. 16) comment that 'the government probably had a closer eye on the revenue consequences...than on achieving the greater improvement in economic efficiency'.

One implication of looking at the diversity of effects of privatization is that it permits analysts to reconsider the policy of privatization in terms of a public choice framework. Within a public choice framework, why would a government be interested in privatization? Selling shares at 'too low' a price will make a government popular with those able to purchase the shares. On the other hand, if those who owned the company when it was in the public sector (i.e. voters) are subject to fiscal illusion, these individuals are not conscious that *their* assets are 'under sold'. Government may improve their popularity re-election chances and especially so if the additional revenue leads to tax cuts or removal of the need to raise taxes. Of course, this advantage happens only once; as a former Prime Minister (Harold Macmillan) noted, it is like 'selling the family silver'. Moving the public owned companies to the public sector would also remove the government from any unpopularity that might be associated with price increases (notwithstanding the responsibility the government has to establish a regulatory mechanism).

As noted above, the process of privatization was also popular with the management of companies that were privatized provided the enterprise was not broken up in the process of privatization. The potential this created for rents may explain criticism of the rewards paid to top management of newly privatized companies. While not an exhaustive list of arguments, it is not difficult to argue that privatization would bring gains to incumbent politicians and to management of companies. A rent-seeking model of privatization can be presented (Jones and Cullis 1988) and the notion that efficiency increases were the only consideration motivating privatization can be contested.

Whether or not privatization has ultimately increased efficiency is difficult to determine. While there are a number of points of reference, none are completely satisfactory. For example, in gauging the impact of privatization it is possible to look at the rate of return (and other accounting ratios) earned within the industry before and after privatization. However, such measures are unlikely to provide all the necessary evidence. For example: rates of return may change because of technological improvement (innovations which reduce costs) quite unconnected with the introduction of privatization; (b) they may reflect the greater use of monopoly power; (c) they may be associated with a reduction in quality of the service; (d) they may result from changes which could have been effected by changing management of publicly owned companies without transfer to the private sector (see Bishop and Kay, 1989). Of course, it is tempting to compare the performance of privatized companies with those that remain within the public sector. Yet, even if a relationship is discovered between 'efficiency' and privatization, it is difficult to determine the causation. Bishop and Kay (1989) argue that, in the case of UK privatization, many improvements in efficiency occurred before privatization. While the 'privatized industries have tended to be faster growing and more profitable...it seems that the causation runs from growth and profitability to privatization, rather than the other way around' (p. 653).

In a recent assessment of privatization in the UK, Bishop *et al.* (1994) stress the importance of using the process of privatization to introduce competition (privatization should be a process which will identify those goods that would be better provided in the private sector). In reflection, they comment: 'The UK privatization programme has not always been as successful at doing this as it should have been and there have been several missed opportunities to introduce competition' (1994, p. 13).

5.7.2 Quasi- (or internal) markets

The push towards more market and less state involvement in the economy has resulted in a relatively new market form—the quasi- (or internal) market. The most important introduction of this market form in the UK is associated with the National Health Service (NHS). The Conservative government, taking advice from an eminent visiting professor from the USA, felt there were both sources of efficiency gains in the NHS and a mechanism for securing them. The sources of the efficiency gains can be partially explored using Fig. 5.13. The figure shows a situation in which the NHS is the victim of excessive vertical integration. In such a situation the production process involves too many successive stages in the supply process being

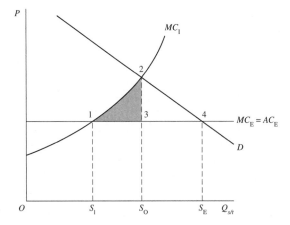

Figure 5.13 'Over' vertical integration.

undertaken internally. In Fig. 5.13 the curve D is the demand for say, units of surgical care per period, Qs/t, and P is their price (implicit pre-reform). The marginal cost of units of surgical care internal to the production unit is represented by MC_I leading to an equilibrium at point 2 and quantity OS_0. If externally there is an alternative production source whose marginal ($=$average) costs are $MC_E(= AC_E)$ two types of efficiency gain arise as equilibrium migrates to point 4 involving OS_E on the quantity axis. The triangle 123 represents a real resource gain from using the external source of supply, whereas triangle 243 is the increased consumer surplus from the quantity increase from OS_0 to OS_E. Note if the over-vertical integration is 'corrected' the quantity of internal supply shrinks from OS_0 to OS_1. If it is accepted that this abstract picture captures the pre-reform NHS, then the second issue of a mechanism for securing the gains becomes relevant. This mechanism became the so called quasi- (or internal) market. The general characteristics of such markets involve:

(i) the state providing the *finance* for the service under discussion, ie. the purchaser;

(ii) the form of the finance may be varied, e.g. ear-marked budget, vouchers distributed to relevant consumers, the use of agents to represent the ultimate consumers, etc.;

(iii) supplier competition to *produce* the services;

(iv) the form of competition may be varied involving competing state, non-profit or for profit (pro-prietary) suppliers.

Fig. 5.14 pictures this process with respect to the reformed NHS. As can be seen the 'purchasers' are fund holding GP's and Health District managers.

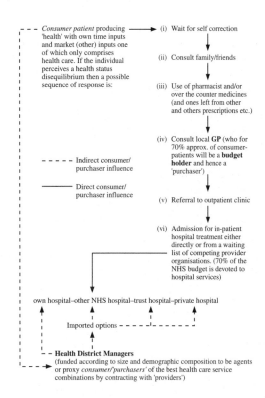

Figure 5.14 The consumer-patient and the reformed NHS.

These individuals are the purchase agents of the con-sumer patient. The four types of hospital listed indi-cate the extent of supply competition. There are a number of sources of interest in this topic motivated by different concerns, e.g. that consumer-patients receive care, the effect of reforms on the size of the public sector, the efficiency characteristics of quasi-market mechanisms, etc. The 'interest' followed here relates to depicting the potential efficiency of quasi-markets.

In section (a) of Fig. 5.15, a four quadrant diagram is used to consider the allocation of a health budget. Beginning in quadrant I of (a), the 'financing' decision is set in the context of a 'political' market. The demand of voters for provision of medical treatment in the NHS (measured on the x axis as 'quantity of medical cases per period of time') is not a 'private' demand for 'own' medical treatment but the demand for facilities provided by the NHS. Questionnaire analysis indi-cates that voters are concerned with the availability of medical care for themselves and for others. Even if, at present, individuals have no demand for medical treatment, they may have an 'option demand' for the availability of treatment. Voters' demand encapsulates

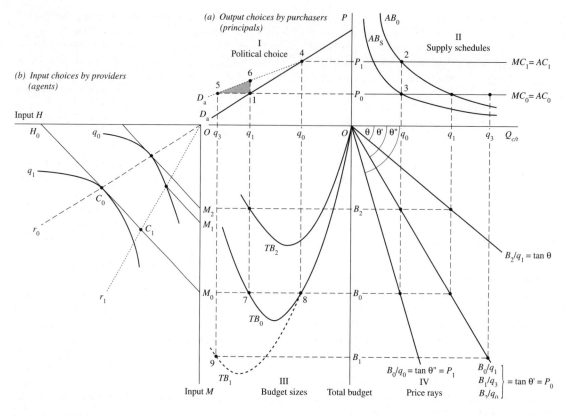

Figure 5.15 The quasi-market.

these broader considerations and, for purposes of exposition, it is helpful if the provision of medical care in the NHS is viewed as the provision of a public good. Hence D_a in part (a) of Fig. 5.15 represents the vertically aggregated demand of individuals for provision of medical services in the NHS. With majority voting, the health budget selected will be that preferred by the median voter. When voters' demand curves are distributed uniformly around the demand curve of the median voter and when each voter faces an equal share of the marginal cost of providing the good, the political market functions in such a way that, at any 'tax-price', the vertically aggregated demand curve depicts the output which is preferred by the median voter.

In part (a) of Fig. 5.15 the determination of a health budget depends on a tax-price (P). Voters' responses to questionnaire surveys reveal that they expect to pay a share of a tax-price when demanding additional publicly provided services (if they did not, their demand for increased spending would be unbounded). Therefore, in quadrant I of part (a) of Fig. 5.15, when the implicit tax price is OP_0 a quantity

Oq_1 is demanded and the preferred budget is initially predetermined as $OP_0 1 q_1$. This is equal to OB_0 in quadrant III at point 7 on the total budget function TB_0 (a locus of points which simply plots total expenditure on the NHS for each quantity per period derived from D_a).

The input choice of providers is investigated in section (b) of Fig. 5.15. The health budget is allocated between two inputs used in a production process designed to treat medical cases. Input H which can be thought of as medical capital (e.g. scanning equipment) and input M, say medical labour (e.g. doctors, nurses) are combined in producing medical treatment. To facilitate the existence of an equilibrium configuration in a quasi-market it is assumed that the production function is linearly homogeneous. Isoquant q_1 illustrates a particular quantity of cases that can be treated with different combinations of inputs H and M. In this figure the price of input M has been normalized, so that the price of one unit of M is £1. This means that the isocost line which intersects the vertical axis at point M_0 is that isocost line associated with expenditure of a budget OB_0 equal to

OP_0/q_1 (as determined in quadrant I of part (a) of Fig. 5.15).

As a reference for future analysis, the framework illustrated in Fig. 5.15 is used, in the first instance, to demonstrate the way in which price signals in a quasi-market might assist decision-makers.

Incentives to providers and to purchasers are assumed consistent with a cost-effective allocation of resources. The analysis will demonstrate that, in such circumstances, a quasi-market has the potential to eradicate the X-inefficiency said to characterize a more vertically integrated organization. In this way the analysis serves to illustrate the potential welfare gain of a quasi-market.

In part (b) of Fig. 5.15, given the relative prices of inputs H and M, output is maximized at the budget constraint $(H_0 - M_0)$ tangency point, C_0, on isoquant q_1. The budget is fixed at OB_0 in quadrant III of part (a) of Fig. 5.15, so that the average cost of medical cases is determined in quadrant IV by the ratio of budget to total number of cases (i.e. as shown by the 'price ray' $B_0/q_1 = \tan \theta' = P_0$). In quadrant II, a rectangular hyperbola, AB_0, maps a locus of points depicting the number of cases (and their implied tax-price) capable of being financed with a fixed budget $OP_0 1 q_1 = B_0$ (ie. it records average budgetary expenditure per case). With average cost equal to marginal cost $(AC_0 = MC_0)$ the supply schedule is defined in quadrant II, the quantity Oq_1 of medical cases is feasible given the pre-determined budget. In this case, cost-effective decisions are made within the quasi-market for the allocation of a fixed pre-determined budget. However, more than this, the implied average budgetary cost is identical with marginal cost and the tax price (P_0) perceived by voters (as illustrated in quadrant I) so that, given the construction, there is no inconsistency.

In a scenario created as the pre-1991 NHS (i.e. in the absence of a quasi-market) a less efficient solution would exist. Observations of excessive vertical integration suggest that inputs used in the NHS were not allocated efficiently. Lack of information with respect to relative prices and lack of incentive to choose an efficient allocation were responsible. With reference to Fig. 5.15, what outcome might be expected if decisions are made in an over-vertically integrated service? With inefficiency, the number of cases dealt with would be less than Oq_1. Assume the number is Oq_0. Production is at point C_1 but, because of inefficiency this is not on isoquant q_0 in part (b) of Fig. 5.15. The health service utilizes an inefficient production technique, i.e. on production ray Or_1. With the same budget (i.e. $OM_0 = OB_0$), X-inefficiency can be iden-

tified. Applying a technique described by Farrell (1957) the categories of X-inefficiency are: (i) technical inefficiency as measured by the distance $OM_0 - OM_1$ (i.e. inputs could be scaled down along Or_1 to achieve this level of budget saving whilst still producing Oq_0 cases) and (ii) input allocative inefficiency as measured by distance $OM_1 - OM_2$ (i.e. a movement to the minimum cost input combinations of providing q_0 in part (b) of Fig. 5.15 at a point on the efficient output expansion path Or_0).

In the absence of a quasi-market, average cost is higher than $AC_0 (= MC_0)$. With a fixed health budget equal to OM_0 in part (b) of Fig. 5.15, average cost per case is to the slope of the price ray $B_0/q_0 (\tan \theta'' = P_1)$ in quadrant IV of part (a). In quadrant II this inefficiency is illustrated by a higher average cost $(= \text{marginal cost})$ of $AC_1 (= MC_1)$. Fewer cases are treated, so that the budget is exhausted at point 2 on AB_0 in quadrant II. The extent of inefficiency per case can be illustrated in quadrant II by determining the minimum average cost for q_0 cases. From part (b) of Fig. 5.15, only a budget of $OM_2 (= OB_2)$ is required to treat q_0 cases if resources are efficiently allocated. In part (a) of Fig. 5.15 the implied average cost would be OB_2/Oq_0 $(= \tan \theta' = P_0)$ in quadrant IV, equal to a price of OP_0 on AB_s in quadrant II. The vertical distance between AB_0 and AB_s at Oq_0 reflects the loss per case from inefficiency (which is equal to 2–3). It distinguishes the efficient resource price of treating cases from the average budget price with which voters are faced.

Therefore, with the introduction of an efficient quasi-market and a movement from C_1 (pre-1991) to C_0 in part (b) of Fig. 5.15, the same budget is more efficiently allocated. However, it would be incorrect to measure the increase in welfare (associated with the introduction of a quasi-market) as the reduction in cost per case multiplied by the number of pre-1991 cases (Oq_0) or post-1991 cases (Oq_1). The welfare gain of moving from an over-vertically integrated health service to a perfectly functioning quasi-market is illustrated by the increase in consumer surplus $P_1 4 1 P_0$ as shown under the demand curve D_a (which exceeds the cost savings on Oq_0 medical cases and is less than the implied cost savings on Oq_1 cases).

The other important consideration which emerges from this analysis is that, while a quasi-market can generate an efficient outcome consistent with a pre-determined budget, this arises only as a result of the most unlikely of coincidences. If government policy is to restrain the health budget, a welfare maximum only emerges if D_a exhibits unitary price elasticity over the relevant range. The construction of quadrant I of part (a) of Fig. 5.15 conveniently illustrates this case, so that $OP_0 1 q_1 = OP_1 4 q_0$ and distance $q_1 - 7 = q_0 - 8 = OB_0$. If the price of treating medical cases fell and if price elasticity exceeds unity, voters prefer a larger health budget as a direct consequence of the introduction of a quasi-market. The introduction of the quasi-market reduces costs, reduces the tax-price of health care and increases the amount that voters wish to spend in order to maximize welfare gains from competition and trade in a quasi-market (which from the political viewpoint may be deemed 'unattractive').

If, for example, the aggregate demand curve were D'_a in quadrant I of part (a) of Fig. 5.15 (implying a total budgetary curve TB_1 in quadrant III), there would be deadweight welfare loss equal to triangle 156 if the health budget were restrained. The budget would be sub-optimal to the extent of $OB_1 - OB_0$ with the equilibrium quantity Oq_3 picking out point 9 on TB_1. Deadweight losses, from either price elasticity or inelasticity arise in a quasi-market (as compared with a conventional market) because of the separation of the 'financing' and 'allocation' decisions. Brazier *et al.* (1990, p. 231) emphasize that the NHS reform 'does not address the highest level of social efficiency, that is the optimal size of the health sector, since the provider operates within a predetermined cash limited budget'. The welfare loss resulting from this failure of a quasi-'competitive' market will be apparent in Fig. 5.15 when demand is anything but unitary price elastic over the relevant range.

Note that the analysis suggests only that a quasi-market has *potential* to increase welfare. Whether it will succeed in increasing welfare depends also on the transactions costs associated with the creation, dissemination and response to information and the ability of actors in the NHS to capture the efficiency gains as rents (see Jones and Cullis 1996).

5.8 Summary

This chapter, unavoidably, has introduced a wide variety of economic themes. At the outset the nature of rent-seeking behaviour was outlined and explored. Many questions can be explored in a rent-seeking context (e.g. see Colombatto and Macey (1996) for an analysis of rent-seeking in the exchange rate regimes of Eastern Europe). However, the main questions asked in this chapter concerned the location of production at the level of both principle and practice.

In considering the case for public production, arguments were extended beyond the welfare economics concepts of 'market failure' to include 'psychological economics'. The capabilities of people are central to both the 'anomalous behaviour' and 'transactions costs economics' approaches.

The economic analysis of the once 'classic' nationalized industry was not only of interest in itself but provided the context for the arguments over the 'return to the market' policies. Here the issues covered are central to current policy debates in many countries all over the world. Indeed, while there is a huge literature on 'privatization' in its many guises, the lack of any real consensus on objectives, methods and performance measurement makes it easy to accept Hensher's comment that: 'The *serious* debate on privatization is yet to begin in most countries' (p. 168). What is more difficult to accept is that a consensus will be easy to come by. Given a fundamental diversity of preferences over public production and the importance of the topic to economists, politicians and individuals at large, this is a debate that is likely always to remain current.

The welfare economics case for privatization is based essentially on competition, but it is not difficult to apply a public choice rationale to explain the popularity of privatization for governments (Jones and Cullis 1988). In the UK the privatization programme has done little to enhance competition. The pattern is one whereby public monopoly has been transferred to the private sector to be controlled by regulatory authorities. Kay and Thompson (1986, p. 29) note that: 'the privatization of large dominant firms is at least pointless and possibly harmful in the absence of effective competition'. Even advocates of the policy of privatization despair that UK privatization has simply shifted the focus towards the regulatory position typical in the USA, rather than significantly enhancing competition (Burton 1987). However, it is not difficult to argue that in a public choice framework government would proceed with privatization even though competition was not necessarily increased. The following examples support this view.

1. Privatization is a policy that is attractive to the members of the electorate if they are able to purchase shares at below-market (subsidized) prizes. Dunleavy and Rhodes (1987, p. 138) comment, with reference to the UK: 'By according small investors privileged access to shares at the discounted stockmarket prices judged necessary to secure a full take-up of the shares on offer, the government can on occasion transfer remarkable cash benefits to a large number of voters as with the British Telecom sale in 1984'. In so far as

members of the electorate suffer from fiscal illusion, they are unable to realize that the value of their share of the capital in public ownership has diminished accordingly. As such, the sale of assets is eagerly awaited and the policy is popular.

2. The receipt of revenue from the sale also reduces the government's borrowing requirement. This may enable policies of tax reduction in the short run which, with a limited time horizon (stretching only to the next election), may be popular with voters.

3. If the gains from the policy are as attractive as outlined for government, then politicians may be less willing to resist the lobbying efforts of those groups who fear competition. In the UK there is evidence that management of nationalized industries has been resistant to the dissipation of their 'empire' in the name of competition. While a simple transfer of a large organization to the private sector may be acceptable, the reduction of the importance of the company may not. The lobbying pressure of management is one factor in explaining the pattern of privatization (see Kay and Thompson 1986). With other gains at stake, it is perhaps not surprising that such lobbying pressures have not been resisted in the name of competition.

Privatization is a policy that emerges from the recommendations of those who are critical of 'big' government because of governmental failure. The paradox is that government failure may mean that this policy is not enacted in the way in which its advocates would wish. Inevitably, the public choice approach is driven to find some constitutional check on government which will limit the abuse of public policy.

In section 5.7.2 a model of the internal market was presented which revealed, if nothing else, that it was a complicated market form that will doubtless be the subject of further economic and political debate.

Appendix: Anomalies

Systematic deviations from economic rationality have been identified in a number of studies. Below they are collected under three headings:

(i) The influence of the *past*. In economics decisions should be about marginal costs and marginal benefits but experiments have indicated that 'history' matters.

(a) *Sunk cost effect*: Individuals tend to take historic/past costs into account in their decisions. Individuals do 'cry over spilt milk' both literally (as children) and figuratively and are willing to throw 'good money after bad'.

(b) *Endowment effect*: Goods in an individual's endowment, i.e. are owned by them, are valued more highly than those not held in the endowment. This suggests a difference between the 'willingness to pay' for a good and the 'willingness to be compensated' for giving up a good. The former is generally smaller than the latter.

(ii) The influence of the *present*. Choices are sensitive to the current context in which they take place.

(c) *Framing effects*: The way a decision problem is formulated and the way the information is presented has a marked effect on individual choices. Framing a decision as a perceived loss or a gain elicits different responses. If identical information is provided as a matrix, decision tree or words different responses are obtained.

(d) *Reference point effect*: Alternatives are evaluated by individuals not in terms of total wealth but relative to a reference point, often the status quo. 'Framing' moves the reference point so that lotteries with the same expected values are treated differently.

(e) *Anchoring effect*: Social states are evaluated from a particular starting-point, the choice of which influences behavioural outcomes. Skilled bargainers, e.g. those at tourist traps set anchors so that you feel successful if you get some way away from the anchor rather than paying or receiving what you initially thought it was worth.

(f) *Overconfidence effect*: Individuals are convinced they know observable facts better than is actually the case. It suggests peoples decisions are to some extent based on false foundations.

(g) *Preference reversal effect*: Individuals tend to choose high probability lotteries with low outcomes over low probability lotteries with high outcomes but are willing to pay more for the latter. It suggests willingness to pay may not reveal preference—the denial of an idea key to much economic thinking.

(h) *Opportunity cost effect*: Out-of-pocket monetary costs are given greater weight in the decision calculus than opportunity costs of the same size. Cash prices are seen as larger than say 'time and trouble' prices of equal size. Forms of prices matter.

(iii) The influence of the *future*. Choices are affected by the way people think about probabilities and this deviates from economic rationality also.

(i) *Certainty effect*: Outcomes obtained with certainty are attributed greater weight in an individual's decisions than those which are uncertain even when the (known) expected utilities are the same. For example, most people prefer a certain £3000 to an 80 per cent chance of £4000 but give up a

25 per cent chance to win £3000 for a 20 per cent chance of £4000. This is anomalous because all that has happened is that the probabilities have been divided by 4.

(j) *Small probability effects*: High and low chance events are treated in a peculiar way—certainty is seen as completely different to high probability and low probabilities overweighted, i.e. the attraction of lotteries is partly that individuals overestimate the actuarial very low probability of winning.

(k) *Availability bias*: Recent spectacular and personally experienced events are systematically overweighted when individuals make choices, e.g. those that have been 'mugged' overestimate the probability of the crime.

(l) *Representativeness bias*: Individuals systematically misconceive the prior probabilities of events and are insensitive to sample size.

References

Abromeit, H. (1988) 'British Privatisation Policy', *Parliamentary Affairs*, 41, 1, pp. 68–85.

Akerlof, G. A. and Dickens, W. T. (1982) 'The Economic Consequences of Cognitive Dissonance', *American Economic Review*, 72, 3, pp. 307–19.

Alchian, A. A. and Demsetz, H. (1972) 'Production, Information Costs and Economic Organisation', *American Economic Review*, 62, 5, pp. 777–95.

Arrow, K. J. (1971) 'The Organisation of Economic Activity: Issues Pertinent to the Choice of Market versus Non-market Allocation', pp. 59–73 in R. H. Haveman and J. Margolis (eds.), *Public Expenditure and Policy Analysis*. Chicago: Markham.

Arrow, K. J. and Lind, R. C. (1970) 'Uncertainty and the Evaluation of Public Investment', *American Economic Review*, 60, 3, pp. 364–78.

Averch, H. and Johnson, L. L. (1962) 'Behaviour of the Firm under Regulatory Constraints', *American Economic Review*, 52, 5, pp. 1052–69.

Bartell, A. and Thomas, L. G. (1985) 'Direct and Indirect Effects of Regulation: a New Look at OSHA's Impact, *Journal of Law and Economics*, 28, 1, pp. 1–25.

Baumol, W. J. (1965) *Welfare Economics and the Theory of the State*, 2nd edn. Cambridge, Mass.: Harvard University Press.

Baumol, W. J. (1984) 'Towards a Theory of Public Enterprise', *Atlantic Economic Journal*, 12, 1, pp. 13–19.

Baysinger, B. and Tollison, R. D. (1980) 'Evaluating the Social Cost of Monopoly and Regulation', *Atlantic Economic Journal*, 8, 4, pp. 22–6.

Bhagwati, J. N. and Srinivason, T. N. (1980) 'Revenue Seeking: A Generalisation of the Theory of Tariffs', *Journal of Political Economy*, 88, 6, pp. 1069–87.

Bhagwati, J. N. and Srinivason, T. N. (1982) 'Revenue Seeking: A Generalisation of the Theory of Tariffs—a Correction', *Journal of Political Economy*, 90, 1, pp. 188–90.

Bishop, M. and Kay. J. (1989) 'Privatisation in the United Kingdom: Lessons from Experience', *World Development*, 17, 5, pp. 643–57.

Bishop, M., Kay, J. and Mayer, C. (1994) 'Introduction: Privatisation and Performance', pp 1–15 in M. Bishop, J. Kay and C. Mayer (eds.), *Privatization and Economic Performance*. Oxford: Oxford University Press.

Boardman, A., Freedman, R. and Eckel, C. (1986) 'The Price of Government Ownership: A Study of the Domtar Takeover', *Journal of Public Economics*, 31, 3, pp. 269–85.

Brazier, J. E. and Normand, C. M. (1993) 'An Economic Review of the NHS White Paper', *Scottish Journal of Political Economy*, 38, 1, pp. 96–105.

Brooks, M. A. and Heijdra, B. J. (1989) 'Exploration of Rent Seeking', *Economic Record*, 65, 188, pp. 32–50.

Burton, J. (1987) 'Privatization: The Thatcher Case', *Managerial and Decision Economics*, 8, 1, pp. 21–9.

Coase, R. H. (1937) 'The Nature of the Firm', *Economica*, 4, pp. 386–405.

Coase, R. H. (1974) 'The Lighthouse in Economics', *Journal of Law and Economics*, 17, 2, pp. 357–76.

Colombatto, E. and Macey, J. (1996) 'Exchange-Rate Management in Eastern Europe: A Public-Choice Perspective', *International Review of Law and Economics*, 16, 2, pp. 195–209.

Culyer, A. J. (1983) 'Public or Private Health Services? A Skeptic's View', *Journal of Policy Analysis and Management*, 2, 3, pp. 386–402.

DiLorenzo, T. J. (1988) 'Property Rights: Information Costs and the Economics of Rent Seeking', *Journal of Institutional and Theoretical Economics*, 144, pp. 318–32.

Dnes, A. W. (1989) 'Rent Seeking Conflict and Property Rights', *Scottish Journal of Political Economy*, 36, 4, pp. 366–74.

Dugger, W. M. (1993) 'Transaction Cost Economics and the State', pp. 188–216 in C. Pitelis (ed.), *Transaction, Markets and Hierarchies*, Oxford: Basil Blackwell.

Dunleavy, P. and Rhodes, R. (1987) 'Government beyond Whitehall', in H. Drucker *et al.* (eds.), *Developments in British Politics*, vol. 2. London: Macmillan.

Farrell, M. J. (1957) 'The Measurement of Productive Efficiency', *Journal of the Royal Statistical Society*, Series A, 120, pp. 253–81.

Farrel, M. J. (1958) 'In Defence of Public Utility Price Theory', *Oxford Economic Papers*, n.s., 10, pp. 109–23.

Forte, F. (1967) 'Should Public Goods be Public?', *Papers on Non Market Decision Making*, 8, pp. 39–46.

Frey, B. S. and Eichenberger, R. (1989) 'Anomalies and Institutions', *Journal of Institutional and Theoretical Economics*, 145, pp. 423–37.

Helm D. R. (1987) 'Mergers, Takeovers and the Enforcement of Profit Maximization', Oxford University Discussion Paper, Oxford University.

Hensher, D. A. (1986) 'Privatisation: An Interpretative Essay', *Australian Economic Papers*, 25, 47, pp. 147–74.

Jackson, P. M. and Price, C. M. (1994) 'Privatisation and Regulation: A Review of the Issues', pp. 1–23 in P. M. Jackson and C. M. Price (eds.), *Privatisation and Regulation: A Review of the Issues*. Longman: London.

Jones, P. R. and Cullis, J. G. (1988) 'Privatisation, Politics and Property Rights', *Biblioteca Della Libertà*, 23, 103, pp. 85–100.

Jones, P. R. and Cullis, J. G. (1996) 'Quasi-Markets: A Public Choice Perspective, University of Bath Discussion Paper.

Kay, J., Meyer, C. and Thompson, D. (eds.) (1986) *Privatisation and Regulation: The UK Experience*. Oxford: Oxford University Press.

Kay, J. A. and Thompson, D. J. (1986) 'Privatization: A Policy in Search of a Rationale', *Economic Journal*, 96, 381, pp. 18–32.

Kelman M (1988) 'On democracy-bashing', *Virginia Law Review*, 47, 2, pp. 199–27.

Knapp, M. R. J. (1984) *The Economics of Social Care*. London: Macmillan.

Leibenstein, H. (1966) 'Allocative Efficiency vs X-Efficiency', *American Economic Review*, 56, 3, pp. 392–415.

Linneman, P. (1980) 'The Effects of Consumer Safety Standards: the 1973 Mattress Flammability Standard' *Journal of Law and Economics*, 23, 2, pp. 461–78.

Lipsey, R. G. and Lancaster, K. (1956) 'General Theory of Second Best', *Review of Economic Studies*, 24, 1, pp. 11–32.

Littlechild, S. (1981) 'Misleading Calculations of the Social Cost of Monopoly Power', *Economic Journal*, 91, 362, pp. 348–63.

Millward, R. and Parker, D. (1983) 'Public and Private enterprise: Comparative Behaviour and Relative Efficiency', pp. 199–274 in R. Millward *et al.* (eds.), *Public Sector Economics*. London and New York: Longman.

Mishan, E. (1988) *Cost Benefit Analysis*. London: Allen & Unwin.

Mundell, R. A. (1962) 'Review of Jansenn's Free Trade Protection and Customs Union', *American Economic Review*, 52, 3, pp. 621–2.

Parker, D. (1993) 'Privatisation Ten Years On: A Critical Analysis of its Rational and Results', pp 174–95 in N. M. Healey (ed.), *Britain's Economic Miracle Myth or Reality*. London: Routledge.

Paul, S. (1985) 'Privatisation and the Public Sector', *Finance and Development*, 22, 4, pp. 42–5.

Peacock, A. T. (1980) 'On the Anatomy of Collective Failure', *Public Finance/Finances Publiques*, 35, 1, pp. 33–43.

Peltzman, S. (1976) 'Towards a More General Theory of Regulation', *Journal of Law and Economics*, 19, pp. 211–40.

Posner, R. A. (1975) 'The Social Costs of Monopoly and Regulation', *Journal of Political Economy*, 83, 4, pp. 807–27.

Quibria, M. S. (1989) 'Neoclassical Political Economy: An Application to Trade Policies', *Journal of Economic Surveys*, 3, 2, pp. 107–31.

Rashid, S. (1988) 'Quality in Contestable Markets: A Historical Problem?', *Quarterly Journal of Economics*, 103, 1, pp. 245–50.

Rees, R. (1976) *Public Enterprise Economics*. London: Weidenfeld & Nicolson.

Rees, R. (1985) 'The Theory of Principal and Agent', *Bulletin of Economic Research*, 37, 1 and 2, pp. 3–25 and 75–94.

Rees, R. (1986) 'Is there an Economic Case for Privatisation?', *Public Money*, 2, 4, pp. 19–26.

Ricketts, M. (1987) 'Rent Seeking Entrepreneurship, Subjectivism and Property Rights', *Journal of Institutional and Theoretical Economics*, 143, pp. 457–66.

Rowley, C. (1978) 'Comment', p. 90 in *The Economics of Politics*, IEA Readings no. 18. London: Institute of Economic Affairs.

Samuels, W. J. and Mercuro, N. (1984) 'A Critique of Rent Seeking Theory', pp. 55–70 in D. C. Colander (ed.), *Neoclassical Political Economy: The Analysis of Rent Seeking and DUP Activities*. Cambridge, Mass.: Ballinger Press.

Schap, D. (1985) 'X-inefficiency in a Rent-Seeking Society: A Graphical Analysis', *Quarterly Review of Economics and Business*, 25, 1, pp. 19–25.

Stigler, G. J. and Fiedland, C. (1962) 'What Can Regulators Regulate? The Case of Electricity', *Journal of Law and Economics*, 5, reprinted as pp. 61–77 in Stigler (1975).

Stigler, G. J. (1975) *The Citizen and the State*. Chicago: University of Chicago Press.

Thaler, R. H. (1988) 'The Winner's Curse', *Journal of Economic Perspectives*, 2, 1, pp. 191–202.

Titmuss, R. M. (1970) *The Gift Relationship—From Human Blood to Social Policy*. London: Allen & Unwin.

Tollison, R. D. (1982) 'Rent Seeking: A Survey', *Kyklos*, 35, 4, pp. 575–602.

Tollison, R. D. and Wagner, R. E. (1991) 'Romance, Realism and Economic Reform', *Kyklos* 44, 1, pp. 57–70.

Tullock, G. (1967) 'The Welfare Costs of Tariffs, Monopolies and Theft', *Western Economic Journal*, 5, 3, pp. 224–32.

Tullock, G. (1971) 'The Charity of the Uncharitable', *Western Economic Journal*, 9, 4, pp. 379–92.

Turvey, R. (1971) *Economic Analysis and Public Enterprises*. London: Allen & Unwin.

Viscusi, W. K. (1985) 'Consumer Behaviour and the Safety Effects of Product Safety Regulations,' *Journal of Law and Economics*, **28**, 3, pp. 527–53.

Webb, M. G. (1976) *Pricing Policies for Public Enterprises.* London: Macmillan.

Weisbrod, B. A. (1975) 'Toward a Theory of the Voluntary Non-Profit Sector in a Three-Sector Economy', pp. 171–95 in E. S. Phelps (ed.), *Altruism, Morality and Economic Theory.* New York: Russell Sage Foundation.

Williamson, O. E. (1985) *The Economic Institutions of Capitalism.* New York: The Free Press.

Wiseman, J. (1978) 'The Political Economy of Nationalised Industry', pp. 73–92 in *The Economics of Politics*, IEA Readings no. 18. London: Institute of Economic Affairs.

Wiseman, J. and Littlechild, S. C. (1986) 'The Political Economy of Restriction of Choice', *Public Choice*, **51**, 2, pp. 161–72.

6 Evaluation of public expenditure: cost–benefit analysis

6.1 Introduction

We have described the 'traditional social optimality approach' to public finance as one that employs the principles of welfare economics to prescribe how government 'should' attain its objectives. There may be no better example of the application of this approach than the theoretical work that underlies the technique of cost–benefit analysis (CBA). Concern in this chapter focuses on how government 'should' appraise alternative expenditure projects. Cost–benefit analysis has been established on the assumption that government seeks benevolently to maximize social welfare. It is a framework for incorporating the multitude of considerations that arise when assessing the desirability of projects. No claim is made that it is a perfect instrument, capable of yielding unambiguously correct estimates of the change in welfare associated with different investment programmes. Rather, it should be seen, more simply, as a method of tackling those questions that are thrown up in appraising public sector investment. It is important then not to expect 'too much' of this technique. On the other hand, the usual riposte to critics of cost–benefit analysis is, How else would you make decisions on public investment, if not by using this technique?

The main objective of this chapter is to present some of the problems that arise in any cost–benefit appraisal of public investment. To deal with these problems, concepts and principles drawn from welfare economics are utilized. Concern here rests mainly with the normative issue of which investment should be chosen, rather than with the positive question of how investments are chosen. The public choice analysis of how investment is chosen is related far more to political costs and benefits. Vote gains and vote losses figure more highly in the considerations of politicians, who look only as far as the next election when considering the 'best' project for investment; in such cases, the projects indicated as desirable by reference

to social welfare may not be the ones that are finally chosen. The fact that government departments invest time and effort when undertaking cost–benefit analysis does not preclude the possibility that they are motivated far more by political factors than by welfare economics. Leff (1988) notes that government departments may reap returns from undertaking the cost–benefit analysis itself, quite independent of the advice that such an analysis provides for project selection. CBA studies may be undertaken to provide data that can be used to defend the bureau's selection of projects (or the politicians' selection). The need to undertake these studies adds to the bureau's size and/or its budget. Olson (1973) notes that the problem of measuring the productivity of bureaus and factors such as the number of CBAs undertaken may prove useful when sustaining the case for the bureau's existence, irrespective of whether they usefully inform decision-making. While this activity is visible, its impact and value is far more difficult to gauge.

The results of cost–benefit analyses may be rejected for many reasons (Leff 1988). Some of these relate to dissatisfaction with the way in which the analysis has been undertaken; others relate to a 'hidden agenda' within which political goals feature more strongly. Before an analysis can be rejected on the grounds that it has been poorly constructed, it is necessary to understand the principles against which any CBA can be judged. Here the intention is to illustrate the way in which welfare economics provides a basis for determining how cost–benefit analysis should be undertaken.

6.2 What is cost–benefit analysis?

Any investment project requires careful consideration, whether the investment is in the private or the public sector. An analysis of an investment project must allow for the fact that some costs are to be experienced in the future. It is well known that individuals will not be indifferent as between receipt of a certain sum of money today and receipt of the same sum of money in the future. Readers can confirm this by responding to the question of whether or not receipt of £100 today means the same as the receipt of £100 in one year's time. Typically, £100 received today is worth more than £100 in one year's time. One reason for believing this is that £100 received today might be invested and thereby earn a rate of interest. If the rate of interest is 8 per cent, in one year's time today's £100 will be worth £108. Another way of making exactly the same comparison would be to say that £108 in one year's time is worth only £100 today. In effect, it is necessary to discount future earnings to make them comparable with earnings received today.

In order to add together future benefits (or costs) that arise from any investment project, it is necessary to recognize that they are incurred at different times. Future benefits (or costs) will have to be discounted to present values. But exactly how does this discounting procedure work? Above it is clear that £108 in one year's time is worth £100 now. In other words, to find the present value of £108 in one year's time we apply the discount factor $1/(1 + r)^n$; i.e. the present value is equal to $108/(1 + r)^n$ where r is the rate of interest or discount and n is the number of years from the present the sum actually arises (in this case $n = 1$). But what about the present value of a sum received in two years' time? Because £100 now is worth £100$(1 + r)$ ($=$ £108) in one year's time, it obviously follows that £108 discounted at $1/(1 + r)$ is equal to a present value of £100. If we had £100 today and invested it at 8 per cent for two years, then after the additional year it would be worth £108$(1 + r) =$ £116.64. By comparison with the original sum, the future value would be $[£100(1 + r)](1 + r) = £100(1 + r)^2$. Therefore, it follows that, to convert a sum of money received in two years' time into present values, it is necessary to discount by $1/(1 + r)^2$.

Suppose that an investment project yields gains in each year of its expected life. If investment were made by a private firm, these gains might be thought of in terms of the addition to revenues brought about as a result of the investment. Within the public sector the benefits are likely to be much wider. Assume that there are estimates of the monetary values of social benefits $(B_1, B_2, \ldots, B_n)$ to be experienced in each of n years of the project's life. It is possible to add these sums, even though they are experienced at different times. Ben-

efits received in each year can be converted into present values and then added. The present value (PV) of this stream of earnings is

$$
PV = \frac{B_1}{(1 + r)} + \frac{B_2}{(1 + r)^2} + \frac{B_3}{(1 + r)^3}
$$
$$
+ \cdots + \frac{B_n}{(1 + r)^n}
$$

(6.1)

Discounted cash flow analysis of investment is well known in business economics. It is required to allow for the fact that the receipts and costs that flow from investment will appear at very different times. The costs of projects are likely to be split between the 'initial' investment (capital) costs (I_0), to be incurred on the project now, i.e. in the present period, and the 'current' costs ($C_1, C_2, C_3, \ldots, C_n$), which will occur during the lifetime of the project. In this way, a capital project will generate a stream of net benefits. During the lifetime of the project annual net benefits ($B - C$) must be discounted in order to evaluate the net present value (NPV) of the project. This is the difference between the discounted sum of the stream of future net earnings and the initial costs of the project. It can be shown as

$$
NPV = -I_0 + \frac{(B - C)_1}{(1 + r)} + \frac{(B - C)_2}{(1 + r)^2}
$$
$$
+ \frac{(B - C)_3}{(1 + r)^3} + \cdots + \frac{(B - C)_n}{(1 + r)^n}
$$

(6.2)

The net present value of an investment, therefore, may be written as

(6.3)
$$
NPV = -I_0 + \sum_{i=1}^{n} \frac{(B - C)_i}{(1 + r)^i}
$$

Investment projects may be ranked according to their net present value. Projects will be worthy of serious consideration if $NPV \geqslant 0$ (unless there are additional capital constraints). The best projects will be those with the highest NPV. Alternatively, projects may be ranked according to their *internal rate of return*. The internal rate of return of a project is the value of r that makes the stream of discounted net benefits equal to the initial capital cost. Those projects, which would record a high net present value, will also typically record a high rate of return. However, there are reasons for preferring one form of ranking to another. Generally it is preferable to rank projects by net present value rather than by rate of return, for the following reasons.

Table 6.1 NPV and internal rates of return

Time	Discounted cash flows
t_0	−£100
t_1	+£230
t_2	−£132
	IRR = 10% or 20%

Source: Webb (1973), p. 23.

First, there may be no unique solution to the internal rate of return. For a particular project, more than one discount rate may reduce a stream of future earnings to zero. In Table 6.1, following Webb (1973), there are *two* internal rates of return (10 and 20 per cent) when the future net benefits take the values shown.

Secondly, with mutually exclusive projects, the internal rate of return may select projects that would not be chosen by the net present value criterion. In Fig. 6.1 the net present value of two projects A and B are shown for various rates of discount. The internal rate of return (that rate of discount which makes $NPV = 0$) is seen to be higher for B than for A. However, if the NPV is considered at discount rates lower than Oc, the project A has a higher NPV than B. If the objective were to maximize the NPV of the project, then for discount rates below c the NPV would indicate the correct project, but to rely on the internal rate of return would indicate the wrong project. The conclusion is that using the NPV by definition leads to the correct choice. While the internal rate of return test may be modified to allow for this problem, the simple NPV test is often regarded as superior.

Therefore, while on face value it seems irrelevant whether projects are ranked according to their internal rate of return or the size of their NPV, there appears reason to prefer the NPV test.

The formula for determining the net present value of a project is helpful in dealing with the question, What is different about cost–benefit analysis? In the public sector, as in the private sector, projects yield returns over a long period and discounting to allow

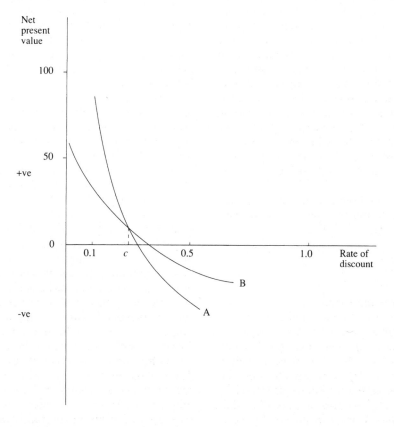

Figure 6.1 Rate of return of mutually exclusive project.

for this is necessary in both cases. So what is special about cost–benefit analysis? The differences between the use of this investment appraisal in the public sector and its usage in the private sector stem from the difference in objectives to be pursued in both sectors. The different objectives mean that:

1. Different costs C and different benefits B are calculated within the formula;
2. Different principles for valuation of these costs and benefits apply in different sectors;
3. Different discount rates r apply in both sectors.

It is usually assumed that in the private sector the objective that firms pursue is profit maximization. Therefore the private firm will interpret B_i as the revenue it earns each year of the lifetime of the project; C_i will be the private cost with which it is faced each year of the lifetime of the project, and I_0 will be the private initial investment that the firm is considering making. These revenues and costs will generally be estimated at market prices. On the other hand, the objective within the public sector is the maximization of welfare, i.e. social welfare. This leads to the inclusion in the investment appraisal of further costs and benefits which would not enter a private investment appraisal. It means that market prices are not always appropriate for estimating costs and benefits. It also means that the discount factor may depend on factors other than the rate of interest. As Mishan (1988, p. xxix) notes, 'The economist engaged in the cost benefit appraisal of a project is not, in essence then, asking a different sort of question from that asked by the accountant of a private firm. Rather, the same sort of question is being asked about a wider group of people—who comprise society—and is being asked more searchingly.'

Prest and Turvey (1965) emphasize that, in looking at the investment criterion, the questions faced by the cost–benefit analyst are:

1. Which costs and benefits are to be included?
2. How are they to be valued?
3. At what rate of discount are they to be discounted?

A consistent theme of this chapter is that the answers to these questions depend on an application of the principles of welfare economics. Public expenditure appraisal is applied welfare economics. For example, it will be argued that, when cost–benefit analysis searches for a positive NPV to justify investment, it is utilizing a Hicks–Kaldor criterion (see chapter 2). That is to say, when the net present value of a public expenditure project is shown to be positive in a cost–benefit analysis, the interpretation should be that, if

the project is undertaken, the beneficiaries from the investment will gain by more than the losers (who forgo the use of the resources involved) will lose. It is a hypothetical test. This interpretation will, however, only be true if the cost–benefit analyst has undertaken the study appropriately. By this we mean that the analyst will need to have made correct decisions with respect to the questions of what to include, how to value costs and benefits, and what discount rate to choose.

6.3 Cost–benefit analysis and externalities: real versus pecuniary impact

One of the distinguishing features of a CBA is the fact that it looks at social costs and social benefits rather than purely private ones. In this respect it recognizes the existence of externalities. It can be recalled from chapter 2 that an external effect is present when the activity of one actor in the economy affects the welfare of another and when that independence is not internalized within the price (or any other) mechanism. For example, in the often cited cost–benefit study of the Victoria Underground Railway Line (Foster and Beesley 1963), the benefits of reduced congestion on the roads of London were added to the revenues of the line in order to establish a measure of the social benefits of the line. In the search for a third London airport, the cost of aeroplane noise is a factor that is directly taken into account (see, e.g. Pearce and Nash 1981). It is possible then to make a distinction between *direct* and *indirect* and *tangible* and *intangible* benefits and costs.

As an example, Musgrave and Musgrave (1989) describe the direct tangible benefits of an irrigation project in terms of the increased marketed farm output of the project, while indirect intangible benefits may be the reduction of soil erosion in nearby hillsides or the preservation of visual amenity. Direct costs of the irrigation scheme may be the costs of pipes, whereas indirect intangible costs may include the destruction of wildlife. In health projects the direct tangible benefits of investment in screening may be the saving of medical costs of treatment, whereas a direct intangible benefit would be the improved lifestyle of the person concerned. Similarly, in education programmes the direct tangible benefit may be the increased future earnings of students and the indirect intangible benefits would be a reduction in the costs of crime or the appearance of a more informed electorate (see, e.g. Blaug 1965).

It is noteworthy that CBA will be concerned with the distinction that has been made between *technical* and *pecuniary* externalities. A technical externality has been defined (Dasgupta and Pearce 1972) as one that occurs 'when the production function of the affected producer or the utility function of the affected consumer is altered' (p. 120). For a consumer, the externality may make it possible that less (more) utility can be obtained from the diseconomy (economy). For a producer, less (more) output may be obtained from a given set of inputs because of the diseconomy (economy). A pecuniary externality is visible in the form of changed prices, wages and profits. However, a pecuniary externality does not alter the technological possibilities of production or consumption. In the normal case, a CBA will not incorporate pecuniary externalities. In general, to include technological and pecuniary externalities would be to double-count. Only if the CBA was explicitly concerned with questions of income distribution would pecuniary externalities be included. The following examples, based on Mishan (1972, 1988), illustrate this distinction.

A CBA of a road project incorporates the following externalities: (a) the external diseconomy generated when the motorway cuts a farmer's holding in two, such that his grazing land is on one part and his cowshed on the other; (b) the external diseconomy generated when a motorway blocks a pleasant view and thereby reduces utility for the consumer. However, it would not incorporate pecuniary externalities, for example when a petrol station on an improved road route finds its trade so expanded that the resale value of the business rises sharply. This additional pecuniary benefit reflects the value of the road scheme to the motorist which will be estimated directly. Pecuniary benefits and costs are the results of changes in relative prices. These changes occur as a response to the public service project, but they tend to be gains (or losses) for some individuals resulting from losses (or gains) experienced by others. They are not net gains or losses to the community as a whole and, while important when considering distributional effects, they are not included when considering efficiency aspects. Typically, then, these pecuniary changes will not enter into the evaluation.

There are, however, many ways of classifying the benefits and costs that can emerge in a cost–benefit analysis. Technical or *real* costs and benefits may be distinguished from *pecuniary* effects. Costs and benefits may also be *tangible* (i.e. where benefits or costs can be measured in the market) or *intangible* (where

Table 6.2 Costs and benefits

	Benefits	Costs
Transport investment project		
Real		
Direct		
Tangible	Saving of fuel cost	Increased vehicle depreciation
Intangible	Saving of time	Increased accidents
Indirect		
Tangible		Reduced farm output
Intangible		Scenic costs
Pecuniary	Gains to owners of garages on the new improved route	Losses to owners of garages on old route
Medical care investment project		
Real		
Direct		
Tangible	Saving of future treatment costs	Current medical costs
Intangible		Time cost to patients
Indirect		
Tangible	Saving of future output of the patients	
Intangible	Improved quality of leisure time	
Pecuniary	Gains to manufacturers of scanning equipment	Losses to the earnings of producers of pharmaceuticals which would have been necessary to ameliorate the symptoms of the complaint

Source: based on Musgrave and Musgrave (1989).

no appropriate market exists and a shadow price is necessary, e.g. an environmental or scenic improvement which results as a consequence of an irrigation project). They are frequently classified as *direct* or *indirect*. This classification may be looked at as the distinction between the primary and secondary costs and benefits. Table 6.2 is based on Musgrave and Musgrave (1989), though it shows different public investment programmes. It is designed to illustrate the different taxonomies that are used to classify, for a number of different programmes, the distinction between direct and indirect benefits and costs, as well as the difference between pecuniary and technical externalities. The examples given in each case are by no means exhaustive and other cases can be imagined. However, readers should consider why the examples have been classified as shown.

In this taxonomy there is a clear distinction between real and pecuniary costs and benefits for the two projects considered. Within the real category, it has also been possible to distinguish between tangible and intangible effects. The taxonomy may assist the cost–benefit analyst in dealing with the many different costs and benefits that stem from any investment project. In this respect, perhaps the most important distinction is between technical (real) effects and pecuniary effects.

6.4 Cost–benefit analysis and consumer surplus: the evaluation of benefits

There is a limited number of sources of information on benefit evaluation. It is possible to appeal to the market, if one exists that is considered satisfactory. However, well-defined markets in all the benefits of public sector projects are often absent. That is not to say that 'adjusted' market data do not (as will be shown below in section 6.5) have a significant role to play, but it is to emphasize that often adjustment is necessary because of market failure. A second source of valuation is individuals. They can be asked directly, in appropriately constructed questionnaires or in experimental contexts, to provide (hypothetical) valuation information. A third behavioural approach, much favoured by economists, is to infer from actual choices what the limits on individual valuations are. For example, assume that 1 hour is saved by a train journey (as opposed to travelling by bus) and that the train fare is £12 more: then, other things equal, it can

be deduced that the train traveller valued a saved travel-hour by at least £12. From such observations maximum and minimum values can be obtained. In extreme circumstances there may be recourse to expert evaluation, but this lacks consistency with the tenets of CBA (i.e. that it is the affected individuals' valuations that should count). The acid test of any valuation, then, is whether it is consistent with the underlying theory. Since CBA is concerned with social costs and social benefits, rather than with the maximization of private profit, there are specific requirements for evaluation. The objective is to derive an estimate of social surplus associated with the project in determining its net worth. A natural starting-point consistent with the Paretian value judgements is, therefore, to ask how much individuals would be prepared to pay for the project. In chapter 2 it was argued that consumer surplus was more than a 'theoretical toy', and here we have an example of its use in cost–benefit analysis.

Let us begin with the example of a project for a road improvement between Bath and Bristol. (Musgrave and Musgrave, 1989, present a similar transport example.) Assume it is proposed that a flyover be introduced on this road, which will enable motorists to make the journey more quickly. Further, assume that prior to the road improvement it takes 1 hour to make the trip, and that after the road improvement it will take just 30 minutes. Suppose that the value of travel time is set at £2 an hour. How much is the improvement worth to individuals in the community? On face value, it seems clear that the gain is the reduction in the time travel (i.e. £1 per trip). Of course, other costs of making the journey may rise; for example, the rate of petrol consumption, wear and tear on the car and the probability of an accident may all increase as a result of the increased speed of the journey. Suppose that these variable costs of time per trip are collectively equal to £1.50 prior to the road improvement and will increase to £2.00 afterward. Before the road improvement the costs of time per trip (£2) and the variable costs per trip (£1.50) total £3.50, while after the road improvement the costs of time and the variable costs per trip will be £3.00. The benefits of the road improvement might then be estimated as the change in the costs of making the trip, i.e. £0.50 per trip.

Before the road improvement there are 1 000 000 trips and after the improvement, because of the fall in costs of travel, it is expected that there will be an increase in the number of trips of 500 000. One way to estimate the welfare effect of these changes is to ask how much individuals would be prepared to pay for them. For the initial number of journeys, the fall in price will be a good estimate of the increase in welfare: 1 000 000 journeys multiplied by £0.50 per trip = £500 000. For the additional traffic this approach would not be satisfactory, as this additional traffic flow would never have made the journey at the old price of £3.50. The marginal user would have paid a price just below £3.50, while after the improvement he pays a price of £3.00. If we assume the demand curve is linear, then the benefits to these 500 000 is $\frac{1}{2}$ (£3.50− £3.00) × (500 000) which is equal to £125 000. The total benefits in any year are estimated to be £500 000 + £125 000 = £625 000.

The point that becomes obvious in this analysis is that estimating the benefits of the projects in this way is tantamount to using the principle of consumer surplus. The cost reduction for the initial users can be seen in Fig. 6.2 to be equal to the area 1352. The value to the additional users is shown by triangle 345. The complete area 1342 is nothing other than the change in consumer surplus which results from the fall in the price of journeys, brought about as a result of the investment in the road project. Having made this analogy, however, it is necessary to bear in mind those reservations that are outlined in chapter 2 regarding the use of consumer surplus.

1. To estimate consumer surplus, the demand curve should be drawn under the assumption that real income is held constant. The area under this demand curve expresses willingness to pay in terms of the more useful measure of compensating variation. The compensated demand curve differs, of course, from the demand curve that is drawn under the assumption of money income held constant. The demand curve identified by the behaviour of individuals will not be the compensated demand curve, as there is no mechanism by which such compensation can be made. The extent to which there is a difference between the Marshallian and the compensated demand curve is debatable. It is quite clear that Marshall himself was conscious of the difference, and in his analysis of consumer surplus he assumed that the good in question was one on which the individual spent little of his income, so that the income effects contingent upon the fall in price would be less significant. Mishan (1972) notes that the statistical problems of simply identifying the Marshallian demand curve (let alone the compensated demand curve) are likely to dwarf the fine distinction that can be made between the Marshallian and the compensated demand curve.

2. The use of the area under the demand curve alone may be an inadequate estimate of consumer surplus. Following the critique of Little (1957), it supposes that there is no change in prices elsewhere. The following example, based on a case outlined by Sugden and Williams (1978), shows how the area may have to be amended to allow for changes in other markets. In

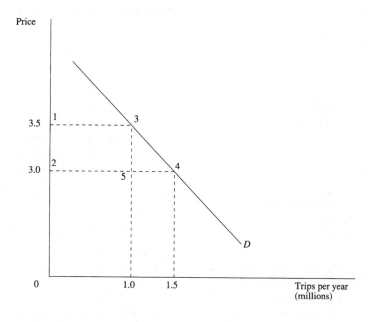

Figure 6.2 Demand for road travel.

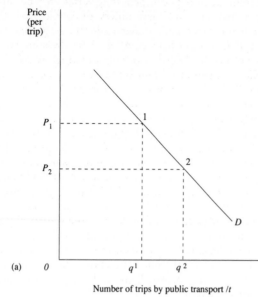

Number of trips by public transport /t

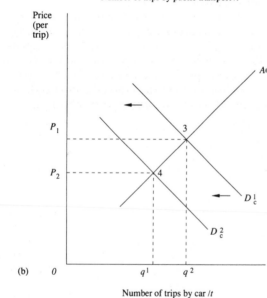

Number of trips by car /t

Figure 6.3 Accounting for benefits in other markets.

Source: Sugden, R. and Williams, A. (1978) *The Principles of Practical Cost Benefit Analysis*, Oxford University Press, Oxford.

this example there is a public sector project which will reduce the price of public sector transport. In Fig. 6.3(a), the demand curve is shown for public sector transport and the effect of the investment programme is to reduce the price from P_1 to P_2. The result of this is

an increase in consumer surplus by $P_1 12 P_2$. However, the fact that the price of public transport has fallen means that some travellers substitute public transport for private transport. In Fig. 6.3(b), the demand curve (D_c) for private transport is shown to shift to the left (D_c^1 to D_c^2). Possibly as a result of a reduction of congestion on the roads, the price of private transport falls. (Note that the price to the road user in this literature is equal to the average cost of a journey, i.e. the price paid per trip, rather than the incremental resource costs created when making an additional trip.) This, of course, creates gains for those motorists who remain in private transport and is a technical externality for the project. The shift in the demand curve traces out, at each point, the gain that comes from the price fall in the market. Though the shift is likely to be marginal, it is magnified in part (b), and the associated gain in consumer surplus to these road users is approximated by the area $P_1 34 P_2$. These gains would clearly need to be added to the gains $P_1 12 P_2$ to record the full gains of the project.

3. There is always the reservation that, after the project has been undertaken, there is no way of checking that the consumer surplus has in fact been increased. Here one can check only that the exercise has been correctly undertaken.

6.5 Shadow pricing: the deficiencies of market prices

It will have become obvious that, in dealing with a cost–benefit analysis, we are applying much of the welfare economics that has been outlined earlier in the book. The theory of second best is another relevant piece of analysis when the analyst is dealing with cost–benefit analysis. Because costs and benefits must be evaluated, it is necessary to utilize prices. Krutilla (1961) argued that, if the outputs of two projects (O_1 and O_2) and the inputs of two projects (I_1 and I_2) could be directly compared, then, provided $O_2 > O_1$ and $I_2 < I_1$, it would be possible to avoid evaluation in terms of pricing outputs O and inputs I; however, if $O_2 > O_1$ and $I_1 < I_2$ this would obviously not be possible. We need to use prices to evaluate output and input, but how reliable are market prices as a measure of benefits and costs?

The message from the theory of second best is that market prices will not be useful when there are known imperfections in the markets. As already noted in chapter 2, the use of the concept of consumer surplus,

and the attempt to use it as an objective to be maximized, relies on the notion that markets are perfect
elsewhere in the economy. The use of market prices to
value the resources used, or as a proxy for the value of
goods to be provided by the public sector, relies on the
belief that the market price records willingness to pay
for the marginal units of the good (or resources) in
question. If everywhere this is true, then market prices
are a useful proxy and the problems associated with
the theory of second best are not relevant. If, however,
this is not true, it will be necessary to eschew market
prices within a cost–benefit analysis and replace them
with shadow prices, which more accurately estimate
the true costs of resources and costs in terms of willingness to pay.

Here we begin by looking at those market distortions that would lead us to make amendments to the
prices we use in any cost–benefit study. The examples
considered are ones where amendment to market
prices will be necessary, but there are other cases
where no market prices exist. If the good to be provided in the public sector is a public good, it may be
unlikely that preferences for this good will be revealed
in a market. There are then no existing prices to
amend. Moreover, for some goods and services there
may be no markets because of the legal framework,
e.g. as slavery is outlawed. It may be difficult on first
consideration to find a market that gives a price for
human life! Even so, the saving of human life may be a
key consideration in transport and other projects.

The following are examples where amendment of
market prices may be recommended. Problems of
shadow pricing, where no prices currently exist, are
considered later.

Monopoly

How is the shadow price of inputs determined when
inputs into a project are provided by a monopolist?
The problem here is that the market price of the input
will not be equal to the marginal social cost of the
inputs. Following Layard (1972), a solution to this
question is provided by considering the alternative
use of the inputs. Suppose cement is required for a
public sector building project (e.g. to build a school)
and that it must be purchased from a monopolist. If
the supply of cement increases in response to the
demand of the project, then the cost of the cement is
the value of resources used to produce it (and in this
case the rental income of the monopolist should not
be included). The pecuniary gain to the monopolist is
not a real cost to the community. However, in other
circumstances the market price would be the relevant
price in a CBA. This would be so if it were impossible

to increase the output of the good. The value of the
good to the public sector should then be set in terms of
the amount that would be paid for it in the private
sector. The key is whether the supply of the good is
elastic. If supply were expanded, we use the value of
the marginal cost of the resources involved. If supply is
inelastic, then the opportunity cost of the resource is
the value that would be paid for the good in the private
sector.

Unemployment

Following this line of argument, the valuation of
labour at the wage rate requires the assumption that
this represents the opportunity cost of labour. But
what if there is unemployment? In these circumstances the appropriate opportunity cost appears to
be zero. Therefore, if project A is to be undertaken in
region I where unemployment is high, this project
may be desirable by comparison with project B undertaken in J where unemployment is low. This may be so
even if the net present value of the project (estimated
for both projects using the wage rate for labour) is
higher for B than for A.

Some would refine this market price adjustment
further. For example, Pearce and Nash (1981) note
that 'it is sometimes argued that unemployment
involves a further social cost—the burden of unemployment benefits on the rest of society' (p. 108). As
they point out, and as readers will now be aware, this is
a mistake. Unemployment benefit is a *transfer* to the
currently unemployed from the rest of the community, not an additional cost. If any refinement were to
be made to the value of zero as the shadow price of
labour, it would be in terms of the social and psychological costs to the unemployed versus the value of
extra leisure time.

The use of leisure may be questioned along the lines
that, if government (accepting the costs of unemployment) has decided not to rectify the problem by
monetary and fiscal steps, there will be no overall
increase in employment by the project. Employment
here will be at the expense of unemployment elsewhere, and the wage rate is appropriate (Haveman
and Krutilla 1968). Pearce and Nash (1981) question
this argument in the context of regional and structural
unemployment which arises from the failure of government to be able to utilize enough instruments to
resolve them.

Taxes

The same principles apply to taxation and to subsidies. Consider again the intermediate goods used in the
project. The output of the industry will be valued at
market prices where the good would otherwise have

been used in some other project; it will be valued at the cost of inputs, net of tax, where they are provided for the project.

International trade and development

A particular form of cost–benefit analysis, associated with developing economies, can be summarized as the Little–Mirrlees–Squire–van der Tak (LMST) approach (see Irwin 1978). For developing countries, market prices are thought to be especially unreliable as guides to accounting (opportunity cost) calculations, because of the presence of very uneven income distribution, market distorting taxes, subsidies, quotas, monopolies and other imperfections such as widespread externalities. The response is an elaborate and complex appraisal mechanism, based on 'border' (international trade) prices. International trade is seen as adding a productive sector to the economy. The mechanism is usually divided into an efficiency calculus and a social calculus. The efficiency calculus for a simple project can be captured in the following equation introduced by Irwin (1978):

$$(6.4) \quad NBP = oer(X - M) - a(SWR.L + NL)$$

where NBP = net benefit of the project
oer = official exchange rate
X = the output of the project which is a good for export
M = imported inputs for the project
SWR = shadow wage rate
L = labour employed on the project
NL = non-labour domestic inputs
a = the conversion factor that converts domestic inputs into 'border' valuations

This schema points up three valuation questions: for internationally traded goods (X and M); for non-traded goods (NL); and for the shadow wage rate (SWR). Once resolved, the project would be said to be evaluated in efficiency accounting prices.

The social calculus involves two wider issues not unfamiliar in this chapter. First, there is an intertemporal question that, if the investment level in a developing economy is thought sub-optimal, say because taxation to finance it is difficult to administer, then that part of NBP that becomes available for investment purposes is viewed as more valuable than the part that goes to consumption benefits now. Second, there is an intertemporal aspect in that, whether it is the poor or the well-off who secure any consumption gains from the project (i.e. a distribution weights question), this yields the net social benefit of the project (NSBP), which looks like

$$(6.5) \qquad NSBP = (NBP - dL) + \sum_{i=1}^{n} \frac{E_i dL_i}{v}$$

where dL = the net gain in earnings from the project that goes to current consumption
E_i = is the equity weight to be attached to the earnings gain of the ith individual (or income class)
v = the weight (> 1) that 'allows' for the lower social value of a unit of extra consumption compared with a unit of extra investment generated by the project

It is impossible to do justice to the LMST system in the space devoted to it here,[1] but enough has been said to argue that, in the developing country context, CBA has all the same valuation, discounting and equity weight issues writ large.

6.6 Shadow pricing: creating prices

The problems of shadow pricing, when no market prices exist, arise in the context of public goods. How can the benefits that emerge from the provision of a public good (with less than perfect preference revelation) be assessed?

6.6.1 Public goods—intangible benefits

In measuring the output of a project, Musgrave (1969) makes the distinction between valuation of an intermediate good and valuation of a final good. In the case of irrigation, the benefits that arise as a result of the irrigation scheme may be measured in terms of the value of the additional output that results from the scheme. The benefits of a flood protection scheme similarly may be estimated by the value of the reduction in damage as a result of the project. When the good enters the utility function as a final good, the benefits are much more difficult to measure. For example, the value of environmental improvement, in terms of the increasing utility that individuals derive from a pleasant view, will be altogether more difficult to assess.

While obvious difficulties exist, attempts have been made to deal with these final goods. Marion Clawson (1959), for example, looked at the benefits derived from a national park. The approach employed in this CBA was to take the travel costs of those people who

---

[1] Interested readers should look at the Overseas Development Administration summary (1988).

visited the park as an estimate of what a visit to the park was worth to them. From areas of varying distance to Yosemite National Park, Clawson estimated the total cost per one-day visit and linked this to the number of people making the visit. Treating the cost of travel as the price of a visit and relating this to the number of visits at that price, it is possible to construct a demand curve for Yosemite National Park. The total benefits from the park would then be proxied by the area under the demand curve. Of course, this approach is open to many criticisms. Should the travel costs be taken as a proxy for price? Did those who travelled to the park also derive utility from the journey itself (so that the travel costs overestimate the price)? Nevertheless, it is an interesting example of a method for teasing out the demand curve for a 'public good' that directly enters utility functions.

6.6.2 The value of human life

One of the key considerations in cost–benefit studies of investment in medical care or road safety is the valuation of human life. While cost effectiveness analysis (effectively, searching for the least-cost method to achieve a stated objective) may be sufficient to choose between alternative projects that save the same number (and quality) of life-years, ultimately the decision must be made regarding how much investment to undertake. To answer this question it is necessary, either implicitly or explicitly, to weigh the costs of the investment against the benefits. To estimate the benefits, the value of human life is a key consideration. For our purposes, the literature that has emerged concerning the estimation of the value of human life is important in so far as it illustrates the main questions that a cost–benefit analyst must have in mind when searching for the 'appropriate' shadow price. It will be argued that central among these considerations is the objective function that is to be maximized.

Various attempts have been made to find a value for human life saved by public sector investment. Mishan (1971) provides a useful classification which is followed here. The first approach to the valuation of human life is concerned with the loss of output that occurs when a life is lost. That is to say, a human life (VL) is valued as

$$(6.6) \qquad VL = \sum_{t=j}^{\infty} Y_t P_j^t (1 + r)^{-(t-j)}$$

where Y_t = expected gross earnings in year t
P_j^t = the probability in the current year j of the person being alive in the tth year
r = the rate of discount

It is possible to use actuarial tables to estimate P_j^t. Estimation of the loss associated with the death of the individual may be more problematical. It is important that the estimate Y represents the marginal product of this individual. To use output per head as a measure of Y would overestimate the value of the marginal product of labour to the extent that this allocated the entire output to labour with no allowance for the use of capital. Use of the wage rate as an estimate of this value is acceptable only if there is perfect competition, for the reasons discussed above. Also, it must be assumed that there is full employment. Moreover, over time productivity may increase, and therefore to estimate future values of Y it would be necessary to make an allowance. For women it would be necessary to allow for the services of housewives; these could be estimated either in terms of the opportunity cost of being a housewife (what women, on average, earn in other jobs) or in terms of the replacement cost, i.e. the cost of a housekeeper.

While these practical problems of estimating appropriate proxies will prove difficult, there is a more fundamental issue. Use of the gross estimate above makes no allowance for the fact that the individual herself would consume some of the output that she produces. A decision has to be made as to whether or not the analyst is concerned with the welfare of the group of individuals that currently exists (including the person whose life is at stake) or the remaining group of individuals who will survive. In the latter case the relevant estimate is net output. That is

$$(6.7) \qquad VL = \sum_{t=j}^{\infty} P_j^t (Y_t - C_t)(1 + r)^{-(t-j)}$$

where C_t is the personal expenditure of the individual during the tth period that is expected at time j.

The distinction rests upon the strong normative decision as to whose welfare is included in the objective function. In the case of net output estimates, we are concerned only about the loss to those who survive the individual. It is possible, of course, that this estimate could lead to very repugnant policy implications. Old age pensioners would be a group at risk, in so far as the product of their labour was near exhaustion and their capital assets would stand to be inherited. More generally, however, it is possible to refer to the value of a human life in average terms, rather than having it targeted upon different groups (see Reynolds 1956, and Dawson 1967).

One of the obvious deficiencies in using the loss of output estimate (either gross or net) as an estimate of the value of life is that it is based entirely on the value of human capital and ignores the consumption aspect of life. Moreover, it says nothing about the pain and discomfort that ill health may create. Klarman (1965) attempts to incorporate this cost by looking at how much individuals spend relieving the symptoms of similar complaints which do not prevent them from working.

While the estimates of human life, constructed in this way, can be augmented and refined, the basis of valuation remains the loss of human capital. To this extent, the approach suggests that the value of life is to be gauged in terms of the objective of *maximizing gross national product*. To make this decision is to make the normative decision that such an objective is 'best'.

An alternative approach to shadow pricing would be to look for values consistent with society's valuation as reflected in the political process. A study by Ghosh, Lees and Seal (1975) illustrates this approach. Ghosh *et al.* look at the speed limit on motorways as reflecting society's decision about the socially optimal speed. They estimate the marginal social benefit from increased speed (in the form of time savings and fuel cost) and argue that this must be just equal to the marginal social cost (in the form of increased casualty rates). For any optimal speed limit it is possible to infer the cost of a casualty. Irrespective of the problems of implementing this approach (in the light of the arguments of chapter 4), readers will be suspicious that the decisions that emerge from the political process accurately reflect society's values. However, it may be assumed that in deferring to government for a valuation individuals choose to forego their preferences in favour of 'expert' opinion. They are not able to make decisions because of inadequate information, and the merit good arguments of chapter 3 again become relevant. As such, so also do the questions raised in chapter 3; i.e. Who are the 'experts' and how are they qualified?

It will be argued later that the principle that economists recognize in a cost–benefit study is the one related to potential Pareto improvement. If a cost–benefit study yields a net present value and if shadow prices have been accurately estimated, this will mean that the gainers from the project could compensate the losers (who forgo the use of the resources) if there were costless redistribution. This means that shadow prices should reflect the values that individuals themselves place on the goods and resources. In any investment in medical care or road safety, the question is how much any individual would pay for a reduction in the probability of the loss of life. Following Jones-Lee (1974), assume that an individual begins with wealth W and a probability of loss of life p (where $0 < p < 1$). His expected utility ($E(U)$) is contingent on the chances that he will live to consume his wealth or that he will die. That is to say,

$$(6.8) \qquad E(U) = (1 - p)L(W) + pD(W)$$

where $L(W)$ and $D(W)$ are the utility of wealth conditional on survival or death respectively.

Imagine that the individual is offered the opportunity to reduce the probability of his death from p to $p^1(< p)$. It is usual to assume that $dL(W)/dW > 0$ while we may assume that $dD(W)/dW \geqslant 0$. Moreover, it would be reasonable to assume that $L(W) > D(W)$, i.e. that the individual prefers to be alive! In such circumstances the individual will pay money to reduce the chances of a loss of life. Therefore, a reduction in the probability of loss of life means that there is a maximum sum V that the individual can give up which leaves his expected utility identical to the position prior to the reduction in the loss of life:

$$(6.9) \qquad \begin{aligned} (1 - p^1)L(W - V) + p^1 D(W - V) \\ = (1 - p)L(W) + pD(W) \end{aligned}$$

The sum V is the compensating variation, i.e. the maximum sum that the individual will be prepared to give up for a reduction in the probability of a loss of life. Under the above assumptions, it is reasonable to suppose that the individual will trade off wealth, as in Fig. 6.4, to pay for a reduction in the probability of death from $\bar{p}$, or will require payment for an increase in the probability of death. If an investment in health care or road safety alters the probability of a loss of life, dV/dp at $\bar{p} = £x$ and this is the marginal valuation of a decrease in risk. Summing this for those at risk will provide a first estimate of the benefits of the investment.

There are at least two ways of estimating this value for use in a cost–benefit study. The first explicit way is to use a questionnaire approach. Jones-Lee (1976) attempts this approach, asking respondents what discount (additional) price they would accept to fly with an airline (B) which has a stipulated worse (better) accident record than an alternative airline (A). On the basis of a survey of some 90 individuals, of whom 31 replied, the evidence suggested that the value of life is £3 million. A second approach is to consider how much individuals actually pay for additional safety. Jones-Lee (1977) examined the implicit valuation that individuals attach to safety according to the frequency with which they incur the costs of changing tyres on their cars.

There are criticisms of this 'willingness to pay' approach to shadow pricing. For behavioural studies,

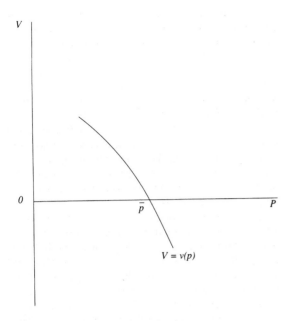

Figure 6.4 The value of human life.

Source: based on Jones-Lee (1976).

it is doubtful that individuals are fully informed about the risks involved when they make choices. Moreover, it may be questioned whether individuals can cope with questionnaire studies, where the probabilities involved are small. Of course, with questionnaire studies there is always the issue of whether or not they will respond honestly or will prefer to overestimate in the hope of additional public expenditure funded by other taxpayers. Perhaps the most conten-

tious criticism, however, is that aimed at the underlying conceptual basis of this form of shadow pricing. Broome (1978) argues that, in the case of human life, compensating variations (CVs) are unacceptable because they rely on ignorance to make the approach operational. The *ex ante* calculation will not approximate the *ex post* outcome and will therefore not be a good policy guide; i.e. those that die would require infinite compensation and the net present value of the project could not remain positive. Broome does not suggest a replacement technique, just that some beneficial projects may involve known deaths.

In summary, it is possible to provide a taxonomy of approaches to determine the shadow price of human life, as outlined in Table 6.3. This summarizes the above discussion and, more importantly, outlines the basis of the principles that may be applied to provide a shadow price in a cost–benefit analysis. It will be clear that, at root, the differences between these approaches depends upon the objective function implied by the analysis. This is a normative decision. However, it would be reasonable to argue that, if a particular shadow price is used, this price should be consistent with the pursuit of a chosen objective function. It might also be noted that, in the context of the application of cost–benefit analysis to select a potential Pareto improvement (see section 6.8), the relevant shadow price would be that which is based on the compensating variation ('willingness to pay'). Brent (1991) attempts to avoid the problems of producing a monetary value of life by using the numeraine of time. However, there is reason to question the underlying objective function (Cullis and Jones, 1996).

In Table 6.3, we draw together a taxonomy which relates the approach to shadow pricing to the

Table 6.3   Conceptual bases of the shadow price of human life

Approach	Source of estimate	Objective function consistent with shadow price	Variations and examples
Human capital livelihood based measures	Market data (e.g. wage rate)	Gross national product	Some court compensations
Political decisions (implicit)	Government legislation	Merit Good: 'Others' are better judges because individuals not fully informed and/or rational	Safety standards—roads, industry
Political decisions (explicit)	Government statements		Department of Environment £ 40 000 (as in 1976)
Willingness to pay (implicit)	Individual market behaviour	Individuals' welfare in terms of their own preferences	Pay premiums for hazardous jobs (army, police, North Sea oil rigs); tyre replacement
Willingness to pay (explicit)	Statements by individuals	Individuals' welfare in terms of their own preferences	Questionnaire surveys

objective function that lies behind it. This highlights the source of the relevant valuation and offers examples of cost–benefit analyses where these estimates have been employed.

6.6.3 Quality adjusted life years ('QALYs')

Given the difficulties of placing a monetary value on human life, analysts have tried to 'duck the issue' by using a non-monetary measure of output. If there is to be investment in medical care the question arises as to where that investment is likely to be most 'productive'. To answer this, a measure of 'quality adjusted life years' (QALYs) has been used. To be consistent with our previous discussion it is important to emphasize that the objective function that underlies investment appraisal should be kept clear when such non-monetary measures are used. Throughout this chapter it has been argued that the objective of a cost–benefit analysis is estimated in terms of potential Pareto improvement and it is important to return to this theme later in this section. But first, what are QALYs?

A QALY is a uni-dimensional scale used to compare different health states. Following Torrance (1976) and Mooney (1992), there are three main ways of attempting to devise QALYs.

(i) *'visual analogue scale' or 'rating scale'* This involves setting out a scale usually with one end equal to 0 (equated with death) and the other end set at 1 (equated with 'perfect' health). If, for example a respondent judged that losing the use of both legs was 0.75 on this scale then this state of health would be assessed as reducing health status (*vis-à-vis* 'perfect' health) by one quarter. Different health statuses become commensurable according to their positions on this scale.

(ii) *'time trade-off'* If, for example, a respondent assessed that 20 years of life with the loss of both legs followed immediately by death were equal to 15 years of life with perfect health followed by immediate death, then if 1 is perfect health the valuation of the health state 'loss of use of both legs' is 0.75.

(iii) *standard gamble* This involves a choice between a certain and a risky situation. The risky situation has a probability (p) of 'perfect' health and a probability $(1 - p)$ of dying immediately. The respondent sets p so as to be indifferent between the risky situation and a certain health status. If the current health state is loss of use of both legs and the individual sets p equal to 0.75, then 0.75 is the valuation of this health state (when again death is 0 and 'perfect health' is 1).

There are difficulties in using these measures. For example, the visual analogue scale does not present respondents with any 'costs' (there is no cost attached to any statement that is made, whereas for decision-makers the problem is in terms of allocating of scarce resources). In the case of the standard gamble, responses may be sensitive to the framing of the questions (Kahneman and Tversky 1979). They may be influenced by individuals' attitudes to risks. They may be difficult for respondents to deal with.

When health statuses can be compared it is possible to measure the benefits of medical care. For example in Fig. 6.5 (Robinson, 1996) until wearing out of the hip joint begins at a particular age (say 65 years) the quality of life is near perfect. After the age of 65 the quality of life depends on a hip replacement operation. With the operation life years are increased (from 72 to 82) and the quality of life is improved. The hatched area minus the dark shaded area between the two lines provides a measure of the quality of life years (QALYs) that are provided by the medical treatment in this case. If 100 such operations with, say, 3 deaths under anaesthetic, 30 people unaffected on recovery and 67 successful outcomes as illustrated above were performed then the 'output' from a typical operation is (in crude symbols):

$$0.67(\ \blacksquare\!\!\diagup\ -\ \blacksquare\ ) - 0.3\ \blacksquare\ - 0.03(\ \equiv\ +\ \blacksquare\ )$$

(i.e. $\dfrac{\text{operation}}{\text{successful}} - \dfrac{\text{operation}}{\text{ineffective}} - \dfrac{\text{operation}}{\text{deadly}}$)

From such estimates it is possible to compare the cost per QALY generated by different treatments for different complaints. Table 6.4 illustrates, for different forms of medical care, the present values of costs per QALY and it may be the case that investment

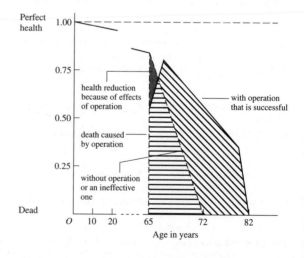

Figure 6.5 QALY construction (scale exaggerated).

Table 6.4   Medical care investment: 'QALY league table'

Intervention	Present value of extra cost per QALY gained (£)
GP advice to stop smoking	170
Pacemaker implantation for heart block	700
Hip replacement	750
GP control of total serum cholesterol	1,700
Kidney transplantation (cadaver)	3,000
Breast cancer screening	3,500
Heart transplantation	5,000
Hospital haemodialysis	14,000

Source: adapted from M. F. Drummond (1991) by Mooney (1992).

programmes with the 'cheapest' QALYs will be given some priority. There are a number of considerations which must be borne in mind when using such measures and when interpreting such 'cost-per-QALY league tables':

(1) Individuals' responses are to hypothetical choices (losing the use of legs may seem very different when fit and well to when seated in a wheelchair). Also relatedly, preferences depend on information. Some studies offer respondents more information concerning health states (e.g. 'you will then be on dialysis') and as a consequence valuation responses are changed. Valuations will be affected by the expected duration of the condition—suffering a chronic condition for two years may be more than twice as bad as for one year. Also, inevitably, individuals' valuations will also depend on other personal characteristics (e.g. their age) and in this context there is a debate as to whether the appropriate respondent should be current patients, past patients, doctors, or members of the general public?

Table 6.5 draws together these issues. It is clear, for example, that dialysis patients rated dialysis not as bad as did the general public. They rated the difference between home and hospital dialysis differently from the general public. Also note that both groups' rating declined as the period of duration asked about was increased (See also Mc Guire *et al*, 1988).

(2) The only output measured is health (there is no allowance for other 'non-health' aspects of treatment, e.g. the information given to patients during treatment, the dignity or privacy provided to patients).

(3) The resource use examined in QALY league tables only have opportunity costs in terms of QALYs. The only outcomes possible (and the only foregone outcomes from the resources that are considered in these tables) are health outcomes.

(4) Different means of estimation of QALYs may yield different results. Comparing values obtained from the three methods, Torrance found that visual analogue scale values were lower than those from time trade-off or from the standard gamble. This may be because the visual analogue approach simply asks individuals to assign relative values (a response that measures the quality of a given health state as $\frac{1}{3}$ of perfect health may not really mean that the individual is willing to trade 3 such years with 1 perfectly healthy year).

(5) Cost-per-QALY values may be reported as average values, while choices to be made are at the margins. The relevant consideration is marginal cost per QALY.

(6) It has been argued that the highly summarized presentation of data, in one cost-per-QALY estimate, is dangerous in that it suggests quick and easy solutions to the decision-maker. This becomes all the more important to the extent that league tables encourage *less* thought by decision-makers about the nature of medical care choices. Moreover, it is questionable that there really is a 'typical case', patients varying widely.

(7) The QALY approach regards each year of (quality adjusted) life gained as equal. For example, one year of additional life for a child who would otherwise die immediately will be counted as the same as two years of 50 per cent quality for an older person who

Table 6.5   Alternative estimates of health status

Duration	Health state	Mean daily health state utility		% difference	Probability that the difference is due to chance
		General population	Dialysis patients		
3 Months	Hospital dialysis	0.62	0.81	31	0.01
8 Years	Hospital dialysis	0.56	0.59	5	NS
8 Years	Home dialysis	0.65	0.72	11	NS
Life	Hospital dialysis	0.32	0.52	62	0.01
Life	Home dialysis	0.39	0.56	44	0.06

Source: Sackett and Torrance (1982).

subsequently recovers from the health complaint and leads a full life in 'perfect' health.

(8) Strict application of the cost-per-QALY league table may imply that some groups of individuals in society, whose treatment have a high cost per QALY, receive no care.

(9) Technological advances and research will affect cost-per-QALY estimates so that they must be continually updated to allow for medical advances.

Return now to our main theme, i.e. that the interpretation of 'shadow prices' is conditional on the objective function. QALYs are not estimates of 'willingness to pay', so, if costs per QALY are compared for investment purposes, what exactly is being maximized?[2] The QALY approach marks a departure from the traditional Paretian welfare economics approach. A QALY is not a measure of utility; the QALY is common for everyone (i.e. two very different people can occupy the same QALY status and yet experience very different utilities).

It follows also that the QALY approach is not to be confused with utilitarianism, i.e. a rule which minimizes the total cost per QALY will not necessarily lead to the maximization of utility for the community. A QALY is regarded as of equal value to everyone but the utility from a QALY may differ. Some commend this. For example, Drummond (1989, p.71) argues that it invokes 'a kind of equality' because it is considered to be worth the same to everyone. It is not the case, for example, that resources should be distributed away from people who (for whatever reason) place a relatively low value on their health.

Using the QALY approach for assessing investment in medical care is tantamount to maximization of *health* for any budget. However, this does not guarantee that all will be treated the same. To illustrate the concept of health maximization (following Wagstaff 1991) consider Figure 6.6. The axes measure health in terms of expected QALYs remaining before death. Consider two individuals (or two groups of similar individuals) A and B who, without treatment, enjoy health status h_a and h_b respectively. Point 1 is an initial

endowment. The potential from medical treatment for A and B is shown by the health frontier 23. The shape of the health frontier and its location are determined by: (i) the total resources available for medical treatment; (ii) the costs to society of the medical care;[3] (iii) the capacity of A and B to benefit from health care. The health frontier is concave to the origin and its slope at any point indicates the marginal cost of a QALY to A in terms of QALYs denied to B. It is concave as it is assumed that health care is subject to a diminishing marginal product. This shows that an individual's (or group's) capacity to benefit at the margin diminishes as more treatment is provided. However, the asymmetry of the frontier reveals either that B can be treated at lower cost than A and/or that B has a greater capacity to benefit from treatment than A.

Allocating resources so as to equate the marginal cost per QALY of medical treatment maximizes health at point 4 on the health frontier (where the cost of a QALY at the margin is the same for A and B). This allocation of resources would increase the health status of B by more than that of A. It is important to emphasize that, while health is maximized, there is no guarantee that all will benefit equally. Capacity to gain from medical treatment matters and also (as noted by Williams 1981) resources will be deployed towards those whose output is highly valued and who as a result of treatment are able to return to work quickly. If A and B have the same capacity to benefit but B's output is more highly valued then allocating resources towards B reduces the net costs to society of treatment. B will receive more QALYs than A.

Of course, there 'should' be some concern about equity. Equity in investment appraisal is to be discussed later in section 6.9. However, here it is possible to illustrate how equity constraints might be introduced when using QALYs. For example, Wagstaff (1991) suggests the adoption of an iso-elastic social welfare function:

$$(6.10) \qquad W = [(\alpha h_a)^{1-\tau} + (\beta h_b)^{1-\tau}]^{1/(1-\tau)}$$

where: W = the level of social welfare associated with the health distribution;

h_a, h_b = the health status;

α = the weight to be attached to A's health;

β = the weight to be attached to B's health.

$\tau \neq 1$

To introduce strong normative constraints then if, for example, A were a young person (or a group of

---

[2] Some have asked individuals how much they would be willing to pay to obtain a particular health improvement, or avoid a health deterioration. Thompson (1986) reports how a group of 247 people, aged between 21 and 66, suffering from chronic rheumatoid arthritis were asked to imagine that a (complete) cure for their condition was available, but only through private purchase. Ninety-six per cent of the subjects responded. Their willingness to pay for the hypothetical cure was 22 per cent of their family's (household) income and willingness to pay as a proportion of income was positively correlated with their degree of impairment in activities of daily living, and negatively correlated with age.

[3] A cost which should include both time and money costs incurred by patients, family and friends, as well as the direct costs incurred by the health service.

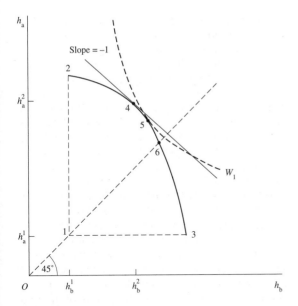

Figure 6.6 QALYs and equity.

Source: adapted from Wagstaff (1991).

young people) and B an elderly person (or a group of elderly people), society might take a view that α should be larger than β. Alternatively, these weights could be set equal and the parameter τ would work simply to emphasize the degree of aversion to inequality in health outcomes. If $\tau > 0$, an aversion to inequality is indicated so that with $\tau < \infty$, the contours of the welfare function (W_1 in Fig. 6.6) are convex to the origin. As $\tau \to \infty$ the welfare contour becomes L-shaped (with its corner on the 45° line) and this is the *Rawlsian* social welfare function (see Chapter 1).

Now in Fig. 6.6 health maximization occurs at 4; (strict) health equality occurs at 6, social welfare (allowing for inequality aversion) is maximized at 5. Note that at 5 (where the slope is less than one) the sum of health statuses will be lower than at 4 but the 'health output loss' is the trade-off that is required for greater equity.

6.7 Discounting and the cost of capital

In the first section of this chapter an explanation was given as to the need for a discount rate for the appraisal of investment projects. The question now is, How

should the discount rate be set? The choice of the discount rate is extremely important. A high discount rate will reduce the value of the stream of net earnings of the project, so as to turn the net present value negative.[4] Moreover, a high discount rate may bias choice between projects: if capital-intensive projects have extremely large initial costs (I_0), then these projects (because of their initial capital costs) are more likely to be ruled out by high values of the discount rate, which reduce future net benefits to a greater extent. Capital-intensive projects that have high set-up costs may rely heavily on those future benefits to be acceptable.

6.7.1 Choice of discount rates

The difficulties that arise in choosing the appropriate discount rate in the public sector may be classed under two headings. First, there is the *conceptual question* of what, in principle, is the right discount rate for public sector projects. Secondly, there is the *practical problem* of finding a suitable proxy for the discount rate that has been selected. To explain the difficulties in determining the social discount rate, it is necessary to understand why there is no obvious rate.

Accepting the value judgements of the Paretian framework, there are clear second-best problems in deciding which rate of discount is appropriate. If all the conditions required for Pareto optimality were to hold (first- and second-order conditions), the difficulty of deciding the appropriate discount rate would be less extreme. If, for example, there were no imperfections in markets, no externalities and no unemployment, then the relevant rate of discount might well be taken to be the rate of interest that exists in the market for loanable funds. The problem arises, however, because there are imperfections that make it impossible for one rate of discount adequately to perform all the functions required of a social discount rate.

On the one hand, the social rate of discount is important because it determines *how much investment* will be undertaken. In this context the rate of

---

[4] It should be clear that at different discount rates some projects will pass and others will fail. What is the correct discount rate to use? If projects are to be recommended on the grounds that the net present value is positive, then it is important that they are calculated on the 'correct' discount rate. Alternatively, if projects are to be accepted according to the internal rate of return on the project (i.e. the rate of discount that makes the NPV zero), then there has to be a test rate of discount which serves as a requirement that must be equalled or surpassed if the project is to look attractive. The choice of discount rate becomes central to the potential acceptability of the project.

discount must reflect society's rate of time preference. That is to say, it will admit projects provided they create a rate of return equal to the rate of interest that society requires in order to forego consumption today for consumption in a future period. By definition, the social time preference discount factor STP is equal to the marginal rate of substitution between consumption in the current period C_t and consumption in the next period C_{t+1}. Use of this discount factor will provide a guide as to the amount of investment that society would choose to invest over time.

On the other hand, the social rate of discount must deal with the *allocation of resources between the private and public sectors*. It will not be defensible if a social rate of discount is used that permits public projects when the opportunity cost is the loss of better investments in the private sector. The social opportunity cost rate of discount SOC is, now, the discount rate that reduces to zero the net present value (in social terms) of the best alternative private use of the funds. If, having used this discount rate, the net present value of a public sector project is positive, then it must imply a greater rate of return than would be experienced had the resources been left in the private sector. Use of the SOC in this way satisfies the objective that no public investment displaces a private investment that has a higher social rate of return.

The difficulty of finding one rate of discount that performs both of these functions can be shown by reference to Fig. 6.7. This figure illustrates the standard treatment of the market for loanable funds. The supply curve S reflects how much individuals will save at different rates of interest. It shows the increase in interest rate required to persuade individuals to save more (and to forgo consumption in this period) in return for additional consumption in a future period. This return reflects the marginal rate of substitution between current and future consumption. By contrast, I shows the demand for investment. It indicates how much individuals would pay to have the use of loanable funds. It acts, therefore, as an index of what the investment is worth in its best alternative use.

When markets are perfect and Pareto optimality conditions apply, the equilibrium rate of interest in the market for loanable funds appears, on first consideration, to satisfy the requirements for the social rate of discount. This equilibrium rate, at one and the same time, acts as an indicator of the social time preference rate and the social opportunity rate of discount. The problem of finding a rate of discount to deal with the two objectives described above seems to be resolved. The equilibrium rate of interest, r_0, will be the appropriate test rate of discount for investment in the public sector.

However, problems arise when there are imperfections in markets. Take for example the impact that a corporation tax may have on this analysis. In Fig. 6.7 it is assumed that a corporation tax applies, so that the amount the project must make, in terms of its rate of return, must be sufficient to pay the tax and to pay the lenders of funds. The result of the tax is to reduce the level of investment, as the rate of return must now be high enough to enable the investor to pay the saver an adequate return and to pay the tax. A wedge is driven between the rate of interest that must be paid to consumers, $r(STP)$—which is the social time preference rate—and the rate of return that the project earns—which is the social opportunity cost rate of discount $r(SOC)$.

In these circumstances a choice between the social time preference rate and the social opportunity cost rate is required. One rate of interest no longer satisfies both definitions. Inevitably, a choice must be made in conceptual terms as to which of these two discount rates is the appropriate one to use for public investment programmes. If emphasis is laid on the allocation of resources between current use in the public and private sectors, then it is appropriate to equalize rates of return in both sectors. That is to say, the higher discount rate is used as a measure of the social opportunity rate of discount. The result of this, however, is that fewer projects will pass the test in the public sector and investment will be lower than if the STP

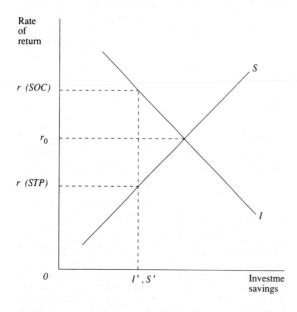

Figure 6.7 Which discount rate?

rate were used. If already there is 'too little' investment in the private sector because of the influence of the tax (see Fig. 6.7), should the lower rate be used in the public sector? Can projects with a lower rate of return be justified here? Though there may be an argument to be mounted in these terms, many economists nevertheless favour the social opportunity cost rate (e.g. Mishan 1988; Webb 1973) because they would not wish to see resources invested in the public sector that can earn a higher rate of return in the public sector. Those who lay emphasis on the allocation of resources through time would support the use of a lower rate.

6.7.2 The social time preference rate of discount: suitable estimates

Having tackled the conceptual choice of the 'appropriate' rate of discount, there is still a need to find a practical estimate of whichever one is chosen. In the case of the social time preference (STP) rate, there are reasons to argue that this rate must be positive. Uncertainty, mortality in the future and the prospect of economic growth with diminishing marginal utility of consumption all support this proposition. For example, as it can be expected that real consumption per head will rise over time, it follows that a given future increase in consumption per head is worth less than an equal present increase. Some economists take each (or all) of these arguments and attempt to pin them down more closely. Henderson (1968), for example, assumes that individuals have a utility function of the Bernoulli form (i.e. individual's utility proportional to the logarithm of consumption so that the marginal utility function has a constant elasticity of -1). Then, with consumption per head growing at 2 per cent per annum, he calculates the social time preference rate to be 3 per cent.

If markets are perfectly competitive, would it be possible to use the market rate of interest as a proxy for the STP rate? In principle, all individuals' time preferences will be the same, as individuals equate them to the market rate of interest. Feldstein (1964) argues, however, that this would require us to assume not only perfect competition throughout the economy, but also perfect forward markets. For the market rate of interest to reflect individuals' choices about present and future consumption, it is necessary that individuals are fully informed.

If this were not enough of a problem, an argument by Marglin (1963a) suggests that the individually determined STP rate may differ from the communally determined rate. He argues that individuals may be better off by undertaking more investment collect-

ively than each would find desirable to undertake privately. He assumes that the individual's decision to invest depends, in part, upon the marginal value placed on consumption by members of the next generation (children and grandchildren), and that there is utility to be had from leaving a capital stock to future generations. The marginal utility from investment will then depend upon the rate of transformation of present consumption into future consumption and on the marginal value of this future generation consumption to the individual compared with the marginal value of the loss of consumption now. As the provision of a capital stock for future generations is an object of the investment, and as the benefits that stem from this bear the characteristics of a public good (non-rival in consumption, non-price-exclusive), there is doubt as to whether anyone individually would invest as much as she would think appropriate from a communal point of view. The provision of a capital stock for future generations is assumed to yield the individual utility, regardless of whether or not she is the one who actually foregoes present consumption. However, Marglin goes on to show that, for certain values of this altruism towards future (as compared with concern for present) generations, there are group sizes such that the individual would be prepared to agree to schemes if *everyone* would make the investment. The result is that communally individuals would be more prepared to invest, and the social rate of time preference would thereby be lower than the market rate of interest which is observed when all individuals act individually.[5] Tullock (1964) has criticized this argument to the extent that it is dubious that individuals should feel altruistic towards future generations who are likely to be wealthier (given technical progress) than many poorer sections of the present generation.

Marglin is not the only person to argue that a communal STP rate would be lower than the market rate of interest. Pigou (1932) suggests that it will be lower because of myopic deficiencies of present generations. The failure of investors in the present generation to see the benefits of investment means that 'too little' is undertaken and the market rate of interest is higher than it might otherwise be.

If markets do not offer the solution to the STP rate, might the answer be found in the collective decision-making of individuals? Perhaps it is possible to turn to

[5] Marglin's argument that investment has public good characteristics presents problems. For example, in the presence of 'crowding out' of private sector investment, the use of a social time preference rate in the public sector will have little impact on the overall total investment.

those representatives of the community who have been democratically elected, in order to find their opinion as to the correct STP rate. Readers, conversant with the arguments of chapter 4, will be sceptical in the extreme about this possibility. The Arrow Impossibility Theorem would indicate that the results from such a constitution rule fail to satisfy certain normative criteria (Arrow 1963). The arguments of Downs (1957) leaves one sceptical that, within a representative democracy, the objectives of politicians can take precedence over those of the 'public interest'. As vote-maximizers, politicians (in the face of electoral myopia) will have a different time-horizon from society at large. Their concern will be that benefits have materialized by the next election. To this end, there may materialize a higher political discount rate than that which might be thought to reflect the STP.

These suggestions as to approximating the STP rate of discount are by no means exhaustive. Marglin (1963a), for example, suggested that, if only the optimal rate of growth for the economy were known, it would be possible to work backwards to derive the rate of discount that gives the 'correct' rate of investment to achieve this rate of growth. This not only assumes a fixed relationship between investment and growth (such that substitution between capital and labour is limited); it also assumes that we can determine the optimum growth rate in the first instance. The problems of determining the STP rate therefore remain.

6.7.3 The social opportunity cost rate of discount: suitable estimates

The task of determining the social opportunity cost is also fraught with difficulties. The obvious starting-point here is to work with the private rate of return that is earned on private investment. Technically, the argument is that resources that are used in the public sector must perform at least as well as those used in the private sector in order to warrant their use in the public sector. But as Baumol (1971) points out, technically we should know which private sector projects are displaced by public sector investment. That is to say, the social opportunity cost rate of discount should reflect a weighted average of the rates of return earned in the private sector projects had the resources been used in the private sector. Therefore

(6.11) $$SOC = x_1(r_1) + x_2(r_2)$$

where r_1, r_2 = the rate of return on private projects 1 and 2

x_1, x_2 = the proportion of resources displaced that would have been invested in projects 1 and 2

When looking at private rates of return, allowance must be made for other factors to gauge the social opportunity cost rate of discount.

Taxation and subsidy

If the private project that is displaced must cover 50 per cent corporation tax, then the SOC rate must be double the rate of return shown on that project in the private sector. Clearly, allowance must be made for the fact that the private project has to generate a return high enough to cover the cost of taxation. Conversely, where the project has enjoyed subsidies, the SOC rate would be below the private rate of return.

Risk

Allowance also must be made for the element of risk that the private project has to cover. It is argued that public projects are less risky than private projects because (a) the law of large numbers applies, and therefore unexpected losses in one project are compensated by unexpected gains in others, and (b) the costs of the projects are split over many taxpayers (Arrow and Lind 1970). However, some economists would argue that, if the private project has to earn a rate of return high enough to make an allowance for the risk with which it is faced, it is 'appropriate' that the public project cover this, if the decision is to transfer resources to the public sector (Webb 1973).

Social costs and benefits

The rate of return on private projects will take no account of externalities and will be evaluated at market prices. It should be noted that the social opportunity cost rate of discount is based on the social rate of return earned by projects in the private sector. For example, assume that a private firm creates pollution. The private rate of return will be estimated after making an allowance for only the private costs on the project. If, however, the social opportunity cost is greater than the market price, the private rate of return will be higher than the social rate of return and the social rate of discount will be lower than the private rate of return.

All these adjustments are necessary for the establishment of the social opportunity cost rate of discount. In the UK, the concept of social opportunity cost appears to have been recognized in analysis of investment in nationalized industries. For example, in 1967 the test rate of discount was set at 8 per cent. The Treasury explained, in a memorandum submitted to the Select Committee on Nationalized Industries in 1968, how this rate was chosen. The basis for the rate was 'the minimum return which would be regarded as acceptable on new investment by a large private firm' (see Webb 1973). As a result of discussions with large private firms, the minimum rate was set at between 6 and 8 per cent after (corporation) tax. However, income for investment may be subject also to income tax. The corresponding before-tax rate of return on the basis of the company taxation system then in force (income tax and profits tax), and allowing for investment and initial allowances, was in the range 8–10 per cent. The chosen figure was 8 per cent. The choice was broadly consistent with the social opportunity cost rate, though many of the fine adjustments noted above are not made.

The difficulties of making full adjustment are obvious. Some cost–benefit analyses have tried to bypass the problems of estimating social opportunity cost by using the government long-term borrowing rate as a proxy for the opportunity cost of funds to the government. Although it is ready and apparent, and although it has been used in the past, it is hardly applicable on theoretical grounds. The more that the government has recourse to taxation as a means of obtaining revenue, the less it needs to borrow and, other things equal, the lower the interest rate that will obtain. In times of war, for example, when the government is forced to raise more funds by borrowing, the long-term borrowing rate increases sharply (Carr 1969). Furthermore, the long-term borrowing rate makes no allowance for the fact that private projects are generally riskier than government loans or that they cover other forms of taxation. In effect, it appears unwise to rely on the long-term borrowing rate as either a proxy for the social opportunity cost rate of discount or for the social time preference rate of discount. It is a rate that is governed more by the needs of the central bank to account for the international flow of short-term capital, and in this way responds to the politically determined interest rate of other countries.

6.7.4 What is opportunity cost?

The question of how opportunity cost is determined has spawned a literature which suggests that the concepts of both social time preference and social opportunity costs are relevant. In theory, there is a fine distinction associated with the definition of opportunity cost. If opportunity cost is the value of the alternative use of the funds used in investment projects, then it has to be conceded that not all of the funds used in public sector investment projects would be used in investment in the private sector. To the extent that such funds are raised by taxation, a large proportion of these funds would have been consumed

had they not been taxed. If there is a distinction between the value of lost consumption in the current period (the STP) and the value of the use of lost private investment (the SOC), then allowance must be made for the proportion of the funds that would otherwise have been consumed and the proportion that would otherwise have been invested.

This argument, based on Marglin (1963b, 1967) and Feldstein (1972), is explained below. The exposition here follows that of Webb (1973). It begins from the argument that the basic criterion for investment should be

$$(6.12) \qquad PV_r(B) > SOC(k)$$

i.e. the present value of benefits discounted at the social time preference rate should exceed the social opportunity cost of the capital used.

It is argued that the social opportunity cost of capital is equal to $Ak(x)$, where A is the opportunity cost discounted at the STP rate per pound of inputs transferred from the private to the public sector, k is total capital outlay of the project incurred in a single period, and x is a scale factor (pounds, dollars). Given the argument above, the value of A is set as

$$(6.13) \qquad A = \theta_1(p/r) + (1 - \theta_1)$$

where θ_1 = the proportion of k that would have been privately invested
$1 - \theta_1$ = proportion of k raised from displaced consumption
p = the rate of return to be earned in perpetuity on a marginal investment in the private sector
r = STP discount rate

The argument says that the opportunity cost of capital should allow for the fact that not all of the resources used in the public sector would represent lost investment in the private sector. The weight used to compensate is based on the proportion that would be consumed and the proportion that would be invested. The present value of the former is its face value; the present value of the latter is the value of the earnings it would generate (p per annum in perpetuity) discounted at the social time preference rate r.

Mishan (1967) would dispute this argument. For him, the opportunity cost is what *could* have been done with the resources rather than what *would* have been done with them. Therefore all the resources could have earned p per annum in perpetuity if invested, and the value of this discounted to the present is p/r. The criterion remains that the net present value must be positive at the social opportunity cost rate of discount.

6.7.5 Discounting and discount rates: is there really a problem?

While there are many difficult questions to be resolved in choosing a social discount rate, there is a line of argument that suggests that there is no requirement at all to discount for investment in the public sector. Goodin (1982) questions both the rationale and the form of discounting. As regards the rationale, he suggests that the psychological approach of pure time preference is a frailty that need not be respected. At the same time, risk and uncertainty are quite different arguments to discounting for time as such (as explained in the next section). The diminishing marginal utility of income argument is accepted as an argument, with the proviso that it should be reversible if the future generation is poorer than the present generation. The opportunity cost argument is seen as a stricture about how discounting might be done, or rather what has to be sacrificed today to secure future benefits, and not as a rationale for making such intertemporal trades.

Similarly, Goodin reflects that, even accepting these four approaches, they do not imply the application of a uniform discount rate over time. Psychologically, some periods are more important than others; diminishing marginal utility will not occur at a constant rate because income growth will vary over time and income itself does not translate into utility at a given rate; opportunities sacrificed in one period are greater than those sacrificed in others.

In this way, having questioned the case for discounting at all, Goodin questions the decision to discount at a uniform rate. He argues that to treat all goods in the same fashion would be inappropriate. Some goods are psychologically more important than others, and this is true with respect to the degree of risk and uncertainty associated with them. The conversion of all goods to the common numeraire money, as in the marginal utility/opportunity cost argument, is viewed as running up against the incommensurability-type argument. Loss of life is one such example which has been introduced elsewhere. Goodin's argument is that such an event cannot sensibly be reduced *ex ante* to a 'money metric' and that 'non-tradables' can be sacrificed now only if the stock of the non-tradable under discussion can be raised in the future—a life for lives. A restricted form of discounting is applicable to non-tradables on this argument with its form and rate reflecting the form and rate of stock growth of the particular non-tradable. Broome (1987), in his approach to discounting in the health care context, also advocates a special form. He sug-

gests a complicated discounting mechanism, justified by reference to the 'psychological connections' between successive periods in an individual's life, and being weaker the more periods are temporally separated.

The question then of how to compare and to add costs and benefits that occur at different times raises more problems the more analysts expose the difficulties of making experiences at different times commensurable. As in most aspects of cost–benefit analysis, the fine-tuning required to do full justice to this problem is itself not without costs, and approximations are applied in the choice of the discount factor. As already noted, uncertainty about the future creates its own problems for estimating the importance of expected events, and it is to this problem that we now turn more specifically.

6.8 Risk and uncertainty

The common saying that only two things in life are certain—death and taxes—highlights both public finance and the question of risk and uncertainty. The omnipresence of risk and uncertainty raises formidable problems in life and hence in economic analysis. An old but not wholly satisfactory distinction can help in outlining the concern with respect to CBA. Risk may be seen as a situation where a probability distribution can be applied to a possible range of outcomes. Risk then rests on the notion that a probability distribution can be attached to some outcomes, and that therefore an expected outcome can be predicted in quantitative terms. In cases of uncertainty this is not possible: knowledge of the relevant probabilities is lacking even though states of nature are assumed to be known. 'True uncertainty' is surely about 'states of the world' arising that cannot be anticipated because they cannot be conceived of in the present period. Cain, the character in the television programme *Kung Fu*, was constantly exhorted to 'expect the unexpected', but, like other aspects of the programme, this does not hold up well. The ability to expect the unexpected makes the future and possible outcomes knowable (in some form) in advance, and this does not adequately capture uncertainty.

For analysis, however, we can deal only with those states of nature that can be anticipated; more formally, by weighting them it is sometimes possible to attribute to each state of nature a probability. There are many strategies that can be proposed for dealing with uncertainty where probabilities cannot be employed (e.g., see Baumol 1965). However, in this section we focus on risk and consider the requirement of talking in terms of probabilistic costs and benefits.

In response to risk, a relatively straightforward procedure is to use the 'expected' value of either the cost or the benefit that is risky, and then discount it in the normal way but at a higher rate of discount. The higher rate reflects the degree of risk aversion. (A lower certain sum may yield more utility than a higher probabilistic sum.) As an example, if a value of work-time saved in ten years' time is likely to be £50 000 or £100 000 with a 50 per cent chance of either one, and if the discount rate used in 'certain' circumstances is 10 per cent, then the procedure would be to discount the expected value at a higher rate:

(6.14)
$$PV(B) = \frac{0.5(£50\,000) + 0.5(£100\,000)}{(1 + 0.1 + r')^{10}}$$
$$= \frac{£75\,000}{(1 + 0.1 + r')^{10}}$$

where r' is an addition to the normal discount rate and varies directly with the degree of risk aversion exhibited. Whether the cost–benefit analyst in the public sector (acting on behalf of society) should follow the private individual's risk aversion is a matter for debate. If he does not, projects rejected in the private

sector will be accepted in the public sector. Arrow and Lind (1970), however, have argued that, where the numbers in the equation are large, so that the risk margins of costs or benefits are very small when associated with individuals, they can safely be treated as certain sums and therefore the additional risk discount r' is not required. One alternative and expedient way of dealing with risk is artificially to shorten the expected life-span of the project, so that risky items that would almost certainly arise in the more distant future are excluded.

There are other ways of dealing with risk and uncertainty outlined in the literature. One approach is to try to calculate the certainty equivalent of the uncertain positive net present value and then rank projects. The decision-maker is seen as trading-off uncertainty (a bad thing)—which can be represented by the variance (σ^2) of the NPV—and the size of the NPV (a good)—expressed as its expected value. Take, as given, the appropriate indifference curves depicted in Fig. 6.6 as I_0, I_1, I_2 and I_3 for a risk-averter who is prepared to accept greater risk only when the expected NPV is also increased. Projects such as A, B, C and D can be placed in the risk-expected NPV space with those on the highest indifference curve being selected first. Their certain equivalents are read off the NPV axis where the project's variance is σ^2, i.e. values A_c, B_c, C_c and D_c respectively for A, B, C and D. It is possible to have projects with negative certain equivalents, which

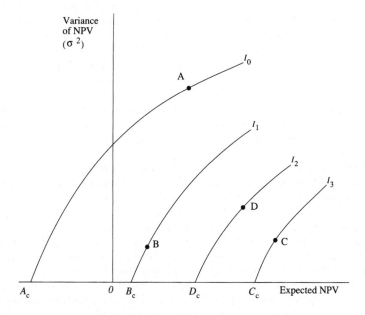

Figure 6.8 Allowing for uncertainty in project selections: the certainty equivalent approach.

clearly should be rejected. In Fig. 6.8 project A should be rejected and the remainder ranked C, D, B. Unfortunately, obtaining the appropriate indifference map is a difficult matter. A more sophisticated discussion of these issues can be found in Dorfman (1962). In the event, the cost–benefit analyst often takes the pragmatic way out, largely ignoring the issue altogether.

A dimension of uncertainty already referred to can be amplified here. In essence, uncertainty occurs because CBA is an aid to the *ex ante* decision-making process concerned with predicting effects on future costs and benefits of a programme, were it to be introduced. A proviso, then, might be added to the identification of a potential improvement. It is that *ex ante* cost–benefit calculations are expected to bear a close correspondence to the *ex post* or realized outcome. Broome (1978), as we have already noted, picks up on this point in relation to human life valuation being treated as the aggregate of the compensations required by individuals to accept an increased risk of premature death. He argues that an *ex ante* statistical death (1000 individuals facing an increase of 0.001 in risk of death) ought to be treated similarly to the *ex ante* death of a known individual. Ignorance of who is to die is a bogus way to make the evaluation mechanism 'work' since for society as a whole there is no uncertainty about the overall distribution of utilities that will arise if the project takes place. This is not to imply that no project involving a death can represent an improvement in welfare, but rather the recommended approach cannot evaluate it as such. Ulph (1982) explores this dilemma and argues that *ex post* and *ex ante* information is relevant for this evaluation.

The author constructs varying rankings of three decisions (projects) using different forms of *ex post* and *ex ante* social welfare function. The main implication is that once CBA is concerned with the distributional consequences of a project, it is no longer the case that it must be based on *ex ante* Pareto improvements alone. In such circumstances both 'before' and 'after' considerations must be incorporated in the decision—a significant departure for the conventional evaluative recipe. This issue has yet to be resolved convincingly.

In Ulph's treatment it is not uncertainty but the known extremely uneven (!) *ex post* distribution of utilities that is the ultimate concern with evaluating life *ex ante* in a probabilistic way. Other, perhaps more tractable, distribution issues are important in the next section.

6.9 Cost–benefit analysis and the potential Pareto improvement criterion

What is to be inferred from a test that looks at the net present value of a project? If, for example, the net present value were £20 000, this does not mean to say that everyone would be better off if the project were undertaken. If, however, the cost–benefit analysis is appropriately undertaken, along the lines described above, the interpretation does bear a direct relationship to the Hicks–Kaldor welfare criteria discussed in chapter 2. If the benefits of the project are estimated in terms of 'willingness to pay' for the project in hand, then they represent an estimate of how well off gainers are made by the proposed change. If the costs are measured in terms of social opportunity, then the value of the resources is that which would emerge from the next best use of the inputs. This value, correctly estimated, is a statement of how much people would pay not to have the proposed change and how much the resources involved are worth if they could be used in the next best alternative way. Thus, for example, if the present value of the benefits of the project were £220 000, this would represent how much better off gainers are by having the project, and if the present value of all the costs are £200 000, this is a statement of how much losers would be prepared to pay not to have the project.

Following Mishan's (1988) framework, and adopting the measures of consumer surplus outlined in chapter 2, we are now in a position to state formally the basic principle of CBA. As the compensating variation for gainers is the maximum sum they are prepared to pay rather than go without the project and the compensating variation of the losers is the minimum sum required for them to put up with the project, then the Hicks–Kaldor criterion is represented by the sum of the compensating variations, ΣV_i. If the NPV of the cost–benefit analysis is positive (£20 000 in the example quoted), then the algebraic sum of CVs is positive and acceptance of the project passes the Hicks/Kaldor or potential Pareto improvement test.

The problems with accepting this criterion in decision-making are twofold.

1. Following Mishan's (1988) critique, it is clear that the use of CBA is constrained to partial equilibrium analysis. It is possible to demonstrate this using the concepts outlined in chapter 2. In Fig. 6.9 the

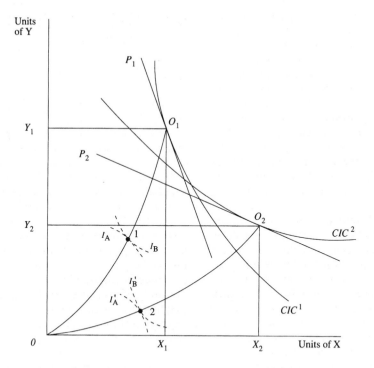

Figure 6.9 The Scitovsky paradox.

Source: Mishan (1988).

initial Edgeworth–Bowley box diagram shows a combination of OY_1 and OX_1 as outputs of two goods in the economy. A cost–benefit analyst is employed to ascertain whether a project should be undertaken. The project would shift resource use such that less of Y and more of X would be produced. There would be a move to $OY_2 - OX_2$. Initially, at O_1, the economy is on the community indifference curve CIC^1. Within the first box, the distribution of income between two representative individuals A and B is given by point 1. It is well known that the community indifference curve is sensitive to the distribution of income. When the project is accepted, there is a movement to O_2, which appears on face value to be a movement to the right of the initial community indifference curve, and therefore an increase in welfare. However, in the resource allocation change, the set of relative prices in the economy changes (see the shift in the slope of P_1 to P_2) and also the distribution of income changes. (Note the change from 1 to 2 which makes A better off and B worse off.) The change in the distribution of income means that a new set of community indifference curves becomes relevant. The shape of these is indicated in this case by CIC^2. It is clear that this

indifference curve crosses with CIC^1. The result therefore is that at O_2 it appears, by reference to the relevant community indifference curve CIC^2, that the move backward from O_2 to O_1 also passes the test of putting the community on a higher community indifference curve! In effect, the shift from O_1 to O_2 passes the Hicks–Kaldor test, but so does the shift back from O_2 to O_1 (see chapter 2). The explanation for this is that, when the project is undertaken, the change in the distribution of income brought about by a change in relative prices is sufficient to alter the initial recommendation because of the effects on the compensated variations.

It is possible to suggest a rather rough and ready example of this analysis which might help readers appreciate what is happening. Imagine there are two groups A and B. A are road-users and B are those who live along the path of a projected road. Initially the net present value of the road project is positive; A can compensate B. However, in the course of the construction of the road, B are employed and their incomes improve relative to A. After the road has been constructed, with B's higher-income levels the cost of the noise (etc.) of the road is valued higher, so that B may be in a position to compensate A (conceptually) not to have the road. The salient fact then is that cost–benefit analysis becomes more vulnerable to this problem the greater the likelihood of significant changes in the distribution of income. Cost–benefit analysis is a technique for partial analysis, not for general equilibrium analysis. It may be appropriate for a small project, e.g. considering a road improvement or the introduction of a new bypass; it is less likely to perform well for major changes, e.g. a whole restructuring of the infrastructure. This point has been well noted; see for example Barlow (1967), who raises the same reservation in the case of CBA of medical care projects.[6]

2. The potential Pareto improvement criterion does not necessarily deal adequately with the problem of interpersonal comparison of welfare. If the net present value is £20 000, then the loss to the poor (£200 000) can be covered by the gains to the rich (£220 000). However, given diminishing marginal utility of income, this need not mean that the utility gains to the rich exceed those losses of the poor. One way of dealing with this problem is to use distributional weights. These may be used to deal with the different marginal utility of income of beneficiaries of projects, or, indeed, they may go further to account for the community's social welfare evaluation of the importance of different individuals. While this may be so in theory, can such weights be estimated? Should such weights be introduced?

There are two ways in which weights can be estimated. The first relies upon the past decisions of society: weights are made explicit from the implicit weights applied by society in different decisions that are made. Secondly, weights can simply be constructed on explicit normative criteria and the decision-maker left to choose whether or not they are significant.

The first approach is perhaps most easily explained by the use of marginal rates of income tax to create distributional weights. Since progressive tax structures are employed by communities, the inference may be that society regards smaller tax payments by the poor as equivalent in sacrifice to higher tax payments by the rich (see chapter 9). The reason would be that the marginal utility of income diminishes as income increases. Assume that there are three income

Table 6.6 Marginal rates of tax and equity weights

Income range (£)	Marginal rate	Equity weight
500–1000	25	4
1000–2000	50	2
2000–3000	75	4/3

groups, as outlined in Table 6.6 (based on Dasgupta and Pearce 1972). In the income range $Y_1(£500-£1000)$ the marginal rate of tax is 25 per cent; in $Y_2(£1000-£2000)$ it is 50 per cent, and in $Y_3(£2000-£3000)$ it is 75 per cent. Using the reciprocal of the marginal rate of income tax, it is possible to construe that the equity weight to be applied to the low-income group is three times greater than that of the higher group and twice as great as that of the middle range.

Perhaps one of the best examples of this approach is the study of Weisbrod (1966). He estimated equity weights from the past decisions of policy-makers with respect to projects that had been accepted. There may arise cases where the project with the highest net present value is not accepted by decision-takers. The reason may well be that policy-makers did not like the distribution of net benefits associated with this project as much as they approved of the distribution of benefits associated with another project. The latter project must, therefore, have a weighted NPV at least equal to the unweighted NPV of the rejected project. Given this assumption, it is possible to establish explicitly the weights that must have been used implicitly in the project selection. By disaggregating the effect of the project with respect to different income groups, it is possible to estimate how much weighting occurred between different groups (when the above assumption applies). Another variant of this approach is that of Brent (1979). He was able to sift out the importance of equity weights in the decision in the UK to close certain railway lines. By assuming that the decision was a function of the costs and benefits enumerated in cost–benefit analysis, he used regression analysis to estimate the importance of these net benefits (as they applied to different groups in the economy) in determining the decision to close or retain railway lines.

The problems with this 'past decision' approach are twofold (Dasgupta and Pearce 1972). First, the implication is that the weights that finally are made explicit would perfectly and uniquely capture society's weights for different groups. With respect to marginal rates of income tax, for example, there are many other ways that society accounts for income distribution

---

[6] The upshot of this discussion is that, with the possibility of the Scitovsky paradox, CBA should be applied to relatively small projects. On 'equity' grounds, projects where the gainers are those that pay for the project, or situations where many projects will be undertaken (so there is a prospect that income effects will cancel) are those to be preferred.

differences (social security measures, for example). With the 'past decision' approach to specific project selection, it would need to be realized that the decisions were taken in the context of other existing measures that existed to deal with the income distribution (progressive tax rates, for example), not all of which may remain constant. Secondly, and perhaps more important, is the criticism that, if past decisions were accurate, why do they need to be made explicit? If policy-makers perfectly accounted for income distribution effects, why do these need to be introduced separately? If they are being made explicit in order to improve the quality of decision-making, then it is not sensible to use weights from past 'imperfect' decisions as the guide for the exercise. In effect, if past decisions are correct the exercise is not needed; if they are incorrect the exercise will be unhelpful.

The second approach does not claim to elicit the equity weights that society has used. Rather, it offers decision-makers alternative weights, which they may or may not choose to employ. Foster (1966) offered one of the most straightforward examples of this approach. Assume there are two income groups, Y_1 and Y_2. Weights may be estimated simply from the ratio of their personal income to the average national personal income. In this case, $w_1 = Y_a/Y_1$, and $w_2 = Y_a/Y_2$. McGuire and Garn (1969) show how this approach may be made more technical. Assume that it is necessary to employ weights to account for the area in which beneficiaries of projects reside. The weight for individual i could be a function of E_i (the area's employment rate for individual i) and Y_i (the individual's income). The precise functional form is, of course, important and open to question. One example may be

$$(6.15) \qquad w_i = a(E/E_i) + b(Y/Y_i)$$

where E = national average employment rate
E_i = area employment rate
Y = national median family income
Y_i = area median family income

The range of possible weights that can be derived from alternative functional forms is extensive.

While it is clear that weights can be estimated explicitly, the use of particular types of weights suggests movements from the simple potential Pareto improvement criterion. It has been argued (Nash et al. 1975) that different objective functions apply depending on whether or not weights are applied and on the nature of the weight applied. Alternatives outlined below allow for the fact that there is diminishing marginal utility of income (utilitarian) and, further, that society may have an additional reason

to prefer a particular treatment of one group of individuals that is different from that of other groups (other forms of social welfare function).

Alternative objective functions and associated CBA weights

Hicks/Kaldor: potential Pareto improvement

$$(6.16) \qquad \max \sum_{i=1}^{g} V_{gi} - \sum_{j=1}^{1} V_{1j}$$

where V_{gi} = compensating variation of the ith gainer
V_{1j} = compensating variation of the jth loser

Utilitarian

$$(6.17) \qquad \max \sum_{i=1}^{g} V_{gi} y_i - \sum_{j=1}^{1} V_{1j} y_j$$

where y_i = marginal utility of income of the ith gainer
y_j = marginal utility of income of the jth loser

Social welfare

$$(6.18) \qquad \max \sum_{i=1}^{g} V_{gi} y_i e_i - \sum_{j=1}^{1} V_{1j} y_j e_j$$

where e_i = equity weight given to the ith gainer
e_j = equity weight given to the jth loser

At minimum, the introduction of equity weights shows the policy-maker how sensitive his decision is to the ranking he gives to individuals in society.[7] It is an additional piece of information for a normative decision, which cannot be avoided. Those analysts who would apply distributional weights argue that not to do so is in fact to apply a weight of one to all involved (Pearce 1983). However, for others it is not considered appropriate to add weights. For Mishan (1988), Harberger (1978) and Musgrave (1969), there is reluctance to accept that the role of the economist is to add distributional weights. They see this role as simply advising the government on how to reach any Pareto-optimal position, and they would leave it to the government to ensure that the outcome (i.e. the choice of the project) is one that is distributionally acceptable. Indeed, for the pursuit of equity there are many different tax/subsidy arrangements that are possible, and it is by no means clear that the best way to adjust for equity is via the selection of different products. As Musgrave (1969) has pointed out, the 'excess burden' (see chapter 7) associated with this

---

[7] Peacock (1973), in an early contribution on the role of the legislature in CBA, identifies a wide area for their influence. The evaluation of externalities, the choice of 'cut-off' period for an appraisal, the choice of the social time preference rate and distributional weights are all viewed as political components in CBA.

form of adjustment may be greater than that associated with a tax arrangement. After all, not to choose the most efficient project is to incur an efficiency loss in *one* market in order to achieve equity, and this may not be the most suitable outcome.

Wagner (1983) provides an example. Chicken farmers are assumed in this example to gain from a flood control project in such a way that 800 chickens are saved. If the distributional weights and the income of chicken farmers make this less attractive than a project that leads to an increase of 100 chickens for the poorer farmers, then the cost of equity weights in efficiency terms can be seen to be large. If the choice was reversed, so that 800 wealthy farmers' chickens were saved, 100 could be given to the poorer farmers to make them no worse off and there would be 700 left to make other individuals better off. The dilemma Wagner alludes to is whether this compensation and possible redistribution would take place. In the absence of actual Pareto improvements guiding policy, society may prefer to temper the recommendations of potential Pareto improvements with equity weights.

6.10 Summary

The principles of welfare economics, previously discussed in a theoretical context, are applied directly when undertaking a cost–benefit analysis. It is clear that a 'serious' cost–benefit analysis requires more than a nodding acquaintance with concepts such as consumer surplus, externalities, the theory of second best, public goods and the Hicks/Kaldor welfare criteria. The theoretical discussion to be found in welfare economics in this way should provide guidance as to:

1. What is to be included in a cost–benefit analysis?
2. How is it to be evaluated?
3. At what rate future costs and benefits are to be discounted?

Choosing costs and benefits requires far more than an ability simply to look for the most 'convenient' or most apparent monetary estimate that may be available. A cost–benefit analyst should be in a position to justify the choice of values and the selection of effects that are compared in any cost–benefit analysis. Welfare economics is directly applied in cost–benefit analyses (for example see Drummond 1981). However, while cost–benefit analysis may inform policymakers, rent-seeking may motivate decisions (see section 5.2 and also Jones and Cullis 1996).

References

Arrow, K. J. (1963) *Social Choice and Individual Values*. New York: John Wiley.

Arrow, K. J. and Lind, R. C. (1970) 'Uncertainty and the Evaluation of Public Investment Decisions', *American Economic Review*, 60, 3, pp. 364–78.

Barlow, R. (1967) 'The Economic Effects of Malaria Eradication', *American Economic Review*, 57, 2, pp. 130–47.

Baumol, W. J. (1965) *Economic Theory and Operations Analysis*, 2nd edn. Englewood Cliffs: Prentice-Hall.

Baumol, W. J. (1971) 'On the Discount Rate for Public Projects', pp. 273–90 in R. H. Haveman and J. Margolis (eds.), *Public Expenditure and Policy Analysis*. Chicago: Markham.

Blaug, M. (1965) 'The Rate of Return on Investment in Education in Great Britain', *The Manchester School*, 33, 3, pp. 205–51.

Brent, R. J. (1979) 'Imputing Weights behind Past Government Expenditure within a Cost–Benefit Framework', *Applied Economics*, 11, 2, pp. 157–70.

Brent, R. J. (1991) 'A New Approach to Valuing a Life', *Journal of Public Economics*, 44, 2, pp. 165–73.

Broome, J. (1978) 'Trying to Value a Life', *Journal of Public Economics*, 9, 1, pp. 91–100.

Broome, J. (1987) 'Good, Fairness and QALYs', in M. Bell and S. Medus (eds.), *The Proceedings of the Royal Institute of Philosophy and Medical Welfare*. Cambridge: Cambridge University Press.

Carr, J. L. (1969) *Investment Economics*. London: Routledge & Kegan Paul.

Cullis, J. G. and Jones, P. R. (1996) ' "What a Difference a Day Makes", Concern about a New Approach to Valuing a Life', *Journal of Public Economics*, 61, 3, pp. 455–7.

Clawson, M. (1959) 'Method of Measuring the Demand for and Value of Outdoor Recreation', in *Resources for the Future*. Washington: Brookings Institution.

Dasgupta, A. K. and Pearce, D. W. (1972) *Cost–Benefit Analysis Theory and Practice*. London: Macmillan.

Dawson, R. F. F. (1967) *Cost of Road Accidents in Great Britain*. London: Road Research Laboratory, Ministry of Transport.

Dorfman, R. (1962) 'Basic Economic and Technological Concepts: a General Statement', pp. 129–58 in A. Maass *et al.*, *Design of Water Resource Systems*. Cambridge, Mass.: Harvard University Press.

Downs, A. (1957) *An Economic Theory of Democracy*. New York: Harper & Row.

Drummond, M. (1981) 'Welfare Economics and CBA in Health Care', *Scottish Journal of Political Economy*, 28, 2, pp. 125–45.

Drummond, M. F. (1991) 'Output Measurement for Resource Allocation Decisions in Health Care', pp. 99–

119 in A. McGuire, P. Fenn and K. Mayhew (eds.), *Providing Health Care: The Economics of Alternative Systems of Finance and Delivery*. Oxford: Oxford University Press.

Feldstein, M. S. (1964) 'The Social Time Preference Discount Rate in Cost Benefit Analysis', *Economic Journal*, 74, 174, pp. 360–79.

Feldstein, M. S. (1972) 'The Inadequacy of Weighted Discount Rates', pp. 245–69, in R. Layard (ed.), *Cost–Benefit Analysis*. Harmondsworth: Penguin.

Foster, C. D. (1966) 'Social Welfare Functions in Cost Benefit Analysis', in M. Lawrence (ed.), *Operational Research in the Social Sciences*. London: Tavistock.

Foster, C. D. and Beesley, M. E. (1963) 'Estimating the Social Benefits of Constructing an Underground Railway in London', *Journal of the Royal Statistical Society* A, 126, pp. 46–58.

Ghosh, D., Lees, D. and Seal, W. (1975) 'Optimal Motorway Speed and Some Valuations of Time and Life', *Manchester School*, 43, 2, pp. 134–43.

Goodin, R. E. (1982) 'Discounting Discounting', *Journal of Public Policy*, 2, 1, pp. 53–72.

Harberger, A. C. (1978) 'On the Use of Distributional Weights in Social Cost Benefit Analysis', *Journal of Political Economy*, 86, 2, pp. 87–120.

Haveman, R. H. and Krutilla, J. V. (1968) 'Unemployment, Idle Capacity and the Evaluation of Public Expenditure', *Resources for the Future*. Washington: Brookings Institution.

Henderson, P. D. (1968) 'Investment Criteria for Public Enterprises', in R. Turvey (ed.), *Public Enterprise*. Harmondsworth: Penguin.

Irwin, G. (1978) *Modern Cost Benefit Methods*. London: Macmillan.

Jones, P. R. and Cullis, J. G. (1996) 'Legitimate and Illegitimate Transfers: Dealing with "Political" Cost Benefit Analysis' *International Review of Law and Economics*, 16, 2, pp. 247–57.

Jones-Lee, M. (1974) 'The Value of Changes in the Probability of Death or Injury', *Journal of Political Economy*, 84, 4, pp. 835–49.

Jones-Lee, M. (1976) *The Value of Human Life: An Economic Analysis*. Oxford: Martin-Robertson.

Jones-Lee, M. (1977) 'An Empirical Procedure for Estimating the Value of Life from Tyre Replacement Data', paper presented to the Health Economics Study Group, Newcastle.

Kahneman, D. and Tverskey, A. (1979) 'Prospect Theory: An Analysis of Decision Under Risk,' *Econometrica*, 47, 2, pp. 263–91.

Klarman, H. E. (1965) 'Syphilis Control Programs', pp. 367–417 in R. Dorfman (ed.), *Measuring Benefits of Government Investments*. Washington: Brookings Institution.

Krutilla, J. V. (1961) 'Welfare Aspects of Benefit–Cost Analysis', *Journal of Political Economy*, 69, 3, pp. 226–35.

Layard, R. (1972) *Cost Benefit Analysis*. Harmondsworth: Penguin.

Leff, N. H. (1988) 'Policy Research for Improved Organizational Performance: A Case from the World Bank', *Journal of Economic Behavior and Organization*, 9, pp. 393–403.

Little, I. M. D. (1957) *A Critique of Welfare Economics*, 2nd edn. Oxford: Oxford University Press.

Marglin, S. A. (1963a) 'The Social Rate of Discount and the Optimum Rate of Investment', *Quarterly Journal of Economics*, 77, 1, pp. 95–111.

Marglin, S. A. (1963b) 'The Opportunity Costs of Public Investment', *Quarterly Journal of Economics*, 77, 2, pp. 274–89.

Marglin, S. A. (1967) *Public Investment Criteria*. London: Allen & Unwin.

McGuire, A. Henderson, J. and Mooney, G. (1988) *The Economics of Health Care: An Introductory Text*. London and New York: Routledge & Kegan Paul.

McGuire, M. and Garn, H. (1969) 'The Integration of Equity and Efficiency Criteria in Public Sector Project Selection', *Economic Journal*, 79, 129, pp. 882–93.

Mishan, E. J. (1967) 'Criteria for Public Investment: Some Simplifying Suggestions', *Journal of Political Economy*, 75, 1, pp. 139–46.

Mishan, E. J. (1971) 'Evaluation of Life and Limb: A Theoretical Approach', *Journal of Political Economy*, 79, 4, pp. 687–705.

Mishan, E. J. (1972) *Elements of Cost Benefit Analysis*. London: Allen & Unwin.

Mishan, E. J. (1988) *Cost Benefit Analysis*. London: Unwin Hyman.

Musgrave, R. A. (1969) 'Cost Benefit Analysis and the Theory of Public Finance', *Journal of Economic Literature*, 7, 3, pp. 797–806.

Mooney, G. and Olsen, J. A. (1991) 'QALYs: Where Next?', pp. 120–40 in A. McGuire, P. Fenn and K. Mayhew (eds.), *Providing Health Care: The Economics of Alternative Systems of Finance and Delivery*, Oxford: Oxford University Press.

Mooney, G. (1992) *Economics, Medicine and Health Care*, 2nd edn. Hemel Hempstead: Harvester Wheatsheaf.

Musgrave, R. A. and Musgrave, P. B. (1989) *Public Finance in Theory and Practice*, 5th edn. New York: McGraw-Hill.

Nash, C. A., Pearce, D. W. and Stanley, J. (1975) 'An Evaluation of Cost Benefit Analysis Criteria', *Scottish Journal of Political Economy*, 22, 2, pp. 121–34.

Olson, M. (1973) 'Evaluating Performance in the Public Sector', pp. 355–384 in Milton Moss (ed.), *The Measurement of Economic and Social Performance*. National Bureau of Economic Research, New York: Columbia University Press.

Overseas Development Administration (1988) *Appraisal of Projects in Developing Countries*, 3rd edn. London: HMSO.

Peacock, A. T. (1973) 'Cost–Benefit Analysis and the Political Control of Public Investment', pp. 17–29 in J. N. Wolfe, *Cost Benefit and Cost Effectiveness*. London: Allen & Unwin.

Pearce, D. W. (1983) *Cost Benefit Analysis*, 2nd edn. London: Macmillan.

Pearce, D. W. and Nash, C. A. (1981) *The Social Appraisal of Projects: A Text in Cost Benefit Analysis*. London: Macmillan.

Pigou, A. (1932) *The Economics of Welfare*, 4th edn. London: Macmillan.

Prest, A. and Turvey, R. (1965) 'Cost Benefit Analysis: A Survey', pp. 155–207 in American Economic Association and Royal Economic Society, *Surveys of Economic Theory*. London: Macmillan.

Reynolds, D. J. (1956) 'The Cost of Road Accidents', *Journal of the Royal Statistical Society* A, **119**, 4, pp. 393–408.

Robinson, M. A. (1996) 'A Picture of Health?', *New Economy*, **3**, 1, pp. 20–4.

Sackett, D. L. and Torrance, G. W. (1978) 'The Utility of Different Health States as Perceived by the General Public', *Journal of Chronic Disease*, **31**, pp. 697–704.

Sugden, R. and Williams, A. (1978) *The Principles of Practical Cost Benefit Analysis*. Oxford: Oxford University Press.

Thompson, M.S. (1986) 'Willingness to Pay and Accept Risks to Cure Chronic Disease', *American Journal of Public Health*, **76**, pp. 392–6.

Torrance, G.W. (1976) 'Social Preferences for health states and empirical evaluation of three measurement techniques', *Socio-Economic Planning Science*, **10**, pp. 129–36.

Tullock, G. (1964) 'The Social Rate of Discount and the Optimal Rate of Investment: Comment', *Quarterly Journal of Economics*, **78**, 2, pp. 331–6.

Ulph, A. (1982) 'The Role of *Ex ante* and *Ex post* Decisions in the Valuation of Life', *Journal of Public Economics*, **18**, 2, pp. 265–76.

Wagner, R. E. (1983) *Public Finance: Revenues and Expenditures in a Democratic Society*. Boston: Little, Brown.

Wagstaff, A. (1991) 'Qalys and the Equity Efficiency Trade-off', *Journal of Health Economics*, **10**, 1 pp. 21–41.

Webb, M. G. (1973) *The Economics of Nationalised Industries: A Theoretical Approach*. London: Nelson.

Weisbrod, B. (1966) 'Income Redistribution Effects and Benefit–Cost Analysis', pp. 177–222 in S. Chase (ed.), *Problems in Public Expenditure Analysis*. Washington: Brookings Institution.

Williams, A. (1981), 'Welfare Economics and Health Status Measurement', pp. 271–81 in J. van der Gaag and M. Perlman (eds.), *Health, Economics and Health Economics*. Amsterdam: North Holland.

7 Tax theory: the basic concepts

7.1 Introduction

Many questions relating to taxation are all too often answered at what might easily be regarded as 'face value'. If we ask, 'What is the cost of taxation?' it would not be surprising if the reply were set in terms of the tax revenue that the government raised. In everyday discussion individuals tend to work on the assumption that the costs of taxation to them are the sums of money that they pay to the Inland Revenue. The 'burden of taxation' is seen purely in terms of the amount of money that is transferred to the government purse. If we ask, 'Who pays a particular tax?' the reply is often set in terms of the individual who actually makes the tax payment to the government. The incidence of taxation is seen to fall on the person legally responsible for meeting the tax bill. Only rarely will there emerge any discussion relating to the 'shifting' of taxation or to the 'distortive' costs of taxation. In debates found in the media and in the political arena, contributors organize their discussion as if their answers to the above questions were both self-evident and apparent. In point of fact, often they are neither.

In this chapter the objective is to investigate these key questions more fully. Both 'social optimizing' public finance theory and public choice analysis utilize concepts outlined in earlier chapters in order to address these kinds of questions. They are obviously essential questions in the context of broader fiscal issues, such as the 'optimum' size of the public sector and the redistributive effects of fiscal policy.

To facilitate an analysis of these questions, it is again helpful to utilize the basic principles of welfare economics. It can be argued, for example, that the cost of a pound (dollar) raised in taxation may exceed one pound (dollar). Moreover, the incidence of taxation may not be at the point of payment of taxation. We intend to highlight the many assumptions that are necessary to provide an answer to the question, 'Who pays a particular tax?' One way to approach this question is by reference to the structure of the neoclassical general equilibrium model—if only to highlight the difficulties of dealing with the above 'self-evident' and 'obvious' questions.

7.2 The excess burden of taxation: partial equilibrium analysis

The 'excess burden' of taxation (or deadweght loss) from a tax has been defined as 'that amount that is lost in excess of what the government collects' (Auerbach 1985, p. 67). In this section concern focuses only on the welfare implications associated with making a tax payment (that is to say that, at this stage there is no discussion of how the revenue raised by the tax collector is spent). It will be shown that while a taxpayer experiences a welfare loss when making a tax payment, this loss usually exceeds the value of the tax payment and it is in this way that there is an 'excess burden'.

To demonstrate the excess burden it is first necessary to estimate the welfare loss experienced as a consequence of paying a tax. In most cases the introduction of a tax (or of a change in the rate of tax) causes relative prices to change. Changes in welfare caused by price changes were discussed in chapter 2. Consumer surplus was used to estimate the impact on welfare of a price change and in chapter 2 the example discussed was the case of a price fall. By contrast, in this section a tax causes an increase in the price of a particular good, good X. Attention focuses on the loss of welfare (as measured by the change in consumer surplus) that is created by the price increase.

In chapter 2 different measures of consumer surplus were described. In this section, to begin, it is helpful to focus on one measure, i.e. *equivalent variation*. When considering the introduction of a tax (and the effect of a price rise), this can be defined as the amount of income which can be taken away from the individual *in the absence* of the introduction of the tax to leave the individual *as well off as if* the tax had

been introduced. It will be shown that the value of the tax payment that an individual makes is usually less than the *equivalent variation* associated with the imposition of a tax. The difference is then referred to as the 'excess burden' (or deadweight loss) of taxation.

In the following example a selective excise tax (of rate t) is levied on the consumption of one particular good X. In Fig. 7.1(a) an individual has a fixed budget

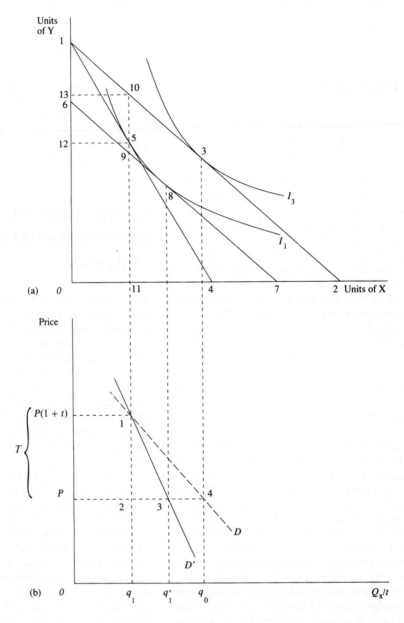

Figure 7.1 The welfare costs of a selective excise tax.

which is allocated between goods X and Y. The initial budget line is 12 and the slope of the budget line reflects the relative price of the two goods $-Px/Py$. Before taxation the individual chooses a combination of the two goods shown by tangency point 3 so as to maximize welfare (i.e. by reaching indifference curve I_3). At this tangency point the individual equates the slope of the indifference curve, i.e. the marginal rate of substitution $(-MU_x/MU_y)$ with the slope of the budget line $(-P_x/P_y)$. As $-MU_x/MU_y$ is equal to $-P_x/P_y$, utility is maximized for the marginal utility per pound spent on good $X(MU_x/P_x)$ is equal to the marginal utility per pound spent on $Y(MU_y/P_y)$.

When the excise tax is introduced on good X (at a rate t), the relative price of X rises and the budget line swivels from 12 to 14. The individual's welfare is reduced to I_1 and the new equilibrium is at tangency point 5. The more of good X the individual purchases the greater the tax that is paid. For example, if the individual were to allocate all income to good X tax revenue, equal to 42 (in units of X), would be paid to the government in taxation. The price of X has now increased to the consumer, for $O4$ units of good X costs $O1$ units of Y (whereas, prior to the tax, $O2$ units of good X cost 01 units of good Y). At tangency point 5 in Fig. 7.1(a) the individual now equates the ratio $-MU_x/MU_y$ (the slope of the indifference curve I_1) with the ratio $-P_x(1 + t)/P_y$ (the slope of 14).

The *equivalent variation* of the tax change can be estimated by shifting the budget line 12 backwards in a parallel fashion to 67 until a new tangency point, i.e. 8 is located on indifference curve I_1. The sum $16(= 10 - 9)$ is the amount that can be taken from the individual *in the absence* of a change (i.e. the imposition of the selective excise tax) to leave the individual with exactly the same welfare *as if* the change in question had taken place. From Fig. 7.1(a) at tangency point 5, if the individual chooses $O–11$ units of good X it will cost $1–12$ units of Y after the tax is imposed. Before the tax was imposed these same units $O–11$ of good X would cost only distance $1–13$ units of Y. It follows that the tax raised is equal to distance $13–12$ (which is equal to $10–5$) in units of Y.

In Fig. 7.1(a) if distance 16 units of Y were taken from the individual it would leave the individual with exactly the same welfare *as if* the selective excise tax had been imposed. This distance 16 units of Y is, of course, the same as distance $10–9$. However, the tax raised is only $10–5$ units of Y and, by comparison with the equivalent variation of the price change, there is an 'excess burden' equal to 59 (i.e. $10–9$ minus $10–5$). This excess burden measured in units of Y is the loss of welfare $(10–9)$ from the price change in excess of

the tax payment $(10–5)$. This loss, 59, is a 'deadweight loss'. The tax paid by the taxpayer is collected by the tax collector and, therefore, is a transfer. However, the additional loss (the excess burden) is an outright loss to the community (i.e. a deadweight loss).[1]

It is important to note in Fig. 7.1(a) that the excess burden depends on the 'substitution effect' of the price change brought about by the tax. For this reason a 'compensated' response (i.e. the movement around the same indifference curve) is the important consideration when discussing excess burden. In Fig. 7.1(a) comparing point 5 with point 8 the marginal rate of substitution has changed (whereas, comparing 3 and 8, the marginal rate of substitution is the same). A distortion of choices affects excess burden. The extent of the loss depends on the extent of this substitution effect created by the change of relative prices.

In order to estimate the welfare loss it is necessary to consider the 'compensated' demand curve. In Fig. 7.1(b) the dashed line D represents the (uncompensated) demand curve of the individual (this is the Marshallian demand curve explained in chapter 2), and D' represents the income-compensated demand curve. The income-compensated demand curve shows how much individuals would demand of the good at the same real income. With reference to Fig. 7.1(a) it shows the substitution effect associated with a price change. A Marshallian demand curve shows the change in quantity demanded when the price

---

[1] Another way in which economists have sought to estimate the 'excess burden' of a tax is to compare the costs associated with that tax with the costs associated with a tax that might perform efficiently (e.g. Musgrave 1959; Allan 1971). Now the approach is to ask the question whether or not it is possible for a government to raise revenue in a less costly fashion. Suppose, that a 'lump–sum tax' were levied, i.e. a tax that required a particular amount to be paid by the taxpayer irrespective of the individual's behaviour. The impact of a lump–sum tax can be illustrated by asking: 'how large must the lump–sum tax be to raise the same tax revenue as raised in the case of the selective excise tax?' In this case, in Fig. 7.1n, the lump–sum tax shifts the budget line in a parallel fashion to the left until it reaches point 6. By reaching point 6 it is clear that tax revenue 16 is identical to that raised by the selective excise tax and the consumer is left able to purchase the same bundle of goods at point 5. However, it is clear in Figure 7.1n that the individual would be better off, as it is possible to choose a tangency between a budget line through 6 and a higher indifference curve at point 8. It therefore follows that the selective excise tax created an 'excess burden' in raising the same revenue. An excess burden that in utility terms is measured by the difference between being on I_2 as opposed to I_1

By reference to any standard microeconomics text (e.g. Henderson and Quandt 1971), students will recognize that in this approach, where the individual is left able to consume the same bundle of goods, there is a 'Slutsky' income adjustment, whereas in the previous analysis, when we shift the budget line so as to raise that tax which would leave the individual on the same welfare level, we are estimating a 'Hicks–Allen' income effect.

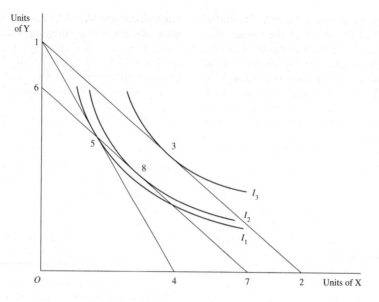

Figure 7.1n Selective excise tax versus lump sum tax.

changes holding money income constant. A compensated demand curve shows the change in quantity demanded holding real income constant, i.e. it shows changes on the same indifference curve.

The excise tax raises the price of good X from P to $P(1 + t)$. In the absence of this tax, the amount of money which it would be possible to take away from the individual to make the individual as well off *as if* the tax were levied (i.e. the equivalent variation) is the area $P(1 + t)13P$. This is a measure of the welfare loss (the consumer surplus loss) that the individual experiences from the imposition of the tax. When the tax is levied the individual purchases Oq_1 and, therefore, pays in taxation an amount equal to the difference between P and $P(1 + t)$ on each unit to the government. In Fig. 7.1(b) $P(1 + t)12P$ is an estimate of the total tax paid. It follows that the tax payment is less than the loss of consumer surplus from taxation $P(1 + t)13P$ (this sum $P(1 + t)13P$ being the amount that could be taken away from the individual in the absence of the price rise to leave the individual as well off as if the price had risen). The difference between the tax cost and the total loss of consumer surplus is the 'excess burden' of the tax, i.e. triangle 123 is a loss over and above the tax payment (hence the term 'excess burden'). The amount $P(1 + t)12P$ is a transfer; the individual loses this but the government receives the revenue. The triangle 123 is not a transfer, it is a 'deadweight loss' (in that there is no offsetting gain elsewhere).

To estimate excess burden (or deadweight loss) it is necessary to estimate the area of triangle 123. The area of any triangle is half the product of the base and the height of the triangle. In this case the area of the triangle is $1/2(dp.dq)$ where dp is the change in price created by the tax (i.e. the difference between $P(1 + t)$ and P) and dq is the difference between q'_1 and q_1. If the income effect is negligible, because the change in price (tax increase) is small, the Marshallian demand curve approximates the linear compensated demand curve. The perceived change in quantity, $q_0 - q_1$ is very similar to $q'_1 - q_1$.

The difference between $P(1 + t)$ and P is tP (which is the the tax paid per unit of the good). In Fig. 7.1(b) area 123 is therefore equal to $1/2tP \, dQ$. If the tax rate and price is known and also the change in demand dQ which will be created by the tax is known then it is a simple matter to estimate the excess burden. Of course, estimates may be required *ex ante*, i.e. before the tax has been imposed. Estimates may be required at the point at which policy is determined. The problem is then to estimate dQ (and ideally this should be estimated with reference to the income-compensated demand curve). The estimate of the change in quantity will depend on the price elasticity of demand. As $e_d = dQ/dP.P/Q$ it follows that:

$$(7.1) \qquad dQ = \frac{e_d \, dP \, Q}{P}$$

and (as $tP = dP$) excess burden (EB) can be estimated as:

$$(7.2) \qquad EB = 1/2\,tP \cdot \frac{(e_d tP\ Q)}{P}$$

or

$$EB = 1/2 e_d t^2 PQ$$

so that excess burden is determined in part by the elasticity of the compensated demand with respect to price.

7.2.1 Compensated demand: must the tax alter demand to create excess burden?

At this stage it is worth emphasizing again that the analysis throughout this section is in terms of the compensated demand curve. This is important because it is not unknown for the impression to be created that, if a tax has no obvious effect on the

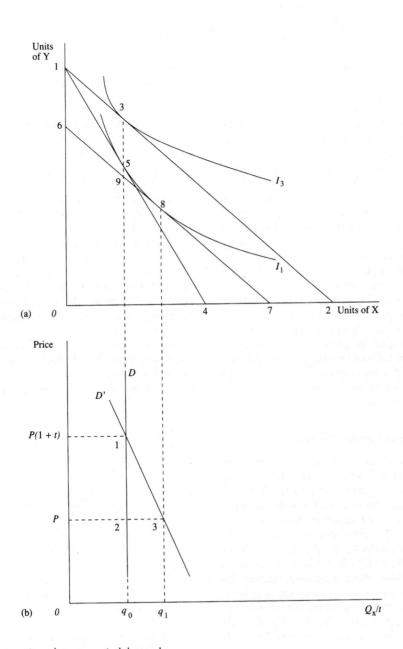

Figure 7.2 Welfare costs and compensated demand.

behaviour of individuals, then there is no excess burden. In Fig. 7.2 we repeat the above analysis for a very specific example (i.e. where there are no obvious effects in demand for the good after the tax has been levied). After the tax has been levied the price to the individual will rise to $P(1 + t)$ but Oq_0 of the good is still consumed. If the tax does not affect quantity demanded can there be an excess demand?

The Marshallian demand curve in Fig. 7.2(b) is a vertical line. It appears that the tax does not distort behaviour and, therefore, will have no efficiency loss. With respect to the Marshallian demand curve (D) there is no welfare loss triangle. However, it is evident from the compensated demand curve (D') that there is still a welfare loss equal to the area of triangle 123.

By reference to Fig. 7.1(a) it is clear that there is still an excess burden. The substitution effect is seen again to be 58 and the excess burden is 59 (estimated in terms of good Y). As such, the appropriate estimate in Fig. 7.1(b) is triangle 123. The difference in this, admittedly unusual circumstance, is that the income effect of the price change leads to less of good X being consumed. Good X is inferior and, in this circumstance, the income effect offsets the substitution effect exactly, leading to the result that no more of the good is demanded after the selective excise tax is imposed (see, for example, Rosen 1988).

Later in this chapter we will have something to say with respect to the welfare costs of an income tax. The reader should note that again the estimate of such losses is with respect to the compensated supply curve of labour. It will not be true to argue that there is no welfare loss if workers do not alter the hours that they work. Once again reference has to be made to the compensated supply curve.

7.2.2 Measures of excess burden

While the analysis of the previous section focused on estimates of *equivalent variation*, it is not the only basis for measuring excess burden. Auerbach (1985) notes alternatives. For example, while Mohring (1971) uses *equivalent variation* as the basis for estimating welfare loss, Diamond and McFadden (1974) use *compensating variation*. The distinction depends on the initial welfare of the individual. In the case of equivalent variation the measure of welfare loss associated with a tax-induced price increase is the amount of money that could be taken from the individual at the existing set of prices to make the individual *as well off as if* the tax had been introduced. The reference point is the level of real income when the tax

is operative. In Fig. 7.3 this sum is shown as area $P(1 + t)12P$.

If instead of using the real income after the tax increase as the reference point, real income prior to the tax increase were used, then the estimate of the change in the welfare effect of a tax will alter. In this case it is possible to ask what is the maximum sum that would compensate an individual when there is a tax so as to return the individual to the welfare level prior to the tax (i.e. how much would be required to make the individual as well off as in the case prior to taxation). As Auerbach (1985, p. 70) puts it, 'how much must come from "outside" the system to compensate for the tax distortion'. This estimate of welfare would be the *compensating variation* estimate of consumer surplus. In Fig. 7.3 this is estimated by the area $P(1 + t)34P$. It is greater than the measure based on equivalent variation because it is associated with a higher level of real income. It is, of course, income (or welfare) effects that mean that estimates associated with the equivalent variation or with the compensating variation differ from estimates based on the Marshallian (uncompensated) demand curve (i.e. $P(1 + t)14P$ in Fig. 7.3).

Comparing the analysis here with the discussion of welfare changes in chapter 2, it will be clear that the compensating variation for a price decrease is the equivalent variation for a price increase and the equivalent variation for a price decrease is the compensating variation for a price increase (see Blaug 1970; Winch 1971).

For the remaining sections of the chapter the equivalent variation of excess burden will generally be used. However, it is important to emphasize that this is not the only conceivable measure. Also, note at

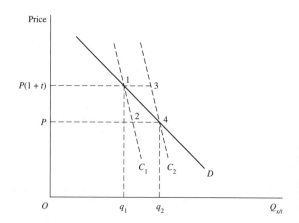

Figure 7.3 Measures of excess burden.

this stage that excess burden has been estimated for a tax payment without any consideration of the welfare effect of government expenditure that this will finance. It should be clear that the estimate of excess burden is premised on the value of real income of the citizen that is used as a reference point (i.e. that real income level after the tax has been introduced as compared to that real income prior to the tax being introduced). This distinction raises some important public choice considerations regarding the responsibility of the citizen within the community. Is the tax part of the real income of the individual or is the relevant real income of the individual that which exists after discharging the responsibility of paying the tax to the community?

7.2.3 Welfare costs with increasing marginal costs

Readers will inevitably be concerned that the analysis we have been using is one in which there are constant costs of production. The marginal costs of the good have been assumed constant and this is a simplification. In the more general case the supply curve may be upward-sloping rather than horizontal. This case is shown in Fig. 7.4, where, following Hyman (1987), it is assumed that a per-unit tax is levied on good

X. The before-tax price is P_0, and with the advent of a per-unit tax the supply curve S shifts to the left, i.e. to S_t. The producer must increase her price in order to pay the tax. In Fig. 7.4, the price that the consumer (demander) pays is P_d and the price that the producer (supplier) receives is P_s. The difference between P_d and P_s is the tax T that is paid per unit on the good. With the tax, the consumer price increases from P_0 to P_d (such an increase is referred to below as dP_d) and the price the producer receives falls to P_s (i.e. by dP_s). This indicates that now the tax is borne by producers and consumers (see section 7.6.1). Before deriving the general formulae for deadweight loss of an excise tax, it is important to be clear about the formulae for price elasticity of demand e_d and price elasticity of supply e_s. These elasticities are, respectively,

$$(7.3) \qquad e_d = \frac{dq/q_0}{dP_d/P_0} \quad \text{and} \quad e_s = \frac{dq/q_0}{dP_s/P_0}$$

so that they may be rewritten as

$$(7.4) \qquad \begin{aligned} e_d &= (dq/q_0)[P_0/(P_d - P_0)] \\ e_s &= (dq/q_0)[P_0/(P_s - P_0)] \end{aligned}$$

As such, the consumer price P_d and the producer price P_s are defined as

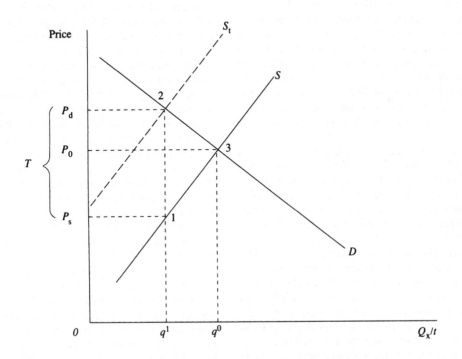

Figure 7.4 Deadweight loss of taxation.

(7.5) $\qquad P_\mathrm{d} = \dfrac{dqP_0}{q_0 e_\mathrm{d}} + P_0 \quad P_\mathrm{s} = \dfrac{dqP_0}{q_0 e_\mathrm{s}} + P_0$

It is clear from Fig. 7.3 that

(7.6) $\qquad\qquad T = P_\mathrm{d} - P_\mathrm{s}$

By substitution,

(7.7) $\qquad T = \left(\dfrac{dqP_0}{q_0}\right)\left(\dfrac{e_\mathrm{s} - e_\mathrm{d}}{e_\mathrm{s} e_\mathrm{d}}\right)$

(7.8) $\qquad dq = T\left(\dfrac{q_0}{P_0}\right)\left(\dfrac{e_\mathrm{s} e_\mathrm{d}}{e_\mathrm{s} - e_\mathrm{d}}\right)$

so that the welfare costs of the tax are

(7.9) $\qquad W = \tfrac{1}{2} T^2 \left(\dfrac{q_0}{P_0}\right)\left(\dfrac{e_\mathrm{s} e_\mathrm{d}}{e_\mathrm{s} - e_\mathrm{d}}\right)$

Noting once again that $T = tP$, if it is necessary to estimate the welfare costs for an *ad valorem* excise tax, this formula can be written as

(7.10) $\qquad W = \tfrac{1}{2} t^2 (P_0 q_0)\left(\dfrac{e_\mathrm{s} e_\mathrm{d}}{e_\mathrm{s} - e_\mathrm{d}}\right)$

This measure provides a more general estimate of the excess burden of taxation. However, it by no means deals with all problems. For example, when a tax is imposed in one market it will have 'knock-on' effects in other markets. Suppose that a selective excise tax is imposed on good X and that good Z is a close substitute. A selective excise tax is already imposed on good Z. When the excise tax is imposed on X, demand for X will fall. As a result of the price increase for X, demand for Z will increase. Because there was originally an excise tax on Z, the excise tax on X now helps improve the allocation of resources, and indeed it reduces the existing excess burden evident in the market for Z. (See chapter 1 and especially section 1.10 on second best.) The estimate for the excess burden that arises when an excise tax is imposed on X is now equal to the excess burden in the X market less the reduction in excess burden in the Z market. (For a precise formulation of the net effect see section 7.5.)

In raising this issue we underline our original observation that the burden of taxation is by no means easy to assess, and this should be kept in mind when considering the redistributive effects of taxation in chapter 9. Also, we have noted the problems of partial equilibrium analysis and the desirability of considering general equilibrium considerations. A general equilibrium analysis of excess burden is discussed next.

7.3 The welfare costs of taxation: general equilibrium analysis

The above analysis was used to suggest that a selective excise tax will be more distortive than an equal-yield income tax. The argument relies on a specific interpretation of Fig. 7.1(a). With goods X and Y on the axes, it appeared that the excise tax would distort relative prices (change the slope of the budget line), whereas a lump sum tax would not distort prices. If an income tax were applied, it might be thought that the budget line would simply be moved inwards in a parallel fashion. (There would be no distortion of relative prices.) This prediction suggests that the income tax (which now appears to act as a lump sum tax) is superior to an excise tax. However, the argument is by no means robust. In particular, such an argument is not satisfactory because the income tax introduces a distortion in the choice between work and leisure. The argument is not necessarily acceptable also because there may be other second-best constraints which apply in other markets. In order to illustrate the significance of these arguments, we use a general equilibrium analysis of the resource allocation costs of taxation. The analysis is set up to deal with the question, Will a selective excise tax create greater resource allocation costs (deadweight losses) than an equal-yield income tax?

The excess burden of taxation can be seen in the context of a simple general equilibrium framework by reference to Fig. 7.5. By definition, the objective here is to consider more than one market. For purposes of exposition, we consider an economy that produces two goods X and Y. In part (a) of the figure, the production possibility frontier (or transformation curve) for the economy is shown as PF. This is a frontier which, as explained in chapter 1, bounds the alternative combinations of the two goods (X and Y) that can be produced in the economy. If the economy is X-efficient it must be producing on the frontier, and for Pareto optimality the best output level for the two goods is shown to be 1. This is a combination of the amounts of the two goods produced at which the marginal rate of transformation (MRT_xy) is equal to the marginal rate of substitution (MRS_xy); that is to say, the slope of the production possibility curve is equal to the slope of the community indifference curve (CIC_3). If markets are perfectly competitive (and there are no elements of market failure, e.g. externalities), 1 may be taken to be the position that

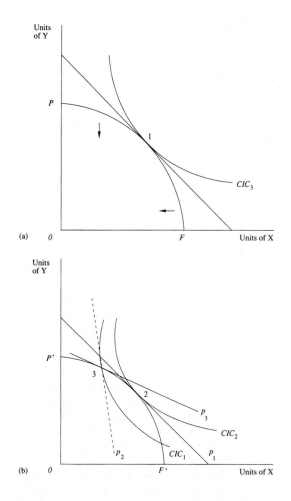

Figure 7.5 The welfare costs of taxation: a general equilibrium analysis.

would emerge in the economy before the introduction of taxation.

Now taxation is necessary to provide government finance. Here we do not discuss how this government revenue is spent. We simply deal with the question of whether, if revenue must be raised, the selective excise tax will create greater resource allocation costs than an equal-yield income tax. Following Allan (1971) and Boadway and Wildasin (1984), in Fig. 7.5 it is assumed that resources are taken from the private sector and that the transformation curve $P'F'$ is, therefore, closer to the origin. (The arrows in part (a) of the figure denote that the production possibility curve for the two goods is moved inwards as resources are taken from the private sector. $P'F'$ shows the available resources, after taxation, for the provision of private

goods. Along $P'F'$ the same distance separates points on this frontier from comparable points on PF. Of course, the alternative exposition would be to assume that the revenue was returned to individuals in a lump sum and that the original production possibility curve was the relevant constraint. We assume, however, that resources have simply been removed by taxation and that both the income tax and the selective excise tax create the same resource loss.) The question now is whether it will matter (in terms of excess burden) which form of tax is used to raise this revenue.

If an income tax is used, the new situation is depicted by point 2. The relative prices of the two goods are not affected by a general income tax and the MRT is still equal to the MRS (though the slope of the production possibility curve $P'F'$ is now equal to the slope of the community indifference curve CIC_2). What if, instead, the revenue were raised by an excise tax on good X?

If the revenue were raised by a selective excise tax, then the relative prices of the two goods would be affected. The set of relative prices, shown by the slope of p_1, would be altered. The prices that consumers face would be equal to $P_x(1 + t)/P_y$. The slope of this price line p_2 is obviously steeper and, as individuals equate the marginal rate of substitution to this set of prices, the new equilibrium would be at 3. At this point the community is at a lower level of welfare, as can be seen from the fact that it is on community indifference curve CIC_1 rather than CIC_2. The tax has driven a wedge between the set of prices for producers and the prices that consumers face. Producers set prices equal to the ratio of marginal costs (MC_x/MC_y) and this is shown by the slope of the transformation curve. Producer prices are therefore shown by p_3. The added distortion of the tax increases the burden felt by the community, i.e. of being on CIC_1 as opposed to CIC_2.

While this analysis appears to conclude that the excise tax creates an additional burden, the important point to note is that such a conclusion is subject to many qualifications.

1. The excess burden arises only if the two goods can be substituted for one another. This should be clear to readers from our discussion of compensated demand curves in the previous sections. (If there were no possibility of substitution between the two goods, the community indifference curve would take the form of a right angle at 2. It would then not matter how much the price ratio changed; there would always be a tangency point at 2. It follows that the greater the degree of substitution, the greater the excess burden.)

2. In the context of the 'second-best' argument it follows that the argument holds only on the assumption that the initial position was one in which perfect competition secured Pareto optimality. If, for example, there was already a tax on good Y, then the selective excise tax might lead to a higher welfare level than a general income tax. If the initial tax on good Y indicated that relatively 'too much' of good X was being produced in comparison with good Y, the second-best solution (i.e. the one in which the original tax on Y continued to exist) might be to put a tax on good X. (See chapter 1 for a related discussion of second-best pricing.)

3. In just the same way, it must be assumed that there are no externalities operating to cause even perfect markets to fail. In such a situation it might indeed be optimal (e.g. if good X created external diseconomies) to put a selective tax on good X rather than to use a general income tax.

4. The elasticity of the compensated supply of labour and the elasticity of the compensated supply of savings must be very low to increase the chances that an income tax will have a lower excess burden. An income tax will affect the return that individuals can expect, in the form of either wages for work effort or interest payments for savings. Take the example of work effort. An income tax affects the allocation of time between work and leisure and thereby creates a distortion in this market. In Table 7.1 (based on Little 1957 and Musgrave 1959), the impact of a selective excise tax on good X is compared with a general income tax. In keeping with the theory of 'second best', there is no way to determine, *a priori*, which tax creates the greatest excess burden. The selective excise tax will drive a wedge between the marginal rate of substitution of X for Y and the marginal rate of transformation between X and Y. It will distort the marginal equivalences between X and L (where L refers to leisure time). However, it has no effect on the equality between the marginal rate of substitution between Y and L and the marginal rate of transformation between Y and L. By contrast, the income tax distorts the marginal equivalences between X and L and Y and L but not between X and Y.

It is impossible to argue that the selective excise tax is worse than the general income tax. We are unable to examine the number of marginal equivalences that are distorted by taxes (Lipsey and Lancaster 1956): we would have to know the distortive impact of the taxes in each of the cases noted. If the supply of work effort were inelastic, the general income tax would not distort decisions with respect to the choice between goods and leisure. (Here we refer to compensated supply as shown in the next section.) It is only, therefore, with this assumption that it is possible to predict that the general income tax is superior to the selective excise tax.

The same argument can be applied in the case of the supply of savings. When an individual chooses to forego current consumption for future consumption, it follows that the choice will depend upon the marginal rate of substitution between consumption of good X now (X_0) and consumption of good X in the next period (X_1) and the marginal rate of transformation between the consumption of X now and the consumption of X in the next period. The income tax will affect such an intertemporal decision because it reduces the rate of interest that the individual can expect to receive from postponed consumption. A wedge is driven between the marginal rate of transformation of current consumption for future consumption (depending on the rate of interest) and the marginal rate of substitution between present and future consumption (which will be set according to the *after-tax* rate of interest).

Readers should be satisfied that they can understand why, in Table 7.1, the distortions of the selective excise tax and the income tax take the form shown. Table 7.2 is based on Musgrave (1959); the same conclusions apply. It is impossible to say, *a priori*, that the selective excise tax creates greater allocation losses than the general income tax. To determine this, far more information would be required about the size of deadweight losses in each case. Therefore, only if the supply of savings is assumed to be unresponsive to the rate of interest (so that the income tax does not distort

Table 7.1 The resource allocation effects of taxes

Selective excise tax (on good X)	Income tax
$MRS_{xy} \neq MRT_{xy}$	$MRS_{xy} = MRT_{xy}$
$MRS_{xl} \neq MRT_{xl}$	$MRS_{xl} \neq MRT_{xl}$
$MRS_{yl} = MRT_{yl}$	$MRS_{yl} \neq MRT_{yl}$

Source: based on Little (1957) and Musgrave (1959).

Table 7.2 Temporal and intertemporal resource allocation effects

Selective excise tax (on good X)	Income tax
$MRS_{xoyo} \neq MRT_{xoyo}$	$MRS_{xoyo} = MRT_{xoyo}$
$MRS_{x1y1} \neq MRT_{x1y1}$	$MRS_{x1y1} = MRT_{x1y1}$
$MRS_{xox1} = MRT_{xox1}$	$MRS_{xox1} \neq MRT_{xox1}$
$MRS_{yoy1} = MRT_{yoy1}$	$MRS_{yoy1} \neq MRT_{yoy1}$

Source: based on Musgrave (1959).

intertemporal choice) will it be possible to conclude that the selective excise tax creates a greater burden (assuming, of course, that the choice between X and Y in each period is responsive to the relative prices).

Selective excise tax versus income tax

It will be evident that there are very many conditions that must apply in order to demonstrate in the above general equilibrium model that the selective excise tax will create greater deadweight resource allocation losses than the general income tax. Those listed above are by no means exhaustive: any other second-best constraints will call this conclusion into question. (For example, readers are left to consider the impact of the assumption that good Y is produced by a monopolist—see also chapter 1.)

7.4 The welfare costs of income taxes

In Fig. 7.6(a) an individual is faced with a choice between work and leisure. The budget line is 12 and its slope illustrates the rate at which leisure time can be transformed into income (i.e. the slope shows the wage rate). The individual is assumed to have a fixed number of hours L (e.g. 24 hours per day) to allocate between work and leisure. Initially she maximizes welfare giving up $2L_0$ hours of leisure and earning $L_0 4 (= OY_1)$ income.

A proportional income tax (at rate t) is introduced which will reduce the after-tax income, so that the budget line shifts to 23. The individual changes the allocation of hours as between work and leisure and (in this example) now will work more (giving up $2L_1$ hours of leisure). In order to estimate the *equivalent variation* it is necessary to reduce the welfare of the individual by as much as the proportional income tax *in the absence of* the proportional income tax. A budget line, 67, is drawn parallel to 12 and tangential to I_1 at point 8. It follows that the reduction in welfare associated with the introduction of the proportional income tax can be estimated as distance 16.

The total tax paid after the income tax has been introduced is equal to the difference between the before-tax income and the after-tax income. From the budget line 12 it is clear that when the individual allocated $2L_1$ hours to work the before-tax income is equal to distance $L_1 - 10$ whereas the after-tax income is shown on the budget line 23 by distance $L_1 - 5$. The tax raised is therefore equal to distance 5–10. The tax raised is less than the welfare loss (as

measured by the equivalent variation). Drawing the parallel line 67 demonstrates that, while the welfare loss of the income tax (i.e. the *equivalent variation*) is distance 16, the tax raised is measured as only distance 10–5. It follows that 59 is a measure of the excess burden (or deadweight loss) created by the proportional income tax.

In Fig. 7.6(a), it is the case that the net effect of the proportional income tax is to reduce the amount of leisure consumed from OL_0 to OL_1 hours (i.e. to increase work effort). In this case, as the relative price of leisure increases, a 'disincentive' effect created by the substitution effect of the price change (the shift from 8 to 5) does not out-weigh a positive 'incentive' effect derived as the income effect (the shift from 4 to 8) and, after the tax, the individual actually works harder. This particular example is useful for it will emphasize the distinction between the *compensated* supply curve for labour and the *uncompensated* supply curve for labour. However, there is, of course, no reason to suppose *a priori* that the substitution effect will be outweighed by the income effect and the uncompensated supply curve might well indicate that fewer hours are worked as after-tax wage decreases. Whatever the outcome, the important point is that the excess burden is measured by reference to the compensated supply curve. Again the excess burden depends on the substitution effect.

In Fig. 7.6(b) the tax changes are described by reference to the supply curves of labour. Before any taxation, the wage rate is assumed to be W.

When the proportional income tax is levied the after-tax wage rate falls to W_t. The shift from 4 to 5 in Fig. 7.6(a) reduces hours of leisure and increases hours of work. This means that there must be a backward sloping supply curve for labour as shown by the (uncompensated) supply curve (S_{lu}). However, the compensated supply curve (S_{lc}) can also be identified. The compensated supply curve shows how the individual would behave if the income of the individual did not change as wage rates are changed. If the individual were held on indifference curve I_1 the response to changes in wage rates can be seen as the substitution effect (moving around I_1). With reference to indifference curve I_1, when considering a change from the wage rate W to the after-tax wage rate W_t the movement would be from point 8 to point 5 in Fig. 7.6(a). This compares directly to a movement from point 8' to point 5' in Fig. 7.6(b) along the compensated supply curve of labour.

It is now possible to identify the 'excess burden' of a proportional income tax in Fig. 7.6(b). In Fig. 7.6(b) when the wage is W the individual is paid a total of

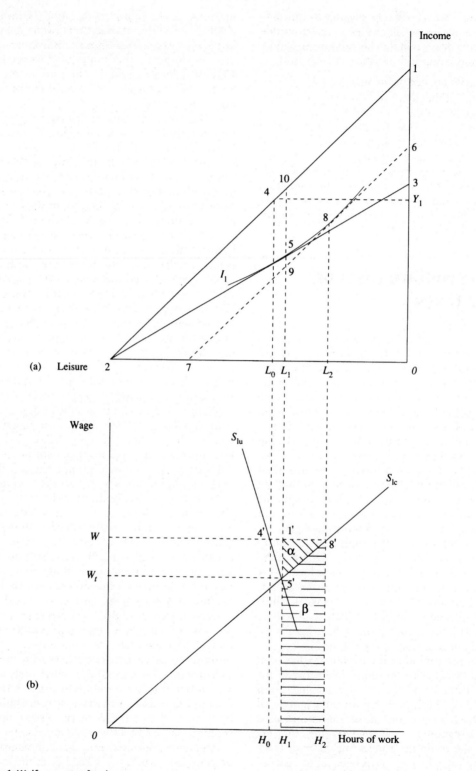

Figure 7.6 Welfare costs of an income tax.

$OW8'H_2$ but only requires, at minimum, $O8'H_2$ to hold real income on the indifference curve constant. The residual being a welfare surplus that is enjoyed. When the tax is levied the supply of hours worked is reduced from OH_2 to OH_1 and the surplus experienced is reduced by an area equal to $W_t W8'5'$ but the amount of tax that is paid is equal to the area $W_t W1'5'$. There is, therefore, an excess burden (or deadweight loss) equal to the triangle $1'5'8'$ (labelled α).[2]

Following the previous discussion relating to excise taxes, the estimation of the excess burden of proportional income taxation seems to be simply an application of the 'standard' Harberger (1964) analysis which takes the elasticity of the compensated supply curve at $8'$ as the starting-point. From Fig. 7.6(b), it is clear that

$$(7.11) \qquad EB = \text{area } 5'1'8' = \tfrac{1}{2} dW dH$$

where EB = the estimate of excess burden
 H = hours worked
 W = the wage rate

The elasticity of the compensated supply of labour is e_s, which is equal to

$$(7.12) \qquad e_s = \frac{dH}{dW} \frac{W}{H}$$

so that

$$(7.13) \qquad dH = \frac{e_s dW H}{W}$$

as $dW = Wt$ (where t is the rate of tax):

$$(7.14) \qquad EB = \tfrac{1}{2} Wt e_s t H$$

or

$$(7.15) \qquad EB = \tfrac{1}{2} t^2 e_s WH$$

[2] The welfare cost of being at $5'$ rather than at $8'$ can also be measured by the difference between the value of the extra income the individual would have received and the maximum amount of income that the individual would have required to give up additional leisure time. The compensated supply curve indicates the wage rate that would have induced the individual to forego another hour of leisure (the least that could be paid to the individual to induce an hour's more work). If there were no tax and the wage were W, then for the additional units of time given up moving from point $5'$ to point $8'$ the individual would receive $H_1 1'8'H_2$, (i.e. the sum of areas alpha and beta). However, at minimum, all that would be required to supply these hours is $H_1 5'8'H_2$, (i.e. area beta). The loss incurred by not working these additional hours (because of the introduction of the tax) can be estimated as area alpha. Note that this is estimated by reference to the *compensated* supply curve of labour—which (because it depends on the substitution effect of the tax) must be positively sloped.

7.5 Partial equilibrium estimates: further considerations

When considering estimates of deadweight losses based on partial equilibrium analysis it is necessary to consider the following:

1. Estimates may be influenced by available data:

The measurement of welfare costs relies on the compensated elasticity but this estimate may differ according to the price at which the estimate is taken. It may be the case, for example, that the estimate of compensated elasticity of supply from empirical work may be one which is estimated at the after-tax wage (point $5'$ in Fig. 7.6, rather than point $8'$). If the supply curve were nonlinear the price elasticities may differ at the two different points. To allow for the difference in the elasticity, Browning (1987) argues that welfare cost (equal $1/2$ (dH) Wt) can be expressed as $1/2$ $[(dH/dW) Wt] Wt$ and if this expression were multiplied by $H_1(1 - t)/H_1(1 - t)$:

$$(7.16) \qquad EB = 1/2 \left(\frac{dH}{dW} \frac{W(1 - t)}{H_1} \right) \frac{t^2}{1 - t} WH_1$$

The term in brackets is the elasticity of the compensated supply curve *at the net of tax wage* (point $5'$). The 'standard' Harberger formula described earlier estimates deadweight loss at the undistorted level (point $8'$). If the estimate of elasticity is that which pertains to a situation when distorting taxes apply, the Browning formula is the appropriate measure.

2. Estimates of welfare costs depend on the existence of other distortions:

As is usual, allowance must be made for 'second-best' considerations (see chapter 1). Rosen (1988) demonstrates this in the case when there are several taxes. Suppose, in Fig. 7.7, that there is a tax (at rate t_j) on a substitute good j, so that excess burden is already equal to triangle 123. Now a tax is imposed on good i, so that demand for good i falls from q_i^1 to q_i^0. While the tax on good i contracts the demand for good i, it also increases the demand for the substitute good j (i.e. the demand curve for good j shifts to the right from Dj to Dj^1). When assessing the welfare loss of a tax on good i it is now necessary to take into account the fact that the tax has increased demand for good j. Consumers in this market now consume additional units of good j (i.e. $q_j^0 - q_j^2$) at a price of $(1 + t_j)P_j$. The additional amount which individuals pay for the

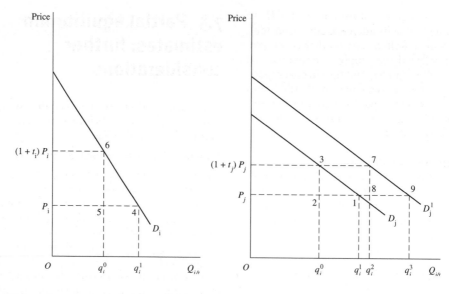

Figure 7.7 Efficiency loss with more than one tax.

good, $q_j^0 3 7 q_j^2$ exceeds the social cost by area 2378 (which is a transfer collected as tax revenue). It follows that there is a social gain (2378) in terms of the value of the additional units of good j over the opportunity cost of providing the additional units of good j. This gain must also be included in any estimate of the deadweight loss of levying a tax on good i. The excess burden of placing the tax on i is equal to the triangle 456 minus area 2378.

When considering the 'overall excess burden' from taxes on several goods Harberger (1974) offers an overview. Not surprisingly, this depends also on the compensated response of one good j for a change in another good i (which is written as S_{ji}). In the example discussed here (and following Rosen 1988) the overall excess burden would be:

$$(7.17) \qquad -1/2(t_i^2 P_i^2 S_{ii} + 2t_i P_i t_j P_j S_{ij} + t_j^2 P_j^2 S_{jj})$$

where: t_i and t_j = the tax rates on goods i and j respectively;

P_i and P_j = the prices of goods i and j respectively;

S_{ij} = the compensated response of good i for a change in good j.

From Fig. 7.7 this includes triangle 456, area 2378 and an area equal to triangle 789.

More recently, Browning (1994) provides another example of a 'second-best' problem. In this case, the existing imperfection is in the labour market. An existing regulation (e.g. for the provision of safety

equipment) affects the wage which is paid to labour, causing it to fall from the marginal value product wage W to W'. Labourers are assumed to place no value on the safety equipment. As such, they adjust their labour supply in response to the wage W'. The difference between W and W' is referred to as the 'non-tax wedge'.[3]

In Fig. 7.8 the existing situation is one in which the wage paid to workers is W'. This wage is below the marginal value product because of the provision of safety equipment. However, an income tax is levied and this reduces the wage rate even further to the after-tax wage W_1 At this after-tax wage the supply of labour is L_1.

It is now the case that there is to be an increase in income tax and the question that arises is how will the deadweight loss of taxation be affected. The increase in the tax reduces the after-tax wage to W_2 and the supply of labour falls to L_2. The initial deadweight welfare loss 123 has increased to 453. That is to say that the welfare costs of the increase in taxation increases the welfare loss associated with the regulation by both area α and by area β.[4] Of course, the former of these areas is the welfare loss associated with the original existence of the 'non-tax wedge'. Therefore, the increase in taxation only serves to make matters

[3] In effect the regulation operates as an implicit marginal tax rate on labour.

[4] Note that the triangle 562 tends to zero for very small increases in the tax.

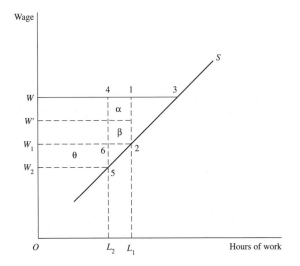

Figure 7.8 Welfare costs on an income tax in a distorted labour market.

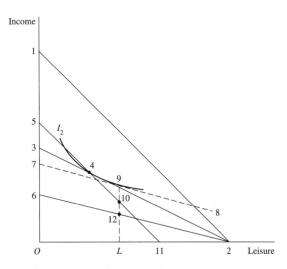

Figure 7.9 Government expenditure and the welfare costs of taxation.

worse, in as much as the original ('non-tax wedge') distortion and original income tax had already created a welfare loss (i.e. causing less than the optimal amount of labour to be employed).

If the objective were to estimate the marginal welfare cost per pound of revenue raised then this would be measured by the ratio of the areas $(\alpha + \beta)/(\theta - \beta)$ in Fig. 7.8. It follows that further marginal welfare loss of an increase of the income tax will be affected by existing non-tax distortions (the 'non-tax wedge'). Existing distortions will influence the marginal welfare costs of raising additional revenue. As Browning (1994, p. 431) concludes, the 'marginal welfare costs of both tax and non-tax policies and institutions are likely to be significantly underestimated by ignoring the interaction between the distortions produced by both phenomena'.

3. Estimates make no allowance for the expenditure of revenues

The partial equilibrium analysis has not allowed for expenditure of the tax revenue. Browning (1987, p. 18) argues that 'the conceptual experiment underlying the notion of marginal welfare costs is a balanced budget operation in which the government spends the increment in tax revenue'. This means that the marginal welfare cost will not only be influenced by changes in taxation but also by how the government spends the funds that are raised.

One assumption that is used is that government spending is a perfect substitute for disposable income

(an assumption which Browning regards as more applicable than it first appears). To account for expenditure assume that the government provides benefits that are perfect substitutes for disposable income (eg. schooling, medical care). In Fig. 7.9 the wage rate is shown by the budget line 12 and the wage is reduced by tax, so that the individual's initial point is assumed to be on the after-tax budget line 32 at point 4. At this point it is clear that tax revenue is raised and this can be measured as distance 15. The line 5–11 is drawn through point 4 to illustrate the amount of tax that will be raised when the individual optimizes at point 4.

Now examine the impact (i.e. the excess burden) of a small increase in the tax rate in relation to the impact of the expenditure it will finance. In Fig. 7.9 the small increase in tax shifts the budget line from 23 to 26. Now, in this case, assume that, via government expenditure, the additional tax receipts are to be returned to the individual. In order to return the individual to her initial indifference curve I_2 it would be necessary that the impact of the expenditure be sufficient to shift the budget line to 78 (i.e. parallel to 26). The new equilibrium would then be at 9. At this point the additional tax revenue is distance 10–12 and, if this is the additional revenue available, it follows that the required benefit from the expenditure must be distance 9–10 greater than the additional tax revenue.

It follows that the marginal welfare cost per unit of revenue of this small tax change (shifting the budget line from 23 to 26) can be measured as 9–10/10–12. The reference position is that which would arise if the individual were returned to her original indifference curve. For this, the marginal benefits from government spending must be more than one plus the marginal welfare cost 9–10/10–12 for the individual to be advantaged by this tax/expenditure action.

4. Partial equilibrium analysis makes no allowance for general equilibrium ('knock on') effects

Killingsworth (1983) notes that the introduction of taxes may affect gross wages and that this 'knock on' effect is ignored in a partial equilibrium discussion that assumes that the individual taxpayer is the only person affected by changes in the tax rate.

Ballard, Shoven and Whalley (1985) consider the question of the marginal excess burden (MEB) or marginal welfare costs of taxation in a general equilibrium context. Their model is a 'multisector, dynamic sequenced numerical general equilibrium' one. The data they used are for the US economy in 1973 and involved 19 producer goods and 15 consumer goods. As noted above, the result of excess burden calculations depend on the relevant elasticity magnitudes. Table 7.3 reproduces their results for their minimum case and their favoured values. The results are available both for taxes and for various parts of the tax system. In this respect the additional use of capital tax tends to be unattractive. Like all general equilibrium models, there are a number of assumptions involved in making the problem tractable, and variations in these assumptions affect the results (a theme that has already been developed and will be amplified below).

Table 7.3 Marginal excess burden from raising £1 extra revenue from specific portions of the tax system

	Uncompensated saving elasticity	
	0.0	0.40
	Uncompensated labour supply elasticity	
	0.0	0.15
All taxes	0.170	0.332
Capital taxes at industry level	0.181	0.463
Labor taxes at industry level	0.121	0.230
Consumer sales taxes	0.256	0.388
Sales taxes on commodities other than alcohol, tobacco, gasoline	0.035	0.115
Income taxes	0.163	0.314
Output taxes	0.147	0.279

Source: C. L. Ballard, J. B. Shoven and J. Whalley, 'General Equilibrium Computations of the Marginal Welfare Costs of Taxes in the United States', *American Economic Review, 75*, 1 (1985), pp. 128–38. Reproduced with the permission of the American Economic Association.

For the moment, it is sufficient to note that the results for this general equilibrium model are in keeping with partial equilibrium results introduced below.

5. The analysis makes no allowance for uncertainty

The discussion above is set in a world of certainty. Easton and Rosen (1980) consider the analysis when there is uncertainty. They argue that if the wage rate were risky, a tax on earnings may be preferable to a lump sum tax as far as taxpayers are concerned. This is because taxation of earnings reduces the variance of earnings and this 'in effect acts as insurance—it lowers risk because the government shares in both losses and gains' (p. 357). In this case, while a pure lump sum taxation entails no excess burden when there is certainty it does cause a comparative burden when wages are uncertain.

7.6 Marginal cost of public funds and policy decisions

The conclusion that the marginal cost of £1 of revenue exceeds £1 is important but is unlikely to be considered by policy-makers. In order to consider the importance of this analysis, we examine Fig. 7.10 (see Browning and Browning 1983). This figure is used to illustrate decision-making with reference to the 'optimum' level of expenditure on government programmes. The demand curve D is taken to express the 'willingness to pay' on the part of taxpayer-voters for the programmes under consideration. If we assume that each additional £1 of revenue costs the community its face value, then the marginal costs of tax revenue will be perceived as constant and equal to 1. In this way the marginal costs of taxation will be seen as $MC(£1 = 1)$ in the figure and the optimum level of government expenditure will be $O12q^1$.

This analysis makes no allowance for the welfare costs of taxation. The marginal costs of taxation are greater than one and are rising. (It should be clear that the welfare costs of taxation increase with increases in the tax rate.[5]) Therefore, in Fig. 7.10 the marginal

---

[5] It is clear that as the rate of tax increases the welfare costs will increase. However, as the tax rate increases, the welfare cost increases by a greater proportion. Figure 7.2n repeats a geometric illustration from Browning and Browning (1983). The tax first increases price from 50 to 60 per unit and the welfare cost is triangle 123. When the tax per unit doubles so that the price to the consumer is 70 per unit, the welfare loss increases by a multiple of 4: welfare loss is now triangle 453. Triangle 453 comprises 461, 615, 152, and 123. Each of these four triangles is equal in area to triangle 123.

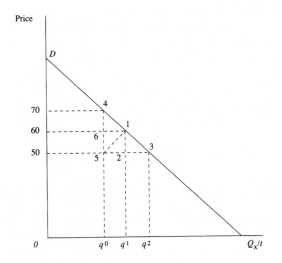

Figure 7.2n Welfare cost and the rate of tax.

Source: adapted by permission of Macmillan Publishing Company from *Public Finance and the Price System* by Edgar K. Browning and Jaqueline M. Browning. Copyright © 1987 by Macmillan Publishing Company.

costs of taxation may be MC_1. The implication is that assuming that £1 of revenue costs £1 will lead to 'excessive' government expenditure. If the welfare costs of taxation are ignored, the marginal costs of

taxation will be misperceived. At a level of q^1 the total costs of taxation will be $O13q^1$ and not $O12q^1$. The optimum level of government expenditure would be Oq^2 and to move to Oq^1 would incur additional welfare losses of 234. Failure of policy-makers to appreciate the full costs of taxation and to equate these with the nominal costs of tax revenue will lead to 'excessive' government expenditure. The excessive expenditure is equal to $O12q^1 - O15q^2$.

From a policy perspective it is, however, important to note that the marginal welfare costs of taxation are not the only costs associated with taxation. Together with the welfare (deadweight) loss, other costs include:

Administrative costs The need to keep records, audit and collect taxes has a real resource cost to the community.

Compliance costs These are the costs passed on to the individual taxpayer in terms, for example, of time spent form-filling and record-keeping. Sandford (1973) suggests that compliance costs are greater than administrative costs in the cases of UK personal income taxation. He reports that the combined total operating costs were at least 3.8 per cent of tax revenue and could be as high as 5.8 per cent of revenue.

Lobbying (rent-seeking) costs Tullock (1967) has noted that the transfer that individuals may receive via the

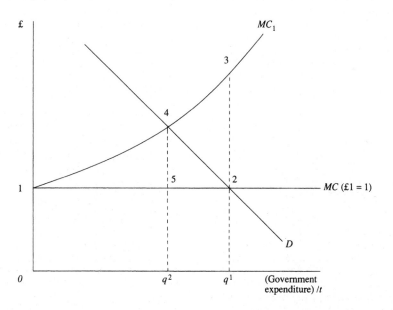

Figure 7.10 The marginal costs of taxation.

Source: based on Browning and Browning (1983).

tax system are a positive increase in income for these individuals and that they would be prepared to spend at least as much in terms of resources to win these transfers by lobbying government officials to introduce new schemes. Such activity turns transfers into real resource losses.

Uncertainty costs Because of the coercive power of taxes, it is always possible that a new redistributive scheme will win electoral consent and that the expected income of an individual may differ from her current income. Even if, on balance, an individual may be a winner as many times as she is a loser in government redistributive schemes, with risk aversion there will be a utility loss (see Jones and Cullis 1986).

7.7 Tax incidence

The preceding discussion of the welfare costs of taxation leads to the conclusion that the costs of taxation may exceed the actual tax revenue raised and that this is an efficiency consideration. In this section the intention is to consider the question who bears the costs of taxation, which is essentially an equity issue. By applying the above welfare analysis of the costs of taxation, it is possible to demonstrate that those who actually pay the tax to the tax collector may not be the

same individuals as those who fully bear the costs of taxation. The economic incidence of taxation can be quite distinct from the statutory incidence (i.e. the individuals legally liable for paying the tax). Once again, it is helpful to demonstrate this argument by reference to both partial and general equilibrium analysis. The argument is very important for any discussion about the effects on real income of particular fiscal regimes.

7.7.1 Partial equilibrium analysis

In Fig. 7.11(a), the producer of the good is legally liable to pay a per-unit tax on output (e.g. a tax that is set as a fixed amount of payment per pound of tobacco, a fixed amount of payment per gallon of petrol, etc.) Because the producer must pay the tax, the producer increases the price of the good to the consumer. This is illustrated in part (a) of the figure by the shift in the supply curve from S to S_t. (The vertical distance between S and S_t measures the tax payment t per unit of the good.) With the upward-sloping supply curve illustrated in the diagram, the impact of the tax varies according to the price elasticity of the demand curve.

When the demand curve D slopes down from left to right, the price of the good to the consumer will rise. However, unless the demand curve is perfectly inelastic, the price of the good will rise by less than the cost of the tax. In Fig. 7.11(a) the price rises from P_0 to P_1.

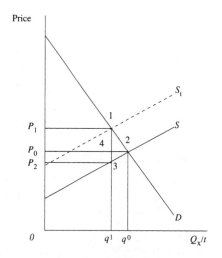

(a) Excise tax imposed on seller

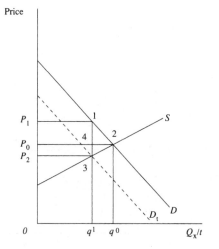

(b) Excise tax imposed on buyer

Figure 7.11 Legal and economic incidence of taxation.

The deadweight losses of the tax are measured as triangle 123 and the tax revenue that is raised is $P_2P_1 13$. Looking at area $P_2P_1 13$, it is clear that part of the revenue is met by a reduction in consumer surplus of $P_1 14P_0$. This part of tax revenue has been paid by consumers in the form of higher prices, enabling the producer to raise the money to pay the tax. The remaining part of the tax revenue $P_0 43P_2$ is a reduction of producer surplus. While technically the producer is legally liable for the tax, part of the cost of the tax has been 'passed on' to consumers.

If the demand for the good were perfectly price-inelastic, then the price of the good would increase by the full amount of the tax and, while legally the producer would be liable for the tax payment, in practice the tax cost would be passed on fully to the consumer.

If the price elasticity of demand were infinity, there would be no increase in price created by the shift in the supply curve.

However, it is not only the price elasticity of demand that is relevant. For example, if the demand curve slopes down from left to right and the price elasticity of supply were infinite, all of the burden of the tax would be met by the consumer in the form of a higher price for the good.

To analyse this relationship, the price that the consumer (demander) pays (P_1 in Fig. 7.11(a)) will be referred to as P_d, while the price that the producer (supplier) would require, if there were no tax to pay (P_2 in Fig. 7.11(a)), will be referred to as P_s. The difference between P_d and P_s is the tax t per unit. Now, following Nicholson (1989),

$$(7.18) \qquad P_d - P_s = t$$

so that

$$(7.19) \qquad dP_d - dP_s = dt$$

In Fig. 7.11(a), it is clear that the distance q^1 to q^0, i.e. the change in quantity demanded, depends upon the change in price to consumers, $P_1 - P_0$ (i.e. dP_d) and the slope of the demand curve, D_p. Similarly, the distance $q^0 - q^1$ can be estimated as the change in the supply price, $P_0 - P_2$ (i.e. dP_s) multiplied by the slope of the supply curve (i.e. S_p). Therefore

$$(7.20) \qquad dQ_d = D_p dP_d$$

$$(7.21) \qquad dQ_s = S_p dP_s = S_p(dP_d - dt)$$

$$(7.22) \qquad dQ_d = dQ_s$$

Therefore

$$(7.23) \qquad D_p dP_d = S_p dP_d - S_p dt$$

$$(7.24) \qquad dP_d(S_p - D_p) = S_p dt$$

$$(7.25) \qquad \frac{dP_d}{dt} = \frac{S_p}{S_p - D_p}$$

Starting from an initial no-tax position and assuming a small tax rate change, this expression can be rewritten. To encompass elasticities, it is necessary to divide the numerator and denominator of this expression by P/Q to get

$$(7.26) \qquad \frac{dP_d}{dt} = \frac{e_s}{e_s - e_d}$$

where e_s and e_d are the price elasticities of supply and demand, respectively.

It is clear then that, if $e_d = 0$ (demand is perfectly inelastic), the rise in price for the consumer is equal to $1 (dP_d/dt = 1)$. If $e_d = $ infinity (demand is infinitely elastic), $dP_s/dt = -1$, since by similar manipulation

$$(7.27) \qquad \frac{dP_s}{dt} = \frac{e_d}{e_s - e_d}$$

The question of who pays the tax cannot then be answered without information about the price elasticity of demand and the price elasticity of supply. The burden of the tax need not fall on the party responsible legally for paying the tax. If the tax is imposed on the seller she adds this tax to her price. She keeps her price net of tax. However, the same outcome occurs if the tax is imposed on the buyer. In Fig. 7.11(b), for the purposes of comparison, we suppose that the consumer must pay the tax. Now the demand curve shifts inward to D_t. At the new equilibrium only part of the payment goes to the seller—the rest goes to the Treasury. It is clear that the share of the tax paid by the consumer and the share paid by the producer is the same in both cases. In Fig. 7.11(b), as we assume that the tax falls on the consumer, the after-tax price received by the producer has fallen by the extent of the per-unit tax. An inspection of the relevant areas in this part of the figure confirms that the burden of the tax between consumers and producers is identical to that in part (a).

7.7.2 Taxes and market structure

In this section the effects of the imposition of a lump sum tax (T) (or equivalently a percentage profits tax) and a specific (excise) tax (t) constant per unit of output are considered under conditions of perfect competition and monopoly. The key to analysing the effects of these two types of tax is isolating the way in which cost curves are affected by the taxes. This is captured in Table 7.4 which records in general form the total cost, marginal cost and average cost for a firm under no tax, lump sum tax and specific tax

Table 7.4 Cost curves and taxation

	No Tax	Lump sum tax (T)	Specific tax per unit (t)
Total cost (C)	$C(q)$	$C(q) + T$	$C(q) + tq$
Marginal cost (MC)	$C'(q)$	$C'(q)$	$C'(q) + t (= MC_t)$
Average cost (C/q)	$\dfrac{C(q)}{q} (= AC)$	$\dfrac{C(q) + T}{q} (= AC_T)$	$\dfrac{C(q) + t}{q} (= AC_t)$

assumptions. For ease of exposition it is assumed that the perfectly competitive industry is a constant cost one (horizontal long run industry supply curve) so that increases or decreases in the number of firms in the industry do not affect input prices and technology that combine to fix the location of a firm's cost structure.

(i) A lump sum (or equivalently a percentage profits tax per period) is easiest to analyse as being, by definition independent of the level of output per period is effectively an increase in fixed costs. Such a change, as can be seen in Table 7.4, leaves short run marginal cost (and also average variable cost) unaltered and therefore the profit maximizing level of output.

However, short run average fixed and therefore average total costs will be raised (AC to AC_T) signalling that some long run adjustments are required. In perfect competition with a starting-point of long run equilibrium with price P_e and industry (market) quantity q_e (see Fig. 7.12(b)) the representative firm in Fig. 7.12(a) would be at point 1 just covering all costs. The impact of the tax is to induce short run losses represented by area 1 2 $P_T P_e$ (i.e. distance 12 is the addition to average fixed cost at output Oq) causing firms to exit from the industry decreasing supply

in Fig. 7.12(b) from S_C to S_T (recall that the supply curves are the horizontal sum of the firms MC curves above AVC) as the number of firms in the industry falls. The process of exits will continue until a new competitive equilibrium is re-established involving an overall lower industry or market output ($q_e > q_{eT}$) coming from a smaller number of firms producing a little more output $q < q_T$. The equilibrium price is raised from p_e to P_{eT}. In monopoly the firm is the industry and the effects of the lump sum tax is to leave the profit maximizing quantity unchanged and economic profit (π) reduced (the economic profit elipse shifts downwards from π to π_T in Fig. 7.13(b)). However, as long as it remains positive there will be no other effect and the producer bears all of the tax. Fig. 7.13 illustrates the marginal case where the monopolist is indifferent between production at Oq_M and not being the industry. The lump sum tax equal to vertical distance 3–4 in Fig. 7.13 panel (b) and area $P_M 2 1 P$ in panel (a) exactly exhausts the economic profit previously enjoyed, i.e. distance 12 is the addition to average fixed cost at output Oq_M.

(ii) A specific (fixed tax per unit) or, more informatively, a variable tax (t) (because, unlike the lump-sum tax, its revenue varies with output) as can be seen from Table 7.4 affects the location of the marginal cost

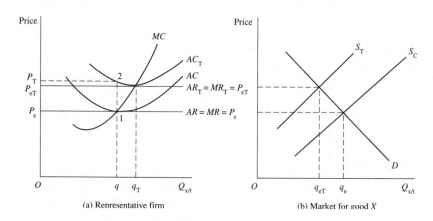

(a) Representative firm (b) Market for good X

Figure 7.12 Lump sum taxation and a constant cost competitive industry.

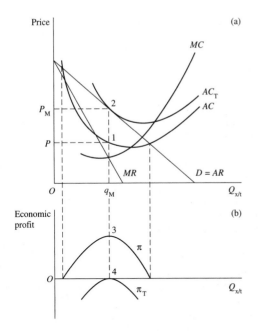

Figure 7.13 Lump sum taxation and monopoly.

run the location of the new 'with tax' marginal cost curve indicates a willingness to supply less at each price level shifting S to S_{SR} in panel (b) and industry and firm output become q_{SI} and q_s respectively and price rises by less than t from P_e to P_S. Such a short run configuration indicates losses for the representative firm in panel (a) equal to area P_S234. Exits are induced in the long run until there are fewer firms each supplying their original quantity per period $q = q_t$ making zero economic profit at price P_{et} which is above P_e by precisely the size of the per unit tax t. Note the supply curves in panel (b) are short run industry ones. Given the constant cost assumption the long run industry supply curves would be horizontal lines emanating from P_e and P_{et} before and after the tax respectively. With a tax of t per unit levied on a monopolist, the MC and AC curves shift upwards to MC_t and AC_t by the amount of the tax in Fig. 7.15(a). As a consequence the profit maximizing output—as determined by the relevant intersections at points 1 and 2 is reduced from Oq_M to Oq_{Mt} and price rises from P_M to P_{Mt}. Panel (b) indicates how economic profit is necessarily reduced by the imposition of the tax from vertical distance $q_M - 3$ to distance $q_{Mt} - 4$ on economic profit elipses π and π_t respectively (The elipses are formed by substracting average costs from average revenue at each quantity per period.) The higher price means the consumer partly bears the burden of tax whereas the lower profit indicates the producer also bears part of the burden. The share of the burden borne by each depends on the own price elasticity of the demand curve(e_d) and the elasticity of the marginal cost curve (e_{mc}). The percentage borne by the consumer (p_d) is given by adjustment of the elasticities formula derived at equation (7.26), namely,

curve and hence the profit maximizing output level. For perfect competition the impact of the tax varies with the shape of the industry long run supply curve; with the change in price ΔP being less, equal or greater than a per unit tax of t depending on whether the industry is an increasing, constant or decreasing cost one. As a constant cost industry has been assumed $\Delta P = t$. The process is illustrated in Fig. 7.14 where the industry and representative firm initial equilibria are points 1 and $1'$ respectively. In the short

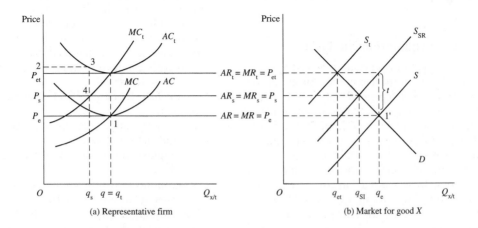

(a) Representative firm   (b) Market for good X

Figure 7.14 Specific taxation and a constant cost competitive industry.

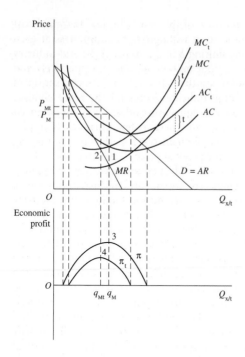

Figure 7.15 Specific taxation and monopoly.

Table 7.5 Summarizing the effects of taxes

	Lump sum taxation	
Under competition:		
Firm		
	Short run	Long run
ΔP	0	+ve
Δq	0	+ve
Industry		
Δq	0	−ve
Under monopoly:		
ΔP	0	
Δq	0	
	Specific (Excise) tax	
Under competition:		
Firm		
ΔP	+ve < t	+ve = t
Δq	−ve	0
Industry		
Δq	−ve	−ve > SR impact
Under monopoly:		
ΔP		+ve(= t when e_d = 0)
Δq		−ve

$e_{mc}/e_{mc} - e_d$ with $e_d \leqslant 0\ p_d \geqslant 0$ and the higher e_{mc} relative to e_d the greater the burden borne by the consumer. Generally the price change is less than the tax imposed i.e. $P_{Mt} - P_M < t$.

The comparative static partial equilibrium results above are summarized in Table 7.5. However, its contents are deceptively clear in that incidence effects vary once the constant cost industry and profit maximizing behaviour assumptions are abandoned. For an analysis of further cases see Brown and Jackson (1990).

7.7.3 General equilibrium analysis

Corporations are a form of business, owned by stockholders who have limited liability for the act of corporation. They are independent legal entitites (i.e. they can sue or be sued) and taxes are often placed on the income of corporations. The economy may be divided between businesses so organized and the unincorporated sector (for not all businesses are run as corporations). Harberger (1962) was interested in the impact of a tax levied only on corporations (the corporate sector). He used a general equilibrium to demonstrate that a tax on the return to capital in the corporate sector may be borne by all owners of capital, whether or not their capital is used in the corporate

sector. This conclusion once again depends sensitively on a number of underlying assumptions. McLure and Thirsk (1975) and Brown and Jackson (1990) deal with this analysis in general equilibrium terms. Hyman (1987) and Musgrave and Musgrave (1989) offer a partial equilibrium illustration. Our intention in this section is to consider the significance of the assumptions used in the model and, more generally, the importance of the Harberger model.

In the Harberger model illustrated below,

1. There are two goods, X and Y, and two factors of production, capital K and labour L. Both factors of production are used in the production of each good, although in the production process each good uses capital and labour in different intensities. (Here good X is assumed to be more capital-intensive in production and good X is produced in the corporate sector.)
2. The total stock of capital and labour are assumed constant.
3. Perfect competition is assumed for both the product and factor markets.
4. Full employment of factors of production is assumed.
5. The economy is assumed to be a closed economy; there is no international trade.
6. Production functions are of Cobb–Douglas form, with constant returns to scale; e.g. for the production of good X, the functional form is

$$(7.28) \qquad X = b_0 L^{b_1} K^{b_2}$$

where X = output of the good X
$\quad L$ = labour
$\quad K$ = capital
$\quad b_0, b_1, b_2$ are the parameters of the production function
$\quad b_1 + b_2 = 1$

from this production function it is possible to derive expressions for the marginal product of labour (MPL) and for the marginal product of capital (MPK). For example, the marginal product of labour is

$$(7.29) \qquad MPL = dX/dL = b_1 b_0 L^{b_1-1} K^{b_2}$$

$$(7.30) \qquad = b_1 (b_0 L^{b_1-1} K^{b_2})$$

$$(7.31) \qquad = b_1 (X/L)$$

The marginal product is equal to a constant (b_1) multiplied by the average product of the factor of production, and it follows that

$$(7.32) \qquad MPK = b_2 (X/K)$$

Using these values of the marginal products, it is possible to show that the elasticity of substitution between factors of production is unity. The elasticity of substitution between factors of production is the proportionate change in the use of factor intensity ratios (e.g. K/L in production) for a proportionate change in factor prices; i.e.

$$(7.33) \qquad s = \frac{\text{proportionate change in factor intensity ratio}}{\text{proportionate change in relative factor prices}}$$

With perfect competition in all markets, producers equate the marginal rate of substitution of factors of production to relative prices. The marginal rate of substitution (or marginal rate of technical substitution, as it is often called) for production functions is the ratio of the marginal products of the factors of production. Therefore

$$(7.34) \qquad s = \frac{d(K/L)/(K/L)}{d(MRS)/(MRS)}$$

MRS is the ratio of the marginal products, so this can be written as

$$(7.35) \qquad s = \frac{d(K/L)/(K/L)}{d[(b_1/b_2)(K/L)]/(b_1/b_2)(K/L)}$$

and

$$(7.36) \qquad s = \frac{d(K/L)(b_1/b_2)}{(b_1/b_2)d(K/L)} = 1$$

As far as the following analysis is concerned, this means:

(a) The total share of output paid to capital and the total share of output paid to labour remains constant with respect to changes in factor rewards. Cost-minimizing producers will substitute factors of production in response to a price change (e.g. if the relative price of capital increases, producers will choose a more labour-intensive form of production). However, with the assumption that the elasticity of substitution is unity, the total payment to capital and the total payment to labour (both before and after such substitution) remains constant. In the case of capital,

$$(7.37) \qquad MPK = b_2 (X/K)$$

$$(7.38) \qquad MPK(K) = b_2 (X)$$

$$(7.39) \qquad \frac{MPK(K)}{X} = b_2$$

(b) The demand for factors of production has a unitary elasticity of demand. With unitary elasticity of substitution, any increase (decrease) in price of the factor will be exactly offset, as far as cost is concerned, by a decrease (increase) in the quantity used of that factor of production. This means also that the demand for each factor of production is unitary-price-elastic, and the demand curve will be a rectangular hyperbola.

(c) There are constant returns to scale. After paying factors their marginal product, there is nothing left over (or under) in terms of output. Production functions exhibit constant returns to scale; e.g. a doubling of factors of production doubles output.

All of these properties of the Cobb–Douglas function become important as the model is analysed.

7. Within the Harberger (1962) model, it is assumed that the owners of capital and the owners of labour spend a constant proportion of their income on good X and on good Y. Utility functions also have the properties of the Cobb–Douglas functional form, which means that demand functions are also unitary-price-elastic. (It does not mean that both the owners of capital and the owners of labour have identical utility functions and identical preferences.)

8. Finally, it is necessary to limit the role of the government in order to predict events. A 'small' tax is levied on the use of capital in industry X which is identified as the corporate sector. It is assumed that there are no other taxes in the economy and that,

when the government spends tax revenue, it is
spent exactly as individual consumers would have
spent the revenue had they not been taxed. (This is
equivalent to assuming that the tax revenues are
returned to the sectors of the community who paid
the tax in a lump-sum fashion.)

With this list of assumptions, it is possible to illustrate
the impact of the corporation tax by using Fig. 7.16.

The number of assumptions required to generate the
analysis is, of course, quite demanding. Throughout,
however, readers should consider how, at any stage,
relaxation or alteration of an assumption would affect
the prediction drawn from the analysis.

In part (a) of the figure the vertical axes are used to
record the rate of return earned by capital in the X
industry (corporate sector) and in the Y industry
(unincorporated sector). The horizontal axis meas-

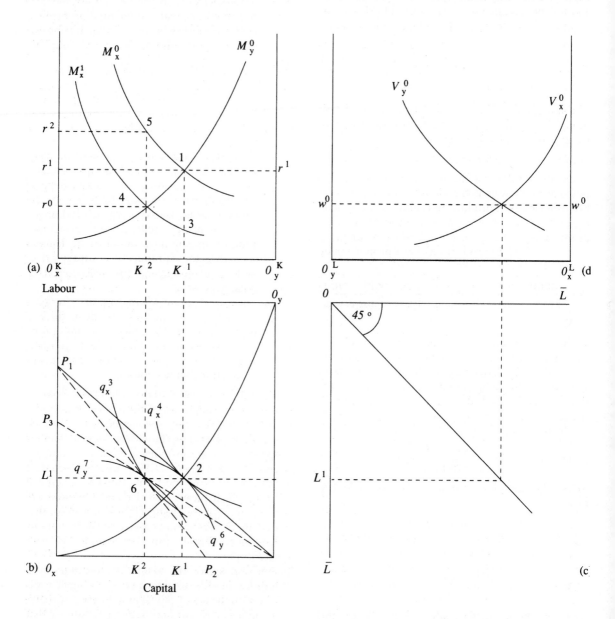

Figure 7.16 The Harberger model.

ures the total stock of capital in the economy. In the initial equilibrium, as perfect competition has been assumed, capital is allocated between the two industries such that the rate of return is equalized (i.e. at r^1). This must be so; for, if the rate of return were higher in one industry than in the other, capital would be moving to the location where its rate of return was higher and there could not be an equilibrium. The initial equilibrium position (point 1), then, is one in which $O_x^K K^1$ is employed in the X industry and the remainder, $O_y^K K^1$, is employed in the Y industry.

In part (b) of the figure, the Edgeworth–Bowley box diagram illustrates the total supply of labour and capital for the economy. In the first instance, again because perfect competition is assumed, the economy allocates its resources so as to be at some point on the contract curve joining $O_x O_y$. The shape of the contract curve indicates that the X industry is everywhere more capital-intensive in production and the Y industry is relatively more labour-intensive in production. The initial allocation of resources is shown at point 2 on the contract curve (i.e., $O_x K^1$ units of capital and $O_x L^1$ units of labour are used in the X industry and the remaining supply of capital and labour are employed in the Y industry). This is clearly a Pareto-efficient allocation. Marginal rates of technical substitution of capital and labour are equal in both industries. This is evident because the isoquants q_x^4 and q_y^6 are tangential at 2. The tangency indicates that producers in the X and the Y industries equate their marginal rate of technical substitution to the same factor–price ratio. This factor–price ratio is shown as the slope of the line P_1. Perfect competition means that producers in both industries face the same set of relative prices for factors of production. Cost-minimizing decisions in each industry means that the initial equilibrium is on the contract curve (and, therefore, on the production possibility frontier).

Part (c) of Fig. 7.16 is simply a device for transferring information from (b) to (d) where the labour market is dealt with. A 45° line lies between two axes, each of which is measured to estimate the initial stock of labour in the economy. Taking the information shown in part (b) around the 45° line, it is possible to see in part (d) how the labour market looks in the initial equilibrium. The marginal value product of labour is shown in each industry as V_x^0 and V_y^0 respectively. We confirm here that, as there is perfect competition and as labour is assumed mobile between industries, the wage rate is initially the same in both industries, i.e. w^0.

To analyse the impact of a corporation tax in the X industry (corporate sector), in part (a) allowance must be made for the fact that the net (after-tax) return to capital will fall. The curves M_x^0 and M_y^0 record respectively the marginal value product of capital in the X and Y industries. The tax causes M_x^0 to shift to M_x^1 as far as the owners of capital are concerned because the difference must now be paid in tax. With the current allocation of capital between industries, the rate of return to holders of capital in the Y industry is $K^1 1$ but that to capital owners in the X industry (after tax) is only $K^1 3$. Capital will move from the X industry to the Y industry. This will continue until the after-tax rate of return in the X industry is equal to the rate of return in the Y industry. Therefore $K^1 - K^2$ units of capital will move from the X to the Y industry to equalize returns (i.e. both are equal to $K^2 4$). The tax has created deadweight losses, and these are shown in part (a) as triangle 145. They can be approximated by the formula $\frac{1}{2} t dK$, where t refers to the rate of corporation tax and dK refers to the capital flow.

That there are deadweight losses is clear from part (b) of the diagram. When $K^1 - K^2$ capital has moved, the economy is no longer on the contract curve in the Edgeworth–Bowley box diagram. In the X industry the relative price of the factors has changed, such that capital is relatively more expensive. This is so because capital must cover the costs of the tax and provide a return to the owners of capital. The relative set of factor prices that is faced by the producers of good X is shown by the slope of the line $P_1 P_2$. The cost-minimizing tangency point that producers choose is shown as point 6, where q_x^3 is tangent to P_2. By contrast, the set of relative prices facing producers in the Y industry is given by P_3. Capital is relatively cheaper in this industry, in so far as only r^0 has to be paid to capital, whereas in the first instance the payment to capital had been r^1. The producers of good Y, therefore, equate the marginal technical rate of substitution of factors of production to the slope of P_3. At point 6, q_y^7 is tangential to P_3 and therefore intersects isoquant q_x^3.

While resource allocation costs are evident, there is no reason for anyone to move from this inefficient outcome. Each industry is in equilibrium, having equated the slope of the isoquant to the price ratio with which it is faced. There is no reason for the allocation of labour to alter. The wage rate remains the same in both industries, as can be confirmed by tracing through parts (c) and (d) of the diagram. Up to this point in the analysis labour does not bear the costs of the tax: the owners of capital bear the costs, *irrespective of whether or not they are in the corporate sector.*

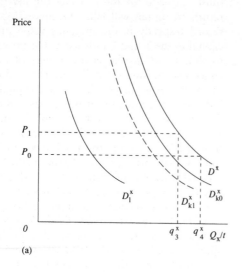
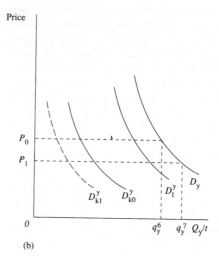

(a)   (b)

Figure 7.17 Tax incidence.

To examine the impact of the corporation tax on prices of commodities, we can consider Fig. 7.17. As noted above, the government is assumed to spend the tax revenues raised in exactly the same way as the owners of the factors of production would have spent them. Therefore, the overall demand curve for good X(D^x) and the overall demand curve for good Y(D^y) does not alter. It is clear, however, that when commodity prices remain constant the output of good Y expands (i.e. shifts from q_y^6 to q_y^7 in part (b) of Fig. 7.16) and the output of good X declines (shifts from q_x^4 to q_x^3 in part (b) of the figure). The result is that, if overall demand for the two goods has not altered, the price of good X must rise and the price of good Y must fall. In Fig. 7.17(a) the market for X is shown. As the output of X has fallen from q_x^4 to q_x^3, price has risen from P_0 to P_1. The demand curve of the owners of capital must shift to the left, as their real income has fallen because of tax payment (i.e. in the diagram D_{k0}^x shifts to D_{k1}^x). Their consumption of this good falls, as a result of both the higher price and their fall in income. There is no reason for the demand curve for the owners of labour (D_l^x) to shift: their consumption of X falls as a result of the increase in the price of the good. In Fig. 7.17(b) the overall demand for good Y, D^y, remains the same. Owners of labour purchase more because of the lower price, whereas owners of capital may purchase less even at the lower price P_1 because the income reduction arising from higher taxes shifts their demand curve (i.e. because D_{k0}^y shifts to D_{k1}^y).

Making reasonable assumptions about the elasticity of substitution between goods and the elasticity of substitution between labour and capital, it is hard to dismiss the conclusion that in the USA (the country under study by Harberger) capital would bear almost all of the burden of taxation. Indeed, assuming that the entire corporate income tax was a tax on the return to capital, Harberger (1962) estimated that the dead-weight cost of corporate taxation in the USA between 1953 and 1959 was between 2.4 and 7.0 per cent of corporate tax revenues. Shoven and Whalley (1972), relaxing Harberger's reliance on linear approximations, provided an alternative calculation. Using similar parameter values, they estimated that the excess burden was between 2.2 and 11.7 per cent of the tax revenues.

Harberger's analysis is useful, in so far as it highlights the various distinctions that need to be kept in mind when considering the incidence of taxation. There is a distinction between the short run and long run. In the very short run, i.e. when capital cannot move, the whole of the burden is borne by capital in the corporate sector. Later, when capital is able to move, the burden of taxation is borne by capital, irrespective of its location.[6] The Harberger

---

[6] As far as consumption by the owners of capital is concerned, the example shows that ultimately the consumption of both X and Y falls. As far as labourers are concerned, the consumption of X has fallen and the consumption of Y has risen. To compare the effect of this it is possible to use either a Laspeyres index (based on pre-tax prices) or a Paasche index (based on post-tax prices).

model, however, is sensitive to the assumptions it incorporates, and, as in all economic models, if you quarrel with the assumptions then you may reject the predictions, as the following examples indicate.

1. The distribution of the burden will depend on the assumed elasticity of substitution between capital and labour. Musgrave and Musgrave (1984) note that the burden on capital is greater and that on labour is smaller, the lower is the elasticity of substitution between labour and capital in X as compared with that in Y. Tresch (1981) shows that, if the elasticity of substitution between capital and labour is zero, the incidence of a corporation tax depends on the relative proportions in which capital and labour are used in the two industries. When labour is used intensively in the taxed industry it may bear the tax more than proportional to its initial contribution to national income. However, results are also sensitive to the elasticity in consumption between the two goods. The burden on capital will also tend to be larger the lower is the elasticity of substitution in consumption of the two goods (Musgrave and Musgrave 1984).

2. If firms in the corporate sector enjoy monopoly profits, then, even though these are reduced by the tax, the owners of capital may still remain within this sector rather than adding to the supply of capital (and thereby bringing down the rate of return) in the non-incorporated sector.

3. Stiglitz (1976) has argued that the tax may work like a pure profits tax, provided that interest payments on both debt and depreciation are tax-deductible. Assume that:

r = the one-period rate of interest
d = the rate of depreciation
t = the rate of corporation tax
m = the incremental increase in profits arising from a marginal increase in the capital stock in the corporate sector

The decision to invest an additional £1 in this sector depends upon the return to this investment (m) less the cost of borrowing the £1 (r) and the cost of depreciation (d). If the interest payments and the economic depreciation are tax-deductible, the net rate of return on the investment is $(m - r - d)(1 - t)$. Hence the firm should invest as long as $(m - d) > r$. The costs of the investment r are independent of the tax t. Before

Musgrave and Musgrave (1984, p. 285) make the general distinction between incidence on the 'sources side' and incidence on the 'uses' side. Consumers of products in the unincorporated sector have the possibility of gaining from the decline in price, though they note that 'these subsequent effects . . . are not likely to over-rule the progressive nature of the tax as reflected in its initial impact on the net return to capital'.

the tax, the firm invests if $m - d - r > 0$, and after the tax is introduced the firm invests if $(m - d - r)(1 - t) > 0$. Hence imposition of the tax leaves the firm's decision unchanged—anything that it would have done before the tax it will do after the tax (as $t < 1$).

Harberger's analysis is more in keeping with a corporate tax without interest deductibility. In that case, the net-of-tax return to a £1 investment is $(m - d)(1 - t) - r$, so that for the investment to be worthwhile it is necessary that $(m - d) > r/(1 - t)$.

4. Rosen (1988) notes that the model is static. If, over time, the tax on corporate capital changes the total amount of capital available to the economy the outcome will differ. If the tax lowers the total amount of capital, the marginal product of labour, and hence the wage rate, will fall. Thus labour will bear a greater share of the burden than otherwise would be the case (Ballentine, 1978).

5. The analysis has been undertaken in the context of a closed economy. Assume, instead, that capital can move internationally. In Fig. 7.18 the marginal product of capital in the corporate sector and in the unincorporated sector is again illustrated. The world price of capital (which is unaffected by the relatively small domestic market in this country) is at r^1. In this case, if a corporation tax is levied and the marginal product curve in the incorporated sector shifts from M_x^0 to M_x^1, capital will move abroad rather than into the unincorporated sector. In Fig. 7.18 this will mean a change in the allocation of capital. Prior to the corporation tax, $O_x^K K^1$ capital was used in the corporate sector and $O_y^K K^1$ capital was employed in the unincorporated sector. After the tax is levied, $O_x^K K^2$ units of capital remain in the corporate sector, $O_y^K K^1$ units are in the unincorporated sector and the remainder, $K^2 - K^1$ units, have gone abroad. Musgrave, Musgrave and Bird (1985) point out that the burden of the tax has now been shifted elsewhere. It is clear that, at this stage in adjustment, the burden of the corporate tax has not been borne by capital. In this case, labour in the corporate sector may bear the burden. Notice that, after deducting the amount paid for capital from the marginal product of capital, the remainder is the payment to labour. In Fig. 7.18 this is reduced by the shaded triangle 123. Of course this is the initial effect of the tax and the other caveats discussed above still apply.[7] However, the example

[7] Musgrave, Musgrave and Bird (1987) note that there are circumstances in which, ultimately, this may lead to less demand for labour and labour in general may bear the burden. Also they note that on the 'uses' side consumers of corporate output may bear the burden.

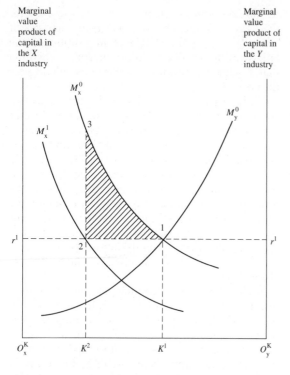

Figure 7.18 Corporation tax in an open economy.
Source: adapted from Musgrave, Musgrave and Bird (1987).

further illustrates the sensitivity of tax incidence to the structure of the economy.

7.8 Tax/subsidy capitalization

Tax (or subsidy) capitalization is a topic that is not only of importance in itself, but also provides a convenient link between concepts of incidence (and hence equity concern) and concepts of allocation (and hence efficiency concern). In addition, the concept once more warns against simply the face value analysis of taxation. To illustrate what is involved, consider Fig. 7.19, which comprises two panels subdivided into two market illustrations. Figure 7.19 (a(ii)) and 7.19(b(ii)) illustrate the overall market for assets, whereas 7.11(a(i)) and 7.11(b(i)) represent the market for a given stock OS_h of asset H (say housing). Panel (a) represents what is labelled the 'small asset' assumption, so that H is a small part of the total sum of assets that can be held, and therefore

nothing in the market for H can affect the rate of return on assets (10 per cent) as determined by the intersection of the total supply curve for assets S and total demand D. Suppose asset H exists in perpetuity and offers an annual return of £10 000. If the equilibrium rate of return on assets is 10 per cent, its capitalized value is £100 000. (The value of an asset in perpetuity is given by the annual return divided by the rate of interest or return.) Now suppose a tax of 1 per cent per annum (equal to £1000 per annum) is imposed on asset H. By definition, H must conform to the 10 per cent rate of return, and with a net annual return (now of £9000) this can arise only if the value of H drops to £90 000 (£9000/0.1 = £90 000). In short, the announcement of a 1 per cent tax on H has been capitalized completely into the price of H the moment it was announced, meaning that all the tax falls on the owners of H. This incidence effect is dramatic and often unappreciated. Irrespective of when tax payments are observed to be made, the total incidence of the tax is felt on its announcement. The movement, D to D_t, captures this tax effect. Additionally, with the overall market for assets, Fig. 7.19(a(ii)), unaffected, there are no allocative consequences, and OS_t remains the equilibrium overall quantity of assets.

Moving to panel (b) of the diagram, the 'large asset' case is illustrated. Suppose a tax on H (which now, by definition, is a large part of the asset market) is sufficient to reduce the net rate of return from 10 to 9 per cent as D effectively shifts to D_t. The equilibrium volume of assets decreases S_t to S'_t, generating an allocative loss equal to the welfare cost triangle 123. But what of the price of the stock of H? With net income of £9000 per annum and a rate of return of 9 per cent, the capitalized value of the asset remains £100 000 (9000/0.09). In the short run, at least, before the adjustment towards equilibrium (involving S_h moving to the left) takes place, the value of the asset H is unchanged. There is no immediate incidence on current owners, and the tax is actually paid as it is observed to be paid. The effects, then, of complete or no capitalization are very different with respect to both equity and efficiency. The complete capitalization of taxes is inequitable to the extent that it creates (unintended?) windfall losses (gains), but it is attractive on efficiency grounds, in that allocative affects appear minimal. No capitalization means the statutory and actual incidences of the tax coincide, which makes equity easy to gauge for tax policy designers; but unfortunately, allocative effects are likely to be significant and need to be analysed.

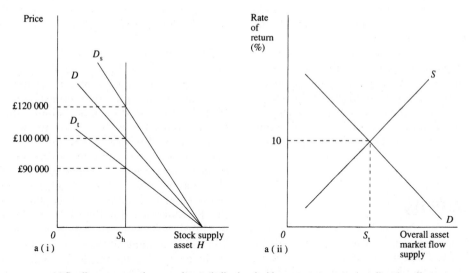

a (i) Stock supply asset *H*

a (ii) Overall asset market flow supply

(a) Small asset assumption; complete capitalization: incidence current owners / no allocative effect

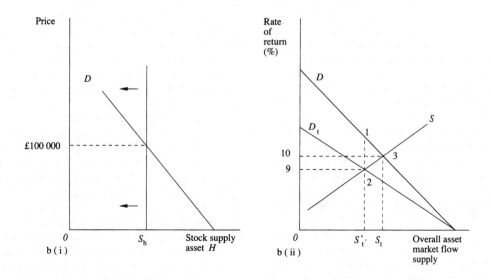

b (i) Stock supply asset *H*

b (ii) Overall asset market flow supply

Figure 7.19 Taxation and capitalization.

Finally, consider the introduction of favourable treatment of asset H to the extent of 2 per cent per annum (compared with other assets). If H conforms to the small asset assumption, the market price will completely capitalize the favourable treatment of H: its price will rise instantaneously to £120 000, so that a net return of £12 000 per annum only means a 10 per cent rate of return on asset H (*D* effectively becomes

D_s in Fig. 7.19(a(i))). The gainers here are the owners of H when the favourable tax treatment is announced. Now further, suppose that some years later a call for an end to the favourable tax treatment of H is heeded and the provision is ended. The value of H drops back on announcement to £100 000. Not only has the subsidy not had a stimulatory effect on the supply of H (which is likely to have been intended, to the extent that owners of H will have changed in the intervening years), but the windfall loss falls on those who did not reap the windfall gain, and, in the absence of other information, this appears unfair.

To firm up ideas, readers may care to think of a possible example of this process. In this context consider the calls from many quarters, including the Church and the Duke of Edinburgh, for the ending of mortgage tax relief. The sense of these calls depends on the extent of mortgage tax relief capitalization, which in turn depends on the small asset–large asset distinction.

7.9 Summary

We began this chapter with a warning that simple questions in fiscal theory require complex answers. With respect to the burden of taxation, it is clear that taxes impose a greater burden than simply the direct burden of the tax revenue that they raise. They impose an *excess burden* on taxpayers, and to ignore this is to compound welfare losses because it will lead to the selection of 'too great' a level of public expenditure. However, the question of the marginal costs of taxation is not divorced from the issue of property rights. Are welfare costs of a particular tax to be estimated by the difference between how much an individual would pay to avoid the tax, less the tax revenue held for her by the state? Or are the welfare costs of taxation the difference between how much you would need to give the individual to make her as well off as she would be in the absence of tax, less the tax revenue held for her by the state? With respect to chapter 2, is the reference point the welfare of the individual when she is taxed (on the argument that the state has a right to tax that income) or the welfare of the individual prior to taxation (on the argument that the individual had a right to her untaxed level of real income)? Before long, the argument on the estimation of the welfare losses of taxation leads to a deeper philosophical discussion concerning the rights of individuals in society.

With respect to the way in which the tax burden is shared by taxpayers, it is quite clear that this burden does not remain simply with the parties legally responsible for making tax payments. Ascertaining the final incidence of taxation requires a quite complex general equilibrium model, or (on the other hand) a number of heroic simplifying assumptions relating to the interaction of different markets. It should be noted, however, that the theoretical niceties

of tax analysis have not precluded applied analysis. In chapter 9 a number of studies that attempt to consider the distributive effects of fiscal policy are discussed.

A key matter in economic or indeed any analysis is the assumptions that are made. Conclusions under one set of incidence assumptions may not carry over to, or be relevant to, another context. In tax analysis, the fuller the context the more complex the analysis, so where possible it is always attractive to choose the simplest context that can handle the problem at hand. The onus is on the analyst to be clear about what is explicitly and implicitly being assumed. Table 7.6 illustrates how the concept of incidence can be generalized much more than has been illustrated in this chapter. Movement down the rows is from a narrower to a broader incidence analysis, providing a description and an example of the type of policy question it might be applied to. Incidence itself is about the change in real income distribution associated with government policy. As you move down column (i), the concept of incidence becomes richer and, as already noted, more complex. Much of the tax analysis in this chapter has been of the type (ii), i.e. the differential kind (e.g. comparison of an excise tax with a lump-sum tax raising the same revenue). However, in chapter 9 redistribution studies carried out by the UK Central Statistical Office are examples of attempts to enact (iv) in Table 7.6.

The kinds of heroic assumptions about how taxes and government benefits are shared by taxpayers (or households) should stand proud by reference to the arguments made in this chapter. Certainly the discussion on capitalization of taxes and subsidies warns against a superficial interpretation of the benefits and costs of such measures. Would those entering the housing market be better off if the government increased mortgage tax allowance, or would they simply pay a higher price for the house they would buy?

In considering the complexities of these issues, readers will have every right to be sceptical that, in practice, all these problems can be addressed prior to policy-making. As in chapter 6 on cost–benefit analysis, the dictates of theory are not always easy to bring into practice. The practical and administrative problems of this theoretical literature are exemplified by the analysis of optimal taxation in chapter 15. But, in any case, do those who play a role in the policy process really worry about these issues? Or are they motivated by other considerations and other vested interests which make the welfare economics discussed in this chapter of far less importance for actual policy-making?

Table 7.6 Incidence scenarios

(i) Incidence type	(ii) Fate of taxation	(iii) Example of a relevant policy question
(i) (Absolute) specific tax incidence	Public expenditure unchanged: tax simply taken out of the economy generating macroeconomic consequences	Raising tax to combat inflation
(ii) Differential tax incidence	Looks at the differences involved in substituting one tax regime for another yielding the same revenue (public expenditure held constant as in (i) above)	Considering covering an expenditure by different taxes
(iii) Budget incidence	Considers not only the tax change but the effect of part of the taxes raised on personal incomes in terms of transfers financed and the effect of expenditures on earnings in the labour market by affecting factor demands	Raising taxes to finance transfer schemes
(iv) Net or budget	Adds to (iii) the benefit of public provision of goods and services (see chapter 9)	Raising taxes to finance public sector transfers and exhaustive expenditures

Source: R. A. Musgrave and P. B. Musgrave (1976) *Public Finance in Theory and Practice*, 2nd edn., McGraw-Hill, New York. Adapted with the permission of McGraw-Hill, Inc.

References

Allan, C. M. (1971) *The Theory of Taxation*. Harmondsworth: Penguin.

Auerbach, A. J. (1985) 'The Theory of Excess Burden and Optimal Taxation', pp. 61–128 in A. J. Auerbach and M. Feldstein (eds.), *Handbook of Public Economics*. Amsterdam: North Holland.

Ballard, C. L., Shoven, J. B. and Whalley, J. (1985) 'General Equilibrium Computations of the Marginal Welfare Costs of Taxes in the United States', *American Economic Review*, 75, 1, pp. 128–38.

Ballentine J. G. (1978) 'The Incidence of a Corporation Income Tax in a Growing Economy', *Journal of Political Economy*, 86, 5, pp. 863–76.

Blaug, M. (1970) *Economic Theory in Retrospect*, 2nd edn. London: Heinemann.

Boadway, R. W. and Wildasin, D. E. (1984) *Public Sector Economics*, 2nd edn. Boston: Little, Brown.

Brown, C. V. and Jackson, P.M. (1990) *Public Sector Economics*, 4th edn. Oxford: Basil Blackwell.

Browning, E. K. (1987) 'Marginal Welfare Cost of Taxation', *American Economic Review*, 77, 1, pp. 11–23.

Browning, E. K. (1994) 'The non-tax wedge', *Journal of Public Economics*, 53, 3, pp. 419–33.

Browning, E. K. and Browning, J. M. (1983) *Public Finance and the Price System*, 2nd edn. New York: Macmillan.

Diamond, P. A. and McFadden, D. L. (1974) 'Some Uses of the Expenditure Function in Public Finance', *Journal of Public Economics*, 3, pp. 3–21.

Easton, J. and Rosen, H. S. (1980), 'Optimal Redistributive Taxation and Uncertainty', *Quarterly Journal of Economics*, 95, 2, pp. 357–64.

Harberger, A. C. (1962) 'The Incidence of the Corporation Income Tax', *Journal of Political Economy*, 70, 3, pp. 215–40.

Harberger, A. C. (1964) 'The Measurement of Waste', *American Economic Review*, 54, 3, pp. 58–76.

Harberger, A. C. (1974) Taxation, Resource Allocation and Welfare, pp. 25–62 in A. C. Harberger (ed.), *Taxation and Welfare*. Boston: Little, Brown.

Henderson, J. M. and Quandt, R. E. (1971) *Microeconomic Theory: A Mathematical Approach*, 2nd edn. New York: McGraw-Hill.

Hyman, D. N. (1987) *Public Finance: A Contemporary Application of Theory to Policy*, 2nd edn. Chicago, Dryden Press.

Jones, P. R. and Cullis, J. G. (1986) 'Is Democracy Regressive? A Comment on Political Participation', *Public Choice*, 51, 1, pp. 101–7.

Killingsworth, M. (1983) *Labour Supply*. Cambridge: Cambridge University Press.

Lipsey, R. G. and Lancaster, K. (1956) 'The General Theory of Second Best,' *Review of Economic Studies*, 24, 63, pp. 11–32.

Little, I. M. D. (1957) *A Critique of Welfare Economics*. Oxford: Oxford University Press.

McLure, C. E. and Thirsk, W. R. (1975) 'A Simplified Exposition of the Harberger Model, I: Tax Incidence', *National Tax Journal*, 28, 1, pp. 1–27.

Mohring, J.A. (1972) 'Alternative Welfare Gain and Loss Measures', *Western Economic Journal*, 9, pp. 349–68.

Musgrave, R. A. (1959) *The Theory of Public Finance*. New York: McGraw-Hill.

Musgrave, R. A. and Musgrave, P. B. (1976) *Public Finance in Theory and Practice*, 2nd edn. New York: McGraw-Hill.

Musgrave, R. A. and Musgrave, P. B. (1984) *Public Finance in Theory and Practice*, 4th edn. New York: McGraw-Hill.

Musgrave, R. A. and Musgrave, P. B. (1989) *Public Finance in Theory and Practice*, 5th edn. New York: McGraw-Hill.

Musgrave, R. A., Musgrave, P. B. and Bird, R. M. (1985) *Public Finance in Theory and Practice: First Canadian Edition*. Toronto: McGraw Hill.

Nicholson, W. (1989) *Microeconomic Theory Basic Principles and Extensions*, 4th edn. Chicago: Dryden Press.

Rosen, H. S. (1988) *Public Finance*, 2nd edn. Homewood, Ill.: Irwin.

Sandford, C. T. (1973) *The Hidden Costs of Taxation*. London: Institute of Fiscal Studies.

Shoven, J. B. and Whalley, J. (1972) 'A General Equilibrium Calculation of the Effects of Differential Taxation of Income from Capital in the US', *Journal of Public Economics*, 1, 3, 4, pp. 281–321.

Stiglitz, J. (1976) 'The Corporation Tax', *Journal of Public Economics*, 5, 3, pp. 1–34.

Tresch, R. W. (1981) *Public Finance: A Normative Theory*. Plano: Irwin-Dorsey.

Tullock, G. (1967) 'The Welfare Costs of Tariffs, Monopolies and Theft', *Western Economic Journal*, 5, 3, pp. 224–32.

Winch, D. M. (1971) *Analytical Welfare Economics*. Harmondsworth: Penguin.

8 Tax evasion and the black economy

8.1 Introduction

From the public bar of the Dog and Muffler to the gin-and-tonic set of the Home Counties, two topics guaranteed to raise blood pressures are tax evasion and transfer (social security) fraud or deception. Tax evasion in particular has recently been analysed because it is a significant part of most definitions of the 'black economy'. Transfer fraud has probably raised more public anger and assertion but has been less well discussed in the economics literature as such.

The words 'black economy' are emotive and pejorative in themselves. Other descriptions for broadly the same set of activities include the 'informal' / 'irregular' / 'underground' / 'subterranean'/ 'hidden' / 'cash' / 'unofficial' / 'dual' / 'unrecorded' / 'moonlight' / 'twilight' / 'second' / 'untaxed' and 'unmeasured economy'. In different contexts different terms may be more or less appropriate. For example, the 'unmeasured' or 'unrecorded economy' draws attention to the implication that official statistics and their use for policy purposes may be suspect if there are measurement failures. This is an issue discussed further below. The term 'black economy' is adopted here, not necessarily because it is the most appropriate but rather because it is the term that has the widest currency. This is not to prejudge the evaluation of the activities labelled as 'black', however, as some economists see such activities in a positive light.

Tanzi (1980) sees the development of the black economy as the product of two main groups of factors: those relating to the desire to evade taxation, and those relating to the desire to avoid government regulations and restrictions. Limits on legal activities include the eligibility requirements for social security payments, whereas limits on illegal activities cover the sale of stolen goods, prostitution (in some countries), drug trafficking, etc. To the extent that resources devoted to these activities might otherwise have been employed generating income in the legal economy, they also serve to reduce tax collections from a given tax rate. In this sense both sets of motivational forces meet at tax evasion.

8.2 Evasion activities

Evasion covers many different types of activity which attract different attitudes from the public at large. Perhaps the most common form of evasion is to claim more deductions or tax exemptions than is warranted or to under-report income. In connection with these activities, different jobs may offer considerable differences of opportunity. Indeed, the ease with which tax evasion can take place is a significant determinant of its volume. For example, casually employed waiters and the self-employed (because their income is not taxed at source) are thought seldom to pay tax at all. It is often believed that different groups are differentially investigated by the tax authorities. In this respect the farming community represents a politically powerful group that is often thought to be 'left alone'. A second such group is those who produce work in both the formal and informal (cash-in-hand) economy: in the formal or market economy they may declare all income and pay tax appropriately; however, for 'on-the-side' jobs, payment may be a strictly cash, no-tax, activity. A third category covers individuals who work only in the cash economy on either a systematic or a casual basis: these individuals may or may not simultaneously draw social security payments.

It is probably the individuals who work only in the cash economy and fraudulently draw social security payments that attract most criticism. The position they are in allows them to make no contributions to social security and to live relatively well while putting in fewer hours of work than the standard working week. In the popular press individuals indulging in 'transfer fraud' are seen as welfare state scroungers and this group seems to attract the worst publicity. Tax dodgers, on the other hand, especially high-income ones, do not always attract much disapproval.[1] Clearly, there are many contexts in which evasion may take place and these seem to be treated differently by the public at large. Furthermore, a popular belief is that high-income individuals may not need to be tax evaders as they can avoid taxation often with the aid of professional legal and accountancy advice.

The distinction between tax avoidance and tax evasion is not an easy one to make. The straightforward answer is that the distinction is one of legality, with avoidance being legal and evasion not. However, legal boundaries are not always precise and there is a grey area of 'avoision', as Lewis (1982) terms it. As to claims that morally certain types of avoidance are indistinguishable from evasion, Cowell (1985) comments that such a distinction based on moral criteria is too vague and not helpful for economic analysis. He argues the case for certainty versus uncertainty as a distinguishing criterion, with avoidance putting the economic actor in a certain context and evasion leaving a degree of uncertainty, as regards the final taxes that will have to be paid. Lewis adds a number of dimensions to evasion and avoidance that can be summarized as follows:

Evasion	By commission	Intentional
		Unintentional
	By omission	Intentional
		Unintentional
Avoidance	Legal 'loopholes' disapproved of by government	
	Tax expenditures as part of approved government policy	

Most of these distinctions are self-explanatory, but it is perhaps worth noting that an economic approach to evasion lends itself best to the intentional kind, where reasoned action dominates. (For a discussion of the definition of the black economy, etc., see MaCaffee 1980.) However, before pursuing evasion in some detail, a short economic account of avoidance is presented.

[1] Lester Piggott, the jockey who as a successful rider made millions of pounds, was imprisoned for tax fraud. This was very unpopular with many sections of the community, and many sent him money to help him out!

8.3 Avoidence: loopholes versus policy weapons

Tax systems have deductions or exclusions which are essentially indirect excise subsidies. These arise either as the result of errors or less than tight drafting of the tax legislation, or as a deliberate policy to encourage activity X. Figure 8.1 can be used to illustrate both these situations. The curve 12 is the initial budget constraint. If both Y (all other goods and services) and X are taxed, the budget constraint moves towards the origin in a parallel fashion (34). The post-tax equilibrium combination of purchases is determined at point 5. If X is exempt, either by accidental or deliberate action, the budget constraint becomes 32 (i.e. if the individual buys all X he will pay no tax at all). In the event, equilibrium is at point 6 with the consumption of X raised. Tax raised is measured by the vertical distance 67. The drawback of X being untaxed is revealed if outcome 6 is compared with one that raises the same tax but with no exemptions. The budget constraint 89 through 6 allows a higher indifference curve (I_2 compared with I_1) at 10 to be achieved and leaves the tax revenue unchanged.

As already indicated, the outcome may be a matter of design or mistake. If X was a good that generated a positive externality, then encouraging its consumption is appropriate. Browning and Browning (1983) suggest that even in these circumstances it may be a doubtful policy tool because of its lack of explicitness

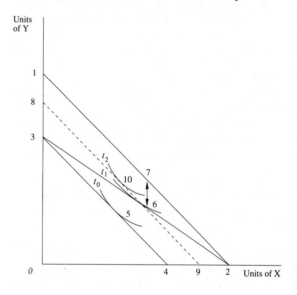

Figure 8.1 Effect of good or service X being untaxed.

may mean that the tax benefits go only to those who are well informed or—more likely in the case of loopholes—to those who have their tax affairs handled by specialist legal/accountancy firms. A further point is that, even if a tax exemption on X is justified it should be the product of explicit public discussion and should not be observed as if it were an inherent part of writing the tax details. The latter situation may well be part of any 'special interest' legislation used to get political support, as discussed in chapter 16.

8.4 Taxation and the informal economy

As a simple starting-point, it is possible to borrow arguments from trade theory to see how the introduction of taxation affects the size of the informal or non-market economy (see Fallon and Verry 1988). Figure 8.2(a) shows a transformation curve TT' which indicates how leisure hours can be reduced to raise output.

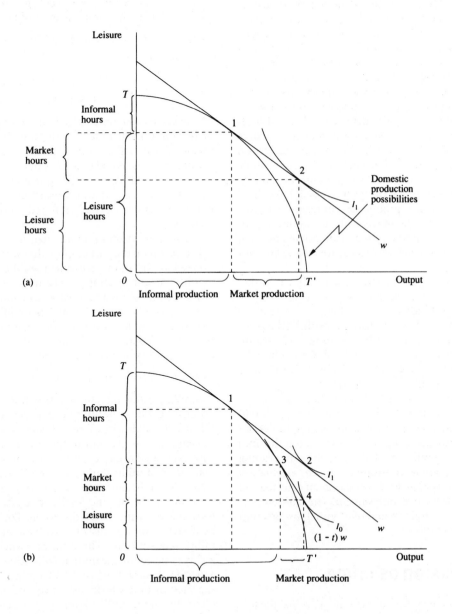

Figure 8.2 Taxation and informal production.

That is, the slope of TT' indicates the rate at which leisure reduction can be converted into output. Suppose the individual begins at point 1: then the hours devoted to leisure and informal production are as indicated. The presence of a market allows the individual to 'trade' with it along the line w (for wage rate). Once market production is an option, the individual finds equilibrium at 2 on I_1 dividing the figure so that informal, market and leisure hours can be distinguished as indicated. In particular, the movement from 1 to 2 involves the introduction of market work-hours and market output. It is of course the latter that is the centre of national income accounting exercises in most countries. Figure 8.2(b) illustrates the impact of the introduction of taxation. The price line labelled w swivels downwards to $(1 - t)w$, reflecting the impact of the tax on wages that are received by hours devoted to market as opposed to non-market or informal production. The depicted individual finds equilibrium at point 4 on the lower indifference curve I_0. Point 3 divides hours into informal production hours, market production hours and leisure hours. The changes in market and leisure hours are ambiguous, but it is clear that the tax has raised the optimal amount of informal production compared with formal production. The movement into informal production is an example of the disincentive effects of taxation reducing the size of measured market output (GNP).

As yet, nothing particularly upsetting has occurred. Certainly there is a welfare loss from distorting the pattern of production, but nothing to warrant the public policy and casual discussions that take place over tax evasion and the 'black' economy. The reason for this is that it is not clear in the above whether the informal hours involve income liable to taxation or simply home production for no renumeration—simply doing things for yourself rather than via a market transaction. It is working for money that should attract positive tax payments, and failing to declare or incorrectly declaring them to the tax authorities that causes conflict. In following this tax-evading path, the individual confronts an uncertain situation in that what is being done is illegal and if detected will involve some form of 'punishment'. The economics of committing a crime should offer initial insights into this decision process.

8.5 Evasion as crime

Tax evasion offers the risk-neutral individual the following type of choice. Assume that taxable income is

Y and the rate of tax is t. Then with certainty the individual can enjoy $(1 - t)Y$ by simply declaring and paying tax. If the individual evades taxes, then further assume that there is a probability p that he will get caught and face a fine or a punishment whose money value is F. The expected value of the evading strategy is given by

$$(8.1) \qquad E(V) = p(Y - F) + (1 - p)Y$$

If this exceeds $(1 - t)Y$ in value, the individual will evade. For example, if $Y = £12\,000, p = 0.5, t = 0.33$ and $F = £5000$, the comparison would be

$$(8.2) \qquad (1 - t)Y = 0.66(12\,000) = £8000$$

as compared with

$$(8.3) \quad p(Y - F) + (1 - p)Y = 0.5(12\,000 - 5000)$$
$$+ 0.5(12\,000) = £9500$$

The expected outcome exceeds the monetary value of the certain outcome and the individual can be predicted to evade. Note that the source of the additional expected income does not affect the decision. The illegal nature of the potential gains offers neither extra nor reduced satisfaction, nor has the uncertain nature of the preferred outcome been included.

A common assumption adopted in economics is risk aversion on the part of individuals, and its inclusion reduces the number of outcomes where evasion is a utility-enhancing strategy. The uncertain prospect has to be differentially attractive to compensate the individual for bearing risk, which is a 'bad' in itself for risk-averse people. Once risk aversion is included, the relevant calculation is utility-based so that the expected utility of evasion becomes

$$(8.4) \qquad E(U) = pU(Y - F) + (1 + p)U(Y)$$

Figure 8.3(b) illustrates the new situation. Y is the pre-tax income and U_0 the utility level associated with it. If the individual declares Y, the certain legal income he can enjoy is $(1 - t)Y$ putting the individual at point 1 with associated utility U_1, which becomes the benchmark level of utility. Suppose initially the monetary value of punishment on detection is F_1, so that $(Y - F_1)$ is the income level and U_2 is the utility level enjoyed with detected evasion. For evasion to be attractive, the act must offer at least as high a level of utility as not evading. This is the case when the probability of detection means that U_1 is achieved with an expected income level of Y^* at point 2. Y^* is the expected income whose certain equivalent $(1 - t)Y$ offers the same utility levels $(Y^* > (1 - t)Y$ is a reflection of risk aversion). Depending on the curva-

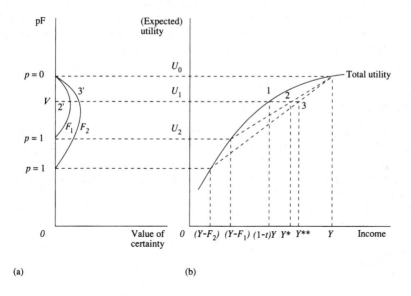

Figure 8.3 Evasion as crime.

ture of the total utility curve, which indicates the extent of risk aversion, Y^* will be much or only just greater than $(1 - t)Y$. The greater the curvature, the greater the risk aversion and the more Y^* must exceed $(1 - t)Y$ to make evasion attractive. Given F_1, this amounts to having a low probability of detection. As p takes values from zero to unity, the expected income position migrates from Y to $(Y - F_1)$. The general point is that if people are risk-averse evasion will be much less than if they are risk-neutral (implicitly contained in an expected value calculation).

Figure 8.3(a) plots the half-moon shapes that indicate the value of certainty to the individual in question. It is simply the horizontal distance between the total utility curve and the expected value line. The distance $V2'$ in 8.3(a) equals 12 in 8.2(b): it represents the money sum that compensates for bearing the uncertainty of a fine F_1 with probability p (at the utility level U_1) associated with the certain income $(1 - t)Y$. The 'top' intercept of the curve labelled F_1 in part (a) occurs when $p = 0$ and the lower one, where $p = 1$ and detection has become a certainty. It is now possible to explore some preliminary policy implications, as follows:

1. The more risk-averse people are, the less evasion there will be.
2. For a given fine F_1, the higher the probability of being detected, the less evasion there will be (p will

vary with resources devoted to detection by the tax authorities and the obligations taxpayers are required to meet.)

3. For a larger fine F_2, Fig. 8.3(a) and (b) need amending as illustrated and Y^{**} becomes the expected income needed to make evasion attractive. $V3' = 13$ is now the appropriate value of certainty and implies that for a larger fine a lower probability of detection will suffice to deter a given evasion decision.

Further discussion of these issues is reserved until a somewhat more sophisticated model of evasion is introduced. In the above framework evasion is an indivisible act, a one-zero choice. In reality, individuals may declare some part of taxable income. A framework that illustrates this has been provided by Cowell (1985)[2] and is introduced below.

8.6 How much to evade and avoid

Individuals are usually faced with the problem of how much of their income to declare for taxation and how much not to declare (rather than whether or not to

[2] Cowell employs a von Neumann–Morgenstern utility function as utilized below.

declare any income at all). Once again, the individual's income is Y and a proportional income tax rate, t, is to be levied on the income that is declared. The probability of detection is p and, if detected, undeclared income will be subject to a fine. If D is the level of income that the individual declares, then when evasion is successful (i.e. the individual is not caught) net income N is:

$$(8.5) \qquad N = Y - tD$$

However, if unsuccessful (and the individual is caught), a fine is levied on the undeclared income $[Y - D]$, so that net income is:

$$(8.6) \qquad C = Y - tD - F[Y - D]$$

As the rate of fine, F, is greater than the tax rate, t, the individual is worse off when caught. The problem that the individual faces is to choose the value of D that maximizes expected utility (EU), where:

$$(8.7) \qquad \begin{aligned} EU &= (1 - p)U(Y - tD) \\ &\quad + pU(Y - tD - F[Y - D]) \end{aligned}$$

or

$$(8.8) \qquad EU = (1 - p)U(N) + pU(C)$$

In Fig. 8.4 the 45° line permits a comparison between units recorded on each axis. As the individual is fined for evasion, all the 'action' in the diagram takes place in the wedge below the 45° line. If the individual is honest and declares all income, then net income is

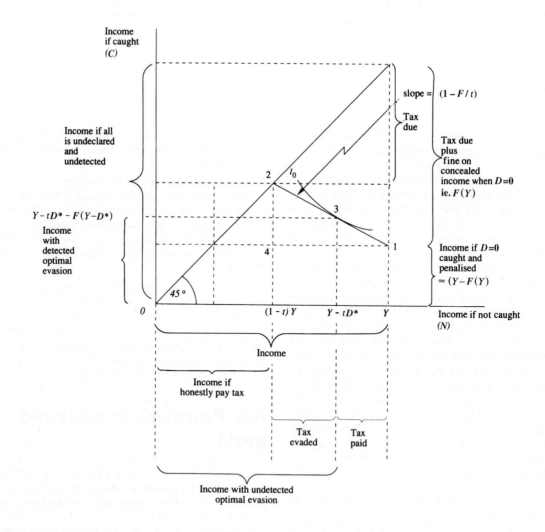

Figure 8.4 Optimal evasion.

$(1 - t)Y$, i.e. at point 2 in the diagram. If the individual is dishonest, income depends on whether the individual is detected. When undetected (the individual is successful as described by N in equation 8.5) the net income of the individual is recorded on the x axis of Fig. 8.4 and if detected net income is recorded on the y axis. Suppose the individual decides to declare only $D^*(< Y)$ of income for taxation. When undetected, the individual is at the position $Y - tD^*$ on the x axis in Fig. 8.4. However, if the individual is detected this strategy leaves a net income (C) at $Y - tD^* - F[Y - D^*]$ on the y axis.

The slope of line 12 in Fig. 8.4 is $(1 - F/t)^3$. This line illustrates the 'price' that the individual will pay if detected as acting dishonestly. At point 2 there is no 'price' to pay as the individual is honest. At point 1 the individual is completely dishonest and, if caught, pays FY to the tax man instead of tY. As the fine F increases relative to the tax rate t, line 12 becomes steeper.

The individual maximizes utility at a point of tangency between the indifference curve and the 'price' line 12. If the individual is risk averse, the indifference curve is convex to the origin. The slope of the indifference curve[4] is:

$$(8.9) \qquad \frac{-(1 - p)}{p} \frac{U'(N)}{U'(C)}$$

where U' is the first derivative of the utility function. An interior optimum (i.e. where some income is undeclared) arises for a risk averse individual when with reference to equation 8.7:

$$\frac{dEU}{dD} = -t(1 - p)U'(N) - (t - F)pU'(C) = 0$$

(8.10)

In Fig. 8.4 the individual solves the problem of how much to declare at tangency point 3. The optimum strategy is to declare D^* and to evade $Y - D^*$ income.

The analysis informs policy-makers if it is able to predict the response of the individual when policy-makers change variables that have been identified. Fig. 8.5 is used to consider the impact of changes in variables. For example:

(a) *The impact of a change in the tax rate*

The slope of line 12 in part (a) of Fig. 8.5 is $(1 - F/t)$. This line illustrates the 'price' that the

individual will pay if detected as acting dishonestly. At point 2 there is no 'price' to pay as the individual is honest. At point 1 the individual is *completely* dishonest and, if caught, pays FY to the tax man instead of tY. As the tax rate increases (relative to the fine) the line 12 becomes less steep, having swivelled to 12'.

In the original situation the individual maximizes utility at a point of tangency between the indifference curve and the 'price' line 12. If the individual is risk averse, the indifference curve is convex to the origin. In part (a) of Fig. 8.5 the optimum solution is to declare D^* and to evade $Y - D^*$ income.

If there were an increase in tax rates intuition might suggest that the individual would be inclined to declare less income (as there is more at stake!). Once again, whether this is the case depends on 'income' and 'substitution' effects. Consider what happens when the tax rate (t) is increased. An increase in the tax rate changes the slope of the 'price' line (point 2 shifts to point 2'). The new 'price' line is 2'1. There is an 'income' (or 'wealth') effect as well as a 'substitution' effect associated with the price change (the movement from point 3 on I_3 to 4 on I_2). Economists usually assume that individuals are risk averse and that absolute aversion is reduced as the individual's income increases. The rise in the tax rate reduces the individual's net income and the 'income' effect in Fig. 8.5 makes the individual more risk averse; $Y - tD^*$ would migrate to the left to point 5. The substitution effect (the movement from 5 to 4) will increase risk-taking (the 'price' of honesty has increased). The income effect works in the opposite direction to the substitution effect and the net effect of an increase in the tax rate depends on the strength of these two effects; *tax evasion may increase or fall*.

Yitzhaki (1974) suggests a way to tackle this ambiguity by considering the case where the penalty on tax evasion is proportional to the evaded tax. In many countries, penalties are levied on evaded tax, ie. $t[Y - D]$ (not on evaded income, $[Y - D]$). In this case, the penalty paid on undeclared income is Ft (where F is now a sur-charge on the tax). The penalty Ft and the tax rate t are now proportional to each other. When there is an increase in t the 'price line' (12) shifts inwards in a parallel way. In Figure 8.5(b) the tax rate is increased by the same amount but now, in the Yitzhaki case, line 12 shifts to 1'2'. The slope of the 'price line' is now $1 - F$ (as it is independent of t). There is now no substitution effect when the tax rate is changed. An increase in tax reduces the taxpayer's income and, with decreasing absolute risk aversion, more income is declared (in order that the taxpayer reduces risk). Myles (1995) shows that if, for example,

---

[3] Distance 15 in Fig. 8.4 is the fall in N, i.e. $-tY$. The slope of 12 is distance 24 divided by distance 14 i.e. $-(tY - FY) / - tY$, or $(1 - F/t)$.

[4] The slope of the indifference curve is determined by dividing the first derivative of (8.8) with respect to N by the first derivative of (8.8) with respect to C.

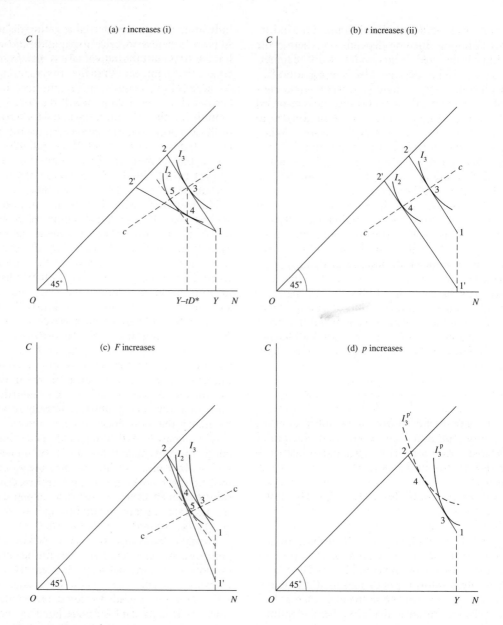

Figure 8.5 Factors affecting tax evasion.

absolute risk aversion R_a (as measured by the Arrow–Pratt definition i.e. $U''(Y)/U'(Y)$) decreases as income increases, higher tax rates will lead to greater income declarations and equilibrium moves from point 3 on I_3 to point 4 on I_2. The result in the case of constant or decreasing absolute risk aversion is unambiguous *but now it is counter-intuitive; an increase in the tax rate causes more income to be honestly declared.* In Fig. 8.5 the locus of points labelled cc

slopes indicate decreasing absolute aversion and as line 12 shifts in it will be clear that tax evasion is reduced. Because some regard the result as counter-intuitive, further refinements of the model have been investigated to determine what is required for tax rate increases to lead to greater tax evasion.[5]

[5] For example, Yaniv (1994) shows that: (a) if the worst that can happen to a detected evader is the confiscation of his entire undeclared income and (b) the *relative* risk aversion is constant and

(b) The impact of a change in the fine

Returning to the original assumptions in part (c) of Fig. 8.5 a change in the fine alters the slope of the 'price' line 12. Point 1 moves down vertically to 1'. In this case, both income (point 3 to point 5) and substitution (point 5 to point 4) effects work in the same direction. As one might imagine, *an increase in the fine discourages evasion* and the price effect is point 3 to point 4.

(c) The impact of a change in the probability of detection

In part (d) of Fig. 8.5 this can be assessed by considering the slope of the indifference curve. The slope has been defined as:

$$\frac{-(1-p)}{p} \frac{U'(N)}{U'(C)}$$

so an increase in p affects the slope of the indifference curve. In Fig. 8.5 the new indifference associated with an increase in probability of detection (i.e. from p to p^1) is shown as the dotted curve $I_3^{p'}$ replacing I_3^p and this is tangent to the original constraint at 4, indicating that *more income is honestly declared as the detection rate increases*.

The theory leads to intuitive results when considering the impact of a change in fine and in probability of detection. However, the results that emerge from the theory with respect to a change in the tax rate are less clear cut. In the Yitzhaki case the theoretical results concerning the impact of an increase in tax rates on the extent of evasion are unambiguous for cases in which the taxpayer has a decreasing or constant absolute risk aversion. But when the taxpayer anticipates that the fine is levied on undeclared income rather than evaded tax there is no clear prediction. It is necessary to consider empirical studies to proceed. This means that analysts must refer to empirical work and to three different kinds of study:

(A) Refer to *surveys of taxpayer attitudes*. For example, Lewis (1979) carried out a survey among 200 male taxpayers in Bath in 1977 and, in general, respondents believed that a reduction in tax would have little effect on evasion. Dean, Keenan and Kerney (1980), based on a survey of 424 adults in Fife (Scotland) in 1977 report that the most popular reason (93 per cent of respondents) for evasion was that the general level of taxation was too high. Mason and

bounded from above by the inverse of the penalty rate then 'when the fruits of evasion become sweeter a rational taxpayer will take a bigger bite' (p. 109). Refinements by way of introducing 'social norms' generates 'solutions' that produce the 'intuitive' result (e.g. Cowell and Gordon 1988). The importance of social norms are discussed below.

Calvin (1984) surveyed 800 taxpayers in Oregon in 1975 and repeated the survey in 1980. Over this time, the percentage who thought that people evaded because taxes are 'too high' rose from 48 per cent to 64 per cent.

(B) Refer to the results of *experimental games*. For example, Friedland, Maital and Rutenberg (1978) involved a sample 15 students in a tax game. They found that when the tax rate increased from 25 per cent to 50 per cent, the probability of under-reporting rose from about 0.5 to 0.8 and overall declarations fell from about 80% to 60%. When the fine was increased from 3 times to 15 times the amount of tax evaded the probability of under-declaration fell, but only marginally. Spicer and Becker (1980) involved a sample of 57 students over a 10-month period. Those who thought they were paying more tax than others evaded nearly 33 per cent of tax payable, those who thought they were paying less evaded only about 12 per cent.

(C) Refer to *statistical analysis of taxpayer behaviour*. Clotfelter (1983) examined the tax returns for about 47,000 individuals (drawn from a survey in 1969 by the Inland Revenue Service in the US). He measured undeclared income as the difference between the amount of income which the IRS auditors determined was due and the amount actually reported by each individual. Honest mistakes ('too much' or 'too little') were expected to average out so that any overall difference would reveal evasion. Evasion was linked to: (i) after tax income; (ii) the individual's marginal tax rate; (iii) wages as a proportion of true gross income; (iv) interest and dividends as a proportion of true gross income; (5) variables for marital status, age, region. Clotfelter concluded that 'higher tax rates tend to stimulate tax evasion' (p. 368); the elasticity of under-reporting with respect to the marginal tax rate ranged from 0.52 to 0.84 depending upon the type of tax return.

For some economists the third of these approaches seems more reliable. When using the results of surveys, there is always a question as to whether respondents have understood the question and/or answered honestly. When considering tax games, there is always a question as to whether or not individuals act differently when they know they are being observed in an experiment and whether the players in the game are representative (e.g. will students with little experience of tax paying act differently to taxpayers?). Nevertheless, an evaluation of all the evidence suggests that it is impossible to rule out the 'intuitive result' that increased tax rates cause more evasion. In particular, note the elasticity estimated by Clotfelter (1983).[6] Further theoretical work is developing to determine what considerations are necessary to generate this result (e.g. see Myles and Naylor 1996).

8.7 Criticisms of economic analysis of tax evasion

Before proceeding to consider the extent to which theory informs policy it is as well to recognize the possible deficiencies of the analysis. Pyle (1991) provides a review of many criticisms of the 'standard' approach (as described in section 8.6). The following list takes this review as a basis. Note, however, it is always easier to criticize than to construct and the important question may be whether or not the analysis described in the previous section can be developed further.

1. The assumption of a constant tax rate is questionable. A progressive income tax schedule needs to be incorporated in the analysis. A progressive income tax system will act as a further disincentive to the declaration of income in the absence of any counteracting incentive (e.g. in terms of an increased likelihood of punishment).

2. The analysis above only considers the raising of revenue and not the use of revenue. One way of dealing with this is to introduce the idea that the revenue is to be used to provide public goods. Cowell and Gordon (1988) explore this. One result is that, if individuals feel that public goods are 'overprovided', then an increase in the tax rate will lead to the intuitive result that there will be increased evasion. The reason is that an increase in tax exacerbates the initial feeling of 'overprovision' and if there were decreasing absolute risk aversion this will lead to increased evasion.

3. Throughout the analysis the assumption is that individuals are amoral utility maximizers. Individuals are expected to deal with tax evasion in exactly the same way as they would deal with any gamble. Is this reasonable? Baldry (1986) reports the results of two sets of experiments. In the first, when tax evasion was the decision some participants never evaded tax (and those who did evade were influenced by the tax schedule). When the experiment was repeated as a

gamble (with identical payoffs) the result was everyone gambled (and each made the maximum bet).

A number of authors have argued that such a difference is created by the existence of psychic or stigma costs which the individual experiences when evading tax. Taxpayers feel badly knowing that they are not discharging their responsibility to the community and surely such costs should be incorporated into the utility function? Spicer (1986) draws attention to 'norms of compliance'. The decision to evade tax will be influenced by factors such as the perceptions of the justice of the fiscal system and the number of individuals' friends who themselves evade tax. In order to incorporate a more 'realistic model of evasion, Spicer amends the decision-making rule to include psychic costs. A taxpayer will evade tax only as long as the expected gains from taxes exceed the expected losses from fines and from the psychic costs associated with evasion. To evade,

$$(8.12) \qquad (1-p)t\theta Y - pst\theta Y - c > 0$$

where t = tax rate;
θ = fraction of taxable income not reported (i.e. $(Y-D)/Y$ in section 8.6);
Y = income;
s = the fine rate imposed on evaded tax (i.e. $st = F$ in section 8.6);
p = the probability of detection;
c = psychic costs of taxation.

The question then becomes, what influences psychic costs and how important are they in the tax evasion decision? Here Spicer notes psychological relationships such as cognitive dissonance, whereby, when an individual acts in a way that is not consistent with his beliefs, feelings of discomfort are created which stimulate changes in beliefs. If taxpayers commit more acts of tax evasion, it is likely that this, in itself, erodes social norms and reduces the psychic costs of evasion. Spicer and Lundstedt (1976) provide econometric evidence that the number of other tax evaders known to the individual make evasion more likely and, in this way, social norms cannot be ignored. How would such analysis affect policy? Take the attraction of tax amnesties whereby evaders are given an opportunity to 'confess'. Malik and Schwab (1991) explore the connections between tax evasion and tax amnesties. Those who find the *ex post* disutility from evasion greater than expected can use the amnesty to achieve the desired honesty level.

4. Returning to the assumption that individuals act immorally, the analysis in section 8.6 is also questionable in so far as it ignores 'compliance costs' of taxation. These are the costs of keeping records, saving

---

[6] Having said this, it should also be noted that this relationship between marginal tax rates and tax evasion is not always found. Geeroms and Wilmots (1985) using Belgian data find precisely the converse conclusion, i.e. that tax increases lead to less evasion.

receipts, filling in forms, etc. that are associated with making declarations to the tax offices. Assume that compliance costs are a fixed cost (incurred whether one declares £1 or £100 000 of income) to the tax offices. Such a cost (if high enough) may act as a deterrent to declaring anything at all. By contrast, assume that compliance costs increase with income (e.g. the number of sources of income may increase as income increases). Now compliance costs are themselves similar to a tax on income (Collard 1989a). Evasion may follow if the costs of acting honestly are significant.

5. But what of the costs of evading? The analysis in section 8.6 suggests that individuals are replete with information. Is it reasonable, for example, to assume that individuals have knowledge of the probabilities of detection. Spicer (1986) argues that 'the tax evasion decision appears to be governed not by maximizing strategies but by rules of thumb or heuristics' (p. 15). In this way, fine calculations based on the probability of detection and the size of punishment are unlikely to be made: available heuristics are more likely to be employed. Research indicates, for example, that past decision experience with audits will bias estimates of audit probabilities. Decision-makers are calculating not the true probability of detection but, instead, the most easy and available guess as to how to order their affairs. Frey and Eichenberger (1989) offer as one example of apparent 'anomalies' the fact that experienced events are systematically over weighted in individual decision-making. These arguments are pertinent in policy discussion of the impact of changes in the probability of detection on the honesty of taxpayers. On the basis of actual probabilities it is difficult to understand why so many taxpayers are honestly rejecting the gamble associated with tax evasion. While psychic costs may help explain, the press coverage given to those found guilty of major evasion may also prove tactically useful. Taxpayers may overestimate the chances of detection as a result of such announcements. Aitken and Bonneville (1980) report that a large survey of nearly 5000 individuals conducted by the Internal Revenue Service in the USA found that the number of tax audits and investigation that actually took place were generally overestimated.

6. The model described in section 8.6 assumed that the individual was a 'price taker'. The individual was too 'small' to have any real impact on the prices that he/she faced. A 'large' taxpayer may influence the behaviour of other taxpayers. A 'large' taxpayer may be so important that how he/she reports income may affect the tax officer's decision to instigate an investigation (i.e. p may now become a function of D).

7. The analysis described in section 8.6 is essentially a static model. Each year the taxpayer enters into a 'new' gamble; a 'new' game with the tax authority. However, for 'large' taxpayers a decision to under declare in one year may affect the decision to evade in a future year (an *erratic* response may attract suspicion). A dynamic model then becomes relevant.

8. The analysis in section 8.6 does not concern decisions related to labour supply. The chances of being undetected may depend on the way in which individuals are remunerated. Wages paid in cash may influence the extent to which individuals will work in the black economy. The extent of tax evasion will then depend on the hours that individuals can spend in the black economy rather than in the formal economy. Cowell (1981) considers the allocation of hours to an official and to an unofficial sector and shows (in the case of a specific utility function) that an increase in the tax rate will reduce the proportion of time spent in the official labour market and increase tax evasion.

9. Analysis of the decision on tax evasion is meant to help tax authorities to recover tax. However, as described in section 8.6 it makes no allowance for the interaction between tax evasion and tax avoidance. An individual could try to avoid her tax legally by changing the allocation of income between sheltered and unsheltered allocations. An increase in the detection rate for evasion might discourage evasion and encourage honesty but it is not clear that it will result in the tax revenue increase that might be expected in the absence of avoidance.

Alm (1988) presents a model along similar lines to Cowell's which has the advantage of a three-activity approach in that tax avoidance is part of the analysis alongside evasion and declaring income to the tax authorities. An insight into the approach taken is offered in Fig. 8.6. Essentially, two stages are involved. The first, the selection of how much evasion, can be taken from Cowell's analysis (so that income net of evaded income equals OO'). The second is the division of legal income between taxable and shelter income, a choice that is independent of that made at stage 1. The relevant variables are the tax structure on legal income, which is progressive (hence its shape OT'). In the case illustrated, positive and increasing marginal costs of avoidance are incurred (AC'). Reported income is measured from O and sheltered income from O' with q^* being the optimal decision point.

One comparative-static result is offered here to illustrate how the model works. An increase in the probability of detection increases legal income at stage 1 (by flattening the indifference map in Fig. 8.4)

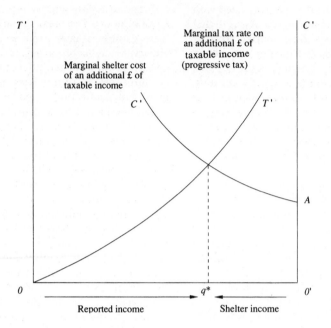

Figure 8.6 Declaration versus avoidance on legal income.

so that OO' becomes OO'' in Fig. 8.7. Curve AC' is bodily moved rightwards by the shift of the vertical axis to O'', and the new optimal decision is around Oq^{**} with both declared and avoided income raised. The effect on the proportions declared is ambiguous. The proportion of declared income changes from

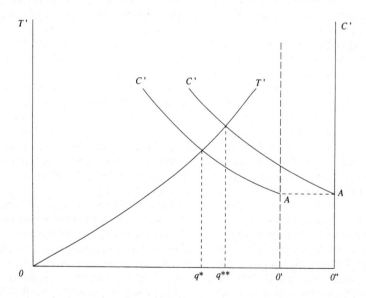

Figure 8.7 Increasing legal income and the effect on declaration and avoidance.

Source: Alm (1988) © Reproduced with permission of Sage Publications Inc., with some additions.

Oq^*/OO' to Oq^{**}/OO''. The proportion will be higher if the marginal shelter cost rises faster than the marginal tax rate as legal income increases; i.e. it depends on the relative slopes of OT' and AC'. (This result is similar in a sense to the informal market—leisure hour choice above in that introducing tax rate t raises informal hours, but the effect on market and leisure hours is ambiguous.) Alm's analysis introduces a 'compliance cost' to avoidance in a way that the analysis of section 8.3 does not.

8.8 Policy to deal with tax evasion

The preceding analysis informs policy-makers if it offers insight into the impact of policy variables such as fines and the probability for detection. Two questions are relevant when considering policy toward tax evasion. First, how much tax evasion is optimal? Secondly, how cost effective are different instruments that can be used to deal with tax evasion?

(a) How much tax evasion is 'optimal'?

In previous sections discussion has been about the optimal level of tax evasion from the point of view of the individual taxpayer. In this section concern focuses on the level of tax evasion that is optimal from the point of view of the community. Taking this perspective it might seem that the answer is obvious; tax evasion is illegal and tax evasion 'should' be eradicated. However, the costs of reducing tax evasion cannot be ignored and it has been argued that continued investment in this activity may eventually commit more additional resources to deterring tax evasion than the additional benefits that such an activity produces. For this reason it might be suggested that the optimal anti-evasion occurs when the marginal costs of reducing tax evasion equals the marginal benefits. If so, the critical consideration is what are the marginal costs and the marginal benefits?

Starting with the marginal benefits of anti-evasion policy, the implication of many policy statements seems to be that the gains from reducing evasion are the tax revenues that are recovered. For example, in evidence to the Public Accounts Committee (1981–2) the Inland Revenue stated that in 1981 the yield (in extra revenue) from investigative work was £92 000 per official (Pyle, 1979). This sum of money would very much exceed the costs of employing a tax investigator. Similarly, Skinner and Slemrod (1985) cite the estimates of the Inland Revenue Service Commis-

sioner to indicate that every extra dollar of resources allocated to the IRS could be expected to bring in more than 10 dollars in tax revenue. If the marginal benefit of tax evasion were additional tax revenue and the marginal cost were the costs of additional tax inspection there is reason to suggest that there has been under-investment.

Two problems arise with such an interpretation. First, there is some reason to doubt that evasion reduces revenue in the 'static' arithmetical way that has been described. In evidence to the Keith Committee (1983) the Inland Revenue calculated the size of the UK's black economy in 1982 as approximately £15 billion per year. If there were a constant income tax rate of 30p per pound of income this suggests a loss of approximately £4–5 billion per annum. Peacock and Shaw (1982) question such analysis. Such a revenue loss would not allow for the expenditure of any revenue earned in the black economy. If there were expenditure on goods and services provided in the formal sector then tax is raised on such expenditure. Nor does it allow for any growth of income in the formal economy. Income generated in the informal sector may ultimately be used to produce employment and income in the formal sector.

Secondly, and more generally, there is reason to question whether or not the revenue that is recovered by anti-evasion policy is a reflection of the benefits of such a policy. This is so because such revenue may be interpreted as a *transfer* rather than a *cost* to the community. Using unrecovered tax revenue as an indicator of social cost may be questionable. Collard (1989b, p. 104) refers to the 'naïve rule' as being that tax investigation be pushed to the point where marginal investigation cost equals marginal tax revenue but questions whether it should 'fall short' of this level because 'investigation costs are real while taxation is simply a transfer'.

So if tax revenue is a transfer where are the benefits of anti-evasion? How does the community benefit? Following Pyle's classification (1979), the following are some of the alleged benefits:

(i) *Output*. Is output reduced by tax evasion? On one hand, a revenue loss may mean that there is less public expenditure and a consequent loss of employment (assuming that the revenue would not have been used in other ways, eg. to cut public borrowing). But, set against this, there is the 'supply side' argument that taxes act as a disincentive. If taxes are a disincentive to work then the output of the economy (formal and informal) may be greater to the extent that some taxpayers are not deterred from work.

(ii) *Equity*: there is an equity/ distribution loss to the extent that the ability to evade is distributed in an arbitrary way across society. The ability to evade depends on opportunity. Collard (1989b) provides an example of how tax evasion increases 'unfairness'. If it is the objective to raise 40 per cent of income in tax and one-third of taxpayers conceal a quarter of their incomes then the required average tax rate will have to be 48 per cent. This will be the effective rate for the honest but the dishonest will only pay 36 per cent. A 'crude' index of unfairness is proposed which is equal to the ratio of the rate paid by honest taxpayers to the rate paid by dishonest taxpayers. In this way one of the benefits of anti-evasion tax policy would be in terms of reducing the index of unfairness. Of course, evasion itself creates unfairness and it may also thwart the government's attempt to re-distribute resources from one section of the community to another because of existing 'unfairness'.

(iii) *Resource misallocation*: Tax evasion affects the allocation of resources. While the effect on reducing the disincentive to work may be positive there is another consideration. For example, if markets are competitive the marginal product of labour and capital mobility is equalized in different sectors of the economy if these resources can move freely from one sector to another. However, if it is difficult to move into the black economy the gross return to labour and capital in the taxed sector may exceed the return in the black economy (to allow for the tax that must be paid in the legal economy). In this way, resources used in the black economy may be more productively used in the formal economy. Alm (1985) estimates the welfare costs arising from the coexistence of an untaxed underground economy and a taxed legitimate sector. He uses a Harberger general equilibrium model (see chapter 7). The welfare cost is approximately 5–10 per cent of GNP.

(iv) *Information bias*: It is argued that the continued existence of tax evasion distorts macroeconomic policy because tax evasion biases information. For example, the government may use official statistics to draw the conclusion that there is a worrying level of unemployment (when, in fact, many so called 'unemployed' are employed in the black economy). A policy to expand the economy may then affect price inflation more than the level of output. One commentator (Feige, 1981) argued that the existence of 'staginflation' (inflation and recession) in the 1970s was no more than a statistical illusion; unemployment appearing to rise as labour moved to the informal economy.

(v) *Tax morality*: As evasion increases it may lead individuals to become more willing to involve themselves in other illegal activities. This may increase crime and increase law enforcement costs.

(vi) *Taxpayer excess burden*: Yitzhaki (1987) argues that tax evasion creates an excess burden. This arises because if the government guaranteed a tax payment that was equal to the tax and expected penalty on evaded income then a risk averse individual could be better off to have an after-tax income *with complete certainty* by not evading income tax.

The list of factors that contribute to the marginal social benefit of anti-evasion policy differs from the ones to which policy-makers most often refer. Of course the effects noted above are difficult to estimate. But equally there are difficulties in addressing issues which arise when considering the marginal cost of anti-evasion. The marginal costs of anti-evasion will be kept to a minimum if policy-makers make best use of the instruments which they can employ.

(b) How should anti-evasion policy be structured?

To illustrate, refer back to the theory in section 8.6. Compare the impact of changes in the probability of detection and in changes in the fine or penalty for evasion. In section 8.6 (following Allingham and Sandmo 1972, Cowell 1984 and Pyle 1989) it was assumed that a taxpayer maximized expected utility (EU) as described in the following equation:

$$EU = (1-p)U(Y-tD) + pU(Y-tD-F[Y-D])$$
(8.12)

From this equation it is possible to state that evasion is worthwhile if when $D = Y$ (i.e. the taxpayer is honest) the marginal expected utility with respect to changes in D is negative. For this will mean that reducing D (the amount declared) will increase expected utility (i.e. the taxpayer gains from dishonesty). What conditions must apply for this to be so? From (8.12) it can be shown that this arises when:

(8.13) $$Fp < t$$

i.e. the expected penalty from evasion must be less than the rate of tax.[7] In so far as this analysis informs

---

[7] When the first derivative *at the point when* $Y = D$ is:

(8.2n)
$$\frac{dEU}{dD} = -t(1-p)U'(Y-tD)$$
$$- (t-F)pU'(Y-tD-F[Y-D]) < 0$$

As $Y = D$, this can be written as:

(8.3n)
$$\frac{dEU}{dD} = -t(1-p)U'[Y-tY]$$
$$- (t-F)pU'[Y-tY]) < 0$$

policy, then to make the taxpayer honest, policy makers must ensure that $Fp > t$.

There are many combinations of p and F that will satisfy the requirement that $pF > t$. Policy-makers may increase p or F. It may appear 'obvious' that, if both p and F deter evasion, increasing F is the appropriate strategy. After all, increasing p requires resource *costs* (tax inspectors, etc.), whereas F is less costly (fines paid by the criminals are *transfers* from the criminals) Why not continue to raise fines to deter? First, justice requires that 'the punishment should fit the crime'. Secondly, to preserve marginal deterrence, fines must increase with the extent of the crime (otherwise individuals may evade everything working on the principle that 'you may as well be hanged for a sh...

...ker is to minimize the ...d this means choosing ...f policy instruments. If ...is possible then to con- ...of anti-evasion policy. ...equal to the marginal ...e 'optimal' level of tax ...complexity of such a ...illustrate how much ...uld be from the more ...ve of equating the ...l tax inspector with ...at the tax inspector

black

...onomy

Almost by definition, any area of concern that contains a significant illegal element is going to be deficient of reliable statistics. Such is the case with the extent of black economies. Overlaid on this inherent data weakness is the fact that different observers have 'axes to grind'. For some, the apparent failure of Keynesian expansionary policies to stimulate GNP can be put down to the fact that it is the black economy that has expanded. For others, the existence of an extensive black economy in which everyone has 'loads of money' justifies the curtailment of social security

or:

$$(8.4n) \qquad = -t(1 - p) - (t - F)p < 0$$

or:

$$(8.5n) \qquad = -t + Fp < 0$$

programmes. For the tax authorities it may represent missed millions and a decline in tax morality. The figures quoted for the black economy are as varied as the methods used to generate them. There are a number of surveys that document these methods and offer criticisms (e.g. O'Higgins 1981, Dilnot and Morris 1981 and Carter 1984). In this section a summary of the main methods summarized in these sources is offered.

It was noted in the chapter on cost–benefit analysis that there is a limited number of sources of valuation information. These sources are market data, behavioural approach, direct enquiry via questionnaires or experiments, and (in exceptional circumstances) the views of experts. This list can be adapted to the measurement methods employed on the black economy to provide an organizing framework.

8.9.1 'Market' data

In this context market data covers a number of official sources of information. In particular, national income accounting offers two approaches. At the 'macro' level MaCaffee (1980) has considered the gap between the income approach to national income calculation and the expenditure approach. Information for the former comes from tax returns, and the argument is that black economy income will not show up as income but will show up on the expenditure side.

Dilnot and Morris (1981) are critical of this approach on the grounds that the basic argument is not all that tight. One example they offer is the renting out of premises that are used as a brothel. The rent paid will probably be included in the income estimate of GDP but the expenditure involved is unrecorded so that the inclusion/exclusion 'goes the wrong way' for the MaCaffee approach. They note that, even if all transactions were entirely legitimate, errors in the sampling used to collect the data and timing inconsistencies would cause the income and expenditure figures to diverge; so they argue that the error between the two approaches is largely that—an error—and advocate the much more disaggregated approach they themselves follow. They use disaggregated income and expenditure figures using the Family Expenditure Survey and find the black economy to be some 2–3 per cent of GNP. O'Higgins (1981) similarly resorts to official statistics. He notes that there is a discrepancy in the Family Expenditure Survey between the expenditure recorded for the self-employed (thought to be significant evaders) and other employed people sharing a similar recorded income. But there is a question over whether the correct comparisons have been made; employee incomes are recorded on a current-period basis, whereas the details for the self-employed are for earlier accounting periods.

It is of course possible to use data that are available to the tax authorities. In the USA the Internal Revenue Service uses detailed audits of a probability sample of individual income tax returns to isolate the characteristics of those likely to under-report taxable income and suggest that 6–9 per cent of legal income goes unreported. O'Higgins is doubtful about a related approach of using official tax enforcement data on the grounds that these will vary with the investigative and prosecution effort made from period to period.

8.9.2 Behavioural approach

Studies listed under this heading are those that rely on the observation that black transactions need to be unrecorded and therefore are differentially cash ones; i.e. they rely almost literally on the behaviour of black economy participants. One such 'indirect' monetary approach relies on the increased circulation of large-denomination notes in the UK economy. However, given inflationary times, transactions at higher prices might be expected to be a significant cause of the observed change in the notes circulating.

Two US studies also rely on the cash-in-hand view of the black economy. Guttman (1977) suggests that legitimate activities involve a fixed ratio of cash to current account (demand deposit) payments so that an increase in this ratio reflects the growth of the black economy. Similarly, Feige (1981; also see 1989) supposes that multiplying the average velocity of circulation with the volume of currency and bank deposits yields the value of total transactions, and if that figure bears a constant relationship (a factor of 10.3) to national income, then this predicted nominal GNP can be compared with that in the actual national accounts to give a measure of the black economy. However, more efficient use of money gives the unexpected ('perverse') result of a shrinking black economy for the UK (see Dilnot and Morris). Both Guttman and Fiege approaches require a 'no underground/black economy' base year or period to compute their results; for Guttman it was 1937–41 and for Fiege, 1939 (both in the USA).

8.9.3 Direct enquiry

Economists have been wary of both questionnaire and experimental evidence because of the strategic and hypothetical elements involved. Most people will underestimate tax evasion on their part when asked, while experimental choices may well not be repeated in 'real-world' situations. However, to ignore the use of questionnaires and experiments is to ignore a growing body of relevant literature. Lewis (1982) details the major studies involved, noting that social surveys concerned with tax attitudes and perceptions have as yet been concerned only indirectly with the extent of tax evasion. However, if low and declining tax morals were combined with an environment in which evasion was thought justifiable, the prediction would be extensive tax evasion. Hakim (1989) is one author who questions the larger estimates of the size of the UK black economy derived from lay opinion. In noting the decline of employment in 'traditional' full-time jobs, she points out that many individuals are not liable for national insurance and/or income tax payments; hence the assumption that an individual with earnings always needs to declare them is false. Given this, anecdotal evidence and questionnaire responses, claiming that millions are working but not paying tax, are true but are not evidence of the hidden economy. Indeed, Hakim estimates that as many as 5 million people in the UK may be misconstrued as being part of the black economy.

8.9.4 Expert opinion

Recourse to expert opinion is distrusted as a source of valuation in economics but may well be relevant as a source of information. In this context one of the best documented opinions is that of Sir William Pile, who is a former chairman of the Board of Inland Revenue and in 1977 guesstimated the black economy as $7\frac{1}{2}$ per cent of GNP.

8.10 Normative significance of the black economy

Many of the points noted above are relevant for the more general question of the overall broader normative significance of the black economy. A development of these arguments indicates why controversy reigns in this area. There are a number of different issues to be considered.

First, because it calls into question the reliability of official statistics, making GNP look 'too low' and unemployment 'too high', it causes considerable policy problems. For those economists who think that

GNP manipulation is possible via discretionary macroeconomic policy, unreliable data on its size and changes over time add a layer of complication to an already difficult task. Furthermore, if much of government expenditure on taxation policy has a redistributive element, then again policy, to the extent that it has to rely on inaccurate official data, is left operating in the dark, perhaps helping those who in reality are not badly placed to the exclusion of more deserving others.

Secondly, there is the question of the 'missing' taxation. Some writers seem to imply that the black economy means that some slice of tax revenue is lost for ever. Presumably a more accurate picture is one in which a given volume of tax revenue has to be raised to meet expenditure commitments, so that evasion by some raises the tax rate faced by others. (Consider the role of the tax rate in the 'excess burden' formulas in chapter 7.) This raises excess burden and equity considerations (raised at 8.8(ii) above). Referring to Fig. 8.1 again, and slightly altering its interpretation, if the vertical distance 67 is the required revenue and some individual manages to get X as an untaxed source of income, then the option of achieving a higher indifference curve at point 10, with all people paying from all income sources, is closed off; i.e. the possibility of untaxed earnings in the black economy distorts choices implying an excess burden. Given that people may have very different opportunities to indulge in untaxed income sources, the tax system may end up receiving a disproportionate amount of its finance from easy sources. This may militate against the equity of the tax system. This of course will depend on how sophisticated the tax authorities are in anticipating where evasion takes place and taking corrective actions in those areas to ensure that the tax burden is distributed equitably.

A third consideration arises if the practice of tax evasion becomes widespread. Weakening 'tax morality' must hinder the efficiency of public sector provision of goods and services—and indeed in the limit make collective activities difficult to finance. It is the coercive powers of the tax authorities that preclude 'free riding'. If their powers cease to be coercive, then the prospect of market failure re-emerges.

By no means all commentators have taken a negative view of the black economy. For the 'Leviathan' state writers it can be seen as 'baulking' by the taxpayer-consumers as the monopoly state tries to maximize tax revenue. Indeed, as noted elsewhere in this text, part of the explanation of the possibility of a Laffer curve is that raising tax rates eventually shrink the tax base to the extent of decreasing the tax revenue collected. In short, those who feel that government expenditure is too high are viewed as containing the state via systematic evasion. In addition, it can be argued that the black economy is a way of offsetting the disincentive effects of taxation in the formal sector. 'I am prepared to work for myself but not for the taxman' is a common rationale for those working for cash-in-hand. When this is work beyond a normal working day in the formal sector, it seldom seems to meet with much moral disapproval.

It has been noted that the more serious studies do not suggest that the black economy is a major problem in the UK. However, what policies are available to keep it in check and reduce it to acceptable levels if it is judged to be out of control? The economic models offer some clear leads. If you increase the probability of detection then evasion will fall, but this involves costly policing and other administrative costs. Placing more compliance costs on the taxpayer also makes detection easier. Furthermore, it was evident in the economic models that increasing the punishment would decrease the extent of evasion, and this initially looks a less expensive avenue to explore. However, at the moral level, most people object to punishments that are out of line with the 'crime', even though it may serve to discourage others from following the same path. Relatedly, punishments that are popularly perceived to be too draconian mean that the willingness to detect and convict evaders is reduced.

Turning to a broader, less fully 'economic', approach to the problem may therefore be fruitful. The probability of detection and fine may be two factors affecting evasion, but the environment of disapproval or approval that is felt from other members of society may also be important. Indeed, there may be interconnections, so that Vogel (1974) found that those who knew others who were tax evaders considered themselves to face a better-than-average chance of successful evasion. While above it was stated that an increased probability of detection reduces evasion, a broader approach may identify a perverse response in that tougher enforcement may decrease compliance by increasing the extent of alienation felt by taxpayers. With a broader approach, it is favourable tax attitudes that are the important basis of reduced evasion. For this to be established, taxpayers need to understand and approve of the policies financed via taxation as well as to feel that they are fairly treated in the implicit contract with government and its agents the tax authorities. In this respect, the introduction of the poll tax/community charge in the UK is a case study of what not to do.

8.11 Summary

The discussion concerning the costs of tax evasion makes it clear that there is dispute as to the 'optimal' level of tax evasion. There may be positive aspects of tax evasion if it reduces the disincentive impact of taxation (which from a 'supply side' point of view creates a greater output level). However, the extent to which tax evasion is thought undesirable also depends on the perception of government. The more likely that government failure causes public funds to be allocated inefficiently, the lower will the 'loss' associated with tax evasion. Some from the 'Leviathan' school perceive tax evasion as 'baulking' by the taxpayer; an opportunity for individuals to resist the monopoly authority that government imposes. Brennan and Buchanan (1977) certainly advocate that a tax constitution should contain opportunities for tax avoidance (if not tax evasion)—as discussed in chapter 16.

While public choice analysis is important in arguing that the 'optimal' level of tax evasion depends on perceptions of government, public choice analysis is also important in an analysis of how much tax evasion is likely to occur. It has been argued in this chapter that the simple approach of equating marginal loss of tax revenue with marginal costs of evasion detection can be misleading and that attention should focus on the marginal social costs and marginal social benefits when defining the 'optimal' level of tax evasion. However, even if this exercise could be successfully undertaken, there is reason (from a public choice perspective) to argue that the level of tax evasion that occurs will be smaller than that which is socially optimal. Frey (1989) emphasizes that the size of the black economy is the outcome of decisions of actors in the political process. The information to which decision-makers are exposed is likely to be biased in favour of reducing the level of the black economy. Producers in the black economy are (for obvious reasons) unable to lobby, whereas producers in the formal economy will be organized and lobby to reduce activity in the black economy. Producers will press for such regulation to reduce the competition which activity in the black economy represents. As far as government administration is concerned there is likely to be an anti-black economy bias. Those involved in public administration lose power and influence as revenues are reduced. For Frey (1989, p. 126) 'the size of the official and unobserved economies are the outcome of the interactions of self interested decision makers'. In so far as those who

present the disadvantages have a stronger voice in the political process the black economy will be smaller. While Frey's discussion raises an important point its relevance can be questioned. For example Collard (1989b, p. 107) argues that 'while the policy maker is interested in net revenue the bureaucracy is interested in gross revenue. On this theory we would expect to find tax bureaucrats pressing for investigation well beyond the "naïve rule"' (that marginal investigation cost equals marginal revenue). However, in practice, he adds that 'pressure for more investigation may well be just as much due to a sense of public responsibility as to bureaucratic imperialism'. Secondly, it is important also to ask the question of just how much influence those involved in the black economy 'should' have on the question of the size of the black economy. Certainly the literature on the economics of crime does not typically include the welfare of criminals when considering policy considerations.

References

Aitken, S. and Bonneville, E. (1980) *A General Taxpayer Opinion Survey*, CSR Inc: Washington, DC.

Allingham, M. G. and Sandmo, A. (1972), Income Tax Evasion: A Theoretical Analysis, *Journal of Public Economics*, **1**, pp. 323–38.

Alm, J. (1988) 'Compliance Costs and the Tax Avoidance: Tax Evasion Decision', *Public Finance Quarterly*, **16**, 1, pp. 31–66.

Alm, J. (1985), 'The Welfare Cost of the Underground Economy', *Economic Inquiry*, **23**, 2, pp. 243–63.

Baldry, J. C. (1984) 'The Enforcement of Income Tax Laws; Efficiency Implications', *Economic Record*, **60**, 169, pp. 156–9.

Brennan, G. and Buchanan, J. M. (1977) 'Towards a Tax Constitution for Leviathan', *Journal of Public Economics*, **8**, 3, pp. 255–73.

Browning, E. K. and Browning, J. M. (1983) *Public Finance and the Price System*, 2nd edn. New York: Macmillan.

Carter, M. (1984) 'Issues in the Hidden Economy: A Survey', *Economic Record*, **60**, 170, pp. 209–21.

Clotfelter, C. T. (1983) 'Tax Evasion and Tax Rates: An Analysis', *Review of Economics and Statistics*, **65**, 3, pp. 363–73.

Collard, D. (1989a) 'Compliance Costs and Efficiency Costs of Taxation', pp 273–77 in C. Sandford, M. Godwin and P. Hardwick, *Administrative and Compliance Costs of Taxation*. Bath: Fiscal Publications.

Collard, D. (1989b) 'How much investigation?', pp. 104–15 in D. Collard (ed.), *Fiscal Policy: Essays in Honour of Cederic Sandford*. Aldershot: Avebury.

Cowell, F. A. (1981) 'Taxation and Labour Supply with Risky Activities', *Economica*, **48**, 192, pp. 365–79.

Cowell, F. (1985) 'The Economic Analysis of Tax Evasion', *Bulletin of Economic Research*, **37**, 3, pp. 163–93.

Cowell, F. A. and Gordon, J. P. F. (1988) 'Unwillingness to Pay', *Journal of Public Economics*, **36**, 3, pp. 305–21.

Dean, P., Keenan, T. and Kenney, F. (1980) 'Taxpayers' Attitudes to Income Tax Evasion: An Empirical Survey,' *British Tax Review*, **1**, pp. 28–44.

Dilnot, A. and Morris, C. N. (1981) 'What Do We Know about the Black Economy?', *Fiscal Studies*, **2**, 1, pp. 58–73.

Fallon, P. and Verry, D. (1988) *The Economics of Labour Markets*. Oxford: Philip Allan.

Fiege, E. L. (1981) 'The UK's Unobserved Economy: A Preliminary Assessment', *Economic Affairs*, **1**, 4, pp. 205–12.

Fiege, E. L. (ed.) (1989) *The Underground Economies: Tax Evasion and Information Distortion*. Cambridge and New York: Cambridge University Press.

Frey, B. S. (1989) 'How Large (or Small) should the Underground Economy Be?' in E. L. Feige, *The Underground Economies; Tax Evasion and Information*. Cambridge: Cambridge University Press.

Frey, B. S. and Eichenberger, R. (1989) 'Anomalies and Institution', *Journal of Institutional and Theoretical Economics*, **145**, 3, pp. 423–37.

Friedland, N., Maital, S., Rutemberg, A. (1978) 'A Simulation Study of Income Taxation', *Journal of Public Economics*, **10**, 1, pp. 107–16.

Geeroms, H. and Wilmots, H. (1985) 'An Empirical Model of Tax Evasion and Tax Avoidance', *Public Finance/Finances Publiques*, **40**, 2, pp. 190–209.

Guttman, P. (1977) 'The Subterranean Economy', *Financial Analyst's Journal*, **33**, pp. 26–7, 34.

Hakim, C. (1989) 'Workforce Restructuring, Social Insurance Coverage and the Black Economy', *Journal of Social Policy*, **18**, 4, pp. 471–503.

Keith Report, *The (1983) Committee on Enforcement Powers of the Revenue Departments*, Cmnd 8822 9120 and 9440, London, HMSO.

Lea, S. E. G., Tarpy, R. M. and Webley, P. (1987) *The Individual in the Economy*. Cambridge: Cambridge University Press.

Lewis, A. (1979) 'An Empirical Analysis of Tax Mentality', *Public Finance/Finances Publiques*, **34**, 2, pp. 245–57.

Lewis, A. (1982) *The Psychology of Taxation*. Oxford: Martin Robertson.

MaCaffee, K. (1980) 'A Glimpse of the Hidden Economy in the National Accounts', *Economic Trends*, **316**, pp. 81–7.

Malik, A. S. and Schwab, R. M. (1991) 'The Economics of Tax Amnesties', *Journal of Public Economics*, **46**, 1, pp. 29–49.

Mason, R. and Calvin, L. D. (1984), 'Public Confidence and Admitted Tax Evasion', *National Tax Journal*, **37**, 4, pp. 489–98.

Myles, G. D. (1995) *Public Economics*. Cambridge: Cambridge University Press.

Myles, G. D. and Naylor, R. A., (1996), 'A Model of Tax Evasion with Group Conformity and Social Customs', *European Journal of Political Economy*, **12**, 3, pp. 49–66.

O'Higgins, M. (1981) *Measuring the Hidden Economy*, Outer Circle Policy Unit, July; reprinted in revised form in two parts in *British Tax Review*, nos. 5 and 6, pp. 286–302 and 367–78.

Peacock, A. T. and Shaw, G. K. (1982) 'Tax Evasion and Tax Revenue Loss', *Public Finance/Finances Publiques*, **37**, 2, pp. 269–78.

Pyle, D. J. (1989) *Tax Evasion and the Black Economy*. London: Macmillan.

Pyle, D. J. (1991) 'The Economics of Taxpayer Compliance', *Journal of Economic Surveys*, 5, 2 pp. 163–198.

Skinner, J. and Slemrod, J. (1985) 'An Economic Perspective on Tax Evasion', *National Tax Journal*, **38**, 3, pp. 345–53.

Spicer, M. W. (1986) 'Civilization at a Discount: The Problem of Tax Evasion', *National Tax Journal*, **39**, 1, pp. 13–20.

Spicer, M. W. and Lundstedt, S. B. (1976) 'Understanding Tax Evasion', *Public Finance/Finances Publiques*, **31**, 2, pp. 295–305.

Spicer, M. W. and Becker, L. A. (1980) 'Fiscal Inequity and Tax Evasion: An Experimental Approach', *National Tax Journal*, **33**, 2, pp. 171–5.

Tanzi, V. (1980) 'The Underground Economy in the United States: Estimates and Implications', *Banca Nazionale del Lavoro Quarterly Review*, **33**, 135, pp. 427–54.

Vogel, J. (1974) 'Taxation and Public Opinion in Sweden: An Interpretation of Recent Survey Data', *National Tax Journal*, **27**, 4, pp. 499–513.

Yaniv, G. (1994) 'Tax Evasion and the Income-Tax Rate—A Theoretical Reexamination', *Public Finance/Finances Publiques*, **49**, 1, pp. 107–112.

Yitzhaki, S. (1974) 'A Note on Income Tax Evasion: A Theoretical Analysis', *Journal of Public Economics*, **3**, 2, pp. 201–2.

Yitzhaki, S. (1987) 'On the Excess Burden of Tax Evasion', *Public Finance Quarterly*, **15**, 2, pp. 123–37.

9 Income (re)distribution

9.1 Introduction

The achievement of economic equity is a stated policy objective in many countries. Assessing the impact of government policies on the income distribution is important not only because the intention of some policies is deliberately to alter it, but also because efficiency-directed policies will invariably have some impact on the distribution of income and wealth. This essentially empirical question is very difficult to answer as it raises a whole host of conceptual, theoretical and practical difficulties that are only partially resolvable. Evaluating the desirability of any change in the income distribution involves 'the' great unresolved question in economics, i.e. How are income distributions to be compared and ranked?

9.2 Overview of income distribution

Economic inequality is a subject that has thrived in the 1970s and 1980s. It is convenient to write as if the appropriate unit of analysis is the individual as opposed to, say, families or households. Households may contain more than one family; for example, there may be a lodger. Additionally, there are the questions of how resources are shared within these units and how to weigh, say children as opposed to adults. Abstracting from these difficult matters, an attractive approach to inequality would be to look at the lifetime purchasing power broadly defined over goods and services enjoyed by individuals, appropriately discounted to give a common basis for comparison. Unfortunately, such longitudinal individual data are only currently being built up. In their absence, attention has been directed towards establishing changes in the distribution of income and wealth that can be attributed to government policy.

Table 9.1 sketches a picture of income and wealth distribution. In part (1) of the top panel all forms of factor prices are listed, their precise values being determined by the supply and demand of the factors in question. This vector of prices, multiplied by individual ownership of factors (here collected under human, physical and financial capital), gives rise to the distribution of income. The fortunate individuals who turn out to be at the top end of the income distribution usually own physical and financial capital as well as their own labour, or human capital.

The middle panel of the table attempts to distinguish the distribution of income from the distribution of wealth. The basic distinction is that income is a *flow* and therefore is measured per unit of time, whereas wealth is a *stock* and is measured at a point in time. In the presence of perfect capital markets and suitably inclusive definitions, wealth would simply be the discounted present value of all future income streams (i.e. including those that might not easily be measured in money terms). As capital markets are not perfect, definitions vary from researcher to researcher and some things are better measured as a stock rather than a flow, so that documented wealth distributions are not simply the present value of all future income streams. The arguments listed under 'Dynamic aspects' indicate how having a favourable position in the current income or wealth distribution makes it likely that you will also have a favourable position in a future income or wealth distribution (inter- and intra-generationally). Current possession of human, physical and financial capital tends to reinforce itself in successive periods, although not completely so.

Having sketched the sources of income and wealth inequality, there is the far from simple matter of how

Table 9.1 Overview of economic inequality

(1) Factor markets determine: Wages Profits Rents Interest Dividends, etc. i.e. *factor prices*	(2) Factor ownership (a) Distribution of human capital (skills, training) among individuals (b) Distribution of physical and financial capital among individuals	(3) Income distribution ((1) × (2)) Distribution of income among individuals; (sometimes divided between (a) earned income from work (b) unearned or investment income from the ownership of property)
Wealth (stock) An attempt to measure (2b) Excludes human capital *Income* (flow) An attempt to measure (3), which is the annual return to both (2a) and (2b) (NB: Definitions vary from study to study, often influenced by data availability.)	Purchasing power net of debts at *one point in time* that an individual derives from cash or bank deposits, plus purchasing power that would be derived from selling all other assets (e.g. house, shares, land) Value of an individual's *increase* in purchasing power obtained from certain sources *in a given period* (usually a year) usually includes earnings from work, interest and rent receipts	Dynamic aspects (i) Rich save and own capital assets which yield future income: poor tend not to save and have little or no income from such assets (ii) More wealthy tend to secure higher rates of return: (a) advantages of scale; (b) better connected to get information and more profitable investments (iii) Applies also to human capital acquisition, e.g. education—educated people encourage their children to acquire education and keep them in the education system longer
	Redistributive policy can take very many forms	
It can attack factor markets directly (i) Minimum wage legislation (ii) Quotas for minorities, e.g. the disabled (iii) Anti-discrimination legislation (e.g. equal pay for women)	It can redistribute the ownership of physical and human capital (i) Death duties and estate taxes (ii) 'Free' education to a high level to reduce the inequality of opportunity to acquire human capital (iii) Creation of a socialist system with state ownership of the means of production	It can attack income distribution directly (i) Tax/transfer policy (e.g. negative income taxation) (ii) Provision of 'merit wants' financed from a progressive tax system

to present the data or, more precisely, what unit of analysis to use. Since money income is the magnitude that underlies the day-to-day standard of living and, depending on the definition, the variable that will (to some extent) reflect wealth, most studies concentrate on this figure. As the different factors are viewed as performing different tasks in the production process, one way to present data would be in terms of so-called functional shares, that is the share of income going to land, labour and capital. If the concern is income inequality, this sort of approach is not very helpful as it tells you nothing about the numbers that have to 'share' each proportion of income. Such an approach makes most sense in a world in which individuals enjoy income from only one source, which in turn was more likely to be the case in earlier historical times. While suggesting that this approach is weak for 'inequality' purposes, the basic framework that is employed in general equilibrium tax analysis, and indeed in much of international trade theory, is cast in terms of the earnings of the different factors (see chapter 13). There is also a sizeable literature on

explaining the size distribution of income which concerns itself with the specific shape this takes (positively skewed (right-hand tail) and leptokurtic (hump-shaped) or leptokurtic lognormal), both over different time periods and in different countries. (See Fig. 9.1 for an illustration.) The unit of analysis for these approximately lognormal distributions is usually individuals or families.

This type of work, associated in the UK with Lydall (1968), offers three main types of explanation for the characteristic shape. Stochastic theories look to the statistics of the situation and ask what type of statistical processes will generate the observed result. If, for example, you take a group of people and give randomly selected individuals within the group increases in income that are a proportion of their existing absolute income size over a succession of periods, a lognormal distribution will result. Such approaches, however sophisticated, generally contain no economic explanation of the characteristic shape.

The 'Chicago' human capital approach (e.g. Becker 1971; also see Mincer 1980) perhaps goes overboard

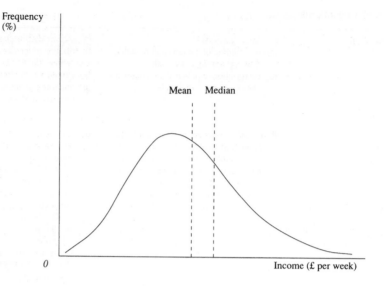

Figure 9.1 Characteristic shape of the personal distribution of incomes.

the other way, seeing observed inequality as simply the reflection of current investments in human capital and returns to past investments. So observed income in period t (Y_t) is a reflection of a base earning from an individual's raw uneducated ability or talent (T_t) and past investments (I_i) times their rates of return (r_i) minus any current investment (which usually is in the form of foregone earnings). Hence

$$(9.1) \qquad Y_t = T_t + \sum_{i=0}^{t-1} r_i I_i - I_t$$

Here the characteristic distribution shape comes from the multiplicative r_i and I_i interaction, which arises even if r_i and I_i are normally distributed in themselves.

Like nearly all the human capital literature, the Chicago approach assumes there is a powerful element of choice. Given basic ability, equality of opportunity to borrow at the market rate of interest to invest in your human capital so as to secure a future return makes observed income inequality a matter of individual choice. However, on the demand side, the influences (whatever their relative strengths) of genetic inheritance and other environmental variables will make individual demands for human capital differ. On the supply side, it is noted in Table 9.1 that high initial income and wealth offer better access to information and financial markets, making the rate of interest different for different groups of individuals in society. Such considerations make the 'voluntary— don't have to worry about income inequality' view

look somewhat forced. The approach does, however, emphasize the importance of time periods. The longer the period, the more the influences of your current position are ironed out, so that students who look (and maybe are!) poor currently over their lifetime will generally look, and be, well off; i.e. cross-section inequality is greater than time-series inequality.

The third approach, which is now more widely adopted, is more eclectic, recognizing both the impacts of human capital (education, training) on individual marginal products (and hence earnings) and other factors, such as individual cognitive ability and personality differences. Such a 'multi-factor' approach[1] (Lydall, 1968) brings inequality policy back into play by recognizing that the unequal and the poor have not simply chosen their lot, but it does retain the emphasis on education and training dominant in the human capital approach.

Other divisions of income, apart from its overall size distribution, suggest themselves as relevant for certain issues; so for example economic growth is associated with changes in shares of income generated in different sectors of the economy (manufacturing, agriculture, etc.); labour market analysis might suggest the relative fates of different economic groups (professional versus manual, architects versus roadsweepers, etc.); regional economists, especially in the

---

[1] It is the summing of the effects of the independent factors that is seen as generating the appropriate characteristic shapes.

current context of the EC, by definition have an interest in regional differences in incomes. All these breakdowns of data are often presented and have a role to play in the analysis of certain questions. However, when considering income inequality, it is the income distribution among individuals that has emerged as most useful. Presentation of the data as a frequency distribution, however, is not very useful for this inequality issue, and other measures have proved more popular.

9.3 Popular measures of inequality and poverty

There is a very large and sophisticated literature on the various measures that could be used to *summarize* economic inequality and make comparisons over time within one country and between countries (see Sen 1973 and Jenkins 1991). The most commonly used measures are quantile shares and Lorenz curves (and associated Gini coefficients). These basic concepts are illustrated in Table 9.2, and in Figs. 9.1 and 9.2. The data given are taken from Jenkins (1990). The quantile shares data are self-explanatory. A weakness of this kind of presentation is that concentrating on how the shares in one part of the distribution compare ignores changes that might be taking place in other parts of the distribution. The Lorenz curve (based on information on incomes ranked in ascending order of size) shows the proportion of income held by each percentage or proportion of the population. Because

of the ranking procedure, shares of income run from 0 to 100 per cent as all income must be held by the total of the income-holding units. The curve sags below the line of complete equality (the 45° line) because incomes are not distributed equally. The proportion of recipients is greater than the proportion of income they hold except at the 'anchor points' on the axes. The Gini coefficient is measured by the ratio of the area from the 'sag' to the 45° line to the area under the 45° line. Figure 9.2 includes the extreme values the coefficient can take and makes it clear that, the closer to unity is the value, the more unequal the income distribution is. The Gini coefficients in Table 9.2 suggest increasing inequality between 1975/6 and 1981/2 and constant inequality between 1981/2 and 1984/5. In addition, the table gives the coefficient of variation for the income distribution, which is a measure of the spread of the distribution relative to the mean of the distribution (i.e. the standard deviation of the distribution divided by its mean).

More recent events are captured in Fig. 9.3 which shows the Gini coefficient (three-year moving average) for the thirty-year period 1961–91 using before-housing-costs (BHC) and after-housing-costs (AHC) income measures. While AHC data suggest greater inequality than BHC data updating the picture from Table 9.2 periods of rising inequality can be seen in the second half of the 1960s and 1980s. For those concerned with inequality the flattening kink in the curve in 1991 looks a hopeful sign.

The 1980s witnessed the domination of the conservative perspective in economic life and the Conservative Party in political life. At the risk of oversimplification conservative philosophy is individualistic, market orientated and not much enamoured of equity as a motivating force for government policy. As such one would expect, as generally confirmed above, the period of the 1980s in the UK to, if anything, be associated with increased income inequality. Jenkins and Cowell (1994) further lend support to this picture. They restage Pen's parade of dwarfs and a few giants where the UK population, scaled for a height that reflects their income, parade past you in one hour. The impact of this mental picture is extremely vivid. With 5 ft. 5 in. corresponding to the average 1988/89 (before-housing-cost) income of £236 per week. (This is the so called equivalized income that uses weights to correct for individual circumstances—see below.) The individual in the middle of the income distribution passing after thirty dizzying minutes is only 4 ft. 8 ins. It is only after 37 minutes that someone of average height (income) passes. The 'basket ball' players then begin to appear

Table 9.2 Changes in the UK income distribution, 1975/6–1984/5

	1975/6	1981/2	1984/5
Income share of the poorest (%)			
20%	6.0	5.5	5.8
40%	16.3	15.7	15.6
60%	33.0	31.3	30.4
80%	57.7	55.2	53.7
100%	100.0	100.0	100.0
Gini coefficient	0.37	0.40	0.40
Coefficient of variation	0.80	0.88	0.90
Average income (£ p.a., 1984/5 prices)	7500	7220	7520

Note: Income is total tax unit income, before tax.

Source: Jenkins (1990); calculations from *Economic Trends*, vols. 295, 369.

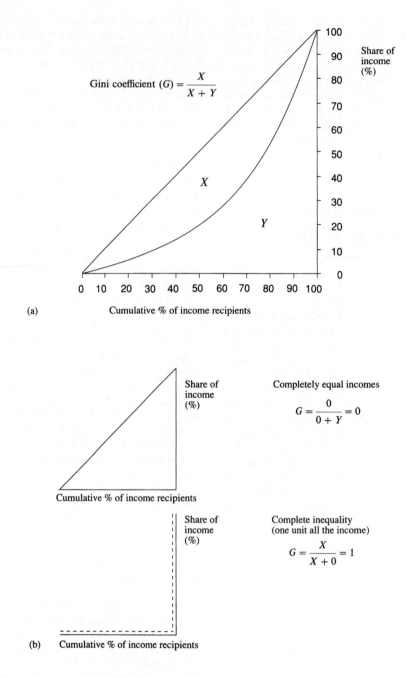

Figure 9.2 (a) The Lorenz curve, (b) Gini coefficients (special cases).

with 11 ft. individuals passing in the fifty-seventh minute. The authors calculations indicate that the last four people to pass you would be 90 ft., 90 ft., 100 yds. and 100 yds. high respectively. Figure 9.4 reduces the impact of the giants by excluding those

with equivalized incomes above £500 per week. As can be seen from the figure the shape of the parade tilted in an anti-clockwise direction between the years recorded. It turns out that the very poorest were actually worse off in 1988/9 than in 1979 but in general real

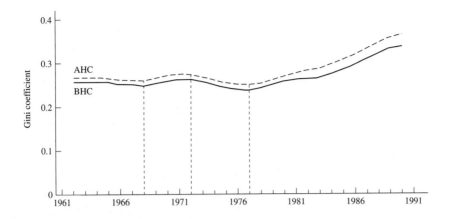

Figure 9.3 Gini coefficient (three-year moving average).

Note: A(B)HC is After (Before) Housing Cost Data.
Source: Goodman and Webb (1994).

incomes rose with points 1 and 2 indicating the respective median values and points 3 and 4 the equivalent means. Overall, however, a stark picture of inequality is presented.

It has already been noted in chapter 1 how efficiency and equity principles are inextricably linked. The existence of a public sector that did not have significant intended distributional consequences would be one that involves universal marginal benefit taxation for each good or service provided in the public sector. Note that an attempt to introduce universal marginal benefit taxation implies the acceptance of the status quo. That is, there is reason to accept the outcome of market processes and avoid interference with them. Such views are discussed further below. While this, with a suitable amount of information, might be the objective of public sector provision, it has, in fact, not been the case. Most taxation is driven by the 'ability to pay' principle (which in itself is meant to be equitable

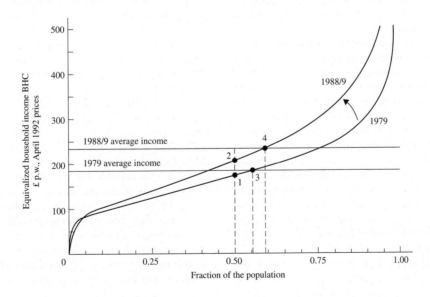

Figure 9.4 Changing 'income parade' since 1979.

Source: Jenkins and Cowell (1994).

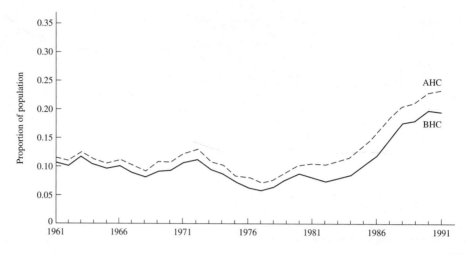

Figure 9.5 The proportion of the total population below half mean income.
Source: Goodman and Webb (1994).

rather than redistributive), and much policy, as suggested above, may be explicitly redistributional. While it is not easy to establish as an empirical matter what the current income-wealth distribution is, even if it could be established, the question of what degree of inequality should be the trigger for government policy remains. While, so far, economic inequality has been discussed in terms of measured command over market resources, there is a connection to poverty when this command is viewed as inadequate. There are two broad approaches to inadequacy that can and have been taken.

The statistical approach follows on from the Lorenz curve type information but recognizes that, for example, studying the income share of the bottom 10 per cent does not indicate how they are doing in relation to the mean or median of the distribution. One way to connect the segments of the distribution is to argue, for example like Fuchs (1965), that a moving poverty line be created if it is accepted that no one should fall below, say, 50 per cent of the mean or median income.

Fig. 9.5 taken from Goodman and Webb (1994) shows the proportion of the population between 1961 and 1991 who on a BHC and an AHC basis 'enjoyed' an income below half the mean income. The overall picture again seems clear with poverty rising on both measures from some 10 per cent or 11 per cent in 1961 to 20 per cent or 24 per cent of the population in 1991, i.e. poverty *on this measure* increased from one-tenth to one-fifth or so of the population. Apart from being important information in itself this type of definition has the attraction that

poverty is a solvable problem, unlike viewing the bottom 10 per cent as perpetually being in poverty. In addition, the approach offers an absolute but moving standard that facilitates research into the characteristics of the poor and measures to move them over the poverty boundary.

The second broad approach is a 'poverty budget' one. The question posed is, What is the minimum acceptable budget below which anyone would be accepted as poor? Rowntree (1901) saw the minimum acceptable as that sufficient to maintain physical efficiency. This apparently concrete and absolute approach involved, once the poverty measure was defined, the distinction between those in primary poverty and those in secondary poverty.[2] The primary poor could not attain the standard whatever they did, while the secondary poor could if they reallocated their income to a different consumption pattern, i.e. if they eliminated some wasteful expenditures. It was realized, however, that physical efficiency depends on the tasks individuals have to perform and in itself is not a Yes–No variable but rather a continuous one. This recognition, combined with the notion that life has to be somehow larger than a physical notion, meant that this approach has been broadened.

A minimal extension is to a labour market approach, which concentrates on the market productive role of human capital and asks what personal budget allows for a growing economy. A wider socio-

---

[2] The repeat of the Rowntree poverty study in York found many families in the same location and relative income bracket.

logical approach poses the question, What command over goods and services is required for individuals to take part in the mainstream of society in which they are a part? The wider the conception of poverty, the greater the number of people who are likely to be viewed as poor and the greater the policy problem in alleviating poverty. However, it is suggested that the definition adopted should imply a 'plausible' number in poverty. Section 9.5.1 strongly questions the picture of inequality and poverty presented here. To facilitate debate and policy formation it is important to isolate as far as is generally possible the impact of the government budget on the Lorenz curve that would otherwise have obtained, and then to consider proposals that are more closely tied to the poverty literature.

9.3.1 Normative principles for redistribution

First, we shall consider the question raised in the introduction regarding the optimal income distribution.

There are a number of distinct approaches to providing the recipe for an optimal distribution of income which take the discussion away from the nuts and bolts of the actual effects of government policies on different income groups. The brief discussion here introduces six such approaches. All can be interpreted as being part of a social optimality approach.

Utilitarianism

Bentham is associated with the maxim of the greatest happiness to the greatest number and would subscribe to the view of maximizing the sum of utility from income. Assume for the moment that utility is not only cardinally measurable but also comparable between individuals. Under such circumstances, the golden rule to maximize social welfare is to equalize the marginal utility from income and set the pattern of income distribution to conform to this. The two Christmas-tree-like drawings in Fig. 9.6 illustrate the point. In part (a) the two depicted individuals have different but diminishing marginal utility of income schedules.[3] With Y_T to distribute, the relevant maximizing allocations are Y_A and Y_B. Any other allocation, e.g. an equal one at Y'_A and Y'_B would be inferior in that the move to Y_A and Y_B would lose $Y'_B 12 Y_B$ of utility for B but raise it by $Y'_A 34 Y_A$ for A, offering a

[3] Tisdell (1972) brings this out vividly in noting that Edgeworth, in *Mathematical Psychics*, had no doubts who were better pleasure machines: these were the upper as opposed to the lower classes, and men as opposed to women!

raised total to the extent of parallelogram 3456 where $Y'_B 12 Y_B = Y'_A 65 Y_A$ by construction. Figure 9.3(b) illustrates the special case where A and B have identical utility functions or, alternatively, where it is accepted that A and B ought always to be treated *as if* they had identical utility functions. In this case the recipe for maximization of social-welfare-like utility is egalitarian; i.e. incomes $Y'_A = Y_A = Y_B = Y'_B$.

Uncertainty

Lerner (1944) derives the egalitarian recipe in a neat and less restrictive manner. He sheds the unrealistic assumptions of cardinality of utility and comparability between the individuals and argues that in an uncertain context the expected sum of utilities will be maximized by an equal distribution. Returning to Fig. 9.3(a) and moving to an equal distribution Y'_A and Y'_B from Y_A and Y_B, the loss of utility has been established as parallelogram 3456. If, however, you had been mistaken about the location of MU_A and MU_B and the assignments had been reversed, the effective starting-points would be $Y_a (= OY_A)$ and $Y_b (= OY_B)$ and the movement towards equality would involve a loss to A of $Y_a 71 Y'_B$ and a gain to B of $Y_b 83 Y'_A$, yielding a net gain of 83-10-9 as $Y_a 71 Y'_B = Y_b 9 - 10 Y'_A$ by construction. (Apart from Y_a and Y_b in Fig. 9.6(a) temporarily read all A's as B's and vice versa.) If you are truly uncertain about the marginal utility schedules (i.e. you do not know which is A's MU schedule and which is B's) and attach a 0.5 probability to the gain and the loss, expected utility is maximized by the equal allocation, because half of 839-10 clearly exceeds half of 3456. Culyer (1980), among others, is critical of this argument because, despite the claim made above, he notes that the argument continues to assume that utilities of the individuals can be summed, which presupposes they can be measured in the same units. In addition, if the probability differs from 0.5, there comes a point where the higher probability of the smaller loss outweighs the lower probability of the larger gain and unequal distributions are prescribed.

Social welfare function

In the so-called 'New' welfare economics, the use of the social welfare function introduced in section 1.5 seemed to 'solve' the equity problem and economic analysis was centred on efficiency. The source of a social welfare function remains a lasting difficulty. To assume it is known is accepted for illustration, but this does not push analysis very far. The Arrow Impossibility Theorem suggests that it may be futile to attempt to build it up from reasonable democratic

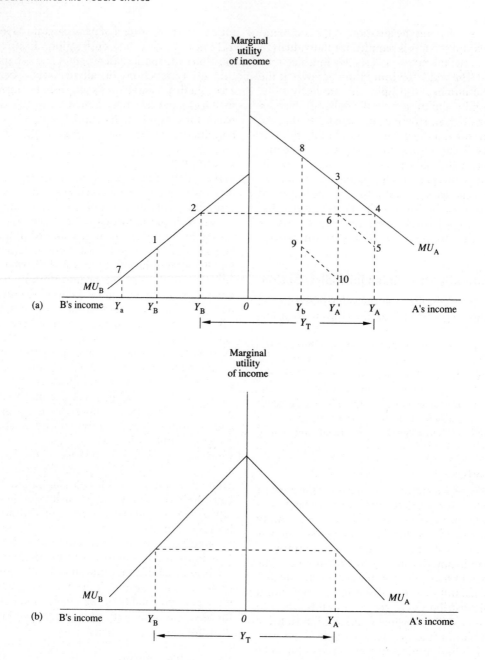

Figure 9.6 Maximizing utility.

assumptions (see chapter 4). In contrast, some sort of appeal to, say, the authority of the government executive (although in practice often the implicit outcome) looks at odds with the individualistic framework of neoclassical economics. Against this background, following the implications of different

formulations has often proved attractive. The 'shapes' introduced in chapter 1 are consistent with the principles of:

(a) maximizing total utility (utilitarianism)
(b) the Rawlsian maximin principle discussed below

(c)
(d) } maximizing the utility of a particular individual

The Nash notion of maximizing the product of individual utilities has been employed by Fair (1971) and although criticized by Ng (1979) is illustrated below.

The 'Rawlsian' social welfare function

John Rawls' *A Theory of Justice* (1971) has been a very influential book. It justifies the use of a fairly radical social welfare function and in a sense combines and rationalizes elements of all three of the above approaches. Rawls suggests that the appropriate way to think about the development of a theory of justice is from the so-called original position behind 'a veil of ignorance'. The idea is to imagine you have been called to a 'convention' to set the rules of the constitution and the social and economic structure of society. In order to make the procedure 'fair', you are imagined to: know little except the most general facts about human society; be ignorant of your own eventual position and role in society; be unaware of your own endowments; be ignorant of where your own best interests will in fact lie, and be ignorant also of the state of development of the society in which you will find yourself. In effect, you are devising the rules for a game of cards (life) in which your particular hand and the game you will eventually play, for some unknown rewards and probabilities, remains unknown. The point is that you do not in this 'original position' know how to be biased and hence have to be fair: justice in this context would have to be 'blind'. Because in Rawls' view we are equal moral beings capable of a sense of justice in this fair starting-point, the rules advocated and accepted would be 'justice as fairness'.

What of the rules that would be derived? Two are proposed:

1. All individuals have the right to the most extensive basic liberty compatible with a similar liberty for others.
2. Deviations from social and economic equality are justified, provided they do not conflict with rule 1 ('equal liberty') and provided
   (a) they are to the advantage of the least well off; i.e. changes that improve the position of the least well off are to be recommended (this is the so-called maximin rule, maximizing the position of the minimum welfare individual), and
   (b) they are attached to positions open to all— equal opportunity conditions.

Much more could be and has been written about this 'difference principle' (2a) and its strengths and weak-

nesses, but enough has been said to, at least, give the flavour of the notion. The ideas of justifying equality, of uncertainty as a major feature and of consensual individual decision-making are links to the elements in this section. A further link can be forged to the discussion of inequality measurement above via the Atkinson (1970) inequality index (AI), which can be related to the isoelastic function discussed in chapter 1 (see also Stratmann 1990). If individual utility of income functions are given the isoelastic form

$$(9.2) \qquad U(Y_i) = \frac{(Y_i)^{1-e}}{1-e} \quad \text{where} \quad e \neq 1$$

then the associated marginal utility of income is

$$(9.3) \qquad dU(Y_i)/dY_i = Y_i^{-e}$$

If social welfare depends on the sum of individual's utility, then social welfare W can be written

$$W(U_1, U_2, \ldots U_n) = \sum_{i=1}^{n} U(Y_i) = \sum_{i=1}^{n} \frac{(Y_i)^{1-e}}{1-e}$$

(9.4)

That is, the aggregate level of welfare in society is given by a welfare function whose arguments are the Von Neumann–Morgenstern 'cardinal' utility of income functions.

Now introduce the concept of equally distributed equivalent level of income (Y_e) as the per capita amount of the smallest total income which if equally distributed offers the same level of welfare as the original distribution, so that

$$(9.5) \qquad \begin{aligned} &W[U_1(Y_e), U_2(Y_e), \ldots, U_n(Y_e)] \\ &= W[U_1(Y_1), U_2(Y_2), \ldots, U_n(Y_n)] \end{aligned}$$

From utility functions of the isoelastic form and the definition of 'equally distributed equivalent income'

$$(9.6) \qquad \frac{(Y_e)^{1-e}}{1-e} = \frac{1}{n} \sum_{i=1}^{n} \frac{(Y_i)^{1-e}}{1-e} \quad \text{where} \quad e \neq 1$$

multiplying by $1 - e$ and taking the $(1 - e^{\text{th}})$ root gives

$$(9.7) \qquad Y_e = \left[\frac{1}{n} \sum_{i=1}^{n} Y_i^{1-e} \right]^{1/1-e}$$

Then the Atkinson index is

$$(9.8) \qquad AI = 1 - (Y_e/\bar{Y})$$

where $Y_e < \bar{Y}$, which becomes in the isoelastic case

$$(9.9) \qquad AI = 1 - \left[\frac{1}{n} \sum_{i=1}^{n} (Y_i/\bar{Y})^{1-e} \right]^{1/1-e}$$

Distributional attitudes to inequality are contained in the parameter e (whose inverse is the elasticity of substitution of the SW curve). In Fig. 9.4 the two-person (A and B) case is illustrated. When $e = 0$ there is indifference about the distribution of income (parallel straight lines with a 45° angle to the x and y axes); $e = \infty$ means that concern is only with the income of the poorest income unit (the Rawlsian case). For any initial income distribution, say at point 1, the line 45° to the x and y axis shows all income allocations attainable from point 1, the initial distribution. The 45° ray from the origin represents equal (average) income for A and B. (For 1 the relevant equal income point is 2.) With an e value of unity, point 1 is on SW_0 and 2 is on SW_1: this represents the difference (gain) in social welfare available by distribution to equality at 2 from 1. Given the definition above, point 3 is the equally distributed equivalent of point 1, Y_e^1. This makes

$$AI = \frac{SW_1 - SW_0}{SW_1} = 1 - \frac{SW_0}{SW_1} = \frac{02 - 03}{02} = \frac{32}{02}$$

(9.10)

The meaning of the index can be seen if a specific value for the index (which runs from 0 to 1) is considered. With $AI = 0.4$, if only 60 per cent of total current income were equally distributed it would be socially valued as equivalent. Rearranging (9.8) yields

(9.11) $\qquad Y_e = \bar{Y}(1 - AI)$

and confirms this. As point 3 in Fig. 9.4 approaches point 2 the index tends to 0, signalling equality of incomes. If 3 approaches the origin the index tends to 1, signalling complete inequality. (For $e = 0$ the index would be zero/02 and for $e = \infty$, the Rawlsian case, 42/02.) The effect of this index is to reduce all the argument about the appropriate shape of the social welfare function to a question of the size of e.

To make what is a complicated mathematical form more approachable a specific two person ($n = 2$) case is explored here for the value of $e = 1$ (the Nash case where the SW curves are rectangular hyperbolas with respect to the Y_B, Y_A axes in Fig. 9.7). Imagine point 1 corresponds to the allocation of a total income $Y = £45$ and that individual B has £40 and individual A has £5. The question is 'What is the value of the AI index in this case?' Adopting the assumption $e = 1$ as indicated by equation 9.2 is 'different' in that it makes the individual utility functions take the form of (see Atkinson 1970, p. 250)

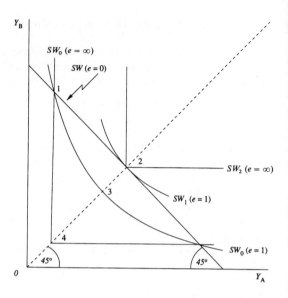

Figure 9.7 The *AI* and equality.

(9.12) $\qquad U(Y_i) = \ln Y_i$

so that for the specific case $e = 1$ (9.6) becomes

(9.13) $\qquad \ln Y_e = \frac{1}{n} \sum_{i=1}^{n} \ln(Y_i)$

(9.14) $\qquad Y_e = \exp^{\frac{1}{n} \sum_{i=1}^{n} \ln(Y_i)}$

where exp is the base of natural logs.

(9.15) $\qquad Y_e = \prod_{i=1}^{n} \exp^{\frac{1}{n} \ln(Y_i)}$

(9.16) $\qquad Y_e = \prod_{i=1}^{n} Y_i^{\frac{1}{n}}$

where Π is the product operator so that the AI index becomes

(9.17) $\qquad AI = 1 - \frac{\prod_{i=1}^{n} Y_i^{\frac{1}{n}}}{\bar{Y}}$

(9.18) $\qquad = 1 - \prod_{i=1}^{n} \left(\frac{Y_i}{\bar{Y}}\right)^{\frac{1}{n}}$

when $n = 2$ (a two person society) and the numbers introduced above substituted in

$$AI = 1 - \left(\sqrt{\frac{40}{22.5}} \times \sqrt{\frac{5}{22.5}} \right)$$

$$= 1 - (\sqrt{1.78} \times \sqrt{0.22})$$

(9.19)

$$= 1 - (1.3 \times 0.47)$$

$$= 1 - 0.627$$

$$= 0.37$$

In terms of Fig. 9.7 point 2 corresponds to $Y_B = Y_A = £22.5$. Point 3 on the SW curve through point 1 for the value $e = 1$ involves (from equation 9.11)

(9.20)
$$Y_e(= Y_B = Y_A) = £22.5(1 - 0.37)$$
$$= £14.17$$

To tie this in with a graphical determination of the AI. If distance 3–2 is 11.77 and 02 is 31.82 then their ratio is 0.37.

Whilst all of this does not make 'e' knowable, it does at a very minimum facilitate discussion of the efficiency-equity trade-off below.

Interdependent utility functions

The above implicitly has individuals gaining utility from their own incomes. There is, however, a consid-

erable literature recognizing that your utility will be affected positively or negatively by the utility achieved by others around you. Other individuals' utility in effect becomes an externality to you, and if Pareto-relevant this would suggest that you would willingly agree to some redistribution.

In Fig. 9.8 B will find himself with income OY_B, and if we assume that A for whatever reason is altruistic towards B, then there exists a demand by A for income for $B(D_A^B)$, which is normally marginally irrelevant. If, however, B falls on hard times, and is prevented from earning OY_B—say, ill health caused unemployment—and his income falls to OY_u, then the externality becomes marginally relevant. As illustrated, the externality is Pareto-relevant over the range $Y_u Y_u^*$ and suggests a welfare-increasing transfer for A and B of that sum.

Concern for others is one way you can gain from giving. Like mercy, it is twice blessed, offering a welfare gain to A of 123 and a gain to B of $Y_u 45 Y_u^*$. The effect of this type of 'everybody gains' argument is, as noted in note 4 in chapter 1, to provide positive sections to the utility possibility frontier as illustrated by UF_1 in Fig. 9.9. This only 'narrows' the efficient area of the frontier to the negatively sloped section between points 1 and 2. Mishan (1972) notes that a

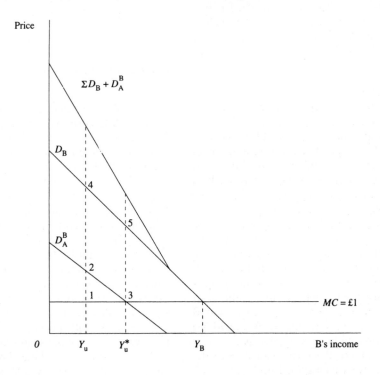

Figure 9.8 Gaining by giving.

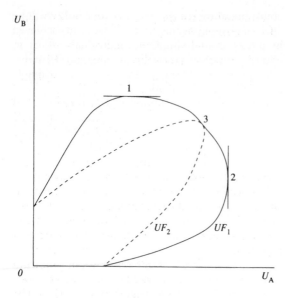

Figure 9.9 Interdependent utilities.

unique result obtains in the unlikely situation of a case like UF_2 where 3 represents an optimal distribution of income. Note that the construction assumes that B is altruistic towards A as well as vice versa. The fact that this explanation can be formulated in an externality/utility possibility frontier context makes clear that the effect of interdependent utility functions is to make equity an 'efficiency' matter.

Equity as non-envy

The 'utility functions' described by equation (9.2) allow the social valuation of the welfare of individuals to be calculated independently of the utility (income) levels of others. This 'separability' is a weakness if an interdependent view of income distribution is deemed crucial (see Sen 1973). Putting yourself in the position of others is the core idea of fairness or equity, being seen as the absence of envy.

The familiar Edgeworth–Bowley trading box can be used to illustrate the argument. In Fig. 9.10(a) point 1 is the centre of the box and, unless individuals have identical preference maps, cannot be on the contract curve. Suppose the contract curve is the continuous curved line between O_A and O_B and point 2 an efficient allocation of X and Y between A and B along it. Now the question is, Does A (B) regard her (his) consumption bundle as attractive as that of B (A)? To find the response, the mirror allocation can be located at point 3 by striking a line from 2 through 1 and extending it for a distance equal to 21; i.e.

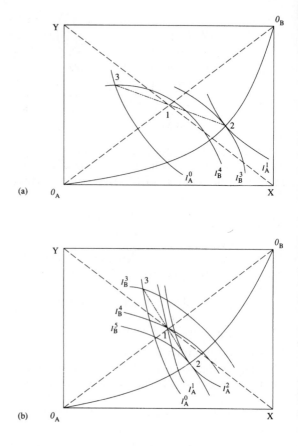

Figure 9.10 Equity as non-envy.

$31 = 12$. As illustrated, B—but not A—can attain a higher indifference curve at 3 than at 2, and therefore B is seen as being envious of A, and therefore point 2 is efficient but unfair in B's terms. One allocation that would be both efficient and equitable in this sense would be an initial endowment at 1 where both A and B have the same X and Y. Since they face the same budget constraint, each can have what the other has so that any trades away from equal allocation to the contract curve must meet the reverse allocation test illustrated as part (b) of the figure. A movement to point 2 raises both A's and B's utility, whereas the reverse assignment at 3 lowers both's utility—they are not envious of each other. The presence of malice or envy is one spur to redistribution and is a theme taken up by those offering the more positive accounts of redistribution (see below).

Before considering these, however, it is worth briefly considering Rein and Miller's (1974) question as to what people mean if they are in favour of income redistribution. Possible interpretations offered include the following.

1. The avoidance of 'income and wealth crystallization' would tend to attack the feedback advantages that high-income high-wealth households enjoy (noted in Table 9.1) with respect to education, health care and the like so that multiple deprivations are avoided. In this context the authors note that 'equalizing' income differentials (higher income to compensate for the lower attractiveness of some jobs) are normally swamped by 'accentuating' differentials (such as status and recognition following high income).

2. A 'social minimum' of income and in-kind provision for all should be achieved.

3. 'One-hundred percentism' refers to *horizontal equity*, whereby quality and level of work effort alone should determine income, and discrimination on the basis of sex, race, social background should be avoided so that all have access to the better posts.

4. 'Lowering the ceiling' involves reducing the concentration of income at the top by the use and enforcement of tax laws.

5. 'Income shares' refers to influencing the share of National Income so that various quantiles in the distribution, e.g. the bottom 20 per cent, must have at least (say) 10 per cent of the income.

6. 'Stratum mobility' is concerned with the narrowing of income differentials among occupational groups. In particular, some feel that occupational groups should enjoy similar *proportional* increases in income which preserve existing differentials, while others, pushing for greater equality, want similar *absolute* increases which have the effect of narrowing differentials.

7. 'Equalization of lifetime income profiles' concerns inequalities in lifetime income growth and involves developing career income profiles that rise with age. Everyone should have a 'proper' job.

8. 'Economic inclusion' involves the notion that income inequalities that exclude individuals from the mainstream of society are to be avoided. This corresponds to the type of poverty line advocated by Fuchs (1965).

9. 'International yardsticks' means that each country must attain as equal a distribution as that achieved by all other countries at the same development stage.

While not exhaustive, these examples indicate how many interpretations can be given to the goal of income redistribution (and may help readers 'spot' their own attitudes!).

9.3.2 Positive accounts of redistribution

Positive accounts of redistribution focus on explaining what, if any, actual redistribution takes place. Whereas the above section was described as being part of the social optimality tradition, this section has elements firmly rooted in the public choice tradition. (The first subsection is the main exception.)

Interdependent utility functions

The analysis of the previous section offered one mechanism whereby individuals would voluntarily redistribute income either in kind or in cash (see Hochman and Rodgers 1969), the cases being those of the specifically and the generally interdependent utility function respectively. The former interdependence is tied to specific goods, e.g. health care and education, whereas the latter relates to general purchasing power. The argument presented is in terms of the 'haves' being concerned for the 'have-nots'. With many 'haves' with similar motivations, a free rider problem emerges to dampen unilateral action. However, in the presence of coercive taxation to solve that problem, the argument suggests that individual net gains from the public sector—the fiscal residual—should vary inversely with original income positions.

There is no requirement, however, for altruism to be the argument causing the interdependence. Redistribution can stem from malice and envy. Brennan (1973a) employs a diagram such as Fig. 9.11 to demonstrate this point. For individual A, her own income Y_A is a good but the other person's income Y_B is a bad, reflecting the presence of malice towards B. (Envy is increasing marginal disutility of the other person's income.) The shape of B's indifference map reflects the same malicious feelings. With initial allocations of income at point 1 on I_B^1 for B and I_A^1 for A, there are clearly gains from trade to be had from the lowering of both incomes as long as adjustment is contained within the usual rugby ball shape. The locus of points between 2 and 3 define the relevant portion of the contract or, more aptly in this case (Boulding's terminology), the conflict curve. An outcome such as 4 raises A's utility to I_A^2 and B's to I_B^2. Intuitively, what is happening is that A's loss of utility from the reduction of her own income is being more than compensated for by the knowledge that B's income is also falling. But how is the income reduction to be achieved? With many A's and B's, the free rider problem arises. Individuals will attempt to allow others to reduce their incomes, gaining in utility from

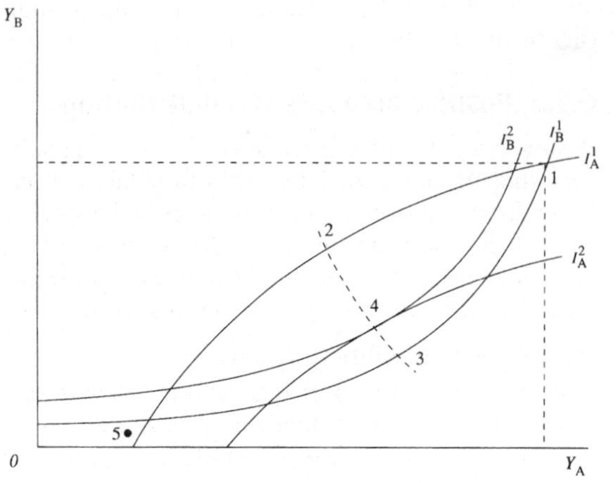

Figure 9.11 Redistribution from malice.

Source: adapted from Brennan (1973) *Journal of Public Economics*, **2**, pp. 173–83, Elsevier, Amsterdam.

that knowledge, while not lowering their own incomes. Additionally, the process could get out of hand. Not all income reductions raise utility. If the cuts become too deep, both A and B can be made worse off, say at 5. These two points suggest the power of government to solve the free rider problem and to referee the process to keep losses in bounds. Brennan now introduces a third actor (or set of actors) C, whose income level Y_C is a neutral good as long as $2Y_C < Y_A$ or Y_B; i.e. they are unconcerned about those with less than half their income. Government redistribution of income from A and B towards C, within limits, raises the utility in this society of some well-off but malicious and envious individuals!

Majority voting

The use of majority voting as the explanation of redistribution has been suggested by Downs (1957) and Meltzer and Richard (1981). The straightforward Downs approach relies on the shape that income distributions typically take. With some very large incomes in the extended tail of the distribution and many small incomes in the 'meaty' body of the distribution, the median voter's income is less than that of the mean voter (see Fig. 9.1). A vote-maximizing political party therefore has an incentive to propose redistribution from the richer segment to the poorer majority. The crude implication, not borne out, is that the poorer 50% + 1 gain from the activities of government. This, however, tends not to be the case in empirical studies.

Tullock (1971), like Disraeli, notes that the top and bottom of the income distribution may have interests in common and that it is the middle (or median) individual, or more loosely groups, who wield the power. After all, the median voter rule suggests that it is the way in which the middle two voters in the income distribution vote that determines the outcome of a rich or poor majority. While siding with the poor is more rewarding because the poor represent less attractive pickings than the rich, they may be able to 'bargain' on the terms on which their support is obtained. Indeed, if the prudent poor are a minority in the majority coalition, then it is possible to see a reason why the middle and lower-middle income ranges appear to come out well in redistributive studies. Le Grand (1982) is one author who documents this view of the effects of UK public expenditure.

Income insurance

Buchanan and Tullock (1965) develop an argument about redistribution based on the idea of income uncertainty and possibilities for insurance. A reinterpretation of Fig. 9.6(a) illustrates the heart of the argument. Given diminishing marginal utility of income, more income in one period cannot compensate for lower income in another period. Suppose Y_A' is individual A's average income but Y_A obtains in a good period and Y_b in a bad period. Individual total utility can be raised if $Y_A'Y_A$ can be removed in good times, leaving Y_A', and added to Y_b to achieve Y_A' also in bad times. The utility lost in good times $Y_A'34Y_A$ is clearly less than that gained in bad times Y_b83Y_A'; i.e. individuals can gain from ensuring an average income in all periods provided the transaction costs of the policy do not fully swamp the potential gain.

Private insurance policies against earning a low income *per se* are hard to find, because once you have paid the premium the moral hazard problem central to Baumol's case for a public enterprise (see chapter 5) would then loom very large indeed. Individually engineered low incomes would be the order of the day for all those insured, and the insurance company would not be able to cover the loss. While some types of income insurance schemes do exist— e.g. pensions—the government, for example stepping in to provide unemployment benefit financed from taxation of the employed, may be a superior provision mechanism. While such intervention is not without a moral hazard problem, it may still remain the best solution for those seeking income insurance; in other words the government can handle the moral hazard problem better than the market can.

Buying protection

Brennan (1973b) picks up on the idea that revolution is a strong possibility in a society with large income disparities. If society is divided between a small, wealthy and politically powerful minority and a majority of poor, politically weak members, the minority have the problem of creating policies to foster stability. The decision to revolt turns on the evaluation of costs (punishment for failure, injury risk, loss of property, etc.) versus the gains of raised income or wealth. The rich and any poor (risk-averse) non-participants cannot expect to gain from any revolution and will be happy to see potential revolutionaries bought off. Here Brennan suggests that revolutionaries will be low-income and risk-loving. Now clearly, one option is to raise the income level of this group in a flat-rate way. However, given their risk-loving nature, greater protection is purchased by a low probability of a large prize rather than a high probability of a modest prize; i.e. a society characterized by a few 'glittering prizes' awarded on the basis of equality of opportunity recommends itself. A policy example consistent with this perspective is a public sector education system based on equality of opportunity with the winners being the academically able irrespective of their income or other background characteristics. Such policies offer the rich some protection as they weaken the resolve of potential revolutionaries.

If there are seeds of truth in the theories outlined in this sub-section, actual redistribution taking place in the public sector will reflect altruistic, malicious, vote-maximizing, insurance- and protection-seeking behaviour. If all or a variety of these motives are present, some redistribution of income or in-kind government provision is expected within limits, although its pattern is likely to be complex. The limits to redistribution captured in these motives are reserved for section 9.6. It is the measurement and pattern of redistribution achieved by the government budget that are the concerns of the next two sections.

9.4 Redistributive impact of the budget

The redistributive impact of the government budget involves numerous problems, which are illustrated below in the form of a convenient list provided by O'Higgins (1980) and Ruggles (1991).

The 'counterfactual' problem

Studies of the impact of the government budget necessarily presuppose what would have been the case in the absence of such a budget. This is the so-called counterfactual problem (common in historical studies) of being able to observe the world of X happening and assessing the impact of X only by trying to suppose what would have happened if X had not happened. In the present context, this amounts to having a market economy outcome and imagining what would happen if there were a mixed economy or, alternatively, imagining taking government activity out of a mixed economy to produce a market- or government-free economy. In the UK the most familiar redistributive budget study is that carried out by the Central Statistical Office and published as *Economic Trends*. The CSO perspective is one that involves producing a market scenario to compare with the observed mixed economy that exists. For some, this fundamental weakness of the created counterfactual makes the whole exercise untenable; for others (see Peacock 1974) it is a question of plausibility; i.e. what you think would have been the case must be plausible. For example, in the absence of state pensions you have to assume that there is some form of post-employment support (presumably private pension schemes), and not that people will have zero income when they retire. Whatever view is adopted, the fact remains that such studies are undertaken and, if for no other reason, some understanding of their possibilities and limitations is desirable.

Extent of coverage

There is the question of what degree of incompleteness is optimal. Having, say, opted for different income groups as the unit of analysis, a calculation along the following lines can be performed for *each group*:

		'Benefits'			'Costs'	
Original pre-budget income	+	In-kind provision of goods and services	+ Transfers −	Direct taxes	− Net indirect taxes	= Post-budget income

Over all groups, the original and post-budget incomes will be the same if there is an economic budget of fixed value to be divided. This corresponds more to economic arithmetic than to economic analysis, and more sophisticated approaches look to evaluation by reference to the tools developed in chapter 6 on cost–benefit analysis. This tension between economic arithmetic and the prescriptions of economic theory shows up in the discussion that follows.

Before moving on, the problem of the counterfactual can be highlighted further. Post-budget income minus real (exhaustive) benefits and transfers plus taxation gives original income. This makes sense at what might be termed an economic arithmetic level, but is flawed at the behavioural level. Virtually all of economics concerns individuals responding in a utility-maximizing way to different economic signals. Changing any of the benefits and any of the taxes will almost certainly generate some behavioural response which will have to be guesstimated if the true original income is to be deduced. Original income calculated by arithmetic is not the original income that would be observed without government intervention. Even if it were possible to model accurately the supply and demand responses to changes in taxes and transfer or benefit provisions of all kinds, it would remain a GNP or market calculation. Affording no weight to extra market considerations, whether good or bad, means that individual or income group economic welfare is being identified with command over market goods or services alone. (Such a criticism can be levelled at most of the discussion of this chapter: see Scitovsky 1986.)

Returning to the question of coverage, this is always less than complete, with more taxes than benefits being allocated to the identified income groups. The asymmetry arises because of the different nature of the benefits provided and taxes levied. Dealing with the benefit side first, it is clear from chapters 3, 4 and 5 that goods and services vary in their 'economic' characteristics and this leads to their different treatment.

In the CSO exercise the majority of public expenditure is ignored because goods or services offering non-rival (or indivisible) benefits are viewed as not conferring benefits on individual households as such. In addition, goods or services that provide benefits to both households and the business sector (but in unknown proportions) are ignored. Even where the benefits can be viewed as almost exclusively attributable to households (e.g. parks), lack of data on patronage leads to them being disregarded. Capital as opposed to current expenditures also raises difficulties because, although the opportunity cost of investment goods is felt now, the benefits will typically arise in the future. One view is that they should be allocated in discounted present value form to individuals who gain from them. However, if these individuals are in a future generation, the problem arises of who gains. Peacock (1974) suggests that the appropriate view is that the current generation is choosing to sacrifice current consumption to internalize its concern for future generations and therefore can be legitimately viewed as gaining from capital expenditure the fruits of which they may not actually sample. As with many aspects of any redistributive exercise, sensitivity calculations are an acceptable if not always convincing way forward.

The 'balanced budget' issue

It was noted above that there is often a disparity between benefits and taxes covered; that is, an unbalanced budget is allocated which creates a distortion in measured net benefits. The word 'balanced' suggests that it would be attractive to equalize allocations on the sides of the budget at either 100 per cent or some other percentage. Ideally, all benefits and taxes should be included, but if this is not possible then Peacock and Shannon (1968) advocated equal allocations of both. For example, a social welfare budget might be created in that the taxes conceived of as paying for programmes could be allocated in line with the volume of social welfare benefits provided. The drawback with equal partial allocation is that it presents a rather arbitrary account of events. Suppose direct taxes and cash transfers are allocated and then cash transfers are increased. Depending on how these increases are financed, different income groups will be affected. A very different picture can be drawn depending on the part of the budget in question. If the 'slice' considered is unaffected by, say, decreased road expenditures or health expenditures and/or the increased indirect taxes required to increase the transfers paid out, then the cash transfers misleadingly appear as a 'free lunch'. In general, less than complete allocations of taxes and benefits, whether matched in size or not, pose problems. (For a distributive study that allocated all taxes and public expenditures in the UK, see O'Higgins and Ruggles 1981.)

The incidence and valuation of expenditures

Chapter 6 on cost–benefit analysis raises the question of the appropriate valuation of costs and benefits, whereas chapter 3 raises the question of different types of goods. Both are relevant under this heading, which concerns itself with the benefit side of the government budget. The exclusion of non-rival expenditures and/or expenditures whose beneficiaries are uncertain by the CSO has already been noted. However, there are other possibilities. For such expenditures, their tax cost can be used as their valuation and can be allocated on a variety of possible bases—per capita, in proportion to household income, rateable value, etc., and where possible actual use of the service by different households. Of course, this is a long way away from the appropriate measures of consumer surplus, and for economic theorists at least looks all too arbitrary.

A good example involves a contribution by Aaron and McGuire (1970). For non-rival goods especially it is tempting to allocate their costs (=benefits) on a per capita basis, but Aaron and McGuire show that this is equivalent to assuming that all individuals have the same marginal utility of income. This can be demonstrated as follows.

The individual demand for good G is given by

$$(9.21) \qquad \frac{dU}{dG} = MU_g = l p_g$$

or

$$(9.22) \qquad \frac{MU_g}{l} = p_g$$

where MU_g = the marginal utility of G to the individual

p_g = the price of G per unit

l = marginal utility of income to the individual

In a two-person economy (A and B), efficient provision involves summation of their marginal benefits, so that

$$(9.23) \qquad \frac{MU_g^A}{l_A} + \frac{MU_g^B}{l_B} = p_g = MC$$
$$(= AC, \text{ assuming a constant cost industry})$$

Assuming that each individual has the same utility of income function and ability to gain from the public good, then with different incomes they will have different l but the same marginal utility from the (equally shared) public good. If Q_g is the efficient quantity of public good provided, then this indicates

$$(9.24) \qquad Q_g \frac{MU_g^A}{l_A} + Q_g \frac{MU_g^B}{l_B} = Q_g AC$$

where $Q_g AC$ is simply the budget expenditure on G. Here the marginal utilities of the public good are the same but the marginal utilities of income are different. In short, for it to be appropriate to allocate $Q_g AC$ equally between A and B, l_A should equal l_B. When this is not the case, benefit allocations are in inverse proportion to A's and B's l. That is, a lower l justifies, on the specified assumptions, a higher share of the expenditure allocated to the provision of G.

The incidence and valuation of taxes

Chapter 7 rehearses the arguments about the direct and indirect (welfare cost) burden of a tax and raises questions of incidence. Both of these issues have a prominent part to play in assessing the impact of taxes on different groups. Except for the cases of perfectly inelastic demand or supply curves, the imposition of taxation will involve an excess burden which will typically (like the incidence itself) be felt in some proportion by consumers and producers alike. Any accurate allocation involves the knowledge of the supply and demand elasticities that drive the welfare cost calculation formulas (see chapter 7). Prest (1968) notes that studies can at least be consistent, so that situations where all income tax is allocated to labour (plausible if Fig. 9.12(a) applies) and all indirect taxation borne by consumers (plausible if Fig. 9.12(b) applies) should be avoided because they involve contradictory pictures of the supply side of the economy. Again, the general way forward is sensitivity analysis.

All the above suggest that income redistribution studies have to be treated with caution and any critical assumptions revealed by sensitivity analysis should be made clear. Table 9.2 gives the inequality information calculated by Jenkins (1990) from CSO 'Blue Book' estimates of the distribution of income. The fact that the overlap of tax payments and transfers in cash and/or kind leaves as much as half the households in a broadly unchanged position has drawn criticism (see Burton 1985). Considerable tax compliance and administrative costs are an aspect of the costs of this ineffective 'fiscal churning'. Furthermore, it is argued by some commentators that, if an attempt were made to trace the redistributive consequences of other types of government policy, e.g. subsidies that are part of industrial policy, then an already very fuzzy picture would become totally confused. In short, the criticism is that we do not really know the redistributive impact of government. The third criticism Burton makes refers to the 'traps' created by the interaction of the tax payment transfer receipt system. This consequence is central to section 9.5.

9.4.1 A dissenting view

Pryke (1995) is one author that disagrees vehemently with the methodology and the nature of the inequality /poverty statistics so far discussed in this chapter. In making his attack on the statistics of section 9.3 he taps into the type of arguments raised by section 9.4. In his view the Department of Social Security in its Households Below Average Income (HBAI) tables and the Institute for Fiscal Studies following their lead give out the wrong message. He describes HBAI data as an 'economic nonsense' and writes 'On balance, HBAI makes a large negative contribution to

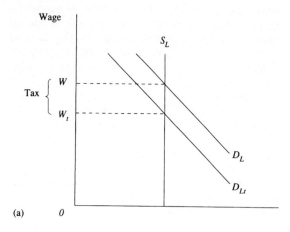

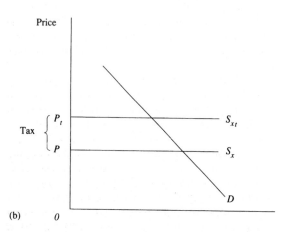

Figure 9.12 Assigning incidence.

knowledge and national debate' (pp. 70–1). How is such a damning criticism supported? The answer to this question involves some of the issues already introduced. His basic argument is that the statistics are grossly misleading in that:

(i) the treatment of housing is flawed in that it fails to include as a benefit to households the services provided by the houses they occupy. For outright houseowners the measure of this benefit is a gross figure (representing interest sacrificed by having capital tied up in housing) while for mortgage payers the appropriate figure is net of the interest payments they make (for renters it is the real or notional rent they pay.);

(ii) the value of leisure is ignored because the exercise is couched in income terms. Someone work-

ing full time for £250 per week is not £100 better off than someone working part time for £150 because the part-timer has more leisure that is of considerable value;

(iii) it is a 'snapshot' cross-section view of the income distribution and therefore says little about a more relevant inequality indicator such as life-time income which is as it happens more equally distributed. The data do not provide information as to whether those in poverty are there temporarily or permanently;

(iv) the amount households save for the longer term should be deducted from income (it will show up as income when households receive their reward from superannuation contributions, personal pension payments and the like);

(v) the weights used to produce what is described as equivalized income are inappropriate. As Jenkins and Cowell (1995) indicate 'the average person might be someone from a family of two adults and two children with "net" unequivalized income of £328, or someone from a childless married couple with a net income of £236 or a single person with a net income of £144.' Recall the average figure is £236 and it applies to the childless married couple because the weights for husband and wife deliberately sum to one (0.61 for a head of household and 0.39 for his or her spouse) hence 0.61 applied to £236 produces the equivalized average income of £144 for a single person. The weights for children reported by Pryke range from 0.09 for those under two to 0.36 for ones of 16 and over. In short the single person household is better off than net income indicates therefore it is 'equivalized up' whereas the two children couple is worse off than net income indicates and is 'equivalized down'. The average equivalized income is found by crediting all members of a household with its equivalized income summing them across households and dividing by the numbers of persons. It represents the income of the household in which the average person lives, on the assumption that it consists of a couple. Pryke sees this as a too narrow and unconvincing form of analysis. It is too narrow in that it identifies welfare with money income available for market goods and services. Surely children are more than simply an additional cost in a household—they must offer some, albeit often intangible, benefits for couples to choose to have them in the first place. The arithmetic is unconvincing in that if children are a cost why would someone with a tenfold increased income from £100 raise their expenditure in a dependent child of 16 from £26.47 (£100 × 0.36/1.36) to £264.71 which is what is implied by the formula;

(vi) finally the HBAI exercise does not include the 'return' from the public sector in the form of in-kind goods and services.

The author follows these arguments with amended calculations which centre particularly on the housing and leisure benefit arguments.

The adjustment of money income to what the author calls real income reduces both the numbers in affluence (the top 10 per cent of the population before any adjustments are made) and poverty (those below half the average equivalized income). For 1988 the numbers and proportion in affluence would fall from 5.6 million and 10 per cent to 4.1 million and 7.4 per cent. The equivalent figures for poverty are 10.3 million and 18.5 per cent falling to 3.6 million and 6.4 per cent. In his final conclusion Pryke notes that 'since mass poverty does not exist, there is no call for the feelings of guilt which are generated by its supposed existence' (p. 75). While the message is a comforting one it will clearly not leave all convinced of its veracity. The helpful point is that the complexity of notions of inequality and poverty are illustrated and the chains of reasoning required to analyse them made more transparent when debate takes a concrete form. In the next section the assumption is that there are some 'less-well-off' people whom the government attempts to help.

9.5 Fiscal measures and the 'less well off'

For a government having to establish a guide to the existing extent of economic inequality and some principles as to when inequality shades to poverty and becomes a policy problem, there is the question of what policy instrument to use. Referring back to Table 9.1, the bottom panel provides some examples of policies collected under three headings: those affecting factor market outcomes directly, those altering the ownership of capital, and those attacking the income distribution directly. The issues discussed in this chapter relate mainly to the second and third options and in particular to proposals to replace a large proportion of them with some type of Citizen's Income

(CI) which is a generic term that covers schemes that involve a complete or partial integration of the tax and benefits system. CI is defined as 'the inalienable right for every citizen regardless of age, sex, race, creed, labour market or marital status to a small but guaranteed income unconditionally' (Citizens Income Bulletin 22 cover page). An increasing number of schemes are canvassed under this banner but the main ones are negative income tax, social dividend, basic income (BI) and participation income. (See Parker and Raven (1996), for a discussion of participation income see Atkinson (1995). For a wider appreciation of the issues related to the UK social security system, see Dilnot and Walker 1989.)

Overlaps in the tax payment transfer receipt system have been a focal point for much discussion in the 1980s with various sorts of 'traps' identified. The major ones are illustrated in Fig. 9.13, which is amended from Atkinson, Flemming and Kay (1983).

OA represents the 'strong' unemployment trap where individuals are financially better off out of rather than in work. This is usually expressed in terms of their having replacement ratios of over 100 per cent. The replacement ratio measures income in and out of work so that it measures net-of-tax earnings minus work-related expenses as compared with out-of-work transfer payments contingent upon the status of being unemployed. Despite much popular misconception, there are relatively few individuals or families that find themselves in this position.

AB, the 'weak' unemployment trap, may be typical of many low-paid workers who face high but less than 100 per cent replacement ratios. It must be noted that no value is being given to the disutility of work in itself. Such a valuation would be controversial; some would want the value of 'leisure' included while others would regard being deprived of work, in a society where people are expected to work, as a cost to the individual. It is this latter consideration that helps explain why many people with high replacement ratios plus the possibility for 'leisure' remain in work rather than opting for unemployment.

BE represents the 'weak' poverty trap, where over a wide range of earned income the effect of explicit taxation plus implicit taxation via the loss of means-tested benefits means that disposable income remains largely unaffected.

CD is the strong poverty trap, where over a range of earned income disposable income actually falls as earned income rises. This is because the explicit tax rate and the means-tested benefit withdrawal rate exceeds unity. One suggestion for avoiding this is to have the explicit tax rate apply only to net-of-transfer

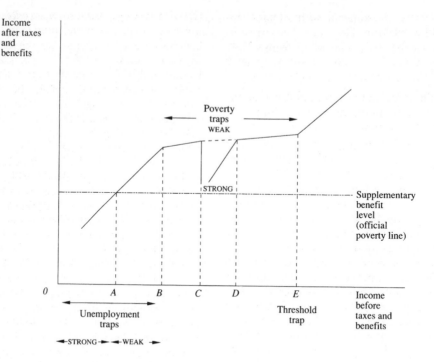

Figure 9.13 A variety of 'traps'.

Source: Atkinson, Flemming and Kay (1983) *The Contemporary Problems of Economic Policy*, Methuen and Co., London.

income earnings, so that if the benefit withdrawal rate *b* is 60 per cent and the explicit tax rate 30 per cent the 'total' tax paid on an additional £1 of earned income would be at a rate $b + t(1 - b)$, which is a sum comprising 60p less means-tested benefit, and 30 per cent of 40p = 12p explicit tax, i.e. 72p. Only if the benefit withdrawal rate exceeded 100 per cent would the individual actually be worse off under such a proposal. But as Collard (1985) points out, this would create a threshold trap around point *E*. If the government were to raise the tax threshold, by say £100 (a common policy to try and help the 'low-paid'), this would be worth £30 to a person to the right of point *E* facing the explicit tax rate above. However, to someone facing the weak poverty trap, and again with the illustrative numbers above, this is worth only 30 per cent of £40, i.e. £12, because the explicit tax rate applies only to the net-of-transfer income; i.e. $t(1 - b) = 0.3$ $(1 - 0.6) = 0.12$.

The simple message is that traps are easy to create even when the object is to ameliorate the effects of one that already exists. As might be expected, high replacement ratios figure in the discussion of unemployment (chapter 10).

Parker (1995) adds to the analysis of traps raising their number to seven. She adds the following to the unemployment and poverty traps:

(i)   The invalidity trap like the unemployment trap is about the erosion of the differential between net income in and out of work but centres on those receiving National Insurance invalidity benefit;

(ii) The lone parent trap arises because lone parents often have low potential wages, high tax rates and high work expenses especially child care;

(iii) The part time trap refers to the reduction of net income between full time and part time work caused by reducing the hours threshold for eligibility to family credit. An example the author provides indicates that in 1994/5 for one of a couple with two children earning £3.75 an hour it made only £5 per week difference whether they worked 16 or 40 hours per week;

(iv) The lack of skills trap concerns the incentives to train so, for example, instead of benefits being contingent on training to qualify for the training for work programme participants have to be unemployed for 26 weeks;

(v) The savings trap is caused by the presence of means-tested benefits. The incentive to save is damaged if individuals anticipate it will reduce their entitlement to benefit in the future.

In Parker's view the upshot of the seven traps is a welfare system that simultaneously fails to cover those most in need and to provide incentives to seek work. The way forward is radical reform involving some form of CI, e.g. a negative income tax system. The basics of CI-type schemes are outlined in the next section.

9.5.1 CI schemes

To avoid the type of problems introduced above, among others, many commentators who accept at least some redistribution as a relevant policy objective advocate some form of automatic tax-transfer system as the only adjunct to an otherwise 'minimum state' guaranteeing law and order and little else. There is a wide variety of possible schemes, ordered below by their varying degrees of generosity to the less well off.

Variations on a tax-transfer theme are presented below, where

Y_e = earned income
Y_d = disposable income, i.e. after any taxes or transfers
Y_p = official poverty line
t = tax rate

(i) With no tax-transfer system,

$$(9.25) \qquad Y_d = Y_e$$

(ii) With a proportional tax system,

$$(9.26) \qquad Y_d = (1 - t)Y_e$$

(iii) With exemptions up to Y_p,

$$(9.27) \qquad Y_d = Y_c \quad \text{for} \quad Y_e < Y_p$$

and

$$(9.28) \qquad Y_d = (1 - t)Y_e + tY_p \quad \text{for} \quad Y_e > Y_p$$

i.e. the no-exemption situation plus the tax no longer levied on Y_p

(iv) With a negative tax system that guarantees tY_p and taxes all Y_e at t,

$$(9.29) \qquad Y_d = tY_p + (1 - t)Y_e$$

(v) With a minimum income guarantee = Y_p,

$$(9.30) \qquad Y_d = Y_p \quad \text{for} \quad Y_e < Y_p$$

$$(9.31) \qquad Y_d = (1 - t)Y_e + tY_p \quad \text{for} \quad Y_e > Y_p$$

(vi) With social dividend (a lump sum to all) equal to Y_p,

$$(9.32) \qquad Y_d = Y_p + (1 - t)Y_e$$

That is, the social dividend differs from the negative income tax scheme only by the higher guarantee when $Y_e = 0$, i.e. $Y_p > tY_p$. (Social Dividend is interpreted now as CI financed out of the profits of industry, e.g. the Alaskan Dividend Distribution Program is financed from Alaskan oil profits.)

Figure 9.14 illustrates the relationship between earned and disposable income described by these schemes up to the break-even point, where $Y_e = Y_d$.

BI is a guaranteed, tax free amount credited automatically, each week or month to every man, woman or child as a right of residence irrespective of marital or work status. The costs and redistributive impact of a Big Bang approach with a BI sufficient to live on suggest it could not be introduced at a stroke hence it is envisaged that it would initially be low and then rise with economic growth and/or the dictates of public opinion. This gradual introduction of BI is called Transitional Basic Income (TBI) (see Parker and Raven 1996). The introduction of the scheme would redistribute income from the top to the bottom of the distribution and in favour of families with children. The finance would come from reducing most benefits apart from TBI and making the tax system more progressive.

One of the vital issues about all these schemes concerns the balance between helping the less well off and the marginal tax rate facing the better off. They are all tax-transfer schemes: the taxes must cover the transfers.

The illustrative figures contained within Meade (1978) suggest that negative income tax proposals are less 'demanding' where guaranteed income is not all that generous. Only if this is the case does the tax rate in the system not climb sharply. However, stronger incentives at all levels of the income structure is a theme in many public policy statements of the 1980s. So for example, if the poverty line Y_p is 40 per cent of average income and 15 per cent of income is required to cover the provision of public sector goods and services, the implied tax rate on earned income for a social dividend at the poverty line is 55 per cent so that individuals would receive 45p of an additional £1 earned! While it is possible to soften this blow by having different tax rates below and above the poverty line, or by having a social dividend that is smaller for those in than those out of work (the two-tier case), once the simplicity and universality of the system is lost, so are most of its advantages. (Dilnot, Kay and

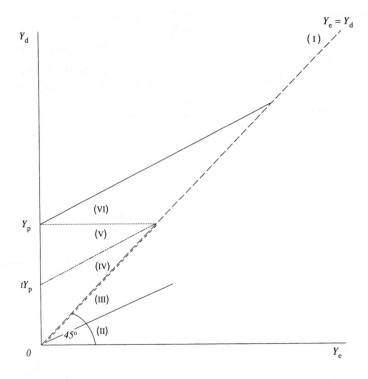

Figure 9.14 Tax-transfer schemes.

Morris (1984) offer a different perspective.) More recently, Atkinson (1989) has calculated the rate of tax to finance two proposed social dividend/tax credit schemes, and he suggests a range of 47.5–51.3 per cent but warns that it is a difficult figure to calculate. For an illustrative TBI see Parker and Raven (1996). A revenue neutral scheme for 1996/7 would involve the guaranteed amount being £17.75 and income tax rates of 26 per cent (no 20 per cent or 24 per cent bands) and two new rates of 45 per cent on incomes above £45,000 and 50 per cent on incomes exceeding £50,000. National Insurance (NI) contributions however could be reduced from 10 per cent to 9 per cent so that the majority of taxpayers would face combined tax and NI contribution rates of 35 per cent compared to the current 34 per cent.

Parker (1995) reports on a combination of BI and income-tested housing benefit. The type of scheme she has in mind is illustrated for a single person in Fig. 9.15 where there is: a partial basic income, Y_g, sufficient for non-householders to live on; a tax discount on the first slice of 'own' income and an income-tested housing benefit making the income schedule Y_p12 and the tax schedule Y_g12, i.e. for non-householders

the tax schedule becomes gently progressive. For low income householders the tax schedule is Y_p12 which is much the same as the conventional negative income tax proposals. Point 1 is the break even point of the scheme. The idea is to combine poverty prevention with work incentives and increased use of discretion (positive as well as negative), by reducing the number of households claiming means-tested and work-tested benefits and bringing back the old-fashioned case officer—instead of relying almost entirely on computers.

In general it is difficult to make the arithmetic of CI look attractive and as Parker and Raven (1996, p. 14) state 'It is important that CI supporters understand that universal benefits are incompatible with very low rates of income tax.' The different consequences of different reform options on future income and hence transfers and tax revenues are difficult to model. However, there is some optimism in the empirical work that finds no strong adverse connection between high social security expenditure and recorded economic growth (see 11.7). Concerning the choice between contingent benefits (those based on a particular status, e.g. being unemployed, a single parent,

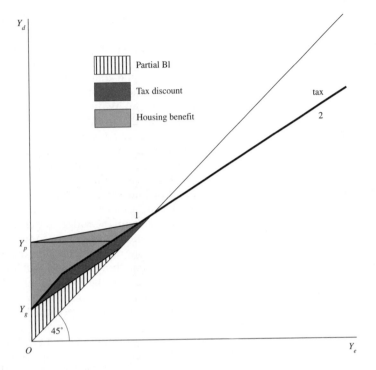

Figure 9.15 Parker's basic income guarantee.

Source: Parker (1995).

disabled) that are associated with typical welfare state provision and the apparently simple income-related means-tested benefits, there is a general point to be made. Contingent benefits have the advantage of picking out groups in society that are in greater need of income and/or in-kind support than other groups. Supporters of this perspective are usually labelled as being 'back to Beveridge'. Supporters of a more means-tested approach are also much more likely to favour some type of CI scheme and argue that within each contingent class there are some who need help and some who do not, so that the rich in 'needy-contingent' categories gain at the expense of the poor in less needy-contingent categories, e.g. the low-paid workers. However, to choose either route is to lose information on either means or status that is helpful to targeting support where it is most required. This is a complex area that is quick to raise controversy and reveal underlying divisions of perspective on the willingness to redistribute income. (Recall the different views outlined in section 9.3.1.) For example, H. Parker concludes the introduction of her book on the integration of the tax and benefit system in the UK as follows:

the real issue concerns human relationships and human values. Do we want to live in a society in which making money is all that matters, or are there other objectives that we hold more dear. (Parker 1989, p. 7)

For her, at least, this is a much bigger issue than the technicalities introduced above.

9.5.2 Cash transfers versus price subsidies and in-kind transfers

One of the standard questions of public finance theory is why redistribution is made to recipients via price subsidies and in-kind transfers rather than through cash transfers. It will become clear that this debate is a mirror-image of the excess burden argument already discussed with respect to taxation. Here there is an excess burden associated with price subsidies or in-kind transfers which would be absent in the case of a cash transfer.

In Fig. 9.16(a) a cash transfer is compared with a price subsidy the objective of which is to make the recipient as well off as possible. The initial price ratio between good X and Y (a composite of all other goods) is shown by the budget line 12. The consumer

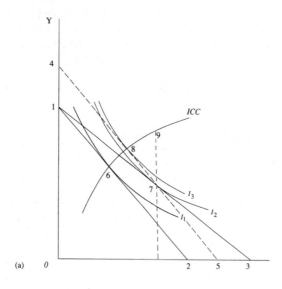

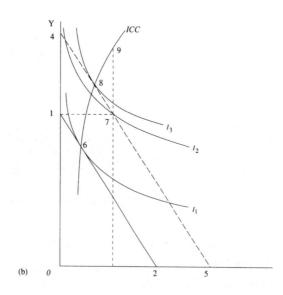

Figure 9.16 Cash transfer versus price subsidies and in-kind transfer.

maximizes welfare at point 6. The government wishes to assist the consumer of product X by reducing its price. A price subsidy causes the budget line to change to 13. The new equilibrium is at point 7 and the consumer is at a higher level of welfare (as can be seen by the tangency point to the higher indifference curve I_2). However, if the government had transferred the cash (sufficient to subsidize good X at point 7), the consumer would face the budget line 45. The new

welfare maximum would be at point 8. The government, at no additional cost to the Exchequer, would have had a greater impact on the individual's welfare. With a cash transfer the recipient of government assistance would attain a welfare level as shown by I_3. In this way the price subsidy scheme is a less efficient instrument for redistribution. It creates an 'excess burden' (as shown by the difference between I_3 and I_2), and this can be estimated (see Laidler 1969). The cash transfer does not distort prices and appears a more efficient redistributive instrument.

In Fig. 9.16(b) the consumer is again initially at point 6 on budget line 12. An in-kind transfer of good X enables her to consume a quantity 17 of good X at no cost. The shape of the budget line changes to 175; after point 7 the individual can consume more of good X, but to do so she must give up some quantity of good Y. In the example shown the new welfare maximum for the individual is on the corner point, 7. The individual would not choose to consume any more of the good than that quantity that is received 'free of charge' from the government. Once again, if the individual is offered the cash equivalent the new budget line is 45. With the cash equivalent of the in-kind subsidy, the consumer can select *any* combination of Y and X. This makes possible a new equilibrium at point 8. Again, the cash transfer leaves the individual less constrained, and the welfare maximum with the cash transfer (point 8) greater than that achieved with the in-kind transfer (point 7).

While these forms of subsidy are not exhaustive, a consistent message appears to be that a cash transfer is the most efficient way of increasing the welfare of the recipient (i.e., for any given transfer, welfare of the recipient may increase to a greater extent). Of course, price subsidies are used for many other purposes; for example, in chapter 3 it was noted that they might be used to tackle the problem of an externality. However, in so far as their purpose is purely redistributive, it seems difficult to provide a rationale for price subsidies or in-kind transfers rather than cash transfers, and yet these latter forms of assistance are extremely important components of public expenditure (see, e.g. Brennan and Pincus 1983).

One attempt to explain the choice of price subsidies and in-kind transfers is to assume a 'goods-specific' externality. In this case concern rests not only with the recipient but also with the donor (who pays the taxes to finance the subsidy). By a 'goods-specific' externality, the important argument in the donor's utility function is not simply the utility of the recipient but also the quantity of a good (e.g. health care or education) consumed by the recipient. The purpose of the subsidy is to increase the recipient's consumption of good X. While the cash transfer appears efficient at increasing the recipient's welfare, it is not the best instrument to stimulate consumption of a particular good. In Fig. 9.16(a) the line ICC is the income consumption curve. It maps a locus of equilibrium welfare maximum points for the consumer as income increases. For the recipient to increase as much of X as shown at point 7, it would be necessary for income to be increased to point 9 on the income consumption curve. That is, the budget line 45 would need to be pushed to the right until it passed through point 9. Obviously this would impose a significant strain on the Exchequer. The cost transfer necessary would be far greater than the cost of the price subsidy. The price subsidy creates a 'substitution' effect as well as an 'income effect', and this substitution effect also encourages consumption of good X. If the objective is to promote the consumption of good X, it is clear that the price subsidy is the more 'efficient' fiscal instrument.

This general conclusion is repeated in Fig. 9.16(b). Here the in-kind transfer encourages consumption of good X at a cheaper cost to the Exchequer than would a cash transfer; for a cash transfer to stimulate consumption of X by as much, it would be necessary to give the individual sufficient cash that the budget line would be pushed out to point 9 on the income consumption curve.

How convincing is the goods-specific externality argument as a rationale for government redistributive policy? Rosenthal (1983) draws together a number of criticisms of the argument which can be listed as follows.

1. For price subsidy schemes to perfectly internalize the goods-specific externality, a great deal of information would be required, of a nature that would be difficult to measure (Browning 1975).

2. Following Lancaster's theory of demand (1966), goods may possess attributes which donors regard as important for donees; e.g. food contains the characteristic nutrition. However, a subsidy on all food may be counterproductive if different types of processed food contain nutrition to a greater or lesser extent. Some foods may be light on 'nutrition' because they are 'time-saving' in preparation. If food is subsidized, then 'convenience foods' may be promoted with perverse results (see, e.g. Johnson 1978). The difficulties of applying the goods-specific externality are in this way compounded.

3. In-kind subsidies are sometimes extremely difficult to police. Certainly vouchers may be provided to consumers to enable them to consume goods at no charge. But there is always the possibility that a black market may develop in the vouchers, as with food stamps in the USA. When the policy and administrative costs of checking this are considered, the advantages of in-kind transfer over cash transfer are reduced. Tullock (1970) refers to such black market trading as a 'crime without a victim', as those who engage in exchange reap gains from trade.

The question of exclusion of non-eligibles from in-kind transfer has been taken up by Toumanoff (1986) and Jones and Cullis (1997). With respect to Fig. 9.16(b) Toumanoff argues that, if the indifference curves shown related to ineligibles, then the utility gain from attempting to consume an inferior good would be less than the utility gain from falsely claiming a cash transfer. Suppose that eligible recipients have lower incomes; then it is arguable that with the transfer they would not be at the corner solution. That is to say, they *would* wish to (and *would* choose to) consume all the in-kind transfer. In this case, for eligible recipients there is no disadvantage in in-kind transfer. But ineligible recipients, with higher incomes, are affected by the kink in the budget line: the attractiveness of the in-kind transfer is less for them, and so the incentives to consume it illegally (and the costs of policing such activity) are reduced. Toumanoff explains that, for the 'hot meal and shelter form of in-kind transfer' (p. 445), the in-kind transfer may be more efficient than hitherto considered. When considering commodities that are 'inferior' (in terms of quantity demanded as income rises), the in-kind transfer may be a more rational choice of instrument, allowing for the possibility that 'ineligible' individuals may attempt to make false claims on government assistance.

4. Because in-kind transfers appear overly paternalistic, 'liberal' economists would shy away from such interference and constraints on the decisions of recipients. (For an examination of the liberal position, see Rowley and Peacock 1975.)

Such arguments as these suggest that price subsidies and in-kind transfers do not possess quite the overwhelming advantage for the stimulation of consumption of goods that appeared to be evident above. Moreover, readers by now will not be surprised to learn that political considerations (rather than goods-specific externalities) have been picked out in order to explain the selection of other forms of subsidies than cash transfers (Browning 1975). Pressure groups in industries that produce selected goods (like good X) have a reason to push for such selective subsidy because it implies a higher demand for their output. Bureaus may require larger budgets and a greater number of staff if they are intermediaries in the provision of in-kind transfers. At the end of the day, the public choice school may offer a more convincing explanation for the choice of redistributive instrument.

9.6 Criticisms of and limits to redistribution

Theories of normative income redistribution set a desirable standard or target, whereas the more positive theories are an attempt to predict something about the nature of redistribution in the empirical world which may or may not be consistent with one or more or any of the views of desirability. The question posed here is what sets the limits to actual and advocated redistribution.

9.6.1 The philosophy of equity

The normative literature reviewed above is the product of a relatively small number of economists (and sociologists) thinking about the notion of an ideal income distribution. It is their value judgement that is largely being presented. The bias in the contributions is towards quite strong views of equity if not egalitarianism, but different income inequality ideologies exist.

While not wishing to set up any cast-iron categorization, Rein and Miller (1974) do establish a loose typology of income inequality ideologies which they view as 'overly smooth' (p. 181) but none the less instructive. The suggestions they make build in the views described in section 9.3.1, as follows:

'Equality of opportunity' involves their possibilities 1–3 (see section 9.3.1) and is seen as a market-orientated approach.
'Lessened inequalities' (possibilities 1–6) is a type of social democratic perspective of retaining the market but reducing the income inequalities it generates in good measure.
'Normative egalitarianism' involves possibilities 1–8 and may entail the establishment of a socialist society.
'Practising egalitarianism' involves equal incomes for all except for allowances for differences in need.

Although Rein and Miller describe themselves as 'normative egalitarians', any of the above positions may not be close to the view of the majority of economists or, more importantly, of the public at large. As the authors themselves comment, 'a dominating concern for redistribution does not exist' (p. 182). The marginal productivity theory of the demand for a factor, which indicates that each factor will be rewarded in line with the value of the marginal contribution of that factor at the margin, may go some way as the basis for an explanation. For many it may be thought that what the market gives you is both fair and rightly yours. Closer inspection tends to undermine this position, which is obviously a comfortable one for the well paid. The influence of the technology you work with, the number and quality of co-operating factors and the product price are all relevant to the theory. However, these are not attributes of an individual as such, which for fairness might be viewed as a necessary condition. The quality of the factor labour itself is perhaps the only variable that is both relevant and an individual attribute. Hence the Chicago human capital school comes closest to diffusing economic inequality as an issue.

Uncertainty features in two of the accounts of seeking an optimal income distribution, but the fact is that decisions about redistributions are made by those who know they are either winners or losers in life's lottery and the unbiased perspective that Rawls is seeking is absent. If feelings of altruism and concern are not as widespread as some would like to think, then the push towards more equality is likely to be a weak one. In short, one limit to redistribution is that the haves are simply not very concerned about the have-nots. Tullock (1971) neatly resolves the apparent paradox of there being much rhetoric about redistribution but very little actual redistribution between income groups. He employs the notion of 'cognitive dissonance', met above in chapter 5, and argues that individuals, e.g. many academics, have to have dissonance between their espousal of equity and their lack of any direct action to alter it. A somewhat superficial way out is to vote for a political party that ascribes to redistribution but does not, when in office, actually take any radical redistributive activities (the past performance of the UK Labour Party, for example, may fit this bill)—that way, you get to salve your conscience and keep your money!

9.6.2 The politics of equity

The voting-oriented positive approaches to redistribution, given the comments above, may seem on stronger ground in explaining policy in that they largely rely on a narrow self-interest motive to make them tick. What prevents the less-well-off majority from really soaking the better-off minority? One explanation is that a one-person one-vote democratic mechanism does not correspond to equal political weight. High-income and wealthy groups have more political influence than lower-income ones.

A number of arguments have been presented in the literature to account for this. Parliaments typically contain a section of people drawn disproportionately from the better-off sections of the community. They share a natural empathy with the concerns of that class which, as we have noted, may not be redistribution towards the less well off. Information is vital to politics and the well off are better placed to acquire and use it. They typically have more education which reinforces this tendency. The wealthy and high-income groups can afford to be part of pressure groups favouring their position and to make donations to political parties to 'buy' influence, broadly speaking. The rich have greater incentive to oppose redistributive policies in that they have much more to lose, and there are arguments that suggest that risk-averse individuals are keener to defend against a loss than to secure a gain (see Jones and Cullis 1986). Reinforcing this differential political power of the rich is the argument above that many poor people may feel they have no reason or right to be part of a redistributive society. Working-class conservatism and Conservatism is a well-known phenomenon. While personal philosophy may be one basis for this observation, the economic limits to distribution that are introduced next provide another.

9.6.3 The economics of equity

One major reason why many individuals may shy away from a very redistributive budget or a generous negative income tax scheme is that they fear that attempts to share the economic cake (GNP) more evenly will reduce its size because of disincentive effects. They may believe that a smaller share of a larger cake is absolutely bigger than a larger share of a smaller cake. Disincentive effects are to many minds the limit to extensive redistributive equity. Even if people stay in the same rank order, the argument runs that the only way to make 'have-nots' into 'haves' is via economic growth, to which high taxation and transfers are seen as inimical. A second line of argument is to see the picture painted so far as too static. It may well be that the overall shape of income distributions is roughly constant, but that is not to say there is not much movement within it intra- and intergenerationally.

Concerning disincentives, the predicted effects of a negative income tax provide an example. High income tax rates above the break-even point of any tax transfer scheme make leisure relatively cheap (the substitution effect) but simultaneously reduce income for buying goods including leisure (the income effect). If the income effect is large for those in high income tax brackets, it may not be implausible to suppose that the overall adverse work consequences are not all that large. Critics, however, argue that you have to measure the impact on the recipients of transfers as well.

The negative income tax case illustrated as Fig. 9.17 shows an initial equilibrium at 1 on I_0, where the individual is assumed simply to face the wage rate implied by the slope of YY'. The introduction of the scheme guarantees tY_p irrespective of actual earnings, so Y'' becomes the origin of the budget constraint. All earned income is taxed at a rate t so that the slope of the budget constraint is reduced along $Y''BY'''$, where B is the break-even point at which earned and disposable income are identical along the poverty line Y_p by construction. Given the illustrations, the negative income tax moves the individual equilibrium to 2, involving a slightly higher income and less work, more leisure and a higher level of utility I_1 as opposed to I_0. The dashed line can be used to decompose this price effect into an income effect 13 (reducing work effort) and the substitution effect of the lowered compensation for each hour of work, 32 (also reducing work effort). Some variation in predictions can be obtained by a different location of the indifference map so that, a priori, the strength of effects cannot be settled.

In the event, empirical work in general (as noted above) does not appear to confirm the presence of large disincentive effects, although for negative income tax (NIT), experiments in the USA undertaken in the 1970s did produce significant negative-work-hours responses of the order of 7 per cent reduction for males, 25 per cent for wives and 15 per cent for female heads of households (see Robins and West 1980). While such estimates are always open to dispute of all kinds, it should be noted that the experiments involved a scheme more like a social dividend, with the income guarantee being set near or at Y_p, and the marginal tax rate was a high one at 50 per cent. Such figures generally exceed what advocates of a negative income tax have in mind.

Turning to movements within the income distribution, mean-variance analysis has been used to illustrate that progressive income taxation will tend to lower the amount of risk-taking it is optimal for a utility-maximizing individual to undertake. The argument runs on to suggest that movements within distributions are significant (e.g. Gallaway 1966) and

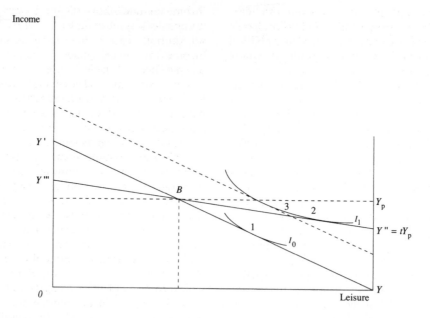

Figure 9.17 Negative income tax and work effort.

that any mechanism, like progressive as opposed to proportional taxation, that impedes the process needs to be considered in this light. As always, there is also contradictory evidence and indeed theory.

While the above arguments are a reflection of 'budget constraints', there is also the question of the preference map used in determining equilibrium work–leisure choices. Okun (1975) notes that high taxation of the rich may be interpreted as an adverse ethical judgement on economic success, altering attitudes (preferences) to it and its attractiveness as a goal. Similarly, at the other end of the spectrum, it is possible that transfer receipts may alter attitudes such that being a 'contributor' to the economic process ceases to be viewed as being part of society. Other causal connections can be argued about; for example, tax transfers may decrease envy, facilitate participation in the mainstream of society and/or foster a sense of unity. While the mainstream of economic analysis is on the whole silent about preference formation (see Lewis and Cullis 1988), these connections between economic policies and preferences are important.

The thrust of the above arguments is the suggestion that there is, or is widely believed to be, a trade-off between efficiency and equity whose precise form is unknown. This trade-off needs to be confronted by those advocating redistribution. One side of the coin is the extent of disincentive effects, while the other side, discussed here, is the willingness to accept these

in order to gain from equity. (These types of calculation arise in project appraisal in developing countries introduced in chapter 6, where the question is the intra-temporal equity one of weighing income/consumption gains for individuals at different points in the income distribution.) The Atkinson index introduced above is fruitful in facilitating the comparison of the marginal social utility gain to, say, a poor person (P) from additional income with that of a rich person (R). The point effectively being made is that, if making a poor person better off by £1 via a redistributive transfer reduces the income of the rich person by more than £1 (because of, say, the necessary administrative costs of the transfer and/or the disincentive effects to earn in the market-place), how much more than the £1 gain to the poor is an acceptable 'price'? It is convenient to think of a valuation ratio of poor to rich, V_p/V_r, which reflects their relative marginal social utilities of income whose form comes from equation (9.3) so that

$$(9.33) \qquad \frac{V_p}{V_r} = \frac{Y_p^{-e}}{Y_r^{-e}} = \left(\frac{Y_p}{Y_r}\right)^{-e} = \left(\frac{Y_r}{Y_p}\right)^{e}$$

Jenkins (1989) and the Overseas Development Administration (1988) provide some convenient calculations for a rich person whose income is four times that of a poor person. These are reproduced with minor modification as Table 9.3.

Table 9.3 Net £1 of transfer income loss sacrifice individuals prepared to accept to raise the income of a poor person under different social welfare functions (captured by *e* values)

e value	Net income loss
0 (= income-maximizer) (allows only costless transfers)	$(£4^0 - 1) = 0$
0.25	$(£4^{0.25} - 1) = 41\,p$
0.5	$(£4^{0.5} - 1) = £1$
1.0	$(£4^1 - 1) = £3$
2.0	$(£4^2 - 1) = £15$
4.0	$(£4^4 - 1) = £255$
(maximize the income of the least-well-off person)	∞

'Leaky bucket' calculations

Of course, this does not resolve the issue of inequality, but it does provide a mechanism through which individuals can focus their view of an acceptable 'trade-off' between redistribution (equity) and efficiency. Okun (1975) characterized this sort of trade-off as a 'leaky bucket', which lost some of its contents (disincentive effects and administration costs) when used to carry income from the rich to the poor. In particular, he frames the question in terms of carrying income from the top 5 per cent of US families in 1974 (average income $45 000 per annum) to the bottom 20 per cent (average income $28 000). A $4000 annual tax on a rich family raises poor families' income by only $1000 each because of their large numbers, but how much beyond that $1000 would you accept as a tolerable loss? For illustration, Okun suggests that Milton Friedman would accept no leakage, characterizing him as an efficiency-maximizer, while the Rawlsian answer is a 99.9 per cent loss, as Rawls is an equality-maximizer. Okun feels that the price set by Rawls on equality is too high but in this context he would be prepared to accept a 60 per cent leak (Okun 1975, p. 94). He further suggests that the chosen acceptable 'leakage' on any particular issue should be the outcome of a collective 'democratic' choice, which, of course, raises the voting issues discussed in chapter 4.

9.7 Summary

This chapter has considered a very large topic not just within public sector/finance economics, but within economics *per se*. As such it is difficult to do more than introduce some issues and concentrate only on the subset of issues that have figured most prominently in the public finance sub-discipline. By way of summary, we contrast some recurring themes in this area of economics.

What types of study are the way forward? It is the 'all'-inclusive macro-redistributive studies that capture most interest in general, but these are the studies that are beset by the most problems at all levels. The more micro-based studies, which focus on a particular expenditure programme or transfer policy, often offer a more tractable research problem, but these are inevitably open to the criticism that they are very partial in nature, giving no real insight into whether government intervention is narrowing or widening the extent of overall economic inequality (assuming we can agree how to measure it!).

Secondly, in redistributive studies there is a wide gulf between the appropriate *cordon bleu* (theoretical) recipe and what the empirical short-order cook is forced to do in practice if any sort of meal is to be forthcoming within a reasonable time period. Data limitations serve to accentuate this gap between theory and practice. In line with this disjuncture, a persistent suggestion in all sorts of studies is to conduct sensitivity analyses to isolate those elements in any assessment that has a significant impact. However, this has its limitations. If, on the one hand, the outcome is insensitive to variation—say, in a valuation—the question arises as to what the study is sensitive to. If on the other hand it is very sensitive to valuation variation, it is difficult to know which valuation is more representative. (Widely varying information may not be very helpful.) After all, if you do not know an appropriate valuation, there may be something arbitrary about knowing what a 'plausible range' for a valuation is. If it is accepted that what motivates interest in redistributive impacts is a desire to be 'fair', then the studies that are carried out using current measures of economic status may often be misleading. To extend an analogy offered by Jenkins (1987), the snapshot/'stills' outside the cinema may not offer a very good guide to the nature of the whole movie. If it is the impact of government intervention over a lifetime or series of lifetimes that matters, then existing work on the snapshot distribution, however sophisticated, may have little of relevance to offer. What may look highly redistributive in a 'still' may be no such thing across a series of time periods.

Regarding the desirable extent of redistribution, there is little consensus. Normative theories tend to be fairly egalitarian, whereas positive theories are generally more pessimistic about redistributive prospects. Finally, it was suggested that widespread philosophical, political and economic beliefs serve to make the relative small amount of measured redistribution that appears to take place the order not only for today but for tomorrow as well.

References

Aaron, H. J. and McGuire, M. C. (1970) 'Public Goods and Income Distribution', *Econometrica*, 38, 6, pp. 907–20.

Atkinson, A. B. (1970) 'On the Measurement of Inequality', *Journal of Economic Theory*, 2, 3, pp. 244–63.

Atkinson, A. B. (1989) *Poverty and Social Security*. Brighton: Wheatsheaf.

Atkinson, A. B. (1995) *Incomes and the Welfare State*. Cambridge: CUP.

Atkinson, A. B., Flemming, J. S. and Kay, J. A. (1983) 'Unemployment, Social Security and Incentives', pp. 99–110 in R. C. O. Matthews and J. R. Sargent (eds.), *Contemporary Problems of Economic Policy*. London and New York: Methuen.

Becker, G. S. (1971) *Economic Theory*. New York: Alfred A. Knopf.

Brennan, G. (1973a) 'Pareto Desirable Redistribution: The Case of Malice and Envy', *Journal of Public Economics*, 2, 2, pp. 173–84.

Brennan, G. (1973b) 'Pareto Desirable Redistribution: The Non-altruistic Dimension', *Public Choice*, 14, pp. 43–67.

Brennan, G. and Pincus, J. M. (1983) 'Government Expenditure Growth and Resource Allocation: The Nebulous Connection', *Oxford Economic Papers*, 35, 3, pp. 351–65.

Browning, E. K. (1975) 'The Externality Argument for In-kind Transfers: Some Critical Remarks', *Kyklos*, 28, 3, pp. 526–44.

Buchanan, J. M. and Tullock, G. (1965) *The Calculus Consent*. Ann Arbor: University of Michigan Press.

Burton, J. (1985) *Why No Cuts?* Hobart Paper no 104. London: Institute of Economic Affairs.

Collard, D. A. (1985) 'Social Security and Work after Fowler', *The Political Quarterly*, 56, 4, pp. 361–73.

Citizen's Income Bulletin, (1996) 22, July.

Culyer, A. J. (1980) *The Political Economy of Social Policy*. Oxford: Martin Robertson.

Dilnot, A. W., Kay, J. A. and Morris, C. N. (1984) *The Reform of Social Security*. Oxford: Oxford University Press.

Dilnot, A. and Walker, I. (eds.) (1989) *The Economics of Social Security*. Oxford: Oxford University Press.

Downs, A. (1957) *An Economic Theory of Democracy*. New York: Harper and Row.

Fair, R. C. (1971) 'The Optimal Distribution of Income', *Quarterly Journal of Economics*, 85, 4, pp. 551–79.

Fuchs, V. R. (1965) 'Toward a Theory of Poverty', pp. 69–92 in *The Concept of Poverty*. Washington DC: Task Force on Economic Growth and Opportunity (US Chamber of Commerce).

Gallaway, L. E. (1966) 'On the Importance of "Picking One's Parents"', *Quarterly Review of Economics and Business*, 6, 2, pp. 7–16.

Goodman, A. and Webb, S. (1994) 'For Richer, for Poorer: the Changing Distribution of Income in the UK, 1961–91, '*Fiscal Studies*, 15, 4, pp. 29–62.

Hochman, H. M. and Rodgers, J. D. (1969) 'Pareto Optimal Redistribution', *American Economic Review*, 57, 3–5, pp. 542–57.

Jenkins, S. P. (1987) 'Snapshots vs. Movies: "Lifecycle Bias" and the Estimation of Intergenerational Earnings Inheritance', *European Economic Review*, 31, 5, pp. 1149–58.

Jenkins, S. P. (1989) 'Recent Trends in UK Income Inequality', in D. Slottje (ed.), *Research on Economic Inequality*, 4, Greenwich: JAI Press.

Jenkins, S. P. (1990) 'Living Standards and Inequality', *Economic Review*, 7, 3, pp. 36–9.

Jenkins, S. P. (1991) 'The Measurement of Income Inequality', in L. Osberg (ed.), *Economic Inequality and Poverty: International Perspectives*. Armonk, NY: M. E. Sharpe.

Jenkins, S. (1995) 'Accounting for Inequality Trends: Decomposition Analysis for the UK 1971–86,' *Economica*, 62, 245, pp. 29–64.

Jenkins, S. P. and Cowell, F. A. (1994) 'Dwarfs and Giants in the 1980's: Trends in the UK Income Distribution', *Fiscal Studies*, 15, 1, pp. 99–118.

Johnson, W. R. (1978) 'Substitution in Household Production and the Efficiency of In-kind Transfers', *Public Finance Quarterly*, 6, 2, pp. 204–10.

Jones, P. R. and Cullis, J. G. (1986) 'Is Democracy Regressive? A Comment on Political Participation', *Public Choice*, 5, 1, pp. 101–7.

Jones, P. R. and Cullis, J. G. (1997) 'In-kind Versus Cash Transfers: Assessing Disbursement,' *Public Finance Review*, 25, 1, pp. 25–43.

Lancaster, K. J. (1966) 'A New Approach to Consumer Theory', *Journal of Political Economy*, 74, 2, pp. 132–57.

Laidler, D. E. (1969) 'Income Tax Incentives for Owner-Occupied Housing', in A. C. Harberger and M. J. Bailey (eds.), *The Taxation of Income from Capital*. Washington DC: Brookings Institution.

Le Grand, J. (1982) *The Strategy of Equality*. London: Allen & Unwin.

Lerner, A. P. (1944) *The Economics of Control*. London: Macmillan.

Lewis, A. and Cullis, J. G. (1988) 'Preferences, Economics and Psychology and the Economic Psychology of Public Sector Preference Formation', *Journal of Behavioural Economics*, 17, 1, pp. 19–32.

Lydall, H. F. (1968) *The Structure of Earnings*. Oxford: Oxford University Press.

Meade, J. E. (1978) *The Structure and Reform of Indirect Taxation*. London: Allen & Unwin.

Meltzer, A. H. and Richard, S. F. (1981) 'A Rational Theory of the Size of Government', *Journal of Political Economy*, 89, 5, pp. 914–25.

Mincer, J. (1980) 'Human Capital and Earnings', pp. 103–28 in A. B. Atkinson (ed.), *Wealth and Income Inequality*, 2nd edn. Oxford: Oxford University Press.

Mishan, E. J. (1972) 'The Futility of Pareto Efficient Distributions', *American Economic Review*, 62, 5, pp. 971–6.

Ng, Y. K. (1979) *Welfare Economics*. London: Macmillan.

O'Higgins, M. (1980) 'The Distributive Effects of Public Expenditure and Taxation: An Agnostic View of the CSO Analysis', pp. 28–46 in C. Sandford, C. Pond and R. Walker (eds.), *Taxation and Social Policy*. London: Heinemann.

O'Higgins, M. and Ruggles, P. (1981) 'The Distribution of Public Expenditures and Taxes among Households in the United Kingdom', *Review of Income and Wealth*, ser. 27, no. 3, pp. 298–326.

Okun, A. M. (1975) *Equality and Efficiency: The Big Trade Off*. Washington DC: Brookings Institution.

Overseas Development Administration (1988) *Appraisal of Projects in Developing Countries*. London: HMSO.

Parker, H. (1989) *Instead of the Dole*. London: Routledge.

Parker, H. (1995) *Taxes, Benefits and Family—the Seven Deadly Traps*. Research Monograph 50. London: Institute of Economic Affairs.

Parker, H. and Raven, S. (1996) 'BI for Intermediates', *Citizens Income Bulletin*, 22, pp. 11–15.

Peacock, A. T. (1974) 'The Treatment of Government Expenditure in Studies of Income Redistribution', in W. L. Smith and J. Culburtson (eds.), *Public Finance and Stabilisation Policy: Essays in Honour of R. A. Musgrave*. Amsterdam: North-Holland.

Peacock, A. T. and Shannon, R. (1968) 'The Welfare State and Redistribution of Income', *Westminster Bank Review*, August, pp. 30–46.

Prest, A. R. (1968) 'The Budget and Interpersonal Distribution', *Public Finance/Finances Publiques*, 23, 1/2, pp. 80–98.

Pryke, R. (1995) *Taking the Measure of Poverty*. Research Monograph 51, London: Institute of Economic Affairs.

Rawls, J. (1971) *A Theory of Justice*. Cambridge, Mass.: Harvard University Press.

Rein, M. and Miller, M. (1974) 'Standards of Income Redistribution', *Challenge*, July/August, pp. 176–82.

Robins, P. K. and West, R. W. (1980) 'Program Participation and Labor Supply Response', *Journal of Human Resources*, 15, 4, pp. 499–523.

Rodgers, J. D. (1974) 'Explaining Income Redistribution', pp. 165–205 in H. M. Hochman and G. Peterson (eds.), *Redistribution Through Public Choice*. New York: Columbia University Press.

Rosenthal, L. (1983) 'Subsidies to the Personal Sector', in R. Millward *et al.* (eds.), *Public Sector Economics*. London and New York: Longman.

Rowley, C. K. and Peacock, A. T. (1975) *Welfare Economics: A Liberal Restatement*. London: Martin Robinson.

Rowntree, B. S. (1901) *Poverty—a Study of Town Life*. London: Macmillan.

Ruggles, P. (1991) 'The Impact of Government Tax and Expenditure Programs on the Distribution of Income in the United States', pp. 220–45 in L. Osberg (ed.), *Economic Inequality and Poverty: International Perspectives*. Armonk, NY: M. E. Sharpe.

Scitovsky, T. (1986) *Human Desire and Economic Satisfaction*. Brighton: Wheatsheaf.

Sen, A. (1973) *On Economic Inequality*. Oxford: Oxford University Press.

Stratmann, T. (1990) 'A Diagrammatic Representation of Inequality', *Public Finance Quarterly*, 18, 1, pp. 47–64.

Tisdell, C. A. (1972) *Microeconomics*. Sydney: John Wiley.

Toumanoff, P. (1986) 'Exclusion Costs and the In-kind Transfer', *Kyklos*, 39, 3, pp. 443–7.

Tullock, G. (1970) 'Subsidized Housing in a Competitive Market: Comment', *American Economic Review*, 61, 1, pp. 218–19.

Tullock, G. (1971) 'The Charity of the Uncharitable', *Western Economic Journal*, 9, 4, pp. 379–92.

10 Central government

10.1 Introduction

The source of finance used to cover the expenditure activities was traditionally the very heart of public finance. The expenditure side has now become much more fully developed but the analysis of the sources of finance, especially taxation, remains very important.

Despite the urging of Wicksell and the modern public choice theorists, in practice the two sectors of the budget are essentially treated separately so that very few expenditure proposals come forward with a specific financial source specified. Traditionally in the UK, the institutional mechanics were broadly that a government's intended expenditure plans for the coming four years were drawn up in the autumn of each year, with the upcoming year being the dominant period for consideration. The process, especially under the expenditure-cutting plans of the Conservative government, is a hard bargaining one between the heads of the various government departments and the Treasury. Once the spending plans are established, the necessary finance was sought, essentially through taxation.

However, since 1993 the UK budget has been a more unified process with expenditure plans and taxation proposals being presented simultaneously in the autumn (November). At each Budget the government provides an estimate of what the spending out-turn will be in the present financial year and plans for the subsequent three financial years. Expected inflation and growth rates are clearly of importance in this process. As with the traditional UK budget revenue analysis is also undertaken and tax changes announced.

10.2 The basic concepts

Despite this element of interdependence in the taxation and expenditure sides of the budget, a focus on revenue raising as such is a sensible pursuit, and this motivated the majority of earlier work in public finance. There are two basic principles to inform the way such taxes should be levied. These are the benefit principle and the 'ability to pay' principle, which have been discussed elsewhere (see chapters 1 and 3). Although some elements of taxation are based on benefit considerations, the bulk of taxation is designed to conform to 'ability to pay', the interpretation of which is no easy matter.

The fundamental choice of tax base is between two flow measures: income and consumption (expenditure), and a single stock measure, wealth. Income is usually defined in terms of the amount of money an individual can spend over a period while leaving his or her net wealth position unaltered. This is the so-called *accretion* concept of income. If an individual earns £20 000 per year and makes a £5000 capital gain over the same period, then her income is £25 000. However, this makes it all too simple. Table 10.1 documents a fuller way to appreciate the notion of income.

It is clearly the elements in panel (a) that are most easily documented and are typically subject to the tax system. If sources of income are not all taxed at equal rates, there is obviously an incentive to convert income into the untaxed form. So, for example, high marginal tax rates encourage fringe benefits in 'remuneration packages' and the growth of the 'cash' economy. Panel (d) would be part of 'imputed' income in a full study of someone's economic position. In developing countries with widespread subsistence farming, it does, by definition, come closer to total income. However, with economic specialization and trade, both intra- and internationally, the existence of market prices and recorded transactions makes the process of taxation much easier. (See the discussion of 'tax handles' in chapter 14.)

The equivalent of income-based taxes on the expenditure side is the personal expenditure

Table 10.1 An income taxonomy

	'Marketed—explicit'	'Non-marketed—implicit'
Visible	(a) Wages, salaries, rent, interest, profits (that may arise as a capital gain) transfer payments (?)	(b) Fringe benefits, e.g. company car, subsidized meals, private health insurance paid for by the employer
Camouflaged	(c) 'Extra' work activities, jobs 'on the side'	(d) Use of part of (e.g.) farmer's own output for domestic consumption

tax,[1] which places a tax on the difference between income receipts during the financial year and savings in the year, i.e. a tax on that part of the income that is consumed. The idea is that tax, payable annually in arrears, would be based on taxable expenditure, which is the difference between net receipts during the year and net savings over the same period. It is often viewed as attractive because the base is that which individuals consume (or their revenue from the economic system) rather than a reflection of what they contribute, i.e. income. It relates to actual consumption rather than possible consumption, and for many the equity of this method of taxation may well be greater than that achieved through income tax.

Personal expenditure taxation was tried in Sri Lanka but was abandoned mainly because of administrative difficulties. It requires that each taxpayer's spendable receipts (i.e. income) be calculated from which savings and investment are deducted, so that consumption is measured as a residual. Hence an expenditure tax is a tax on the difference between net income (gross income minus the costs of securing that income) and the change in net worth (net change in the value of liabilities minus the net change in the value of assets).

Whether, in operation, such a tax would have lower administrative costs than a personal income tax depends on the details of the tax. Such a tax is often claimed to encourage saving but the argument can cut both ways. The taxing of consumption does make current saving more attractive. However, if the scheme is viewed as one that does not tax interest on savings, then more consumption in the future can be financed from a given volume of savings and those seeking a target future consumption can meet it with a lower level of current savings. Given the limited experience with actual personal expenditure taxation, empirical evidence is lacking. A general point to be kept in mind throughout this chapter is that any tax reform involves the costs of transition from one scheme to another. Changes falsify individual expectations and inevitably create windfall gains and losses and other undesigned consequences which are likely to affect equity adversely. The design and administration of transitional rules in themselves suggest high short-run costs that may well outweigh discounted long-run benefits.

In principle, there is no significant difference between income (a flow) and wealth (a stock) since the value of an individual's wealth is simply the discounted present value of the individual's net income stream, i.e. the stock value of the flow. If income is part of 'ability to pay', then it would seem clear that wealth is also. The difference between these tax bases arises at the practical level in that some things are more easily measured as a stock than as a flow, for example the value of a painting. As a consequence, individuals (and many measures) tend not to think of wealth and income as two sides of the same coin, but rather as different segments of that coin.

As with all taxation bases, there are the usual coarse and fine questions of definition. Americans especially distinguish between 'realty' (land, housing, property-type wealth) and 'personalty', the latter being subdivided further into tangibles (physical-type personal wealth, e.g. cars) and intangibles (financial-asset-type wealth, e.g. share certificates). In practice, it is those elements of economic worth that are most easily measured (because of their marketable nature as an asset value, which is easily detectable) that attract taxation. These types of tax take the form of annual wealth taxes, gift taxes and inheritance taxes. Taxation of sales is also common, in the form of specific (so much per physical unit of measurement) or *ad valorem* (percentage of money valuation) taxes on goods and services. Taxation of income, personal expenditure and wealth are usually viewed as direct taxation, whereas taxes on the sale of goods and services are seen as indirect taxation. (For some fairly

[1] The reason why personal expenditure can be viewed as an income tax that exempts interest on savings can be seen from the following. If all income Y is saved under a tax system that has a tax allowance for interest on savings, consumption becomes $Y(1-t)(1+i)^n$, where i is the rate of interest and n the number of years. Under an expenditure tax the same outcome is obtained with tax being paid when consumption takes place, yielding $Y(1+i)^n(1-t)$, an equivalent result. (See Kay and King (1983) for a discussion of other points raised in relation to a personal expenditure tax.)

recent comparative material, see Pechman 1987.) But what does this distinction mean?

Atkinson (1977) provides an account of traditional and modern themes in the debate, central to early public finance, between the use of direct and indirect taxation. At the outset he reviews a number of definitions, the main two economic ones being to associate taxes with 'shifting' and with 'tailor-making'. In the first, direct taxes are seen as being paid by those on whom the formal incidence sits, e.g. income tax, whereas indirect taxes are those that are shifted so that the formal or statutory and actual or effective incidence diverges. The second, 'tailor-making', definition relies on whether the tax is sensitive to the particular (economic) characteristics of the taxpayer, so in this definition sales taxes of varying rates on different goods and services would be indirect, i.e. independent of who is the buyer or seller. Atkinson himself favours this second approach and contrasts it with direct taxation (a tax on total income or expenditure with varying marginal rates) by considering what he calls 'transitional' taxes.

The background to the tax-mix debate is seen as having two major schools of thought:

1. the targets-instruments approach, with the instrument of direct taxation being suitable to equity and indirect taxation to efficiency: while tailor-making is the link in the case of equity, visibility is the apparent link for the efficiency (disincentives) assignment;
2. the superiority of direct taxation on both the equity and efficiency scores.

Neither view comes out unscathed, and the conditions under which each holds more water is explored in chapter 15.

10.3 Tax theory and tax practice

Although theory and practice are meant to go together in most accounts of economic endeavour, one area where there seems to be an alarming gap is between tax theory and tax practice. At one extreme there is the abstract tax theorist who analyses with great sophistication the introduction of subtle variations on '$(1 - t)$' into his or her equations, while at the other there are those applying the percentage of an academic's book purchase price that is tax-deductible. Tax administrators often see tax theory as a luxury to be indulged in in any odd moment they might have to look up from their files, while tax theorists tend to see the administration and practical aspects of taxation as an easily coped with minor irritant, or deviation, from their 'grand design'. (See the Ricketts (1981) critique of optimal tax theory discussed in chapter 15.)

Most would find Adam Smith's canons or basic principles of taxation attractive. These are:

1. *Equity* Individuals ought to contribute 'as nearly as possible in proportion to their respective abilities' (Smith 1776, p. 310).
2. *Certainty* Tax liabilities should not be arbitrary or uncertain (visibility and compliance cost considerations).
3. *Convenience* The manner and timing of tax payments should be convenient to the taxpayer. (Here the question of compliance costs also arises.)
4. *Economy or efficiency* The excess burdens (or welfare costs) of taxation should be minimized. (Included under this heading are the administrative, collection and psychic compliance costs of taxation.) (For further discussion see Sandford, Godwin and Hardwick 1989.)

Putting the principles above into an analytical and practical context is difficult, not least because they may well conflict with each other. In the UK the Inland Revenue Department and the Customs and Excise Department administer income tax and sales taxes respectively. The major Inland Revenue tax is personal income taxation whose yield is a quarter of total revenue raised. The other main 'income' taxes are: national insurance contributions (NIC); corporation tax (a tax on the gross profits of companies); petroleum tax (comprising three levies on UK gas and oil production); capital gains tax (a tax on the gain from the sale of certain assets); and a gifts tax (in the form of the capital transfer tax which applies to transfers between individuals). The relative importance of these revenue sources can be seen in Fig. 10.1.

Where the Customs and Excise Department is concerned, the valued added tax (VAT) compulsory in all EC countries, vies with excise duties as the most significant revenue source. VAT is a general sales tax which applies to the value added at each stage in the production chain with its formal incidence being on consumers, as the tax is included in the sales price at each 'intermediate' stage. Excise duties are taxes on specific home-produced or imported goods, with 'cigarettes, booze and petrol' being the usual UK suspects to be rounded up on each Budget day.

The income sources (see Fig. 10.1) and expenditure patterns of the government sector are reported in official statistics but are not widely appreciated. In

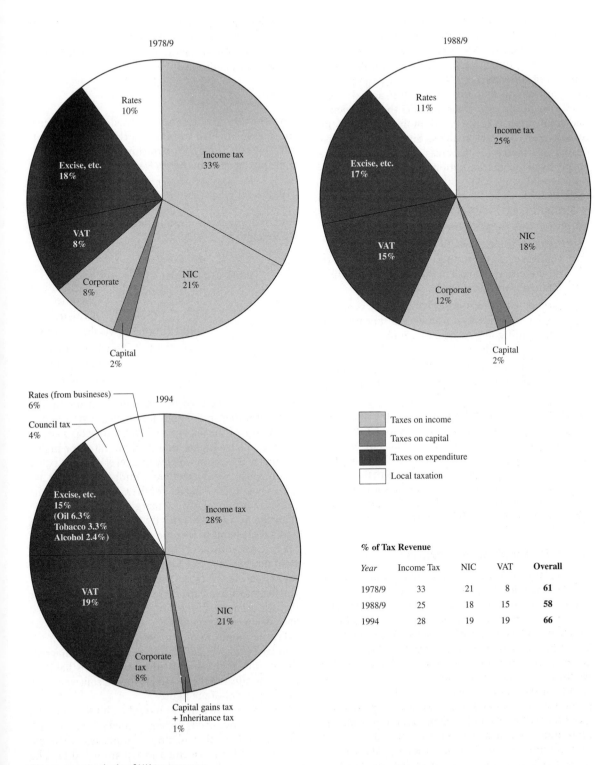

Figure 10.1 Analysis of UK tax revenue.

Source: 'Financial Statistics', *Financial Statement and Budgets Report 1989/90*, and 'Financial Statistics', May 1995.

an area where the costs of being well informed are high compared with the benefits, this is not surprising. However, it does mean that misconceptions are common. Tracing out the efficiency and equity consequences of different tax tools forms a large part of the purpose of this text. Here the actual taxes employed are briefly reviewed and their efficiency and equity aspects commented on in the light of the earlier, more abstract analysis. Since rates are discussed in chapter 12, the areas for discussion here are personal income tax, national insurance contributions, excise taxes, VAT, corporation tax and capital taxation.

Slemrod (1994) suggests behavioural responses to tax reform take three forms:

(i) *timing* responses where changes in the tax incentives cause the timing of a course of action to be altered in response to the new tax regulation on their impending implementation;

(ii) *form or nature* responses where there is an incentive to reclassify a transaction that was due and is still going to take place into a different category of activity;

(iii) *real* responses where work—leisure, saving—consumption etc. choices have been altered by a tax change.

Slemrod suggests, from his experience, the incidence of these responses dwindle as you move from (i) to (iii). It reverses the general economic notion that long-run adjustment is greater than short-run adjustment. Here the longer-run fundamental consequences are less than the superficial shorter ones would led to expect. It is the issue of responses that motivates much of the analysis below.

10.3.1 Personal income taxation

The effects of personal income taxation are usually viewed in relation to the aggregate supply of hours of market work and the associated welfare costs. The presence of income tax at high marginal rates should also induce movements into untaxed areas: jobs with high non-monetary returns/attributes, fringe benefits as opposed to recorded cash payments, and work in the 'black economy' (see chapter 8).

One of the most heavily researched areas in economics is the response of labour supply (hours) to income taxation. An outline of the basic approach can be found in Killingsworth (1983). The object is to establish the change in hours supply to the labour market ∂H as a result of a change in wages ∂W, which, other things equal, generates an income effect (y) and a substitution effect (s), as follows (assuming that the only tax is the introduction of a *proportional* one on labour income and it is this that is causing the change in W):

$$(10.1) \qquad \frac{\partial H}{\partial W} = \frac{\partial H_s}{\partial W} + \frac{\partial H_y}{\partial W}$$

Now the term ∂W can be expressed as the change in income ∂Y divided by hours worked H, so that substituting $\partial Y/H$ for ∂W in the final term of (10.1) and multiplying all terms by W/H yields

$$(10.2) \qquad \frac{\partial H}{\partial W}\frac{W}{H} = \frac{\partial H_s}{\partial W}\frac{W}{H} + \frac{\partial H_y}{(\partial Y/H)}\frac{W}{H}$$

And multiplying the top and bottom of the final terms by Y yields

$$(10.3) \qquad \frac{\partial H}{\partial W}\frac{W}{H} = \frac{\partial H_s}{\partial W}\frac{W}{H} + \frac{\partial H_y}{\partial Y}\frac{Y}{H}\frac{WH}{Y}$$

Uncompensated wage elasticity = substitution elasticity + income elasticity weighted by the share of income coming from hours of work.

The effect of the income tax system on the budget constraint that individuals face depends on the precise nature of the tax system. Progressive tax systems usually involve higher marginal tax rates for higher earnings. This, combined with a level of non-taxable income (Y_e), would generate a budget constraint like 123 in Fig. 10.2(a). In fact, for the UK the tax structure achieves progressivity (a marginal tax rate greater than the average tax rate) by having tax allowances and a wide band of income over which the marginal tax rate is a constant. There is a second, higher, constant marginal tax rate for those who earn more than, say, Y_h in Fig. 10.2(b). This replaces the curvilinear constraint with one that has several angled flats. More realistic accounts of the budget constraint allow for a level of unearned income Y_u and the presence of an overtime premium on the basic wage rate when the standard work week $O'H_s$ is exceeded. (In the diagram this occurs after the individual involved is liable to tax.) The effect of these is to produce a constraint like that in part (c) of the figure.

Hausman (1985) notes how the Slutsky equation discussed above needs to be modified in the presence of a tax system that is more complicated than the proportional one assumed in equation (10.1). The presence of nonlinearities create so-called virtual incomes like those illustrated as Y_1 and Y_2 in Fig.

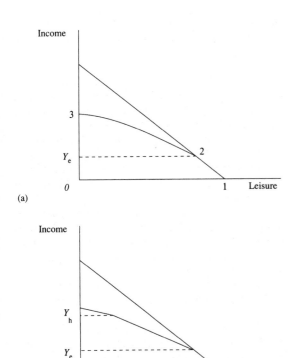

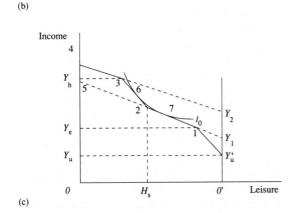

Figure 10.2 Income taxation and budget constraints.

of the segments. However, in the non-proportional tax rate case, the virtual income is also altered (except for the first segment), generating a further income effect which will serve to alter labour supply. Under a system of progressive income taxation, there are few *a priori* sustainable generalizations about the labour supply consequences of taxation. While this reinforces the empirical nature of the question, there is a further empirically relevant problem raised by nonlinear budget constraints. If the tax-transfer system creates a budget constraint that is nonlinear and nonconvex, then it is possible for more than one tangency with an indifference curve to arise, and indeed for the same indifference curve to have two tangency points, and small changes in the budget constraint can cause the chosen number of hours to jump from one segment of the constraint to another (e.g. points 6 and 7 in Fig. 10.2(c)). The consequences of changes in the budget constraint for hours of work again become generally unpredictable *a priori*. In the case of two tangencies for the same indifference curve illustrated by I_0 in the figure, a 'gap' is created in labour supply as there is no wage at which the individual will choose the number of hours associated with the 'kink' point 2. Hausman (1985) explains how specifying a utility function and searching the segments econometrically for the tangency offering highest utility provides an empirical answer to the problems posed by nonlinearity. Analysis of how individuals respond to a change in tax allowances and/or tax rates is now a much more complex affair. (For further discussion of these constraints and other issues see Brown 1981.)

Empirical work on labour supply can be briefly explored here. Atkinson and Stiglitz (1980) provide a survey of the various approaches and methods employed. Surveys of attitudes have been popular with some researchers. Basically, individuals are asked what their responses to higher taxes on earnings are. However, such surveys, even if couched in sophisticated designs, have the weaknesses of all surveys: they are 'hypothetical' and do not correspond to actual behaviour. Respondents may act 'strategically' or tell the interviewer what they think he or she wants to hear. Results are often open to many interpretations and extension to a reliable quantitative answer is difficult. Experimental work, as in the various American negative income tax experiments, is also open to many of these criticisms. Those under study are aware they are part of a short-run experiment and therefore are less likely to act 'naturally' and signal their long-run responses. In addition, experimental design in any area of research is always open to criticisms concerning sample size, composition and interpretation

10.2(c). They are established by the extension of any of the budget segments backwards to the right-side vertical axis. Such 'linearization' establishes an 'as if' budget constraint for an individual. An individual finding a tangency on the segment 12 of the Y'_u1234 'kinked' budget constraint would choose the same number of hours of work if she faced the linear budget constraint Y_1125. Changes in tax rates generate income and substitution effects by altering the slope of the results. Neuberg (1989) is an author who has considered this type of work in detail.

As with the quest for compensating variations in cost–benefit analysis, economists are happier with data on observed behaviour. The evidence, whether in the form of a time series or a cross-section of individuals, industries or regions, comes not from taxation directly but from hours of work supplied at different wages net of tax—which, of course, is not quite the question at hand. People may act differently in response to changes in taxation than to variations in earnings *per se*. The use of large datasets and sophisticated econometric techniques is impressive but invariably proceeds only in the face of technical difficulties that weaken confidence in the results.

One type of regression equation that has been employed to give empirical content to the question of taxation and labour supply hours (H) is

$$(10.4) \quad H = a_0 + a_1 W + a_2 N + \sum_{i=3}^{n} a_i X_i + u$$

where $a_0, \ldots, a_n$ = coefficients to be estimated
$\quad W$ = wage rate
$\quad N$ = income from non-labour sources
$\quad X_i$ = a vector of variables introduced to allow for other differences between individuals in the sample apart from their wage and non-labour income
$\quad u$ = randomly distributed error term

The estimates of a_1 and a_2 are a source of the substitution and income derivatives in equation (10.1), which, when combined with the mean values for H, W and Y in the sample, can give the three elasticities in (10.3).

Table 10.2 taken from Blundell (1992) provides a range of the empirical evidence for the relevant elasticities for married women, husbands and lone mothers. The total income elasticities (which capture the total income effect and are the difference between the uncompensated and the compensated wage elasticities) are all negative confirming leisure as a normal good (as income rises more leisure is 'bought' and fewer hours of work supplied). The compensated wage elasticities reflect the substitution effect so that increases in taxation induce a higher opportunity cost of leisure and less leisure and more work hours being chosen, i.e. a positive elasticity is generated. Given the arrangement of signs it is their relative magnitudes that matter in determining the overall impact of tax changes on work effort. Most of the studies are for married women with the positive uncompensated

elasticity indicating increased work effort if tax rates were lowered. As illustrated in chapter 7 it is the substitution effect that dictates the magnitude of the welfare costs of taxation and given the size of compensated wage elasticities for women these would appear to be significant here. Often the estimated uncompensated wage elasticities for husbands (males generally) are small and negative, i.e. a mildly backward-bending aggregate labour supply curve. The results for lone mothers suggest large uncompensated elasticities which are mainly thought to reflect a labour force participation rather than work hour adjustment effect.

Blundell (1992) adds to this by emphasizing the importance of microsimulation analysis which via the use of a very large number of datapoints allows the consideration of different individuals with different marginal effective tax rates and other incomes, i.e. associating individual labour supply responses with their corresponding marginal effective tax rates.

The results of this type of work have always been less dramatic than people are often comfortable with. There seems to be a feeling that labour supply ought to be very sensitive to taxation so that the disincentive effects of income taxation are large. The evidence does not appear to confirm this, especially in the case of full-time male workers. It must be noted, however, that the supply of labour is a multi-dimensional concept, so that the effect of taxation on labour supply may show up as: less effort while at work, emigration, longer holidays, shorter working lives, different occupational choices and associated human capital acquisition, etc. These other possible connections to income taxation require separate investigation for a fuller picture to be painted.

Having said this, there are reasons to suppose that labour supply would not be as responsive to tax changes as is, perhaps, expected. First, individuals do not work only for pecuniary rewards. Job satisfaction or the prestige associated with a particular occupation may be important in their decision-making, and these factors are typically ignored. Secondly, individuals rarely have the control over their work-hours that is typically assumed in the theoretical literature. Hours of work are set for certain occupations (e.g. 40 hours a week) and overtime may or may not be an option. For professional workers like solicitors and accountants, there may be greater discretion, but typically the individual's work/leisure choice may be far more constrained. Third, the assumption is that individuals are fully aware of tax rates. Empirical work has long cast doubt on this (see, e.g. Brown 1968). Again, solicitors and accountants may have greater aware-

Table 10.2 Some elasticities for labour supply

Author	Sample	Uncompensated wage	Compensated wage	Income (total)
Married Women				
Cogan (1981)	US	0.65	0.68	−0.03
Hausman (1981)	US	0.45	0.9	−0.45
Arrufat and Zabalza (1986)	UK	0.62	0.68	−0.06
Blundell and Walker (1982)	UK			
	No children	0.43	0.65	−0.22
	One child	0.10	0.32	−0.22
Arellano and Meghir (1989)	UK			
	No children	0.37	0.44	−0.13
	Young children	0.29	0.50	−0.40
	Old children	0.71	0.82	−0.21
Husbands				
Hausman (1981)	US	−0.03	0.95	−0.98
Ashworth and Ulph (1981)	UK	−0.33	0.29	−0.62
Blundell and Walker (1982)	UK	−0.23	0.13	−0.36
Lone Mothers				
Hausman (1980)	US	0.53	0.65	−0.18
Bingley, Symons and Walker (1992)	UK	0.76	1.28	−0.52
Jenkins (1992)	UK	1.44	−	−0.24

Sources: Killingsworth (1983) and Blundell (1992) as recorded in Blundell (1992) with permission of the Institute for Fiscal Studies.

ness of tax rates, but this is less likely for the man in the street. In Brown's 1968 survey only 3 per cent of workers knew the standard rate of tax and only 6 per cent of managers were able to estimate their marginal rate of tax. While Brown's survey indicated that people overestimated the amount of tax paid, a more recent survey by Lewis (1978) confirmed the misperceptions but indicated a general underestimation. Both studies cast doubt on individuals' awareness of *tax changes* and therefore suggest a low labour response.

Despite the evidence, the Conservative government in the 1980s was determined to lower income taxation to offset its disincentive effects. It is possible as a matter of deduction to gain some insight into the likely consequences of cuts in the basic rates of tax. Ulph (1987) points out that those who earn close to the tax threshold will enjoy little or no income effect from the tax cut so that the substitution effect should dominate, causing them to work more hours. In contrast, those at the top end of the earnings distribution will enjoy a substantial change in their after-tax income so that the income effect will be large, causing the high-income earners (the dynamic entrepreneurs?) to work less. Ulph emphasizes the need to consider different groups in the labour force separately—e.g. those who work at the tax threshold (mainly part-time married women) and the currently unemployed—so that their particular incentives can be analysed.

Finally, it is worth considering the incidence of personal income taxation. As noted elsewhere, it is the relevant supply and demand elasticities that matter. In Fig. 10.3 the demand for labour in the absence and presence of a proportional income tax is depicted as D and D_T respectively. Two labour supply curves are depicted, one perfectly inelastic (S_{LI}), the other with a

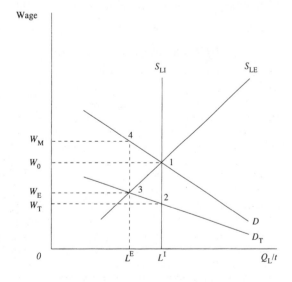

Figure 10.3 The incidence of proportional income taxation.

positive slope (S_{LE}), reflecting that in aggregate the substitution effect of an increasing wage rate dominates the income effect and more hours are supplied. In the case where the inelastic curve S_{LI} applies, the initial market wage W_0 and supply of hours L^I obtain but the net of tax wage becomes W_T and the whole of the tax paid (distance 12) is paid by the factor labour. With some elasticity in the labour supply curve S_{LE} the effect of the tax is to reduce employment to OL^E so that the market wage rises to OW_M and the net-of-tax wage received by workers becomes OW_E. In this case only part of the tax paid in total (distance 34) is paid by the workers (W_0W_e): the remainder of the tax (W_0W_M) finds its incidence on consumers in the form of higher labour input costs. If, as generally seems to be accepted, the supply of labour (especially for male heads of households) is overall fairly inelastic, it is safe to assume in redistributive studies that personal income taxes stay where they are put and that forward shifting is insignificant.

10.3.2 National Insurance Contributions

National Insurance contributions (NICs) represent some 18 per cent of total tax revenue in the UK. Their tax base is employment incomes. The most significant tax reform in the UK 1989 budget involved changes in the way that the employee share of NICs was levied (the employer's share was unchanged), and it is interesting to compare the old and the reformed system. In Table 10.3 we can see that the rate up to the lower limit was cut to 2 per cent from 5, 7 or 9 per cent, depending on what employees' pay level was. The 'Employee gain' column illustrates how much this

'helps' payers. Compared with the old system, increases in the marginal tax rate (MTR) are seen to occur for the £75–£115 weekly pay band with the average tax rate (ATR) falling, indicating that both substitution and income effects should pull in this range towards *less* work. However, for those not currently working the attraction of paid employment is enhanced. The nature of the old system also illustrates the way 'notches' or 'traps' are introduced into the pay system in that as an employee moved from, say, £74 to £75 a week, NICs went from 2 to 7 per cent of all income. (£43 and £115 were obviously the other notches.)

More recently it has been employers' national insurance contributions that have been the centre of criticism as it produces discreet steps up in contributions due from employers' at £58, £105, £150 and £205 gross income per week (see Fig. 10.4 reproduced from the Institute of Fiscal Studies 'Green Budget' (1995)). The effect of these steps or notches is to cause the distribution of earnings to cluster just below the steps and reduce flexibility of the labour market especially for those at the lower end of the earnings distribution. It has to be remembered, however, that despite NIC's being labelled employers' and employees' the actual incidence is, given the argument captured in Fig. 10.3, on employees, so that movements in contribution rates should show up in workers 'take home' pay.

10.3.3 Excise taxes

Revenue from excise duties on home-produced goods and services and imports comes mainly from three

Table 10.3 Change in employee NICs

Contracted-in, weekly amounts

Weekly pay £	Old system MTR = ATR	New system MTR	ATR (%)	Employee gain	
				%	£
43	5% = £2.15	2% = 86 p	2	3	1.29
75	7% = £5.25	9% of £(75 − 43) = £2.88 + £0.86 = £3.74	5	2	1.51
115	9% = £10.35	9% of £(115 − 43) = £6.48 + £0.86 = £7.34	6.4	2.6	3.01
325	9% = £29.25	9% of £(325 − 43) = £25.38 + £0.86 = £26.24	8.1	0.9	3.01

Source: Lloyds Bank Economic Bulletin, no. 124, April 1989. Reproduced with the permission of Lloyds Bank.

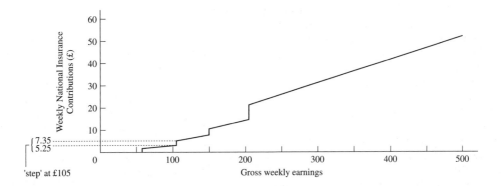

Figure 10.4 Employer National Insurance contributions (in SERPS).

Source: Institute of Fiscal Studies 'The Green Budget' (1995).

sources: tobacco, alcoholic drinks and hydrocarbon oil (predominantly petrol and diesel oil). In the UK, tobacco, for example, is taxed as a specific duty per unit of quantity and an *ad valorem* element based on the recommended retail price of 21 per cent. In 1986 this accounted for nearly 12 per cent of revenue raised by expenditure taxes and 4 per cent of total government revenue (see Godfrey and Maynard 1988). At one level an attractive feature of goods subject to excise taxes is that they are relatively price-inelastic in demand, so that it is possible to raise taxation appreciably and increase revenue, because with only a modest effect on the level of consumption there is a small excess burden. At another level, however, this inelasticity feature is unattractive, because on a merit good, and some 'externality' arguments, the objective of government policy should be to reduce consumption, and owing to the price inelasticity tax rises will not have a very significant impact on the level of consumption. Given the price inelasticity argument, changes in duties in the annual budget are probably best seen as motivated by revenue-raising considerations.

Merriman (1994) tests the public choice proposition developed by Buchanan and Lee (1982) that politicians intent on setting taxes simply to maximize tax revenue may result in an equilibrium that involves a tax rate greater than the one that actually maximizes tax revenue. The context of the investigation is the excise taxation of cigarettes in the USA. High cigarette excise taxes can be justified either on the basis of a market failure argument (merit want or externality-type arguments might be adduced) or an optimal tax argument that recognizes that excess burdens are smallest where demand elasticities are lowest. Using Fig. 10.5 panel (a) connects the quantity of cigarettes

purchased per period (Qc/t) to the tax rate on them (t) whereas panel (b) connects the tax rate to the amount of revenue raised. Full or long-run adjustment is depicted by D_{LR} and R_{LR} respectively and dictate outcomes that are feasible in the sense they can be sustained beyond the short period. The revenue maximizing tax rate is t^*. Short-run adjustment to excise tax imposition, however, is slow and hence politicians with attenuated time horizons may well opt for a 'myopic' equilibrium. With t^* set they are tempted to adjust along $D_{SR(t1)}$ and $R_{SR(t1)}$ increasing tax revenue temporarily by say, choosing tax rate $t1$ moving from $1'$ to 2 and increasing revenue from $r(t^*)$ to $r(t1)$. Given the construction the short-run achievement of point 2 results in the longer period in outcome associated with point 3 as $D_{SR(t1)}$ rotates clockwise around point 1 to coincide with D_{LR} when there is an incentive to exploit the short-run inelastic demand curve through point 4. This process of adjustment ends when preferences of the politician as represented in the shape of an indifference curve in panel (b) (vertical for a revenue maximizing politician, convex to the origin if tax revenue and high tax rates on cigarettes are both 'goods' to the politician and concave from below in the 'good–bad' case actually illustrated as I^*) is tangent to a short-run revenue curve $R_{SR(t2)}$ on the long-run feasible tax rate–tax revenue trade-off represented by R_{LR}, i.e. point 5 with tax rate $t2$. The inference is that politicians have chosen excise tax rates on cigarettes that are too high by reference to a revenue maximizing rate ($t2 > t^*$).

While the inference is clear what of the empirical evidence? The 'myopic' equilibrium or politicians treating excise taxes on cigarettes as a good (convex indifference curves) establishes equilibrium on the negatively sloped section of R_{LR} indicating that

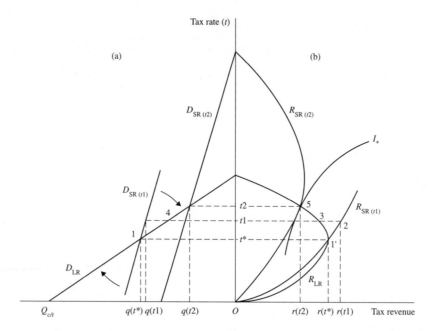

Figure 10.5 Revenue maximizing excise taxes?

marginal tax revenue from a change in the excise tax should be negative (an increase in t should decrease r). The results of estimating the change in revenue from separately increasing excise taxes in the individual states of the USA offered strongly contradicting evidence. For example it was estimated for Alaska that a permanent one cent increase in excise taxes from 2.53 to 3.53 cents per packet would reduce sales by 3.34 packs per capita per annum from 128.9 suggesting an increase in revenue per capita per annum of $1.20 $((128.9 \times 1) - (3.34 \times 2.53))$. The conclusion seems to suggest strongly an equilibrium on the positively sloped section of R_{LR} and that politicians: (i) do not treat excise taxes on cigarettes as a 'good' (which would be the case if they disliked cigarette consumption themselves or thought it was a net vote gainer because of market failure correction); (ii) do not revenue maximize in their choice of t. Whether actual excise tax rates in the various states are part of normatively optimal packages is another matter.

10.3.4 Value added tax

Value added tax is important in the UK because of its EC membership. It is a general sales (domestic consumption) tax covering a very wide range of goods and, as its name suggests, is a tax on the value added at each production stage (the difference between the value of sales and purchased inputs). The difference between formal and actual incidence is important and is emphasized by the 'shifting' definition of an indirect tax.

The bread sale example in Table 10.4 has four production stages, each 'adding' £200 in value and facing a 15 per cent tax rate. Until a sale is made to a non-registered person, all VAT paid is redeemable by the next registered trader in the chain. (Note the incentive to be registered for VAT.) At each stage the gross (output) tax due (OT) is included in the price as the inputs (intermediate outputs) are passed on. Tax paid at an earlier stage is deducted to produce the net tax due at each stage. Registered VAT payers have to present a three-monthly return (not synchronized between stages) on which all output tax and input tax is declared for the period and the net tax paid.[2] That is, the baker declares £90 worth of output tax, and with £60 deductible input tax pays £30 net. (This has been recovered by him in the price to the retailer of £690.) At first sight all the tax is paid by the final purchaser. However, the simple analysis of chapter 7 dealing with excise taxes suggests that this can be the

---

[2] It is possible to receive tax back if, for example, you are stock-building. With, say, £500 worth of inputs deductible, input tax would be £75, but if outputs were £300, output tax would be £45 and net tax, minus £30.

Table 10.4 Simplified VAT example

| | Inputs (Deductable) | | Outputs (Value added) | | Net tax |
| | Inputs | Input tax (IT) | Output | Output tax (OT) | (OT − IT) |
	£	£	£	£	£
Stage 1 (farmer)	0	0	200	30	30
Stage 2 (miller)	200	30	400	60	30
Stage 3 (baker)	400	60	600	90	30
Stage 4 (retailer)	600	90	800	120	30
Consumer price = £800 + £120 = £920					

case only if demand is completely inelastic or supply is completely elastic. In the other cases, part of the tax is felt by the producers or suppliers in the form of the lower prices that would have obtained if VAT did not apply.

VAT provides a buoyant revenue source and covers about 60 per cent of consumers expenditure in the UK. However, it has disadvantages in that it tends to be regressive which may need to be offset in other parts of the tax-benefit system. Further it has high administrative and compliance costs. Raising more revenue by VAT involves either extending the tax base and/or increasing the VAT rate which is relatively low in the UK compared to Europe (see chapter 13). However, shifting away from direct to this form of indirect taxation at minimum has a one-off effect on the retail price-index and this may prove an impetus to an inflationary process.

10.3.5 Corporation tax

Taxation of income earned from corporations is not a simple issue. There are two broad views about the object of the exercise (see Musgrave and Musgrave 1989). On the so-called *integrationist* view, corporation tax is a device to include corporation income within the personal income tax base. The second, *absolutist*, view is that it is an additional 'absolute' tax on corporate income independent of the operation of the personal income tax system. If the integrationist position is accepted, then the one-time perennial exam question of whether 'corporation taxation' is double taxation is brought to the fore. If all profits from corporations were distributed to shareholders, then on the integrationist view all that is required is a mechanism by which individuals can pay their tax on this income source at their personal marginal rate. The absolutist view is that this would not be a sufficient appreciation of the matter and that

corporations have a separate liability to tax. While not denying that only individuals can ultimately feel the burden of taxation, absolutists feel that the corporation is a legal entity, an economic organism in and of itself. In this respect any shifting of corporation tax would counter this argument to tax corporations *per se*.

The general line of argument developed by Musgrave and Musgrave (1989) is that, while there may be a case for a separate tax policy in relation to corporations, it is not evident that the type of corporation tax system enacted fits the bill. All businesses, not just incorporated ones, gain from the public-good and quasi-public-good provisions of the public sector, especially the legal framework in which limited liability is enjoyed. While this is a benefit, it is difficult to establish the cost of securing it, and it is not obvious what the appropriate tax base for each public-good or quasi-public-good gain should be. In the absence of perfect competition, tax policy may be justified in influencing industrial structure, and microeconomic theory describes the impact of different types of taxes on monopoly firms' decisions. Again, however, a specific objective needs to be established and a suitable tax instrument selected. Alongside concerns about the benefits enjoyed from public sector provision and the structure of industry, there is also the desire to influence the pattern of expenditure in the economy. Levels of investment are important to economic growth, and it is often considered a 'good thing' to stimulate growth by inducing a higher level of investment. The use of investment tax credits, so that firms can offset some of the cost of capital equipment against corporation tax liability, is one instrument that could be assigned to this target.

Corporation tax systems fall into different categories. Under the 'classical' system company profits are taxed and then any dividends paid out are taxed as unearned income by the recipients at their marginal tax rate. This is the *double taxation* case (in comparison with income from non-incorporated businesses) and tends to encourage profit retention rather than dividend payment. The *imputation* system in the limit corresponds to integrationist views and offsets the double taxation effect by imputing corporation tax paid to dividend recipients as an offset to their personal liability to tax from that source. Such imputation can be complete or partial. The partial imputation shades into the *split rate* system, which treats distributed income in a more favourable tax manner than income retained by the corporation. For recent discussion of this topic see Mintz (1995).

The incidence and welfare costs of corporation tax have been discussed in chapter 7 in a general equilibrium context.

The rationale for corporation tax as such has always been a matter of dispute in traditional public finance. However, for those following a public choice line there is a more clear response. The corporation is a legal entity and it is easy to foster the illusion that this entity can pay tax independent of individuals so that the cost of the public sector becomes less transparent and hence reduced in size. In reality only people can bear the burden of a tax so that corporation tax must reduce someone's income. The tax must either be passed forward to consumers in higher prices or back to factor owners in lower factor rewards (lower wages for labour or lower returns to capital). Where the incidence of corporation tax actually lies is still a matter of debate with support for both forward and backward shifting. (In the Harberger model discussed in chapter 7 the corporation tax is largely paid by the owners of capital.) In all events uncertainty as to where the actual tax falls allows politicians to select a biased account favourable to the bulk of their supporters if faced with voters who are not illuded.

The Labour Party proposal to impose a one-off (retrospective) windfall tax on the 'privatized' utilities can be considered in this light. Following the Institute of Fiscal Studies (1995) the public choice aspect is clear in that the tax will apparently raise revenue from the 'fat cat' running often inefficient electricity and water companies and therefore be a vote gainer. The logic behind the tax is that the Conservatives privatized the utilities in an unacceptable way. As noted in chapter 5 offer prices were set sufficiently low so that there were instant capital gains to initial investors and the continued high profits reflect unsuccessful regulation through Oftel, Ofwat and the like. However, it is difficult to correct past errors and the imposition of a windfall tax would:

(i) be either felt by consumers or shareholders of the companies (the capacity to shift the burden forward depends on the stringency of regulation);

(ii) inequitable to the extent that if the burden falls on shareholders only a subset of them will be the original shareholders many of whom will have encashed their capital gain through share sales;

(iii) retrospective taxation offends the rules of revenue raising as generally played seeming to reflect the exercise of arbitrary power introducing 'extra' uncertainty into economic decision-taking reducing utility;

(iv) related to point (iii) the proposal by the Labour Party does serve to underline their claims of Conservative mismanagement as well as making investors wary of further 'privatization' offers, i.e. public choice voter popularity gains.

10.3.6 Capital taxation

There are two main UK taxes under this heading: capital gains tax and capital transfer tax.

Capital gains tax is levied on the difference between the selling price and the buying price of an asset. There are a number of exemptions, including a sole or main residence, a private car and life insurance policies. Capital losses can be offset against capital gains tax liability, and there is a tax-free element before capital gains tax is levied at the individual's personal marginal tax rate.

One of the purposes of capital gains taxes is to prevent individuals from avoiding tax by converting their income into a capital gain: individual choices could be distorted and people might, for example, seek assets like oil paintings as opposed to bonds. The return of the former when realized on sale represents a capital gain, and if untaxed would be much more attractive than interest payments which would be taxed as part of income. Variations in the ability to convert income to a capital gain, plus the fact that such gains are more significant in higher than lower income brackets, means that any favourable treatment they might receive would be inequitable. Despite this the Conservative government has expressed a desire to abolish this tax.

Capital transfer tax (since the 1986 Budget inheritance tax) has undergone a number of changes. Originally it covered all gifts, but since 1986 it is restricted to gifts on death or those made within seven years of death. Again, there is a tax-free element, and there are exemptions which include transfers between husbands and wives and gifts to charities. James, Lewis and Allison (1987) document the growth of concessions related to capital transfer tax and conclude that, like its predecessor estate duty, it is 'a voluntary tax paid only by those who dislike[d] their relatives even more than they disliked paying tax' (p. 45). Whilst this is the only UK major tax on wealth John Major made it clear that he disliked this tax.

10.3.7 Taxation in aggregate

So far the discussion has considered the separate elements in the UK tax system in isolation, but a common query concerns the burden of the tax system as a whole, say as between countries or across income ranges. There is no easy way to answer this type of question. With regard to the first part of the question, 'league tables' of the most taxed countries is a common response. Table 10.5 reproduces some recent relevant data for a number of countries. For the sample of countries chosen, it is clear that the UK is not the most heavily taxed overall. However, despite political rhetoric, it is impossible to draw any 'robust' normative conclusions from such estimates (see Cullis and Jones 1987).

Table 10.5 Tax as a percentage of GDP, 1994

	Total	Income and profits	Social security	Goods and services	Other
France	44.1	7.8	19.1	12.0	5.2
UK	34.1	12.1	6.1	12.0	3.8
Germany	39.3	11.5	15.4	11.3	1.1
Italy	41.7	14.5	13.0	11.8	2.4
USA	27.6	12.3	7.0	5.0	3.3
Japan	27.8	10.5	9.8	4.3	3.3

Source: OECD Revenue Statistics, 1965–95, tables 3 and 6.

With respect to the effects of the overall tax system at each income level, Dilnot, Kay and Morris (1984) provide an insight. To put their approach crudely, they attempt to summarize the tax system in a complicated version of the following equation:

$$(10.5) \qquad T = T_a + bY$$

where T = aggregate tax payments
T_a = tax payments that can be viewed as independent of income (autonomous)
Y = taxable income
b = effective marginal rate of tax

This is more than a summary of the descriptions of each tax introduced above: rather, an economic picture captured by econometric estimation. The authors introduce a methodology for describing a whole tax system that is useful here as a summary device. The essentially degressive structure of UK personal income taxation (tax allowances plus a single marginal tax rate which together serve to make the tax system progressive) allows it to be represented as

$$(10.6) \qquad t = bY - a$$

where t = tax paid
a = tax allowance expressed as a tax credit
b = marginal tax rate on income
Y = gross income

Next, income-related deductions are introduced. These comprise mainly mortgage interest, pension fund contributions and life insurance premiums and are captured in the form of

$$(10.7) \qquad M = M_1 + M_2 Y$$

where M is mortgage interest payment. Equation (10.1) becomes

$$(10.8) \qquad t = b(Y - M) - a$$

so that

$$(10.9) \qquad t = b(Y - [M_1 + M_2 Y]) - a$$

and

$$(10.10) \qquad t = b(1 - M_2)Y - (a + bM_1)$$

so that the effect of mortgage interest deductions is to alter the effective marginal tax rate to $b(1 - M_2)$ and raise the value of the tax credit by bM_1. (Other deductions are treated similarly: see Table 10.5.)

The favourable treatment of mortgages, pensions and life insurance in the UK tax system has not gone without comment. Kay and King (1983) note that, because of the advantages associated with these assets, they dominate net personal savings in the UK. The authors describe them as 'civil servant' assets rather than 'entrepreneurial' ones, because they suit those with settled plans who do not wish to move geographically or occupationally. Additionally, because of their contractual nature, they have elements of 'forced' savings about them in times when individuals may need greater flexibility.

With regard to expenditure taxes, Dilnot, Kay and Morris use a linear Engel curve for the ith commodity (X_i) as follows:

$$(10.11) \qquad X_i = Z_i + x_i Y$$

where X_i = consumption expenditure on the ith commodity
x_i = marginal propensity to consume X

Introducing t_i as the tax per unit on i, aggregate tax T becomes

$$(10.12) \quad \begin{aligned} T = t + t_i X_i &= [b(1 - M_2) + t_i x_i]Y \\ &\quad - (a + bM_1 - t_i Z_i) \end{aligned}$$

In words, the effective marginal tax rate is raised by $t_i x_i$ and the tax credit is reduced by $t_i Z_i$. The NICs discussed above are introduced at a rate n_2 and gross employee renumeration Y_r is given by

$$(10.13) \quad \begin{aligned} Y_r &= (1 + n_2)Y \\ Y &= \frac{1}{1 + n_2} Y_r \end{aligned}$$

Equation (10.11) becomes

$$\begin{aligned} T &= t + t_i X_i + n_2 Y \\ &= \frac{[b(1 - M_2) + t_i x_i + n_2]Y_r}{1 + n_2} - (a + bM_1 - t_i Z_i) \end{aligned}$$

(10.14)

All the adjustments made are summarized in Table 10.6.

To recap the method, direct taxes have a legal framework facilitating the assessment of the overall effective marginal tax rates. However, marginal income tax rates would be overestimated if income-related deductions were ignored. Here the assumption is that mortgage and other deductible payments, including (half) of life insurance premia, are 'caused' by high incomes. As for indirect taxation, estimated Engel curves relate the expenditure of groups of households on taxed goods to total expenditure. The application of the structure of the indirect tax system to the estimated consumption patterns in each group enables the integration of the indirect with the direct tax system. The third and final step is the inclusion of payroll-based taxes.

The results suggest that in 1981, for a married couple with two children (wife not in paid work) in the basic band for income tax and below the national insurance ceiling, the *overall* marginal tax rate on gross employee remuneration (GER) was 53 per cent with an associated tax credit of £1437. For the average GER in this group the average tax rate would have been 38.3 per cent. For other groups the authors note that the overall marginal tax rate was at an historically high level in excess of 60 per cent. Such calculations clearly lend credibility to the claims of Mrs Thatcher

Table 10.6 A descriptive model of the UK tax system

	Tax credit	Marginal rate	
Income tax	$b\left(A + M_1 + P_1 + \frac{L_1}{2}\right)$	$b\left(1 - M_2 - P_2 - \frac{L_2}{2}\right)\left(\frac{1}{1 + n_2}\right)$	(1)
Employer NI	—	$\frac{n_2}{1 + n_2}$	(2)
Employee NI	—	$\frac{n_1}{1 + n_2}$	(3)
All direct taxes	(1)	(1) + (2) + (3)	(4)
VAT	a_{1i}	$a_{2i}\left\{1 - b\left[\left(1 - M_2 - P_2 - \frac{L_2}{2}\right) - (P_2 + L_2 + S_2) - n_1\right]\left(\frac{1}{1 + n_2}\right)\right\}$	(5)
Excise duties	↓	↓	(6)
Intermediate taxes	↓	↓	(7)
All indirect taxes	(5) + (6) + (7)	(5) + (6) + (7)	(8)
Total, all taxes	(4) + (8)	(4) + (8)	(9)

Tax base = gross employee remuneration
$M_1 + M_2 Y$ = mortgage interest payments
$P_1 + P_2 Y$ = pension contributions
$L_1 + L_2 Y$ = life insurance premia
A = tax allowance
b = basic rate of income tax
n_1 = employee NI contributions, contracted-in
n_2 = employer NI contributions, contracted-in
$a_{1i} + a_{2i}E$ = coefficients relating indirect tax i to expenditure
$S_1 + S_2 Y$ = savings other than pension, life insurance
Source: A Dilnot, J. Kay and N. Morris, 'The UK Tax System, Structure and Progressivity, 1948–1982', *Scandinavian Journal of Economics*, 83, 2 (1984), pp. 150–65.

in the early Conservative 'era' that the population was 'over'-taxed. The pros and cons of this are discussed elsewhere; the main purpose here is to offer an insight into how a whole complex tax system can be summarized by condensation into a 'tax credit' and a single 'marginal rate'.

10.3.8 Public debt

When government expenditure exceeds government revenue (e.g. from taxation) the government runs a budget deficit. One way to finance this deficit is to borrow from the public by selling bonds.[3] The government's deficit is the annual shortfall between spending and tax revenue. Public debt is the total of unpaid deficits (i.e. a total which includes the sum that the government owes from past years). For public choice economists the existence of deficit financing and the creation of public debt causes problems. First, it is argued that debt creates a a burden for future generations, i.e. for those who will be faced with servicing and redeeming the public debt. Secondly, it is alleged that deficit financing makes the 'tax price' of goods and services provided in the public sector appear lower than the true 'tax price'. Borrowing reduces the amount that is paid for public sector goods and services and leads the community to commit an 'excessive' allocation of resources to the public sector.

By contrast, other economists argue that raising finance by borrowing is simply 'equivalent' to raising revenue by taxation and, therefore, there can be no additional burden from borrowing. The argument that borrowing is 'equivalent' to taxation stems from the writings of David Ricardo (1772–1832). With the 'enormous' deficit incurred by Great Britain during the Napoleonic Wars, Ricardo took an interest in public debt. He considered the proposition 'that if people take full account of the future tax burden that will have to be imposed in order to pay the interest on public debt then financing government purchases with current taxes is equivalent to financing it with debt and paying the interest on that debt in perpetuity' (Parkin and King 1992, p. 929). The implication being that, if a government were to borrow to cover the deficit that emerged between taxation and spending, rather than covering this by additional taxation, the impact would be equivalent as far as individuals

were concerned. Whether Ricardo actually believed that tax finance and borrowing were equivalent is a matter of dispute (O'Driscoll 1977). Ever since, economists have devoted energy to identify conditions in which they would be equivalent. The basic argument is that taxation directly reduces the taxpayer's net worth (because he/she must pay the tax now) but an equivalent amount of government debt creates an equal reduction in the taxpayer's net worth (as the taxpayer will be faced with the liability to repay the tax in the future). When considering public debt, a taxpayer's net worth is equally reduced by the capitalization of future tax liabilities which are required to service and to redeem the debt.[4] The conclusion is then that both forms of finance are equivalent. This result is often referred to as the Ricardian Equivalence Theorem.

Here the objective is to examine the conditions under which Ricardian equivalence will hold and then to reconsider the public choice case against public debt.

10.3.8a Ricardian equivalence

The Ricardian Equivalence Theorem can be illustrated by an analysis of an individual's consumption and saving decision.[5] In Fig. 10.6 an individual is assumed to have an after-tax income of $Y_1 - T_1$ in period 1 and an after-tax income of $Y_2 - T_2$ in period 2. The individual may not wish to consume all after tax income in period 1; preferring to save some of the income for consumption in period 2. The budget line 12 illustrates the way in which consumption possibilities can be transferred between the two periods. The slope of the budget line is $(1 + r)$, where r is the rate of interest. Any income saved in period 1 will earn this rate of interest. So, for example, in a very extreme scenario, if the individual consumed nothing in period 1 then the sum available for consumption in period 2 would be equal to $[Y_2 - T_2 + (Y_1 - T_1)(1 + r)]$. This sum is represented by the distance $O2$ in Fig. 10.6. Conversely, if the individual could borrow against future income (ie. $Y_2 - T_2$) for consumption in period 1, the present value of $Y_2 - T_2$ would be $(Y_2 - T_2)/(1 + r)$ and together with $Y_1 - T_1$ this would be equal to the distance $O1$ in Fig. 10.6. In this way, both the slope and the position of the line 12 can be determined.

---

[3] Interest-yielding bonds are attractive to those individuals who chose to purchase them. The excess of spending over revenue could be financed by printing money rather than selling bonds to the public though the implications for inflation might deter choice of this option.

[4] Following Buchanan and Wagner (1978, p. 98): 'Suppose …that the rate of interest is 10 per cent and that a tax of \$100 on a person is replaced by an identical share of public debt issue with the debt obligation to be met with a payment of \$110 in one year. This shift does not affect the taxpayer's net worth.'

[5] See, for example, Browning and Browning (1991) and Hoover (1994).

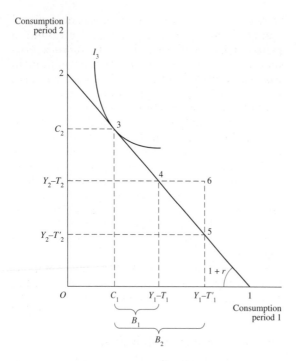

Figure 10.6 Ricardian equivalence.

Source: adapted from Hoover (1994).

The indifference curve I_3 in Fig. 10.6 shows the rate at which the individual would be prepared to forego consumption in one period for additional consumption in the other period. At any point on the indifference curve, the slope of the indifference curve reveals the individual's marginal rate of time preference (the rate at which the individual would substitute present consumption for future consumption). Of course, the individual will maximize welfare by attaining the highest possible indifference curve. This means allocating consumption between the two periods so as to attain a tangency position between the indifference curve and the budget line 12. In Fig. 10.6, the individual maximizes welfare at point 3 on indifference curve I_3. At this point the decision is to consume OC_1 in period 1 and OC_2 in period 2. This means saving in period 1 an amount equal to $(Y_1 - T_1) - C_1 (= B_1)$ for future consumption in period 2.

The government now decides to finance some existing expenditure programmes by borrowing in period 1 and is able to reduce taxes accordingly. The tax cut increases the consumer's after-tax income in period 1 to $Y_1 - T_1'$. If this were all, the individual might assume an income effect (or net worth effect), i.e. it would seem as if the budget line moved out to the

right and that the relevant position was not point 4 on budget line 12 but point 6 on a budget line (not drawn) further to the right. However, the individual is assumed to be fiscally aware. The government will have to pay off the debt-financed tax cut in the future. As long as this is fully anticipated, in period 2 it will follow that taxation will increase from T_2 to T_2' (where $T_2' - T_2$ is equal to the future value of the tax cut $T_1 - T_1'$). The increase in taxes in period 2 reduces after-tax income to $Y_2 - T_2'$; the tax increase will be equal to the tax reduction received in period 1 plus the interest payable for one period. Therefore, in Fig. 10.6 the tax increase in period 2 will be equal to $T_2 - T_2'$ and the combined effect is to move the individual's endowment point from 4 to point 5 on the initial budget line (i.e. there is no income or 'net worth' effect).

As the interest rate remains the same, the individual remains in equilibrium at point 3, i.e. the point chosen when financing in period 1 was more heavily reliant on taxation. Saving will increase from B_1 to B_2 in period 1. Note that the increase in saving equals the amount of the tax reduction in year 1. It has increased to allow for the additional tax liability in period 2. The solution to the individual's maximization problem remains unchanged (at point 3) and the individual remains on budget line 12. Taxation and government borrowing are equivalent and it follows that no additional burden can be created by borrowing. However, the result is fragile. While the following list is not exhaustive, it is illustrative of the assumptions required to maintain equivalence.

(*a*) *Infinite lifetime*: In this example the individual expects to be alive to pay the tax when the debt is redeemed. If the individual were to die before the debt was redeemed then, during the individual's lifetime, it would appear that an income effect had been experienced and the equivalence theorem would not apply.

While some rely on the artifact of infinitely long-life people to present the case for Ricardian equivalence, there is an alternative. Barro (1976) has demonstrated that, when individuals' own time horizons are finite, Ricardian equivalence may still hold if individuals in the present generation are concerned about the welfare of their children. An individual in the present generation may acquire utility both from the consumption of goods and services and also from safeguarding his/her children's welfare. The children of the present generation are similarly concerned about their children. The implication is that an individual in the present generation makes decisions in the same way as a single individual (or dynasty) facing an infinite time horizon.

In Fig. 10.6 assume that consumption in period 1 is by a member of the present generation and consumption in period 2 is by this individual's children. The indifference curve signifies the extent of altruism, i.e. the extent to which the individual will trade-off present-day consumption for her children's future consumption. In this situation, instead of B representing saving by the individual for personal consumption in the next period, now B_1 is the bequest that the individual wishes to make for her children. Individuals in the present generation recognize that the future redemption of borrowing will impose a tax liability on their successors. Therefore, to compensate the children, the individual increases the bequest of assets by sufficient to service and redeem the debt (i.e. from B_1 to B_2). Once again, an addition to public debt causes an equal increase in saving.

That parent's leave bequests for their children is evident. However, that such bequests are motivated only by concern for the welfare of children is questionable. Bequests may arise, in part, because of the uncertainty associated with determining the time of death. They may arise for strategic reasons, to ensure care and consideration from siblings (e.g. see the survey article by Seater 1992). Barro's model can be questioned in many different ways (e.g. Feldstein, 1976). Together with the original idea of Ricardian equivalence it is also sensitive to the arguments that follow.

(b) *Perfect capital markets where individuals can borrow and lend at the same rate as the government*: There are two examples to note. First, if the government was able to borrow at an interest rate lower than that available to individuals the present value of the government debt issue would be less than the value of the current tax reduction (leading to an increase in net wealth). The impact of this is easy to see. In Fig. 10.7 the lower costs of borrowing mean that the amount to repay is lower in period 2. Therefore, instead of increasing taxes from T_2 to T_2' in the second period, taxes are increased only from T_2 to T_2''. The effect of this is to allow individuals to experience an income (or 'net worth') effect. Comparing point 5 on the original budget line 12 with point 7 (the new combination of consumption in both periods that is now available), it is as if the budget line has moved to the right to 89. Individuals are better off having been able to borrow at the lower government borrowing rate.

Secondly, if there were a difference in the capital market between the rate of interest at which individuals could lend and the interest rate at which they

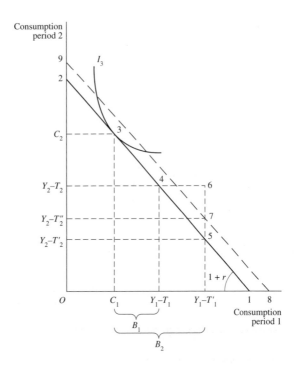

Figure 10.7 Costs of borrowing.

Source: adapted from Hoover (1994).

could borrow this distortion would be sufficient to offset the equivalence between tax and debt finance. In Fig. 10.8 the individual can lend at r_l (which is assumed equal to the government borrowing rate) but the rate at which individuals can borrow is the higher rate r_b. Some individuals may find themselves at equilibria at the kink that now exists in the relevant budget line 243. An individual at point 4 saves nothing (or leaves no bequest) for the next period. After a switch to deficit financing and a reduction in taxes the kink of the budget constraint shifts to point 5. If (as is possible) the new optimum is at the new kink (point 5) then there is no increase in saving (or bequest) to meet the future tax costs.

(c) *Lump-sum taxation*: Brennan and Buchanan (1987) demonstrate that, if future taxes are not lump sum, individuals are affected by the decision to finance by debt rather than by taxation. For example, suppose in the future the tax were to be a proportional tax on consumption. Individuals will be likely to switch more consumption into the current period and, therefore, save less than would be predicted by Ricardian equivalence (i.e. when there was lump-sum taxation). Consider Fig. 10.9. An individual faces a budget constraint 12 but debt has been raised (D) and

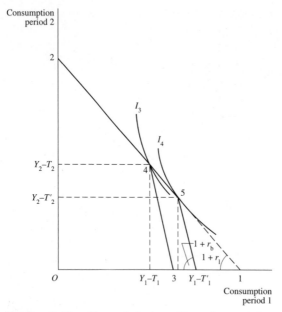

Figure 10.8 Ricardian equivalence and imperfect capital markets.

Source: adapted from Hoover (1994).

the individual will be expected to pay his/her contribution (D/n). If a lump-sum tax were raised the budget line would shift back in a parallel way to 34 and the new optimum would be at point 5. However, suppose

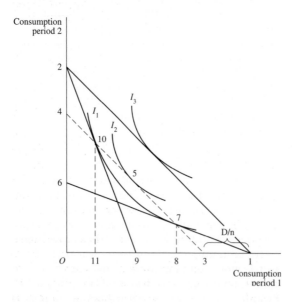

Figure 10.9 Financing a deficit.

Source: adapted from Brennan and Buchanan (1987).

that a tax (set to raise $D/n = 13$) in revenue were to be imposed on future consumption so that the budget line swivels to 16. Individuals would be rational to bring forward their consumption and the optimum would be at point 7. After allowing for the tax, saving out of after-tax income would be equal to distance 38. However, instead suppose that tax is raised on present consumption so that the budget line swivels from 12 to 29. Now the optimum position would be at 10 and the level of saving would be far greater at 3–11, as individuals push their consumption into a future period. The point is that saving will be affected by the way in which the tax is raised to deal with the deficit

(d) *No uncertainty*: In the above illustration the individual was certain as to both current and future period income earning prospects. To the extent that consumers save more as a precaution against uncertainty, if deficits create uncertainty about future income they may have a greater impact on savings which actually 'crowds in' investment (Chan 1983).[6]

(e) *Allowance for economic growth*: If the growth rate of the economy exceeds the interest rate no generation need ever actually pay a portion of the postponed taxes.

This list of assumptions (illustrative rather than comprehensive) is formidable and the Ricardian equivalence result appears very fragile. But is it relevant? Do people behave as Barro suggests? Is Ricardian equivalence relevant for policy-makers? How can it be tested?

While the following list (based on Seater 1992) is again by no means exhaustive it illustrates the various tests that have been applied:

(i) *A direct test.* For example Feldstein (1982) estimates the following equation for period t:

$$(10.15) \quad \begin{aligned} C_t &= a_0 + a_1 Y_t + a_2 W_t + a_3 SSW_t + a_4 G_t \\ &\quad + a_5 T_t + a_6 TR_t + a_7 D_t + e_t \end{aligned}$$

where: C = total consumer expenditure;
Y = current income;
W = privately owned wealth at the beginning of the period;
SSW = a measure of the value of future social security benefits;
G = total government purchases;
T = total tax revenues;
TR = government transfers to individuals;
D = net total government debt at the beginning of the period;
e = the residual.

---

[6] This argument has been criticized by Bernheim (1987).

The implication of Ricardian equivalence is that an increase in government expenditure, other things constant, implies a tax cost in the future and so a_4 should be negative as taxpayers save more for future taxes. Similarly it follows that a_3 should equal zero (an increase in social security benefits would have to be paid for by taxation) and also $a_5 = 0$ and $a_6 = 0$, while $a_2 = a_7$.

(ii) Interest rate tests: Ricardian equivalence suggest that interest rates should be unaffected by the issue of new government debt (see, for example, Barro 1987).

(iii) International finance tests: A possible problem of interest rate tests is that if international capital markets are perfect a ('small') country would show no effect on interest rates irrespective of Ricardian equivalence. However, if Ricardian equivalence were false the incipient rise in interest rates would cause an offsetting inward flow of foreign capital and therefore an appreciation of the domestic currency (see Evans 1986).

(iv) Growth rates: If Ricardian equivalence does not apply, government deficits 'crowd out' private investment and reduce growth rates. The test is whether government deficits affect growth (see Kormendi 1985).

(v) Public choice tests: Lipford and Dougan (1995) attempt a test based on the voting behaviour of legislators. Their argument is that the decision of a legislator to vote to raise social security benefits will only be affected by the age composition of his/her constituency if the effects of the social security programme are not offset by inter-generational transfers from parents to children. Empirical evidence from 1972 when Congress raised social security benefits by 20 per cent yielded no evidence that legislators were influenced by their state or district population aged 45 (or 65) and above.

It is clear that Ricardian equivalence requires many restrictions and many would view these as unlikely in practise. However, Ricardian equivalence can not be summarily dismissed. It has been considered important in terms of its ability to explain data[7] and after assessing alternative empirical tests Seater (1992, p. 182) concludes that: 'Although tests of Ricardian equivalence do not quite give an unambiguous verdict on that proposition's validity, I think it reasonable to

conclude that Ricardian equivalence is strongly supported by the data.'

10.3.8b Public choice and public debt

The Ricardian Equivalence Theorem and its interpretation by Barro would suggest that reliance on borrowing will incur no further costs than those that would be incurred had taxation been used to finance government. However, perhaps because the requirements for equivalence are so demanding, economists have suggested that borrowing will cause problems. The first of these relates to the argument that borrowing passes on a 'burden' for future generations. The second relates to the allocation of resources at any moment of time; borrowing may lead to an 'excessive' public sector.

(a) A burden on future generations?
The debate concerning the intergenerational 'burden' created by public debt has a long history. In a review article, Cooper (1988) notes that in the 'classical' view there were two ways by which a burden could be passed to future generations. First, a direct route, by which individuals in the present generation feel better off and, therefore, increase their consumption (not recognizing that the debt would need to be repaid and not saving in anticipation). Feeling that their net worth had increased, they enjoy greater consumption and the capital stock for future generations is reduced. The second, indirect, 'classical' mechanism focused on interest rates. Increased government borrowing causes interest rates to increase as bonds are made more attractive to purchasers. Higher interest payments will decrease (or 'crowd out') private investment. Of course, both of these effects would be impossible if Ricardian equivalence held because, in such circumstances, individuals would be perfectly aware of future liabilities and increase saving accordingly.

By contrast, Keynesian economists tend to be critical of the view that public debt could create a burden on future generations. In this case 'burden' is defined in terms of resources. The burden of the debt must be borne by the present generation because resources are withdrawn from the private sector for use in the public sector at the time the debt is created. Present generations could hardly draw on resources which had yet to be created. Furthermore, when the debt is repaid (or serviced) one section of the community (taxpayers) pays another section of the community (bondholders). The answer appeared to be that, in the case of public debt held by national citizens, 'we owe it to ourselves' and there can be no burden to the

---

[7] For example although results are mixed savings do appear to rise in response to budget deficits (e.g. see Friedman 1982). In the US, despite a falling rate of national savings since the 1980s, there is support for the Ricardian equivalence proposition over very long periods of US history.

community as a whole (see Lerner 1948). A distinction is made between debt held internal and debt held external to the country. When debt is held externally (i.e. borrowing from abroad), taxpayers in future years must pay back to 'others' who are outside the community in question. However, if debt is internal it appears, on this definition of 'burden' and 'generation', 'that there can be no burden; a future generation simply repays itself.

From a public choice perspective, Buchanan (1958) criticized this 'new orthodoxy' arguing that, while the decision to finance the debt is voluntary, the decision to repay the debt is coercive. If future generations are not party to the original decision and are forced to pay taxes to redeem the debt they suffer a burden (in public choice terms). Of course, now the issue of whether the burden is held internally or externally is irrelevant. Buchanan (1989, p. 6) emphasizes that: 'Taxes, which are by their very nature coercive, must be levied against persons in order to generate the revenues that are required to finance the interest charges on the debt.' While not ignoring the importance of the criticism that government borrowing 'crowds out' private investment, this is a 'secondary' problem to the issue of coercion. Even if the supply of savings is not reduced for future generations, their exposure to coercion to finance the debt would still constitute a burden.[8]

Mishan (1963) criticized Buchanan's analysis. First, if a burden is created by the need to raise taxes to pay off the debt, then it is taxation that causes the burden. If further borrowing were undertaken to pay off the debt it would seem that a burden might be avoided. Secondly, if taxation reflects a voluntary agreement by members of a future generation to pay off the debt then there is no 'coercion'. Thirdly, if the present generation invested resources it may be possible to earn a rate of return sufficient to pay off the debt. In this case there would be no necessity to raise taxation and no burden in the future period.

Mishan notes that Buchanan's contribution stimulated other contributions, including that of Bowen, Davis and Kopf (1960). These authors refer to 'generations' in terms of age. The essence of their argument can be summarily described as follows. Suppose the community comprise three generations: the young (Y), the middle aged (M) and the old (O).

The government raise finance of say £24 000 by borrowing. The resources are to finance a consumption activity. The young and the middle aged agree to lend the money while the old refuse (as the debt will not be repaid for another twenty years). All three generations enjoy the consumption activity financed via the public sector. Twenty years on Y is now the 'new' middle aged (M_1) and M is now the 'new' old generation (O_1), O having 'passed on'. There is of course a new generation Y_1 to replace Y but these did not exist twenty years ago. The government now raises a tax to repay the debt. It follows that Y_1 will be taxed to pay their contribution for a consumption activity some twenty years ago from which they gained nothing. The 'new' young generation (Y_1) pays £8000 and the 'new' middle aged (M_1) pay £8000 and the 'new' old (O_1) pay £8000. This is used to repay the existing middle aged ($M_1 = Y$) and existing old ($O_1 = M$) generations. It follows that a burden has fallen on the 'new' young (Y_1) who enjoyed none of the consumption benefits financed by borrowing and yet are liable for the tax costs. The old generation (O) of some twenty years earlier have enjoyed a consumption event and 'escaped' the costs. A burden has been inherited by the young (Y_1).

These examples of arguments concerning intergenerational burden are not exhaustive. However, the important point to note when assessing contributions to the debate is that, to a large extent, the debate is dependent on semantics. Consider closely the definition of 'burden' and 'generation'. Notice, for example, that the use of the word burden by the Keynesians is in terms of the *use of resources* whereas in Buchanan's example it has to do with the disutility of *coercion*. Compare the definition of the word 'generation'. To the Keynesians a generation comprises *everyone alive at a given date*. To Bowen, Davis and Kopf a generation is *age related* (and might be seen as a subset of the generation described by the Keynesians).

Surveys are available. For example, West (1975) develops a taxonomy which depends on:

(i) the definition of the word 'burden'—which can be considered as subjective (opportunity-utility-based) cost or objective (outlay-commodity-based);

(ii) individual and aggregate (national) burdens;

(iii) flow payments of costs and their capitalization into current net worth.

His general point is that the debt burden is resolved when each of its aspects is placed in its appropriate 'cost' category. Perhaps like all long-running debates, this issue is one that is sustained by participants writing about rather different concepts.

---

[8] Writing in the *Financial Times*, 20 March 1993, Barry Ridley commented that: 'This week Norman Lamont required future generations of British taxpayers to assume the burden of the nearly £1000 a head by which we propose, as a nation, to live beyond our means in 1993–94. Those future taxpayers have not had the opportunity to give their consent...'

(b) Borrowing and the size of the public sector

One distinct, public choice criticism of government borrowing depends on the existence of fiscal illusion. When government borrows, the 'tax price' for additional units of goods and services supplied in the public sector can easily seem lower than the true marginal opportunity cost. Buchanan and Wagner (1978) consider the case of a full employment economy where currently the government finances a unit of a public expenditure by a tax of $1. What happens if tax income were to fall, so that only 90 cents were collected and the remaining 10 cents were raised by borrowing? Of course, the government is still able to spend $1 in order to to provide the good or service. However, the 'tax price' per unit of output from the public sector now appears to be only 90 per cent of its former level. Demand for the good or service will increase and if 'tax price' elasticity were greater than zero, equilibrium would only be restored by an increase in the quantity of the public good beyond one unit. The 'apparent' price fall caused by borrowing increases the momentum for public sector growth. (Consider the discussion in chapter 4 of Fig. 4.10. In that case the 'tax price' which appears to face voters—MC/N—would appear to be reduced by 10 per cent as a consequence of borrowing. The median voter would require an output of the public sector which is larger than in the absence of borrowing.)

For the public choice school, the public sector 'Leviathan' is unleashed by borrowing. By comparison, in the case of Ricardian equivalence where individuals are not illuded, individuals are fully aware that the costs of borrowing must be met in the future and this stimulus from borrowing is not evident.

Public choice scholars argue that a failing of democratic processes is that politicians have an incentive to exploit the fiscal illusion. This arises because borrowing offers politicians the opportunity of appearing to offer goods and services via the public sector at lower tax costs in order to improve their chances in elections. Politicians court popularity by offering greater services at reduced tax costs. Expenditure increases are attractive to vote-seeking politicians and, as political competition increases, it is predicted that reliance on budget deficits will increase.

In fact, Buchanan and Wagner (1978, p. 85) go so far as to blame Keynesians for making budget deficits appear respectable:

Keynesian policy is centred on the use of the government's budget as the primary instrument for insuring the maintenance of high employment and output. The implementation of Keynesian policy therefore, required both the destruction of former principles of balanced public budgets and the replacement of these principles by principles that permitted the imbalance that was necessary for Keynesian budgetary manipulation.

In the above example, if there were a shortfall in demand (so that full employment was not maintained) some Keynesians would defend the use of a budget deficit to increase aggregate demand (in order to restore full employment). However, if voters then mistake the 'tax price' of publicly provided services the resource allocation between private and public sectors is distorted and there is an over-expansion of the public sector. The criticism of Keynes is essentially that he did not allow for mis-application of his work by politicians. This illustrates the distinction at the heart of this text, i.e. between an approach to public finance which assumes that politicians act in the 'public interest' and an approach which begins from the assumption that imperfections within the political process are important. Buchanan and Wagner (1978, p. 84) quote Keynes's biographer, R. F. Harrod, who stated that Keynes assumed that economic policy would be made by 'a small group of enlightened men ... in accordance with the "public interest"'.

So, how valid is this criticism of public borrowing? Does political competition create greater reliance on government borrowing and will this expand the public sector? Mueller (1989, p. 301) notes that: 'Although not necessarily concurring in the dire conclusions and predictions reached by Buchanan and Wagner, the political business cycle literature concurs in emphasizing the backwardly myopic, if not naïve, behavior of voters.' There is reason for concern. Examining government deficits in OECD countries over the period 1951 to 1985, Mueller argues that macroeconomic outcomes must be seen as a consequence of political competition. With respect to government borrowing, Mueller (1989, p. 306) concludes: 'The only two countries in the early eighties with budget deficits of less than 1 per cent of GDP are oil rich Norway (which ran a slight surplus) and Switzerland. Switzerland is the only country in the table for which parties do not compete for the privilege of controlling the central government.'

If deficits increase when there is more virilant political competition, will borrowing increase the size of the public sector? Multiple regression analysis is used to estimate the impact of different socio-economic variables on the size of the public sector. Variables such as the level of real income, the size of the population, etc. are likely to increase the demand for government-provided services and, to these variables, researchers have added the size of the budget deficit as an explanatory variable (e.g. see Niskanen 1978). Tridimas (1992) provides a critique of such studies. However, after allowing for the deficiencies of previous work, his own conclusion with respect to United Kingdom data between 1955 and 1988 is that 'similar to previous studies, the results show that deficit finance increases the demand for government spending...' (p. 275).

For the public choice school the solution to this problem is constitutional constraint (see, for example, Niskanen 1992). Politicians must be constrained to ensure that the government budget is balanced. There are obvious problems that arise in determining and in monitoring the precise constitutional constraint (see chapters 14 and 16). However, the 'explosion' in government borrowing in the US in the 1980s saw demands for a balanced budget constraint. In 1980 the US government public sector deficit was $59 bn and by 1986 it was $221 bn. In 1980 US national debt stood at $914 bn but some five years later it had doubled (Healey 1989). The Gramm–Rudman–Hollings Bill (named after the sponsors of the bill) was passed in 1986. It called for specific budget deficit targets and hoped to bring about a balanced budget by 1991. If planned expenditures exceeded targets, a preset formula cut back expenditures on each programme. The Supreme Court regarded this procedure as unconstitutional and Congress was forced to take alternative steps in 1987. The example illustrates both the concern that can arise over government borrowing and the difficulties of enforcing constitutional constraints.

In conclusion, it would be wrong to ignore this theory of public sector expansion. However, not everyone shares the public choice view that fiscal illusion (associated with government borrowing) will necessarily create 'excessive' deficits. For example, Alessina and Perotti (1995) draw attention to several problems associated with the public choice explanation of deficit financing. First, they emphasize that in the public choice discussion fiscal illusion is more than simply the difficulty for the electorate to understand the complexity of the government budget. It may be difficult for the public to estimate correctly both benefits and costs of public expenditure programmes. In the public choice case it is not that the public make uncorrelated errors concerning the costs and benefits associated with the government budget for, if this were so, then, on average, overestimates and underestimates would cancel. While they accept that voters make errors, they question whether, given the difficulty of understanding the government budget,

there will always be a bias in the direction of underestimation of costs. Moreover, they question the value of the public choice analysis in explaining changes in deficits. For example, why was there such an expansion of borrowing in the US in the 1980s? Was it really that 'fiscal illusion' had become more prolific in the US in the 1980s than in the 1970s? Also, how can cross-country differences be explained? Why are voters more illuded in some countries than in others? Buchanan and Wagner (1977) would suggest that different tax structures and different fiscal institutions explain differences in fiscal complexity and differences in illusion but Alessina and Perotti stress that there is no empirical evidence to support this.

Holcombe and Mills (1995) also note the comparatively recent growth of deficit finance in the US and, in assessing Buchanan and Wagner's (1977) identification of Keynesian principles, they also argue that 'a relatively small percentage of voters are familiar with Keynesian economic principles' (p. 62). They explain the growth in deficits in the US as resulting from the increased electoral security of incumbents in Congress which lowers their accountability to voters and relaxes the political constraint on deficit finance.

10.4 Tax reform

Tax reform is a subject that cuts across general disciplines and can have a number of motives. Approaches can be divided between (1) those following an implicit social optimality approach, looking at the pros and cons of a reform from the viewpoint of all affected individuals rather than reflecting sectional interests, (2) those looking to political philosophy, and (3) those, for example in the public choice tradition, who are sceptical of reform proposals, regarding them as an attempt at 'rent-seeking' (Buchanan 1987, Tullock 1988). The following examples correspond to these views.

10.4.1 Annual wealth tax

As an example of the first approach, the case of an annual wealth tax discussed in Sandford, Willis and Ironside (1975) can be considered. The volume they produced contains sections on economic perspectives, case studies from other countries and a series of nine chapters centring on the precise details and pitfalls of a possible wealth tax for the UK. (For these authors, wealth is the value of the stock of physical and financial assets held by an individual, company, asso-

Table 10.7 Objectives and structure of a wealth tax

	(1) Objectives	(2) Appropriate threshold	(3) Appropriate rates	(4) Ceiling	(5) Additive or substitutive
(a)	Efficiency	Low	Low: proportional or mildly progressive	None or 'notional'	Substitutive
(b)	Horizontal equity	Low	Low: proportional or mildly progressive	None or 'notional'	Substitutive
(c)	Reduction in inequality				
	(a) Limited (relative)	Could be high	Mildly progressive	High	Substitutive
	(b) Radical (absolute)	Could be high	Progressive	None or 'restricted'	Additive
(d)	Control	Low	Immaterial	Immaterial	Immaterial

Source: C. T. Sandford, J. R. M. Willis and D. J. Ironside, *An Annual Wealth Tax*, Heinemann, London, 1975 (with minor alterations). Reproduced with the permission of the Institute for Fiscal Studies, London.

ciation or institution less liabilities.) Table 10.7 provides a useful framework to structure the discussion. Column (1) deals with the objectives of a wealth tax and can be summarized as follows from the related paragraphs in their work.

1. Efficiency is discussed in relation to the wealth tax replacing some income tax or a projected increase in income taxes. Such a tax is seen as having lower disincentive effects than an income tax because it relates to past effort; i.e. there is no disincentive effect to work for additional income that is to be consumed. Second, the imposition of a wealth tax creates an incentive for wealth holders to seek money returns on their wealth (otherwise the tax generates a tax liability and no money income to meet it) and indeed to maximize them; for example, investment in valuable picture collections looks relatively unattractive. (High progressive rates would deter savings and investment, so low proportional or weakly progressive rates are advocated.)

2. Horizontal equity is met more nearly by a wealth tax than by a higher income tax rate on unearned income (income from property) or than on income from work. This is because the wealth base recognizes the additional economic power and hence taxable capacity offered by wealth ownership, even if no money income is derived, as for example with the ownership of jewels, or where an identical money income is secured from two very different capital values. The money income-less wealth holder is not in the same position as the money income-less street dweller. Again, a low wealth tax rate is suggested as a supplement to income tax.

3. Inequality reduction is treated at two levels. The first views a wealth tax as in paragraphs 1 or 2, as a way of capturing income, with the object under this heading being to reduce the feedback effect of large wealth holders enjoying higher incomes and therefore adding to their wealth by saving. This suggests the 'substitutive' wealth tax, which can be paid from income leaving wealth intact as opposed to the 'additive' wealth tax, which necessarily involves the sale of assets and corresponds to a strong aim of reducing wealth inequality. The views correspond to relative versus absolute wealth reduction and the implied rates can be seen from Table 10.7 and guessed easily.

4. Administrative control refers to the data that are gained by the presence of a wealth tax, enabling the cross-checking of statistics and facilitating good tax administration and reduced evasion.

The discussion in the original work is obviously much fuller than this, but here the interest is in the approach. Possible criteria are outlined and the implications of the criteria for thresholds, rates, ceilings and the tax type are presented. While the authors have a view, readers are given the options and the relevant costs and benefits. The authors are broadly following the 'textbook' approach to economic policy—setting up the 'facts of the situation', laying out the alternatives and predicting or assessing their likely consequences. Before considering another approach, it is interesting to note that the objectives broadly correspond to Sandmo's (1976) introductory discussion of what might be meant by an optimal tax with the efficiency (excess burdens) approach being identified with the economist, the equity considerations with the 'man in the street' and the 'control' point with the tax administrator's viewpoint. In this way the eclectic nature of the approach is clear.

10.4.2 Family taxation

This section is based on an article by Wilkinson (1982), which is very useful as it exposes the underlying ideologies/philosophies or interests that are at stake in this kind of reform. In particular, the author isolates three perspectives: conservative, radical and moderate. It is assumed that income taxation of the family unit should correspond to principles of 'ability to pay', i.e. horizontal equity and the minimization of 'excess burdens'. Essentially, in the UK the schedule of non-zero tax bands is the same for most individuals so that progression (a marginal tax rate that exceeds the average tax rate) is achieved by the exempt income band.

Traditionally, the tax system was constructed on the basis of a family with one 'breadwinner' and with the husband assumed to be that 'winner'. It offered married men a tax allowance of some one-and-a-half times the single person's allowance to which working wives were entitled. By the 1980s the increased labour force participation by women, combined with the desire for equity of married men and women, provided the spur to reform.

This suggested two elements of concern in the existing system. First, the 'aggregation' principle meant that on marriage the husband and wife were treated as a single tax unit, with any income earned by the wife being added to that of the husband for tax purposes. For most couples this made little difference in terms of tax actually paid, but, as feminists were quick to point out, it treated the wife as a dependant and not a separate entity. Relatedly, it afforded the wife no financial privacy (except by couples opting to be taxed as two single persons, which 'paid' financially only if the loss of the husband's allowance could be compensated for by a lower amount of income subject to a tax band higher than the basic rate). Secondly, the rationale of the married man's (husband's) allowance looked doubtful. Working wives had a single person's allowance in their own right and, while 'non-working' wives had no money income, it was felt that the imputed income from non-market home production needed to be part of the picture. The existence of economies of scale in family life (bulk buying, spreading fixed costs, etc.) means that, although two cannot live as cheaply as one (it seems to us at least), cohabitation means that a given per capita standard can be maintained for two at less than double the expenditure for one.

If anything, these considerations suggest that the 'allowance' was in the wrong direction. The 1980 Green Paper, *The Taxation of Husband and Wife*, had as a central proposal the scrapping of the married man's allowance to be replaced by a single person's allowance each for husband and wife. However, for a non-working partner this allowance could be partially or wholly transferable to the working partner; i.e. there was transferability of tax allowances. Against this background, Wilkinson explores the positions noted above.

Conservatives would like to preserve traditional family roles so that women are discouraged from market-based work. Whole or partial transferability encourages this, favouring in tax terms one-earner couples over two-earner couples. However, having a wife and protecting the traditional family are not quite the same thing, and the system is really an indiscriminate subsidy to all married men. If the object is to encourage mothers to stay at home, the use of child benefits would have been a superior policy. Furthermore, if the problem is seen to be women taking men's jobs, making them unemployed, the problem is one of macroeconomic policy, and is not to be solved by effectively concentrating it in a disguised fashion among non-working wives.

Moderates tend to favour single allowances that are non-transferable with a cash benefit payable for dependent children. (Note that tax allowances offer least to low-income individuals who may not be liable to tax and most to those paying the highest marginal tax rates.) This approach tends to have a neutral effect on a decision about whether to be part of home or market production, avoiding women's role being institutionalized as dependants.

Radicals fully recognize the point of the common phrase, 'can afford to have a wife and children at home'. Against this background of a wife who was willing to work on the market, the choice to work at home must involve a higher (or at least as high a) level of utility. That is, there is an imputed income that might be proxied by the market wage required to buy in the domestic work of the wife or, more appropriately, the necessary compensating variation (the minimum sum acceptable to compensate for the loss of the services of a non-(market) working wife). Radicals would end the married man's allowance, would tax 'imputed' income and would recycle the increased tax revenue as child benefits. Although this seems equitable, it is claimed that imputed income is not an everyday concept so that the tax of income that is not a money flow would be politically unpopular as it would have to be paid from the working partner's income. Of the three broad proposals considered, this would encourage women to work on the market. Political feasibility was adduced as one of the pluses of the moderate scheme of family tax reform.

In April 1990 reforms came into operation which addressed the first but not the second elements of concern outlined above. The element of sexism in the tax system was corrected to the extent that the income of the wife is now taxed independently so that her income is no longer viewed as belonging to her husband. However, there remained horizontal inequities in that married couples are entitled to the 'married couple's allowance' (equal to 0.6 of a single person's allowance (SA)), offering them tax gains compared with unmarried couples. Furthermore, two-earner couples enjoy greater allowances (2.6SA) than single-earner couples (1.6SA), a provision that dates from the Second World War when there was a policy to encourage married women to work. In a context in which the majority of married women now work and the reason for a single-earner couple is often related to having children, this looks inequitable to the extent that those with more responsibilities are less favourably treated (see Johnson and Stark 1990). Leaving the tax details aside, the importance of this example of tax reform approach is the clear way in which choices of tax system reflect the personal (political) philosophy that is held implicitly or explicitly by individuals.

The Institute of Fiscal Studies 'Green Budget 1996' (1995) points out that the often publicized fiscal incentives to marry, divorce or become a single parent are so small as to be only relevant at the margin of indifference in these choices—a situation that surely applies to very few. However there remains a significant point about the taxation of family in the light of falls in 'married couple's allowance' since 1990. The 'Green Budget 1996' study suggests there are two principles (implicit in the discussion above) that could be followed. Either joint taxation (the couple is treated as a single unit for tax purposes) or independent taxation (each partner is treated as an individual taxpayer) are the options analysed. The joint taxation principle leads back into the conservative approach above with fully transferable or partially transferable tax allowances between couples to minimize their tax liabilities. A reform in the other direction would be to move to fully independent taxation which would involve the removal of what is left from 'married couple's allowance' and the 'additional personal allowance' so that horizontal equity would be completely achieved in that post tax income would be the same for all taxpayers with identical pre-tax income. In this 'independent' scenario any help to families in difficult circumstances would be achieved by other means, e.g. raising child benefit. To repeat the point made above no system is free from an implied and explicit view as to the value of the family as an institution.

10.4.3 Tax reform movements: electic view

Sandford (1993) writes about the tax reform movement of the 1980s emphasizing the notion that many countries instituted widespread reforms of a very similar nature. The origins of the movement he associates with six arguments:

(i) the extent of tax avoidance, through the use of tax loopholes, and tax evasion was both widespread and growing undermining tax morality;

(ii) relatedly high marginal tax rates were not helping achieve equity as high income or wealthy individuals could easily circumvent the tax code and therefore the rates lacked a rationale;

(iii) estimates of the disincentive effects and welfare losses associated with the tax system suggested these impacts were significant;

(iv) almost global inflation meant that with largely non-indexed tax systems there was considerable 'fiscal-drag' redistributing income towards governments which were under the criticism of having overexpanded public sectors;

(v) increasing 'internationalization' of different economies meant countries had to follow the trend and adopt more similar tax regimes;

(vi) there was a change of philosophy in that the positive claims for planning and state intervention in market economies began to look unsupported so that a return to the market mechanism and the 'roll back' of large public sectors became popular.

Against this background the general nature of the widespread reforms (that broadly left tax revenues unchanged) seem reasonable. So that:

(a) broadening the personal and corporate income tax base and

(b) improved tax administration are consistent with (i)

(c) reductions in the rate of personal and corporate income taxes and

(d) fewer steps in the tax scale correspond to arguments (ii) and (iii)

(e) a change in the tax mix towards much greater reliance on indirect taxes especially VAT was given a considerable push by the requirements of actual and potential EC membership (point (vi))

(f) the tenor of most of arguments (i)–(vi) is either explicitly or implicitly consistent with a more right-wing then left-wing philosophy ('getting governments off the backs of people', 'no new taxes', 'getting incentives right', etc. became and to an extent remains

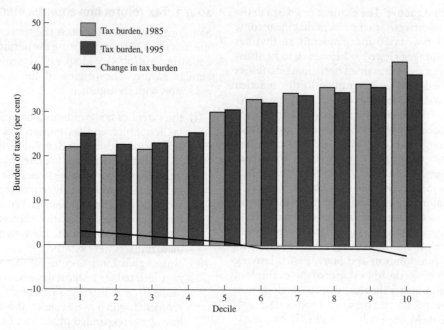

Figure 10.10 Proportions of income taken in personal tax, by decile.

Source: Giles and Johnson (1994) with permission of the Institute for Fiscal Studies.

the 'sound bite' phrases of the day). The converse of this emphasis on the efficiency properties of the market economy is a decreased interest in equity as a motivating force in taxing (and spending).

How closely does the UK pattern of tax reform reflect these general characteristics? An answer can be found in Giles and Johnson (1994). Table 10.8 documents the main tax changes over the decade since the mid-1980s when the Sandford tax reform movement was mainly observed. The money values in the figures are in 1993 constant prices, i.e. they are corrected for inflation. The general pattern of lowering income tax rates and the switch towards indirect taxation is indicated by the direction of the arrows. The net revenue effects indicated in the last column confirm the switch of emphasis. The major changes not included in the table are those related to corporation tax. As regards the progressivity (equity) impacts of the tax changes Fig. 10.10 is instructive. Here the continuous black line sloping downwards illustrates a regressive change between 1985 and 1995 and the fact that it crosses the bottom axis from positive to negative values indicates more tax being paid by the lower-income deciles and less by the upper-ones. As indicated in Table 10.8 there has been some reduction in the overall amount of tax paid; however, the net gainers have been those with high incomes and the losers

at the bottom. It is the switch from progressive direct taxation to regressive indirect taxation that causes this effect. Although it must be noted that from the second decile onwards the overall tax system remains progressive it is difficult to escape the conclusion that equity has not been a motivating force in the changes. Sandford comments on the tax reform movement noting: 'With hardly an exception, vertical equity, if it entered at all, was seen as a constraint rather than an objective' (Sandford 1993, p. 22). Whilst the picture painted by the statistics so far conforms with the tax reform movement argument, their authors Giles and Johnson (1994) put a more pragmatic interpretation on the tax events they describe. They point out that between 1985 and 1990 the economy was growing and therefore tax revenues were buoyant, facilitating massive tax cuts mainly in the form of income tax rate reductions. However, the recession of the early 1990s increased the PSBR considerably signalling that tax revenues would have to be increased. The two, mainly indirect tax increasing, UK budgets of 1993 are then viewed as the response to recessionary effects reversing the initial tax cuts. There is agreement that the change in the balance of sources of tax revenues did sum to 'substantial reform' but as described it looks less like a coherent strategy than perhaps is implied by Sandford.

Table 10.8 Main tax changes between 1985 and 1995

	1985		1995	Net revenue effects (£ billion raised)	
Income tax					
Basic rate	30%	↓	25%	−10.3	
Highest rate	60%	↓	40%	−3.8	
Lowest rate	30%	↓	20%	−3.5	
Personal allowance	£3,445	=	£3,445	1.9	Other income tax
MCA level	£1,950	↓	£1,720	2.5	MCA restriction
MCA rate	Marginal rate		15%		
Basic rate limit	£25,300	↓	£23,700		
MIRAS ceiling	£46,800	↓	£30,000	3.2	MIRAS reductions
MIRAS rate	Marginal rate		15%		
National Insurance contributions					
Main rate	9%	↑	10%	−1.3	
Indirect taxes					
VAT rate	15%	↑	17.5%	2.7	
VAT rate on domestic fuel	0%	↑	17.5% ⎫		
Excise duty on a gallon of petrol	£1.27	↑	£1.69 ⎪		
Excise duty on 20 cigarettes	£0.81	↑	£1.13 ⎬	4.2	
Excise duty on a pint of beer	£0.28	↓	£0.24 ⎪		
Excise duty on a bottle of wine	£1.15	↓	£1.01 ⎪		
Excise duty on a bottle of spirits	£7.38	↓	£5.55 ⎭		
Local tax changes				−1.1	
Insurance tax				0.3	
			Total	−5.2	

Source: Giles and Johnson (1994) with permission of the Institute for Fiscal Studies.

10.4.4 Tax reform: public choice view

Tullock (1988) defines rent-seeking as 'using resources to gain rents for people where the rents themselves come from something with *negative social value*' (p. 37; emphasis ours). (See the discussion on rent-seeking in chapter 5.) Tax reform, essentially about changes to the tax code to meet an efficiency criterion, is argued by Tullock to have two other characteristics as viewed by the ordinary individual: first, that a tax reform is about taxes going down, and second, that it is about the closing of loopholes, since they are viewed as mechanisms allowing the rich to avoid taxes (a distribution/equity motive as compared with the resource efficiency argument of economic theory outlined in chapters 7 and 8). Lott (1988) questions Tullock's definition of rent-seeking, seeing as unhelpful the attempt to tie it to whether or not its consequences are improvements. He considers the notion of the 'competition to obtain rents' (p. 48). Whatever the rights and wrongs of this particular definitional dispute, there is clearly some purchase in the approach.

Buchanan (1987), not surprisingly, provides an example. He offers a public choice model of the US 1986 tax changes, which involved both rate reduction and base broadening for individual and corporate taxpayers with overall the same revenue being raised. While acknowledging that there may be a combination of tax broadening and rate reductions that raises the utility of all, he sees this as unlikely. This consensus approach is then compared with a Downsian median voter set-up in which three groups are identified: those with lower tax payments and higher utility; the median group, i.e. those with higher tax payments and higher utility (because of reduced excess burdens); and those with higher tax payments and lower utility. Here tax legislation can be seen as reflecting majority preferences, with the trick being that the tax reduction accompanying the broader base must be sufficient to induce a higher utility level for the median group. The shortcoming is that no role is assigned to political agents, who are seen as maximizing rents subject to legal and re-election constraints. Rents are seen as positively correlated with the level of public expenditure and the frequency of changes in finance and expenditure patterns.

With expenditure maximization, most individuals should be at the highest point on the individual Laffer curves (point 3 on *ILC* in Fig. 10.11), with some

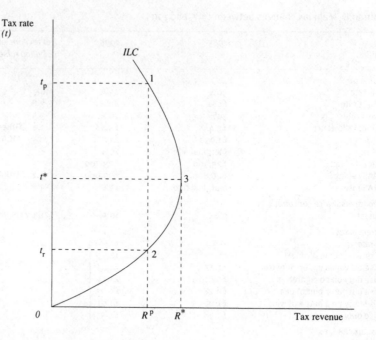

Figure 10.11 Frequent tax reform as revenue maximization.

beyond the maximum facing, say, tax rate t_p at point 1, generating revenue R_p. The 1986 reforms are seen as interim adjustments needed to relocate individuals on the upward-sloping part of their tax rate–tax revenue curves, making them ripe for the 'fleecing' of more revenue in the future. It is a process of moving this group from point 1 to 2 by lowering the tax rate to t_r, preserving revenue at R_p and subsequently increasing the tax rate to t^*, raising maximum revenue R^* at point 3. The closing of political loopholes in the short run offers possible rents in the future, as renegotiation between political agents occurs over the longer period.

The lesson for rent-seekers in this scenario is that a change is better than a rest. The normative evaluation of the reforms is seen as ambiguous as the broader base, reducing excess burdens, offers a plus that has to be offset against the optimistic fiscal illusion ('tax-free' public expenditure) induced by the switch from visible income tax to less visible corporation tax.

The brief accounts of tax reform here provide views of reform that are motivated by an attempt to secure 'welfare'-improving changes, impose a particular political philosophy, or an attempt to pursue rent-seeking by political agents. While it is tempting to suggest that all proposed or actual tax reforms contain elements of all these perspectives, the major point is that these authors take a different view as to what (predominantly) motivates tax reform.

10.5 Summary

The basic concepts considered in this chapter introduced the distinctions made in tax applications and pointed out some of the issues of definition. Tax systems are usually designed independently of the purposes for which the finance is raised. From the point of view of economic theory, it is desirable that the tax system reflect both efficiency and equity considerations. Under the heading of 'Tax theory and tax practice' an overview of the basic UK taxes was provided and each tax was briefly featured in turn. A different aspect of each tax was generally given emphasis to avoid repetition (and hence to introduce a wider variety of considerations relevant to a tax discussion and analysis). There were:

Personal income taxation—the shape of the budget constraint in more complex tax contexts
National insurance contributions—marginal and average tax rates and 'traps'
Excise taxes—revenue raising versus resource allocation
Value added tax—tax shifting, calculation and compliance costs of taxes
Corporation tax—the basis for a tax liability
Capital taxation—capturing non-income aspects of economic power

Taxation in aggregate—describing overall tax systems
Debt finance—burdens and visibility

In the final section tax reform proposals were summarized, with three different perspectives illustrating that different economists and commentators take different positions and perspectives. Traditional social optimality analysis, political philosophy and rent-seeking approaches all have something to offer but do not lend themselves to ready synthesis into an overview. Finally it is worth noting that Johnson and Stark (1993) highlight how easy it is for political parties to present tax information in a way that will foster voting support. They note that the impact of any tax change could be assessed with respect to:

(i) the system of taxation currently in place;

(ii) the system of taxation that would obtain if it was updated for inflation, i.e. an indexed tax system;

(iii) the proposals of political opponents.

With different possible comparitors, different units of analysis (individuals or families or households) it is all too easy to make almost anything look the case (making for low-quality public debate).

References

Alessina, A. and Perotti R. (1995) 'Political Economy of Budget Deficits,' *International Monetary Fund Staff Papers*, **42**, 1, pp. 1–31.

Atkinson, A. B. (1977) 'Optimal Taxation and the Direct versus Indirect Tax Controversy', *Canadian Journal of Economics*, **10**, 4, pp. 590–606.

Atkinson, A. B. and Stiglitz, J. E. (1980) *Lectures on Public Economics*. New York: McGraw-Hill.

Barro, R. J. (1974) 'Are Government Bonds Net Worth', *Journal of Political Economy*, **82**, 6, pp. 1095–117.

Barro, R. J. (1987) 'Government Spending, Interest Rates and Prices, and Budget Deficits in the United Kingdom, 1701–1918', *Journal of Monetary Economics*, **20**, 2, pp. 221–47.

Barro, R. J. (1989) 'The Ricardian Approach to Budget Deficits', *Journal of Economic Perspectives*, **3**, 2, pp. 37–54.

Bernheim, B. D. (1987) 'Ricardian Equivalence: An Evaluation of Theory and Evidence', pp. 263–304 in *Macroeconomics Annual*, vol. 2. Washington DC: National Bureau of Economic Research.

Blundell, R. (1992) 'Labour Supply and Taxation: a Survey', *Fiscal Studies*, **13**, 3, pp. 15–40.

Bowen, H. R. (1943) 'The Interpretation of Voting in the Allocation of Economic Resources', *Quarterly Journal of Economics*, **58**, 1, pp. 27–48.

Bowen, W. G., Davis, R. and Kopf, D. (1960) 'The Public Debt: A Burden on Future Generations?', *American Economic Review*, **50**, 4, 701–6.

Brennan, H. G. and Buchanan, J. M. (1987) 'The Logic of the Ricardian Equivalence Theorem', pp. 79–92 in J. M. Buchanan, C. K. Rowley and R. D. Tollison (eds.), *Deficits*. Oxford: Basil Blackwell.

Brown, C. V. (1968) 'Misconceptions about Income Tax and Incentives', *Scottish Journal of Political Economy*, **15**, pp. 1–21.

Brown, C. V. (ed.) (1981) *Taxation and Labour Supply*. London: Allen & Unwin.

Browning, E. K. and Browning, J. M. (1983) *Public Finance and the Price System*, 2nd edn. New York: Macmillan.

Browning, E. G. and Browning, J. M. (1991) *Microeconomic Theory and Applications*, 4th edn. New York: Harper Collins.

Buchanan, J. M. (1958) *Public Principles of Public Debt*. Homewood, Ill.: Richard D. Irwin.

Buchanan, J. M. (1965) *The Demand and Supply of Public Goods*. Chicago: Rand McNally.

Buchanan, J. M. (1969) *Cost and Choice: An Inquiry into Economic Theory*. Chicago: Markham.

Buchanan, J. M. (1987) 'Tax Reform as Political Choice', *Economic Perspectives*, **1**, 1, pp. 29–35.

Buchanan, J. M. (1989) 'The Political Economy of the Budget Deficit', pp. 1–12 in J. M. Buchanan, (ed.), *Essays on the Political Economy*. Honolulu: University of Hawaii Press.

Buchanan, J. M. and Wagner, R. E. (1977) *Democracy in Deficit: the Political Legacy of Lord Keynes*. New York: Academic Press.

Buchanan, J. M. and Wagner, R. E. (1978) *Fiscal Responsibility in Constitutional Democracy*. Boston: Leiden.

Chan, L. K. C. (1983) 'Uncertainty and the Neutrality of Government Financing Policy', *Journal of Monetary Economics*, **11**, 3, pp. 351–72.

Cooper, J. (1988) 'The Burden of the Public Debt: A Review', *South African Journal of Economics*, **56**, 4, pp. 278–91.

Cullis, J. G. and Jones, P. R. (1987) *Microeconomics and the Public Economy: A Defence of Leviathan*. Oxford: Basil Blackwell.

Dilnot, A., Kay, J. and Morris, N. (1984) 'The UK Tax System, Structure and Progressivity, 1948–1982', *Scandinavian Journal of Economics*, **86**, 2, pp. 150–65.

Evans, P. (1986) 'Is the Dollar High Because of Large Budget Deficits?', *Journal of Monetary Economics*, **18**, 3, pp. 227–49.

Feldstein, M. S. (1982) 'Government Deficits and Aggregate Demand', *Journal of Monetary Economics*, **9**, 2, pp. 1–20.

Giles, C. and Johnson, P. (1994) 'Tax Reform in the UK and Changes in Progressivity of the Tax System, 1985–95', *Fiscal Studies*, **15**, 3, pp. 64–86.

Godfrey, C. and Maynard, A. (1988) 'Economic Aspects of Tobacco Use and Taxation Policy', *British Medical Journal*, 297, pp. 339–43.

Hausman, J. A. (1985) 'Taxes and Labour Supply', pp. 213–64 in A. J. Auerbach and M. Feldstein (eds.), *Handbook of Public Economics*, vol. 1. Amsterdam: North-Holland.

Healey, N. M. (1989) 'Should the US Budget Deficit be Cut?', *Economic Review*, 7, 2, pp. 24–31.

Holcombe, R. G. and Mills, J. A. (1995) 'Politics and Deficit Finance', *Public Finance Quarterly*, 23, 4, pp. 448–56.

Hoover, K. D. (1994) *The New Classical Macroeconomics*. Oxford: Basil Blackwell.

Institute for Fiscal Studies (1995) *Institute of Fiscal Studies Options for 1996: The Green Budget*. London: Institute for Fiscal Studies.

James, S., Lewis, A. and Allison, F. (1987) *The Comprehensibility of Taxation*. Aldershot: Avebury.

Johnson, P. and Stark, G. (1990) 'The Taxation of Husband and Wife', *Economic Review*, 7, 3, pp. 27–8.

Johnson, P. and Stark, G. (1993) 'Assessing the Impact of Tax Changes', *Fiscal Studies*, 14, 3, pp. 131–40.

Kay, J. K. and King, M. A. (1983) *The British Tax System*, 3rd edn. Oxford: Oxford University Press.

Killingsworth, M. R. (1983) *Labour Supply*. Cambridge: Cambridge University Press.

Kormendi, R. C. (1985) 'Does Deficit Financing Affect Economic Growth? Cross Country Evidence', *Journal of Banking and Finance Supplement; Studies in Banking and Finance*, 2, pp. 243–55.

Lerner, A. P. (1948) 'The Burden of the National Debt', in L. A. Metzler *et al.* (ed.), *Income, Employment and Public Policy: Essays in Honor of Alvin H. Hansen*. New York: W. W. Norton.

Lewis, A. (1978) 'Perception of Tax Rates', *British Tax Review*, 6, pp. 358–66.

Lewis, A. (1982) *The Psychology of Taxation*. Oxford: Martin Robertson.

Lipford, J. W. and Dougan, W. R. (1995) 'A Public Choice-Theoretic Test of Ricardian Equivalence', *Public Finance Quarterly*, 23, 4, pp. 591–602.

Lott, J. R. (1988) 'Some Thoughts on Tullock's New Definition of Rent Seeking', *Contemporary Policy Issues*, 6, 4, pp. 48–9.

Merriman, D. (1994) 'Do Cigarette Excise Tax Rates Maximise Revenue', *Economic Inquiry*, 32, pp. 419–28.

Mintz, J. (1995) 'The Corporation Tax: A Survey', *Fiscal Studies*, 16, 4, pp. 23–68.

Mishan, E. J. (1963) 'How to Make a Burden of the Public Debt', *Journal of Political Economy*, 71, pp. 529–42.

Mueller, D. (1989) *Public Choice II*. Cambridge University Press: Cambridge, 1989.

Musgrave, R. A. and Musgrave, P. B. (1989) *Public Finance in Theory and Practice*, 5th edn. New York: McGraw-Hill.

Neuberg, L. G. (1989) *Conceptual Anomolies in Economics and Statistics: The Negative Income Tax Experiments*. Cambridge: Cambridge University Press.

Niskanen, W. A. (1978) 'Deficits, Government Spending and Inflation', *Journal of Monetary Economics*, 4, 3, pp. 591–602.

Niskanen, W. A. (1992) 'The Case for a New Fiscal Constitution', *Journal of Economic Perspectives*, 6, 2, pp. 13–24.

O'Driscoll, G. P. Jr. (1977) 'The Ricardian Non-equivalence Theorem', *Journal of Political Economy*, 85, 1, pp. 207–10.

Parkin, M. and King, D. (1992) *Economics*. Addison Wesley: Wokingham.

Pechman, J. A. (ed.) (1987) *Comparative Tax Systems: Europe, Canada and Japan*. Arlington, Va.: Tax Analysts.

Ricardo, D. (1951) *The Principles of Political Economy and Taxation Works and Correspondence*, vol. 1, ed. P. Sraffa. Cambridge: Cambridge University Press.

Ricketts, M. (1981) 'Tax Theory and Tax Policy', pp. 31–46 in A. T. Peacock and F. Forte (eds.), *The Political Economy of Taxation*. Oxford: Basil Blackwell.

Rosen, H. S. (1988) *Public Finance*, 2nd edn. Homewood Ill.: Irwin.

Sandford, C. T. (1993) *Successful Tax Reform*. Bath: Fiscal Publications.

Sandford, C. T., Godwin, M. R. and Hardwick, P. J. W. (1989) *Administrative and Compliance Costs of Taxation*. Bath: Fiscal Publications.

Sandford, C. T., Willis, J. R. M. and Ironside, D. J. (1975) *An Annual Wealth Tax*. London: Heinemann for the Institute for Fiscal Studies.

Sandmo, A. (1976) 'Optimal Taxation: An Introduction to the Literature', *Journal of Public Economics*, 6, 1, 2, pp. 37–54.

Seater, J. J. (1992) 'Ricardian Equivalence', *Journal of Economic Literature*, 31, 1, pp. 142–90.

Slemrod, J. (1994) 'Three Challenges for Public Finance', *International Tax and Public Finance*, 1, 2, pp. 189–95.

Smith, A. (1776) *The Wealth of Nations*. New York: Random House, 1937.

Tridimas, G. (1992) 'Budgetary Deficits and Government Expenditure Growth: Toward a More Accurate Empirical Specification', *Public Finance Quarterly*, 20, 3, pp. 275–302.

Tullock, G. (1988) 'Rent Seeking and Tax Reform', *Contemporary Policy Issues*, 6, 4, pp. 37–47.

Ulph, D. (1987) 'Tax Cuts—Will they Work?', *Economic Review*, 4, 4, pp. 35–9.

West, E. G. (1975) 'Public Debt Burden and Cost Theory', *Economic Inquiry*, 13, 2, pp. 179–90.

Wilkinson, M. (1982) 'The Discriminatory System of Personal Taxation: Some Proposals for Reform', *Journal of Social Policy*, 11, 3, pp. 307–34.

11 Public choice aspects of macroeconomic policies

11.1 Introduction

In traditional public finance texts, a considerable proportion of chapters were devoted to fiscal policy in a macro context. This can be justified by the fact that Keynesianism was the accepted dominant macro-intellectual tradition and that in this tradition a key role, if not *the* key role, is government manipulation of fiscal policy weapons to achieve economy-wide targets. In the 1960s, 1970s and 1980s many macroeconomists have seen different lights on the road to an economic Damascus. Each has attracted his or her share of supporters who could also see the light once it was pointed out to them. Some theories have enjoyed more academic success than success in terms of policy adoption, while others have been very influential at the policy level but not within the circles of academic economists.

Given that there has been no consensus at the academic level about the superior way to model the macroeconomy, the best way forward, with regard to the role of government in the macro world, is to review its significance in the context of different schools of thought. It can be noted that the 'Keynesian' perspective has links with the social optimality approach to public finance as it incorporates market (economy) failure and hence a role for government. The other perspectives of 'monetarism'—'new classical' and 'supply side'—have found more favour with the public choice school with its University of Chicago connections. In this way, the contrast of view that is a theme of the microeconomics chapters is sustained in this macroeconomics one.

There is also a second sense in which the theme of the other chapters is sustained here. The social optimality approach models government as a benign and unselfinterested neutral actor in the way in which it takes macroeconomic decisions. The public choice school, however, sees individuals in government as self-interested actors in their own right. In this setting the government is not the referee in the macro economic game judging the winner of the struggle between competing schools of macro thought rather it is one of the key players. As a player the government has at least two sources of utility. Following Frey (1978) one is ideological. Certain schools of thought are more attractive to some ideologies than others (the implications of Keynesianism are other things equal more attractive to those on the left of the political spectrum than to those on the right). The second is instrumental in that governments only have power in democracies when they can command a majority of voters at an election. This raises the question of vote maximizing macroeconomic policy. In this chapter we address these two sources of utility to those in government. With respect to the details of the macroeconomic theories characterized (characatured!) here readers should look to explicit macroeconomic texts, e.g. Blanchard and Fischer (1989), Leslie (1993).

11.2 Macro theories, policies and political incentives

Once the public choice perspective is introduced, a relevant question becomes, What is in each theory for the political actors? They are not neutral with respect to what is seen to be the current orthodoxy. Some theories endorse their own ideologies while others do not. Taking each in turn, their basic tenets and relative political attractions can be highlighted. At the risk of oversimplification,[1] only four 'schools of thought' are discussed: the Keynesians, the monetarists, the 'new classicals' and the supply-siders. Their typical profiles are summarized in Table 11.1.

[1] Cross (1982), for example, discusses four 'brands' of Keynesianism. Also see Cross (1991).

Table 11.1 Macro schools of thought

	Keynesian	Monetarist	New classical	Supply-siders
Attitude to monetary and fiscal policy	Discretionary intervention advocated, especially fiscal policy	Opposed to discretionary intervention but if adopted effective policy is monetary-based	No systematic economic policy can alter the real course of the economy	Minimize the distortionary impact of fiscal policy in markets
Position advocated	Discretionary policy to 'fine-tune' the economy	Stable monetary rule	Any stable economic policy will have the same effect	Low tax rates, tight monetary stance
'View of world'	Emphasis on the short run: people live in the short run and it is possible to reduce economic misery	Emphasis on the long run: while recognizing short-run disequilibrium, doubt ability of government to improve the situation	The short run equals the long run because the economy is (apart from unanticipated events) always in its equilibrium configuration: there are no policies that can improve the speed of adjustment in the economy	Change tax-transfer provisions to affect individuals' actions
Political implications	Government intervention of an extensive kind with short-run policy action; major role for government	Minimum government and little discretion with economic policy; small and inactive role for government	Implies stable government policy to reflect long-run growth pattern	'Get government off the backs of the people' by decreasing taxation
Public choice	Keynesian budget deficits a 'terrible legacy'	More attractive because it limits the discretionary action of government (and the absolute size of its intervention)		

11.2.1 The Keynesian tradition

The Keynesian tradition, at least in its popular form, is a short-run aggregate demand-driven analysis which suggests that there is no reason to suppose that the equilibrium level of output consistent with total planned spending will be consistent with full employment in the labour market. Deflationary and inflationary gaps can be closed by discretionary monetary and/or fiscal policy. With the ability to learn from past policy mistakes, Keynesians often argue for 'fine-tuning' of the economy to avoid the misery of unemployment and inflation, with more benefits (and hence weight) being associated with the relief of unemployment. The emphasis in this tradition is very much on the limitations of the market mechanism. Disequilibrium is seen as the order of the day, with markets on the real side (goods and services, labour) being slow to adjust. If prices are moving only slowly towards their equilibrium values, then they are currently 'too high' or 'too low', and in either case too few transactions will take place. If prices are 'too high', demand is choked off, and if 'too low', supply is choked off. The short side of the market is said to dominate. Given this view of market allocation, there is no incentive to 'respect' the market and intervention is fully justified.

The market for labour may be a convenient way to separate the schools of thought. Figure 11.1 has four panels. In part (a) the demand and supply of labour for the economy is depicted. The real wage rate is on the y axis and the quantity of labour is on the x axis. The demand for labour is its marginal product (derived from the aggregate production function in part (b)). The supply curve represents the outcome of the income-leisure choices of individuals who are utility-maximizing. At the equilibrium point 1 the real wage is W_1/P_1 and L_1 is the quantity of labour employed generating Y_1 of real output. The 45° line in part (c) projects this level of output to part (d), where the level of output at the price level P_1 can be plotted. With different price levels it is possible to derive the level of output that will obtain and hence an aggregate supply curve is derived. If the price level rises to P_2 (falls to P_0) when the nominal wage remains constant, the real wage falls (rises). If on the other hand all prices, including wages, rise or fall together, the nominal wage will rise to W_2 (fall to W_0), leaving the real wage unchanged and equilibrium in the labour market (and the level of output) completely unaffected—a completely inelastic aggregate supply curve AS.

The Keynesian tradition in particular does not view W and P as moving completely in sympathy. Wages are seen as flexible upwards but 'sticky' downwards, so

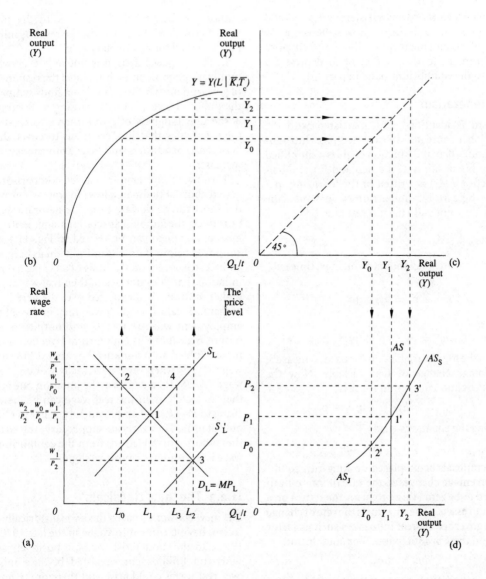

Figure 11.1 Derivation of an aggregate supply curve.

that rises in P cannot decrease the real wage rate but falls in P can increase it (illustrated in Fig. 11.1 as W_1/P_0). Downwardly sticky wages gives a J shape to the AS curve, labelled AS_J, with the curve beginning at the existing price level P_1. A further combination is possible if wages are 'sticky' upwards (for whatever reason) and price level P_2 lowers the real wage rate. The double-'sticky' case yields the positively sloped AS curve throughout its length, labelled AS_S in the figure.

It is AS_J that is usually attributed to the Keynesians. Nominal wages that will not fall allowing situations where the real wage gets too high to clear the market. With no inherent mechanism to correct this disequilibrium outcome, the economy can stay on the lower curve of the J with considerable unemployment; i.e. with the real wage W_1/P_0 the economy might stick at $2'$ on AS_J in part (d) with L_0–L_3 unemployed in part (a). Increasing aggregate demand along AS_J with expansionary fiscal policy—lower taxes, raised government expenditures on transfers and goods and services—looks attractive as it moves the economy towards full employment at $1'$. The implied price level rise from P_0 to P_1 is sufficient to depress the real wage to the equilibrium value in part (a).

11.2.2 Monetarism

Monetarism is identified and associated with the work of Nobel Laureate Milton Friedman. Introducing the money demand function enables a simplified account of his position. If the demand for real balances function (M_d) is written in the following specific form where M_n is nominal money demand, P the price level Y output and i the interest rate,

$$(11.1) \qquad M_d = \frac{M_n}{P} = Y^h i^{-j}$$

then, taking natural logs and introducing a time subscript,

$$(11.2) \qquad m_{nt} - p_t = hy_t - ji_t$$

and

$$(11.3) \qquad m_{nt} = hy_t - ji_t + p_t$$

Changes in the log of variables can be used to measure the percentage change of that variable. Now the equivalent equation for period $t + 1$ is

$$(11.4) \qquad m_{n(t+1)} = hy_{t+1} - ji_{t+1} + p_{t+1}$$

Differencing the equations yields

$$(11.5) \qquad dm_n = hdy - jdi + dp$$

With the emphasis being placed on long-run equilibrium, percentage changes in the rate of interest can be expected to be zero (i is a proxy for the return on a wide range of assets). The dy term is the rate of change of output governed by real influences such as factor supplies and their productivities. For equilibrium,

$$(11.6) \qquad dm_s = dm_n$$

where dm_s is the rate of change of the nominal money supply set by the monetary authorities. Substituting,

$$(11.7) \qquad dm_s = hdy + dp$$

or

$$dp = dm_s - hdy$$

This is the familiar result that the rate of change of prices, i.e. the inflation rate, is the difference between the rate of growth of the money supply and the rate of growth of the demand for money for transaction purposes. (dy is the natural or equilibrium rate of growth of output and h is the income elasticity of demand for nominal cash balances.) In the long run, if the rate of growth of the money supply set by the

authorities outstrips that warranted by the 'natural' rate of growth of the economy, the result is inflation; hence the call for a 'monetary rule'.

In this respect inflation is not only everywhere a monetary phenomenon, but is also the responsibility of government. This is a chord that finds sympathy in the public choice school. According to Friedman, it is the unwillingness of governments to tax-finance their activities that induces them to cover the gap between expenditures and taxes with money supply increases.

Turning to the labour market comparison suggested above, Friedman allows for rates of growth in the short run to deviate from the natural rate. This introduces the famous expectations-augmented Phillips curve, which can be related to Fig. 11.1 and is employed below. If unions or individuals bargain for, and receive, wages on the basis of an expected rate of inflation that does not occur, then real wages will be higher or lower than expected over the period of the bargain. If real wages are lower, then in the short run employment will rise to OL_2 and output to Y_2; i.e. output rises above its equilibrium level because people are 'fooled' into thinking they are working for real wage W_4/P_1 when they are actually working for real wage W_1/P_2. If, in contrast, the inflation rate is lower than expected, then the real wage can be viewed as rising to W_1/P_0 and employment will fall to OL_0 and output to Y_0. The aggregate supply curve traced out by these short-run deviations from the equilibrium real wage is AS_s and has a positive slope.

11.2.3 The 'new classicals'

The 'new classicals' macro theory is historically fairly recent, having come into vogue in the late 1970s and 1980s. In the monetarist world, a positively sloped short-run Phillips curve existed because mistakes over real wages could arise and therefore temporary deviations from equilibrium existed. In the long run the Phillips curve is vertical because consistent expectations and outturns are established so that the equilibrium real wage and the natural rate of output obtain. For the 'new classicals' there are no systematic mistakes, and the long-run equilibrium position is always established except for random errors. This powerful and eyecatching result is obtained by postulating a world in which:

1. all prices, including wages, are perfectly flexible upwards and downwards;

2. economic agents suffer no systematic misperceptions, money illusions, etc., so it is the unforeseen

and unexpected that have influence on the economy;

3. economic agents can be modelled as if they simultaneously employ an economic model of the economy and use all available information, the expected marginal benefits of which equal or exceed its marginal cost, to make predictions about economic outcomes.

In this 'rational expectations' type of world (see Sheffrin 1983) everyone can rapidly appreciate both the consequences of economic policy and the fact that the underlying equilibrium values for real variables will be unaltered by policy. Once again, returning to part (a) in Fig 11.1 there will be no deviations from the equilibrium value of the real wage rate: any price changes will be appropriately compensated for by wage changes and OL_1 individuals will be employed producing Y_1 level of output, irrespective of the price level. The aggregate supply curve AS is vertical in the short run as well as in the long run, so the 'natural' rate of employment (and hence unemployment) and output are always achieved as long as changes can be foreseen and are expected. The incomplete, sluggish and/or mistaken adjustments to changing economic signals that can be found in the Keynesian and monetarist short-run situations are removed from the new classical world by economic agents' incentives and their ability to use full information to adjust to any new configuration of nominal variables as rapidly as possible. Any attempt, for example, to engineer a rate of unemployment except that associated with the natural rate of output Y_1 will be thwarted. If the government increases the money supply to increase the price level to engineer a fall in the real wage, actors can be expected to be fully aware of this and hence to adjust the nominal wage so that no real purchase on the economy can be obtained. As noted above, there can be exceptions to the vertical aggregate supply curve when changes are unanticipated.

With stable macro policies of either a monetary or a fiscal kind, rational expectations on behalf of economic agents mean that such agents fully appreciate the signals that trigger government policy and the prescriptions that follow, internalizing this into their behaviour. Apart from making random forecasting errors, the only way to affect real variables is to continually surprise people by deliberately fostering 'unstable' macro policies; but this is counterproductive.

With the inability of stable monetary and/or fiscal policy to alter the real course of the economy, it is the determinants of the 'natural rates' that are the source of concern, and this is where the supply-siders would say they come in; by highlighting the way existing government policy provisions affect utility-maximizing choices, they concern themselves with the location of the various functions involved.

11.2.4 Supply-side economics

Supply-side economics is probably the perspective that had least credibility academically but most credibility politically. After all, by conforming with the prejudices of many voters, it must offer something close to a 'dream' economic platform for the politicians.

The recipe of supply-side economics can be illustrated by reference to Fig. 11.2. Suppose the wage rate for the economy is W_0; then at the individual level in Fig. 11.2(a) the equilibrium income leisure choice is at point 1. This is associated at the macro level with an overall income level $Y_a(W_0)$ and, given a zero tax rate (in our example, for simplicity, the tax rate t is a proportional one so that average and marginal tax rates coincide), the level of recorded income will be close to if not identical with it at $Y_r(W_0)$. With the introduction of higher tax rates t_1, t_2 and t_3, the effect is to move the equilibrium income leisure choice to points 2, 3 and 4 respectively. Initially, the income effect of the taxes makes the individual 'buy' less of all normal goods including leisure. Work-hours increase and the actual level of income rises. At all points, however, the substitution effect associated with taxes makes the opportunity cost of leisure less. More leisure hours are taken. The relative strengths of the income and substitution effects dictate the outcome. The tax rate where actual income is maximized is t_a^* in part (b) of the figure. With higher marginal tax rates the incentive to evade and not declare income increases, so that the discrepancy between actual and recorded income widens as t increases. The lower tax rate t_r^* is the tax rate at which recorded income is maximized.

Tax revenue is the product of the tax rate and recorded income, and this generates the Laffer curve, LC_r in Fig. 11.2(c). The Laffer curve LC_a in the same part of the diagram relates to actual income. Note that the products tY_r and tY_a are not maximized where $Y_a(W_0)$ and $Y_r(W_0)$ are maximized, because over a range a bigger share of a smaller income will represent a higher total tax revenue than a smaller share of a larger income.

Laffer argued that with a high tax rate, say t_3, a move to a lower one, say t_2, would raise actual income,

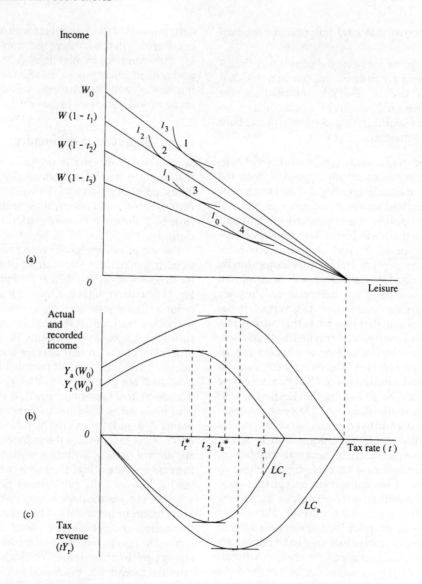

Figure 11.2 The Laffer-supply-side position.

recorded income and tax revenue. Getting the government 'off the backs of the people' by offsetting the incentives to leisure and evasion would offer something for everyone. The government would have more to spend, at the same time as real output would have risen offsetting unemployment. If the rise in real output takes place against a background of a tight money or explicit 'monetarist' policy, there will be downward pressure on the inflation rate and an already attractive package is further enhanced.

While the logical steps in the argument are acceptable, there are a number of difficulties. Not least

among these is that you have to be beyond the peak of the Laffer curve to begin with. The account of Buchanan and Lee (1982), relying on the distinction between short-run and long-run Laffer curves in this respect, is crucial (see chapter 16). In terms of Fig. 11.1 'supply-side' macroeconomics can be viewed as shifting the aggregate supply curve to the right. The evidence of labour supply responses to tax cuts is that they are undramatic (see chapter 10). If they are to occur, it is likely to be in the long run when economic actors can adjust to the new situation. In the short run it is generally argued that tax cuts will simply stimulate aggregate demand and, with aggregate supply largely unaffected, will be inflationary. Such a consideration raises the prospect of having to run a surplus budget at the same time as cutting taxes. It is the difference between the expected short-run and long-run consequences of macroeconomic policy changes that leads into the instrumental attraction of different macroeconomic policies as opposed to schools of thought. The focus being not so much on which macro 'school of thought' is ideologically attractive, but rather on what macro actions will capture the voters. In this sense the literature discussed next is about the political process and macroeconomics rather than macroeconomics *per se.*

11.3 Political business cycles

The presence or absence of political business cycles is an area of contention in the realm of macroeconomic policy. The basic idea is a simple one and follows in the Downsian vote-maximizing tradition, suggesting that those in office, conscious of election dates, manipulate the economy to achieve political popularity. The cost of such actions is that individual welfare is lowered by such manipulation. Broadly speaking, expansionary monetary and fiscal policies before an election will lower rates of interest and levels of unemployment while raising national income. After an election, this policy has to be reversed to avoid the likely inflationary consequences. Many models built around this basic theme are surveyed by Alt and Chrystal (1983). They build up a taxonomy that relies on whether the preferences of the electorate are seen as fixed or varying and whether government capability is seen as strategic or responsive. Responsive government seeks to follow the preferences of its supporters, whereas strategic government action seeks to vote-maximize irrespective of the party's own supporters' preferences. Fixed and variable voter preferences are self-explanatory labels. Here we make no attempt to survey as many models as in the Alt and Chrystal taxonomy, but seek rather to highlight some examples. (For an alternative taxonomy see Alesina 1988.)

The first model considered is one of the best articulated ones and assumes fixed preferences and strategic government. It is the model developed by Nordhaus (1975) and it adopted the then current views of the shape of the Phillips curves. In particular, there is a long-run Phillips curve ($LRPC_e$ ('e' for 'early')) that is negatively sloped. The basic picture is represented by

Fig. 11.3(a), where a family of short-run Phillips curves ($SRPC$) are also illustrated. The hypothetical numbers attached to short-run curves indicate that the point on a short-run Phillips curve that is on a long-run Phillips curve is where expected and actual inflation rate coincide. To the left of $LRPC_e$ inflation is greater than expected or anticipated, and vice versa to the right.

To bring this picture into line with the earlier ('new classical') part of this chapter, a vertical $LRPC$ has been added labelled $LRPC_c$ (c for current as opposed to e for the early version). Part (b) of the figure represents the iso-vote curves and indicates combinations of two 'bads', namely inflation and unemployment, that yield equal votes from the electorate where the labels indicate more votes as you move towards the origin. Putting the iso-vote 'preferences' on the Phillips curve constraints yields the 'equilibrium' path of the model (see Fig. 11.4). Attempts to trade on the location of the short-run Phillips curves means the equilibria that governments try to engineer are successively found at 1, 2 and 3, assuming that $SRPC_1$ incorporates the initially expected inflation rate. The trade-off possibilities worsen because to the left of $LRPC_e$ people's expectations about inflation are falsified with the actual rate exceeding the expected rate. Trade union bargaining and other attempts to 'catch up' with reality serve only to raise inflation (and unemployment) until point 3 is achieved and expected and actual inflation rates coincide. The reverse pattern would obtain to the right of $LRPC_e$ and a move from a point such as 4 to point 3 can be anticipated. The highest long-run sustainable popularity is achieved where the $LRPC_e$ is tangential to the iso-vote curve V_2 at point 5.

The burden of Nordhaus's model is to suggest that a democratic economy will exhibit an inflationary bias with the gains from exploiting a 'fooled' electorate being a higher rate of inflation at point 3 than at point 5. (Note that this also involves a lower rate of unemployment than the long-run equilibrium would suggest.) Of course, the possibility of lower unemployment at point 3 in Fig. 11.4(b) is precluded as the natural rate r_n will obtain. The long-run sustainable position that maximizes votes is now an axis 'solution' at point $5'$, where the natural rate is combined with zero inflation. However, short-run political considerations suggest that point 3 will be the outcome. Among the criticisms levelled at the Nordhaus model is the assumption it contains that voters are systematically 'fooled': they do not appear to learn that costly post-election recession follows beneficial pre-election boom.

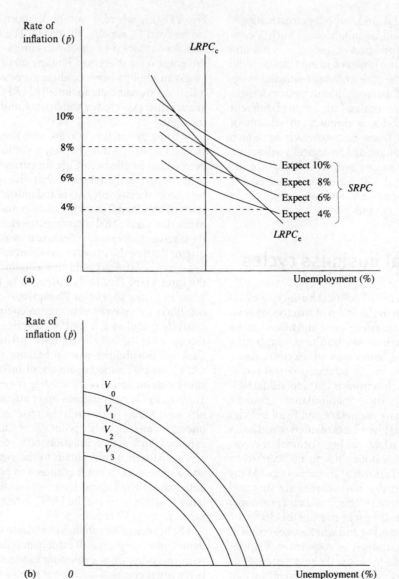

Figure 11.3 Ingredients of the Nordhaus model.

As noted above, one of the most influential schools of macro thought in recent years is that associated with rational expectations, which involves actors internalizing all available information in a model to anticipate now the consequences of, say, increasing the money supply. If accepted, then the short-run Phillips curves disappear and there is only the vertical location on the long-run one to argue about. Such an outcome seems to cut the ground from under the Nordhaus model, with point 5' in Fig. 11.4(b) being the equilibrium outcome. The point of this criticism, however, has been dulled somewhat by models offering somewhat similar predictions that replace myopic voters with voters who have less information than those who shape policy (e.g. Rogoff and Sibert 1988).

Another model allows for partisan effects to occur even in the presence of rational expectations. In a US setting, Republicans are associated with keeping inflation in check at a greater cost in terms of unemployment than the Democrats will accept; to put it,

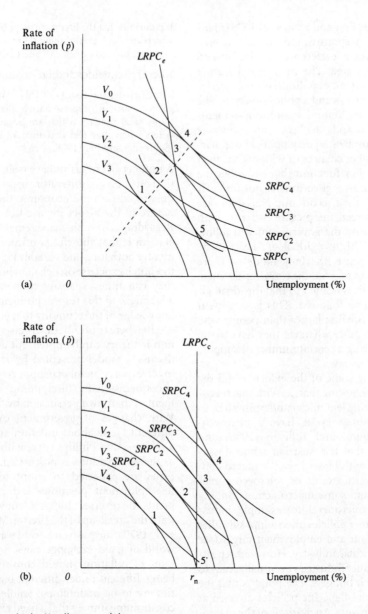

Figure 11.4 Equilibrium in the Nordhaus model.

perhaps, too strongly, one is the party of unemployment and the other the party of inflation. Before an election, voters uncertain of the outcome are viewed as assigning probabilities to the result, allowing wage-setters to negotiate on the basis of the average expected post-election monetary growth rate—the average being a weighted one with the weights the assigned probabilities of each party's success. On this basis, if the Republicans win the monetary growth rate will be lower than 'averaged for' and a recession will

occur. The reverse will apply if the Democrats win. Sheffrin (1989) considers empirical evidence relating to this proposition and finds it lacking. One of his main pieces of evidence is the failure of the 'announcement' effect of the result on the stock exchange to be strongly supportive with the theory. (The stock market should, for example, internalize a Republican success with instantaneously lowered prices, reflecting the expected depressed profit streams because of the result; see also chapter 5.)

Frey (1978; also see Frey and Schneider 1978) manages to combine both responsive and strategic government with fixed voter preferences in his several contributions to this area. The main novel feature exploited is a two-level test of political business cycles with a popularity function and a policy function. The first function connects economic conditions—unemployment, inflation and the rate of economic growth—to the incumbent's party political popularity and hence his or her chances of winning the next election. It is the policy function that embodies the strategic and responsive government positions. If popularity is low then economic variables are manipulated to 'correct' the picture, whereas with comfortable popularity the government will follow its supporters' and its own ideology, i.e. will be responsive. In this sense, the Frey model is more utility-maximizing than vote-maximizing as such. Popularity in the polls is wanted so that the ideological programme can be followed. This is consistent both with politicians being larger than people who simply wish to be in office whatever they have to do, and with parties having a central number of supporters who share an ideology.

Before mentioning some of the evidence and the criticisms, it is worth noting that, as with macroeconomics in general being lent micro underpinnings, so macro-political business cycles have a microeconomic aspect. Ekelund and Tollison (1986) and Lewin (1988) note that the Austrian school (associated in particular with Hayek) see the macro consequences as being the result of microeconomic-motivated actions and some macro actions finding their impact at the micro level; for example, industrial, regional and other policies often adopt subsidies to maintain an output and employment target (see chapter 5) in a particular industry. However, repeating the process for other industries eventually leads to the running of deficit budgets. The point is that the deficits are the result of specific policies directed at specific groups of workers. An example of the macro-to-micro arguments is that politically inspired monetary relaxations and contractions serve to alter the nominal rate of interest, giving the wrong investment signals. If losses are made by investors acting misguidedly, this results in macro output and employment reductions. Again, the point is the micro connections through 'wrong' relative prices having macro consequences.

Most authors of political business cycle models subject their models to econometric or other forms of testing. The results tend to be very mixed. Alt and Chrystal comment that

It is curious that the literature on political business cycles is widely invoked, even though there is little evidence for the existence of such cycles. (Alt and Chrystal, 1983, p. 103)

whereas Schneider and Frey comment:

Summarizing the results of this part, we clearly see that governments in representative democracies undertake those fiscal policies which are popular for a majority of voters when they feel that their re-election is in danger. (Schneider and Frey 1988, p. 262).

A number of criticisms have been levelled at the political business cycle literature in general. Some relate to queries concerning economic theory, others to the nature of the actors involved in political processes. Regarding economic management, one tenet of monetarism is that the effects of money supply changes involve both long and variable lags, so that it assumes too much expertise on behalf of politicians to imagine they can time expansive monetary policy to their advantage. In this respect politicians apparently have knowledge of the economy that economists do not.

Elsewhere contradictions between models and economic theory can be noted. Alt and Chrystal (1983) discuss a model presented by Hibbs (1977) which involves party members/supporters with fixed preferences occasionally 'disciplining' a wayward government of their own persuasion by failing to vote for it. With changes of government over time reflecting different views about inflation and unemployment, a cross-section Phillips curve with different countries as the observations is postulated. Left-wing incumbents are expected to adopt high-inflation, low-unemployment positions and right-wing governments the reverse. One problem with this is that, up until the break-up of the Bretton Woods system in the early 1970s, the postwar period was characterized by a world of fixed exchange rates, which suggests that rates of inflation should converge, as opposed to being different under different regimes, if fixed parities are to be maintained. Laidler (1987) notes the constraining impact that a fixed exchange rate regime will have on politicians:

Increased government borrowing tends, under such a monetary policy regime, to lead to increased domestic credit expansion and hence ensures that current account difficulties quickly become overall balance of payments problems. So long therefore as the central country of the Bretton Woods system pursued responsible policies, fiscal deficits in a peripheral country such as the United Kingdom generated balance of payments problems for that country, and any government seriously committed to maintaining a fixed exchange rate on the US dollar found its freedom to run such deficits severely curtailed by the commitment. (Laidler 1987, p. 345)

(One argument for the UK fully joining the European Monetary System is that in order to maintain parity the UK would have to have the same (low) inflation rate as Germany, see section 11.4 below.)

It has already been noted that most models have a view of politicians as people who follow overly narrow self-interested behaviour to the detriment of interests of the electorate and presumably their own long-run reputations. A similar point can be made with respect to voters who, despite what some economists might like to think, will have views beyond the fate of major economic indicators and will be concerned about the conduct of foreign and domestic policy at large. Kelman (1988) in particular takes this kind of line, pointing out that those most opposed to the Vietnam war were those who had no chance of actually going there and being in danger. Ideology is apparently a better predictor of attitudes of American voters to the introduction of a national health insurance programme than the personal benefits that individuals can expect to receive. In general, Kelman points out that voting surveys, despite the predictions of many of the political business cycle models, suggest no significant connection between personal fortune and voting behaviour. Those who tend to vote against an incumbent government are not those who have become unemployed; rather, they are those who see the government as a weak and incompetent one. All this is not to suggest that political advantage has not had and does not have any effect on the conduct of macro policy, but rather that the evidence and theory presented is consistent with its having a small rather than dominating impact. As with any relatively recent field of investigation, this conclusion needs to be viewed as interim rather than final.

11.4 Macroeconomic policies and political incentives in 'Europe'

'Europe' as a topic within economics has in recent years been a major issue for obvious reasons. Certain aspects of the European debate merit inclusion in a public finance–public choice book in the context of this chapter. In particular the 'new' optimum currency area theory draws on a Nordhaus type model as part of its analysis and is specifically relevant to the UK's short spell in the Exchange Rate Mechanism (ERM). Furthermore any move towards European Monetary Union (EMU) raises public choice and

public finance questions with respect to its rationale and role for fiscal policy. These topics are discussed in turn below.

As intimated above there is now a split between 'old' and 'new' optimum currency area literature. The question being addressed is that of the optimum area over which exchange rates should be fixed with the idea being that this 'area' will be decided by economic forces rather than historically derived borders that define countries. The initial classic (now 'old') contributions to this debate centred on issues of factor mobility, degree of openness of the economy and extent of diversification amongst other criteria (see Ishiyama 1975). The new optimum currency area theory is discussed in Tavlas (1993) and reflects issues that have surfaced in more recent macroeconomics. Two issues combine in Fig. 11.5 to illustrate this process. The first is that although short-run Phillips curves may exhibit a negative relationship between inflation and unemployment the long-run Phillips curve is vertical. The case illustrated is for Germany (panel (a)) and the UK (panel (b)). It is instructive to concentrate on panel (a) initially. The long-run Phillips curve for Germany (LR_g) is vertical at the German natural rate of unemployment u_{ng}. As above short-run Phillips curves cross the long-run one, LR_g, when the actual rate of inflation as recorded on the vertical axis equals the constant expected inflation rate ($\dot{p}_g^e$) along each short-run curve. In panel (a) $\dot{p}_g^e$ equals $\dot{p}_g$ at point 1. The remaining curve in panel (a) reflects the second issue and is the 'German' indifference curve between the two 'bads' inflation and unemployment. The 'flat' shape of this, concave to the origin curve, indicates the Germans' 'hard-nosed' preferences concerning inflation allegedly stemming from Germany's hyper inflation experiences in the interwar years. It suggests a willingness to 'trade' a large increase in unemployment for a small decrease in inflation. The tangency of the indifference curve I_g^* and the short-run Phillips curve $\dot{p}_g^e$ on the long-run Phillips curve LR_g indicates that point 1 is a full equilibrium from a political (preferences) and an economic (Phillips curves configurations) viewpoint. The outcome is the almost legendary low German inflation rate of recent years.

The third issue relates to the notions of reputation, credibility and time inconsistency. Modern governments are viewed as having credibility if official announcements about economic policy accord with the beliefs of the public about the policy that will be followed. Reputation (the governments historical track record) is one way of securing or failing to secure credibility. If governments repeatedly renege on their

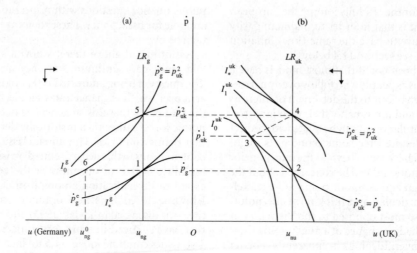

Figure 11.5 Importing credibility and political equilibrium.

policy statements it will lower its average credibility and push its marginal credibility towards zero where the announcement of a policy change will have no impact on the public's expectations.

The UK having earned a 'soft-nosed' reputation over inflation can be viewed as having 'steep' indifference curves in panel (b) of Fig. 11.5 as illustrated in I_0^{UK}, I_1^{UK} and I_*^{UK}. In the 1970s, 1980s and early 1990s low inflation became almost the sole UK macro economic objective and the question was how to achieve it when the government lacked credibility with respect to achieving low inflation. One answer was to 'import' credibility by fixing the nominal exchange rate to that of Germany indicating that a hard-nosed monetary policy like that of Germany's would have to be adopted in the UK. In effect joining a currency area to lower domestic inflation to the German level was the objective. In terms of Fig. 11.5 joining the Exchange Rate Mechanism (ERM) in October 1990 was telling the public that the economy was going to be at point 2 in panel (b). But is this credible? The answer is no as the so-called 'tying ones hands' policy is 'time inconsistent'. A time consistent policy is one such that political preferences and economic constraints dictate that the economic actors do not have an incentive to alter their actions in the future. At point 2 this is clearly not the case—there is time inconsistency. Given the directions of preference, shown by the arrows, point 2 on I_1^{uk} is a lower level of utility than point 3 on I_0^{uk} which could be achieved by the government 'surprise engineering' an increase in inflation to $\dot{p}_{uk}^1 (> \dot{p}_{uk}^e = \dot{p}_g)$. In a similar method to

the Nordhaus adjustment this 'Barro-Grossman' model results in the UK adjusting to point 4 where political and economic equilibrium coincide with an expected and actual inflation rate of $\dot{p}_{uk}^2 > \dot{p}_g$. This politico economic model of the desires to join the currency area suggests a similarity of preferences over inflation and unemployment is a prerequisite for its ultimate success. That credibility is an attractive attribute for government can be seen if it is assumed that an economic shock occurred that placed Germany at point 5 with the same high inflation rate as that of the UK. The indifference curve through $5I_0^g$ is inferior to I_*^g and a statement by the German government that it will re-establish point 1 is credible and economic actors would set wages and prices accordingly and more from 5 to point 1. If such a statement were not credible and the government went ahead to re-establish $\dot{p}_g$ the German unemployment-level would have to rise to U_{ng}^0, associated with point 6, as an intermediate step. The distance U_{ng} to U_{ng}^0 is the unemployment cost of not being credible. It is the important issue of unemployment in this macro economic setting that motivates section 11.6 whereas the next section picks up another inflation-related theme.

11.5 Inflation taxation and 'Europe'

Rebelo (1994) explores the public finance dimension of inflation highlighting the revenue raised from an

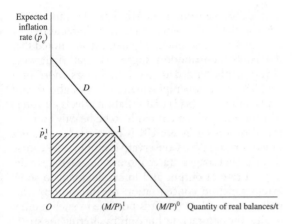

Figure 11.6 Size and welfare cost of an inflation tax.

inflation tax. If inflation is unanticipated, individuals holding assets denominated in money terms will suffer a loss in the real value of their assets, and in this sense they will be taxed. However, the analysis of inflation as a tax normally involves individuals who correctly anticipate the actual rate of inflation. Following Dornbusch and Fischer (1978), if the level of real income is fixed, then the quantity of real balances individuals desire is given by $(M/P)^0$ in Fig. 11.6 (i.e. that quantity demanded when the actual and expected inflation rates are zero). D is the demand curve for real balances showing how individuals seek to reduce their holdings of real balances as the inflation rate rises. With real incomes constant, individuals will desire to add to their cash balances in line with the rate of inflation (this is the amount of nominal balances required to make the volume of real balances constant). The real value of an inflation tax Tr is given by:

$$(11.8) \qquad Tr = \frac{\Delta M}{P}$$

(the so called cash flow measure of seigniorage) where ΔM is the change in nominal balances and P is the price level. Dividing and multiplying the right-hand side by M yields

$$(11.9) \qquad Tr = \frac{\Delta M}{M} \cdot \frac{M}{P}$$

with, *ceteris paribus*, $\Delta M/M$ being equal to the rate of inflation ($\dot{p}$). In the short run the inflation tax is equal to $\dot{p}(M/P)$. In Fig. 11.6 if the actual and expected inflation rates are $\dot{p}_e^1$ the desired level of real balances is $(M/P)^1$ and the tax paid equal to the hatched rectangle. The tax raised in this way is collected by the government buying private sector goods and ser-

vices with the 'created' volume of nominal balances which individuals wish to add to their money balances to keep the value of real balances constant in each period.

Like most taxes this involves a welfare cost. In this case, in the absence of inflation, the additional services of real money balances individuals would demand is represented by triangle $(M/P)^1 \, 1(M/P)^0$ and hence this is the distortion induced by the systematic use of inflation as a tax. Dornbusch and Fischer (1978) note that for developed economies there is relatively little recourse to money creation as a tax raiser. That said, for the poorer European economies (Portugal, Greece, Spain) 'seigniorage' or inflation tax amounted to some 10 per cent of the total tax revenue between 1979 and 1987 (Giovazzi and Giovannini 1989).

Given that government revenue raising involves welfare costs it can be expected there is an optimal inflation tax. Rebelo points out two gains from an inflation tax. First, it taxes black market and other illegal activities that otherwise escape. Secondly, it taxes the holdings of domestic currency held by foreigners. Against this background is it appropriate to have a single low inflation rate (and tax) in all the European countries?. Rebelo's answer is no because the countries have different preferences over public sector size; tax collection costs; labour taxes, capital taxes, property taxes; VATs and black markets. With all these differences it is unlikely that a single inflation tax for all European countries is part of an optimal tax package. Having viewed the common inflation tax as broadly inappropriate the author turns to what he describes as political economy arguments that support monetary union. It is in the light of Wagner's Law (see chapter 14) of increasing relative public sector size overtime that Rebelo finds the true evil of inflation tax. Surprise bouts of 'printing money' especially before elections expands public spending and eventually reduces the real value of public debt denominated in nominal terms when inflation occurs. Without recourse to money creation the costs of government spending have to become more visible or transparent. Consumer voter awareness is raised and therefore more government discipline obtains.

Given the above, the fiscal aspects of the convergence criteria may have nothing much to do with optimum currency areas but a great deal to do with optimal public choice. But why would politicians seek monetary union at the cost of spending limitations generated by the budgetary constraints? The case of Germany is not so paradoxical because of their 'hard-nosed' preference map but what about the other countries? The answer seems to be that to preserve the system of transfers, that is key to the EC stable exchange rates is vital. Hence countries willingness to bear the costs of reduced freedom to spend. Despite Rebelo's endorsement of EMU as a check on Wagner's Law, it seems to imply the politicians who want it are not quite finding their self-interest.

The convergence criteria (part of the Maastricht Treaty) for joining the European Monetary Union involve three monetary and two fiscal criteria.

The three monetary criteria are:

(i) the rate of inflation in the year prior to joining must not exceed by more than 1.5 per cent the three lowest inflation rates in the Union;

(ii) the long-run interest rate in the year before joining must not exceed by more than 2 per cent the three lowest long-run interest rates in the Union;

(iii) the country must have participated for two years in the 'normal' fluctuation band of the ERM (a generous ±15 per cent since August 1993) without a currency devaluation.

The two fiscal criteria are:

(iv) its budget deficit must not exceed 3 per cent of its GDP;

(v) the national debt to GDP ratio must not exceed 60 per cent.

De Grauwe (1994, p. 161) notes that 'The remarkable thing about the Maastrict entry conditions is that they have so little to do with economics.' Furthermore as indicated above different conditions are emphasized by 'old' optimum currency area theory, e.g. high degree of factor mobility.

Earlier it was stressed that the process of being part of a currency union involves the similarity of monetary policy between countries otherwise inflation rate differences places pressure on the fixed nominal exchange rate, i.e. there can only be a single monetary policy stance. This loss of a policy instrument becomes complete in a monetary union with irrevocably fixed nominal exchange rates or a single currency and a single central bank. An implication of this is that the focus falls on fiscal policy.

11.6 Unemployment

As a crude approximation, the 1930s saw unemployment as a dominant issue, while the 1950s and early 1960s saw the operation of the Keynesian consensus with full (or some say over-full) employment. Infla-

tion as a problem dominated the late 1960s and 1970s, whereas the 1980s seem to have been characterized by both inflation and unemployment. It was noted that the Hibbs contribution suggested that right-wing governments tended to see inflation as more of a problem than unemployment. A straightforward explanation for this is that inflation affects all voters whereas unemployment tends to be heavily concentrated on (as far as the UK is concerned) areas not noted for extensive Conservative support. Of course theories that suggest the economy will gravitate to the natural rate of output and unemployment to some extent sanction concentration on inflation as 'the' policy issue. (Note that it is possible in such models to alter the natural rate, but only by altering the structure of the labour market.) In this respect the concentration of the Nordhaus model on inflationary bias is appropriate to its context. However, the purpose of this section is to focus on unemployment, its measurement and some explanations of its ominous presence. The account is not exhaustive but is outlined with a view to drawing out alternative perspectives.

Measuring unemployment, like measuring the size of the public sector, at first seems an obvious exercise, but in fact is far from being so. While there has been a world recession to contend with on top of the problems the UK would otherwise have faced since 1979, public choice theorists would not be surprised that the Conservative government has sought to minimize the level of reported unemployment. By the same token, the public choice school would not be surprised to find that the Labour Party opposition regarded the official unemployment figures as underestimates. The arguments that divided them are illustrated in Table 11.2 which reproduces in a slightly amended form a table that appeared in *The Sunday Times* (6 November 1983).

Whilst 'gerrymandering' is the name given to redefining political boundaries to improve your vote 'Thatchering' may become the name given to redefining statistical boundaries. Between 1979 and 1994 there were nine major changes in the method of constructing the UK unemployment statistics (only the last of which was in the 1990s). Two observations raise suspicions about the motivations of such changes. First, only the initial change raised the unemployment statistics (by a modest 20 000) whilst the next eight all served to reduce the numbers recorded as unemployed. Secondly, whilst the Department of Employment have been willing to rewrite history in the backwards direction by compiling unemployment figures on the new more politically favourable basis they have not been willing to provide figures on the

Table 11.2 Measuring the unemployed

(1983 official total: 3 million plus)

Left-wing additions		Right-wing substractions	
Unemployed excluded by changes in the form of the unemployed statistics	189 000	School-leavers	168 000
		Claimants not really looking for work	490 000
Unemployed over the age of 60 (no longer required to register)	199 000	Severely disabled	23 000
Short-time working	43 000	Unemployables (severely physically or mentally incapacitated)	135 000
Students on vacation	27 000	Job changers' (unemployed for less than a week)	360 000
Effect of special employment measures	395 000	'Black economy' workers illegally claiming benefit	
Unregistered unemployed	490 000	(see chapter 8)	250 000
New total (approx.)	4.4 m	New total (approx.)	1.7 m

Source: David Lipsey, 'Jobless—the Great Divide', *The Sunday Times*, 6 November 1983.

assumption of continuing the 'old' definition forward. Such an exercise has been carried out elsewhere suggesting the official first quarter 1994 unemployment figures of 2.75 million (10 per cent unemployment approximately) would have been 3.8 million (almost 14 per cent unemployed). For the detailed changes and a discussion of measuring unemployment see Johnson and Briscoe (1995). While not wishing to examine the pros and cons further, enough is presented to establish that the much vaunted 'facts' of any situation are seldom that. Furthermore, whatever reducing arguments are accepted, nearly all commentators acknowledge that Britain did have an unemployment problem of some considerable dimensions in the 1980s (which was heavily age- and geographically concentrated). How is this accounted for? We offer some forms of explanation, the first two of which are Keynesian in orientation (see Blinder 1988) while the third is based on a public choice approach.

11.6.1 Real wage stickiness

There are an increasing number of theories about why the market-clearing real wage is not attained. In terms of Fig. 11.1, if (W_1/P_0) is established, how is it that the number of workers recorded as unemployed is measured between points 2 and 4 rather than the real wage falling so that labour market equilibrium is established at OL_1? Trade union power is an obvious explanation and is explored further in the context of coalitions below. A less strongly related argument is that contained in a version of the 'insider–outsider' accounts of unemployment (see Linbeck and Snower 1986). Here, even in the absence of unions, those currently in employment have power. The realization that it is a very costly option for a firm to try and lay off

all employees and replace them allows 'insiders' to bargain for a continuing employment relationship and to achieve a greater than labour-market-clearing wage. Employers know that 'insiders' will not cooperate with any undercutting 'outsiders' if they employ them, while on the other side of the market would-be undercutting outsiders can expect to be 'harassed' by insiders if they are successful in gaining employment. Linbeck and Snower (1990) respond to Fehr's (1990) comment on their work by explaining why firms will not replace all insiders with undercutting outsiders. Their explanation relies on the 'turnover costs' that would be involved: the fact that

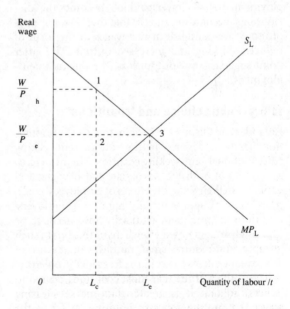

Figure 11.7 Unemployment caused by rent-seeking.

insiders are more productive because they have had more on-the-job training; that such training may well come from insiders who on being sacked will not be there to supply it; that harassment via picket lines, the 'angry silence', etc., can be employed even by displaced insiders, that the unpopular act of replacing a whole work-force is likely to cost the firm in terms of lost 'good-will'. If this argument is accepted, then insider–outsider theory still has some purchase despite Fehr's objections.

11.6.2 'Efficiency' wage theories

Efficiency wage theories tie back with the rationale of the firm as a form of productive organization. The Alchian–Demsetz (1972) approach suggests that team production outproduces isolated individual production, providing a necessary but not sufficient condition for firm formation. The trouble with firms is that 'team' production gains are bought at the cost of opportunities to 'shirk'. An employer might respond to this by offering his workers higher wages to foster effort so that they will fear losing their jobs because the alternative jobs are less well paid (see Greenwald and Stiglitz 1987). However, if this is a rational response for one employer, it is likely to be a rational response for all of them, so that all firms will pay more. The consequence of this is that the real wage level exceeds the equilibrium one so that there is, simultaneously, high real wages and unemployment. The main implications are (a) that the fear of unemployment, not of a lower paid job, becomes the 'disciplining' mechanism, and (b) that there is some 'pay-off' to above-equilibrium real wages in the form of reduced shirking and increased output. The latter point suggests some output loss to reducing unemployment.

11.6.3 Public choice and 'coalitions'

Colander and Olson (1984) claim that too little attention has been devoted to the role of rent-seeking (distributional gain-seeking coalitions) in the macroeconomics of both the Keynesian and new classical varieties. In their view, the effects of employees' coalitions keeping wages artificially 'high' or of employers' coalitions keeping them artificially 'low' needs to be fully analysed. As noted elsewhere in this book, such group action requires small numbers or the use of selective incentives to avoid the free rider problem.

The authors argue that most coalitions related to 'sellers', so that it is greater-than-market-clearing wages that are the concern, resulting, as far as the labour market is concerned, in excess supply (unemployment) rather than excess demand (vacancies). In Fig. 11.7 the area $(W/P)_h 12 (W/P)_e$ represents the coalition gain from a higher-than-equilibrium wage $(W/P)_e$. The coalition reduces employment to OL_c from OL_e. In a wider context a quantity of labour $L_c L_e$ will be forced into the sectors of the economy where there is less rigidity. However, if the rent-seeking coalitions are extensive, this may well reduce wages elsewhere to the point where reservation wages are not met and unemployment and/or underemployment is commonplace. The return to being on the inside of the charmed circle entails potential employees extending their search and queuing to join the successful rent-seekers; i.e. search unemployment is raised.

Colander and Olson contend that the effect of coalition power is to reduce the speed and quality of adjustment to changing economic circumstances. The time and trouble costs of getting an agreement rise once you move from individual private decisions to group ones. Regarding quality, the incentive for group members to be well informed is less than for private individuals because of the opportunity to try and free-ride on the information of others. Incomplete information guides the outcome. Slowly adjusting, ill-informed rent-seekers can, to some extent, be traded upon by vote-seeking politicians who want a growing economy with falling unemployment. Expanding aggregate demand to raise prices will unexpectedly lower real wages, pushing employment away from 1 and towards 3 in Fig. 11.7 while simultaneously increasing output. While empirical evidence relating unemployment levels to the unionization level in the USA provides some support for the analysis, the major point the authors offer is that the explicit or implicit adoption of price-taking competitive behaviour in macro modelling is misleading.

11.7 Public sector size and economic growth

The quest for economic growth is a third target seen as central to macro economics. Despite a large amount of theorizing and empirical research the process of and recipe for economic growth has remained elusive. The focus of this section is rather more limited and is concerned with the connection between public sector size and economic growth. Clearly economists of the Leviathan public choice school tend to support a view that sees a large public sector as detrimental to economic growth. In contrast evidence of a correlation between GDP growth and the growth rate of government and more weakly between GDP growth and the size of government have been associated with the argument that there is a strong positive externality between the public and private sectors. As discussed in chapter 5 in relation to transactions costs economics the state is a vital participant in a market economy. Property rights establishment, provision of information channels, standards of weight, measure and product alongside market infrastructure and human capital investments are all likely to be positive additional inputs in private sector production. But as emphasized throughout this text the public sector has to be financed either through taxes, borrowing or inflation taxes. All forms of revenue raising have potential disincentive effects, for example, via relative price changes, rate of interest increases and price level uncertainty respectively. The size of these 'costs' are open to dispute but clearly can affect work effort and the level of investment in the economy. The latter effect being one form of 'crowding out'.

Two studies, coming to different conclusions, concerning the relationship between economic growth and public sector size (if any) are Landau (1985) and Saunders (1985). They are illustrative of work in this area. Both Landau and Saunders recognize there are reasons for believing that large public sectors can both stimulate or hinder economic growth, making the question essentially an empirical one. Landau, who has the more econometrically sophisticated approach, acknowledges that the evidence will always be open to different interpretations. In this context is it that public sectors have growth consequences or vice versa? In the absence of fully articulated growth models, which include the effects of government spending, both investigators opt for an unashamedly empirical approach. Landau is specific about his approach. He relates economic growth to levels of physical and human capital and changes in their productivity. One important set of variables affecting the productivity of investment deals with the share of government expenditure in national income. Additional variables employed included a time trend, contraction and expansion year dummies, and the percentage change in the terms of trade. Several specifications of the growth rate and public sector measures were used in the regressions.

The results indicate a detrimental impact on economic growth of government sectors. (The data are a pooled time series over the years 1952–76 involving 16 developed economies including the UK and USA.) A 10 per cent increase in the government share in national income implies in the regression a 0.6–1.6 per cent decline in per capita growth national income. Conclusions drawn by Landau include that both the consumption and investment expenditures by government exhibit a negative correlation with growth, although transfers do not. That transfers may be given a clean bill of health on growth grounds may be significant for the UK where considerable public sector growth can be attributed to transfers.

Saunders (1985), considered the impact on economic growth (percentage change in real GDP) of total government outlays as a proportion of GDP, and to allow for other growth influences, the share of gross fixed capital formation in GDP (a constant was also part of the linear regression equation). Although for both periods studied the government share variable is negatively related to economic growth, it is only significant at the conventional level for the early (1960–73) period. The same variables were used in an attempt to explain differences in economic growth between the two periods, but provided no evidence that the post-1973 decline in economic growth bears any systematic relation to public expenditure growth. In addition, the hypothesis that economies with large public sectors were better equipped to withstand the supply-side shocks of the middle 1970s was tested by replacing the government growth variable by the level of the government expenditure share in 1975. The evidence gave some, but not overwhelming, support for the notion that the decline in economic growth after 1975 was slightly less in those countries with larger public expenditure shares.

Saunders reflects that his work, like that of many others, identifies no simple relationships, either adverse or beneficial, between overall economic performance and the size and growth of public sectors. He argues that the way forward is a more disaggregated approach, so that the influences of the structure of different revenue and expenditure policies can be isolated.

This is a message echoed in Dowrick (1993) who tested two equations one of the general form:

$$\begin{matrix} \text{Growth} \\ \text{rate of} \\ \text{aggregate} \\ \text{output} \end{matrix} = \begin{matrix} \text{Factor} \\ \text{input} \\ \text{growth} \end{matrix} + \begin{matrix} \text{Private} \\ \text{sector} \\ \text{innovation} \\ \text{rate} \end{matrix} + \begin{matrix} \text{Factor} \\ \text{productivity} \\ \text{effect} \end{matrix}$$

$$+ \begin{matrix} \text{Production} \\ \text{externality} \\ \text{effect} \end{matrix} + \begin{matrix} \text{Innovation} \\ \text{effect} \end{matrix}$$

The production externality effect is captured by assuming that government output affects private sector production. The factor productivity term allows determination of whether at the margin government growth that attracts factor inputs from the private sector increases or decreases aggregate growth, i.e. if and how marginal factor productivities differ between the public and private sectors. The final term tests whether technical progress is greater in the public than the private sector. Using data running to 1988 on twenty-four OECD countries with six observations for each country the regression coefficients on the final three terms suggested a positive connection between government consumption growth and GDP growth. Unfortunately for the anti-Leviathan school the econometric tests suggested the results were spurious in that the direction of causality was at least partially from GDP growth to government consumption growth and not vice versa. Furthermore econometric testing of an investment equation indicated that for every dollar of additional government consumption, investment spending fell by 40 cents, i.e. the level of government consumption affects adversely aggregate investment. However, this is very much an average picture and this section is illustrative and not an exhaustive survey of the evidence.

Atkinson (1996) picks up on the point flagged above that social security transfer expenditure is often the largest element of public sector expenditure and as such the target for the 'high social security transfers-low economic growth' school of thought. He echoes points also made above:

(i) the empirical evidence is mixed (of ten studies reported two found an insignificant impact, four a positive impact and four a negative impact);

(ii) in the absence of explicit theoretical models the interpretation of any evidence takes place in somewhat of a vacuum as directions of causality become ambiguous or spurious. Ambiguous because high social security spending may lower economic growth or low economic growth may cause social security spending to be high. Spurious if economic growth falls after the initial industrialization of an economy while social security expenditures expand with the maturity of an economy.

The key question is whether disincentives are inherently embedded in welfare states, or are functions of specific types of transfer or are insignificant (this of course ties back to the discussion of section 9.5). For example, it is claimed that the presence of state pensions decreases private savings and that a policy to reduce state pensions to means-tested forms of assistance would raise private saving and hence invest-

ment. However, this would create a 'savings trap' in that for many the incentive would be to decrease savings to zero to ensure maximum qualification for the means-tested assistance on offer at retirement. Further a switch to private savings and the consequent increased share holding by pension and insurance companies may distort the capital market in such a way as to decrease investment undertaken by publicly quoted companies. A pension fund dominated equity market, it is argued, tightens the 'take over constraint' on firm-growth-maximizing managers and hence decreases their willingness to invest in research and development and capital projects. In short the point is that reforms set up disincentive effects of their own which must be part of any overall evaluation. In the meantime Atkinson (1996, p. 186) concludes there is 'no overwhelming evidence that high spending on social security leads to lower growth rates'.

Overall it is likely that different revenue raising and expenditure policies have different effects and the trick is to identify those that have a positive economic growth impact.

11.8 Summary

In this chapter thumbnail sketches of the major 'schools' of macro thought have been presented. By definition the nuances of each have been ignored. This sacrifice was made in order to bring out their relevance for government in ideological and instrumental settings. Keynesianism, with its blessing for both policy intervention and unbalanced budgets, is a *bête noir* of the public choice economists (see Buchanan and Wagner 1977). A perspective of well-working markets (therefore the need for minimal government intervention) and a balanced budget make the competing schools of thought more attractive to this group. It was argued that supply-side economics offered most to the politicians, whereas theories of political business cycles suggest an 'incentive' but perhaps little real ability to instrumentally manipulate the economy to secure re-election. Applying a similar analytical framework to 'Europe' allowed credibility and time inconsistency to be explored in the context of fixing your exchange rate to a low inflation economy. As for unemployment, arguments about the statistics cannot mask the realization that the UK had considerable unemployment in the 1980s. The public choice approach suggested that coalitions and rent-seeking were central to understanding this.

With respect to economic growth the role of governmental aspects seem uncertain. There is a case for the growth and size of the public sector having a positive or negative impact on the rate of growth of the economy. Whilst Keynesians are likely to prefer the former public choice economists find the latter more convincing. Attempts to put the two cases before an empirical judge have produced mixed results but this is probably a reflection of the difficulties of adequately econometrically modelling the growth process alongside a too aggregated level of analysis. On this issue it is probably fair to say the jury is still out.

Interestingly, Blinder (1988) connects the success of the new classicals over the Keynesians in the 1970s with: the need to be both different and technical to succeed as a (US) academic economist; Keynesian lack of microeconomic underpinnings; and the rise of a right-wing ideology in the USA. In this respect, the 'trick' was to make macroeconomics look like neoclassical microeconomics. Blinder argues that the resurgence of Keynesian economics is based on the reverse process of making microeconomics look more like (Keynesian) macroeconomics. This resurgence involves pervasive monopoly, externality and other 'market failure' arguments which connects the 'social optimality' approach to public finance with modern Keynesianism.

References

Alchian, A. A. and Demsetz, H. (1972) 'Production, Information Costs and Economic Organisation', *American Economic Review*, 65, 5, pp. 777–95.

Alesina, A. (1988) 'Macroeconomics and Politics', pp. 13–52 in S. Fischer (ed.), *Macroeconomics Annual 1988*, vol. 3. Cambridge, Mass.: MIT Press/National Bureau of Economic Research.

Alt, J. E. and Chrystal, A. K. (1983) *Political Economics*. Brighton: Wheatsheaf.

Atkinson. A. B. (1996) 'Growth and the Welfare State', *New Economy*, 3, 3, pp. 182–6.

Blanchard, O. J. and Fischer, S. (1989) *Lectures on Macroeconomics*. Cambridge, Mass.: MIT Press.

Blinder, A. S. (1988) 'The Fall and Rise of Keynesian Economics', *Economic Record*, 64, 187, pp. 278–93.

Buchanan, J. M. and Lee, D. R. (1982) 'Politics, Time and the Laffer Curve', *Journal of Political Economy*, 90, 4, pp. 816–19.

Buchanan, J. M. and Wagner, R. E. (1977) *Democracy in Deficit, the Political Legacy of Lord Keynes*. New York: Academic Press.

Cairncross, F. and Keeley, P. (1981) *The Guardian Guide to the Economy*. London and New York: Methuen.

Colander, D. C. and Olson, M. (1984) 'Coalitions and Macroeconomics', pp. 115–28 in D. Collander (ed.), *Neo-Classical Political Economy*. Cambridge, Mass.: Ballinger.

Cross, R. (1982) *Economic Theory and Policy in the UK*. Oxford: Martin Robertson.

Cross, R. (1991) 'Macroeconomics into the 1990's', *Scottish Journal of Political Economy*, 38, 2, pp. 293–301.

De Grauwe, P. (1994) 'Towards European Monetary Union without the EMS', *Economic Policy*, 18, pp. 149–74.

Dornbusch, R. and Fischer S. (1978) *Macro-economics*. New York: McGraw-Hill.

Dowrick, S. (1993) 'Government Consumption: Its Effect on Productivity, Growth and Investment', pp. 134–52 in N. Gemmell (ed.) *The Growth of the Public Sector—Theories and International Evidence*. Aldershot: Edward Elgar.

Ekelund, R. B. Jr. and Tollison, R. D. (1986) *Economics*. Boston: Little, Brown.

Fehr, E. (1990) 'Co-operation, Harassment and Involuntary Unemployment: Comment', *American Economic Review*, 80, 3, pp. 624–30.

Frey, B. S. (1978) 'Politico-Economic Cycles and Models', *Journal of Public Economics*, 9, 2, pp. 203–20.

Frey, B. S. and Schneider, F. (1978) 'A Politico-Economic Model of the United Kingdom', *Economic Journal*, 88, 350, pp. 243–53.

Giovazzi, F. and Giovannini, A. (1989) *Limiting Exchange Rate Flexibility: The European Monetary System*. Cambridge, Mass.: MIT Press.

Greenwald, B. and Stiglitz, J. E. (1987) 'Keynesianism, New Keynesianism and New Classical Economics', *Oxford Economic Papers*, 39, 1, pp. 119–33.

Hibbs, D. A. (1977) 'Political Parties and Macroeconomic Policy', *American Political Science Review*, 71, 4, pp. 1467–87.

Ishiyama, Y. (1975) 'The Theory of Optimum Currency Areas: A Survey', *International Monetary Fund Staff Papers*, 22, 2 pp. 344–83.

Johnson, C. and Briscoe, S. (1995) *Measuring the Economy*. Harmondsworth: Penguin.

Kelman, M. (1988) 'On Democracy Bashing: A Sceptical Look at the Theoretical and "Empirical" Practice of the Public Choice Movement', *Virginia Law Review*, 74, 2, pp. 199–273.

Laidler, D. (1987) 'International Monetary Institutions and Deficits', pp. 338–57 in J. M. Buchanan, C. K. Rowley and R. D. Tollison (eds.), *Deficits*. Oxford: Basil Blackwell.

Landau, D. L. (1985) 'Government Expenditures in and Economic Growth in the Developed Countries: 1952–76', *Public Choice*, 47, 3, pp. 459–78.

Leslie, D. L. (1993) *Advanced Macroeconomics: Beyond IS-LM.* London: McGraw-Hill.

Lewin, P. (1988) 'Political Business Cycles and the Capital Stock: Variations on an Austrian Theme', pp. 294–7 in T. D. Willett (ed.), *Political Business Cycles.* Durham, NC: Duke University Press.

Linbeck, A. and Snower, D. (1986) 'Wage Setting, Unemployment and Insider–Outsider Relations', *American Economic Review*, 76, 2, pp. 235–9.

Linbeck, A. and Snower, D. (1990) 'Co-operation, Harassment and Involuntary Unemployment: Reply', *American Economic Review*, 80, 3, pp. 631–6.

Nordhaus, W. (1975) 'The Political Business Cycle', *Review of Economic Studies*, 42, 130, pp. 169–90.

Rebelo, S. (1994) 'Discussion of De Grauwe (1994),' *Economic Policy*, 18, pp. 174–8.

Rogoff, K. and Sibert, A. (1988) 'Equilibrium Political Business Cycles', *Review of Economic Studies*, 55, 1, pp. 1–16.

Saunders, P. (1985) 'Public Expenditure and Economic Performance in OECD Countries,' *Journal of Public Policy*, 5, 1, pp. 1–21.

Schneider, F. and Frey, B. S. (1988) 'Politico-Economic Models of Macroeconomic Policy: A Review of the Empirical Evidence', pp. 239–75 in T. D. Willett (ed.), *Political Business Cycles.* Durham, NC: Duke University Press.

Sheffrin, S. M. (1983) *Rational Expectations.* Cambridge: Cambridge University Press.

Sheffrin, S. M. (1989) 'Evaluating Rational Partisan Business Cycle Theory', *Economics and Politics*, 1, 3, pp. 239–59.

Tavlas, G. S. (1993) 'The "New" Theory of Optimum Currency Areas', *The World Economy*, 16, 6, pp. 663–85.

12 Local government

12.1 Introduction

In this chapter we focus on some fundamental questions pertaining to the fiscal activities of local authorities. In particular, two related questions are, How large should local authorities be? and What gains, if any, are derived from fiscal decision-making at a local level? Traditionally, public finance theory has approached these issues using the assumption that government is motivated by pursuit of the 'public interest'.

The intention again is to illustrate the difference between the traditional theory of public finance and the public choice approach. The literature on the impact of intergovernmental grants is particularly useful for this purpose. The public choice school once more offers explanations for economic phenomena that cannot be easily explained by traditional public finance theory. It is left to readers to assess whether such explanations appear reasonable or contrived.

12.2 The welfare gains from multiple fiscal units: the decentralization theorem

The welfare gains from decentralization are often considered by reference to those deadweight losses that result from centralization (Oates 1972). Assume that the population of a particular nation-state is divided into two distinct localities. A local public good is to be provided in each locality and it is assumed that there are no inter-jurisdictional spillovers. The cost is to be shared equally by residents. In Fig. 12.1 we illustrate the demand for the local public good of two 'representative' individuals, one

from each locality. D_A represents the demand of individuals in locality A and D_B represents the demand of individuals in B. The marginal costs of providing this particular local public good G are assumed to be constant. The price each individual is asked to pay is shown as $P = MC$ in the diagram. (This would be each individual's share of the overall marginal costs.)

In this diagram, if a centralized regime provided a single uniform level of the good, the level of output provided could be shown as a compromise between the demands of the individuals in each locality, i.e. a level of $O\bar{q}$. Such a quantity is lower than the amount that would be demanded by the representative individual A but more than would be demanded by the representative individual B. Inevitably, welfare losses are experienced by each of these two individuals. The losses are shown as triangles 123 and 145. Triangle 123 indicates the loss that arises because individual A does not consume as much as she would choose if there were no need to compromise. She would gladly pay

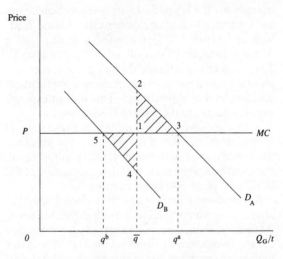

Figure 12.1 The welfare loss of centralization.

$\bar{q}23q^a$ for the additional units $\bar{q}q^a$, but these would cost only $\bar{q}13q^a$ to be made available. Triangle 145 indicates the welfare losses that are experienced by individual B because he is consuming more than he would otherwise choose. He pays $q^b51\bar{q}$ for the additional units $q^b\bar{q}$ but he values them at only $q^b54\bar{q}$.

If each area could provide itself with just the quantity of the good that it requires, these deadweight losses could be avoided. Decentralization permits each locality to provide itself with the quantity of the good it prefers. This illustrates the 'decentralization theorem', which is described by Oates as follows:

For a public good—the consumption of which is defined over geographic subsets of the total population and for which the costs of providing each level of output of the good in each jurisdiction are the same for the central government or the respective local government—it will always be more efficient or at least as efficient for local government to provide the Pareto-efficient levels of output for their respective jurisdictions than for central government to provide any specified and uniform level of output across all jurisdictions. (Oates 1972, p. 35)

There are, however, a number of points to add.

1. As Oates (1979a) notes, in Fig. 12.1, if q^a and q^b were close, then $\bar{q}$ would provide a close approximation. It is evident that the greater the difference in tastes and preferences, the greater the welfare losses. Welfare losses from centralized provision increase with *heterogeneity*.

2. As in other cases, the deadweight welfare loss depends on the *price elasticity of demand*. The more inelastic the demand curves (the steeper the demand curves at points 5 and 3 in Fig. 12.1), the larger will be the area of the shaded triangles. The sizes of the triangles are the key to the losses from centralization. In an attempt to estimate these welfare losses, Bradford and Oates (1974) estimated a multiplicative demand function (for local school expenditures). They used this to estimate the loss in consumer surplus that would rise from adherence to a hypothetical uniform level of expenditure. (This was an expenditure level equal to the existing average level.)

3. In the above analysis, if there are *economies of scale* in the production of the good, this will influence the optimum size of the locality. Other things equal, there will be a greater case for taking advantage of the lower average costs of larger communities.

4. The above efficient gains from decentralization arise as government deals with its allocative functions. By contrast, there is more widespread agreement that the *macroeconomic stabilization function* will be better performed by central government than by local governments. Because of the openness of small local economies, the government expenditure multiplier will be low and fiscal policy will have less impact for stabilization purposes. In this case the effect of local fiscal expansion, for example, will fall on the 'imports' from other local economies. The fiscal multiplier in the expansionary locality will then be reduced. Any particular local government may be forced to incur an extremely large budget deficit in order to have an expansionary effect on the local economy.

5. Similarly, a local economy may not prove effective for the operation of *redistribution policy*. When individuals are mobile between local authorities, a local economy seeking to impose a higher tax on its upper-income residents would simply create an incentive for such residents to move to another locale. If individuals are less mobile internationally, a central government is more able to effect redistribution policies. The rich tend to want to be away from the poor, but the poor want to be in the same jurisdiction as the rich.

12.3 The optimum size of local authorities: an application of the theory of clubs

In chapter 4 an analysis of consumption-sharing arrangements was based on Buchanan's (1965) theory of clubs. Here, following Musgrave and Musgrave (1989), our objective is to show how this theory can be applied to the question of the optimum size of local authorities. By 'optimum' we mean efficient, and by size we refer to the number of residents and the total expenditure on local public goods. In order to discuss the analysis of Musgrave and Musgrave, it is helpful to set it in a four-quadrant diagram, similar to that used by Sandler and Tschirhart (1980).

The question of how many individuals N should be resident in a local authority is considered in quadrant II of Fig. 12.2. The costs per capita of providing a particular local public good (e.g. street lighting, fire service, education) depend on the number of residents who share the total cost. The curve A illustrates costs per capita; as more people live in the locality, there is a reduction in the share that each resident pays of the total cost T incurred by providing some service level of the good in question. If we assume that the total cost is constant, then curve A will be a rectangular hyperbola. It is an average cost curve for citizens for a constant level of output. However, by comparison, the

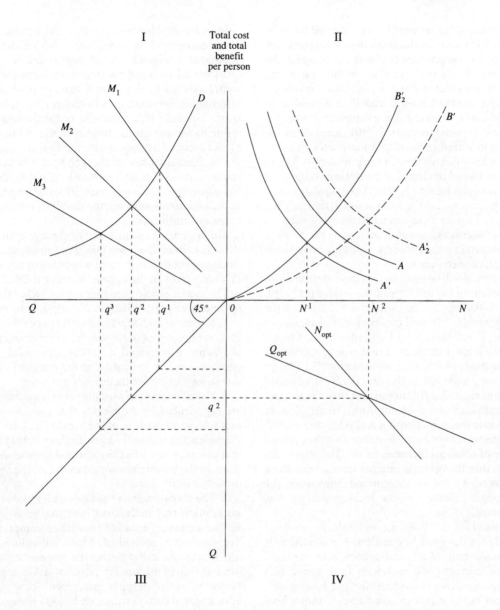

Figure 12.2 'Optimum' local community.

Source: adapted from Sandler and Tschirhart (1980) 'Theory of Clubs: An Evaluative Survey', *Journal of Economic Literature*, xviii, p. 1486.

curve A' shows the *marginal savings in per capita cost* as the number of residents increases. The curve measures the amount by which A falls as the population of the locality increases. It shows the fall in average costs as numbers increase by one additional individual. If T is the total cost of providing the good, then the change in per capita costs of providing the good is

(12.1) $\qquad d(T/N)/dN = T/N^2$

This is the marginal cost savings experienced as a consequence of increasing the number in the locality.

Increasing the number of residents reduces the costs of a fixed level of the public good. On the other hand, as more individuals settle in the locality, costs of crowding will be experienced by the residents. The public good in question is not a pure public good (see chapter 4) but one whereby congestion costs are experienced as capacity levels are reached. The B

curves indicate the per capita crowding cost for individuals. Such costs increase as the population size increases. By comparison, B' shows the *marginal per capita crowding* costs, i.e. the amount by which crowding costs increase as the population increases. In interpreting the curves A' and B', it is possible to think of curve A' as a marginal benefit curve (i.e. reduction in costs) associated with increases in the population and of curve B' as a marginal cost curve associated with an increase in the population. In this context it should be clear that the optimal number of residents in the locality is N^1. (The population size should be increased to the point at which the marginal gains to residents are made equal to the marginal costs to club residents as a result of increasing the number in the locality; i.e. the property rights are vested with existing club members.)

However, it will be obvious that this solution is not independent of the total size of the service provided. For example, suppose that the level of output of the good increased. The total cost may as a consequence increase. The A' curve would be shifted upward to A'_2. It is possible also that the increased expenditure might alleviate the crowding cost associated with a greater number of people, and in this case the B' curve would shift to the right, thereby increasing the optimal number of individuals for the community. In the diagram we illustrate the shift in both A and B functions to A'_2 and B'_2 respectively. It is evident then that the optimal number of residents increases to N^2. The important point is that the optimal number of residents for a local authority can be determined only when the 'appropriate' quantity of the local public good is determined.

In quadrant I, D is an individual's demand schedule for the good in question. For simplicity it is assumed that tastes and income are identical between residents, and therefore, once again, this is a 'representative individual' for the locality. M_1 is the per capita marginal cost curve. It shows how costs increase for each resident as the quantity of the local public good increases. On face value, the question of what output of the good to produce appears quite easy to resolve. The solution would appear to be Oq^1. Yet it has already been argued that the marginal costs of the good will be a function of the number of people in the community, and therefore M_1, M_2, M_3 relate to different numbers (e.g. 100, 200, 300 residents in the community). It is obvious then that, until the question of the optimal number of individuals in the community is resolved, it is impossible to determine how much of the good should be provided.

In so far as both these questions have to be solved simultaneously, it is important to utilize the other quadrants in Fig. 12.2. A 45 degree line is used in quadrant III to transpose quantities from the horizontal axis on to the vertical axis. In quadrant IV information derived from quadrants I and II are collated. The line N_{opt} plots the optimal number of residents for any given quantity of the public good. (This is derived from quadrant II.) The line Q_{opt} plots the optimal quantity of the good for any number resident in the neighbourhood. (This is derived from quadrant I, via quadrant III.) The intersection of the two curves indicates the simultaneous solution to the two problems.

Moving back from quadrant IV through quandrant III to quadrant I, we see that this implies that Oq^2 should be produced. Tracing upwards from quadrant IV to quadrant II, the optimal number is ON^2.

The model as discussed may appear rather simplistic, and there are qualifications that might be made.

1. Musgrave and Musgrave (1989) note that technical economies of scale may be experienced in the provision of increased quantities of a local public good. Above it is assumed that the marginal costs of increasing output are themselves increasing.

2. Not all benefits of a locally provided public good are experienced by the locality that provides it. For example, some portion of the benefits may spill over to residents in another locality. Topham (1983) argues that this may not affect the optimal number of residents in the locality but would influence the optimal provision of the good.

3. The above analysis has been undertaken on the assumption that individuals have similar tastes and similar incomes; i.e. we have used the assumption of a 'representative' individual. Since individuals have different tastes, it may be that the efficient solution is for individuals of similar taste to group together. However, with multiple groupings, some of the advantages of cost-sharing may be lost. The question of how groupings occur will be considered in the next section.

4. If individuals of similar income were grouped together, the outcome might be unstable. If the taxes that individuals pay for a local public good were higher as a consequence of higher income, the poor might enjoy a greater quantity of a local public good if they were resident in a high-income area. There may well be a tendency for zoning on the part of high-income groups in order to exclude the poor.

5. The optimal size of the local authority depends on the kind of public good under consideration. It will be evident to the reader that it is the element of

congestion that occurs in a local public good which determines that the size of the locality should be restricted. If the good were a pure public good then there would be no limit to the size of the locality. If there were no congestion costs the optimal size of a locality would be infinite. However, a given locality may be responsible for the provision of more than one local public good, and local public goods will differ according to their capacity limits and the congestion costs thereby created. It may be impractical to have local authorities of different sizes for each and every local public good that any locality may provide.

12.4 The Tiebout hypothesis: 'voting with your feet'

Following a discussion of the optimal size of clubs, it is appropriate to consider how individuals take up club membership, i.e. how they choose a local authority in which to reside. Tiebout (1956) argued that individuals select the local community whose provision of local public goods and tax prices best satisfies their preferences. Tiebout's analysis was framed as a direct response to Samuelson's (1954) conclusion that individuals would not reveal their preferences for public goods. Tiebout, however, argued that in a local community context individuals would reveal their preferences, by moving to the locality that best reflected their tastes and offered the preferred tax–benefit mix (if mobility was relatively costless). As Hughes has observed,

we may assume that households will move so as, in effect, to subscribe to the clubs (local governments) whose policies most closely match their own preferences. This is equivalent to the competitive processes of matching consumer preferences and cost conditions in a market with many buyers and sellers and it is possible to show that under appropriate conditions similar efficiency properties will characterise the ultimate equilibrium of the distribution of households across local authorities. (Hughes 1987, p. 5)

Samuelson (1954) noted the problem for the provision of public goods by large groups, i.e. the problem of preference revelation. The Tiebout hypothesis appears to mitigate this, in so far as individuals reveal their preferences by 'voting with their feet'. For example, those who like expenditure on libraries and the arts can reside with others of the same persuasion. Those with a preference for other forms of fiscal expenditure will join their respective local 'club' elsewhere. If each local community offered a different menu of public goods expenditures, then each individual could be thought to select the local community that provided a level of output corresponding to his or her preferences.

It should be clear, with respect to the decentralization theorem, that the Tiebout effect increases the welfare gains from decentralization:

household mobility means that differences in local preferences and in the policies of local government may reinforce each other ... In other words household mobility shifts the trade-off between local autonomy and national standard decisively in favour of local autonomy because it increases the homogeneity of such preferences between local jurisdictions. (Hughes 1987, p. 5)

Holcombe (1983) illustrates the Tiebout equilibrium using a diagram similar to Fig. 12.3. In part (b) of the figure the vertical sum of three individuals with different demand curves (D_1, D_2 and D_3) for a local public good G is ΣD. With a marginal cost of provision of G equal to OT and equal tax shares, the equilibrium quantity (either on a $\Sigma D = MC$ or a median voter argument) is Oq^2. For this outcome for individual 1, whose demand curve is D_1, there is a welfare loss from over-provision of triangle 145. For individual 3 the welfare loss from under-provision is triangle 123. If there are competing local jurisdictions, individual 1 can 'exit' to a community of like-minded individuals, and similarly for individual 3. In an ideal outcome there would be three communities with equilibrium as in parts (a), (b) and (c) of the figure. If in each community there are (three) identical individuals (each enjoying a situation where their demand equals OP_t) there are no welfare loss triangles. In each community there is a different level of provision of local public goods Oq^1, Oq^2 and Oq^3. Given fiscal migration, welfare losses from allocatively different outcomes from some individuals' equilibrium quantities can be avoided. Individual 3 has expressed preferences for a greater provision of the local public good by moving to a jurisdiction which offers greater provision of the local public good. Voting with their feet, both individual 1 and individual 3 no longer experience the welfare loss of consuming a level of provision of a local public good which is different to that which they would prefer.

In this way the 'Tiebout hypothesis' is obviously of considerable theoretical importance. It stands as a qualification to the problems of public good provision. But, in practice, how likely is it to act as an equilibrating mechanism? To answer this question it is possible to refer to at least two areas of discussion. First, there is the restrictiveness of the assumptions

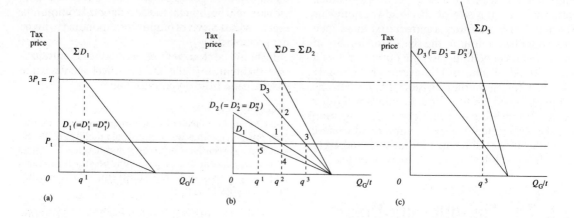

Figure 12.3 Tiebout adjustments.

Source: based upon Holcombe (1983) *Public Finance and the Political Process*, Southern Illinois University Press, Illinois.

that underly the Tiebout mechanism. On the basis of analysis by Tresch (1981), Hughes (1987), Musgrave and Musgrave (1989) and Boadway (1979), attention can be drawn to the assumptions required to make mobility efficient. Secondly, there is empirical work which looks for evidence that fiscal considerations play any part at all in the decision of individuals to reside in a particular locality.

12.4.1 The Tiebout mechanism: underlying assumptions

The following list of assumptions, which is by no means exhaustive, adds a note of scepticism to the claim that individuals can easily locate in the local communities that reflect their preferences.

Full knowledge of all the communities' characteristics

It is assumed that the individual has complete information of the local taxes and expenditures.

Costless mobility

The mechanism functions only if fiscal considerations play a decisive role in location choice. Of course, other factors, such as job opportunities, friendship and family ties, typically play their part. It has been alleged that the assumption that only fiscal considerations are important 'makes the voting by feet hypothesis somewhat unrealistic, except in a setting where people work in the inner city and may choose among the suburbs for residence' (Musgrave and Musgrave 1989, p. 453). Costless mobility implies that there are no work problems, i.e. that households can move without having to

obtain alternative jobs or without having to worry about transport costs to their place of work. Housing considerations are also important. In the UK, for example, there is evidence that the local authority council house system has reduced mobility over long distances for those who seek housing in this sector (Hughes and McCormick 1981).

Externalities

The movement of a household from one locality to another may cause externalities in the form of added congestion. For a welfare-maximizing equilibrium, the Tiebout mechanism must create a situation whereby it is impossible for any individual to increase utility as a result of changing communities. However, when there are externalities even costless mobility may not be sufficient to attain this result. As individuals migrate, externalities are experienced by those already resident in the community.

This literature (see, for example, Buchanan and Wagner 1970, Buchanan and Goetz 1972, Flatters, Henderson and Mieszkowski 1974) has been discussed by Boadway (1979). Assume that individuals migrate between districts until the benefit they derive from being resident in one locality is equal to the benefit they derive from being in another. If total benefit (utility) derived from being in locality X is denoted by TB_x and total benefit from being in Y is TB_y, then equilibrium occurs where

$$(12.2) \qquad TB_x = TB_y$$

But will this prove a welfare maximum? When an individual moves to a region, she may add congestion costs to already crowded facilities. If MC_x represents marginal congestion costs of adding one more person to region X, then a welfare maximum requires that

$$(12.3) \qquad TB_x - MC_x = TB_y - MC_y$$

Because the individual moving into a local community is not concerned with the congestion costs that this implies for existing residents, her decision to move will be determined by the difference between TB_x and TB_y and there will be no incentive to move at a point when TB_x is equal to TB_y. Equilibrium occurs when equation (12.2) rather than (12.3) is satisfied. (Note that now the property right is with the entrant, who is able to join any club she wishes.)

One variant of this argument which Boadway (1979) discusses relates to the impact of migration on tax costs. The share of local taxes (which has already been taken into account in TB_x) is relevant for other existing members of the locality. As noted in our discussion of the optimum size of clubs, the arrival of an additional individual reduces the taxes that existing residents have to pay to finance a given level of expenditure. As a result, the benefit of one more resident in X (to the new *and* existing residents) is $TB_x + t_x$ where t_x is the tax paid by the marginal immigrant. Ignoring problems of congestion, it is argued that a welfare optimum requires

$$(12.4) \qquad TB_x + t_x = TB_y + t_y$$

Free migration will result in an optimum only if $t_x = t_y$, that is, if the total tax bill for a marginal individual is the same in the two regions. *A priori*, there is no reason to expect that the tax bill per person will be the same in both regions. However, Topham (1983) raises a question-mark over this criticism. If there were a divergence in tax bills, then, other things equal, there would be a preference to reside in the locality where the tax bill is lower. If one area were to turn out to be a tax haven, property and house prices would rise (capitalizing the favourable tax bill) in this area, so reducing its *TB*.

Economies of scale

When there are diverse preferences for public goods, the number of local communities required to produce an equilibrium would be extremely large. This might imply many small communities, thereby missing out on possible gains that would arise from the existence of economies of scale in the production of local output.

Benefit spillover

In the analysis above, the assumption was that all of the benefits were experienced by those residents in the locality (i.e. in the club). Benefits provided by one locality may spill over into another jurisdiction. The two localities may 'internalize' this spillover by a process of direct bargaining. Alternatively, there may be a role for a central government. (This is discussed later in this chapter.) Either way, there will be a modification to the analysis outlined above.

Non-static preferences

If preferences for local public services change during the life-cycle, there are added strains for the Tiebout mechanism. At certain ages individuals have a priority for educational facilities for children: later they will be more concerned with facilities for old-age pensioners. The implication is that either households move as circumstances change, or local communities consist of individual households whose needs change simultaneously.

12.4.2 The Tiebout hypothesis: empirical tests

The improbability of all the above assumptions obtaining casts doubt on the Tiebout proposition. So how can we test whether fiscal conditions play any role in the decision to reside in a local community?

Oates (1969) focused on education expenditures per pupil and used this as a measure of the quality of public services in 53 northern New Jersey municipalities. If property is fixed, then, as people move into an area that has a superior set of public services, they will drive up property prices in that area. Oates found that property values were negatively correlated to the tax rate. He also found that school expenditures per pupil and property values were positively related, i.e. that additional fiscal spending attracted an inflow to the locality. These results support the hypothesis that individuals are willing to pay more in order to live in communities that provide high-quality services.

While Oates interprets the relationship between capitalization and effective local taxes/expenditure to indicate the explanatory power of the Tiebout hypothesis, Edel and Sclar (1974) and Hamilton (1976) are sceptical. If the Tiebout mechanism worked, then no capitalization of taxes/expenditure would be expected. If the Tiebout mechanism worked and individuals were mobile, then local communities would contain individuals with the same fiscal preferences and the tax/expenditure patterns would perfectly reflect these preferences. In effect, there would be no reason to move in a Tiebout equilibrium. Therefore the existence of tax and expenditure capitalization would reflect a disequilibrium; i.e., the Tiebout equilibrium would not have been attained. (More-

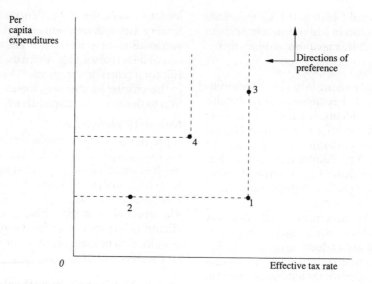

Figure 12.4 Migratory incentives.

over, it is not sufficient to argue that the Tiebout equilibrium is being reached if capitalization falls over time—see Pauly (1976) and Chaudry-Shah (1988).)

Aronson (1974) and Aronson and Schwartz (1973) develop a framework that indicates relatively attractive destinations. In Fig. 12.4 the axes measure a 'bad' effective tax rate (x axis) and 'good' per capita local government expenditures (y axis). For anyone in jurisdiction 1, any location to the north (3), west (2) or north-west (4) generally must be superior (less of a bad, more of a good or both). Hence jurisdictions should gain population relative to 1 if they are at, say, 2, 3 or 4. The process can be repeated for jurisdiction 4. The test the authors apply is that destination jurisdictions 2, 3 and 4 should gain residents relative to the origin town 1. Evidence from local government areas in both the UK and the USA offered empirical support.

A minor extension to this would be to imagine an efficient jurisdiction's frontier, EJF in Fig. 12.5, which offers the higher per capita expenditure for any effective tax rate or, equivalently, the lowest effective tax rate for any given per capita expenditure. Imposing individual i's indifference curve on the figure, i's 'ideal home' is jurisdiction H, achieving utility I_*.

Another approach to testing the Tiebout hypothesis was suggested by Gramlich and Rubinfeld (1982). They considered homogeneity of preferences by reference to responses to survey questions. If the Tiebout mechanism is relevant, then there should be some effect of the costs of moving on the pattern of preferences; that is, when there are many localities it is easy

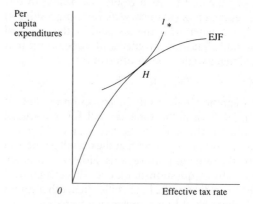

Figure 12.5 Optimal location.

for individuals to move to the one they most prefer, and hence there should be a greater homogeneity of preferences within those localities. They confirmed there was substantially greater homogeneity of demand within suburbs located near many other communities. By contrast, where there were few other communities exit was less easy and there was more heterogeneity.

12.4.3 The EC budget: public finance vs. public choice

In this section the objective is to compare the prescriptions of traditional public finance for the operation of the EC budget with those that might be derived from a public choice analysis. Lessons from the literature on fiscal federalism may be applied when formulating the role of the budget in the European Community. Fiscal federalism literature offers prescriptions concerning the assignment of fiscal tasks to the EC budget. However, the role of the budget might be quite different if a public choice critique of government were relevant? Once again, the objective is to contrast arguments from traditional (social optimality) public finance (as to how public policy *should* be pursued) with explanations from public choice theory (of how public policy actually *is* pursued). In this section concern focuses on expenditure and redistribution (as the macroeconomic functions of the EC budget are discussed in section 11.4).

In 1957 the Treaty of Rome provided that expenditure of EC institutions would be financed by a general budget. The budget has grown significantly since 1957. Today it remains small in relation to the national budgets of member states, accounting for about 1.1 per cent of EC GDP in 1992 (by comparison with the budgets of member states' national governments which averaged 30 per cent of national GDP). However, in absolute terms the Community budget is almost equal to Greece's GDP (Hitiris 1994). The growth of the budget is shown in Fig. 12.6. The main area of EC expenditure has been on agricultural policy (particularly to guarantee prices) by the European

Agricultural Guidance and Guarantee Fund but this has been falling as a share of the budget (see Table 12.1 for details of expenditure in 1991).

Until 1970 the EC budget was funded by direct contributions made by member states. Since 1970 it has been financed from the 'own resources' of the EC. 'Own resources' are those taxes that member states have agreed should be deemed the resources of the EC. Initially (in 1970) they comprised three elements: (i) customs duties levied on goods imported from outside the EC, (ii) agricultural and sugar levies, (iii) a share of the VAT revenue raised in each country. The VAT contribution is the amount of revenue that would be raised from levying a specific VAT rate (e.g. 1 per cent VAT rate) on a standardized or 'harmonized' base.

In recent years the finances of the budget have been reformed. The 'Delors package' was meant to apply throughout the period 1988–92. It proposed that: (i) the VAT resource continue with a ceiling of 1.4 per cent (with the assessment base not exceeding 55 per cent of each member states GNP at market prices, measured uniformly under a Commission Directive so that high consumption and low income member states would not be unreasonably charged) (Hitiris 1994) and (ii) that a new, 'fourth resource' be added to 'own resources'. This new source of finance would provide the revenue required to cover expenditure in excess of the traditional 'own resources' (including VAT receipts). The budget would be subject to an overall

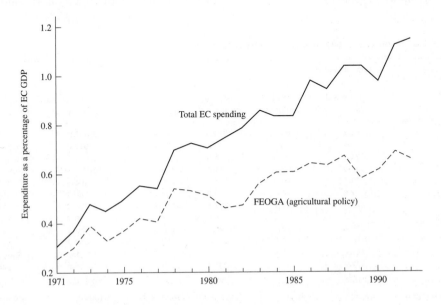

Figure 12.6 The European Community budget in relation to member state's GDP, 1971–92.

Source: Smith (1992) with permission of the Institute for Fiscal Studies.

Table 12.1 Expenditures made in 1991, by sector and recipient member states (Ecu m.)

Member state	EAGGF Guarantee	EAGGF Guidance	Regional Fund	Social Fund	Repayment by Member States	Other	Total[a]
Belgium	1,459.4	11.3	46.4	65.3	12.5	1,039.1	2,634.0 (4.9%)
Denmark	1,215.6	14.1	11.3	45.8	4.2	88.8	1,379.8 (2.6%)
France	6,332.7	362.9	323.2	513.5	63.2	556.0	8,152.5 (15.2%)
Germany	4,990.5	181.0	94.8	239.7	252.9	838.5	6,597.4 (12.3%)
Greece	2,211.8	223.4	537.2	349.1	—	367.0	3,688.5 (6.9%)
Irish Republic	1,628.7	153.6	411.9	403.8	101.5	110.3	2,809.7 (5.2%)
Italy	5,347.0	203.8	710.8	414.5	5.7	629.5	7,311.2 (13.6%)
Luxemburg	2.8	5.5	18.3	1.8	—	240.2	268.5 (0.5%)
Netherlands	2,469.8	15.2	34.6	122.5	211.6	146.0	2,999.8 (5.6%)
Portugal	316.4	196.9	971.2	379.3	49.4	315.1	2,228.2 (4.1%)
Spain	3,300.3	420.3	1,488.8	697.0	482.3	486.0	6,874.8 (12.8%)
UK	2,252.7	98.5	530.1	636.9	137.6	413.6	4,069.5 (7.6%)
TOTAL	31,527.8	1,886.4	5,178.6	3,869.3	1,320.8	5,231.0	49,008.5 (91.9%)

[a] Figures in parentheses show the percentage of the total budget allocated. The remaining 8.9% unallocated includes payments for overseas aid and administration.
Source: Bladen-Hovell and Symons (1994).

ceiling for the total of all own resources of 1.2 per cent of EC GNP. The proportion of farm spending in the budget was expected to decline from two-thirds to 56 per cent by 1992, with a rise in the share of the structural funds financing regional and social policy (Hitiris 1994). From an equity point of view, the effect of introducing the GNP-based resource would be to make the EC tax system more closely tied to the principle of 'ability to pay'. Contributions in 1992 of member states are shown in Table 12.2.

In February 1992 the Commission published a document referred to as the 'Delors II' package. This proposed further reform. The real value (in 1992 prices) of EC expenditure was to be increased from ECU 67 billion in 1992 to ECU 87.5 billion in 1997. Priority should be given to (i) additional expenditure on economic and social cohesion, (ii) promotion of 'a favourable environment for competitiveness', and (iii) foreign aid. Agricultural spending was permitted to increase in real terms but it was to continue falling

Table 12.2 Own resources in 1992 by member state (Ecu m.)

Member State	Type of resource					
	Agricultural levies	Sugar and isoglucose	Customs duties	GNP-based own resource	VAT-based own resource	Total own resources
Belgium	84.1	69.4	832.5	294.3	1,108.1	2,388.4
Denmark	6.3	39.1	222.3	189.3	618.0	1,074.9
France	74.7	321.8	1,548.9	1,719.0	7,505.7	11,170.2
Germany	142.0	333.0	3,546.0	2,413.3	10,162.2	16,596.5
Greece	16.2	16.9	178.1	111.5	508.5	831.2
Ireland	2.0	12.0	153.2	54.4	248.2	469.7
Italy	346.1	124.2	1,037.4	1,787.2	5,278.0	8,572.9
Luxemburg	0.1	—	11.5	17.4	79.2	108.2
Netherlands	108.4	78.2	1,160.7	400.1	1,700.4	3,447.8
Portugal	117.2	0.1	117.0	103.0	469.7	806.9
Spain	141.3	50.0	555.8	774.2	3,531.5	5,052.8
UK	177.9	67.7	2,236.5	1,459.3	3,456.6	7,398.0
TOTAL	1,216.2	1,112.4	11,599.9	9,323.1	34,666.0	57,917.6
(% of total budget)	(2.1)	(1.9)	(20.0)	(16.1)	(60.0)	(100.0)

Source: Bladen-Hovell and Symons (1994).

as a proportion of the total budget (from 51 to 46 per cent of total appropriations). The structural funds would increase from 28 to 32 per cent (Hitiris 1994). It was proposed that the ceiling on 'own resources' be increased from 1.2 to 1.37 per cent of EC GNP by 1997. This would be achieved mainly by extending the GNP-based contributions to finance the budget and at the same time reducing VAT-based finance. The maximum VAT rate would be reduced from 1.4 per cent to 1 per cent over the period 1995–9. For countries with a per capita GNP of less than 90 per cent of the Community average, the assessment base would be reduced from 55 to 50 per cent of their GNP as from 1995 (Hitiris 1994). The Edinburgh European Council (December 1992) adopted the new proposals but subsequent events (e.g. the uncertainty surrounding the ratification of the Maastricht Treaty) led to the Delors II package being shelved.

Changes since 1957 and proposed changes in the Delors II package indicate the direction of change in the EC budget. The question is, 'are these changes consistent with recommendations that might arise from the (traditional) social optimality public finance literature or, instead, are they predictable from a public choice approach?' At this stage of development the EC budget is still very small but, if steps were taken towards a pre-federal arrangement, how should fiscal policy be assigned between EC and national budgets?

12.4.3a   Lessons from fiscal federalism

Why should member states assign more responsibility to a central budget (i.e. move toward the direction of federation)? Oates (1972) was concerned with why there should be a movement to decentralization and, in answering this question, different budgetary functions were considered. Some fiscal responsibilities appeared the prerogative of a central government, while others were better set under the control of lower levels of government. For example, as a summary, Oates suggested that an 'attractive solution' would be to:

Let the central government resolve the distribution problem and allow decentralized levels of government to provide public services. (Oates 1972: p. 150)

Following the fiscal federalism analysis in this chapter, begin by asking the question which of the following tasks should be assigned to an EC budget:

(a) *Expenditure*

Oates (1972) offers *a decentralization theorem*. When a central government is constrained to supply uniform quantities of any service and when preferences for quantities of public goods differ systematically between member states, there will be welfare loss if a central government is unable to meet the different requirements for local public goods.[1] Of course there are qualifications. For example, joint action may be preferable if it offers gains via economies of scale. However, notwithstanding such considerations, the argument for centralization of expenditure policy is open to question. To the extent that individuals may become more mobile in the EC the Tiebout hypothesis (see section 12.3) supports the argument against centralizing expenditure policy. If individuals can express their preference over more 'locally provided' public goods by voting 'with their feet' there are welfare gains from decentralization.

Applying the decentalization theorem to the EC would suggest that only public goods or 'supranational' public goods be financed by a European Community. Defence and foreign relations are usually cited as examples of supranational public goods. In fact, the decentralization theorem appears to offer support for the principle of subsidiarity, i.e. that (broadly speaking) no government intervention at the central level is justified if activities undertaken at member-state level involves no significant cross border spill-over effect. Indeed, only when such spill-over effects cannot be resolved easily by negotiation between member states should the central government become involved (i.e. when transaction costs are reduced by intervention from the centre). The subsidiarity principle (Bureau and Champseur 1992) states that budgetary intervention at an EC level should be admitted only in the presence of cross-border externalities or economies of scale which cannot be properly alleviated by simple co-ordination between concerned national governments.[2]

(b) *Income redistribution*

It is usually argued that the task of redistribution should be assigned to a central (or federal) government (Musgrave 1959). This is because of the import-

---

[1] Tiebout (1956) provided analysis that would support this.

[2] While currently, EC budget support of the Common Agricultural Policy might not easily be defensible by reference to public good theory it has been suggested that to shift income support for agriculture to member states would only result in greater distortion. This might arise if national governments were to compete in offering subsidies to increase the share of the European market for their own farmers. Of course the idea that such competition would necessarily prove harmful is questionable. However, the comparison again is between welfare with and without centralization (Walsh 1992).

ance of mobility when considering the effectiveness of income redistribution measures. Musgrave (1983) summarizes the principles which underlie the assignment of taxation between central (federal) and state government. First, highly progressive taxes are to be allocated to higher levels of government. Secondly, taxes on company incomes should be allocated to higher levels. Thirdly, taxes on an immobile base (e.g. land) should be raised by lower-level government. In this discussion the mobility of taxpayers is important. With high marginal rates of tax in one member state workers and capital might be provided with an incentive to leave the jurisdiction. This would reduce the effectiveness of any attempt at redistribution. The question is then, how important is the issue of mobility when dealing with the assignment of fiscal tasks between EC and member states' national budgets? To answer this, first consider more closely the arguments concerning redistribution and mobility and second compare these arguments with other arguments which support moving the task of redistribution to the EC budget.

(i) Redistribution and mobility

If individuals are mobile between local jurisdictions, an 'aggressive' policy to redistribute income from wealthy to poor households within any one local jurisdiction faces the risk that low-income individuals will be attracted to the locality and that high-income individuals will be driven out. Evidence in the US reveals that household mobility would cause under provision of assistance to low income families in a wholly decentralized system (Brown and Oates 1987). Inman and Rubinfeld (1991) advise that redistribution should be implemented in the EC as a 'central government transfer program'. They note that: 'With mobile households and a common citizenship, the marginal tax costs of income redistribution within each member state is increased as each member dollar transferred by an upper income household to a lower income resident will likely attract new low income residents from neighboring states' (p. 7).

As high-income factors of production become more mobile it will prove increasingly difficult for any state jurisdiction to achieve redistribution goals independently of other jurisdictions; attempts to redistribute within a jurisdiction will simply drive out mobile factors. Even if it were to remain possible, increased mobility increases the price elasticity of supply of factors and, as Sinn (1994) demonstrates, when a tax levied on mobile factors causes movement between jurisdictions, taxation creates higher deadweight losses. Does this then mean that a central government should take over the task of redistribution?

Some qualifications should be noted. First, fiscal federalism analysis does not reach the conclusion that *all* redistribution should be assigned to the central government. Some arguments (e.g. Pauly 1973) suggest that there is often much greater concern in a community for the local indigent poor than for the poor elsewhere. In a local community, redistribution can be viewed as a 'local public good' and it can be demonstrated that this might be better achieved by local than by central government. Secondly, the prescriptions of fiscal federalism are called into question by public choice scholars who attach importance to 'tax competition' between different local jurisdictions. Such economists dismiss the assumption that government acts benignly in pursuit of the 'public interest' and replace it with a view of government as a 'Leviathan' (Brennan and Buchanan 1980). If centralization of fiscal policy weakens the constraints that limit the growth of public expenditure then transferring fiscal responsibility to the centre is to be resisted. Decentralization offers competition in so far as taxpayers are mobile and able to chose their preferred jurisdiction. Mobility provides a rationale for retaining fiscal authority at the local level because mobility intensifies competition between lower-level governments.

While these theoretical doubts are present, there is also significant doubt as to whether or not the extent of mobility in Europe warrants providing a greater role for redistribution to the EC budget. Eichenberger (1994) questions the importance of mobility in Europe. He regards the mobility argument as 'not compelling'; citing empirical work that suggests that lower-level government is successful at redistributing income (e.g. of Gold (1991), for the US and of Kirchgassner and Pommerehne (1993), for Switzerland). He argues that 'lower level governments are indeed actively and successfully redistributing income...' (Eichenberger 1994, p. 406). On the other hand, while the importance of mobility is questionable, there is reason to suggest that mobility has had an increasing effect on national fiscal policy in the 1980s and 1990s. With reference to the 1980s, Hoeller and Louppe (1995, p. 82) note that 'while the cross border flow of people has remained very low, capital flows have surged'. Mobility increased in the 1980s and national tax policy in European countries was affected. One reason for the wave of 'supply-side' tax reform (covering reduction of basic rates of income tax and reduction of the number of income tax bands) was the increased mobility of capital and skilled labour which made it difficult for any country to resist unilaterally (Dilnot 1994).

While the main thrust of the argument concerns the effect that mobility has on the capacity for national redistribution there are also efficiency considerations. Inman and Rubinfeld (1991, p. 6) note: 'In the simplest case of identical private economies, public good levels and tax structures on mobile residents (requiring therefore equal populations for an optimal allocation), any state with a marginally lower population will attract additional residents because of its lower per resident public goods costs'. Other things equal, mobility will mean that citizens will move to those states where the tax costs of public goods are lower. Boadway and Wildasin (1984) show that, if the marginal product of factors were equal prior to any factor movement, the attraction of less expensive public goods in some jurisdictions would cause efficiency losses. Hence the prescription by Inman and Rubinfeld (1991, p. 6) is that 'natural resource rich member states should be taxed and natural resource poor states should be subsidized'. This efficiency argument only serves to support the proposition that increased mobility should be associated with a more redistributive EC budget.

(ii) Social cohesion

Another reason for expecting that the EC budget might play a greater role in redistribution has to do with the pursuit of social cohesion. The process of integration may create more problems for some countries than for others. For example, when a country becomes a member of the EC it relinquishes the ability to use external protection if domestic industries and domestic employment appear threatened (so that the benefits of membership are called into question). Redistribution to deal with problems of cohesion may apply on a short-term or on a long-term basis. On a short-term basis, transfers from the EC budget to 'weaker' countries are transitional assistance for states with severe adjustment policies (Smith, 1992). On a long-term basis, some manufacturing countries (e.g. Germany) may do relatively better when other member countries open their markets to each other and to compensate weaker nations, who may do less well from the customs union arrangement, redistribution may be required. Sinn (1994, p. 95) notes 'it is often feared that the EC's function is to help Germany dominate Europe's economy. Regardless of how dubious such a fear may seem from a German perspective the true aspect of it is that a manufacturing country like Germany needs large markets to fully exploit the economies of scale'.

This kind of argument can be set in an even broader context. For example, it might be argued that economic union enhances international relations. A reduction in the threat of military conflict brings resource saving to member states and, even if some member states have to compensate (redistribute to) others to integrate, the costs are recovered via a reduction in military expenditure. Commenting on budget redistribution, Sinn (1994, p. 95) notes that: 'Even if the poorer countries benefit more from Europe than the richer ones do, the premium may well be worth paying if it avoids the risk of returning to Europe's horrible past. The saving in military expenditure alone dwarfs the EC expenditure.' Once again, 'problems of social cohesion' suggests that increased integration will be linked to an increased redistributive role via the EC budget and this may be required on a long-term basis.

(iii) Insurance

A third reason to expect that the EC budget may include 'redistributive' features has to do with the need to offer the budget a greater insurance role. Uncertainty is associated with integrated economic development and EC budgetary rules, defined in terms of pre-set criteria (e.g. net transfers related to unemployment or low income), are of value to all countries. While, in the main, the weaker and poorer member states may benefit from direct financial transfers, it is possible that even richer states may feel better off to know that such protection is available. Of course, on occasion richer states may also receive financial assistance; Sinn (1994) notes the transfers received by Germany to assist with re-unification.

If further uncertainty accompanies increased integration a more redistributive EC budget may be expected. Policy discussion concerning movement towards monetary union raises the prospect that, as capital and skilled labour become more mobile, they will be attracted to 'a central block of economic activity and prosperity which stretches from south-east England, Denmark and the Netherlands... to south east France and northern Italy' (Swan 1995, p. 284). Countries on the periphery of the EC may fare less well and an even more active redistributive policy has been prescribed. The MacDougall Committee in 1977 argued that, if exchange rate stability reduced the ability for weaker, less prosperous member states to devalue, fiscal transfers would be necessary to stabilize income divergences between nations (CEC 1977). The Committee envisaged three stages: (i) pre-federal with a community public sector taking up 2–2.5 per cent of GDP; (ii) federation with a small community public sector 5 to 7 per cent of EC GDP; (iii) federation with a large community public sector 20–25 per cent GDP (Hitiris 1994). More recent estimates, based on the Commission's calculations, challenge the projections of the MacDougall Committee. Bladen-Hovell and Symons (1994, p. 385) report that: 'On the assumption that income support would be triggered once unemployment differentials reach 2 per cent, the programme would be able to offset approximately 20 per cent of a decline in a region's relative income at a cost to the EC budget of only 0.25 per cent of EC GDP.' Once again, the analysis is consistent; while there is dispute as to the precise budgetary requirements all parties suggests a more redistributive budget as integration increases.

Present arrangements restrain the extent to which the EC budget can achieve redistribution:

First, estimates of the extent to which it affects redistribution only make sense by reference to net tax payments from member states. Some might prefer that the EC budget were focused on interpersonal redistribution (eg. Smith 1988) but administrative costs mean that inter-country redistribution remains the critical consideration. Transfers occur between the EC budget and national government budgets; 'there are relatively few areas where existing Community policies deal directly with private sector agents' (Smith 1988, p. 111).

Secondly, Wildasin (1990) discussed the problems of dealing with redistribution when national governments also deal with redistribution. If the EC wanted to help individuals in say a southern region of Italy, there is always the problem that the Italian govern-

ment might take such assistance into consideration when considering how much assistance it should give to that region. In this way EC redistribution would simply 'crowd out' assistance by national governments.

To what extent then has the EC proved able to redistribute? Figure 12.7 records the net contributions of the EC budget and, in general, suggests that poorer countries gain most (e.g. Ireland, Portugal and Greece) and richer countries (e.g. Germany) contribute most. However, there are many difficulties in answering this question (see Bowles and Jones 1992):

(i) When looking at the budget it must be remembered that the focus of attention is simply on financial flows. Countries also gain differentially by their access to the large market within the EC.

(ii) Some of the policies which the budget supports creates redistribution effects which are not captured in financial flows. For example, agricultural price support causes consumers in some states to pay more for goods from agricultural producers in other member states. If lamb is imported to the UK from New Zealand a tax is paid on imports into the UK which is forwarded to Brussels. However, if lamb is bought from France at a price higher than New Zealand lamb but less than the price of New Zealand lamb plus the tariff, an 'implicit' tax is placed on UK consumers. Prest (1985) refers to an Institute of Fiscal Studies (1983) report that estimated such implicit taxation for the UK at £4 billion. These implicit taxes are seldom estimated or considered in any formal analysis.

(iii) It is difficult to interpret the 'own resources' of the EC. Are these contributions made by member

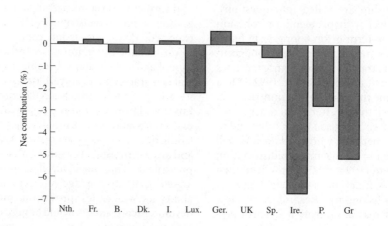

Figure 12.7 Net contributions as a proportion of GDP.
Source: Smith (1992) with permission of the Institute for Fiscal Studies.

states or are they genuinely the 'own resources' of the EC? Those committed to the EC argue the latter. They refer to the 'Rotterdam Principle'. For example, taxes paid on imports into the port of Rotterdam may be transferred to the budget by the Netherlands but, as the goods may be consumed ultimately in other EC countries, it is citizens of other EC countries who actually pay the tax. As such, these are not contributions by the Netherlands but 'own resources' of the EC (see Bowles and Jones (1992) for further discussion).

(iv) In interpreting the transfer of funds there is a difference between transfer payments and payments for real resources. For example, some part of expenditures in Belgium will be for administrative expenditures carried out for the EC (Reichenbach 1983).

In conclusion, the scope for inter-personal redistribution in the EC is limited and assessments of the extent of international redistribution via the budget must be qualified. However, the predictions of literature on fiscal federalism suggest that there will be greater scope for redistribution via the EC budget in the future. This does not only depend on the argument that mobility in the EC may increase. It also depends on the arguments in favour of increased social cohesion and the provision of mutual insurance. By comparison, the scope for expenditure may be far more limited in the future. Only when collaboration between countries is impossible should the EC budget deal with issues of cross-border spill-over and with the provision of 'supranational' public goods (where free rider problems may be relevant).

As far as intergovernmental grants are concerned, literature on fiscal federalism might support unconditional or equalizing grants from the more prosperous to the poorer jurisdictions to promote the 'redistribution goal' of horizontal equity. It would support matching grants to decentralized governments for programmes that involve external benefits to other jurisdictions (Hitiris 1994).

12.4.3b Lesson's from public choice

Having illustrated the way in which the traditional approach to public finance offers advice now compare the advice that would stem from public choice. Note again, how the perception of failings in the political process create a difference.

(*i*) *Allocation*

The public choice school is more alarmed at the prospect of assigning greater responsibility for allocation to a higher-level government authority because it is expected that the problems of 'government failure' will be greater. The fear is then that expenditure policies would bear even less relation to voters' preferences than if decision-making was assigned to 'lower' levels of government.

Downs (1957) highlights the costs which voters face when acquiring information. It can be argued that problems of information are greater the more tiers of government exist and the more that decision-making is referred to higher tiers of government. Again, a case for decentralization of allocation decisions is made but this time the emphasis is on problems within the political decision-making process. Vaubel (1994) argues that the EC is attractive to national politicians precisely because it increases information costs for voters. He reviews empirical work which indicates that voters are less informed about EC policies than about national policies in their home country. It is argued that politicians are then able to transfer potentially unpopular policies to the EC where less is understood by voters (e.g. agricultural price support). Also rent-seeking producers will prefer that allocation decisions are made at a higher tier of government as it makes it more difficult for voters to perceive the additional costs. As another tier of government obfuscates, Vaubel also argues that the EC community serves as an 'alibi' or 'scapegoat' for national politicians who want to introduce policies which might threaten electoral support. Such policies may be at variance with the wishes of the median voter at home. However, as the division of powers in the Community are blurred to voters, national politicians can argue that they are 'compelled' to introduce such changes. Assigning greater responsibility to the centre reduces the ability of voters to monitor government and increases the scope for national politicians to respond to the demands for inefficient expenditure programmes that generate rents for producers.

Buchanan and Tullock (1962) have noted that log-rolling may lead to 'excessive' expenditure the more that finance is available from a central budget. In the US there have been allegations of 'pork-barrel' deals, where a representative from one jurisdiction agrees to vote for expenditure in another jurisdiction in return for a similar pledge. Such discussion suggests that total expenditure from a central budget may be expanded beyond the optimum. For this reason, leaving more responsibility to finance expenditure at state level may prove one way of mitigating failure. The more that tax costs are felt elsewhere (other jurisdictions) the more that states are likely to fail to internalize the full costs of expenditure programmes (Weingast *et al.* 1981—see section 12.9). Olson (1971) notes that 'excessive' public sector spending is likely when the benefits of programmes are limited to only a few while costs are widely spread over all the population. If expenditure programmes in a (local) jurisdiction were to be financed by taxes raised within the (local) jurisdiction the possibility for cost spreading would be reduced.

For empirical support, Schneider (1995) refers to earlier research which shows that institutional differences matter with respect to the growth of government. Pommerehne (1978) looks at public expenditure in 111 Swiss municipalities. It was expected that the introduction of representatives into the democratic decision-making process would create distortion between the preferences of the median voter and the actual outcome of collective decision-making. Support for this proposition emerges in Pommerehne (1978) and in Pommerehne and Schneider (1978, 1982). Schneider (1995, p. 9) concludes—'the representative form of government substantially changes (the nature of) the outcome of the political process, i.e. it increases government activity to a level greater than would be reached if it were directly determined by voters/tax payers'. From this Schneider argues that, while 'the removal of intra European barriers to the movement of people, goods capital and services might weaken the influence of special interest groups and bureaucracies in member states . . .', 'a growth at the federal European level has to be expected as soon as Europe wide interest groups and parties have been fully established . . .' The implication is that an additional layer of 'representation' (with decisions removed to higher levels of government) will only compound problems. Schneider proposes a strict European constitution to constrain decision-making at the EC level.

(ii) Redistribution

The argument of Brennan and Buchanan (1980) in favour of decentralization is that, within a decentralized structure, governments are forced to compete. Just as competition in the private sector exercises its disciplinary force, so competition among different units of government at a decentralized level of government can break the monopolistic hold of a large government. Collusion reduces the possibility of exit for voters. Brennan and Buchanan (1980, p. 182) note the possibilities of collusion between separate government units:

In return for an appropriate share of the additional revenue, the central government would act as an enforcer of the agreement between governments, doling out financial penalties to those jurisdictions which attempted to breach the agreement. Appropriate 'fiscal effort' would become an important criterion for determining the share of total revenue that went to each lower level government: If some state/province levied a low rate of tax in relation to some instrument over which it retained jurisdiction, other states would need to be able to penalize it by means of its grant appropriation by central government.

This 'collusion hypothesis' suggests an absence of fiscal competition. It suggests size of government should vary inversely with decentralization. Oates (1985) explored this in his empirical study of forty-four countries (including the US) but was unable to find any evidence of a significant negative relationship. Nelson (1987) also finds no support for the proposition that the less centralized the federation the greater the degree of intensity of competition between component governments and the smaller the share of aggregate government expenditure in the GNP *ceteris paribus* (nor also has Heil (1991)). However, Eberts and Gronberg (1988) and Zax (1989) find that both greater decentralization and greater fragmentation at the county level of government contributes to smaller government.

Grossman and West (1994) attempt to test the collusion proposition directly by reference to experience in Canada. They argue that bureaucrats are concerned with the security of their position and that this security is threatened if taxpayer-citizens migrate. It is suggested that there is a great incentive for the low income to migrate and, as this threatens the position of bureaucrats, equalization grants are used to assist low-income jurisdictions. Grossman and West suggest that in Canada tax-price fixing occurred when (during the Second World War) the central government took responsibility for tax collection (income and corporation taxes). In their interpretation, the programme of equalization (installed gradually since the late 1940s) was not strictly for equity purposes. If it had been, there would be no reason to expect (as the 'collusion hypothesis' would predict) the rise in the expenditure of government as a *whole* relative to GNP. Moreover, the use of intergovernmental grants cannot be explained by efficiency considerations (internalizing externalities between local government units) for there was also evidence of grants generating a growth of federal *own purpose expenditures*.

Summary

The purpose of this section has been to consider the way in which arguments drawn from traditional public finance and arguments drawn from public choice

Table 12.3 Fiscal federalism, public choice and the EC budget

Fiscal federalism:	Public choice:
Allocation: heterogeneous preferences	**Allocation:** taxpayer-consumer information
Oates Decentralization theorem suggests that local public goods should be at the state level	*Downs*—voters are 'rationally ignorant' and are likely to know less, given the complexity of different tiers of government
Tiebout hypothesis supports the presumption that goods are provided more efficiently at a lower level of government as individuals are able to move to locations that suit their fiscal preferences	*Pommerhene and Schneider* argue that shifts from direct democracy to levels of representation distort public sector provision
	Buchanan and Tullock log rolling can increase/cause 'excessive' public expenditure. Tax costs are not fully internalized
Redistribution:	**Redistribution:**
Mobility: *Musgrave* indicates the taxes that should be assigned to the 'federal' level	*Brennan and Buchanan's* collusion hypothesis suggests that central government use grants to ensure collusion on tax (collusion intended to stop fiscal competition)
Social cohesion: movement towards further integration requires a mechanism for distributing the gains from integration	*Grossman and West* argue that grants have been used to restrain movement of taxpayers (which might threaten bureaucrats' security)
Insurance: all states can gain if 'regional' assistance is available to deal with problems	
Intergovernmental grants: Lump-sum grants to be used for redistribution purposes; matching grants for efficiency purposes	**Intergovernmental grants:** Lump-sum grants have efficiency costs because of the possibility of a 'flypaper effect'—money sticks where it hits

might be used to inform policy with respect to the assignment of expenditure and redistribution functions to the EC budget. It should be clear that, while the literature from traditional public finance is sceptical about assigning 'too many' powers to a central government, the prescriptions drawn from public choice are even more firmly in favour of decentralization. Table 12.3 compares the main arguments in summary form and illustrates the greater bias in favour of decentralization that arises when the failings of the political process are brought into consideration. When considering responsibility for allocation, the fiscal federalism literature gives emphasis to heterogeneous preferences in calling for greater decentralization. By contrast, arguments from the public choice school point to the political decision-making problems of having higher tiers of government. When considering responsibility for redistribution, the fiscal federalism literature considers the efficacy of taxes at different government levels but the public choice approach also gives emphasis to the dangers that can arise if a 'Leviathan' government controls distribution.

As a final comparison, note that while in the fiscal federalism literature lump-sum intergovernmental grants are defensible for redistribution, the public choice school would be sceptical as such grants are subject to a 'flypaper effect' (see section 12.8).

12.5 The sources of local government revenue: local domestic rates versus the 'poll' tax

While the 'decentralization theorem', the theory of clubs and the Tiebout hypothesis focus on the gains to be had from leaving decision-making in the hands of a local authority, central government exerts an important influence on local authorities when limiting their choice of local taxation. In this section attention turns to the question of which source of finance is preferable for a local authority. The importance of local (domestic) taxes and of central government grants in local government expenditure is shown in Fig. 12.8 for the UK. Before April 1990 local taxation was in terms mainly of domestic rates (a property tax) but in the early 1990s the UK government introduced a poll tax (based on individuals over the age of eighteen years). There are many tax options available for local authorities but it is impossible to consider all possibilities thoroughly within this chapter. As an illustration of the significance of the different approaches to public finance, we consider the debate in the UK about whether or not a poll tax ('community charge') should

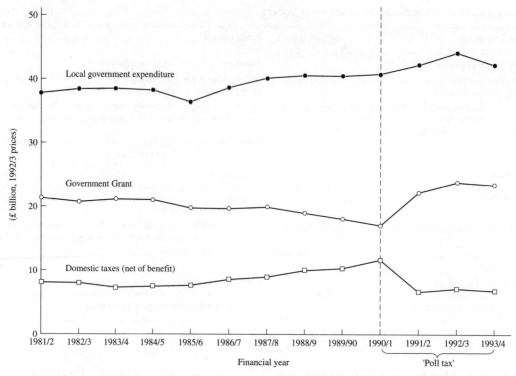

Figure 12.8 Real local authority expenditure, real government grant and real local domestic tax revenues (net of benefit), 1981–2 to 1993–4.

Source: Local Government Financial Statistics. England No. 4.

have replaced a system of domestic rates. The aim is to illustrate the emphasis in the debate on public choice considerations.

In a broader political economy model, this question would be tackled with respect to a large number of criteria. Sandford (1984) suggests a set of 'criteria for local taxes' as follows.

1. The tax base should be widely and fairly evenly dispersed.
2. It should be economical to administer.
3. There should be localized incidence of the tax.
4. The tax should raise high and reliable yields.
5. It should have an equitable impact.
6. The tax should be perceptible.
7. It should promote local accountability.

This set of criteria is really very broad but it could be even broader. Through their impact on property prices, local taxes can have important implications for mobility of labour. Muellbauer (1987, p. 9), therefore, considers local tax reform 'from the point of view of the UK economy's supply side, in particular of a less

inflationary, better functioning labour market base . . .'.

Central government in the UK in the late 1980s sought to place greater emphasis on the criteria of local tax perceptibility and accountability. This may have been an example of popular expression of those worries that arise from the criticism that is engendered by the public choice approach. Public choice analysis would suggest that local government expenditure may be in danger of 'excessive growth' if tax perceptibility and accountability are not characteristics of the tax system (see chapter 14). In the UK, the Conservative government introduced a reform of local taxation which replaced domestic rates with the so-called 'community charge' or 'poll tax'.

Domestic rates were a tax on the rateable value of real estate (land and buildings). They were payable by the occupiers of the property, and the rateable value was assessed on the annual letting value of the property. By contrast, the community charge was a poll tax levied on *all* individuals aged 18 or over. The switch was planned to occur in Scotland in 1989 and in England and Wales in 1990. While the debate surrounding this reform was extensive, there was reason to argue that 'Most of the debate has been about controlling local authority expenditure, about the altered political incentive for voters, about redistribution among households and about administrative issues' (Muellbauer 1987, p. 7). While not exclusive, public choice considerations stood proud in this list.

In this section our intention is to look briefly at the nature of debate surrounding this local tax reform. We acknowledge that there were well-known problems with the domestic rate system in the UK, but leave it to readers to discern whether the emphasis on constraining local authority growth warranted this change of taxation. The intention is to indicate the degree of ambiguity and the general lack of information that can characterize debate on tax reform. This, of course, creates considerable leeway for the input of political influence which stems from the basic approach to taxation that individuals take. While it is difficult to argue convincingly that one system of taxation is superior to another, strong positions are still taken according to ideological commitment.

12.5.1 Criticisms of domestic rate system

Among the most quoted (though controversial) criticisms of domestic rates were the following.

Regressive between taxpayers

Reflecting the importance of housing in the household budget, domestic rates fell most heavily on the low-income groups. Sandford (1984) quoted the *Report of the [Allen] Committee of Inquiry into the Impact of Rates on Households*. It showed that in England and Wales the lowest income groups paid 8.1 per cent of household income in rates, whereas the highest income group paid under 2 per cent.

Distortion of business investment

The rate of tax (the 'poundage') differed; it was higher where the property values were lower and where the needs for local expenditure were greater. High rates may have been a locational disincentive for both businesses and households.

Arbitrary assessment/administrative costs

Because rateable valuations were expensive to undertake, they were done infrequently and irregularly. The result was that the valuations could be outdated and appear arbitrary. Revaluations were costly though other costs of administration were relatively low.

Tax awareness

Muellbauer (1987, p. 11) argued that 'Dominating the recent debate . . . is a fourth set of objections against domestic rates. This is that of "no representation without taxation". . . .' In the UK rates did not provide a close link between those who voted for expenditure increases and those who paid the costs of local services. Only about one-third of potential voters paid full domestic rates. Rates were paid by the head of the household, and some households received rate rebates.

Rates and the benefits of local services

Rates did not relate to the costs of providing services to different residents. This was obviously linked to the issue of cost awareness. Even between those who paid the tax, the link was weak. For example, a family of four occupying a semi-detached house may consume more local services than the single occupier next door, but would still pay the same rates. There was no relation between the services consumed and the costs of them to individuals, and the central government appeared to wish to introduce a benefit-related tax for local authorities.

12.5.2 Criticisms of the poll tax

While the objections to rates are well known, it would be difficult to be very confident that a switch to a poll tax would adequately redress these problems.

Regressive tax

The community charge would operate as a poll tax and would be paid irrespective of income. Obviously the tax would be regressive. As Kay and King (1986) stressed, 'what matters from the point of view of social and economic policy is not the progressive or regressive impact of every individual element of the tax system but the impact of that system as a whole' (p. 150). However, the same qualification applies to domestic rates.

Administrative costs

To avoid the full regressive impact of the poll tax, it was possible to introduce rebates for old-age pensioners, low-income individuals, single-parent families, the disabled, etc. It should be clear, however, that the more that a tax is tailored to the characteristics of the taxpayers, the greater the administrative costs will be. It is possible that, while the administrative costs incurred by property valuation were avoided, they could be replaced with the valuations of the poll tax for many different households.

Tax awareness

While the above arguments suggested that the link between payment of the domestic rates and services received would lead to greater expenditure, it should be noted that domestic rates are one of the more obvious and most easily perceived of all taxes. Kay and King (1986, p. 150) noted that 'Domestic rates occasion much criticism. Often this criticism is less than coherent, and it sometimes seems that a principal reason for the volume of protest is simply that rates are an unusually transparent tax; there are few other cases where individuals are personally and directly responsible for making payments.' Tax transparency should be a feature that serves to resist 'excessive' local government growth. In the USA this experience has been evident when there are movements to restrain the growth of state spending. For example, Proposition 13, which sought to curtail local government expenditure, can be related to antipathy towards property taxation. (For a fuller account, see the review of literature in Cullis and Jones 1987.)

The poll tax and the benefits of local services

The government in the UK made much of the case that a poll tax related to the benefit principle of taxation. On face value, this argument appeared justified. However, when the recipients of local government services were identified, there was reason to question this argument. A study by Bramley, Le Grand and Low (1989) analysed evidence on usage of services carried out by 'a major and representative' local authority. Only about 10 per cent of expenditure went on services that were clearly pro poor and about 20 per cent were biased toward those services (e.g. education, roads, leisure services) that favoured the better off. They estimated that, overall, it could be said that the better off use services costing 45–70 per cent more than those used by the least well off. By comparison with the rating system, the poll tax incidence deviated even more systematically from service usage. The poll tax did not prove to be a good benefit-related tax. The authors of the report concluded: 'the Government is mistaken in its assertions about the use of local services... the retention of the rating system is a more attractive option if indeed a benefit tax is what is being sought' (p. 28).

A comparison of the pros and cons of the poll tax concluded, not surprisingly, that:

The argument between domestic rates and the community charge (CC) is finely balanced ... They share many defects. Neither is fair, in the sense of being related to income, and thus ability to pay. They are both regressive taxes, in that they fall in relation to income as income rises, except where the complex rebate system helps lower incomes. Neither is buoyant as a source of revenue, without unpopular increases in poundage or amounts. Neither has much relation to local services used by the taxpayer. Neither achieves greater accountability of local authorities to the voters, in spite of claims made for the CC ... (Johnson 1990)

What then was the purpose of reform? Commentators emphasized that the poll tax was ultimately concerned with reducing local government revenue. Sandford (1990) presents a humorous discussion how replacing the poll tax by a local sales tax on salt might perform this better. Local governments with high tax rates would be forced to reduce the rate of tax on salt to that pertaining in lower-rate localities, or else lose revenue by seeing their residents travel to purchase salt elsewhere. Perhaps the real purpose was then a response to fears of a Leviathan in local government.

The discussion here as to the relative merits of domestic rates and the poll tax has been introductory. (See Morrissey, Cullis and Jones 1990 for further analysis.) At this juncture the aim is simply to note that, in this debate, public choice arguments concerning tax awareness and the growth of local government were important. Muellbauer (1987) questioned the tax awareness argument. He noted that the 'argument against rates rests on the shaky premise that, in local elections, individuals vote as individuals and are little influenced by the costs and benefits to the household of a policy change by the local authority' (p. 11). However, in the absence of clear evidence and when the fiscal debate is difficult to resolve, it is possible that those who begin with a public choice framework may be led to quite different reform proposals from those who approach the issue from a more traditional framework. As Mitchell (1988, p. 50) notes, 'At bottom the gap between public choice and conventional political science reflects a conflict of values and beliefs—in other words, ideology.' This same conflict also plays its part in the distinction between public choice analysis and traditional public finance.

Before drawing this discussion to a close, it is worth noting briefly that there are, of course, other tax alternatives for a local authority. (For further discussion see Foster *et al.* 1980.) They might, for example, raise revenue by a local sales tax or a local income tax. In the UK local income taxes were recommended by the Layfield Committee (1976), to operate alongside domestic rates. Local income taxes might be thought capable of performing better against the criterion of equity, but it was argued that they would be difficult to administer in the UK, for the reasons outlined by Kay and King (1986). However, the public choice approach, in terms of *explaining* policy developments, may have a more clear-cut analytical impact again when it comes to analysing the acceptability of this tax. As George Jones, a member of the Layfield Committee, noted,

A study of the Layfield Committee . . . provides an intriguing irony. Although set up in 1974 in response to outcries about huge increases in domestic rates, it never came near to recommending their abolition or even their substantial replacement with another tax. Indeed, it proposed that they be retained and further, that in addition to this unpopular tax there should be a new unpopular tax local income tax—a prospect of little attraction to most politicians. (Quoted in Sandford 1984, p. 262)

The likely unpopularity of the local income tax may explain resistance to this tax. Certainly the demise of the poll tax can be explained by its impact on political popularity polls. Despite desperate attempts to make it palatable (Cullis, Jones and Morrissey 1993), the tax was finally deemed unworkable. It contributed to a significant extent to the unpopularity and fall from office of Mrs Thatcher[3] and John Major was soon to replace the poll tax.

In April 1993 the Community Charge was replaced by a hybrid local tax, the 'Council Tax'. It is basically a banded property tax but it has a personal element (e.g. giving discounts to single adults living in properties and to empty properties) and an income element (e.g. giving discounts if certain categories of individuals—such as those in receipt of income support from the government and students in full time education—reside in the property). Each dwelling is allocated to one of eight valuation bands (through A to H) based on market value of the property. The amount payable in each band is determined in ratio terms by central government (e.g. the amount payable in band A will be 66 per cent of what is charged in band D). When the tax for the property is estimated any allowance (for number of individuals in residence or for income of residents) is made and the Council Tax bill is sent as a single request for payment to each dwelling. The tax reform made greater allowance for taxpayer's circumstances and (being based on property) was easier to collect than was the poll tax (based on individuals). The effect on income distribution was to ease the burden of tax for the poor (those below the seventh income decile) but further up the income distribution the two taxes 'are almost equally regressive' (Giles and Ridge 1993, p. 15).

12.6 User charges

In recent years there has been growing interest in another form of finance which has been particularly important for local government. User charges for excludable goods offer another revenue source. Application of user charges appears to be a reaffirmation of the benefit principle of taxation (see chapter 3). User charges can reflect the marginal benefit to taxpayers of the goods and services that have been provided within the public sector. They appear to offer a way of extending the principle of consumer sovereignty within the public sector.

In the late 1980s the UK levied user charges to help finance around 600 individual services. Bailey (1994) notes the following examples: 7 per cent of the accounting cost for education (mainly vocational college courses—cookery, woodwork, etc.); 11 per cent of costs of social services (e.g. charges for residential care of the elderly, meals on wheels, day nurseries, etc.); 13 per cent of road and transport expenditure (mainly parking fees); 12 per cent of local environmental services (e.g. burial charges, public conveniences); libraries and museums covered 6 per cent of local environmental services; 4 per cent of the costs of police services (e.g. charges for crowd control in sporting events). In the UK, rents for municipal housing were the largest single source of user-charge revenue. Some advocate greater use of this revenue source for other services (e.g. to finance the National Health Service).[4]

Table 12.4 reveals an increased reliance on user charges in OECD countries. Table 12.5 shows that between 1980 and 1989 local government in all OECD countries (with the exception of Canada) increased the ratio of user charges to grants. In all countries there was an increase of the ratio of user charges to local taxes. Usually, countries with the highest percentage increases in user charge revenues also have the largest proportionate increases in both grants and user charges, and also the largest increases in local taxation. This suggests that user charges were not simply replacing local taxes or grants during the 1980s, i.e. it is not simply a fiscal substitution strategy.

12.6.1 The case for and against user charges

Why might a government rely on user charges as a revenue source? While not exhaustive, the following arguments have been used to justify user charges:

(i) User charges are an application of the 'benefit principle' for public sector goods and services. The analysis of 'first best' (as described in chapter 1) indicates that there are circumstances in which welfare can

---

[3] A poll tax was introduced in England by Henry II (1154–89). The tax, which did make some small allowance for income, was unpopular and proved a contributory factor to the Peasants' Revolt, led by Wat Tyler in 1381.

[4] For a discussion of how greater use may be made of user charges in the UK health service see Bailey and Bruce (1994).

Table 12.4 The growth of local government user charges, 1980–9

Country	Increase in grants received		Increase in user-charge revenues		Increase in local tax revenues	
	Percentage	Rank	Percentage	Rank	Percentage	Rank
Australia	145	2	425	1	149	2
Canada	81	6	109	8	111	7
Denmark	51	8	153	5	127	5
France	130	3	247	4	190	1
Germany	19	10	55	10	44	10
Ireland	108	4	266	3	110	8
The Netherlands	33	9	91	9	64	9
Norway	180	1	334	2	139	3
UK	95	5	116	7	138	4
US	70	7	124	6	113	6

Notes: Data for Germany relate to the period 1980–8, except for local taxation. Grants received by local governments include those paid by other levels of government and by international or supranational authorities.
Source: OECD (1992).

Table 12.5 Ratios of income sources, 1980–9 (in percentages)

Country	Ratio of user charges to grants		Ratio of user charges to local taxes	
	1980	1989	1980	1989
Australia	63	135	27	56
Canada	20	23	26	26
Denmark	8	13	11	12
France	31	47	31	38
Germany	65	85	54	60
Ireland	10	17	92	160
The Netherlands	5	7	77	90
Norway	15	23	11	19
UK	13	14	20	18
US	22	28	25	26

Source: OECD (1992).

be enhanced when consumers respond to 'prices' set equal to marginal costs (and user charges offer this possibility).

(ii) User fees can be 'tailored' according to circumstances in which taxes would involve an element of cross subsidization. For example, consider the financing of local amenities by taxpayers. Those living in high population density locations (urban areas) are often faced with subsidizing the cost of services to taxpayers living in low population density locations (rural areas). If taxes are replaced by user charges the charges can be designed so as to force the recipients of services to pay more for their services when the marginal cost of provision (for them) is higher. The element of cross subsidization is removed.

(iii) User charges produce feedback from consumers to policy-makers in the public sector. For example, if there is excess supply at a specific user charge then this would indicate 'over production' of the good or service and inform policy-makers that less of particular services is required (at the user charge that has been set).

(iv) If a local government finances services through taxation it may be the case that residents are left subsidizing consumption of services by non-residents. For example, if local services were financed by taxes on permanent residents, students in Bath University (who are not permanent residents in Bath) would be able to consume services financed by residents in Bath. User charges for locally provided goods and services reduce this element of subsidy.

(v) User charges may offer an additional revenue source which allows local government to respond to changing circumstances. If taxpayers in a local authority are unwilling to accept a cut in existing services, the ability of a local authority to adapt to changing socioeconomic conditions is severely constrained in the absence of an alternative revenue source.

The **case against** user charges can be described as:

(i) It is not necessarily the case that user costs should be set at marginal cost. Setting the user charge is far more difficult when allowing for 'second-best' considerations (i.e. adjusting for the existence of externalities and/or monopoly in other markets). Moreover, user charges may not be set at marginal cost when the Paretian criterion is not the only consideration and when further equity considerations are relevant. However, as well as these conceptual problems there are more basic practical problems. At a practical level local authority cost data are seldom in a form which would permit marginal cost pricing (accounting costs tend to identify the *sources* of funds rather than their *opportunity costs*). Setting user charge at marginal cost is not easy and sometimes not appropriate.

(ii) It is easier to set user charges for some services which, by their characteristics, are 'excludable' (e.g. swimming pools). However, it would be difficult to set user chargers for other less excludable goods, e.g. street lighting.

(iii) While there are advantages in 'tailoring' user charges to suit different conditions, different charges for different categories can be confusing and lead to resentment.

(iv) There are administrative costs (transactions costs) in relying on user charges (e.g. administering toll booths on bridges or roads). These may make user costs expensive. Not only are there administrative costs in financing expenditures on road and bridges by user charges but delays involved may also add to traffic congestion and to these congestion costs. In such circumstances it might be better to rely on earmarked taxes. Moreover, user charges may simply shift costs elsewhere. The tolls on the Severn Bridge in the UK are said to simply increase traffic density of alternative routes for which tolls do not apply.

(v) Equity considerations may work against the use of user charges. This is likely to be more important when user charges are set for necessities (e.g. gas, electricity, water supply, sewerage, waste removal, hospital care). In such circumstances relying on user charges may be regressive.

An assessment of the case for and the case against suggests broad principles. Whether there 'should' be reliance on user charges depends on considerations of feasibility (i.e. whether or not the good is in large part 'private' (e.g. as in the case of a tennis court); 'mixed' (e.g. trash removal) or 'collective' (e.g. mosquito abatement). From a public choice view, user charges seems to offer a potential remedy for the failings of the political process in so far as it introduces a measure of 'consumer sovereignty' or 'taxpayer sovereignty'. However, whether or not user charges can restrain government failure is not obvious. Everything depends on how user charges are set, as the following discussion reveals.

One of the inherent problems in public choice is the ability of self-interested decision-makers to distort potentially helpful reforms (see, for example, the discussion of privatization and of quasi-markets in chapter 5). User charges are vulnerable to the self-interest of those responsible for setting the charges. For example:

(i) User fees may be (and may have been) set 'too low' by politicians. This distortion is introduced in order that politicians might attract electoral support from the recipient group (McChesney 1991).

(ii) On the other hand, Anderson (1991) argues that, when electoral considerations are not paramount, user charges might be 'over priced' in order to produce monopoly rents for those associated with the supply of the service in the public sector.

(iii) User charges fail to restrain adequately the alleged indulgences of bureaucrats. In the Niskanen (1968) model, bureaus' finance comes from a budget approved by politicians and the introduction of user charges would seem an obvious restraint. It might be thought that a bureaucratic empire would be difficult to build if bureaucrats had to rely on finance from user charges in so far as it would be difficult to supply services beyond the point at which consumers would pay for them. However, Lee (1991) reveals that even when user charges are used there is no guarantee that bureaus will supply the 'optimum' level of the good.

The message is similar to that which emerged in chapter 5. There is no easy way to guarantee a restraint of government failure. In the case of user charges there is no guaranteed increase in efficiency—everything depends on how they are introduced.

12.7 Intergovernmental grants

The traditional public finance approach to intergovernmental grants (or grants-in-aid) which flow from central (or federal) government to local (or state) authorities has been concerned with the question of what form the grant should take. Central government can use grants to change both the distribution of income and the pattern of spending between local authorities. In order to know how to structure the grant, it is necessary to predict the response of the local authority to different kinds of grant. In this way, the impact of alternative forms of grant on local fiscal decisions becomes an important consideration when choosing the 'appropriate' form of grant to use. The results of some empirical studies suggest that the theoretical predictions that emerge from traditional public finance are, in this respect, at odds

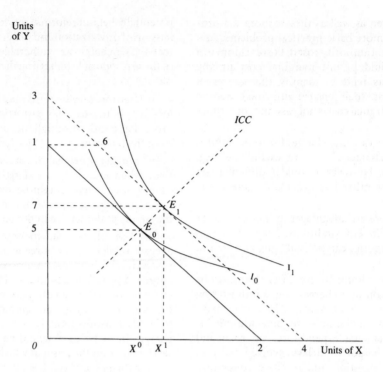

Figure 12.9 Unconditional non-matching grant.

with experience. The public choice school again has the opportunity to explain this inconsistency. A public choice appraisal indicates that the whole question of central–local budgetary arrangements can assume considerable importance in explaining the growth of the public sector in general.

12.7.1 The effect on local authority spending

Intergovernmental grants are used for a number of efficiency and/or equity purposes. Topham (1983) notes that in the USA state grants finance about a third of local public expenditure, while in the UK grants-in-aid account for about half the revenue of local authorities. In this section some basic microeconomic theory is applied in order to analyse the likely response of local authorities to the receipt of different types of grants.

Intergovernmental grants may be *conditional* or *unconditional*. Conditional grants are dependent (in some way) on the behaviour of the recipient local authority; for example, central government may require that the grant be spent on some particular expenditure programme (health, education, transport). Conditional grants can come in the form of *matching* or *non-matching* grants. In the case of matching grants the central government agrees to

match a certain proportion of the expenditures of the local authority; for example, central government may pay x per cent of the total cost of providing a service at the local level. Moreover, grants may be *open* or *closed*; there may or may not be an upper limit beyond which the central government will not go.

In traditional public finance, the form in which the grant is made will influence the expenditure of local authorities. In keeping with this, the analysis utilizes the assumption that a local authority maximizes a utility function, in exactly the same way as would an individual in neoclassical microeconomic theory. The relevant indifference curve may be considered to be that of a 'representative voter'. As Rubinfeld (1987) notes, this is all right if everyone in the community is identical, but it causes an obvious problem if there is heterogeneity. (Alternatively, therefore, the indifference curve has sometimes been taken to reflect the preferences of the median voter inasmuch as there are circumstances in which, when the majority voting rule applies, the decision from the local community will be that of the median voter.[5]) In the following analysis an initial budget line (12 in Fig. 12.9) repres-

---

[5] For cases where it may be appropriate to utilize the indifference curve of the 'median voter', see chapter 4.

ents a constraint prior to any grant assistance from a federal government. It limits the consumption possibilities between one good X (provided by the local authority) and all other goods Y. The local authority ('representative' individual) seeks to maximize utility. The impact of the grant is then captured by changes in the position and/or slope of the budget line. Wilde (1968) exemplifies the approach on which the following analysis is based.

Unconditional, non-matching closed grants

In Fig. 12.9 the line 12 illustrates the trade-off faced by a 'representative' individual prior to grant assistance. With no grant aid, the local authority prefers (at point E_0) to pay taxes of 15 (in units of Y) and provide OX^0 of the publicly provided good. If the authority receives a fixed sum 31, then it is able to purchase more of the publicly provided good. The budget line moves out to the right and the individual elects to purchase more of X if the publicly provided good is a normal good. *ICC*

is the income consumption curve, and it is clear that the total provision of the good will increase as the local authority receives the grant. (The new equilibrium point is E_1.) In the locality, the welfare of individuals is increased (a shift from I_0 to I_1). More of the local publicly provided good is consumed, but not all of the grant is used to increase consumption of this good (i.e. consumption of Y also increases—distance 57).

Conditional, non-matching closed grant

In Fig. 12.10 it is possible to consider the impact of a conditional, non-matching grant. In this case the total of the amount received by the local authority must be spent on the provision of good X. In the case shown, the budget line now looks like 154 and the conditional constraint forces the local authority to a corner solution 5. The local authority would have moved from E_0 to E_1 had the grant not had any conditions binding. It is evident that, by comparison with an unconditional grant, it is on a lower level of welfare (shown by

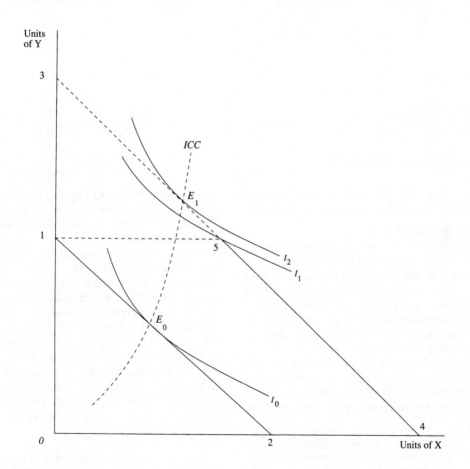

Figure 12.10 Conditional non-matching grant.

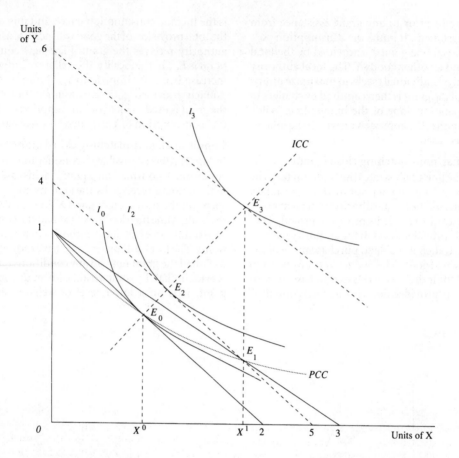

Figure 12.11 Matching open-ended grant.

indifference curve I_1) as a result of spending more than it would otherwise choose to spend on good X.[6]

Matching open-ended grant

In this example, for every pound spent by the recipient authority, a specified sum must be spent by the central government. This means that the grant operates like a price subsidy for good X and the budget line for the local authority changes slope from 12 to 13 in Fig. 12.11. As a consequence, the local authority shifts from the initial equilibrium E_0 to E_1. There is a movement along the price consumption curve (PCC) to a point where OX^1 of the good is demanded. The matching open-ended grant (price subsidy) will always lead the authority to consume more of the good than an unconditional non-matching grant

(lump-sum subsidy). In Fig. 12.11 a comparison is made of the two grants. To enable the authority to consume (if it should choose) OX^1 (the equilibrium with the matching open-ended grant), the central government must offer an unconditional non-matching grant of 14. In this case the new equilibrium point would be E_2. With an unconditional non-matching grant the impact is simply that of an 'income effect' (a shift along the income consumption curve ICC). In the case of the matching open-ended grant the effect is that of a price reduction, which incorporates both a substitution effect and an income effect; hence the shift along the price consumption path PCC. It may be noted that in this diagram, to be sure that there is an increase of the consumption of the good X by a similar amount (i.e. to OX^1), the grant must be much greater (i.e. equal to 16).[7]

---

[6] If the tangency point E_1 is below point 5 in Fig. 12.10, there is no difference as far as the local authority is concerned. The constraint that the grant must be spent on the service is not relevant, as the locality would choose to spend more than this on the service. An illustration would be the constraint 164 in Fig. 12.9.

[7] If the price elasticity of demand of the recipient authority is greater than unity, a matching grant will induce it to spend more of its own resources on the local public good.

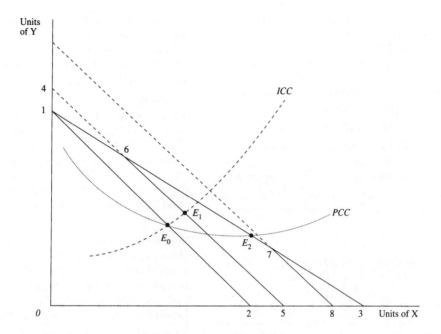

Figure 12.12 Matching closed-ended grant.

Source: based on King (1984).

Matching closed-ended grant

With a closed-ended matching grant the budget line will be kinked. In Fig. 12.12, assume initially that the conditions of the matching grant are such as to reduce the price of good X; i.e. the grantor will match at a rate of 23 to O2. The budget line changes from 12 to 13. However, now assume that there is an upper limit on this grant of 25 (in units of X). In this case the relevant budget line becomes 165, as the most that will be forthcoming from the central government is 25 (in units of X). The grant will now have the same effect as a non-distorting conditional non-matching grant of amount 25 (in units of X) and the individual will choose to move from E_0 to E_1 along the income consumption curve *ICC*. By comparison, if the upper limit for spending were 28 (in units of X), then the matching rate is relevant. The budget line is now 178, and the individual will choose to move along the price consumption curve to point E_2. Clearly, everything depends on the way in which the grant is closed. (For other examples, see King 1984.)

The above examples of intergovernmental grants are by no means exhaustive, but enough has been said to indicate that, when the form of grant aid is specified, the nature of the amendment of the budget line for local authorities is specified. One point that is obvious is that a matching grant is generally more successful than a non-matching grant in stimulating local expenditure on a particular good or service. With this analysis in mind, it is now useful to consider alternative forms of grants in the context of the objectives that underlie the use of intergovernmental grants. It is already clear that, for example, if the objective of the central government is to encourage local authority spending on some service, a matching grant will be preferred to a lump-sum grant, even though the lump-sum may increase the welfare of the local authority residents by more than a matching grant. This is just one example of the interrelationship between the form of grant and the objective of the central authority.

12.7.2 The case for intergovernmental grants

In this section the objective is to consider the rationale for intergovernmental grants and the particular form they should take.

Inter-jurisdictional spillovers

It has already been noted that there may be external benefits for neighbouring localities as a result of any one jurisdiction's expenditures. The fact that the spillovers are external benefits implies that the local authority responsible for such activity takes no account of it in its decision-making. If region R undertakes programmes that create spillovers for region S, then, following Boadway and Wildasin (1984), the optimal decision is to set the provision of that good at the quantity where

$$(12.5) \qquad MB_r + MB_s = MC$$

where MB_r = the marginal benefit to residents of R
$\quad\quad MB_s$ = the marginal benefit to residents of S
$\quad\quad MC$ = the marginal cost of the programme

However, if the local authority does not include the spillover benefits in its decision-making calculations, it will provide only to the point where

$$(12.6) \qquad MB_r = MC$$

In such circumstances a subsidy granted at the per-unit rate of $MB_s/(MB_r + MB_s)$ would lead the authority to the optimal point. The marginal cost of expansion to R would then be set equal to $MC[1 - MB_s/(MB_r + MB_s)]$ and the authority would increase its provision of this good. Matching grants are better in this context because, in altering the price, they stimulate a greater provision of the good at a lower cost to the grant donor. The fact that the donor is better off, because the recipient demands more of the good, makes a grant that changes prices better than one that simply changes income for the donee.

Promoting a merit good

Central government may, on merit good grounds, think it appropriate that a local authority provide more of a particular service. From the analysis above, it would be reasonable to recommend the use of open matching specific grants for each individual service that it wanted expanded. However, it might use closed lump-sum grants if there were simply some relatively high level of consumption which it felt was 'desirable and adequate'. General grants would be appropriate only if the grantor felt that all local services were merit goods.

Revenue sharing

Local authorities in aggregate may suffer a fiscal imbalance inasmuch as they are unable to finance all those expenditure programmes that are considered desirable. Central government may encourage local governments to raise more tax revenue by introducing new taxes, levying charges or borrowing. However, one alternative way in which central government may play a role is to collect the tax revenue on behalf of local governments and then simply to turn the rev-

enue over to them. If the central government plays a role purely in terms of revenue raising, then an unconditional grant would seem the most appropriate instrument from the point of view of benefiting the recipient local authority.

Equalization

While there may be no fiscal imbalance in aggregate, some authorities may be unable to finance programmes that other authorities find easy to handle. In this case the objective is to close the fiscal gap between revenue sources and expenditure responsibilities between different authorities. The reason could be based on considerations of either equity or efficiency.

Horizontal equity   When there is no mobility of labour across jurisdictions, it is possible that two identical individuals residing in two different jurisdictions may obtain different net fiscal benefits. Buchanan refers to fiscal equity being attained when there is horizontal equity across different states:

> Individuals of a given level residing in a high income state will obtain a larger net benefit from the state fiscal activities than will a similar person residing in a different state. This source of horizontal inequity can be removed by a set of interstate transfers that equalize the fiscal residua across states. (Buchanan 1950, p. 588)

Whether central government chooses to remove this is, however, dependent on value judgements and a decision to attain horizontal equity (Grewal, Buchanan and Matthews 1980).

Efficiency   With labour mobility, inefficiency can arise from fiscal spending in different localities. To attain efficiency, it would be expected that factors of production would be allocated so that their marginal products would be equal. Here, following Boadway and Wildasin (1984), it is possible to illustrate how different fiscal residua create inefficiency when labour is mobile. Assume that R is a high-income locality and S is a low-income locality. In Fig. 12.13 the wage rates for labour in the two localities are shown on the vertical axis. The marginal value product of labour in the two locations is illustrated by M^r and M^s, respectively. The total supply of labour is shown by the distance on the horizontal axis; if initially there is an efficient allocation of resources, then O_rL_0 labour is in locality R and O_sL_0 is in locality S. At this point the marginal products of labour are identical at point 1 in the two localities (assuming that wages are set equal to marginal value product).

Now suppose that in locality R revenue can be raised from resource taxes t_r (e.g. taxes on land) and

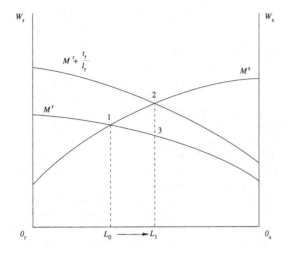

Figure 12.13 Inefficient location and fiscal residuum.
Source: based on Boadway and Wildasin (1984).

that this is available to be shared by the resident population l_r. In S (now the 'poor' state) there is no such revenue. In the figure $M^r + (t_r/l_r)$ is the wage rate (the 'social' wage, i.e. inclusive of the marginal value product and the fiscal residuum) and there is migration from R to S to the extent of $L_0 L_1$, leading to an output loss measured by triangle 123. Unless there is any redress to this distortion, the marginal products of labour will not be equal. While the higher wage rate compensates the marginal worker for the lack of amenities in S, there is an equilibrium where the marginal products of labour are no longer equal. In this way output is lower than it would otherwise be and there is an 'efficiency' cost in terms of this output loss.

Sufficient has been said to suggest that there may be good reason to utilize intergovernmental grants and that, in order to choose the appropriate grant, it is necessary to consider both the objective and the likely response of the local authority to the grant. However, while the theoretical analyses yield precise predictions, these have not always been found in empirical analysis. While there is some evidence that matching grants are more stimulative than unconditional grants, the prediction that unconditional grants have the same effects as a lump-sum increase in income is not confirmed. Once again, the door is open for public choice explanations as to the impact of grants on decision-makers in local authorities.

12.8 Public choice and intergovernmental grants: the 'flypaper effect'

In the analysis outlined above, it should not matter whether a central government cuts taxes or gives lump-sum grants to local authorities. In either case, public spending should increase by the income elasticity of demand. With reference to the previous discussion of an unconditional, non-matching grant, it was illustrated that the effect on local spending is just the same as that which arises as a result of an increase in income. If central government cuts taxes, so that the income of a representative individual increased by the same amount, the increase in local spending should be identical. (Again, the effect would be illustrated by a parallel shift of the budget line and by the movement along the income consumption curve.) A review of empirical work by Gramlich (1977) indicates that this is not the case in the USA. Lump-sum grants from a central government stimulate greater local authority spending than would occur as a result of an equivalent cut in taxes by a central government. Whereas a $100 increase in the net income of individuals leads to an increase in a recipient authority's spending by $5–$10, a lump-sum grant raises spending by $40–$100. Gramlich and Galper (1973) estimated that in the USA an additional $1 of unconditional aid to state and local governments induced, on average, a $0.43 increase in spending. This phenomenon has been referred to as the 'flypaper effect', so named because money will stick in the sector that it hits—grants to the local public economy will be spent in the local public economy.

In order to explain the 'flypaper effect', it is again possible to examine public choice theory. The traditional model assumes harmony between the interests of voters and their representatives in the political process. The public choice approach, however, disputes this assumption. In particular, the role of bureaucrats and the impact of fiscal illusion has been considered. However, such arguments are not the only ones made to explain the 'flypaper effect'. Following King (1984) we contrast some alternatives.

12.8.1 The role of bureaucracy

The Niskanen (1968) model of bureaucracy has been applied by King (1984) to explain the flypaper effect. In Fig. 12.14 the demand for the output of a good provided by a bureau is D and this can be viewed as the

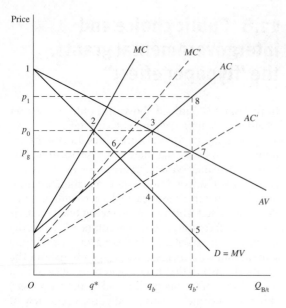

Figure 12.14 The Niskanen model.

Source: based on King (1984).

marginal valuation (*MV*) of the good. The minimum average cost of producing the good is shown as *AC* and the associated marginal cost is *MC*. The bureaucrat is assumed to be concerned with maximizing the size of the budget (because the bureaucrat's salary, power, prestige is assumed to depend on budget size). In this process the bureaucrat is assumed to enjoy a mono-poly position based on an asymmetry of information. The bureaucrat has information of both the demand for the good and also of the costs of supplying it. When requesting a budget to provide the good the bureaucrat is aware that the sponsors (i.e. politicians) have only information about the demand for the good. To maximize budget size, the bureaucrat will ask for a budget whereby total cost of providing the good is as great as the total benefit to voters provided by the good (to exceed this is impossible as politicians would recognize that total cost exceeds total benefit). In Fig. 12.14 AV is the average valuation of voters for the good and it follows that the bureau would produce an output of Oq_b (whereby $AC = AV$ and the triangle $P_012 = 234$). The output of the bureau exceeds the output that would be forthcoming in a competitive market, i.e. Oq^*. (For an elaboration of Niskanen's analysis see chapter 14).

Suppose that the bureau produces its service for a local (or state) authority and that this receives an open matching specific grant which reduces the costs of the service for local voters by one-third. The average costs

to the local authority of providing the service will shift down to AC'. Under these conditions the bureau will enjoy support from local sponsors for an output of $Oq_{b'}$ where $AC' = AV$ so that triangle $P_g16 = $ triangle 567. The initial total cost covering local authority budget is OP_03q_b whereas after the grant total costs are $OP^18q_{b'}$ of which $OP_g7q_{b'}$ is raised locally and P_gP_187 takes the form of the central government grant. Additional output is $Oq_{b'} - Oq_b$ and as total benefit increases by $q_b45q_{b'}$, this permits an increase of the budget (from local sources) by the same amount. As King (1984, p. 106) notes, the bureau's 'budget rises by more than the amount of the grant'.

King (1984, p. 107) argues: 'for this theory to explain the flypaper effect, it is sufficient for it to show that the effect of a rise in citizens' incomes could be to raise the budget by less...'. He notes that if the good were normal 'the *MV* and *AV* sche-dules 'would shift to the right, and outputs and bud-gets would rise, but the increase in the budget need not equal the value of the grant let alone exceed it...'. For a 'flypaper effect' as described above the bureau per-suades the sponsor to act as if a lump-sum grant is 'an open matching specific grant'. It is unlikely that a rise in incomes would shift the *AV* and *MV* schedules significantly. It follows that receipt of a lump-sum grant would have a far greater impact on local (or state) spending than would an equivalent increase in income.

The Romer–Rosenthal model

Romer and Rosenthal (1980) have presented an alter-native model of the operation of bureaux. This is referred to as the 'setter model'. In this model bureau-crats in local authorities propose a level of agency funding which is put before the electorate in a refer-endum. If a majority of voters accept the proposal, it is enacted; if not, the local expenditure is set at a legally specified *reversion* level. Examples of such reversion levels are evident in some states of the USA (e.g. Colorado, Oregon, Michigan). Romer and Rosenthal assume that the reversion level is exogenous. Should the budget proposed by the local bureau be rejected, expenditure will revert to a specified level which is known to the voter. One objective of the analysis is to show that this institutional arrangement will cause local authority spending to differ from the usual pre-dictions of the traditional model.

In Fig. 12.15 the preferences of the median voter over a private good and the local public good are illustrated. Each voter pays a tax price for the good and this is implicit in the slope of the budget line 12. It is clear that the most preferred position for the med-

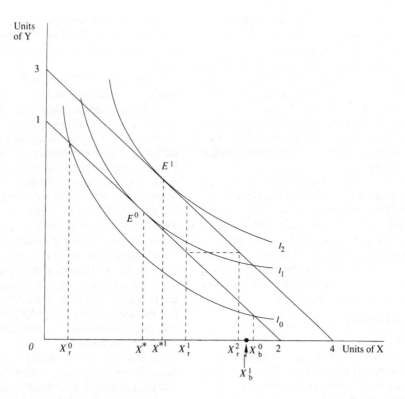

Figure 12.15 The Romer–Rosenthal model.

ian voter is X^*. If the reversion level were set at X_r^0, it should be evident that the median voter would vote for any level of the output *between* X_r^0 and an output just below X_b^0 (e.g. X_b^1) in preference to X_r^0. Any such level of output will put the median voter on a higher indifference curve than would the reversion level X_r^0.

Given this choice two situations are possible:

1. If the reversion level is X_r^0, the median voter may vote for an output of *almost* X_b^0. This is a higher output than would be preferred if the only constraint were that shown by the budget line 12 (i.e. output X^*).

2. If X_r^* is greater than X^*, the bureau will propose a level of spending that *is* the reversion level. This, again, would mean that output is greater than preferred by the median voter when this institutional constraint does not apply.

Assume case 2, i.e. that the level of expenditure most preferred by the median voter (X^*) is less than the reversion level. In Fig. 12.15 assume that the reversion level is X_r^1. If the incomes of voters increase, this will shift the budget line in the figure to 34. The most preferred expenditure level of the median voter

increases to X^{*1} (assuming the local publicly provided goods are normal). The equilibrium allocation for the median voter shifts from point E^0 on indifference curve I_1 to E^1 on I_2. However, if the institutional arrangement described by Roemer and Rosenthal applies, the individual does not freely choose to move from E^0 to E^1. If the median voter's most preferred point X^{*1} remains less than the reversion level, the level of spending remains unchanged at the reversion level X_r^1. The bureau still enacts the legally specified reversion level, which is still greater than the median voter's most preferred choice. In this case, there is no increase in spending as a result of an increase in the level of income of the median voter.

In contrast to this, if the local authority receives a lump-sum grant, equivalent in size to the increase in income, this will have an effect on the local authority's spending on X. The bureau takes full account of the grant to increase the reversion level of output by exactly the size of the grant, e.g. to X_r^2 in Fig. 12.15. Just as the setter is legally obligated to spend fully at the reversion level (should his proposal fail), so he is obliged to spend the whole of the grant in addition to the reversion level of spending (an assumption consistent with the institutional arrangements of some states in the USA). Thus, if the median voter's preferred point X^{*1} is less than the reversion level, a lump-sum grant will put the new equilibrium level of public spending at a new higher reversion level. (The increase is equal to the full amount of the grant.) This particular case vividly illustrates the possibility of a 'flypaper' effect. With an increase in income there is no increase in local provision of the good, but when the increase comes via a lump-sum grant there is a full increase in spending.

Of course, this particular case depends on the assumption that the reversion level exceeds (and continues to exceed) the most preferred level. Romer and Rosenthal (1980) consider alternative relationships between these levels of spending. For our purposes, however, enough has been said to describe how the institutional setting can cause expenditure patterns of local authorities to deviate in the direction indicated by empirical work of Gramlich.

12.8.2 Fiscal illusion

Oates's model

Another means of explaining the 'flypaper' effect depends on the assumption of fiscal illusion. Voters are given only part of the story when making their decisions. They make their decisions on the basis of two pieces of information: the level of output Q and the associated tax liability T. This means that they may have an idea of the *average tax price* Q/T of such services.

In Fig. 12.16 the D curve is the demand curve of the median voter for the locally provided good. The tax price to the median voter is P_m. Without any grant from central government, the preferred position is output Oq^0 (i.e. where marginal benefit for the median voter is equal to marginal cost to the median voter of providing the good). On receipt of the lump-sum grant, the authority could pass it on, as an income increase, to voters. In this case the D curve moves to the right, to D^1, and the quantity demanded is Oq^1. The effect is similar to a change in income and depends upon the income elasticity of demand.

By contrast, the authority, on receipt of the lump-sum grant, could simply offer to produce the good at a lower 'subsidized' price P_s. For example, in Fig. 12.16, the new tax price for the good may be thought to look like the curve B (instead of MC). Now the impact on spending depends on the price elasticity of demand. Demand becomes Oq^2.

Whether or not a 'flypaper' effect is prevalent depends on the relative size of the price and the income elasticities of demand. Oates (1979b) considers the relative size of these elasticities as indicated by

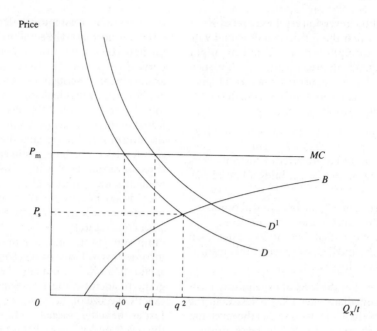

Figure 12.16 Fiscal illusion and the 'flypaper effect'.

Source: based on Oates (1979).

empirical work (see Bergstrom and Goodman 1973). He calculates that the marginal increase in public expenditure for a rise in incomes is 0.1, while the marginal increase in public expenditure for an increase in intergovernmental grants is 0.4. This is quite close to the empirical results that suggest a 'flypaper' effect.

12.8.3 Adaptation of the 'traditional' model

As well as public choice arguments, there are a number of explanations for the flypaper effect ('money sticks where it hits') which can be drawn from the 'traditional' social optimality approach and which by comparison might be considered 'benign' (Quigley and Smolensky 1992).

One explanation would question the empirical analysis. It is argued that lump-sum grants (and matching grants) are typically awarded after application by a potential beneficiary and after a period of negotiation between governmental agents. In this process 'grantors' hope to ensure that recipients increase spending on a particular sector. Therefore, what may appear to econometricians to be an 'untied block grant' may in fact be a grant conditional upon increased spending.

A second explanation relates to transactions costs. Changes in tax are costly. In response to a lump-sum grant grant, it would take time and effort to revise and reduce tax rates to the new level demanded by the median voter. Such resources might be wasted if it is thought that growth in income will require that tax rates will soon have to be increased again. A tax reduction would be transitory and costs involved could be saved if expected income increases (or expected increases in the costs of service) mean that there would have to be future increases in taxes to meet the demands of the median voter.

A third explanation depends on the share of the median voter in national and in local tax (Heins 1971 and Fisher 1979). For example, suppose the median voter's share of local taxes is smaller than her share of the increase in national taxes paid by the local jurisdiction in financing a grant. The median voter would be better off as a result of the intergovernmental grant and an additional increase in spending (or flypaper effect) might be observed. This would be so even when the median voter determines outcomes (though critics, e.g. Fisher 1982 argue that in practice this 'tax substitution' effect is quite small).

A fourth explanation relies on altruism. King (1984) continues with the assumption that decisions reflect the demand of the median voter and makes no allowance for governmental failure. However, he assumes that, when the median voter votes, she will not accept proposals that imply that the local tax rate leaves the poorest citizens in the locality with a net private income below some specified level. In Fig. 12.17 the median voter is constrained to vote for an output combination along 18 of the budget line 12 because otherwise the local authority would set tax rates that left the poorest citizens with a minimum income level lower than that regarded as acceptable; i.e. they would set a tax greater than 19. The initial equilibrium chosen along this range is E_0. In the diagram 12 is the budget line prior to receipt of a grant. A lump-sum specific grant would change the budget line to 145.[8] If the voter were unconstrained by concern for the poorest individual she would move to E_1. (She may feel no such constraint because spending all the grant does not increase taxes in the locality.)

A cut in taxes that raised residents' incomes by the same amount as the lump-sum grant would be expected to produce the same amount as the lump-sum grant. If there were such an identical cut in taxes, the relevant budget line for the median voter would be 65. Unperturbed about the taxes of others, the individual would prefer to be at E_1. However, if the additional constraint is binding, the median voter would no longer be able to choose E_1. For example, assume that, as a part of the cut in tax introduced by central government, the poorest citizens in this locality enjoyed no benefit (possibly because their incomes were previously too low for them to be required to pay the central government tax). The median voter, concerned about the welfare of the poorest in her locality, would not want local authority spending to increase if this increased the tax on the poorest members of the locality. Therefore, in Fig. 12.17 the total tax raised from each individual could not exceed 6–10 (equal to 19): the median voter is constrained, by concern for the poor, to keep taxes payment at 6–10. On the new budget line, 65, the best position to be chosen now is point 7 (vertically above 8). In these circumstances the output selected would be OX^1 and this is less than the output OX^2 which was selected when the median voter was unconstrained by concern for the poor. The result is that there is no increase in provision of the good when there is a cut in taxes, even though when the lump-sum grant applies there was an increase in provision. Once again, the 'flypaper' effect is evident.

---

[8] In Fig. 12.17a matching grant would change the budget line 12 to say 13. The new equilibrium would be on the price consumption curve beyond E_0.

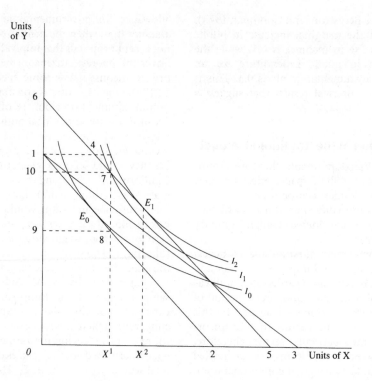

Figure 12.17 The 'traditional' approach with a minimum income constraint.
Source: based on King (1984).

This is an extreme example. If we assume, instead, that the poorest in the locality benefits (though not fully) from the cuts in central tax, a higher output will be chosen as a result of the cut in taxes, though this will be less than output OX^2, the output that would be chosen if an equivalent lump-sum grant had been received. Of course, the analysis is sensitive to the impact of the central government tax cuts: if these were actually targeted on the poor, they might reduce the initial constraint on local taxation to which the median voter adheres.

Has public choice theory satisfactorily explained the flypaper effect? The flypaper effect may appear something of a curiosity, but it illustrates another example of the distinction between what we have referred to as the 'traditional' approach and the public choice approach to public finance. With so many explanations, readers may be forgiven for thinking that, in theory, 'anything goes'. We would simply note that, for those instances where empirical evidence clashes with traditional public finance, there may be explanations other than governmental failure. The 'social optimality' approach can be refined to deal with the problem without necessarily resorting to the

conclusion that 'self-interest' on the part of politicians and bureaucrats is proven. Of course, in the last example it is questionable whether voters in local authorities are as concerned with the plight of the poor as is suggested in King's approach. Even so, King argues that his theory has the advantage of also explaining why a lump-sum grant has less of an impact on local spending than does an equal value-matching grant—another result evident in empirical work.

12.9 Decentralization and the growth of the public sector

One of the arguments that comprise the 'Leviathan' school of the 'over-expanded' public sector relates to the extent of decentralization. Brennan and Buchanan (1980) argue that, where there are competing political jurisdictions, 'exit' possibilities will act as an effective constraining mechanism; i.e. public expenditures should vary with the extent of fiscal decentralization.

Oates (1985), among others, offers some counter-arguments and finds the empirical evidence lacking both at the international level and in the state–local sectors in the USA. This material will be discussed alongside other related material in chapter 16.

Although the 'Leviathan' school see centralized government as constrained, another line of argument would draw attention to the potential expansionary impact of central government. Weingast, Shepsle and Johnsen (1981) explore the implications of projects, programmes and grants that concentrate their benefits on specific geographical constituencies but are financed through general taxation. This is what is understood in their paper by a 'distributive policy'. It is an 'over-expansion' scenario with political costs and benefits dominating economic ones. The total economic costs (TC_e) of a project are divided into

C_1 = real resource expenditures on the project in the constituency in which the project is located

C_2 = real resource expenditures outside the project constituency

C_3 = non-expenditure real resource costs located in the project constituency, e.g. non-pecuniary externalities such as environmental pollution

The total benefit of the project in a given locality, TB_e, is the sum of the present value of the economic benefits of the project. This is enough information to identify the efficient benchmark project size as OE in

Fig. 12.18, where the difference between TB_e and TC_e is maximized. The expenditure costs T of the project $C_1 + C_2$ are assumed to be allocated over n districts so that

$$(12.7) \qquad T = C_1 + C_2$$

and the tax bill for the ith district is

$$(12.8) \qquad t_i(C_1 + C_2) = t_i T$$

where $\sum_{i=1}^{n} t_i = 1$.

With these data, the analysis of the selection of a project size can proceed. The authors isolate three processes or mechanisms.

1. *The politicization of expenditures* involves the recognition that C_1 expenditures result in local pecuniary gains for factor owners as increased demand raises factor prices so that large C_1-type costs of the project are transferred to the benefit side of the equation.

In order to analyse and isolate the impact of local districts in the analysis, the authors initially assume one district, j, so that *all* real resource expenditures ($C_1 + C_2$) take place in j and $t_j = 1$. The object then becomes to maximize the difference between $TB_e + C_1 + C_2$ and $C_1 + C_2 + C_3$ (which is the maximum difference between TB_e and C_3 that occurs at project size OP in Fig. 12.18).

2. *The districting mechanism* allows the expenditure costs of the project to be diffused, so that $t_j \neq 1$. The

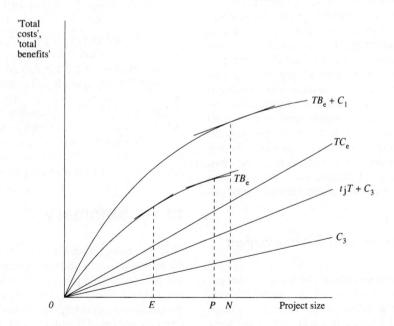

Figure 12.18 Political determination of distributive projects.

relevant difference to maximize for those legislators who see maximizing their district's private benefits as a way to seek re-election is between $(TB_e + C_1)$ and $(t_jT + C_3)$, which occurs at project size ON in the diagram. The requirement for ON to exceed OP is that the rate of growth of C_1 (local real resource expenditures) with respect to 'size' exceeds the rate of growth of the local tax bill as size increases. This is not a very demanding condition. If, for example, there are 20 districts, it means that C_1 can grow at just a shade over one-twentieth the rate of growth of total expenditures and the condition for ON to exceed OP will be met.

3. *The taxation mechanism* has already been introduced. However, it is worth noting that, as long as taxes in each locality are a declining function of the number of districts, as for example with equal shares, the optimum size of project for each locality increases with the number of districts, other things equal. That is, t_jT will tend to fall in Fig. 12.18 and point N will tend to migrate to the right.

In some ways this is the 'tyranny of the majority' argument (met in chapter 4) described in a different way. However, the authors have a more concrete institutional context for their analysis, noting that the US Congress is characterized by universalism and reciprocity when this type of distributive project arises. Universalism tends to guarantee all districts a project and reciprocity allows the recognition that different districts will have different project priorities. In such a setting, the 'logrolling' process is easily established. This type of argument presents a link between local government districts (or areas), central government representation and central government expenditure. It apparently adds a 'twist' to the public choice argument that local Leviathans are in chains with many competing districts. It suggests that the cost is an over-expanded higher level of representative government. Decreasing local government spending autonomy, in circumstances where there is a close connection in j between tax costs and benefits, will tend to replace OP-sized local projects with ON-sized centrally provided and generally financed ones.

12.9.1 Union power and local government expenditure

Union power, or otherwise, is the subject of much debate both in economics and in general. Valletta (1989) provides a public choice avenue through which *unionized* municipal workers increase their wage/employment opportunities. One way for

unions to avoid the unemployment consequences that are likely to attend pushing up wages is to shift their own demand curve to the right. If successful both increased wages and employment are possible. The mechanisms through which they can achieve this are of interest. Moving from the general to the particular:

(i) unions can issue information and generate publicity to foster public support for their particular departments, e.g. refuse collection. Increased expenditure on their department may then become popular or at least not resisted;

(ii) because they are organized into a union they can form a natural voting bloc willing to support candidates for any locally elected offices who are prepared to do their bidding;

(iii) internally to local government the political environment may enable union officials to employ what the author calls 'end run bargaining'! This involves an 'over your head' approach to the legislators or supervisors as a way of outflanking administrators who may oppose their expansionist designs. Similarly 'double-deck' bargaining involves negotiating a collective bargain with one level of local government and then appealing to a higher legislative level for a better bargain. In circumstances where more than one level of local government has responsibility for public policy unions tend to be given more concessions than when faced with a unified opposition.

With the aid of regression analysis and data from 700 US cities Valletta found that union power exercised in this way, on average increased expenditure on unionized municipal departments. The increased expenditures mainly took the form of more workers consistent with (ii) above. However, the argument did not appear to be consistent with a municipal Wagner's Law (see chapter 14) as the increased expenditure on unionized departments appeared to come as a reallocation from non-unionized departments.

12.10 Summary

That the theory of local public goods, together with the analysis of clubs and the Tiebout mechanism, are less than perfect explanations of local government responsibility does not mean that these concepts should have no part to play in shaping future policy. Of course, in and of themselves, they are unlikely to do justice to all the complexities that influence policy change. Yet there are ways in which other more practical considerations can be brought into consideration. Helm and Smith (1987), for example, introduce an administrative rationale for local government. They argue that '... the local/central government relationship with respect to administration is ... an example of the general principal/agent problem— how to provide necessarily decentralized (to maximize information) agents with incentives to pursue the central government principal's objectives' (p. ix). In keeping with the literature on fiscal federalism, local preferences are more readily apparent to local government; however, more than this, local government provides a more suitable hierarchical pattern for administration. Instead of central boards to oversee services, such as education, fire protection, etc., it may be better to have a decentralized pattern. One of the administrative advantages is that central government can ameliorate the monopoly of information which may be possessed by such agents. By creating 'yardsticks', central government may find the task of monitoring quality of service more manageable (e.g. 'if more dustbins are emptied per kilometre for a lower cost in Scotland than Gateshead, central government has useful information for appraisal': Helm and Smith 1987, p. x).

Local government, then, is better informed and easier to monitor than are national bureaucracies established to provide particular services. That they are able to raise revenue is a 'safety valve' to correct decisions by a less perfectly informed central government. Administrative considerations, which look for the best assignment of tasks within a hierarchical structure, can in this way augment other considerations outlined above. The result is that tasks such as redistribution, which in the fiscal federalism literature are seen as a prerogative of central government, may (given the imperfections of the Tiebout mechanism and the informational requirements of administration) be shown to be better pursued at a lower level of government when broader considerations are taken into account.

While such considerations as those outlined by Helm and Smith may amend the prescriptions of basic fiscal federalism theory, it is a matter of concern when some of the staple prescriptions are flaunted. In the UK, since 1979, central government has tightened control over local authority spending. There have been changes in the block grant from central government; rate-capping; the abolition of the Greater London Council; the forced introduction of greater tendering; and changes in local authority finance. Moreover, in the 1986 Green Paper it is stated that

'The main task of central government is to establish national policies and priorities for defence, foreign affairs and the economy as well as for public services—such as education—which are provided locally, but where there is a national interest in standards.'

To set national standards and seek to restrain local expenditure are not policy prescriptions that easily emerge from fiscal federalism. While such theory may indicate that local voters should be made aware of costs, the case for differences in spending patterns and in standards of services is rooted in the reduction in welfare losses indicated by the decentralization theorem. Also, in the context of Helm and Smith's (1987) case for local government, 'The notion that central government can make judgements about local "overspending" sits very uneasily with the rationale for decentralising redistributive functions to local governments in the first place' (p. xix).

References

Anderson, G. M. (1991) 'The Fiscal Significance of User Charges and Earmarked Taxes: A Survey', pp. 13–33 in R. E. Wagner (ed.), *Charging for Government: User Charges and Earmarked Taxes in Principle and Practice*. London and New York: Routledge.

Aronson, J. R. (1974) 'Financing Public Goods and the Distribution of Population in Metropolitan Areas: An Analysis of Fiscal Migration in the US and England', pp. 313–41 in A. J. Culyer (ed.), *Economic Policies and Social Goals*. London: Martin Robertson.

Aronson, J. R. and Schwartz, E. (1973) 'Financing Public Goods and the Distribution of Population in a System of Local Governments', *National Tax Journal*, **26**, 2, pp. 137–60.

Bailey, S. J. (1994) 'User Charges for Urban Services', *Urban Studies*, **31**, 4–5, pp. 745–65.

Bailey, S. J. and Bruce, A. (1994) 'Funding the National Health Service: the Continuing Search for Alternatives', *Journal of Social Policy*, **23**, 4, pp. 489–516.

Bergstrom, T. and Goodman, R. (1973) 'Private Demands for Public Goods', *American Economic Review*, **63**, 3, pp. 280–96.

Bladen-Hovell, R. and Symons, E. (1994) 'The EC budget', pp. 368–87 in M. J. Artis and N. Lee (eds.), *The Economics of the European Union*. Oxford: Oxford University Press.

Boadway, R. W. (1979) *Public Sector Economics*. Cambridge, Mass.: Winthrop Publishers.

Boadway, R. W. and Wildasin, D. E. (1984) *Public Sector Economics*, 2nd edn. Boston: Little, Brown.

Bowles, R. and Jones, P. (1992) 'Equity and EC Budget: A Pooled Cross Section Time Series Analysis', *Journal of European Social Policy*, 2, 2, pp. 87–106.

Bradford, D. and Oates, W. (1974) 'Suburban Exploitation of Central Cities and Governmental Structure', pp. 43–90 in H. Hochman and G. Peterson, *Redistribution through Public Choice*. New York: Columbia University Press.

Bramley, G., Le Grand, J. and Low, W. (1989) *How far is the Poll Tax a 'Community Charge'? The Implications of Service Usage Evidence*, Welfare State Programme, Discussion Paper, WSP/42, London School of Economics.

Break, G. F. (1980) *Financing Government in a Federal System: Studies of Government Finance*. Washington DC: Brookings Institution.

Brennan, G. and Buchanan, J. M. (1980) *The Power to Tax: Analytical Foundations of a Fiscal Constitution*. Cambridge: Cambridge University Press.

Brown, C. E. and Oates, W. E. (1987), 'Assistance to the poor in a Federal System', *Journal of Public Economics*, 32, 3, pp. 307–30.

Buchanan, J. M. (1950) 'Federalism and Fiscal Equity', *American Economic Review*, 40, 4, pp. 583–99.

Buchanan, J. M. (1965) 'An Economic Theory of Clubs', *Economica*, 32, 125, pp. 1–14.

Buchanan, J. M. and Goetz, C. J. (1972) 'Efficiency Limits of Fiscal Mobility: An Assessment of the Tiebout Model', *Journal of Public Economics*, 1, pp. 25–43.

Buchanan, J. M. and Wagner, R. (1970) 'An Efficiency Basis for Federal Fiscal Equalisation', in J. Margolis (ed.), *The Analysis of Public Output*. New York: Columbia University Press.

Bureau, D. and Champseur, P. (1992) 'Fiscal Federalism and European Economic Unification', *American Economic Review*, 82, 2, pp. 88–92.

CEC (1977) Commission of the European Communities, *Report of the Study Group on the Role of Public Finance in European Integration i. General Report ii. Individual Contributions and Working Papers* (the MacDougall Report) (Economic and Financial Series Nos A13 and B13 Brussels CEC).

Chaudry-Shah, A. (1988) 'Capitalisation and the Theory of Public Finance: An Interpretive Essay' *Journal of Economic Surveys*, 2, 3, pp. 209–45.

Cullis, J. G. and Jones, P. R. (1987) *Microeconomics and the Public Economy: A Defence of Leviathan*. Oxford: Basil Blackwell.

Cullis, J. G. Jones, P. R. and Morrissey, O. (1993) 'The Charge of the Tax Brigade', *European Journal of Political Economy*, 9, 3, pp. 407–26.

Eberts, R. W. and Gronberg, T. J. (1988) 'Can Competition among Local Governments Constrain Government Spending', *Economic Review*, (Federal Reserve Bank of Cleveland) 24.

Edel, M. and Sclar, E. (1974) 'Taxes, Spending and Property Values: Supply Adjustment in a Tiebout–Oates Model', *Journal of Political Economy*, 82, 5, pp. 941–54.

Eichenberger, R. (1994) 'The Benefits of Federalism and the Risk of Overcentralization', *Kyklos*, 47, 3, pp. 403–20.

Fischer, R. C. (1979) 'A Theoretical View of Revenue Sharing Grants', *National Tax Journal*, 32, 2, pp. 173–84.

Fischer, R. C. (1982) 'Income and Grant Effect on Local Expenditure: The Flypaper Effect and Other Difficulties', *Journal of Urban Economics*, 12, pp. 324–45.

Flatters, F. R., Henderson, V. and Miezkowski, P. (1974) 'Public Goods, Efficiency and Regional Fiscal Equalisation', *Journal of Public Economics*, 3, 2, pp. 99–112.

Foster, C. D., Jackman, R. A. and Perlman, M. (1980) *Local Government Finance in a Unitary State*. London: Allen & Unwin.

Giles, C. and Ridge, M. (1993) 'The Impact on Households of the 1993 Budget and the Council Tax', *Fiscal Studies*, 14, 3, pp. 1–20.

Gold, S. D. (1991) 'Interstate Competition and State Personal Income Tax in the 1980s', pp. 205–17 in D. A. Kenyon and J. Kincaid (eds.), *Competition among States and Local Governments*. Washington DC: Urban Institute Press.

Gramlich, E. M. (1977) 'Intergovernmental Grants: A Review of the Empirical Literature', pp. 219–39 in W. E. Oates (ed.), *The Political Economy of Fiscal Federalism*. Lexington, Mass.: Lexington Books.

Gramlich, E. M. and Galper, H. (1973) 'State and Local Fiscal Behaviour and Federal Grant Policy', pp. 15–58 in *Brookings Papers on Economic Activity*, vol. 1. Washington DC: Brookings Institution.

Gramlich, E. M. and Rubinfeld, D. L. (1982) 'Microestimates of Public Spending Demand Functions and Tests of the Tiebout and Median Voter Hypotheses', *Journal of Political Economy*, 90, 3, pp. 536–60.

Grewal, B. S., Buchanan, J. M. and Matthews, R. L. (1980) *The Economics of Federalism*. Canberra: Australian National University Press.

Grossman, P. J. and West, E. G. (1994) 'Federalism and the Growth of Government Revisited', *Public Choice*, 79, 1–2, pp. 19–32.

Hamilton, B. W. (1976) 'The Effects of Property Taxes and Local Public Spending on Property Values: A Theoretical Comment', *Journal of Political Economy*, 86, 3, pp. 647–50.

Heil, J. B. (1991) 'The Search for Leviathan Revisited', *Public Finance Quarterly*, 19, 3 pp. 334–46.

Heins, A. J. (1971) 'State and Local Response to Fiscal Decentralization', *American Economic Review*, 61, pp. 449–55.

Helm, D. and Smith, S. (1987) 'The Assessment: Decentralisation and the Economics of Local Government', *Oxford Review of Economic Policy*, 3, 2, pp. i–xix.

Hoeller, P. and Louppe, M. (1994) 'The EC's Internal Market: Implementation and Economic Effects', OECD Economic Studies, 23, pp. 55–108.

Hughes, G. (1987) 'Fiscal Federalism in the UK', Oxford Review of Economic Policy, 3, 2, pp. 1–23.

Hughes, G. and McCormick, B. (1981) 'Do Council Housing Policies Reduce Migration Between Regions?', Department of Economics Discussion Paper no. 8104. Southampton: University of Southampton.

Inman, R. P. and Rubinfeld, D. L. (1991) 'Fiscal Federalism in Europe: Lessons from the United States Experience', Working Paper No. 91–15, Program in Law and Economics, Centre for the Study of Law and Society, University of California: Berkely, Ca.

Johnson, C. (1990) 'Pros and Cons of Poll Tax', Lloyds Bank Bulletin, no. 137, pp. 1–4.

Kay, J. and King, M. (1986) The British Tax System. Oxford: Oxford University Press.

King, D. (1984) Fiscal Tiers: The Economics of Multi-level Government. London: Allen & Unwin.

Kirchgassner, G. and Pommerehne, W. W. (1993) 'Tax Harmonisation and Tax Competition in the European Community: Lessons from Switzerland', Paper presented at the ISPE-Meeting, Linz, Austria, 19–21 August.

Layfield Report (1976) Local Government Finance, Cmnd, 6453. London: HMSO.

Lee, D. R. (1991) 'The Political Economy of User Charges: Some Bureaucratic Implications', pp. 60–74 in R. E. Wagner (ed.), Charging for Government: User Charges and Earmarked Taxes in Principle and Practice. London and New York: Routledge.

McChesney, F. S. (1991) 'Excises, Earmarked Taxes, and Government User Charges in a Rent Seeking Model', pp. 163–78 in R. E. Wagner (ed.), Charging for Government: User Charges and Earmarked Taxes in Principle and Practice. London and New York: Routledge.

Mitchell, W. C. (1988) Government As It Is: The Impact of Public Choice Economics on the Judgement of Collective Decision Making by Government and on the Teaching of Political Science, Hobart Papers no. 109. London: Institute of Economic Affairs.

Morrisey, O., Cullis, J. G. and Jones, P. R. (1990) 'Poll Tax Paradoxes and the Analysis of Tax Reform', Discussion Paper no. 90/5, Department of Economics, University of Nottingham.

Muellbauer, J. (1987) 'The Community Charge, Rates and Tax Reform', Lloyds Bank Review, no. 166, pp. 7–20.

Musgrave, R. A. (1959) The Theory of Public Finance. New York: McGraw Hill.

Musgrave, R. A. (1983) 'Who Should Tax Where and What', in C McClure Jr. (ed.), Tax Assignment in Federal Countries. Canberra: ANU Press.

Musgrave, R. A. and Musgrave, P. B. (1989) Public Finance in Theory and Practice. New York: McGraw-Hill.

Nelson, M. A. (1987) 'Searching for Leviathan; Comment and Extension', American Economic Review, 77, 1, pp. 198–204.

Niskanen, W. A. (1968) 'The Peculiar Economics of Bureaucracy', American Economic Review (Papers and Proceedings), 57, 2, pp. 293–321.

Oates, W. E. (1969) 'The Effects of Property Taxes and Local Public Spending on Property Values: An Empirical Study of Tax Capitalization and the Tiebout Hypothesis', Journal of Political Economy, 77, 6, pp. 957–71.

Oates, W. E. (1972) Fiscal Federalism. New York: Harcourt Brace Jovanovich.

Oates, W. E. (1979a) 'An Economist's Perspective on Fiscal Federalism', in W. E. Oates (ed.), The Political Economy of Fiscal Federalism. Lexington, Mass.: Lexington Books.

Oates, W. E. (1979b) 'Lump-sum Intergovernmental Grants Have Price Effects', pp. 22–30 in P. Mieszkowski and W. H. Oakland (eds.), Fiscal Federalism and Grants in Aid, Coupe Papers on Public Economics. Washington DC: Urban Institute.

Oates, W. E. (1985) 'Searching for Leviathan', American Economic Review, 75, 4, pp. 748–57.

Oates, W. E. (1989) 'Searching for Leviathan; A Reply and Some Further Reflections', American Economic Review, 79, pp. 578–83.

Pauly, M. V. (1976) 'A Model of Local Government Expenditure and Tax Capitalisation', Journal of Public Economics, 6, 3, pp. 231–42.

Pommerehne, W. H. (1978) 'Institutional Approaches to Public Expenditure; Empirical Evidence from Swiss Municipalities', Journal of Public Economics, 9, 2, pp. 255–80.

Pommerehne, W. H. and Schneider, F. (1982) 'Unbalanced Growth between Public and Private Sector and Empirical Examination', pp. 309–26 in Haveman, R. H. (eds.), Public Finance and Public Employment. Detroit: Wayne State University Press.

Prest, A. R. (1985) 'Implicit Taxes', The Royal Bank of Scotland Review, 147, 3, pp. 10–26.

Quigley, J. M. and Smolensky, E. (1992) 'Conflicts Among Levels of Government in a Federal System', Public Finance/Finances Publiques, 41, pp. 202–15.

Reichenbach, H. (1983) 'EC Budgetary Imbalances; A Conceptual Framework', Finanzarchiv, 41, pp. 452–65.

Romer, T. and Rosenthal, H. (1980) 'An Institutional Theory of the Effect of Intergovernmental Grants', National Tax Journal, 33, 4, pp. 451–8.

Rubinfeld, D. L. (1987) 'The Economics of the Local Public Sector', pp. 571–639 in A. J. Auerbach and M. Feldstein (eds.), Handbook of Public Economics, Vol. II. Amsterdam: North-Holland.

Samuelson, P. (1954) 'The Pure Theory of Public Expenditure', Review of Economics and Statistics, 36, 4, pp. 387–9.

Sandford, C. T. (1984) *Economics of Public Finance*, 3rd edn. Oxford: Pergamon Press.

Sandford, C. T. (1990) 'The Poll Tax with a Pinch of Salt', *Accountancy*, June, p. 27.

Sandler, T. and Tschirhart, J. (1980) 'The Economic Theory of Clubs: An Evaluative Survey', *Journal of Economic Literature*, 18, 4, pp. 1481–521.

Schneider F. (1995) 'Some Elements of A European Federal Union: A Public Choice Approach', Arbeitspapier 9518, September, Institut fur Volkswirtschaftslehre, Johannes Kepler Universitat, Linz.

Sinn, H.-W. (1994) 'How much Europe? Subsidiarity, Centralization and Fiscal Competition', *Scottish Journal of Political Economy*, 41, 1, pp. 85–107.

Smith, S. (1992) 'Financing the European Community: A Review of Options for the Future', *Fiscal Studies*, 13, 4, pp. 98–127.

Swan, D. (1995) *The Economics of the Common Market*. Harmondsworth: Penguin.

Tiebout, C. M. (1956) 'A Pure Theory of Local Expenditures', *Journal of Political Economy*, 64, 5, pp. 416–24.

Topham, N. (1983) 'Local Government Economics', pp. 129–98, in R. Millward *et al.*, *Public Sector Economics*. Harlow: Longman.

Tresch, R. W. (1981) *Public Finance: A Normative Theory*. Plano, Texas: Business Publications Inc.

Valletta, R. G. (1989) 'The Impact of Unionism on Municipal Expenditures and Revenues', *Industrial and Labour Relations Review*, 42, 3, pp. 430–42.

Vaubel, R. (1994) 'The Public Choice Analysis of European Integration; A Survey', *European Journal of Political Economy*, 10, 1, pp. 227–49.

Walsh, C. (1992) 'Fiscal Federalism; An Overview of Issues and a Discussion of their Relevance to the European Community', Working Paper No. 12, Federalism Research Centre, Australian National University, February.

Weingast, B. R., Shepsle, K. A. and Johnsen, C. (1981) 'The Political Economy of Benefits and Costs: A Neoclassical Approach to Distribution Politics', *Journal of Political Economy*, 89, 4, pp. 642–64.

Wildasin, D. (1990) 'Budgetary Pressures in the EEC; A Fiscal Federalism Perspective', *American Economic Review*, 80, 2, pp. 69–74.

Wilde, J. A. (1968) 'The Expenditure Effects of Grants-in-Aid Programs', *National Tax Journal*, 21, pp. 340–8.

Zax, J. S. (1989) 'Is There a Leviathan in Your Neighborhood?' *American Economic Review*, 79, 3, pp. 560–7.

13 International issues in public finance

13.1 Introduction

Trade taxes are a far more important component of central government revenue for less developed countries than they are for developed countries. Table 13.1 shows the percentage of total government revenues raised by trade taxes for a sample of quite different countries. It is clear that this can be quite a substantial proportion; for example, Gambia, Yemen, Swaziland, Rwanda and Chad all raised more than half their total revenue by this form of taxation.

An examination of this table suggests a relationship between the proportion of revenue raised from trade taxes and the level of development of the country. The fact that less developed countries rely far more heavily on trade taxation is borne out by statistical analysis (see, e.g. Lewis 1963; Greenaway 1980). By reference to conventional economic theory, this reliance on trade taxes is a costly way of raising revenue. It can be demonstrated that the welfare costs of raising revenue by trade taxes are likely to be much greater per pound raised than by alternative forms of taxation. Hence the question must be asked, Why would any country rely on this form of revenue?

This question is a perfect starting-point for a consideration of the distinctive approaches of 'traditional' public finance theory and the public choice school. In the early sections of this chapter the objective is to examine the case for trade taxes by reference to the Paretian model, which, as already demonstrated, underlies traditional public finance theory. What case could there be, by reference to this model, for restrictions on import or export markets and government intervention in the trade sector? It will be demonstrated that, if revenue is to be raised, then the use of 'efficiency' arguments does not point to import taxes. Other considerations may be relevant when the standard comparative-static model is explored more closely. But for the public choice

school the explanation, as usual, lies in the failings of the political process and the impact of rent-seeking pressure groups. Which set of arguments is more persuasive?

13.2 Trade versus non-trade taxes: an economic appraisal

If we were to compare the welfare costs of raising revenue by a tax on imports and by a consumption tax, the analysis would appear to favour the more general consumption tax. In Fig. 13.1 the home supply curve for a product (good X) is shown as S. The domestic demand curve is shown as D. The world

Table 13.1 Trade taxes, openness and income per capita

Country	TT[a]	NM[b]	GNP[c]
Gambia	62.56[d]	91.7	378
Yemen	60.51	50.8	442
Swaziland	59.44	127.5	903
Rwanda	53.52	28	233
Chad	52.43[d]	56.4	125
India	19.85	12.0	204
Spain	8.50	20.9	5043
Canada	6.75	43.5	11017
USA	1.54	14.7	12451
UK	0.17	46.1	8954
France	0.04	32.5	10684
Germany	0.02	41.4	11398

[a] TT = trade taxes as a percentage of total government revenues — average of seven-year period 1976–82
[b] NM = exports plus imports as a percentage of GDP
[c] GNP = per capita of mid-year population in $US 1980 market prices; average of seven-year period 1976–82
[d] Data incomplete for seven-year period.
Source: based on G. K. Shaw, 'Revenue Implications of Trade Taxes', in D. Greenaway, *Economic Development and International Trade*, Macmillan, London, 1988, pp. 175–6. Reproduced with the permission of Macmillan Publishers Ltd.

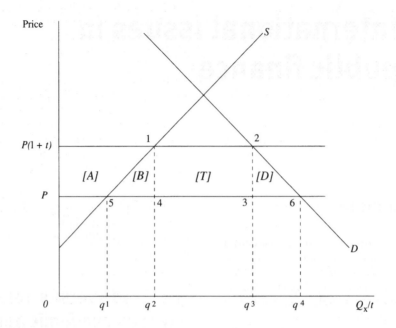

Figure 13.1 The welfare effect of a tax on imports.

price of imports is OP, so that up to quantity Oq^1 it is cheaper to produce the good at home than to import (i.e. S is below OP). After this point, it is cheaper to import the good than to use resources producing an additional unit at home. At the price OP a total of Oq^4 is demanded so that imports are q^1q^4.

If an *ad valorem* import tariff of rate t is applied to imports, the price of imports rises from OP to $OP(1 + t)$. The quantity of imports falls to q^2q^3. Home production, protected by the tariff, rises from Oq^1 to Oq^2, whereas overall demand for the product falls from Oq^4 to Oq^3 as the price to the consumer rises. The tariff revenue is given by area 1234 (i.e. area $[T]$). The welfare losses incurred in raising this revenue are shown by triangles 145 ($[B]$) and triangle 263 ($[D]$). When the import tariff is introduced, the loss $[B]$ occurs because the country uses up resources producing goods that are more cheaply imported. As the supply curve is above OP for units q^1 to q^2, it is evident that the marginal costs associated with producing these goods are greater than the costs (OP) of importing them. The welfare loss $[D]$ arises because consumers reduce their demand for the good, even though they would willingly pay more than the free trade price for it. For units q^3 to q^4 willingness to pay exceeds OP, yet these units are still not consumed. The welfare cost arises because the tax distorts signals.

Consumers are made to believe that imports cost $OP(1 + t)$; a production loss arises from expanded home production, and a consumption loss results from reduced demand. The welfare losses are borne, of course, by the consumer. The tariff leads to a reduction in consumer surplus of ($[A] + [B] + [T] + [D]$). The home producer gains $[A]$ as an increase in producer surplus, created by the fact that he can now charge $OP(1 + t)$ for his product and still compete with imports. The area $[T]$ is a loss of consumer surplus but a gain to individuals as taxpayers; this tax revenue makes possible some public expenditure or a cut in taxes elsewhere. Therefore it also is a transfer within the community. The areas $[B]$ and $[D]$, however, are deadweight losses. This is the cost of raising $[T]$ revenue. Each unit of revenue incurs on average $[B + D]/[T]$ in welfare costs.

Compare this means of raising government revenue with a general consumption tax of rate t. The important point to note is that the consumption tax is applied to both home production and imports; i.e., it is less discriminatory. In the example shown in Fig. 13.1, the price of goods rises to $OP(1 + t)$ and hence demand is reduced from Oq^4 to Oq^3. However, there is no fiscal incentive for home production to expand: home production is not artificially favoured by a general consumption tax. Therefore there is no loss of area $[B]$. Total tax revenue is now equal to $([A] + [B] + [T])$. Clearly, the welfare losses per unit of revenue raised have decreased greatly to $[D]/([A] + [B] + [T])$.

From this comparison, the decision to rely upon trade taxes as a revenue raiser is difficult to explain by the use of conventional economic theory. However, on closer inspection there are arguments that emerge to explain why any country might use trade taxes as a revenue raiser. Moreover, these arguments often relate more closely to the circumstances of less developed countries.

13.2.1 The 'optimum tariff' argument

The case for the use of tariff restriction to international trade has been established in international economics when the objective is to maximize the welfare of the country concerned (rather than world welfare). The argument relies on the assumption that a country may have an effect upon the *terms of trade* as a result of its own trading activity. In the case of an importing country, it may be possible for the country to reduce the price of imports as a result of reducing its demand for imports.

In the analysis above, it was assumed that the country had no impact upon the terms of trade. When it introduced a tariff, this did not affect the price of imports to the country. The country was a price-taker and, to this extent, it can be described as a 'small country'. In the case of a 'large country', the nation has international bargaining power with respect to a particular commodity. For such a country the supply price of imports will not be constant, and in Fig. 13.2 this is shown by the fact that the supply of imports S_m is upward-sloping. The demand for imports is shown as D_m, and if there were free trade the total quantity of imports of commodity X would be Oq_m^1 at a price of OP_1. If a tax were introduced, there would be a difference between the price at which imports were bought (P_3) and the price at which consumers purchased the good (P_2). Assume a tax at rate t_1, so that the price to consumers is P_2 (i.e. the import price OP_3 multiplied by $(1 + t_1)$). Imports will be Oq_m^2, the price to consumers becomes OP_2 and the price of imports to the country is OP_3. It is apparent that cutting the demand for imports has reduced the price of imports to the country from OP_1 to OP_3. There are deadweight losses associated with this tax, as shown by triangles $[A]$ and $[B]$. The

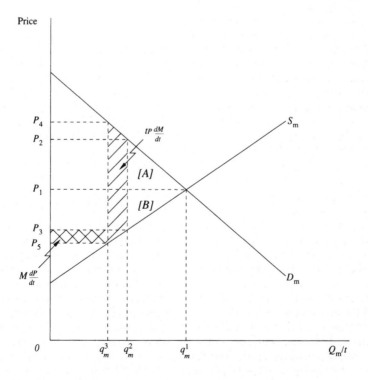

Figure 13.2 An 'optimum' import tax.

Source: adapted from Lindert, P. (1986) *International Economics*, 8th edn., Irwin, Homewood, Illinois.

first of these is a loss to the country that imposes the tax, in so far as residents of that country have lost consumer surplus on the units of imports no longer imported. The second triangle [B] is a loss to the exporting country, which no longer sells these units. Of course, the importing country has lost [A] but, set against this, it has gained the remaining imports at a lower price; i.e. there is a cost reduction of $(OP_1 - OP_3)(Oq_m^2)$ and this outweighs [A]. It should be borne in mind that this sum is a transfer from the exporting country, which now receives less revenue for its exports. In terms of world welfare, the sum of [A] and [B] is the total deadweight loss.

The importing country, nevertheless, has a reason to introduce the tax. The question that now arises is, How will the 'optimum' rate of tax be set? In Fig. 13.2, it is assumed (following Lindert 1986) that the suggestion has been made to raise the rate of tax to t_2. The implication is that the wedge between import prices and consumer prices will increase to $OP_4 - OP_5$. In the diagram there are additional losses borne by the country (in terms of the consumer surplus loss on the units no longer imported, i.e. $Oq_m^2 - Oq_m^3$). These additional losses are approximated by the expression $[tP(dM/dt)]$, where tP is the tax paid on the import reduction (dM/dt) brought about by the increase in tax. The additional gains are equal to the change in the import price (created by the tax increase) multiplied by the remaining imports—which can be written as $M(dP/dt)$. It is obvious that it is worth changing the tax as long as the net marginal gains in welfare are positive; indeed, only when they are equal to zero can we argue that the existing tax rate is the optimal rate t^*. Therefore

$$(13.1) \qquad M(dP/dt) - t^*P(dM/dt) = 0$$

so that

$$(13.2) \qquad t^* = \frac{dP/dt}{dM/dt}\frac{M}{P}$$

and

$$(13.3) \qquad t^* = (dP/dM)(M/P) = 1/e_s$$

where e_s is the elasticity of supply of imports to the country.

It is clear therefore that, for any country, tax revenue may be raised by the country while at the same time the welfare of the country is improved. The excess burden (deadweight losses) of the tax in this case is outweighed by the terms-of-trade improvement which the country experiences. The tariff rate that maximizes this welfare for the country is that which equals the reciprocal of the elasticity of supply

of imports. It should be noted, however, that this is so, provided there is no retaliation from the supplier of exports to the country. From the analysis above, exporters abroad stand to lose, and therefore they may be tempted to retaliate by reducing their demand for imports from this country. The prospect of a tariff war does not imply that the country which initiates the import tariff will necessarily lose (Johnson 1953–4), but it is an important consideration. At the end of a tariff war the terms of trade could still favour the instigator of the war, though the possibility that *all* would be worse off as a result is a very real threat.

Why is it that government intervention is now justified in the import sector? Why is free trade not maximizing the welfare of the country? The answer to these questions lies in the fact that the supply price of imports does not represent the marginal cost to the country of additional imports. The total cost of imports is equal to the import price P, multiplied by the quantity of imports M. As Layard and Walters (1978) note, the marginal cost of imports is

$$(13.4) \qquad \frac{d(PM)}{dM} = P + M\frac{dP}{dM}$$

which can be written[1] as

$$(13.5) \qquad \frac{d(PM)}{dM} = P\left(1 + \frac{1}{e_s}\right)$$

where e_s is the import price elasticity of supply of imports.

When an importer buys an additional import, the price to him is the cost of the import P, but the price to the country is this P plus the impact that the additional purchase has on the price of all other imports, i.e. $M(dP/dM)$. In a sense, then, the effects of decisions of an importer spill over to others who import the good. This is the distortion in the import sector that is corrected by the government.

13.2.2 Administrative costs of tax collection

The above discussion of the merits of different taxes for raising revenue has totally neglected the costs of administering and collecting taxes. This point is of special importance to less developed countries. For tax collection it is important that the taxpayer and the tax base be readily identifiable. In countries that have substantial subsistence sectors, how can income be distinguished from consumption? For economies where there are many traders who are to be found in

---

[1] From equation (13.4)

$$(13.1n) \qquad \frac{d(PM)}{dM} = P\left(1 + \frac{MdP}{PdM}\right)$$

informal street markets and who may be itinerant, how are traders to be identified and checked? Far easier to concentrate upon a smaller number of importers who, at least, should have invoices relating to their business. For less developed countries this must surely be an important consideration. (This relates to the 'tax handles' argument introduced in chapter 14.)

13.2.3 Tariff policy in developing countries

There are other considerations (outlined by Greenaway 1981, 1982) which may lead to an explanation of the reliance of the developing countries on trade taxes, as the following examples indicate.

International/revenue constraints

It is argued that, as income per capita grows, countries are likely to come under increasing pressure to reduce their use of trade restrictions. The General Agreement on Trade and Tariffs (GATT) was designed to reduce tariffs generally, and at various tariff negotiations attempts have been made to achieve this goal. (The Kennedy Round, for example, refers to such negotiations between 1962 and 1967.) Countries are less prepared to condone high tariffs when they are less subject to the problems experienced by developing countries. Moreover, it is argued that, as the revenue yield of trade taxes is inelastic with respect to the growth of income, countries inevitably may be forced to turn to other forms of revenue as they grow.

Import substitution policy

One of the oldest arguments in favour of tariffs is the 'infant industry' argument, which maintains that temporary protection may be necessary for new domestic industries which, after a period of 'learning', will acquire the skills necessary to make them viable competitors internationally. However, while this argument is readily put forward to defend the use of trade restrictions, there are very many problems with it. First, the argument needs to be presented in such a way as to warrant government intervention. For example, are there market imperfections that require attention? Are there external economies associated with assistance to certain industries? Secondly, if there is a case for government intervention, should support to industry take other forms than import protection, e.g. industrial subsidies? Thirdly, if it can be shown that import tariffs are the best approach, will the potential benefits outweigh the costs of protection to be experienced during the period of protection? These arguments are well known (see, e.g. Corden 1974). Yet, given considerations such as the weakness of capital markets and the difficulties of financing industrial subsidies in developing countries, import substitution may become an objective of developing countries.

There are, then, reasons why any country would use a tax on trade as a source of revenue. The traditional approach can rationalize this by developing caveats in the Paretian framework. For example, the terms-of-trade argument rationalizes import (or export) taxes on the grounds that they can be Pareto-optimal for the country concerned even though they would not be Pareto-optimal for the world as a whole. The infant-industry argument rationalizes import taxation on the grounds that there are dynamic considerations which the original Paretian analysis did not address. That is (by reference to Fig. 13.1), the home supply curve S would shift to the right, thereby reducing deadweight losses and leading to a replacement of some imports (at price OP) with even cheaper home-produced goods. Later the arguments of the public choice school will be considered, but first it is worth considering the problems that countries would experience if they were to try to maximize revenue from trade taxes.

13.3 Maximizing government revenue and smuggling

In chapter 8 the problem of tax evasion was discussed. Smuggling is another example of this same problem. One argument that could be made in its favour is that, if typically trade taxes create welfare losses, then smuggling must be welfare-enhancing. Is this so? Will smugglers enhance welfare if their activity reduces the deadweight losses associated with taxation? This is another version of the argument that a black economy need not be wholly a bad thing. Here we seek to show that smuggling will reduce welfare in circumstances where legal and illegal trade co-exist.[2] Our reference point, however, does not include the well-being of the smuggler himself. Typically, in the economic analysis of crime the well-being of the perpetrator of the crime is not included (Anderson 1976): to do so would lead to very curious results.[3]

---

[2] In circumstances where there is no legal trade, smuggling inevitably increases welfare in the Paretian model by increasing choice.

[3] Robbery, in this scenario, could look like an efficient redistribution mechanism!

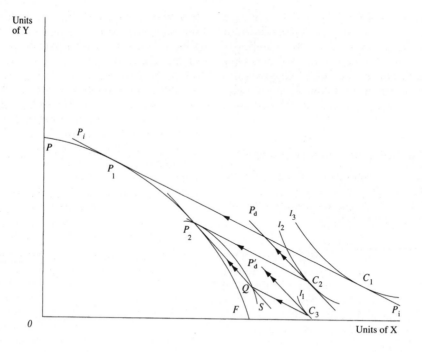

Figure 13.3 The welfare effects of smuggling.

Source: adapted from Bhagwati, J. N. and Srinivason, T. N. (1983).

The following analysis is based on a discussion of one possible case considered by Bhagwati and Hansen (1973). It goes a long way to confirm the belief that it is worth spending resources to deal with smuggling. In Fig. 13.3, *PF* is the transformation (production possibility) curve for a country. If free trade exists, the country will produce that combination of goods Y and X shown at point P_1. It will export some of good Y in order to import units of good X, and residents of the country will consume at C_1. The country will be able to exchange good Y for good X at the international terms of trade P_i and this will permit consumption at C_1 (a point outside the production frontier shown by *PF*). This is the welfare maximum that will be reached when there is a free trade policy.

The introduction of a tariff means that the domestic prices change to P_d. (The slope of $P_d = (P_x/P_y)$ $(1 + t)$, where P_x/P_y is the free trade set of relative prices shown by P_i.) This, of course, protects home production of the importable good X and production shifts in the economy to point P_2. If legal trade takes place there is still some increase in welfare over and above the position of no trade. Utility-maximizing consumers equate their MRS_{xy} to the internal set of

prices, and consumption now takes place at C_2.[4] Obviously, the difference between welfare on community indifference curves I_3 and I_2 is an estimate of the welfare loss (i.e. the deadweight loss in Fig. 13.1) incurred by the movement away from free trade (namely, triangles [B] and [D]).

If smuggling should co-exist with legal trade, then consumers would have an incentive to purchase the smuggled good up to the point at which the price of the smuggled good was just equal to the price of the legal import plus the tax on the legal import. Assume that the smuggler has increasing costs. (That is, the more he smuggles, the greater is the cost per item of getting the smuggled merchandise into the country.) Assume that the transformation function with smuggling takes the shape P_2S; this shows how Y can be exchanged for X—starting from P_2—when dealing with a smuggler. The average terms of trade in dealing with a smuggler is then P_2Q. At this price, the maximum that it is worth buying from a smuggler is set at point Q. Beyond Q the price of imports from a smug-

[4] The legal trade is still at a consumption point outside the production possibility curve because, although there are deadweight losses, the tariff is not prohibitive and the country still gains, to some extent, from trade.

gler is actually greater than the price of legal imports inclusive of the tax. Thus, after point Q consumers will buy the legally imported goods and pay the tax. The additional legal trade is shown by the difference between Q and C_3. The point C_3 on I_1 is the consumption point that will emerge when legal trade and smuggling co-exist. Ultimately, consumers equate their MRS_{xy} with the domestic set of prices.

It is now possible to compare the welfare position of the country when there is both smuggling and legal trade and when there is simply legal trade. Obviously, there is a welfare loss associated with the smuggling and this is measured by the difference between I_1 and I_2. The welfare loss arises because consumer trade has been diverted by the tax to a more expensive supplier. While the smuggler can match the legal price, this is only because of the effect of the tax. At least if the consumer bought the import legally the tax paid would be available for the government to use in the economy. While the consumer does not perceive this advantage, it would, of course, be an advantage to the economy as a whole and far better than simply covering the additional costs assisted with smuggling. The analysis by Bhagwati and Hansen has spawned a literature looking into the effects of smuggling. (See e.g. Bhagwati and Srinivasan (1983) for a review of other contributions.) However, it is reassuring, at least on the above analysis, to see that there is a case for expenditure of resources to deter smugglers.[5]

Smuggling is just one of many considerations that a government must evaluate when deciding how to set tariffs so as to maximize revenue.

13.4 Trade taxes and public choice: pressure-group analysis and rent-seeking

The above analysis examines the use of trade taxes as a source of revenue and argues that it is only in quite specific circumstances that tariffs would be relied upon as a source of revenue because there are other more general taxes which raise revenue at a lower cost in terms of deadweight loss. Indeed, economic theory is consistent in advocating international trade and the

benefits that can arise if each country concentrates on the production of the good in which it has a comparative advantage. For a country (rather than for the world as a whole), it has been shown that there are welfare gains to be had from the introduction of an optimum tariff, while in other circumstances (e.g. infant industry arguments) the case for protection is by no means clear-cut. The question arises, therefore, as to whether it is economic considerations or public choice explanations that better explain a country's use of trade taxes.

A number of studies point to the importance of pressure groups in explaining the use of trade taxes.

1. A study of the US Tariff Act of 1824 by Pincus (1975) found that high protection tended to go to those industries that were most concentrated, where communication among producers was easiest, and which had a presence in a sizeable area.

2. Richard Caves (1976) examined the Canadian tariff structure and found it best explained by a pressure-group theory, predicting, for example, that protection would be highest in those industries where producers were the most concentrated and buyers the least concentrated.

3. Baldwin (1976) performed a statistical test of congressional voting on the 1974 US Trade Act. He found that protectionist votes were positively related to political party membership (because of party loyalty—the bill was sponsored by a Republican administration), to the prominence of protectionist industries in congressional districts and to the receipt of campaign contributions from trade unions which were protectionist.

Such evidence accords with the predictions of Olson (1971), who argues that smaller groups are more easily mobilized than larger groups. In this way, producer groups for any product can organize more easily and are likely to be more influential (politically) than consumers (who, for any product, are likely to be a large group). It is the consumers who would lose from protection of any product. With reference to Fig. 13.1, it is clear that the losses of consumers are much greater ($[A] + [B] + [T] + [D]$) than the gains $[A]$ that producers are likely to experience.[6]

However, consumers are likely to be less aware of the particular tax rates on the imports of certain goods; and they are far less likely to mobilize to oppose these rates even if they are aware of their existence. Producer groups (e.g. trade unions, trade associa-

---

[5] While this conclusion is subject to the constraints noted above, there are other ways of justifying expenditure on customs and excise policing. For example, there are products that are kept out of the country on merit good arguments, e.g. drugs. Measures to deter drug smugglers may be far more widely justified by reference to merit good arguments.

[6] Note, however, that consumers as taxpayers may receive back $[T]$ as a tax reduction elsewhere or in the form of public expenditure.

tions) have already mobilized for other reasons. Their representatives are well informed; and, in the context of the discussion so far, if politicians can win votes by agreeing to the introduction of taxes on imports because the losers are unaware of the tax costs, then it is likely that such taxes will be introduced, regardless of whether or not there is a case for them in conventional neoclassical welfare economics.

Magee (1982) provides evidence as to the nature of political support or opposition for trade taxes. He shows that this is industry-based. In Table 13.2 the position of labour and of capital (represented by the managers) in the USA was identified with respect to the president's trade bill in 1973. If factors of production shared opinions and lobbying took place along industry lines, all of the observations would be in the upper left–lower right diagonal. According to the Table 19 of the 21 industries indicate industry lines.

Applying an analysis explained by Williamson (1983), it is not difficult to explain this result. If we invoke the concept of economic rents associated with government activity, it is possible to explain why political pressure would be industry-based. In Fig. 13.4(a) the Edgeworth–Bowley box diagram shows

Table 13.2 A classification of 21 US industries according to their protectionist or free trade position on the president's trade bill, 1973

Position of capital	Position of labour	
	Protectionist	Free trade
Protectionist	Distilling	Tobacco
	Textiles	
	Apparel	
	Chemicals	
	Plastics	
	Rubber shoes	
	Leather	
	Shoes	
	Stone, etc.	
	Iron/steel	
	Cutlery	
	Hardware	
	Bearings	
	Watches	
Free trade	Petroleum	Paper
		Machinery
		Tractors
		Trucks
		Aviation

Source: S. P. Magee, 'Protectionism in the United States', in P. Oppenheimer (ed.), *Issues in International Economics*, Oriel Press, London, 1982. Reproduced with the permission of Routledge.

the quantities of capital and labour available to a particular economy. Initially the economy is at an equilibrium on the contract curve $O_x O_m$ at point 1. At this point $O_x K_1$ of the capital stock is employed in the X industry and the remainder $(O_x \bar{K} - O_x K_1)$ is employed in the Y industry. $O_x L_1$ of the labour supply is employed in the X industry and the remainder $(O_x \bar{L} - O_x L_1)$ is employed in the Y industry. Of the two goods, M is imported into the country and X is the good that the country exports. However, it is clear that there is an active import-competing industry making use of capital and labour.

In Fig. 13.4(b) V_m is the value of the marginal product of labour in industry M. That is to say,

$$(13.6) \qquad V_m = P_m \frac{dM}{dL}$$

Initially the labour market is in equilibrium at

$$(13.7) \qquad V_m^0 = V_x^0 = W_0$$

There is, therefore, no incentive for labour to move between industries and the total supply of labour is such that $O_L^x L_1$ is in the X industry and $O_L^m L_1$ is in the M industry. It is assumed that factors of production can eventually move between the industries but that this takes time. In the very short run, neither factor of production can move: they have skills or characteristics that are specific to the industry in which they are located. It is assumed that labour is relatively more mobile than capital. Only in the very long run can capital be transferred from one industry to another.

With these assumptions relating to factor specificity, it is possible to outline the likely course of events were a tariff to be placed on the import good M. With a tariff imposed on good M, its price will rise, causing V_m^0 to shift to V_m^1. The marginal value product of labour will therefore increase in the import-competing industry. If factors of production do not move in response, the wage in the M industry will rise to W_1. In the very short run, the owners of labour in the M industry can possibly benefit as a result of the introduction of the import tax: the real wage in industry M will be higher in terms of good X.

If labour (but not capital) is mobile, then workers move to industry M and the wage rate falls to W_2. This is shown by the movement from L_1 to L_2 in the figure. Notice that in part (a) it is evident that the capital stock allocation is fixed and this means that the economy moves off the contract curve from 1 to 2. The wage rate to labour is still higher (in terms of good X—though lower in terms of good M, as the shift in the wage rate now is not as great as the vertical distance between V_m^0 and V_m^1 which is created by the

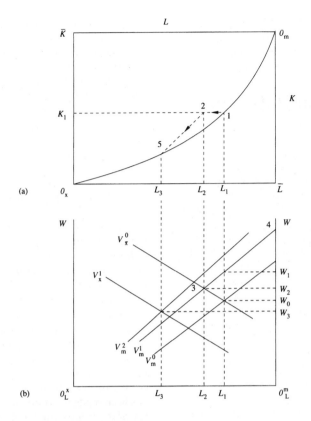

Figure 13.4 Industry-based pressure for import taxation.

Source: Williamson, John (1983) *The Open Economy and the World Economy*, Basic Books, New York.

increase in the price of M). Depending on consumption patterns, labour in this industry may yet be better off. However, the real return to capital will be higher in the M industry. The return to capital is now shown by triangle $W_2 34$. The total output of labour is the integral under the marginal value product curve V_m^1 between O_L^m and L_2. Each unit of labour is paid W_2 so that total labour costs are $O_L^m W_2 3 L_2$. The remaining triangle $W_2 34$ is the return to capital. This triangle under the V_m^1 function is obviously greater than the corresponding triangle under V_m^0 at the wage of W_0. It is still possible, then, at this stage for *both* labour and capital in the M industry to be better off as a result of tariff protection. (For further discussion of this short-run adjustment analysis, see Mussa 1974; Williamson 1983; Neary 1985.)

In the long run, when capital is mobile, it too moves to industry M. Labour will have moved from the X industry until the wage rate was equalized in the two industries at W_2. As capital did not move in the first instance, the rate of return to capital in the X industry

must have fallen. (The triangle under the V_x^0 function at L_1 when the wage rate is W_0 is greater than the triangle under V_x^0 at L_2 when the wage rate is W_2.) Now, as capital moves to industry M, the marginal value product of labour function (V_x^0) shifts to the left (to V_x^1) as each unit of labour has fewer units of capital to work with. By analogy, V_m^1 shifts to the left. Eventually a new long-run equilibrium emerges where the wage rate has fallen to W_3. Labour in both industries is worse off after the full long-run adjustment, but until this time both labour and capital in the M industry have reason to press for import taxation of good M. Inasmuch as short-run (or sector-specific) considerations are dominant, it is likely that pressure for protection will be industry-based.

The conclusions that emerge as to why tariffs are introduced are in keeping with those of chapter 16. The design of taxation has more to do with public choice considerations than with conventional economic theory. Pressure-group activity can be well described by a politico-economic model that focuses on rent-seeking, and lobbying will be industry-based. (See Frey 1984 for a useful discussion of the application of public choice theory to trade policy.)

13.5 The harmonization of indirect taxes

Tax harmonization has usually been designed in terms of the objective of keeping taxes neutral with respect to trade. The aim being to ensure that national taxation does not influence the choice which consumers make between goods from different countries. It 'should' not be the case that goods from country A are preferred simply because they carry a lower rate of sales tax in country A than the goods in country B. If country B were the most efficient producer of a particular good but also the country with the higher tax, consumers may see it as preferable to purchase the good from country A even though the costs of producing the good were greater in country A. The higher rate of sales tax, in this way, distorts international trade between countries A and B.

One of the functions of border tax adjustments is to equalize the conditions of competition between different producers. There are two principles of border tax adjustment that are relevant:

1. *The origin principle*: here the good is taxed in the country in which it is produced and it continues to bear the tax of the country of origin, even though it is sold and consumed in another country—in effect there is no border tax adjustment.

2. *The destination principle*: here there is a border tax adjustment. The same sales tax will be imposed on imported goods as is imposed on domestically produced goods. Under this arrangement, goods which are exported are exempted from tax, so that, in turn, ultimately they will bear only the same sales tax as that imposed on other goods produced in the country to which exports are destined for consumption. This arrangement requires adjustment to taxes at national frontiers. Exported goods enjoy a rebate of tax in the country from which they are exported and then are taxed according to the rate of sales tax in the country to which they are destined.

Is there any difference as far as the allocation of resources or the trade balance is concerned if the origin principle, rather than the destination principle, applies?

Consider two countries A and B with no import taxes between them. Initially there is a situation of *internal* and *external* equilibria; i.e. there is full employment (with no price inflation) and there is an equilibrium on the balance of trade. Now assume that country A imposes an indirect tax on sales, the result of which is that the price index in country A is raised by 10 per cent. If the destination principle applies, country A's exports compete in country B on exactly the same terms and country B's exports compete in country A on exactly the same terms. There is no impact on resource allocation or on the balance of trade. There is, however, the need to make the tax adjustment. Fiscal frontiers must exist and their existence implies a real resource loss incurred in computing exemptions, rebates, etc.

If the origin principle of indirect taxation applied, goods from country A sold in country B would carry the additional tax cost of the tax imposed in country A. They would, therefore, become uncompetitive. By contrast, goods from country B, sold in country A, would be more attractive, in so far as they would not carry the tax cost. If wages and prices were inflexible, so that prices in A could not fall (to be competitive) there would be no *internal* mechanism by which A's competitiveness would be restored. While country A has been made uncompetitive, the resulting tendency towards a trade deficit will place downward pressure on the value of country A's currency. How much will A's currency fall in terms of B's currency? It will continue to fall until the tendency for a trade deficit is brought to an end, i.e. until the goods from country A are once more competitive at home and abroad. At this new equilibrium, trade patterns between A and B are the same as before country A imposed the tax. The balance of trade for both countries is once more in equilibrium and there is full employment in both countries. Resource allocation is unchanged, even though the origin principle applies. Note, however, that there is no requirement here for fiscal frontiers.

Following Lockwood *et al.* (1995) the equivalence of the destination and origin principle can be shown by reference to Table 13.3. Country A produces good X and country B produces good Y under conditions of constant returns to scale. There is a single factor of production, labour (which is in a completely price inelastic supply). In each country one unit of labour is used to produce one unit of the good. Labour in country A is taken as the numeraire, so that $w_a = 1$ and $w_b = w$. A uniform tax rate in A is denoted by t_a and in B it is denoted by t_b. The two regimes (origin and destination) can be regarded as equivalent if the prices in the Table 13.3 are the same in both regimes.

Table 13.3 Consumer prices relative to the wage in different tax regimes

Regime	Good X	Good Y
Origin		
Country A	$1 + t_a$	$(1 + t_b)w^o$
Country B	$\dfrac{1 + t_a}{w^o}$	$1 + t_b$
Destination		
Country A	$1 + t_a$	$(1 + t_a)w^d$
Country B	$\dfrac{1 + t_b}{w^d}$	$1 + t_b$

Source: Lockwood *et al.* (1995) with permission of the Institute for Fiscal Studies.

Inspection of Table 13.3 reveals that this will be so if $w^d = w^o(1 + t_b)/(1 + t_a)$ (where w^d refers to wages in the destination regime and w^o refers to wages in the origin regime). For this equality to arise then either wages need to be flexible or, more practically, exchange rates must adjust. On the face of it, this analysis seems to suggest that there is no difference, as far as resource allocation is concerned, whether the destination or the origin principle of taxation are operative. This conclusion is, however, dependent on some important assumptions. For example:

(a) *Exchange rates are flexible.* In our analysis of the origin principle, the mechanism which made the tax non-distortive was the change in the exchange rate of A's currency. If there are fixed exchange rates (even if only in the short run) this equilibrating mechanism is inoperative. (Note that here we are assuming throughout that wage and price adjustment does not occur in the two countries.) If exchange rates were fixed, it would matter which principle of border tax adjustment applied. When exchange rates are fixed, a change from the origin principle to the destination principle by a country, acts as a subsidy to exports and implies a tax on imports. The result should be an improvement in the balance of trade (as long as the prices of factors of production remain unchanged).

(b) *The tax is general.* In their analysis of the 'origin v. destination principle' argument, Johnson and Krauss (1973, p. 242) argue that: 'It makes no difference to the exploitation of comparative advantage through trade which principle of border tax adjustment is applied provided the tax is a truly general one.' The importance of the assumption that the tax be general can be seen by working through the following example of Musgrave and Musgrave (1989). Assume again that there are two countries A and B but now both produce goods X and Y.

If country A imposes a *general* sales tax then it has been shown that, under the destination principle, there are no trade effects. If country A had applied a *selective* tax to one good, Y, the result would be that, domestically, consumers would consume more of good X and reduce their consumption of good Y. This adjustment may affect the level of trade in both of these commodities but it will not affect the location of production for both products. The destination principle will ensure that country A is not put at a competitive disadvantage in terms of good Y. The result is that there is a distortion created as far as consumption patterns between X and Y are concerned but there is no distortion in production.

If country A imposes a *general* production tax on goods X and Y and, if there is the origin principle, prices in A rise but, with a change in the value of the currency, there are no distortive losses. However, if A put a production tax on one good Y, consumers in country B of good Y will see that the price of the good from A has risen and will substitute in favour of domestic production. As B imports less, the price of A's currency will fall. Therefore, in A consumers find that the price of imports has increased and they import less. A new equilibrium is established. There is a lower level of trade and there is also an effect upon the location of production. Country A now produces more X and country B produces more Y.

It is perhaps worth noting that, even if taxes were general across all consumption goods, the equivalence between regimes would not hold unless the tax was general across both consumption and investment goods. Following Sinn (1990), two countries A and B produce a homogeneous consumption good C and a homogeneous investment good I. Let P_C^A and P_C^B be the country-specific producer prices of consumption goods with $P_I^A P_I^B$ the corresponding producer prices of investment goods; t_a and t_b are VAT rates and $t_b > t_a$. Free trade in investing goods implies $P_I^A = P_I^B$ and, with the destination principle, trade in consumption goods implies $P_C^A = P_C^B$, or $P_C^A/P_I^A = P_C^B/P_I^B$. On the other hand, under the origin principle $P_C^A(1 + t_a) = P_C^B(1 + t_b)$ so that $P_C^A/P_I^A > P_C^B/P_I^B$.

(c) *No other factors affecting exchange rates.* Jones (1991) lists the assumptions required for equivalence. Exchange rates must change only in reponse to competitiveness in trade. Therefore, from the initially balanced trade position exchange rates must be determined only by prices. There should be no net transfer payments, such as interest on debt, between countries. There should be no net flow of capital to one country. In this way the change in exchange rates will maintain equivalence in a world in which there is complete international immobility of factors of production.

(d) *Different principles applied to different products.* There is a difference which results as a consequence of choosing to apply the origin and the destination principle on different commodities. Consider the case outlined by Robson (1984). Once again, assume that a tax of 20 per cent will be applied to all goods in country A. But in this case assume that A applies the origin principle to trade in Y and the destination principle to trade in X. A has a comparative advantage in Y but with the origin principle applying this will make its exports of Y more expensive and imports of Y (from countries with no such sales tax) less expensive. By contrast, imports of X will carry the same sales tax as domestically produced units of X. The result is that this may distort the comparative cost position and, in the extreme, it could lead A to import Y and export X (for X will get the tax rebate when exported under the destination principle).

It is clear that as with other equivalence theorems in economics a host of assumptions are required to maintain equivalence (Johnson and Krauss 1973).

13.6 Current policy in the European Community for harmonization of indirect taxes: progress so far

Policy for tax harmonization in the EC was based on the Neumark Report of 1963 (i.e. the Report of the Fiscal and Financial Committee). This set three main requirements for member states to attain tax harmonization:

1. the EC countries should harmonize by the adoption in each member country of value added tax as *the* sales tax;
2. member countries should equalize value added tax (VAT) rates;
3. the abolition of fiscal frontiers for intra-EC trade.

The report proposed, in effect, that the Community should adopt the *restricted origin principle*. This meant that the Community would operate a destination principle for trade outside the community and an origin principle for trade within the Community (Hitiris 1994). The recommendation appeared to be based on the experience of federal states. However, in practice until 1992 the Community simply accepted

that VAT should be the sales tax for member countries and, by operating a system of fiscal frontiers (i.e. a destination system) the EC in effect continued a *selective destination* principle (whereby each country set its own VAT rates).

The choice of the VAT as the sales tax was based on the feature of the tax that, by comparison to some alternative sales taxes, it did not distort production. The goal, in this exercise, was clearly that of tax neutrality. The value added tax and the cascade tax were considered for adoption in the EEC. The cascade tax is levied on the *gross* value of output at each stage in the process of production. If a product is in an intermediary stage and passed on for finishing by another firm, the price of the good to the other firm will include the sales tax. Ultimately when the final firm sells the finished good it will carry the tax again. Under the cascade tax the total tax paid will depend on the number of times that the product changes hands. It creates an in-built incentive for vertical integration between firms. This may discourage specialization and create an artificial competitive advantage for those firms already in operation (see chapter 10). By comparison, the value added tax is paid at each stage of production on the value added at each point in the production process and not, as in the cascade tax, on the selling price or gross value at each stage. There is, therefore, no inducement created to make vertical integration attractive. Moreover, it is easier at each stage of production to ascertain how much tax has been paid, and this is important in the context of the destination principle.

Each country set its own VAT rates and set its own VAT tax base. These could differ as fiscal frontiers enabled the destination principle to apply. However, there were pressures to move to a Single Market and to remove border controls (fiscal frontiers). These were costly to administer. The Cecchini Report (1986) estimated that frontier delays added 1.8 per cent to the prices of traded goods to the EC. Cnossen (1983) reported that the costs of administering border controls were 7.5 per cent of the value of intra-EC trade. The Single European Act committed the members of the EC to achieve a common market by 1992 which required the removal of fiscal frontiers. But how could the system survive when fiscal frontiers were abolished?

The solution for the EC is to replace the administration of fiscal frontiers with administration of a 'Clearing House' system. Instead of adjusting at the borders, adjustment would take place at a later stage. Under the destination system taxes were removed on exports of goods from a member state and the VAT on the importing member state would be levied. The proposed system would mean that goods which were exported from one member state would carry their VAT. Following Lockwood *et al.* (1995), assume that a good valued at £20 in country A is exported to country B. If the VAT is 17.5 per cent in Country A then the importer will pay £3.50 as the tax element of the good imported from Country A. If the good were then sold for, say the equivalent of £30 in Country B (where the VAT is 20 per cent) the tax to be paid to tax authorities would be the equivalent of £6. However, a credit is given for the £3.50 already paid and so only £2.50 is paid to the tax authorities in B. It is as if the importer had imported the good with no VAT charged from Country A. The tax authorities in Country B would recover the additional £3.50 from tax authorities in Country A so that, in total, the equivalent of £6 tax revenue would be paid to authorities in Country B and zero to authorities in Country A (which would have been the outcome had there been fiscal frontiers). The settlement of each claim between authorities is not required as a clearing house system operates and focuses on the net liabilities between tax authorities (just as in the case of the operation of the clearing house system between commercial banks). While the clearing house has to be formally established[7], the prospect of this system permits countries some element of freedom in setting tax rates (see Smith 1993 for a discussion of these proposals).

VAT tax rates are quite different in different EC countries as can be seen in Table 13.4. Note that there are also differences in the tax bases. For example, as a result of different exemptions the VAT coverage of private consumption is 35 per cent in Ireland; 44 per cent in the UK and, in many other member states, about 90 per cent (Hitiris 1994).

The proposed system has been criticized by Lockwood *et al.* (1995). It is said to be: (a) administratively cumbersome; (b) subject to problems of exchange rate variation which creates uncertainty about revenue and (c) it would create quite complex arrangements if the good were re-exported from the Community to a third country. The authors suggest another solution, i.e. the introduction of a non-reciprocal restricted origin (NRRO) system. This is described in Table 13.5. While a destination system is not equivalent to a restricted origin system (as suggested by the Neumark Committee) the authors argue that when exchange rates are flexible, moving from a destination approach to a NRRO system is equivalent. Under a NRRO system, within the customs union, member states (countries A and B) operate the origin system but, when goods are exported to non-member countries (e.g. country C), they are taxed both at the exporting country's tax rate and again at the rate of country C. As far as country C is concerned, country C charges its tax rate on imports. However, when country C's goods are moved to country A or B they are tax free upon import to A or B and only carry the tax of the country of destination. Lockwood *et al.* show that exchange rates

Table 13.4 Value added tax rates (%) in EC member states in 1993

Country	Reduced rate	Standard rate	Increased rate
Belgium	1, 6 and 12	19.0	
Denmark		25.0	
France	2.1 and 5.5	18.6	
Germany	7.0	15.0	
Greece	4 and 8.0	18.0	
Ireland	0, 2.7, 10.0, 12.5, 16	21.0	
Italy	4, 9 and 12.0	19.0	38.0
Luxemburg	3.0 and 6.0	15.0	
Netherlands	6.0	18.5	
Portugal	5.0	16.0	30.0
Spain	6.0	15.0	28.0
UK		17.5	

Source: reprinted with permission from Hitiris (1994)

[7] The present system is one whereby instead of VAT of the country of destination being added at the frontier it is added by the purchaser. This system is due to expire on 31 Dec. 1996 and be replaced by the clearing house system (Westaway 1992).

Table 13.5 Consumer prices relative to the wage

Destination regime

	Good X	Good Y	Good Z
Country A	$1 + t_a$	$\dfrac{w_b^d(1 + t_a)}{w_a^d}$	$\dfrac{1 + t_a}{w_a^d}$
Country B	$\dfrac{w_a^d(1 + t_b)}{w_b^d}$	$1 + t_b$	$\dfrac{1 + t_b}{w_b^d}$
Country C	$w_a^d(1 + t_c)$	$w_b^d(1 + t_c)$	$1 + t_c$

NRRO regime

	Good X	Good Y	Good Z
Country A	$1 + t_a$	$\dfrac{w_b^o(1 + t_b)}{w_a^o}$	$\dfrac{1}{w_a^o}$
Country B	$\dfrac{w_a^o(1 + t_a)}{w_b^o}$	$1 + t_b$	$\dfrac{1}{w_b^o}$
Country C	$w_a^o(1 + t_a)(1 + t_c)$	$w_b^o(1 + t_b)(1 + t_c)$	$1 + t_c$

Source: Lockwood *et al.* (1995) with permission of the Institute for Fiscal Studies.

can change so as to make prices the same under this system as they would be if a destination system applied. When $w_a^d = w_a^0(1 + t_a)$ and $w_b^d = w_b^0 (1 + t_b)$ a switch from the destination regime to the non-reciprocal restricted origin regime has no effects on resource allocation.

It is clear (by a process of substitution) that when the exchange rates have changed, as described above, the system produces prices that are equivalent to those that operate with the destination system. The authors argue that their proposal would be administratively simpler but recognize that: (a) it may be politically unpalatable (it would seem that imports and exports from the customs union would be treated differently); (b) as nominal wages are not flexible the introduction of fixed exchange rates would remove the mechanism for equivalence. The second of these problems is very important given the plans (of some) for monetary union in the EC.

While a system for dealing with the removal of fiscal frontiers has been devised, the Commission 1985 White Paper concluded that there would be the need also to equalize approximately national VAT rates. They intended to cut the number of VAT rates to a standard and a reduced rate. Countries would then set the standard rate between 14 and 20 per cent and the reduced rate between 4 and 9 per cent. The 5 per cent margin was considered sufficient to match the likely transport costs associated with attempting to purchase goods in low VAT countries for resale in high VAT countries. While the Commission wish to stipulate these margins some countries (e.g. the UK) have argued that convergence of VAT rates would emerge less formally. The argument is that 'harmonization' would emerge via the free play of market forces (high tax rate countries being forced to come in line or else lose markets for their goods) (see also Bos and Nelson, 1988).

Loss of sovereignty to set VAT rates will affect different member countries differently. For example, Denmark has a high level of final consumption tax (16 per cent of GDP compared to 8 per cent or 11 per cent for other member countries). This means that Denmark would experience a revenue loss, or a revenue shift towards direct taxes (Guieu and Bonnet 1987). However, while there may be some loss of sovereignty, the gains are said to be (Emerson 1988) in terms of: (a) eradicating the resource cost associated with fiscal frontiers; (b) creating psychological gains that individuals derive from being a part of a common market; (c) greater competition; (d) greater predictability of indirect taxation.

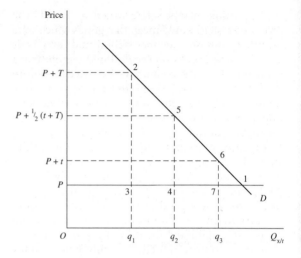

Figure 13.5 Welfare gains from tax equalization.

Keen (1993) argues that the case for moving towards uniformity is robust in so far as the welfare gains to high tax countries will exceed the welfare loss to low tax countries when VAT rates are averaged and the destination principle is applied. In Fig. 13.5 two countries have identical linear demand curves (D). The world price is P. In country A the tax is initially t and in country B it is initially higher at T. For purposes of harmonization the tax is to be averaged, i.e. set at $1/2(t + T)$. The distance $q_1 q_2$ is the same as $q_3 q_2$, as with the linear demand curve the same absolute change in price in the two countries creates the same absolute change in demand. This means that the reduction in excess burden in the high tax country 2345 exceeds the increase in country A 6745 and collectively the two countries are better off.[8]

Of course, there are arguments in favour of diversity. Cnossen (1990) asks how much 'tax harmonization' there should be and presents arguments in favour of diversity. He argues that the objective should not be an average of existing practices for:

(a) Tax coordination like tax reform should proceed from widely argued criteria (equity, efficiency).[9]

---

[8] The argument is very general—demands can differ across the two countries and they can have any logical possible shape, there can be any number of taxed goods and world prices may respond to changes in the pattern and amount of trade.

[9] When considering income distribution Symons and Walker (1990) use family expenditure survey data to look at the effects of EC indirect taxes (VAT and excise duties) on prices in the UK. Using own price and cross elasticities of demand they indicate a fall in expenditure on fuel, clothing, tobacco and increased expenditure on beer, wine and spirits. The effect of harmonization proposals was regressive.

(b) To equalize nominal taxes is futile in so far as taxes that appear identical on paper may diverge widely in practice. Cnossen argues that the Danish value added tax (scrupulously administered) is a 'world apart' from the Italian value added tax (which reportedly is widely evaded).

(c) Even if taxes are equalized, differences in subsidy arrangements will affect trade.

(d) Federations survive with diversity (e.g. in the US forty-three states out of fifty have their own personal income tax) and there is room for tax diversity.

(e) With monetary union likely in the EC there is greater need to retain some independence for social and economic policies.

(f) Cnossen recognizes the possibility of spillover effects for other states (i.e. that in the absence of border controls consumers move to low tax states and low tax member states could look attractive to residents of high tax states). It can be argued that diversity is welfare enhancing even if it entails economic and administrative costs. The imposition of higher taxes on wine may prove as unpopular in Germany and Italy as the imposition of higher taxes on beer in the UK.

Tax harmonization would be unattractive to public choice scholars to the extent that it 'smacked of' tax coordination. Excessive tax coordination would be comparable to cartelization. It may prove the opportunity for member states to collaborate to 'secure a monopoly on the level of taxation' with the possibility that they would raise tax burdens.

These criticisms of tax harmonization suggest that too much emphasis may be placed on the pursuit of tax neutrality. Dosser (1973) argued that EC policy was too narrowly defined and that it would fail to the extent that the focus of attention was on the equalization of nominal rates rather than the equalization of effective rate. He described the loss of ability to change taxes to deal with distributional and stabilization issues as costs of such an interpretation of harmonization. More broadly, he related the concept of harmonization to the degree of international integration which is under consideration (see also Dosser *et al.* 1982) and, to the extent that the common market aspires to promote common policies via the EC budget. He considered that tax harmonization should reflect the wider considerations of 'traditional' public finance in the context of financing the EC budget.

The EC has taken further steps in a programme of tax harmonization as a result of its desire to remove border controls (fiscal frontiers). Whether or not it has been preoccupied with issues of tax neutrality is, however, a moot point.

13.7 Taxation of income from overseas: multinationals

The harmonization of product taxes has been considered from the standpoint of making taxation neutral. The objective of harmonization has been to ensure that taxes do not distort an outcome in which the most efficient producer-country is the country that supplies the good. In the same way, it might be argued that taxes on income should be harmonized, so that factors of production can be used where they are most productive. Focusing on the return to overseas investment, the aim here is to consider the principles of taxation to be applied when dealing with the taxation of multinational companies. In particular, we look at tax policy with respect to parent firms who have subsidiaries in other countries, in order to illustrate the possible distortions that may arise as a result of taxation of overseas income. The question posed is, What considerations will tax authorities be likely to take into account when taxing the return to investment in foreign countries?

As Musgrave (1969) has pointed out, to answer this question it is important to begin with a statement of the objectives of tax policy. With respect to efficiency, which is our primary concern, it is necessary again to distinguish between *world* efficiency and *national* efficiency. If concern is with world efficiency, then the objective is an international allocation of capital at which the rate of return on investment has been equalized between countries. If the rate of return is higher in one country than in another, then clearly it is efficient for capital to move internationally to the location where the rate of return is highest. However, it can be shown that this need not be required to maximize the welfare of the country from which investment stems; for that country, the national welfare is increased by maximizing the return *to the country*.

In Fig. 13.6, the vertical axes measure the marginal product of capital in the home country and in the foreign country. The total stock of capital in this two-country model is shown by the horizontal axis. The initial allocation of capital is such that OK_1 is at home and O^*K_1 is in the foreign country. Therefore the rate of return at home r_h is lower than the rate of return abroad, r_f. In these circumstances, if there is no barrier

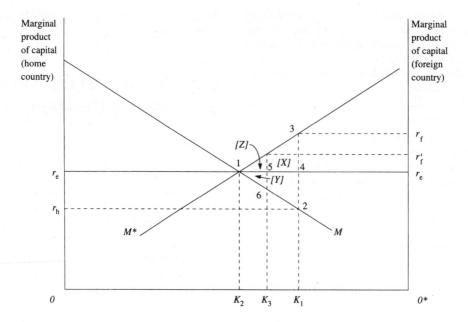

Figure 13.6 Taxation of overseas investment.

to the international movement of capital, $K_1 K_2$ of capital will move to the foreign country. This movement will occur until the rates of return to capital in both countries are equalized. It is clear that, at this point, an efficient world allocation of resources has been achieved. It is impossible to increase the return to capital in one country without reducing it by a greater amount in the other country. Initially (when OK_1 of capital was in the home country) this had been possible. When capital moved, output in the home country fell by $K_1 21 K_2$ (i.e. the area under the marginal product curve for the home country) while output abroad increased by a greater amount, i.e. $K_1 31 K_2$. Now, however, if the home country receives the rate of return from the investment abroad, then it will receive r_e on each unit of capital (a total of $r_e(K_1 K_2)$), which improves its welfare by triangle 142 over and above what the home country would have earned on this capital had it remained at home. By comparison, even if the foreign country were to pay $r_e(K_1 K_2)$, i.e. $K_1 41 K_2$, it would still be better off to extent of triangle 431. Both countries gain when there is free international movement of capital. Welfare for the world as a whole is maximized when the rates of return are equalized.

While world welfare is maximized, it is also clear that the home country might have done better *for itself* had it restricted the flow of capital abroad. In the figure, had the home country restricted the flow of investment abroad to $K_1 K_3$, then the rate of return on capital in the foreign country would not have fallen by as much. The rate of return would have fallen only from r_f to r_f'. As a result, the home country would have received $r_f'(K_1 K_3)$ on the capital that still went abroad. However, it would have lost the net return on the capital that stayed at home (i.e. $K_3 51 K_2 - K_3 61 K_2$). Since area [X] exceeds area [Y], this must mean that the net gain from restricting the flow of capital is positive. However, for the world as a whole, the loss from such a restriction is equal to areas [Z] and [Y].

Therein lies the dilemma. As far as the home country is concerned, welfare is maximized by a restriction of the flow of capital, but as far as world welfare is concerned, there is no case for restriction of capital flows. Note, however, that here the source of the gain to the home country arises because its capital movement to the host country reduces the return on capital in the host country. Where the capital movement is too small to have such an effect, there is no case for restriction, even in terms of national welfare considerations. Where the flow of capital has the effect on the rates of return as shown here, there will obviously be an optimum limited flow of capital abroad. (See Kemp (1969) for a discussion of the *optimal tax rate* on overseas investment.) Also, in a general equilibrium framework, the flow of capital abroad may affect the terms of trade, and this is a consideration that has been ignored. (See Jones (1963) for a discussion of the optimum tax rate when the terms of trade are affected by the flow of capital abroad.)

The question of maximizing national welfare or world welfare carries over into the treatment of *double taxation*. If the foreign (host) country applies a tax to the profits of the multinational, should the home country tax these profits again? Here again, the distinction of national versus world welfare is important. If world welfare is to be maximized, it is clear that there should be no restriction to the flow of investment and a *credit* rule should be applied; that is, the home country should credit the company for taxes already paid. If the home country's corporation tax exceeds the foreign country's corporation tax, the company simply pays the difference to the home country. (In the extreme, if the foreign corporation tax exceeds the home corporation tax, the home country should make good the difference from its Exchequer.) The credit rule implies export neutrality; i.e. there is no tax incentive to invest at home rather than abroad. It does not guarantee import neutrality; i.e. the overseas investor in the home country is still treated differently from the domestic supplier of savings.

Operation of the credit rule, in response to the problem of double taxation, implies that there is no advantage in keeping capital at home. Capital flows to the locations where its rate of return is greatest. From the national point of view this is not optimal. The response, in this case, is the *deduction* approach, whereby no credit is given (Musgrave 1969). The home country (country H) will maximize its national welfare when the after- (foreign) tax return to overseas capital in country H is equal to the rate of return on capital invested at home. Thus, investors face the return of $(1 - t_h)r_h$ (where r_h is the rate of return at home) or $(1 - t_h)(1 - t_f)r_f$ (where r_f is the rate of return abroad). When

$$(13.8) \qquad (1 - t_h)r_h = (1 - t_h)(1 - t_f)r_f$$

the home country (following this deduction approach) maximizes national welfare. Companies investing abroad must face the home country's corporation tax on their after-tax profits abroad because the only thing that matters to the home country in maximizing welfare is the rate of return that comes 'home'.

Tax policy with respect to overseas investment in this way is subject to the decision about whether world welfare or national welfare is the objective. Of course, there are more complications than we have space to describe. Caves (1996) provides a good survey of the literature on taxation of multinational enterprises, including the response of the multinational enterprises themselves. It is quite clear that, by adjusting prices of goods between the parent and subsidiary firms, multinationals can engage in a policy of reducing the tax burden that they may face from import and corporation taxes. These internal prices, referred to as 'transfer prices', in this way may respond to the tax policy of countries towards overseas investment. The importance of taxes on the decisions of companies to undertake investment abroad is also covered in Caves (1996), but note that political factors (e.g. stability of the government, risks of *coup d'état*, street demonstrations) may be as important as economic considerations in multinationals' investment strategies (see Schneider and Frey 1985).

13.8 Summary

This chapter has addressed several issues.[10] Perhaps the most important, in the context of the main theme of this text, is the relationship between 'traditional' public finance analysis and public choice theory in the analysis of trade taxes. Once again, these have been presented as competing theories which can be used to rationalize the use of import taxes. Within the traditional framework, the rationale for such intervention relied upon specific adaptations of the Paretian model—for example the introduction of distortions in trade, which, in the 'optimum' tariff literature, creates a difference between the marginal cost of imports and their supply price. By contrast, the public choice approach would not necessarily look to government intervention as a response to market distortion, but rather would look to the failings in government and the political process. The impact of pressure groups on the decision-making of politicians is an argument that appears empirically to play a more important role in explaining trade policy.

While up to now we have stressed the differences between the two approaches, it is possible, from the analysis of this chapter, to highlight some possible complementarity between these analytical approaches. By introducing the assumption of factor specificity into the basic neoclassical model, it is possible to explain the source of rent-seeking. The factors

---

[10] There are, of course, many other areas where public finance theory and international trade theory overlap. One obvious example is in the case of defence. Public good theory provides a natural starting-point for the study of alliances and for an analysis of trade in defence goods (see, e.g. Jones 1988).

of production (labour and capital) were shown to share an interest in protection according to the industry in which they worked. Industry-based pressure was more likely than pressure relating simply to social class or to ownership of factors of production. In this way the same neoclassical model that is the heart of the traditional approach is readily adapted to predict the source of the political pressure that the public choice literature perceives as a determinant of trade policy. In a review of the work of Musgrave, Buchanan (1989) calls for a greater interaction between the two approaches to public finance theory. This kind of example, applied in other areas of public finance, may well offer a fruitful interdependency between the two approaches.

The second aspect of this chapter that is worth highlighting is the way in which the 'traditional' approach to public finance has been applied to international issues. The Paretian model can be applied, but now there is an additional dimension. This is created, in some cases, by the need to decide whether tax policy is directed at the maximization of national or world welfare. Musgrave's (1969) treatise on *Fiscal Systems* highlights the importance of this distinction in issues such as tax harmonization and the taxation of overseas investment. It is, of course, a logical extension of the analysis of the optimum import or export tax. In so far as the framework is Paretian, the focus of tax harmonization is on 'efficiency' and 'neutrality of taxation' (as appears evident in EC indirect taxation policy). It is left to Dosser (1973) to remind us that there are other goals of taxation, distribution and stabilization within the 'traditional' three-sector public household approach of Musgrave (1959).

References

Anderson, R. W. (1976) *The Economics of Crime*. London: Macmillan.

Baldwin, R. E. (1976) *The Political Economy of US Postwar Trade Policy*, Bulletin no. 4. New York: Centre for the Study of Financial Institutions, Graduate School of Business Administration, New York University.

Bhagwati, J. N. and Hansen, B. (1973) 'A Theoretical Analysis of Smuggling', *Quarterly Journal of Economics*, **87**, 2, pp. 172–87.

Bhagwati, J. N. and Srinivason, T. N. (1983) *Lectures on International Trade*. Cambridge, Mass.: MIT Press.

Bos, M. and Nelson, H. (1988) 'Indirect Taxation and the Completion of the Internal Market of the EC', *Journal of Common Market Studies*, **27**, 1, pp. 27–44.

Buchanan, J. M. (1989) 'Richard Musgrave, Public Finance, and Public Choice', *Public Choice*, **63**, 3, pp. 289–91.

Caves, R. E. (1976) 'Economic Models of Political Choice: Canada's Tariff Structure', *Canadian Journal of Economics*, **9**, 2, pp. 278–300.

Caves, R. E. (1996) *Economic Analysis and the Multinational Enterprise*. 2nd edn. Cambridge: Cambridge University Press.

Cecchini, P. (1988) *The European Challenge*. Aldershot: Wildwood House.

Cnossen, S. (1983) 'Harmonisation of Indirect Taxes in the EEC', *British Tax Review*, **6**, 4, pp. 232–53.

Cnossen, S. (1990) 'The Case for Tax Diversity in the European Community', *European Economic Review*, **34**, 3, pp. 471–9.

Corden, W. M. (1974) *Trade Policy and Economic Welfare*. Oxford: Oxford University Press.

Dosser, D. (1973) 'Tax Harmonization in the European Community', *Three Banks Review*, no. 98, pp. 49–64.

Dosser, D., Gowland, D. and Hartley, K. (1982) *The Collaboration of Nations: A Study of European Economic Policy*. Oxford: Martin Robertson.

Emerson, M. (1988) *The Economics of 1992: The EC Commission's Assessment of the Economic Effects of Completing the Internal Market*. Oxford: Oxford University Press.

Frey, B. S. (1984) *International Political Economics*. Oxford: Basil Blackwell.

Greenaway, D. (1980) 'Trade Taxes as a Source of Government Revenue: An International Comparison', *Scottish Journal of Political Economy*, **27**, 2, pp. 175–82.

Greenaway, D. (1981) 'Taxes on International Trade and Economic Development', in A. Peacock and F. Forte (eds.), *The Political Economy of Taxation*. Oxford: Basil Blackwell.

Greenaway, D. (1982) 'Maximum Revenue Tariffs and Optimal Revenue Tariffs: Concepts', *Public Finance/Finances Publiques*, **37**, 1, pp. 67–79.

Guieu, P. and Bonnet, C. (1987) 'Completion of the Internal Market and Indirect Taxation', *Journal of Common Market Studies*, **25**, 3, pp. 209–22.

Hitiris, T. (1994) *European Community Economics*, 3rd edn. New York and London: Harvester Wheatsheaf.

Johnson, H. G. (1953–4) 'Optimum Tariffs and Retaliation', *Review of Economic Studies*, **21**, pp. 142–53.

Johnson, H. G. and Krauss, M. B. (1973) 'Border Taxes, Border Adjustments, Comparative Advantage and the Balance of Payments', *Canadian Journal of Economics*, **3**, 4, pp. 595–602; reprinted as pp. 239–54 in M. B. Krauss (ed.), *The Economics of Integration*. London: Allen & Unwin.

Jones, A. M. (1991) 'Tax Harmonization in the European Community', pp. 73–113 in D. Gowland and S. James, (eds.), *Economic Policy After 1992*. Aldershot: Avebury.

Jones, P. R. (1988) 'Defense Alliances and International Trade', *Journal of Conflict Resolution*, **32**, 1, 123–41.

Jones, R. W. (1963) 'International Capital Movements and the Theory of Tariffs and Trade', *Quarterly Journal of Economics*, **81**, 1, pp. 1–38.

Kemp, M. C. (1969) *The Pure Theory of International Trade*. Englewood Cliffs, NJ: Prentice-Hall.

Keen, M. (1993) 'The Welfare Economics of Tax Co-ordination in the European Community: a Survey', *Fiscal Studies*, **14**, 2, pp. 15–36.

Layard, P. R. G. and Walters, A. A. (1978) *Micro-Economic Theory*. New York: McGraw-Hill.

Lewis, S. R. Jr. (1963) 'Government Revenue from Foreign Trade: An International Comparison', *Manchester School*, **31**, pp. 39–46.

Lindert, P. H. (1986) *International Economics*, 8th edn. Homewood, Ill.: Richard D. Irwin.

Lockwood, B, de Meza, D. and Myles, D. (1995) 'On the European Union VAT Proposals: The Superiority of Origin over Destination Taxation', *Fiscal Studies*, **16**, 1, pp. 1–17.

Magee, S. P. (1982) 'Protectionism in the United States', in P. Oppenheimer (ed.), *Issues in International Economics*. Stocksfield: Oriel Press.

Musgrave, R. A. (1959) *The Theory of Public Finance*. New York: McGraw-Hill.

Musgrave, R. A. (1969) *Fiscal Systems*. New Haven, Conn., and London: Yale University Press.

Musgrave, R. A. and Musgrave, P. B. (1989) *Public Finance: Theory and Practice*, 5th edn. New York: McGraw-Hill.

Mussa, M. (1974) 'Tariffs and the Distribution of Income: The Importance of Factor Specificity, Substitutability and Intensity in the Short Run', *Journal of Political Economy*, **82**, 6, pp. 1191–205.

Neary, P. J. (1985) 'Theory and Policy of Adjustment in an Open Economy', pp. 43–61 in D. Greenaway (ed.), *Current Issues in International Trade*. London: Macmillan.

Olson, M. Jr. (1971) *The Logic of Collective Action: Public Goods and the Theory of Groups*. Cambridge, Mass.: Harvard University Press.

Pincus, J. J. (1975) 'Pressure Groups and the Pattern of Tariffs', *Journal of Political Economy*, **83**, 4, pp. 757–78.

Robson, P. (1984) *The Economics of International Integration*, 2nd edn. London: Allen & Unwin.

Schneider, F. and Frey, B. S. (1985) 'Economic and Political Determinants of Foreign Direct Investment', *World Development*, **13**, 2, pp. 161–75.

Shaw, G. K. (1988) 'Revenue Implications of Trade Taxes', in D. Greenaway (ed.), *Economic Development and International Trade*. London: Macmillan.

Sinn, H. W. (1989) 'Tax Harmonization and Tax Competition in Europe', *European Economic Review*, **34**, pp. 489–504.

Smith, S (1993) ' "Subsidiarity" and the Co-ordination of Indirect Taxes in the European Community', *Oxford Review of Economic Policy*, **19**, 1, pp. 67–94.

Symons, E. and Walker, I. (1990) 'Fiscal Harmonisation: Implications for the UK', *Economic Review*, **7**, 5, pp. 10–15.

Westaway, T. (1992) 'The Fiscal Dimension of 1992', pp. 81–105 in D. Swann (ed.), *The Single European Market and Beyond*. London, New York: Routledge.

Williamson, J. (1983) *The Open Economy and the World Economy*. New York: Basic Books.

14 Public sector failure and public expenditure growth

14.1 Introduction

Much has been said so far about the limitations of market allocation mechanisms. Markets tend to offer unsatisfactory outcomes where: benefits are non-rival and/or non-excludable; property rights are unassigned or communally assigned; transaction costs are large; and information is limited. However, the public choice economists argue that for too long the policy implications of this list and variations on it have remained unscrutinized. Furthermore, they have argued that much past debate has implicitly compared an imperfect market context with an ideal and fictional view of non-market or government allocation processes and outcomes. There is a parallel literature on non-market failure which is most explicitly presented in the writings of Wolf (1979, 1987). It is these contributions that underlie the next three sections. They have an important connection with debates about the growth of the public sector, as it is the non-market failure arguments that are employed to explain the 'unwarranted' growth of government.

14.2 Non-market demand conditions

While it is generally argued that market failure results from the under-provision of certain types of goods and services, the opposite view is taken when considering non-market failure. Here, a number of arguments place the blame on the inflation of demand for public sector activities. First, there is a lowered tolerance of shortcomings of the market. Population growth and its attendant congestion coupled with a generally increased awareness of markets' limitations is seen as an important cause of this. Secondly, insti-

tutional changes have encouraged political actions of adjustment. The type of innovation Wolf has in mind is the development of contingent lawyers' fees and class actions in courts.

A third point, perhaps more telling, is the incentives and priorities adopted by most politicians. It has been noted by many that successful politicians are those who act on or react to a topical issue in the short run at the expense of the implementation of actual policies and their long-run consequences. UK Prime Minister Harold Wilson coined the phrase, 'A week is a long time in politics.' In general, with a time horizon as short as the next election, it pays politicians to discount the future heavily. If politicians had a saleable property right in their office as do owners of firms, this myopic push to action would be avoided, because the impact of too many bad decisions would be internalized and would adversely affect the value of the property right. Capitalization as a disciplining mechanism is absent for politicians.

The separation of the costs and benefits of decisions is seen as a major source of inflated demands and it accounts for the appeal of Wicksell's advocation of simultaneous voting on a project and its source of finance. Micro-level decoupling of costs and benefits can be seen in 'special interest' effects when a small number gain a significant amount from legislation and a large number lose a small amount which they are (induced to be) unaware of or which is too small to offer the incentive of trying to oppose the legislation. Macro-level decoupling of costs and benefits shows up in the redistributions to the less-well-off majority from the minority who are relatively well off. The problem these processes cause is a possible inefficiency in 'special interests' in that costs may, in total, exceed the benefits and disincentives to earn more in the market-place.

One element often ignored in the demand function is the role of preferences or tastes. Wolf sees these as distorted towards increased public sector demand by a number of mechanisms. First, there are issues associated with a biased sample of information. Market failures (bads) make better news than market successes (goods). Publicists are a self-selecting sample of the currently disenchanted who compound the effect of pressure groups in calling for changes. Second, those in government have a natural tendency to be pessimistic about the market and optimistic about their ability to intervene and improve matters. Finally, there is the element of the past. Wolf sees the cultural and intellectual legacy of a socialist ideology to be found in Western democracies as a determinant of preferences.

The upshot of the arguments briefly rehearsed in this section is a demand context that very much favours or induces public sector action in many and varied forms.

14.3 Non-market supply conditions

The supply of non-market situations is also seen to be riddled with sources of inefficiently large provision. The insights are derived by comparison with the neoclassical theory of the firm. The output or product of the public sector is easily talked about in abstract discussion, but developing definitions and units of measurement is a difficult and complex matter. Additionally, there is often no competitive market test of the consumer valuation of the 'outputs' of the public sector. The output is produced under (near) monopoly circumstances and cannot easily be rejected by consumer-voters. (This element of non-rejectability makes the concept of a demand curve tenuous.) Supply curves are derived in neoclassical theory from well-defined production functions. However, for public sector activities the relationship between the inputs and outputs is either vague and uncertain or unknown. What produces good education services or good health care services is not readily reduced to a repeatable, mechanical recipe. Again with reference to neoclassical theory, the first-year student knows that the 'shut-down' point of a firm is a market price that does not cover the average variable cost of production in the period. Given these points, it is evident that a ready signal as to when to cease *non-market* activity is not present. In short, the elements familiar in the market supply of private goods are either vague or unspecified in the equivalent public sector context of the provision of a good; i.e. there is a considerable

slack in which governmental decision-makers can operate without fear of discipline. However, for an opposing view to Wolf see Wittman (1989).

14.4 A typology of non-market failure to match market failure

Given the above, Wolf outlines parallel sources of failure in the non-market as well as the market context.

1. The equivalent of public goods and externality is seen to be *redundant and rising costs* attendant on the disjunction between costs and benefit/revenue receipt, with little incentive because of the lack of competition to be X-efficient. Compounding this lack of incentive is the realization that change is onerous and the benefits to be secured uncertain, i.e. government or public producer inertia is likely to be observed. Even if these pitfalls can be avoided, there remains the problem of allocative inefficiency. Even if least marginal cost is achieved, the incentives to equate least marginal cost with the median voter demand curve may be missing. The economics of bureaucracy discussed in the next section is especially relevant here. To this can be added Lindsay's (1976) argument of bias towards visibility of output. Stated briefly, the argument is that government departments or agencies recognize that they will require some sort of indicator of their output that is monitorable by any monitor or monitors the government chooses to appoint—the rational response to this incentive is to bias output towards visible outputs at the expense of invisible or less visible ones which may nevertheless be part of the efficient output mix.

2. The equivalence of increasing returns/extensive economies of scale resulting in the decreasing-cost industry case is the presence of 'internalities' and *private organizational goals*. In the absence of ready performance indicators and a shut-down point, internal rewards and penalties that have little to do with the public purpose of the agency prevail.

3. The equivalent of market imperfections is so-called *derived externalities*. The argument relates to the notion that each government intervention, for example, comes with the imposition of unintended, unanticipated and uncompensated costs. The political incentive both to act quickly and to evaluate costs and benefits over only a short time horizon are prime movers in bringing about this outcome.

4. Distributional inequality of income and wealth has its counterpart in distributional inequalities based

on power and prestige. Actions to correct market failures give officials, politicians and bureaucrats generally the power not only to set the rules, but also, importantly, to choose how they will be interpreted at the day-to-day level.

While it is possible to argue how these equivalencies have been made, the main aim is to put non-market or governmental failure on an equal footing with the historically longer recognized market failure.

14.5 Bureaucratic economics

One of the most rehearsed pieces of public sector economics in recent years has been that of bureaucracy as developed by Niskanen (1968, 1971), among others. The simplest scenario is set up in terms of a constant long-run marginal and average cost curve illustrated in Fig. 14.1. The bureau is modelled as a monopoly seller of its services to the government. In this monopoly context it is thought safe to concentrate on the bureaucrats because they will have the upper hand in any bargaining. The reasons for this are the actual location of the long-run marginal cost (LRMC) curve and the median voter's demand curve D_v. Regarding the demand curve, it pays bureaucrats to investigate its location by monitoring public opinion polls and the like. While for the government executive negotiating about budgets is only

one of its many tasks, and therefore it devotes only a small proportion of its time to this activity, for the bureaucrats the incentive is different; their budget can be expected to engage their attention fully. Against this background, what can bureaucrats be expected to maximize with their monopoly power?

Niskanen postulates a utility function containing all the P's—power, prestige, pay and promotion. All these, he argues, are a function of the size of a bureau so that, in circumstances where bureaux cannot be seen to be making a monopoly profit in cash, they will opt to raise the size of their department. In Fig. 14.1 Oq^E is the efficient level of provision offering consumer surplus gains of triangle 123. The powerful monopoly bureau can in effect use this surplus to subsidize an inefficiently large volume of bureaucratic activity. In this case the maximum level of output sustainable is Oq^B where total costs $O34q^B$ equal total benefits $O25q^B$; i.e. $O315q^B$ is common and triangle 123 equals triangle 145. This is the classic bureau that is too big by a factor of 2. The policy implications that arise in this context stem from attempts to decrease monopoly power. Increasing competition by forcing bureaux to compete with each other and/or with outside organizations is advocated alongside better definitions of bureaucratic tasks to facilitate monitoring. Changing incentives, by allowing civil servants to keep a proportion of any genuine cost savings they can make, is also attractive in this context.

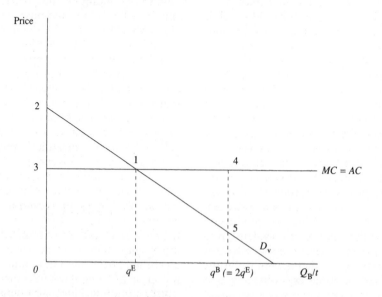

Figure 14.1 The 'x2' bureau.

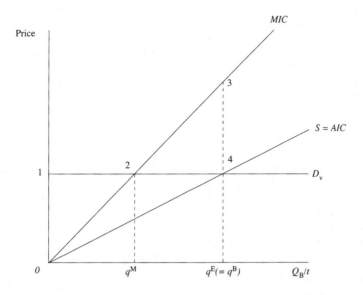

Figure 14.2 The 'optimal' bureau.

Despite this approach having captured the public's imagination via television programmes like *Yes Minister*, there are other perspectives to consider. Indeed, by adopting some strong reverse assumptions it is possible to convert bureaucratic allocative inefficiency into allocative efficiency. Consider now Fig. 14.2, where the median voters' demand curve D_v is perfectly elastic and the bureau is now seen as monopsonist in the input market. If it has monopsony power there is a divergence between the supply of the input ($S = AIC$), its average input cost, and the marginal input cost (MIC). Indeed, given a linear supply curve, MIC will rise twice as fast as AIC. The normal monopsony result is too little employment of that input at Oq^M, offering surplus 012 which can be employed if the bureau wishes to maximize its output to raise employment to $Oq^E (= Oq^B)$, with triangle 012 equalling triangle 234. In this case a bureaucratic input employment will be either *too low* by a factor of 2 or allocatively efficient. While not suggesting that this is typical, it may contain a similar amount of truth as the 'times 2' scenario. (Note that one case for state provision is the exploitation of monopsony power: see chapter 5.)

Bohm (1987) offers some countervailing arguments to the widely advocated view of the inefficient bureaucracy. Three points, he suggests, make the extreme view implausible. First, not all areas of economic policy are readily adaptable to the self-interested behaviour of bureaucrats. Secondly, the bureaucratic exploitation literature is rather longer on theory than on empirical evidence; indeed, the latter is not easy to discern. Bohm conjectures that there are as many good and bad bureaucrats as there are doctors, scientists, etc. Jackson (1982) notes, for example, that there are cases where bureaucrats operate in exactly the opposite way: James Schlesinger of the US Defense Department, for example, advanced his career by cutting budgets. Third, there is the question of the media. In democracies the 'power of the media' may well act as a strong discipline on bureaux that are blatantly inefficient. In this respect it is interesting to note Sen's (1983) comment on famines to the effect that political factors are very important. The presence of the media and mass communication and political competition, he argues, ensures that governments must exert themselves to avoid famines in India. In contrast, where communication about famines and political competition are absent as in China, they tend to occur.

14.6 Measuring the public sector: a debate within a debate

All long-running debates by definition are multi-faceted. One facet of the debate on the size of the public sector is precisely to do with its size. Nothing comes unquestionably measured, and what is understood by the 'public sector' is no exception. What is commonly sought is a proportionate measure of the size of the public sector in relation to the output of the economy. The output of the economy is the province of national income accountants, who offer a number of measures. The main questions are: Whether a figure net or gross of depreciation is best employed? Is it domestic or national income? or product? that is to matter (the domestic figure excludes net income from abroad). Should the chosen measure be presented at market prices or at factor cost, i.e. net of indirect taxes and subsidies? In different contexts, each of the eight possible denominators implied by these questions might have a role to play.

As for the numerator, matters are controversial. There are three broad possibilities:

1. Count all public expenditure that involves the raising of finance, on the grounds that it is generally the use of tax instruments that causes disincentive effects in the market and consequent allocative/welfare cost effects. Those implicitly focusing on the market output in particular as the appropriate maximand for the economy find this measure attractive.

2. Count only the expenditures that are real. These 'exhaustive' expenditures are to be distinguished from transfer payments (mainly social security and debt interest) because they represent the area over which government sovereignty over expenditure replaces consumer sovereignty. The implicit view here is that it is government (imposed) decision-taking that is the source of worry.

3. Count only those exhaustive expenditures that are not in the form of purchases from the market. This lower option may be justified if you feel that what matters is the extent to which the government organizes production. The implicit view here is that market-produced output 'bought in' is least-cost production, whereas the public sector has a different (the usual implication is inferior) efficiency level from that of the market.

The significance of these arguments for what is seen as 'the' public sector can be appreciated from Fig. 14.3 with, for example, social security being near a third of general government expenditure. Choice of definition makes large differences.

There are other elements that need to be considered in a fuller discussion. Should nationalized industries be excluded on the grounds that they are largely autonomous? Should all 'financial assets' expenditure

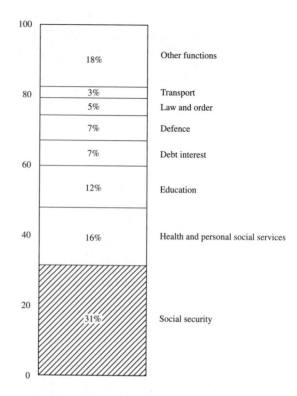

Figure 14.3 General government expenditure by function (estimated 1995–6).

Source: Public Expenditure Statistical Analyses 1996–97, Table 1.2.

be excluded on the grounds that it is simply government acting as a financial intermediary? And so on. Enough has been written to establish that it may not be an easy matter to establish the appropriate nominal data to collect. The word 'nominal' is important because this may paint a different picture from that of real data. Beck (1976, 1985) in particular has argued that the price (cost) index for public sector activities rose faster than the general price index. The implication is that to establish a 'real' measure the numerator must be deflated by a larger index than the denominator.

Note that it is the role of government in its tax-transfer/real-expenditure guise that is being documented here, but there are many influences of government on the economy that are missed in such a measure, such as tax expenditures that exempt, say, good X from the tax base (see chapter 8), and the use of direct regulations to represent methods of implicit taxation that are in many cases not dissimilar in nature from their explicit counterparts and as such should be counted fully (see Cullis and Jones 1987). The reason for their general relegation to subsidiary

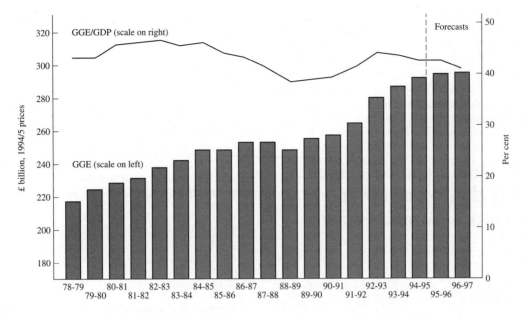

Figure 14.4 General government expenditure (GGE) excluding privatization proceeds, in real terms and as a proportion of GDP, 1978–9 and 1996–7.

Note: The out-turn for 1994–5 and forecasts for 1995–6 and 1996–7 are based on the Government's latest estimate,

contained in the Summer Economic Forecast published in June 1995.

Source: Financial Statement and Budget Report 1995–96 Revised Tables, and Summer Economic Forecast 1995.

importance is the fact that routine data on these elements are less often available in most economies.

14.7 Wagner's law

In public finance literature 'Wagner's law' forms a corner-stone of any discussion of the public sector growth. Adolf Wagner (1883; see Wagner 1958) noted a tendency in Western industrializing countries for the public sector (as measured by total public expenditure) to increase in absolute terms and also relative to the rest of the economy. His 'law of increasing state activities' predicts that the relationship would continue. In support, he argued: (i) the state would need to expand administration and law and order services, (ii) there would be an increased concern with distribution issues and (iii) there would be a greater need to control private monopolies. The 'modern formulation of Wagner's law' is that 'as per capita income rises in industrializing nations, their public sectors will grow in relative importance' (Bird 1971, p. 2) and, set in these terms, it has found considerable empirical support. Reviewing a plethora of empirical

studies, Gemmell (1993, p. 118) concluded that 'there is strong evidence across a wide and remarkably diverse range of countries that the progress of time is associated with rises in per capita income and ratios of nominal government expenditure to income'. Yet, despite the importance attached to the 'law', critics view Wagner's predictions as essentially teleological and argue that the relationship lacks a firm theoretical basis (e.g. Thompson 1979).

Musgrave (1969) attempted to explain the relationship between public sector growth and increased per capita income by an analysis of whether or not the demand for goods and services provided in the public sector was income elastic. He distinguished between government consumption, investment spending and transfers (or welfare benefits). However, in each case there is no unequivocal reason for expecting income elastic demand for all levels of income and he reached the conclusion that: 'The theory of expenditure growth remains a fascinating but somewhat elusive problem. Even if economic factors only are considered, it is difficult to arrive at an expenditure law...' (Musgrave 1969, p. 122). This conclusion casts obvious doubt on the value of Wagner's law for forecasting and similar criticism has also been made by

Bird (1971) and Herber (1975).[1] However, even if it had been concluded that income elasticity of demand continually exceeded unity, it might be argued that such an explanation of the relationship described by Wagner's law would simply be tautological. In this chapter a great deal of effort is devoted to explaining why the relationship referred to as Wagner's law has been observed.

14.8 'Public choice' versus public choice and other accounts of Wagner's law

To state the position baldly, government sector growth is to the expenditure side of public economics what labour supply and taxation are to the finance side: both represent extremely heavily researched areas where personal prejudice on one side or the other is much closer to the surface than in most areas of economics. That is, both represent areas where, clearly, people believe different things and these beliefs shape their arguments. In many respects the evidence produced speaks only to the few uncommitted. As for the committed, evidence in their favour is sound and other evidence, flawed.

Against this background of a large volume of controversial literature, it is difficult to proceed without, almost by definition, doing injustice to some positions. What is at stake for the protagonists is the success or otherwise of an unaided market economy. The dominant paradigm in economics is the neoclassical one, which in good measure can be identified with the operation of unfettered market forces. If market economies are far from being such, i.e. if they are so-called 'mixed' economies, then two competing explanations arise. Either actual market economies do not work anything like as well as their often frictionless textbook counterparts, or else the mechanism has become fouled, blocked or perverted by self-interested actors whose actions are unfortunately not constrained by a fundamental fiscal and/or expenditure constitution. Large government sectors

seem visible evidence that markets either cannot work or have been prevented from working. Implicit in the above must be a notion of what are or are not legitimate matters for collective concern and acceptable methods for operationalizing that concern. In summary, the public sector growth debate is the practical outcrop of fundamental issues that divide individuals. It is the battleground for deeply conflicting and strongly held viewpoints.

Of necessity, any survey must be selective. Regarding the 'facts', it was noted above that measurement problems of a conceptual and practical kind abound. Two quotations suggest different 'pictures':

That government has grown, and grown dramatically, cannot be questioned. (Mueller 1987, p. 115)

The fact to be explained is not the high variability of government expenditure, but rather its remarkable stability with respect to the trend growth of national income. (Alt and Chrystal 1983, p. 220)

Although it is true the respective authors are talking about two different Western democracies (the USA and UK respectively), the contrast remains striking.

Saying that the government sector is 'too big' (or too small!) is the objective of the theoretical and empirical contributions that have been made. It is an area where the difficulty of attempting to sustain a distinction between so-called normative and positive economics becomes apparent.[2] The seemingly positive exercise of assessing the causes of growth carries normative overtones. If government sector growth could be tied to the monopoly power of bureaucrats, it is tantamount to saying that such monopoly power should be circumscribed.

More fundamentally, any apparently positive statements about the public sector presuppose that a normative question of what is an optimal or desirable level of government expenditure has already been answered. As Wiseman (1980) discusses in relation to social expenditures, this is by no means an easy matter to decide. First, there is the question of the framework or paradigm in which the question is to be analysed, as this determines what views are relevant. Wiseman favours the approach that underlies neoclassical economic theory, which is methodological individualism. Adopting the value judgement that it

---

[1] Herber (1975) argued that as Wagner's law was related to periods of industrialization it was not clear what would occur after periods of industrialization. Some, however, questioned that even if there were continued industrialization, the relative size of the public sector could keep on expanding. Clarke (1945) actually set a figure to the limits of taxation at 25 per cent of national income; a limit that might be breached only with dire consequences for inflation and freedom (see also Clarke 1977).

[2] In the larger context of this book, it is interesting to note Buchanan's comment: 'I share with Musgrave the frustration at the efforts of many of our peers in economics when they make too much of the positive–normative distinction in our inquiry. The way that we look at, or model, the complexities of social interaction depends upon our ultimate normative ideals, and, in turn these ideas, themselves are shaped, in part, by the way we look at the interaction process (1989, p. 290).

is individual preferences that should matter precludes so-called organic conceptions of society in which society is more than the sum of its individual elements. In an organic conception it is the decisions of those best able to articulate the general will and interests of the organism that should be decisive. A Marxist approach, on the other hand, would see conflicting and exploited classes of individuals reflecting the underlying technology of society as the relevant elements to consider, and might argue for the size of government that would accelerate the pace of progress towards the final socialist state as the optimum. The fact that the latter two approaches may seem less familiar to readers should not downgrade their significance.

If only to pursue the argument further, let it be accepted that the individualistic approach wins the day. At first sight the optimal level of public expenditure is the value that corresponds most closely to individual preferences. But these preferences would be contingent upon the specific set of property rights that currently exist. Individuals also have preferences about what the property right structure should be and about mechanisms to change it. With a change in the system of rights would come a change in the expression of individual preferences. Wiseman's answer to the question of 'optimal social expenditures' is as follows:

If we begin from the prescriptions of methodological individualism [don't forget, you can begin elsewhere], then the optimal social organisation for a community would be one whose decision rules and procedures (property and contract laws, etc.) and rules for changing those rules (constitutional, etc. arrangements, laws affecting the behaviour of groups) generate the most efficient reflection of individual preferences. (Wiseman 1980, p. 256; comment in square brackets ours)

While this discussion may appear to be abstract, it is unavoidable if a genuine appreciation is to be gained of what is involved in determining the optimal size of public expenditures. Against this background, statements like that of Burton (1985), advocating an Economic Bill of Rights and a constitutional government spending limit of 25 per cent of GNP ('Twenty-five per cent of GNP is 25 per cent of GNP—full-stop!' (p. 100)), look rather too strong.

If this question is accepted as a difficult one to answer, how has the debate proceeded? First, debates proceed best when there is considerable ambiguity about what is being said. Second, most (but not all) protagonists have accepted the individualistic perspectives as defining the rules of the game. Given this, establishing deviations from what individual

preferences would be has become the acid test of 'too big'/'too small'. More specifically, it is the mechanisms that are used to explain public sector growth that carry the positive/normative message. Such mechanisms may be notionally classified on a scale of red for inefficient ones to green for efficient ones with ambiguous amber ones in between.

Table 14.1 offers a taxonomy based on Berry and Lowery (1987) with some modifications. The focus of the discussion will be the arguments or mechanisms that put upward pressure on the *level* of public expenditure. As Mueller clearly points out, the dependent variable in Wagner's law is the growth of the *share of* public sector and not its level. Indeed, Berry and Lowery in their empirical work seem to be subject to this criticism. The problem is that more work needs to be done to relate these arguments to the growth of public sector expenditures as a share of output. This point should be borne in mind. Where possible, the arguments are illustrated by reference to a consumer equilibrium diagram which can be thought of as pertaining to the median voter.

(1) Leviathan bureaucratic monopolies
The Niskanen model is discussed in more detail above and predicts that bureaucrats have monopoly power such that they can make an all-or-nothing offer of bureaucratic services (G in Fig. 14.5) that exhausts any consumer surplus (measured by the vertical difference between the parallel lines) on a deprivation measure (the amount that can be taken off the individual at the current quantity of G) that would make the individual indifferent between that quantity of G and no G (all Y); i.e. points 3 and 4 are both on indifference curve I_0. The all-or-nothing offer the bureaucrat makes is a higher quantity of G (that associated with point 5), involving an expenditure 56, which leaves the individual indifferent between this quantity of G and no G at all. Such an offer allows no consumer surplus.

Agenda setting is another aspect of bureaucratic behaviour. Romer and Rosenthal (1978) develop arguments that rely on the ability of bureaucrats to decide upon the votes that may be taken to exert 'growth' pressure. Suppose the constitution has a decision mechanism that specifies a default position if the bureaucrat-inspired level of provision is rejected by the electorate. Again using Fig. 14.5, the median voter, facing the tax price for good G incorporated in the budget constraint, would prefer the quantity of G associated with 1. Suppose for simplicity that the default position is no G at all. The bureaucrat can offer a quantity anywhere between 1 and 5 confident

Table 14.1 Public sector growth: a taxonomy of causes

	Leviathan excessive government		Responsive government
Source of growth momentum	Endogenous	Exogenous	Exogenous
Colour code	Red(-ish)	Amber(-ish)	Green(-ish)
Role of political actors	Political actors actively pursuing their self-interest and initiating action	Political actors passively persuing their self-interest, with other individuals initiating action	Political actors' passive responses to individuals initiating action
Specific arguments used	(1) Bureaucratic monopolies (2) Fiscal illusion (3) Bureaucratic voting power	(4) Party competition, electoral timing and redistribution (5) Interest/pressure-group activity (6) Centralization (fewer government tiers)	*Micro perspectives* (8) Demand function arguments (9) Supply function arguments (10) Internalization of economies (11) Information
	Temporal perspectives (15) Constitutional decline	(7) Taxation considerations	*Temporal perspectives* (12) Displacement effects (13) Social security growth (14) Marxist approach

Source: adapted from Berry and Lowery (1987).

that the median voter will accept it. For example, an offer of point 7 on I_1 will be preferable to point 4 on I_0 so that, even though 1 is optimal, 7, a 'too large' a quantity of G, will be supported by the median voter. The mechanism illustrates another avenue of influence open to the bureaucrat.

(2) Fiscal illusion

This topic is also discussed in connection with political actors and tax design. In the context of public

sector growth, three broad effects of illusion would be attractive to those trying to manipulate the median voter. First (by reference to Fig. 14.6), they would try to make the tax price of the public sector good G appear lower than it actually is. With optimist illusion over the relative price of G, the individual will move from 1 to 2, enjoying the same level of utility but with a higher quantity of G in the combination chosen. Second, it might be desirable to foster the idea that the median voter is in receipt of a real income increase as a result of tax expenditure decisions. This

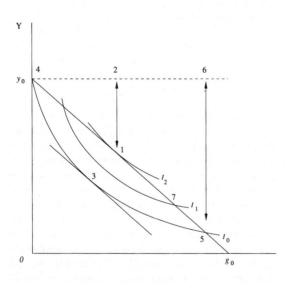

Figure 14.5 Bureaucratic power and the consumer surplus of the median voter.

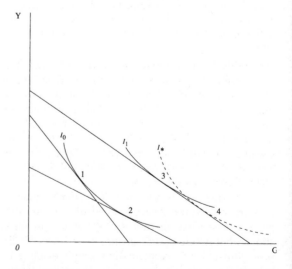

Figure 14.6 Fiscal illusion (realities).

would give the median voter the idea that she can achieve 3 on I_1. Third, an attempt could be made to alter the preferences of the voter to raise the absolute value of the marginal rate of substitution between Y and G (MRS_{gy}). Such a change would move the individual from 3 on I_1 to 4 on I_*.

To summarize, political actors who identify their self-interest with a larger rather than a smaller quantity of G should foster substitution, income and preference effects to raise G in illuded equilibrium 'enjoyed' by the median voter.

(3) Bureaucratic voting power

This argument simply draws attention to the fact that those who work in government are effectively a producer group with a direct interest in the size of their industry. If such a producer group can make itself a decisive segment of the voting population, it is then in a position to ask for and receive favourable public policies. Musgrave (1981) notes that, as the families of those who work in the public sector are likely to support propositions for public sector growth, this voting block can be quite significant. For example, in the USA, with employed voters making up about two-thirds of eligible voters, public employees account for 12 per cent of total eligible voters; allowing for their families, this public employee voting block reaches 18 per cent of eligible voters.

(4) Party competition, electoral timing and redistribution

In competitive political conditions, the party or parties not in power must form a majority winning platform. Given that it is the poor who offer the largest source of as yet untapped political power, the suggestion is that government programmes favouring the poor will be offered as a *quid pro quo* for political support. This effect, it is argued, is intensified at election times. The manipulation of policy near elections to engineer a majority is also central to the literature on political business cycles (see chapter 11).

However, the contribution that makes most use of suffrage and redistributive considerations is that of Meltzer and Richard (1981). In their model, government uses a proportional tax rate to raise revenue to finance lump-sum transfers to individuals. In Fig. 14.7, transfer size is simply $t\bar{Y}$ where t is the tax rate and $\bar{Y}$ is mean per capita income. Beyond t^* the disincentive effects of the tax reduces work hours and hence $\bar{Y}$. Given that ability varies within the population, the least able will be taxed out of work first. Now high-ability (-income) individuals will find

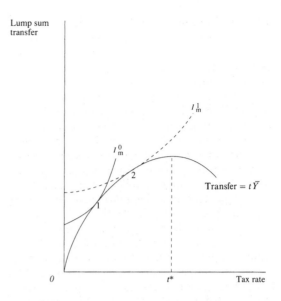

Figure 14.7 Redistribution and suffrage extension.

the tax rate more of a 'bad' than will the less able. For those not working, the tax rate becomes neutral. The driving force of the model is that growing suffrage often implies the addition of low-income (-ability) individuals. So the median voter indifference curve will tend to flatten over time and raise the tax-transfer activity of government over time. The movement 1 to 2 in the figure illustrates this. I_m^0 and I_m^1 are the indifference curves of the median voter under two suffrage regimes with the wider one being represented by I_m^1. Growing inequality in the distribution of income will increase the distance of the median below the mean income individual and this has the same effect (see Fig. 9.1).

(5) Interest/pressure group activity

The role of interest or pressure groups in government sector growth has been examined by many commentators. As noted elsewhere (p. 339), it is producers as opposed to consumers who are likely to find such a group attractive to organize. The argument is then that political actors will take up their cause as a 'special interest'. The motives behind the special interest may well condition views on the legitimacy of the cause. If the object is simply to achieve redistributive gains that have no particular rationale, then such activity seems unattractive. If, however, it is a mechanism through which public goods preferences are revealed or externalities internalized, judgements would presumably be less harsh.

(6) Centralization

Centralization tends to be favoured by those seeking to keep government expenditures in check. The argument is that, as a rule, the spending and tax-raising authority should be continuous. Where this is not the case, as with many tiers of government, the possibility of grants from other levels of government encourages spending that does have to be matched by increased finances in the spending jurisdiction. Furthermore, many tiers of government offer increased numbers of political actors who may be responsive to pressure groups wanting more public expenditure. Lower levels of government in themselves may see their role as putting pressure on other levels of government to (part-) finance their expenditure. Sandford and Robinson (1975) argued that the growth of local government expenditure in the UK was attributable to the growth of grant-supported expenditures at the local level, creating local representatives who could spend resources that they did not have to raise or be accountable for.

(7) Taxation considerations

One view of government argues that taxation causes expenditure so that government expenditure will grow as the tax take increases. Over time increasing numbers of activities are undertaken in the formal sector of the economy subject to the tax regulations, hence raising tax revenue. Similarly the increasing incorporation of productive enterprises makes them subject to corporation tax. On this account changes that yield increased tax would allow tax rate cuts, but these are not attractive to political agents. The argument can take less sinister overtones if the lack of taxes is constraining responsible government action. Musgrave (1969) suggests that the development process with its accompanying growth of specialization and trade offers 'tax handles' that facilitate public expenditure.

(8) Demand function arguments

The standard 'median' demand function approach would explain the quantity of G demanded per period as a function of own price P_g, prices of other goods P_y, income I, and changes in tastes or preferences. As Mueller (1987) notes, relative growth of G then arises where:

1. the own-price elasticity of demand has $|e_d| < 1$ and P_g rises compared with P_y;
2. the own-price elasticity of demand has $|e_d| > 1$ and P_y rises compared with P_g;
3. income has been rising and G has an income elasticity $E_I > 1$;

4. there has been a change in preferences towards G and away from other goods.

Wagner's (1958) own explanation of his 'law' of rising public expenditures can be incorporated under these headings. Increasing urbanization and interdependencies accompanying industrialization suggests that congestion and other externalities may shift preferences towards G. However, Galbraith (1962) has argued in the opposite direction, suggesting that individuals emulate each other with respect to private goods and that their preferences are shaped by intensive private goods advertising. Other things equal, if the median voter has a shift of preference towards public sector provision, it would be expected that left-wing or liberal parties would obtain office and enact that preference. Although the evidence for party-political influence has not been great. Wagner felt that G-type goods would exhibit positive income elasticities greater than unity and thus would be classified as luxury goods. Services like education and health care may conform to this, but others may not. Relatedly, a prerequisite of industrialization may be heavy investment in capital goods, especially those of a sunk kind undertaken by government. In terms of Fig. 14.6 the income effect and the preference shift are now real rather than the product of illusion. As for price elasticities, the own-price elasticity of G is often regarded as having an absolute value of less than unity. To make this argument work in explaining public sector growth, a consistent rise in the cost and hence price of G-type goods is required. This part of the argument is presented below.

(9) Supply function arguments

Baumol (1967) has argued that a given unit of G will rise in price relative to a given unit of other goods Y over time. This is because the G activity is labour-intensive and less subject to productivity increases than capital-intensive manufacturing enterprise. If unions cause wages to rise in the public sector alongside productivity-induced wage rises in the private sector, then costs per unit will rise relatively. A similar result obtains if the public sector has to bid labour away from the private sector. While some have argued that low productivity is the consequence rather than the cause of public sector provision, this argument, known as the relative price effect or hypothesis, has been accepted by many. For a discussion, see West (1991).

(10) Internationalization of economies

Some commentators have noted the increasing 'openness' of economies as a source of instability. Countries

may be increasingly vulnerable to importing inflation, unemployment and supply disruptions. On
this argument, Cameron (1978) sees increasing government intervention as a response to exogenous
shocks. The 'openness' or otherwise of economies
ties in with the case for optimum currency areas.
McKinnon (1963) argues that open economies will
find it easier to adopt a fixed exchange rate regime
than closed ones. It has been noted by some commentators that adjustment under a fixed exchange rate
regime involves price-level and rate-of-interest effects
felt by the whole community.[3] A conjecture is that,
with the UK fully in the European Monetary System
(essentially a permanently fixed exchange rate
regime), pressure to intervene will continue if not
intensify.

(11) Information

An inequality-driven account of public expenditure
growth is offered by Tarschys (1975). His argument is
that individuals have in mind an acceptable level of
inequality with respect to income or a good. The
cutting edge is provided by differences between the
actual and assumed position. If information becomes
available that makes it clear that actual inequality is
greater than that supposed, then there will be both
demand- and supply-side pressure for redistributive
government activity. On the supply side, the better-
off, who are the ones keenest to act on this 'caring'
externality, can be expected to push for lessening
inequality. On the demand side, those who realize
how deprived they are can similarly be expected to
agitate for remedial action on the part of the government.

(12) Displacement effects

The presence of displacement effects has been the core
of many academic articles around the world and ori-
ginates in work by Peacock and Wiseman (1961).
Their basic argument is that in normal times there is
a politically acceptable tax threshold that can be over-
ridden only at the cost of political suicide. However,
when a crisis such as war arises, some normal or
peace-related government expenditures are 'displaced', or more than replaced, by crisis- or war-
related expenditures, financed by a new higher tax
threshold made acceptable by the 'crisis'. With the
passing of the crisis, it is always possible for the old
tax threshold to be re-established, but this option is
not generally taken up. War-related public expenditure tends to be replaced by almost as much public

<hr>

[3] Under flexible rates, adjustment tends to be concentrated on
importers and exporters rather than on the public at large.

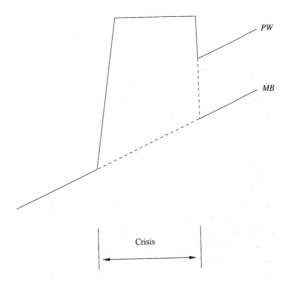

Figure 14.8 Displacement effect.

expenditure devoted to long-standing problems that
have been made more visible by the onset of the crisis.
This occurs as a result of an 'inspection' effect.

This displacement thesis rests upon an empirical
examination of public sector growth in the UK and
suggests a crisis path like the one labelled PW in Fig.
14.8, with government expenditure remaining at a
higher level after the crisis has passed. The weight of
the explanation falls on the financing side of public
expenditure and on a relaxation in this constraint.
The hypothesis has come under criticism as a result
of much econometric testing (see Diamond 1977).
Bird (1971) believes that, over the period of crisis
there is a replacement of peace-related expenditure
by war-related expenditure, together with a growth
in public expenditure as a fraction of output. However, after the crisis G/GNP slowly reverts to the same
trend rate of increase experienced before the crisis.
The question is therefore whether Peacock and Wiseman have established a displacement effect of permanent or long-run significance. The Musgrave (1969)–
Bird (1971) position is that after the crisis defence
expenditure falls and overall total expenditure
(together with civilian expenditure) returns to the
same trend experienced before the crisis. The effect,
a short-run (temporary) one, is labelled MB in the
figure.

(13) Social security growth

Whilst the headings so far are about different types of
factors in general this heading deals with a specific

element of government expenditure. Commentators would note that social security spending is the type of transfer spending that dominates the UK 'public sector' (see Fig. 14.3) among many others and therefore is worthy of separate consideration. It also serves to pick up on a number of arguments in earlier chapters. Social security is a vast and important topic; however, here the emphasis will be placed on its economic rationale, nature and temporal characteristics.

In the social optimality tradition the justification for the provision of unemployment pay, old age pensions and the like must be found in 'market failure'. As regards pensions in chapter 5 when considering Akerlof and Dickens' (1982) use of the psychological notion of 'cognitive dissonance' it was noted that it might provide a case for a state/public pension scheme. Individuals are often uncomfortable thinking about their own deaths and therefore 'manage it' out of their minds and try and act as though they will live and be earning forever. In such circumstances it would cause dissonance to be saving for your retirement and your approaching death. Given this mind set it can be seen that people may well end up by not having saved enough for their retirement and hence a compulsory state scheme may be a reasonable response. Furthermore there may be a direct equity argument that the low paid simply cannot save sufficient for their retirement and deserve help in later life especially if they have been seen to work hard.

Unemployment payments highlight the difficulty facing risk-averse people in insuring certain types of events. Consider Fig. 14.9 which depicts the marginal utility of income schedule for someone who is risk averse (i.e. diminishing marginal utility of income). Suppose 'good' and 'bad' times are equally likely and the individual secures an income of £5000 in a 'good' working period (hence Y_g) and only £1000—Y_b in a 'bad' working period. In a bad period the marginal utility of income is the distance $Y_b - 2$ which is considerably greater than the marginal utility of income in a good period which is distance $Y_g - 1$. This risk-averse individual would enjoy higher utility if he or she could secure the average income £3000 = Y_a with a constant marginal utility of income equal to $Y_a - 3$. The utility loss from not having the 'good times' is $Y_a 3 1 Y_g$ and the utility gain from not having 'bad times' is $Y_b 2 3 Y_a$ which exceeds $Y_a 3 1 Y_b$ by area 2 3 4 5, i.e. there is a utility gain from income smoothing. In effect the individual would like to insure against bad times by paying a premium in good times. In these circumstances and assuming a 'frictionless' world the potential income loss is £4000 with a half chance of it occurring and hence the fair premium would be

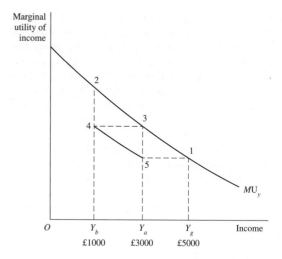

Figure 14.9 Gains from income 'smoothing'.

£2000. The illustrated individual would be happy to give up £2000 of income if good times arise for the guarantee of a £2000 addition to his income if bad times occur. In short, risk-averse individuals would like to ensure a constant income at a fair premium. Unfortunately insurance mechanisms are beset with problems one of which is the notion of 'moral hazard' (also met in chapter 5). If an insurance company accepted the type of deal outlined above it tends to find the insuree hits bad times more often than 50 per cent of the time, after all why work hard in good times? It is better to save the effort and claim bad times have occurred and have the insurance company make good £2000 of income. In such circumstances the 'moral hazard' behaviour causes the scheme to quickly collapse. (There are of course frictions in any real scheme, e.g. the need to have the required premium in the initial period and for insurance companies to cover administrative costs and make a normal rate of return.) Effectively collectivizing the risk with a social security scheme that involves unemployment pay cannot solve these problems (witness the debate on the effect of high 'replacement ratios' on the incentives to find a job) but it may nevertheless reduce them. In the event, whatever the rationale, state pensions, unemployment benefits and other social security transfer payments are a feature of most Western democracies.

Creedy (1993) is one author who addresses the great growth of social security budgets in many countries. He reports Beck's (1979) finding that typical growth rate of such expenditures in the 1950s was 10 per cent compared to 18 per cent in the 1970s. The dynamics of such growth are complex but a number of simple points can be made. First, as noted in chapter 9, social security payments are 'contingent' benefits, i.e. based on a particular status—being unemployed, a single parent, past retirement age, disabled, etc. The incidence of such contingencies are only, at best, partly controllable by government action (macroeconomic policy, work safety legislation, etc.) and once the eligibility criteria are chosen the number of individuals in each contingent category is to a large extent uncertain. Secondly, the expenditure increasing moral hazard effect of all forms of insurance schemes has been noted above. Thirdly, the scale of payments to eligible individuals is clearly important with indexed benefit payments in a period of 'stagflation' being a 'nightmare' for those trying to control public expenditure. Fourthly, there is the question of how long people remain in each contingent category. For example, increasing longevity combined with state retirement pensions almost 'automatically' increases the size of public expenditure. This latter consideration raises the current concerns over state transfer payment schemes.

State schemes are said to be unfunded or pay-as-you-go which means they are straightforward transfers from the current taxpayers to the current eligible individuals. The payments received do not come from the investment of 'premiums' in income generating assets which would occur in a funded scheme. Wagner (1976) notes the fragility of this 'contract' between taxpayers and benefit recipients. If state pensions are considered there is an intergenerational compact between current taxpayers and pension recipients such that current taxpayers will become pension recipients in their turn from the taxes of the then current taxpayers and so it goes on. Wagner argues that the real rate of return on tax contributions to current pensioners is the sum of the real rate of growth of per capita income and the rate of growth of the labour force. In a two 'activity' model one of which is working the second of which is retirement, suppose real income and labour force growth are both 5 per cent. Further assume the mean worker income is initially £25 000 which is taxed at 5 per cent to finance pensions. In the second period mean income will be £26 250 and the labour force will have increased by 5 per cent. In this case paying £1250 (£25 000 × 0.05) in the working period generates £1378.13 in the retirement period (£25 000 × 1.05 × 0.05 × 1.05) a return of 10.25 per cent. Whilst this looks attractive if the rate of growth of the labour force and real income growth both halve in the next (third) period those paying

£1312.50 in period two feeling entitled to a 10.25 per cent return and hence £1447 in their retirement period would need to tax the then working cohort at a rate of 5.2 per cent. The more dramatically the postulated growth rates change the more penal the implied tax rate will seem. (Readers can verify this by placing their own numbers in the formula for the required tax rate derived in Table 14.2, e.g. suppose the growth of the working population is negative in period 3.) Add to this longer retirement periods and shorter working lives and the arithmetic looks all too daunting. It is in this context that current concerns about the future viability of state pensions in the UK and other countries arises.

Enough has been written to give some indication of the dynamics of social security payments (see Creedy (1993) for a formal model) to see why they: form such a large proportion of general government expenditure; are difficult to control and generate a concern to 'return to the market' especially with respect to pension provision (a current UK government policy theme). Finally this account of a simple unfunded pension scheme highlights the point made in conclusion to chapter 9 that what looks like redistribution (from richer to poorer) within a period (a 'snapshot') is simply income smoothing over a lifetime (the 'movie')—a series of periods.

Table 14.2 Unfunded pensions and the tax rate

	Workers earn	Retirees receive
Period 1	w	tw
Period 2	$w(1 + g_Y)(1 + g_F)$	$tw(1 + g_Y)(1 + g_F)$
Letting	$(1 + g_Y)(1 + g_F) = 1 + g$	

the rate of return to period 1 workers is

$$\frac{tw(1 + g) - tw}{tw} = g$$

If g falls to g' then in

| Period 3 | $w(1 + g)(1 + g')$ | $\tau w(1 + g)(1 + g')$ |

(where τ is the tax rate required to offer other period 2 workers a rate of return equal to period 1 workers, namely, g)

solving for τ

$$\frac{\tau w(1 + g)(1 + g') - tw(1 + g)}{tw(1 + g)} = g$$

$$\frac{\tau}{t}(1 + g') - 1 = g$$

$$\frac{\tau}{t} = \frac{1 + g}{1 + g'}$$

with $g > g'$ then $\tau > t$

Symbols: w = initial wage, g_Y = rate of income growth, g_F = rate of labour force growth and t = initial tax rate.

(14) Marxist approach

Another general approach comes from the Marxists. Their explanations of the increasing role of the public sector receive little attention in the popular texts on public finance and the economics of the public sector because of the different paradigm employed. Nevertheless, they put forward an explanation of the operation of Wagner's law that merits consideration. One contribution is discussed here by way of illustration.

It is to be remembered that in the Marxist schema the state is the agent of the capitalist class. O'Connor (1973)[4] begins by outlining the two often contradictory roles of the state in the capitalist world: to maintain conditions that make profitable capital accumulation possible, and to create and maintain conditions for social harmony. The second is a legitimating role. Contradiction arises if the state uses its power to help one class at the expense of another: then it is clearly in danger of losing legitimacy. On the other hand, if it does not make capital accumulation profitable, the source of its power (the tax on the surplus value produced) is endangered. Finding itself on Morton's fork, the state must tread a difficult path, mystifying its activities whenever possible.

Corresponding to the state's two functions are two types of expenditures, for the provision of social capital and social expenses. The former are expenditures required for profitable accumulation and are subdivided into social investment and social consumption. Social investment consists of projects and services that increase the productivity of a given amount of labour power and *ceteris paribus* increase the rate of profit. Social consumption consists of projects and services that lower the reproduction costs of labour and *ceteris paribus* increase the rate of profit. The second type of expenditure, on social expenses, concerns those projects and services that are required to maintain social harmony.

O'Connor argues that nearly every state agency is involved in both of these functions, and he offers two basic theses. First, growth of the state sector and state spending is functioning increasingly as the basis for the growth of the monopoly sector and total production; simultaneously, the growth of state spending is the result of growth of the monopoly sector. In short, the growth of the (American) state is both the cause and the effect of the expansion of monopoly capital. Second, accumulation of social capital and social expenses is a contradictory process that tends to generate crises of all types. Under Marxist accounts, similarly, the government has the task of providing profit opportunities against a background where consumer demand in developed economies would be largely sated. To offset this effect, the government must encourage wasteful consumerism and offer profit opportunities in the public sector; hence large defence and construction programmes. The feature of defence programmes in particular is that they do not have to face a market test—their provision is an end in itself, which is largely non-rejectable by consumer voters. This is very close to one of Wolf's supply-side points introduced in section 14.3.

(15) Constitutional decline

The constitution sets out the rules by which *processes*, both economic and political, operate over time. The basic dilemma in constitutional economics is the old one of 'Who guards the guards?' The constitution gives coercive power to governments, yet the population wishes to contain or constrain the use of that power.

One of the themes in the public choice literature on constitutions is their propensity to 'decay' and come to require fundamental reform. Constitutions facilitate co-operation between individuals and therefore raise the utility possibilities achievable by individuals as compared with an anarchistic result, where outcomes reflect the underlying distribution of natural abilities among individuals. In the arguments developed by Buchanan (1975) and Holcombe (1985), each generation tacitly agrees to the 'social contract' that is the constitution by not indulging in civil unrest. This argument is captured in Fig. 14.10 developed by Holcombe (1983), which shows the utility levels achievable by individuals G and B. The anarchistic initial position is represented by point 1. By accepting the 'social contract' and co-operation, both B and G expect to gain, say, at a minimum to points 2 and 3 respectively. A point such as 4 on *UF* might be the initial co-operative equilibrium. The cost of civil unrest is the difference between the anarchistic equilibrium to which society would revert and the current utility level enjoyed; i.e. initially 4 is compared with 1. Now suppose G becomes a member of government and is in a position to exploit to her own advantage the 'slackness' in any constitution that is required to allow for the uncertainty of events. Pictorially, this can be represented by a move away from 4 towards 5 in the interior of the frontier as gains to G at the expense of B involve some inefficiency. In a dynamic context, constitutions unwind for the following reasons:

1. Checks and balances do less checking and balancing as methods of scrutiny are limited and the

---

[4] Foley (1978) offers an alternative Marxist approach to government expenditures in a mainstream economics journal.

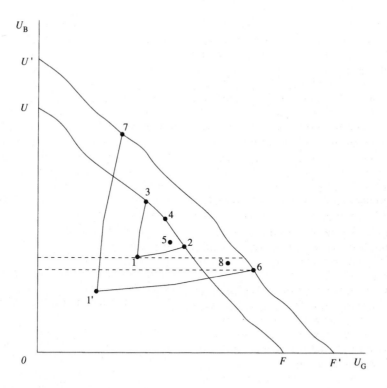

Figure 14.10 The 'eroding' constitution.

Source: based upon Holcombe (1983) *Public Finance and the Political Process,* Southern Illinois University Press, Illinois.

majority have a mandate to impose legislation on all individuals.

2. Those in political power become adept at maintaining it (see, e.g. the section on political business cycles in chapter 11) and grow immune to consumer voter preferences.

3. Constitutions can become the victims of their own success in that, by facilitating net investment and economic growth, the comparison with the anarchistic equilibrium increases, making the opportunity cost of dissent very high. Hence, despite the fact that you may feel and be the victim of excessive government, you do not 'revolt'.

In terms of Fig. 14.10, economic growth shifts the utility frontier *UF* to *U'F'* while the increased interdependence of individuals reduces the 'reversion' anarchistic equilibrium from 1 to 1'. The 'baulking' level of utility for B and G now becomes 6 for B and 7 for G, i.e. lower than points 2 and 3. Given the capacity of G to exploit her position, point 5 migrates towards a point such as 8; i.e. the outcome is the recognition of B that, although he is 'exploited' by more and more overtime, it still remains optimal to keep the 'social

contract'. (The utility enjoyed by B is lower at 8 than at 1 but higher than at 1' and above the 'revolt' trigger utility point 6.)

The tools of excessive government that are a feature of the eroded constitution have already been met: forced riding, special interest effects, logrolling, bureaucratic slack, etc. The aim of constitutional reform is to eradicate many of the deleterious effects that are central to the Leviathan government argument. The context here, however, is that overtime constitutions decay and the growth of government is the odour that results from that decay.

As noted above, much empirical work has centred around these various arguments, which need to be formulated in terms of the growth of the public sector share in output rather than simply the level or size of the public sector. Mueller (1987) is emphatic on this point. He notes that many of the arguments put forward to explain Wagner's law actually predict a *level* of the public sector that is too large, rather than the required outcome, i.e. that the proportion of the public sector in national income that will grow over time. He reviews the following public choice arguments:

1. Government responding to 'market failure'-type arguments, e.g. public goods, externality correction, etc.—a demand function approach, 'normative' in stance;
2. Government responding to majority income redistribution desires, e.g the Meltzer–Richard (1981) suffrage extension approach;
3. Government responding to special interest groups, e.g. the price effect of majority voting, pressure group formation;
4. Bureaucratic monopoly power exploited by those in government;
5. Fiscal illusion effects induced and manipulated by those in government.

While arguments 1–3 represent, as the descriptions suggest, 'responsive' government action, 4 and 5 represent initiating government action only vaguely constrained by the electorate. Mueller (1987), in describing all this as part of a public choice perspective, is using the term in a wider sense than generally employed in this book. Approach 1 is expressly normative and part of traditional social optimality approach, while 2–5 and especially 4 and 5 are more 'public choice' in orientation as well as carrying negative connotations.

However, it is with respect to bureaucracies that Mueller saves the 'levels' argument summarized in Fig. 14.1 and the related text. To 'nail down' the argument as supporting Wagner's law, he postulates that bureaucratic power depends on the absolute size of the bureau. Arguments consistent with this are that (a) outside monitoring difficulties increase with the size of the bureau, and (b) there are more insiders working to increase the size of the bureau, the larger the bureau is already. Given this, the budget in period $t(B_t)$ can be the product of a coefficient a_t (greater than 1) and G_t, the true demand for publicly provided goods. Hence

$$(14.1) \qquad B_t = a_t G_t$$

if

$$(14.2) \qquad a_t = e^{aB_t}$$

and

$$(14.3) \qquad G_t = ce^{nt}$$

where c is a constant, n is the rate of growth of national income and t is time.

Substituting (14.3) and (14.2) into (14.1) yields

$$(14.4) \qquad B_t = ce^{aB_t}e^{nt}$$

Given this, the growth g of the budget is

$$(14.5) \qquad g = \ln B_t - \ln B_{t-1}$$

$$(14.6) \qquad \ln B_t = \ln c + aB_t + nt$$

$$(14.7) \qquad \ln B_{t-1} = \ln c + aB_{t-1} + n(t-1)$$

therefore

$$(14.8) \qquad g = a(B_t - B_{t-1}) + n$$

In words, the growth rate is greater than n and increases with the absolute difference between the current and last period's budget.

Berry and Lowery (1987) call for greater integration of the explanations, which at one level is attractive. However, caution needs to be exercised. If the explanations are not couched within similar frameworks, then pushing arguments together may well not be adding like with like. This is especially true of, say, a Marxist/class approach and a neoclassical, individualistic explanation. However, it is also a relevant consideration in a narrower context. Many public expenditure analyses operate via the median voter, but as Buchanan points out, there are other alternatives.

Putting all the possible explanations together may create a ragbag of independent variables that have no overall coherence unless spheres of influence are clearly specified. One way to save this outcome then, is for greater explicitness in the formulation of the argument. In such circumstances, those sections of the public expenditure to which arguments about public sector growth are meant to apply would be clear. Similarly, the context, whether redistributory, the provision of non-rival goods etc. is often implicit and fuzzy. Finally, as noted by Berry and Lowery, searches for mono-causal explanations of complex economic phenomena may be attractive but are fruitless.

A study, edited by Lybeck and Henrekson (1988), tried to establish whether it was possible to develop a common 'super-model' to explain the growth of government. Cross-country comparisons of the growth of government in European countries were undertaken to establish whether the growth and size of government could be related to common models. While particular models of government growth performed well in some economies, they were rejected in the analyses of other countries.

One result of this study is to throw greater emphasis on a study of specific institutional arrangements in particular countries. As Lybeck concludes, 'Obviously and perhaps inevitably, we are still a long way from deriving a common model that can explain the growth of the Government sector in several countries' (p. 44). Somewhere between the search for mono-causal explanations and a common 'super-model' may lie the less ambitious middle ground of a consistent framework. Some such suggested frameworks are outlined in the Appendix to this chapter.

14.9 Summary

[Expenditure growth should at least start from the assumption that] a theory of public expenditures will take a stable share of national income in the long term. (Alt and Chrystal 1983, p. 228)

A striking phenomenon of modern times has been the steady growth of the government sector. Despite the hot political debates that have greeted the successive steps of government expansion, there is surprisingly little scientific understanding of the forces tending to bring it about. (Hirschleifer 1984, p. 529)

These two quotations cover a number of controversial debates in economics that have been outlined in this chapter. Like all 'big issues', that of government growth offers something for everyone. For the economic statistician there is the debate about how the government sector is to be defined, and indeed whether, once a different price index is allowed for in public expenditures, there has been any significant growth at all (Beck 1976, 1985). For those interested in political economy the 'hot political debates' are the attraction. The public choice theorists of the Virginia/libertarian/anti-Leviathan school manage to see almost everything that is economically evil manifest in the public sectors of Western democracies. For those following a positivist methodology there is the question of predicting and/or explaining growth or non-growth.

Against this background of a topic in which a wide cross-section of economic arguments, approaches and techniques are employed, the later sections of the chapter outlined different approaches in which the individual arguments can be synthesized, although no formal models as such were offered.

The main purpose of distinguishing between the three broad approaches outlined in the Appendix, apart from curiosity, is to determine how to view any changes in the level of observed public expenditure. If the factors offered in the microeconomic approach are valid, then that approach offers a measure of normative sanction to public expenditure; the factors outlined are those that form the basis of market analysis, and markets (competitive) are sufficient for efficiency (in the absence of market failure). By contrast, the 'public choice' approach centres almost exclusively on inefficient allocative mechanisms,

and a recognition that these arguments carry weight leaves the public sector condemned. The developmental time-series approach is painted with a broad brush, and without more detailed analysis the approach has a positive role but seems to lack any necessary normative implications; hence its amber colour code.

Five main points arise:

1. There is a counterpart collection of arguments to parallel market failure arguments.
2. Bureaucratic economics has been developed in a manner that makes the bureau an unattractive economic form, but this is not an unanswerable or unassailable case.
3. Wagner's law centres on the growth of the public sector as a share in the economy over time, but measuring its presence or absence raises both conceptual and practical issues.
4. Arguments explaining or justifying Wagner's law are legion, and it is important to isolate the normative implications they carry.
5. To date it is the negative connotations of large and growing public sectors that have dominated in the so-called Leviathan debate. However, there are arguments 'going the other way' (see Cullis and Jones 1987).

Appendix

(a) A microeconomic approach (green)

A basic premise here is that private–public sector allocation decisions are carried out in an efficient manner, so that the mix of goods and services produced reflects the quantities of each that individuals demand when each good or service is priced at its marginal cost of production. A stylized demand-side model might be represented by

$$G = aP^b Y^c Q^d T^e D^f$$

where G is a public sector provision measure, P is a tax price variable, Y is income, Q is the provision of complementary or substitute goods, T is preferences and D is demographic factors. (Terms b, c, d, e and f would be elasticity values if the equation were econometrically estimated in log form.) An equivalent account on the supply side would give emphasis to Baumol's productivity lag argument (Baumol 1967), which is concerned with supply in the production function/costs of inputs context. However, income can also be interpreted in a supply-side guise (see Thompson 1979). This is because of the connection between income and tax revenues that governments can raise to finance expenditures (e.g. Cooper's (1975) model of the National Health Service).

(b) A 'public choice' approach (red)

Paradoxically, a 'public choice' approach suggests that the one variable the level of public expenditure does not reflect is choices of the public. Three broad sources of distortion can be identified in this approach.

Political process and government expenditure bias

Political process bias, favouring an inefficiently large public sector, centres on arguments about consumer-voters who are 'rationally ignorant', majority voting mechanisms that create forced riders and permit logrolling, and special interest legislation. In addition, some researchers (e.g. Wagner 1976) have models in which consumer-voters are fiscally illuded into underestimating the true cost of public expenditure programmes. An *implicit* agreement to vote favourably on increased public expenditure is also said to arise within the political process as more and more individuals become dependent upon the public sector for their employment. The livelihood of many families then becomes dependent on resisting cuts and promoting increases in public expenditure. To the extent that these may operate as a block vote, there is clearly the potential for a snowball effect. The more the public sector grows, the greater it ties the fortunes of voters to its future, and the greater the dependency, the more favourably voters react to a maintenance or increase in public sector activity (see Busch and Denzau 1977). Recently the role of interest (pressure) groups has been emphasized (see Becker 1985; Mueller and Murrell 1986).

Governmental process and government expenditure bias

Here focus is on the structure and incentive mechanisms in the executive and administrative branches of government. Niskanen's (1968, 1971) work on the monopoly bureau, combined with the argument of the preceding paragraph, offers one line of argument. However, the simplest approach to explaining government expenditure would rely on the 'incrementalist' model of budgetary determination outlined by Davis, Dempster and Wildavsky (1966) and Wildavsky (1964, 1975).

The difficulties of government decision-making are further illustrated by what might be termed a 'system'

argument. This approach would argue that rules, processes and procedures take over from people as organizations become more complex. In terms of the growth of public expenditure, this amounts to ascribing the changes that take place to changes in administrative and planning procedures of public expenditure, for example the Public Expenditure Survey Committee.

Constitutional decay and government expenditure bias

Recently the public choice economists have stressed constitutional reform as a way of checking the Leviathan state. They develop a number of lines of argument listed by Burton (1985). Gradual shifts of power from the courts to administrative bodies foster the public sector via regulation designed to favour powerful interest groups. Such regulation involves both bureaux and subsidies. Hayek (1979) emphasizes the gradual way in which it has become legitimate for governments to exercise unlimited power, which has resulted in favourable expenditure policies being demanded and enacted. Buchanan and Wagner (1977, 1978) argue that the legacy of Keynesian theory has been to legitimate unbalanced deficit budgets, again leading to greater public expenditure. Finally, the extension of the franchise has also been seen to be the source of public sector growth. With an extended franchise and an unequal income distribution, the government is faced with demands to redistribute income towards the poor majority.[5] For various reasons, then, constitutions are seen as decaying over time; hence the reform demands that involve statutory limits to the size of government and compulsory balanced budgets.

(c) Developmental/time-series approach (amber)

By far the most quoted explanation of the relative growth of the government sector over time is that of Peacock and Wiseman (1961; also 1979). Their essential observation was to note that the public sector, as measured by government expenditure as a percentage of GNP, grew over time in a stepwise rather than a smooth manner.

The essence of the Peacock–Wiseman approach is the limit of taxation that a community is prepared to tolerate and discrete changes in tolerance induced by 'crises'. Musgrave and Musgrave (1976) present an explanation of the operation of Wagner's law which rests on the availability of tax handles. These, they

---

[5] Paradoxically, Peltzman (1980) has a model in which greater equality of private income increases the demand for government redistribution.

argue, come with increased economic specialization and trade, both intra- and internationally. Hence the argument becomes that the more a country develops, the easier it is for the public sector to grow. Also, they mention the less hostile attitude towards taxation that may be part and parcel of the development process. The argument that generally it may be easier to find funds for any given programme over time is consistent with findings that spending on social security as a proportion of GNP is strongly correlated with the length of operation of the system (see Pryor 1968). The Musgraves, however, have been criticized as outlining a facilitating process for growth rather than an explanation of the instigating process. The counterpart of the Musgraves' 'tax handles' study may be, for example, the funding of 'spending handles' by bureaucracies.

Alt and Chrystal (1983) offer a rather different perspective on the public expenditure debate. They note the *stability* of the ratios to GDP of the annual values of three categories of public expenditure (consumption, transfers and investment) in Britain for the period 1955–79. The explanatory model offered by Alt and Chrystal draws on Friedman's (1957) 'permanent income hypothesis' account of personal consumption spending. The authors hypothesize that public expenditures are planned to grow in proportion to expected or trend national income. The rationale for such an argument is a planning context in which expenditure growth is targeted on the expected growth of national income. Although there are errors in such expectations, the broad picture is one of sluggish government expenditures, largely independent of short-term income fluctuations responding to changes in trend or permanent national income only. Alt and Chrystal offer supporting econometric evidence for the UK and the USA for the three types of expenditure noted above.

References

Akerlof, G. A. and Dickens, W. J. (1982) 'The Economic Consequences of Cognitive Dissonance', *American Economic Review*, 62, 5, pp. 777–95.

Alt, J. E. and Chrystal, K. A. (1983) *Political Economics*. Brighton: Wheatsheaf.

Baumol, W. J. (1967) 'The Macroeconomics of Unbalanced Growth', *American Economic Review*, 57, 3, pp. 415–26.

Beck, M. (1976) 'The Expanding Public Sector: Some Contrary Evidence', *National Tax Journal*, 29, 1, pp. 15–21.

Beck, M. (1979) 'Public Sector Growth: A Real Perspective', *Public Finance/Finances Publiques*, 34, 3, pp. 313–56.

Beck, M. (1985) 'Public Expenditure, Relative Prices and Resource Allocation', *Public Finance/Finances Publiques*, 4, 1, pp. 17–34.

Becker, G. S. (1985) 'Public Policies, Pressure Groups and Dead Weight Costs', *Journal of Public Economics*, 28, 3, pp. 329–47.

Berry, W. D. and Lowery, D. (1987) *Understanding United States Government Growth: An Empirical Analysis of the Postwar Era*. New York and London: Praeger.

Bird, R. M. (1971) 'Wagner's Law of Expanding State Activity', *Public Finance/Finances Publiques*, 26, 1, pp. 1–26.

Bohm, P. (1987) *Social Efficiency*, 2nd edn. London: Macmillan.

Borcherding, T. E. (1985) 'The Causes of Government Expenditure Growth: A Survey of the US Evidence', *Journal of Public Economics*, 28, 3, pp. 359–82.

Buchanan, J. M. (1958) *Public Principles of Public Debt*. Homewood, Ill.: Irwin.

Buchanan, J. M. (1975) *The Limits to Liberty: Between Anarchy and Leviathan*. Chicago: University of Chicago Press.

Buchanan, J. M. (1989) 'Richard Musgrave, Public Finance, Public Choice', *Public Choice*, 61, 3, pp. 289–91.

Buchanan, J. M. and Wagner, R. E. (1977) *Democracy in Deficit*. New York: Academic Press.

Buchanan, J. M. and Wagner, R. E. (1978) *Fiscal Responsibility in Constitutional Democracy*. Leiden/Boston: Martinus Nijhoff.

Burton, J. (1985) *Why No Cuts?* Hobart Paper no. 104. London: Institute of Economic Affairs.

Busch, W. C. and Denzau, A. T. (1977) 'The Voting Behaviour of Bureaucrats and Public Sector Growth', in T. E. Borcherding (ed.), *Budgets and Bureaucrats: The Sources of Government Growth*. Durham, NC: Duke University Press.

Cameron, D. (1978) 'The Expansion of the Public Economy: A Comparative Analysis', *American Political Science Review*, 72, 4, pp. 1243–61.

Clarke, C. (1945) 'Public Finance and Changes in the Value of Money', *Economic Journal*, 55, 220, pp. 371–89.

Clarke, C. (1977) 'The Scope and Limits of Taxation', pp. 19–28 in A. R. Prest *et al.* (eds.), *The State of Taxation*. London: Institute of Economic Affairs.

Cooper, M. H. (1975) *Rationing Health Care*. London: Croom-Helm.

Creedy, J. (1993) 'Social Security Expenditure', pp. 155–83 in N. Gemmell (ed.), *The Growth of the Public Sector— Theories and International Evidence*. Aldershot: Edward Elgar.

Cullis, J. G. and Jones, P. R. (1987) *Microeconomics and Public Economy: A Defense of Leviathan.* Oxford: Basil Blackwell.

Davis, O. A., Dempster, M. A. H. and Wildavsky, A. (1966) 'On the Process of Budgeting: An Empirical Study of Congressional Appropriation', *Public Choice*, 1, pp. 63–132.

Diamond, J. (1977) 'Econometric Testing of the Displacement Effect: A Reconsideration', *Finanz Archiv*, 35, 3, pp. 387–404.

Foley, D. K. (1978) 'State Expenditure from a Marxist Perspective', *Journal of Public Economics*, 9, 2, pp. 221–38.

Friedman, M. (1957) *A Theory of the Consumption Function.* Cambridge, Mass.: National Bureau of Economic Research.

Galbraith, J. K. (1962) *The Affluent Society.* Harmondsworth: Penguin.

Gemmell, N. (1993) 'Wagner's Law and Musgrave's Hypothesis', pp. 103–18 in N. Gemmell (ed.), *The Growth of the Public Sector—Theories and International Evidence.* Aldershot: Edward Elgar.

Hayek, F. A. (1979) *Law, Legislation and Liberty*, Vol. III. London: Routledge & Kegan Paul.

Herber, B. P. (1975) *Modern Public Finance*, 3rd edn. Homewood, Ill.: Richard D. Irwin.

Hirschleifer, J. (1984) *Price Theory and Applications*, 3rd edn. Englewood Cliffs, NJ: Prentice Hall.

Holcombe, R. G. (1985) *An Economic Analysis of Democracy.* Carbondale and Edwardsville: Southern Illinois University Press.

Jackson, P. M. (1982) *The Political Economy of Bureaucracy.* Oxford: Philip Allan.

Lindsay, C. M. (1976) 'A Theory of Government Enterprise', *Journal of Political Economy*, 84, 5, pp. 31–7.

Lybeck, J. A. and Henrekson, M. (eds.) (1988) *Explaining the Growth of Government.* Amsterdam: North-Holland.

McKinnon, R. I. (1963) 'Optimum Currency Areas', *American Economic Review*, 53, 4, pp. 717–25.

Meltzer, A. H. and Richard, S. F. (1981) 'A Rational Theory of the Size of Government', *Journal of Political Economy*, 89, 5, pp. 914–25.

Mueller, D. C. (1987) 'The Growth of Government: A Public Choice Perspective', *International Monetary Fund Staff Papers*, 34, 1, pp. 115–49.

Mueller, D. C. and Murrell, P. (1986) 'Interest Groups and the Size of Government', *Public Choice*, 48, 2, pp. 125–45.

Musgrave, R. A. (1969) *Fiscal Systems.* New Haven, Conn.: Yale University Press.

Musgrave, R. A. (1981) 'Leviathan Cometh—or Does He?', pp. 77–120 in H. Ladd and N. Tideman (eds.), *Tax and Expenditure Limitations*, COUPE Papers on Public Economics 5. Washington: Urban Institute.

Musgrave, R. A. and Musgrave, P. B. (1976) *Public Finance in Theory and Practice.* New York: McGraw-Hill.

Niskanen, W. A. (1968) 'The Peculiar Economics of Bureaucracy', *American Economic Review* (Papers and Proceedings), 57, 2, pp. 293–321.

Niskanen, W. A. (1971) *Bureaucracy and Representative Government.* New York: Aldine-Atherton.

O'Connor, J. (1973) *The Fiscal Crisis of the State.* New York: St Martin's Press.

Peacock, A. T. (1978) 'Comment', pp. 115–16 in J. M. Buchanan *et al.*, *The Economics of Politics*, IEA Readings no. 18. London: Institute of Economic Affairs.

Peacock, A. T. and Wiseman, J. (1961) *The Growth of Public Expenditure in the United Kingdom.* London: Allen & Unwin.

Peacock, A. T. and Wiseman, J. (1979) 'Approaches to the Analysis of Government Expenditure Growth', *Public Finance Quarterly*, 7, 1, pp. 3–23.

Peltzman, S. (1980) 'The Growth of Government', *Journal of Law and Economics*, 23, 2, pp. 209–87.

Pryor, F. L. (1968) *Public Expenditures in Communist and Capitalist Nations.* London: Allen & Unwin.

Romer, T. and Rosenthal, H. (1978) 'Political Resource Allocation: Controlled Agendas and the Status Quo', *Public Choice*, 33, 4, pp. 27–43.

Sandford, C. T. and Robinson, A. (1975) 'Public Spending', *The Banker*, 125, pp. 1241–56.

Sen, A. K. (1983) 'Development: Which Way Now?', *Economic Journal*, 93, 372, pp. 745–63.

Tarschys, D. (1975) 'The Growth of Public Expenditures', *Scandinavian Political Studies*, 10, pp. 9–13.

Thompson, G. (1979) *The Growth of the Government Sector.* Milton Keynes: Open University Press.

Wagner, A. (1958) 'Three Extracts on Public Finance', in R. A. Musgrave and A. T. Peacock (eds.), *Classics in the Theory of Public Finance.* London: Macmillan.

Wagner, R. E. (1976) 'Revenue Structure, Fiscal Illusion and Budgetary Choice', *Public Choice*, 25, pp. 45–61.

West, E. G. (1991) 'Secular Cost Changes and the Size of Government: Towards a Generalized Theory', *Journal of Public Economics*, 45, 3, pp. 363–81.

Wildavsky, A. (1964) *The Politics of the Budgetary Process.* Boston: Little, Brown.

Wildavsky, A. (1975) *Budgeting: A Comparative Theory of Budgetary Processes.* Boston: Little, Brown.

Wiseman, J. (1980) 'The Choice of Optimal Social Expenditures', pp. 249–61 in K. Roskamp (ed.), *Public Choice and Public Finance.* Paris: Editions Cujas.

Wittman, D. (1989) 'Why Democracies Produce Efficient Results', *Journal of Political Economy*, 97, 6, pp. 1395–424.

Wolf, C. Jr. (1979) 'A Theory of Non-market Behaviour: Framework for Implementation Analysis', *Journal of Law and Economics*, 22, 1, pp. 107–40.

Wolf, C. Jr. (1987) 'Market and Non-market Failures: Comparison and Assessment', *Journal of Public Policy*, 7, 1, pp. 43–70.

15 'Normative' optimal taxation

15.1 Introduction

In chapter 7 the concept of the 'excess burden' of taxation was introduced and explored. It was noted that taxes might be ranked according to their resource allocation costs. For example, a selective excise tax on any good that is price-inelastic in demand, other things equal, will have a lower excess burden than a selective excise tax on a good that is price-elastic in demand. Similarly, an income tax would be expected to generate a lower excess burden if the compensated supply curve of labour were inelastic. General consumption taxes may create a lower excess burden than would a plethora of narrow-based discriminatory taxes randomly set so as to raise the same total tax revenue.

While these facts are important, it should be emphasized that traditional public finance is not only concerned with the goal of resource allocation. In an important work that set out the objectives of policy, Musgrave (1959) outlined a number of alternative goals that are relevant within traditional public finance. Musgrave (1959, 1989) develops the much followed three functions of the public household, namely allocation, distribution and stabilization. The distinctions he makes are justified 'as a framework, designed to draw attention to the distinct goals involved and, following the insight thus gained, to take feasible steps towards avoiding conflict and a more efficient fiscal process' (Musgrave 1989, p. 6). The importance of this division then is that, if fiscal policy is designed for revenue-raising or allocative purposes (or, indeed, for stabilization purposes), it must also be concerned with income distribution. While taxes on goods that are price-inelastic in demand create a lower excess burden than equal-rate taxes on goods that are price-elastic in demand, such taxes often prove highly regressive. If, for example, the range of price-inelastic goods

includes food, the poor will be hardest hit by this tax, because they spend a greater proportion of their income on food. In chapter 7 it was demonstrated that a lump-sum tax does not create an excess burden. However, such taxes (e.g. a poll tax) are paid at the same rate irrespective of income, and therefore are likely to be far more regressive than taxes that are linked to income. A central theme of the traditional approach to public finance is that there is a trade-off between the effect that taxes (and subsidies) have on different objectives. That a tax performs less well in terms of resource allocation (or efficiency) considerations may be more than compensated for if it performs well in terms of equity considerations.

In this chapter the first question to be addressed is, How should taxes be set so as to minimize efficiency losses? A first analysis of the literature on optimal commodity taxation highlights the difficulties of achieving this objective when leisure, as one of the goods that individuals consume, is not taxable. Later in this chapter the attention turns to the need to attain a desired income distribution while still minimizing welfare losses. The trade-off between equity and efficiency loss is at the heart of the quest for what has become known as 'optimal taxation'.

The implications for this 'normative' issue of optimal taxation, which stem from the public choice literature, are explored in a final critique of the optimal taxation literature. However, it should be noted that a completely different interpretation of the concept of 'optimal taxation' can be based on the approach of public choice scholars, and this is examined in chapter 16. In that chapter optimum taxation is based not on what is 'best' for the community but, rather, on what is best for actors in the political process and on how a tax system can constrain the self-seeking behaviour of those who get to design it.

15.2 Optimal commodity taxes

Assume that a government wishes to raise a sum of revenue. The sum required is a fixed amount of revenue R, and the revenue is to be raised by the taxation of commodities. As already demonstrated, in principle, a lump-sum tax will not affect consumers' decisions and will, therefore, avoid deadweight losses. Why then are lump-sum taxes not used more generally to raise tax revenue?

Lump-sum taxes (such as a poll tax) are a useful *theoretical* ploy for economists. However, in practice it is difficult to establish a tax that might have no effect at all on any individual behaviour. (For example, even a poll tax may affect the choice of family size under certain conditions.) Moreover, as already noted, lump-sum taxes may be deemed highly regressive. Heady argues:

In principle, this distributional disadvantage of lump-sum taxes could be avoided by setting lump-sum taxes that differed between individuals in such a way that the wealthy paid higher taxes. However, if such a scheme is to be truly non-distortionary it cannot be based on actual income, only on potential income, and this involves the impossible task of measuring people's potential income (a task which is made even more difficult by the fact that it would be each person's self-interest to understate his or her earning ability).[1] (Heady 1988, p. 187)

For such reasons as these, we begin by ruling out the lump-sum tax alternative. To begin, tax revenue will depend on taxes that are to be levied on commodities. However, in the first case discussed, it will be shown that commodity taxes can be made to work like a lump-sum tax provided that leisure is taxable.

15.2.1 Optimal commodity taxes: leisure taxable

A basic starting-point is to consider the introduction of the need for government revenue R in an otherwise two-good world (one of which is leisure L and the other is labelled X). If the government is to raise the revenue in this context the prices of the goods (P_1 and P_x must be raised above their initial marginal cost levels (MC_1 and MC_x). To make the issues concrete, assume that the resource constraint is 20 hours of potential leisure, whose initial marginal cost price is unity. It is possible to convert leisure into good X at a rate of 2 units of leisure for 1 unit of X; i.e. $MC_x = 2$.

[1] Hence the interest in truth-revealing mechanisms which have been met above in chapter 3 on public goods.

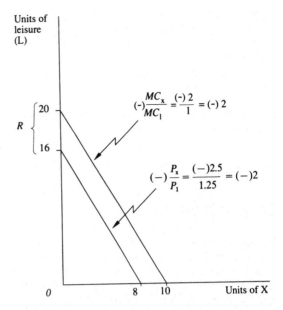

Figure 15.1 Optimal commodity taxation: leisure taxable.

These assumptions determine the location of the budget constraint (20–10) in Fig. 15.1. The overall budget constraint is

$$(15.1) \qquad I = MC_1 L + MC_x X$$

where I is 'total income' and the other terms are as indicated above.

The question is, How should government increase the prices of the goods to raise the (assumed) necessary revenue of 4 units of leisure? While nothing can be done to offset this direct burden, it is possible to minimize the indirect or excess burden. If the government raises the prices of each good above its marginal cost by an equiproportional rate determined as

$$(15.2) \qquad \frac{P}{MC} = \frac{I}{I - R} = \frac{20}{20 - 4} = 1.25$$

with the new price ratio implied by a 25 per cent tax rate, it is possible to choose between $20/1.25 = 16$ units of leisure or $10/1.25 = 8$ units of good X; i.e. household resources fall. In the figure, such a policy of equiproportional taxation involves a parallel shift inwards in the budget constraint, leaving price ratios unchanged. In the construction it does not matter where the indifference curve tangency with the two budget constraints is met. There is no excess burden in this special case because no marginal equivalence is affected. There has in effect been a lump-sum reduction in the value of time endowment by 20 per cent. Layard and Walters (1978) evaluate this point.

As long as leisure is taxable, then, there are grounds for choosing *equiproportional taxation* of all commodities if the objective is to minimize excess burden. The problem is that in practice leisure is non-taxable. It is extremely difficult to measure leisure time accurately as a basis for tax.

15.2.2 Optimal commodity taxation: leisure non-taxable

If leisure is not taxable there remains a solution. Remember that the objective is still to minimize the overall excess burden of collecting tax revenues. However, the context is a 'second-best' one, so that, with the inability to tax leisure, it may not be desirable to tax all other goods equiproportionally.

The Ramsey Rule

[A] small uniform intensification of the optimal taxes (that increase all taxes by the same proportion) will produce equal proportionate reductions in demand for all goods if the consumer is compensated to stay on the same indifference curve. (Heady 1988, p. 212)

It can be shown that, in certain quite specific circumstances, this result is attained when tax rates are set inversely proportional to the price elasticity of demand. How can this be proved?

Following Rosen (1988), assume there are two goods X and Y. In order to determine that tax rates should be set inversely proportional to price elasticity, it is important to stress at the outset that there are no cross-effects between these goods. This means that the goods are assumed to be unrelated—neither substitutes nor complements. That is, $\partial X/\partial P_y = 0$ and $\partial Y/\partial P_x = 0$ (the so-called 'independents').

In chapter 7 we derived the Harberger (1964) formula and showed that the excess burden of a selective excise tax on a commodity X would be

$$(15.3) \qquad EB_x = \frac{1}{2} e_x P_x X t_x^2$$

where e_x = price elasticity of the compensated
demand for good X
P_x = price of good X
X = quantity of the good X consumed
t_x = the rate of tax on good X

Therefore, it follows that the excess burden on commodity Y would be

$$(15.4) \qquad EB_y = \frac{1}{2} e_y P_y Y t_y^2$$

Assume, once again, that the total revenue to be raised is R. Total revenue is equal, by definition, to the tax raised on good X (i.e. $P_x X t_x$) and the tax raised on

good Y (i.e. $P_y Y t_y$). For any tax revenue raised, we wish to minimize the sum of $\frac{1}{2} e_x P_x X t_x^2$ and $\frac{1}{2} e_y P_y Y t_y^2$ and at the same time to satisfy the constraint that R is raised. More formally, we seek to

$$(15.5) \qquad \min \left(\frac{1}{2} e_x P_x X t_x^2 + \frac{1}{2} e_y P_y Y t_y^2 \right)$$

subject to

$$(15.6) \qquad R = P_x X t_x + P_y Y t_y$$

so that, forming the Lagrangean expression

$$(15.7) \qquad \begin{aligned} L &= \frac{1}{2} e_x P_x X t_x^2 + \frac{1}{2} e_y P_y Y t_y^2 \\ &\quad + \lambda (R - P_x X t_x - P_y Y t_y), \end{aligned}$$

$$(15.8) \qquad \partial L/\partial t_x = e_x P_x X t_x - \lambda P_x X = 0$$

$$(15.9) \qquad \partial L/\partial t_y = e_y P_y Y t_y - \lambda P_y Y = 0$$

so that (to minimize excess burden)

$$(15.10) \qquad t_x/t_y = e_y/e_x$$

This result is known as the *inverse elasticity rule*. It tells us that, to minimize the excess burden, tax rates should be set inversely proportional to price elasticities of the goods, and it satisfies the Ramsey rule as described above (Ramsey 1927).

To minimize total excess burden, it should be noted that excess burden is a consequence of distortions in quantities. Therefore, the proportional reduction in X should be equal to the proportional reduction in Y, and this is what the Ramsey rule implies. We have shown that the Ramsey rule implies that $t_x e_x = t_y e_y$. As t_x and t_y are the percentage increases in the prices of the two goods, then

$$(15.11) \qquad t_x \frac{(dq_x/q_x)}{t_x} = t_y \frac{(dq_y/q_y)}{t_y}$$

so that it is necessary that

$$(15.12) \qquad dq_x/q_x = dq_y/q_y$$

To consider further the rationale for this expression, in Fig. 15.2 we illustrate the demand curves for two products X and Y which (as noted in chapter 7) are income-compensated. Following Hyman (1987) and Rosen (1988), this implies that the excess burden associated with taxes t_x and t_y on the two goods X and Y increases as the price elasticity of demand increases. Therefore, a tax on X is optimal if it makes the proportional reduction in demand for good X equal to the proportional reduction in demand for good Y created by the tax on Y. To put the same tax rate on the two goods irrespective of price elasticity of demand would be a mistake, as can be shown in the figure. Revenue could be raised from taxing

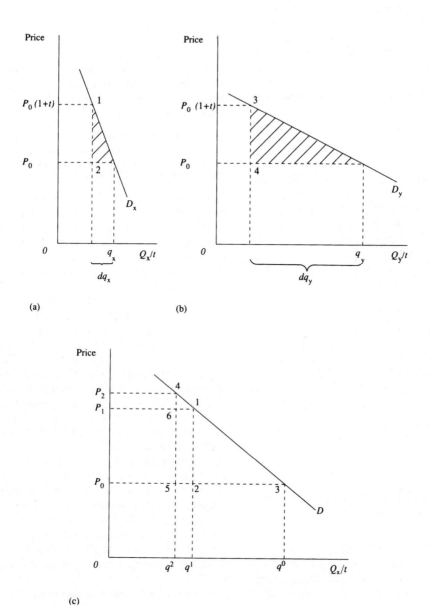

Figure 15.2 Comparing excess burden.

Source: based on Rosen (1988) and Heady (1988)

good X with a consequent smaller cost in terms of excess burden. As things stand, the same tax revenue is raised from the tax on X as from the tax on Y $(P_0 - P_0(1 + t)12 = P_0 - P_0(1 + t)34)$. However, the efficiency costs in raising revenue from the tax on X is the shaded triangle in part (a) of the figure,

and this is less than the shaded triangle in part (b). It makes sense therefore to put the higher tax rate on the good with the lower price elasticity of demand.

While this exposition emphasizes the need to consider welfare costs across different products, it can be noted that, when setting the tax rates, the analysis must be carried out in terms of equalizing the *marginal* excess burden per unit of revenue raised on different products. Using a partial equilibrium approach, Heady (1988) derives the optimal commodity tax explicitly in this way. In Fig. 15.2(c) the income-compensated demand for good X is illustrated. A commodity tax raises price from P_0 to P_1 and indeed we can assume that $(P_1 - P_0)$ is the same fraction of P_0 for all goods. Let

(15.13) $(P_1 - P_0) = zP_1$

If the tax is increased, so that price rises to P_2, excess burden will increase by area 4125. For a very small tax change this approximates to zP_1 (i.e. distance P_1P_2) multiplied by $(dQ/dP)dP$ (i.e. distance 52). This latter distance is the change in quantity resulting from the increase in price caused by the increase in tax. (The remaining triangle 461 approximates to zero.) Additional excess burden is then

(15.14) $zP_1(-dQ/dP)dP$

or

(15.15) $ze\,dPQ$

where e = price elasticity of demand.

Extra revenue raised from the tax increase is the difference between the area P_1P_246 (the additional revenue on remaining quantity sold) and 6125 (the lost revenue on the quantity that is no longer purchased as a result of the tax). This extra revenue can be written as

(15.16) $dPQ - zP_1(-dQ/dP)dP$

or

(15.17) $(1 - ze)dPQ$

so that the increase in excess burden per unit of revenue raised is the ratio of (15.15) to (15.17), i.e.

(15.18) $\dfrac{ze}{1 - ze}$

which is smaller for goods with a lower price elasticity. Therefore, starting from a position of uniform taxation, it is appropriate to increase tax on goods with a low price elasticity of demand and to lower tax rates on goods with a high price elasticity. Total revenue would thereby be maintained but total excess burden would be reduced. If we wish to equalize the excess burden per unit of revenue raised for all goods, then we require that

(15.19) $z_ie_i/(1 - z_ie_i) = k$ for all i

where k is a constant and the subscript i ties the values of z and e to each good i. Therefore, when this condition holds

(15.20) $z_i = k/[e_i(1 + k)]$ for all i

and

(15.21) $z_ie_i = k/(1 + k)$ for all i

As e refers to the income-compensated price elasticity of demand for a linear demand curve, this equation tells us that the proportional increase in demand that follows the removal of the optimal commodity taxes will be the same for all goods.

The Corlett and Hague rule

Goods which are complementary to leisure should be taxed more heavily than goods which are substitutes for leisure. (Brown and Jackson 1986, p. 341)

From Corlett and Hague (1953), it can be argued that, in a situation of one consumer and two consumption goods (as discussed above), revenue can be increased most efficiently by taxing more heavily the good that is more complementary (or less substitutable) with leisure. Following Heady (1987), it is possible to capture something of the intuition that lies behind a rule that would tax complements to leisure at a higher rate.

It is usual to consider the impact of income tax on labour supply, but here leisure is seen as one of the goods enjoyed by individuals and commodity taxation is shown to affect the supply of labour. In Fig. 15.3(a) the importance of the supply of labour to the determination of the optimal commodity tax is considered. On the vertical axis the output of a good is shown and on the horizontal axis an individual's input of labour is measured. Initially the dotted line *OPF* shows how the individual can transform labour input into output: it is the production possibility curve for this individual. If a commodity tax is to be introduced that raises R, then, when the utility-maximizing individual adjusts to it, the after-tax budget constraint looks like *OB* and the relevant equilibrium is point 1. Here I_0 is tangent to the after-tax trade-off *OB* and labour input is OL_1, total output is OGY_1, revenue is R and post-tax output for the individual is ONY_1.

There is a distortion created by this tax, as is evident by comparison with the use of a lump-sum tax. The lump-sum tax can raise the same revenue R without changing the slope of the production possibility curve (as with B', parallel to PF). In this case the optimum position for the individual is point 2 on I_1 (where L_{opt} units of labour are supplied and output of commodities is GY_{opt}). For the individual, post-tax output is NY_{opt}. Therefore, with a non-distortionary tax the optimum would be one where the consumer supplies *more* input and consumes more output. Heady (1987, p. 254) therefore argues that, by reference to the ori-

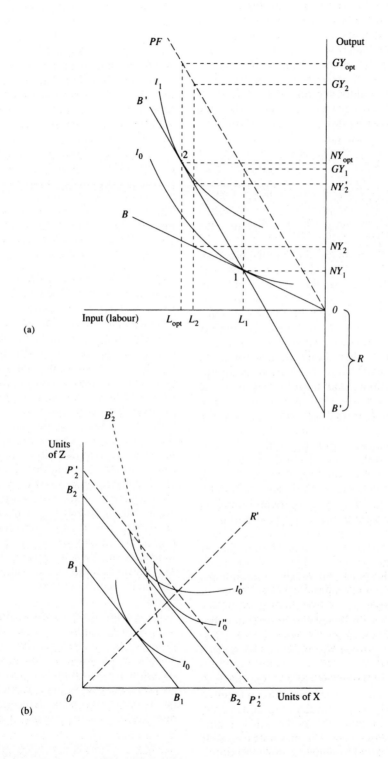

Figure 15.3 Optimal commodity taxation and labour supply.

ginal point 1, whether or not the equilibrium is at welfare maximum 'can be viewed as part of a question of whether it is possible to induce the consumer to supply more input (such as L_2) and thus participate more in the market economy...' (producing GY_2).

The output axis can be taken to represent the aggregate of two goods (valued at producer prices) as long as the two goods are equally taxed. In this case, tax revenue would be independent of the proportion the consumer spent on each good. If there is equal taxation, the question is whether the tax rates can be altered so as to induce the consumer to participate in supplying greater output. It is clear from part (a) of the figure that output, at GY_2, is more than enough to keep the individual on indifference curve I_0 (as well as raising the necessary revenue R), but that after tax rewards NY_2 are not sufficient.

In part (b) of the figure the indifference map between the two goods X and Z is illustrated. The initial equilibrium is on I_0, where a total of $B_1 (= NY_1)$ units are available. The line B_2 represents consumption possibilities available to the individual if L_2 units of labour were supplied (i.e. when after-tax consumption is NY_2). Of course, if L_2 units were supplied, the individual would actually produce GY_2. How much would the individual require to supply L_2 units of labour and keep on I_0 in part (a)? Obviously, it would be more than NY_2 but less than NY_2', the output generated net of the tax revenue constraint R. In part (b), the indifference curve I_0 tells us the amount of the goods that the individual would require in order to hold her welfare constant if L_2 units of labour were supplied. Note then that the welfare of the individual is *exactly the same* on I_0 and I_0' (and indeed on I_0''). This apparent paradox is resolved if it is recognized that there is a third good, leisure, so that I_0 and I_0' are different parts of a sphere of indifference. (See the treatment of second best in chapter 1.) On I_0' more goods are available for consumption than on I_0, but also more units of labour are supplied and hence less leisure is enjoyed. Obviously, the fact that B_2 is not tangent with I_0' explains why the individual remains at the initial equilibrium and does not choose to supply more units of labour. However, if B_2 were to intersect I_0', the individual would be induced to supply more labour.

A change in tax rates can be made to alter the slope of B_2 so as to intersect I_0'. The intersection is required to allow a higher level of utility than I_0 to be achieved. If the individual consumes the good in equal proportions, i.e. moving along OR', this may not be possible and therefore equal commodity taxation will be optimal. (That is to say, if the pattern of indifference

curves looks like I_0 and I_0'', equal commodity taxation may be recommended.) However, what if the pattern of indifference curves looks like I_0 and I_0'? Here, by increasing the tax on good X and decreasing the tax on good Z, the slope of the line B_2 could be altered so as to cut I_0', which means that the individual would be induced to supply more labour. The slope of B_2' illustrates this possibility.

From the particular shape of I_0', it is clear that Z is a good for which demand increases more when labour supply increases (whereas good X is a good whose demand increases less when labour supply increases). It is not unreasonable, then, to think of good X as being more complementary to leisure than good Z. The recommendation is to move from equal commodity taxation to greater taxation of the good more complementary to leisure. In this way the general rule of Corlett and Hague has been illustrated.[2]

The Ramsey rule reconsidered

Explicit in the above discussion of the Ramsey rule is the assumption that the goods are unrelated; that is to say, $\partial X / \partial P_y = 0$. Consider a tax on a good that has a price-elastic compensated demand. The large reduction in consumption of this good must be offset by a significant increase in consumption elsewhere. However, as the compensated demand curves for the consumption goods are independent ($\partial X / \partial P_y = 0$), the increase that occurs must be an increase in leisure sufficient to make up the balance. In prescribing that, for unrelated goods, the tax rate should be set inversely to price elasticity of demand, the Ramsey rule is, in effect, saying that the tax rate should be relatively lower on goods that are more substitutable with leisure (i.e. are price-elastic). Conversely, to argue that a relatively higher tax should be set on a good that is price-inelastic is to argue that a relatively higher tax should be set on a good that is less substitutable (more complementary) with leisure. This means that the Ramsey rule is a specific case of the more general analysis of Corlett and Hague (1953).

It is possible to relate the second-best rule, which suggests that commodity taxes should be inversely proportional to the elasticity of demand (higher where there is inelasticity for the good or service) to the influence of cross-price effects. In a world where leisure is not a taxable good, the argument is that those goods that are complements of leisure should be taxed more highly. But how can this be achieved when ele-

---

[2] Equal commodity taxation remains optimal when the shape of the indifference curves take the shape shown by I_0'', and here an equal proportionate tax rule must be satisfied.

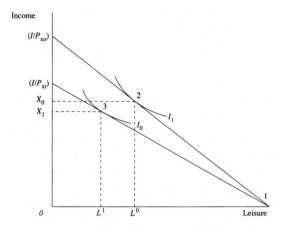

Figure 15.4 Inelasticity and complementarity.

ments of complementarity and substitutability have been assumed away above?

Figure 15.4 offers an intuitive appreciation of the response. The x axis measures leisure and the y axis income, expressed in terms of units of good X, a gross complement of leisure (i.e. it is individual income I divided by P_x). At the initial budget constraint shown by $1 - I/P_{x0}$ the individual finds equilibrium at point 2 with L^0 leisure and X_0 unit of good X. If a tax is now imposed on good X, price rises to $P_{xt}(> P_{x0})$ and the budget constraint swivels, with the individual finding equilibrium at point 3. If the demand for good X is price-inelastic more will be spent on it, even though the quantity of X chosen has fallen from X_0 to X_1. Now if there are no price cross-effects (complementarity and substitutability), spending on all other goods must remain unchanged. To allow spending on good X to rise, leisure must be sacrificed ($L^0 L^1$). Hence, with zero cross-effects, a good like X, whose demand is inelastic, acts like a gross complement of leisure, and the 'inverse elasticities' rule amounts to taxing the complements of leisure more highly.

The Ramsey rule makes no explicit allowance for income distribution but optimal tax literature attempts to include both equity and efficiency considerations. Diamond and Mirrlees (1971) demonstrate that distributional considerations alter the equal proportional reductions rule substantially. In particular, they show that it is optimal that goods consumed particularly heavily by the poor should experience a lower than average proportional reduction. The amendment to the Ramsey rule (i.e. equal proportional reductions demand as a consequence of taxation) depends on the level of concern for the poor

and differences in consumption patterns between rich and poor. In the case of 'independent' goods, Diamond and Mirrlees show that the optimal tax rate on a good depends both on the inverse of its price elasticity of demand and on its income elasticity (which reflects how the individual's budget share of a good changes as income rises). Many goods with low price elasticities also have low-income elasticities (such goods are regarded as necessities; they are not very responsive to changes in either price or income). For such goods, efficiency arguments (in favour of high tax rates) must be balanced against distributional arguments (in favour of low taxation) and the question arises as to whether differential taxation really is appropriate.

Atkinson and Stiglitz (1980) argue that, when there are normal goods (goods which are consumed in larger quantities as individuals have higher income), the poor benefits from an increase in uniform payment more than from a policy which used an equivalent sum of money to reduce the sales tax on a particular good (as the reduction in sales taxes would benefit the rich more because they buy more of the good). In the analysis, the uniform payment deals with redistribution and, if this is set optimally, the issue of whether or not to use differential sales taxes becomes one of efficiency. If a uniform payment is set optimally and if there is weak separability between goods and leisure,[3] uniform taxation is optimal.

When applying Atkinson and Stiglitz's result for a country such as the UK it must be noted that their analysis ignores differences in preferences between households (differences that might arise, for example, from different demographic characteristics). Heady (1993) argues that if these differences are especially significant there is an argument in favour of VAT zero rating for some goods; such goods form a large part of the budget of particular demographic groups. Zero rating of food and children's clothing is defended by the observation that poor families with large numbers of children spend a high proportion of their budgets on these items. Deaton and Stern (1986) consider Atkinson and Stiglitz's result when the economy has different demographic groups. They show that uniform taxation is desirable if preferences are weakly separable and if households in each demographic

---

[3] A utility function that is weakly separable between goods and leisure can be written as

(15.1n) $U = U(L, C(X_1 \ldots \ldots X_4, \ldots X_n)$

where L = leisure
   $C(\cdot)$ = a function of the X_i
   X_i = the consumption of the ith good.

group receive an optimally chosen government transfer (uniform within each group). The argument is that redistribution between groups is accomplished most efficiently by the use of direct payments to households (and the sales tax is left to deal with the problem of efficiency). Ebrahimi and Heady (1988) use a numerical analysis to consider whether it would be better to abolish zero rating of food and use the additional fund to finance an increase in child benefit. Their analysis highlights the difficulties of determining the child benefit but they conclude that, to achieve distributional goals, direct payments are more effective than non-uniform sales taxes.

15.3 Optimal linear income tax

If the government wishes to make income transfers from the rich to the poor, one means of transfer is via a negative income tax (see chapter 9). In its simplest form, a negative income tax system would comprise a lump-sum payment made to everybody, and thereafter a tax levied on all other income. (See Meade (1978) for a discussion of such arrangements.) It is claimed that a negative income tax is efficient, and it has been possible to incorporate this tax arrangement into the literature on optimal taxation. Here, the arrangement is reflected in the tax schedule under consideration. In Fig. 15.5 a linear income tax sche-

dule is illustrated which implies a lump-sum transfer (negative tax handout of $-a$) and, thereafter, a constant rate of tax on income. Tax revenues are a function of a constant $(-a)$ and the marginal rate of tax t:

$$(15.22) \qquad \text{tax revenues} = -a + tY$$

The value of $-a$ corresponds to the lump-sum payment that a government would make to individuals with zero income. However, as income increases the tax payments increase at constant rate t. The slope of this function is labelled t in the figure and the schedule is linear, showing that t is always constant irrespective of income level. Point b would be a break-even point: at this point the taxpayer would pay in tax an amount equal to the lump-sum payment already received.

The objective in this section is to consider how the values for t and for a should be set. To determine the optimal linear income tax, it is necessary to minimize the excess burden associated with achieving a desired redistribution of income. How much redistribution is required depends on the nature of the social welfare function. One social welfare function might be a 'utilitarian' social welfare function:

$$(15.23) \qquad \text{Social welfare} = \Sigma u^h$$

where u^h is the utility of individual h.

However, this social welfare function takes no account of income distribution which is the focus of attention here. So to amend the function to allow for income distribution one formulation (see chapter 1) is:

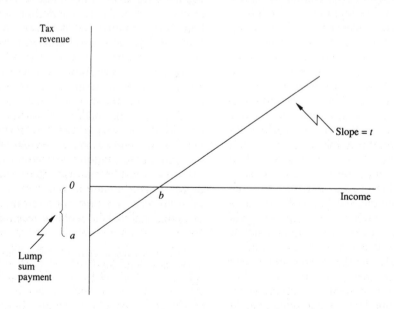

Figure 15.5 Linear income tax.

(15.24) social welfare $= \dfrac{1}{1-e}\Sigma(u^h)^{1-e}$ for $e \neq 1$

If $e = 0$ this expression is the same as (15.23) but if e is positive, increases in u^h are transformed into less than proportional increases of:

(15.25) $$\frac{1}{1-e}(u^h)^{1-e}$$

i.e. less weight is attached to a given absolute increase of utility to somebody with a high utility than to somebody with a low utility. This social welfare function demonstrates a preference for equalizing utility and the strength of this preference for equalizing utility increases with the value of e. When e approaches infinity, the degree of preference for equality becomes very strong, so that only the utility level of the worst off household has any weight in the social welfare function (i.e. the social welfare function proposed by Rawls 1971).

Optimal tax depends on the gains in social welfare from redistributing income and the costs associated with taxation. The cost of income redistribution is the effect that the tax has on the supply of labour. The higher the marginal rate of tax, the greater the deadweight losses created in the labour market. The problem then is to determine a tax schedule which minimizes these costs for any income distribution objective. While the optimal income tax literature is quite technical, it is possible to utilize a simple illustration so as to highlight those factors which are important in determining an optimal rate of taxation. In the following example we follow: Collard (1978), Brown, (1983), and Brown and Jackson (1986).

Individual A is assumed to be more 'able' than individual B, so that A's wage rate w^a exceeds that of B, w^b. In Fig. 15.6(a) the wage rate w^a determines the slope of the budget line 12. Individual A is at an initial equilibrium E_A^1. At this point she has chosen that combination of leisure and work that would maximize her utility, given the constraint shown by 12. By comparison, in part (b) a wage rate of only w^b for individual B means that the budget line 34 is not so steep. Individual B is at an equilibrium at point E_B^1. For simplicity of exposition, we assume that there are only two individuals and that their tastes or preferences are identical. The difference in the two equilibria of indifference curves in parts (a) and (b) of the figure relate only to the fact that the two individuals are at different income levels.

Starting from this initial situation, the objective is to determine a linear income tax that will minimize efficiency losses and lead to the 'best' distribution of income. In the analysis it is assumed that the government has no other revenue objective; i.e., the revenue is required only for redistribution. The objective then is to find a tax structure (which incorporates the negative income tax format) and to raise sufficient revenue for redistribution to maximize a social welfare function and minimize efficiency losses in the labour market.

In Fig. 15.6 we illustrate one example of a specific linear income tax with a marginal rate of tax t and a lump-sum transfer LT. The particular marginal rate is shown as $t = 25/02$ (in part (a)) $= 46/04$ (in part (b)), for the effect of the income tax is to alter the slope of the budget line to the same extent for both individuals. With this tax rate, the new equilibrium for A would be E_A^2 and for B, E_B^2. However, the tax proceeds are redistributed to each party via a lump-sum transfer shown as LT. Therefore, after the transfer the individual's relevant budget line moves out to the right in both cases. For individual A it is 78 and for individual B it is 9–10. The result is that the new equilibrium for individual A, accounting for the tax on income and the lump-sum transfer, is E_A^3, and for B it is E_B^3.

It is evident that individual A is a net payer of tax. Her income *before tax* is BTY^a and *after* both tax and transfer is ATY^a. By comparison, individual B is a net recipient from this tax-transfer arrangement, his before-tax income of BTY^b being less than his after-tax income of ATY^b. The marginal rate of tax is equal for the two individuals and the lump-sum payment is also fixed and equal, so that this corresponds to the description of the linear income tax shown in Fig. 15.5. The question remains, however, as to whether or not the redistribution generated by this linear income tax is deemed a 'good' or a 'bad' result.

In terms of a *Rawlsian* social welfare function (see chapter 9)—which focuses on increasing the welfare of the worse-off individual—it would be considered a 'good' result, as the welfare of the worse-off individual, B, has increased. However, as Brown and Jackson (1986) note, against a *Paretian* social welfare function—which required that welfare improve only if someone could be made better off and no one else be made worse off—this outcome would be unacceptable. If concern rests with maximizing total welfare, the acceptability of the outcome depends on whether A's loss of welfare is less than (or greater than) B's welfare gain. (And here, of course, there would be all the difficulties of measurement of welfare.)

In Fig. 15.6(c), where the utilities of the two individuals are shown on the two axes, it is clear that to maximize welfare a particular distribution of income is required in the post-tax position. Here the social

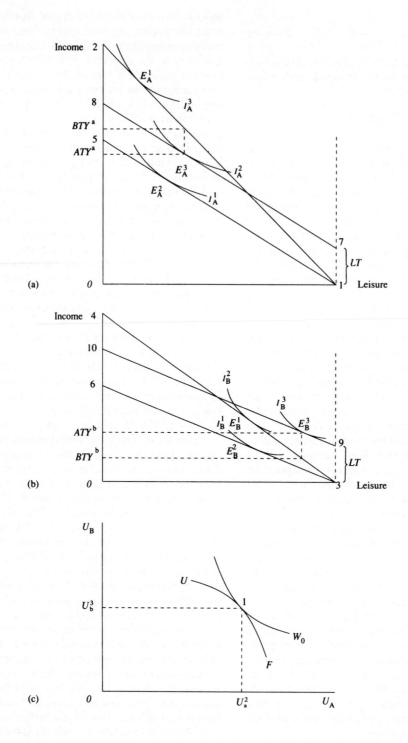

Figure 15.6 Optimal linear income tax.

Source: based on Collard (1978)

welfare function has been illustrated as W_0. The curve UF is a utility feasibility curve which maps those points that are available to the two individuals when there are alternative linear income tax schedules in operation. Obviously, those schedules that minimize deadweight losses will be depicted *on* the boundary of UF. Note that the boundary UF is not the same as the Pareto utility frontier described in chapter 1, because there it was supposed that lump-sum taxes with no efficiency losses were possible. In general, points on the line UF in Fig. 15.6(c) are likely to be nearer the origin, as an income tax rather than a lump-sum tax is being applied for redistributive purposes. (See Stiglitz (1988) for a discussion of such utility feasibility curves.) In part (c) the optimal marginal rate of tax will be that which enables the two individuals to enjoy a real income of U_a^2 and U_b^3 respectively (i.e. at tangency point 1).

Following Collard (1978), it is possible to integrate and review these considerations more closely by using a four-quadrant diagram. Essentially the same argument is repeated here, but a re-run may help to fit together the ingredients of the optimal tax approach. In quadrants III and IV of Fig. 15.7, parts (a) and (b) of Fig. 15.6 have been brought together, and they now stand on their sides, sharing the same common vertical axis for leisure. The horizontal axes at the base of the figure now measure income, and the length of the vertical axis for these lower quadrants is determined by the physical constraint of available time. The original budget lines are drawn as 12 and 34 respectively. Without repeating all of the above discussion, we begin here from the post-tax equilibria for the two individuals. These are shown as E_A^3 and E_B^3 respectively. (NB: the solution to this social welfare maximization approach has been kept the same in Fig. 15.7 as in 15.6 for simplicity. It is as if in 15.7 we happened to illustrate the 'optimal' case by chance.)

In order to compare the distribution of welfare that this position implies, it is helpful to cardinalize the utility enjoyed by the two individuals. Utility is measured in Fig. 15.7 in terms of the amount of income that each individual would require to be as well off as if he or she had no work whatsoever. This will be the point at which the indifference curve, which measures the after-tax and transfer welfare for each individual, cuts the horizontal utility axes drawn midway in the figure. Therefore, the horizontal axis midway measures in a cardinal way the utility of the two individuals.

In quadrant I a 45° line transfers estimates from the horizontal U_B axis to the vertical U_B axis, while in quadrant II the UF function defines the utility feas-

ibility curve for the individuals. If an efficient tax-transfer mechanism were applied, then this curve would demarcate the highest utility that could be experienced for any distribution of welfare between the individuals. Inside this feasibility curve, an 'inefficient' tax-transfer arrangement would be in operation.

In quadrant II W_0 is the relevant social welfare function, and it is clear that at the tangency point with UF the optimal linear tax is determined. Readers may now go back through the quadrants of this diagram to discover the value of the lump-sum transfer $(-a)$ and the value of the rate of tax t which determines the optimum outcome at the tangency E in quadrant II. The diagram tells us that, of all the 'efficient' (i.e. efficiency-loss-minimizing) tax-transfer arrangements, the one illustrated is preferred because it performs better in terms of equity considerations. In this way the questions of both efficiency and equity have been addressed. The optimal linear tax is one where $a = 17 = 39$ and $t = 25/02 = 46/04$.

From chapter 7 it should be evident that the elasticity of labour supply plays an important role in the determination of the optimal marginal income tax rate because this elasticity helps determine welfare losses. Stern (1976) calculates optimal (linear) tax rates using simulation analysis. As with much economic analysis, equity and efficiency put pressure in opposite directions. The equity coefficient e indicates that the higher its absolute value, the greater is the preference for equity and the higher is the required tax rate. An e value of zero indicates no preference for equality, whereas $e = \infty$ is the Rawlsian formulation of maximizing the position of the least well off. Potential efficiency loss is implied by the shape of the indifference map between income and labour captured in the elasticity of substitution. The preferences of all individuals are assumed common with a constant elasticity of substitution. (Different values of this constant are explored.) For example, a value of zero is the no-substitution case, whereas a value of 1 is the Cobb–Douglas case. The higher the elasticity value, the greater the efficiency costs associated with each tax rate; i.e. the less individuals will work at each tax rate. In addition, a certain amount of revenue (R) is required to cover the purchase of public sector goods and services in some of the simulations.

Fig. 15.8 captures these ideas. The higher the elasticity value, the lower is the t rate for any equity view incorporated in the e value. For any elasticity value, a higher t value is associated with a greater preference for equity.

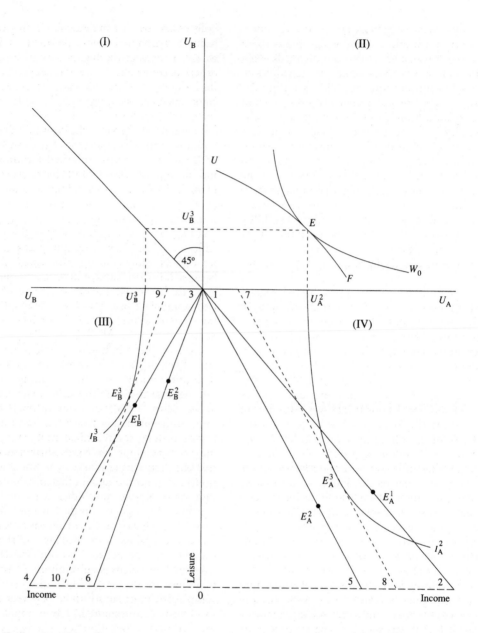

Figure 15.7 Finding an optimum linear tax.

One way in which this formulation of the optimal tax problem can be utilized can be seen by assessing the policy-maker's chosen e^* as the appropriate equity value; if he is advised that E^* is the best current empirical estimate of the elasticity of substitution, then the optimal linear income tax to promulgate is t^*. Another way to use the figure is to assume that the current tax system involves t^*, and, with E^* accepted, e^* could be presented to decision-takers to 'check' that

this is what they have in mind in their tax policy (Stern's own 'selection' at the time of writing the article was $R = 0.05$, $E^* = 0.4$, $e^* = 2$ implying $t^* = 0.54$). Stern is well aware of the limitations of his work and does not 'oversell' it. However, even if all the problems with producing a 'clean' version of Fig. 15.8 could be avoided, many would argue that the concept it addresses is far too restricted (see section 15.6 and chapter 16).

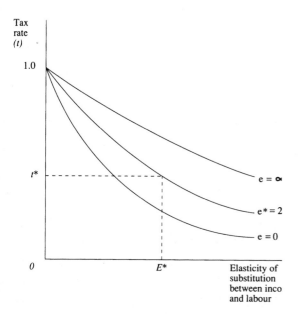

Tax
rate
(t)

1.0

t*

e = ∞

e* = 2

e = 0

0   E*   Elasticity of
                          substitution
                          between inco
                          and labour

Figure 15.8 Stern's 'trade-offs'.

15.4 Optimal nonlinear income tax

If the marginal rate of tax can vary with income, it may be usual to expect, from an 'ability to pay' argument, that the marginal rate of income tax 'should' increase as income increases (notwithstanding the limitations of such an argument—as discussed in chapter 1). Progressive income taxes, with the highest income-earner paying the highest marginal rate of tax, may appear 'fair' and 'appropriate'. If the argument is that individuals with higher levels of income 'should' pay a greater percentage of each additional pound earned, then it will be surprising that some of the results that emerge from the literature on optimal nonlinear taxation dissent from this conclusion. Instead, this literature can prescribe a tax function of quite a different character. For example, it has been argued that the individual with the highest income should be paying a rate of tax of zero on the last pound earned (Seade 1977). The objective of this section is to explain the rationale of this argument.

In the UK marginal rates of tax are high at the top levels of income and also at the lowest levels of income. At the bottom income levels the marginal tax rates in the UK are high (see chapter 9) because

individuals lose means-tested benefits when they begin to earn more income; in the extreme, the marginal rate of tax (including the loss of benefits) could conceivably exceed 1 and people could be caught in a 'strong poverty' trap, with no incentive to work for higher income. The design of a function that represented marginal rates of tax to income would, therefore, appear U-shaped, with high marginal rates at both the top and the bottom. By contrast, the prescriptions of optimal tax theory is that this should be altered and, indeed, should become an inverted U-shape. Referring to such prescriptions, Kay and King note:

The principles that emerge—that marginal tax rates should be low at both the highest and the lowest levels of income—contrast sharply with what most people have prevously believed (ourselved included). They also suggest a pattern different from that observed in the UK.... But the arguments that lie behind them are in fact rather familiar.... High marginal tax rates on the largest incomes bring in very little revenue, and are not worth pursuing if they have adverse consequences. Measures of support for low income families achieve rather less than nothing if their receipts are recouped by marginal rates of tax.... (Kay and King 1986, p. 214)

Such arguments weigh the welfare losses created by high marginal rates of tax against the potential gains in redistribution of tax revenue. To highlight this argument, it is helpful to focus on the top end of the income schedule. Here it can be demonstrated, for example, that the marginal rate of tax of the highest income-earner can be made zero (a) without a loss of tax revenue for redistribution to the poor, or (b) with an actual increase of tax revenue to redistribute to the poor. This means that the welfare of the top income-earner can either increase or be held constant with no necessary loss of welfare to others. In either of the circumstances described, there are no costs in terms of loss of revenue for redistribution to the poorer section of the community when the government elects to impose a zero marginal rate of tax for the top income-earner.

In Fig. 15.9(a) the budget line, 12, refers to the trade-off between leisure and income for the individual with the highest ability, i.e. in this context the individual who earns the highest wage rate. His net-of-tax budget line is shown by 13 (which, being curvilinear as illustrated, indicates that he is subject to higher marginal rates of tax at higher levels of income). The shape of the after-tax income schedule $1E_13$ reflects the assumption that there is a progressive income tax in operation. In this context, the individual maximizes utility at an equilibrium of E_1 on I_3,

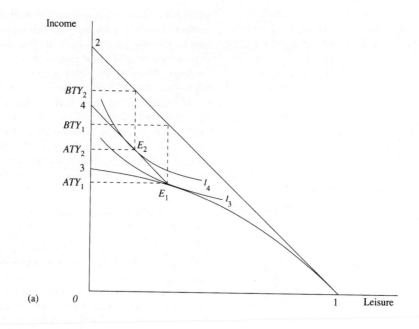

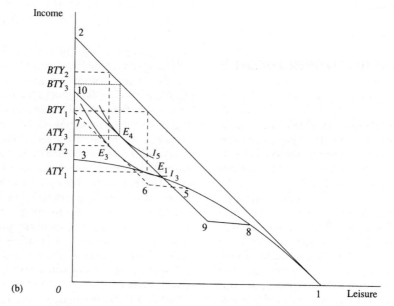

Figure 15.9 Optimal nonlinear income tax.

Source: based on Brown and Jackson (1986).

where the total amount of tax paid is the difference between his before-tax income BTY_1 and his after-tax income ATY_1. To demonstrate that a zero rate of tax might make this wage-earner better off, without at the same time reducing the total tax revenue for redistribution, set the marginal rate of tax to zero at the

before-tax income of BTY_1. This means that any income earned after point E_1 on the after-tax budget line is untaxed. Therefore, the net of tax budget line looks like $1E_14$. (In other words, after point E_1 the after-tax budget line, E_14, has the same slope as 12, reflecting the fact that the income tax rate is zero.) The new equilibrium allocation of hours for the wage-earner is E_2 on I_4, where he increases his work effort, giving up more hours of leisure and earning a higher before-tax income BTY_2. The total tax paid remains the same, i.e. $(BTY_2 - ATY_2) = (BTY_1 - ATY_1)$ (both represent the vertical distance between parallel lines 12 and $E_1 4$), but the individual is better off, with the higher after-tax income of ATY_2 being on I_4 as opposed to I_3. (In the same way, if the marginal rate of tax were positive it would still improve welfare if the slopes were steeper than $E_1 3$ but less steep than $E_1 4$.)

Alternatively, in Fig. 15.9(b) a tax function has been introduced which changes the net-of-tax budget line from $1E_1 3$ to 1567. This new after-tax budget line hits a point, 6, where the marginal rate of tax becomes zero. However, this tax arrangement leads the individual to a new equilibrium point E_3, where the total tax paid exceeds the amount previously paid but the taxpayer is no worse off. The amount of tax paid on the old schedule is $(BTY_1 - ATY_1)$ and this is less than the amount paid at E_3, i.e. $(BTY_2 - ATY_2)$. The individual, in moving from E_1 to E_3, has clearly held personal welfare constant, by remaining on the same indifference curve I_3. Therefore a tax function with a zero marginal rate at the top level of income can be introduced, so as to increase the total amount of tax available for redistribution without reducing the welfare of the top income-earner.

It almost goes without saying, however, that the marginal rate of zero must apply to the *top* income level. Suppose in Fig. 15.9(b) that the zero rate of tax was operative at a lower level of income. In this case the after tax budget line (now passing through a point below E_1) could look like 189–10. The *top* income-earner now shifts from point E_3 to point E_4 so as to maximize welfare on I_5. The result of this is that, as far as this individual is concerned, less tax is paid. Here it can be seen that $(BTY_3 - ATY_3) < (BTY_1 - ATY_1)$.

In these circumstances the top income earner pays less tax. But below the top income earner high-income earners could be induced to new equilibrium points where (compared to their original equilibria) they pay more tax. In certain cases total tax raised may still increase. However, a far more robust conclusion is that reducing the top income-earner's marginal income tax to zero would improve welfare with no necessary loss in revenue for redistribution.[4]

One aspect of the analysis so far is that, while it identifies the top wage-earner as paying a zero mar-ginal rate of tax, it has not provided information about what the tax schedule would look like at income levels up to the top level. Following Seade (1977) and Brown and Jackson (1986), consider Fig. 15.10, where the preference of a high (though not top) wage-earner is illustrated. If the high wage-earner had a zero marginal tax operative at her chosen equilibrium (EH_1), there would be a reallocation of hours so that EH_3 would be the new preferred equilibrium. In this case the after-tax wage schedule is such that there is a zero rate at the top income level (exactly that illustrated in Fig. 15.9(b) as 189–10) and the problem would be the loss of tax revenue from the top wage-earner who locates at E_4. If, however, there is a zero marginal tax rate for the *top* income-earner, then there can be some positive tax payment by other *high* wage-earners. If the high income-earner is to be at a point where she pays the same tax as in the original equilibrium position (EH_1) and the top earner is to achieve point E_2 in Fig. 15.9(a), then the tax schedule must be set so as to induce her to pick a tangency point along the stretch $EH_1 3$. The only way to do this (given that the indifference curves are convex to the origin and a zero or negative rate of tax is ruled out) is to ensure that the after-tax budget line is convex also. In this way it is possible that the individual may be led to a point such as EH_2, where the indifference curve is tangent to the after-tax budget line. However, for this to occur, it should be evident that the marginal rate of tax must be falling as income increases so as to make the after-tax budget line tangent to the indifference curve and thereby permit a tangency solution. The after-tax schedule should be convex, like $4E_2$, in the relevant range of Fig. 15.10 so as to ensure a tangency point with the individual's indifference curve I_2, whereby the same tax is paid although the marginal rate of tax is not zero. In Fig. 15.10 the top income earner has a zero marginal rate of income tax and hence is at equilibrium E_2 (see Fig. 15.8). The after-tax budget line for the high-income earner is $E_2 4$. It is clear then that, rather than increase with income, marginal rates of tax must fall as income increases over a range up to the *top* income earner.

Though these conclusions appear curious at first sight, it should be clear that they are necessarily implied by the attempt to attain a redistribution goal and minimize efficiency losses. Will they prove influential in altering the shape of the schedule of marginal rates of tax in the UK? Here we must note (as do Brown and Jackson 1986, and Heady 1988) that there are wider problems in modelling taxpayer behaviour, such as the problems of dealing with uncertainty, and the difficulty of dealing with variation in

---

[4] There are occasions when precise requirements of particular social welfare functions may make this appropriate, but these would be rather contrived.

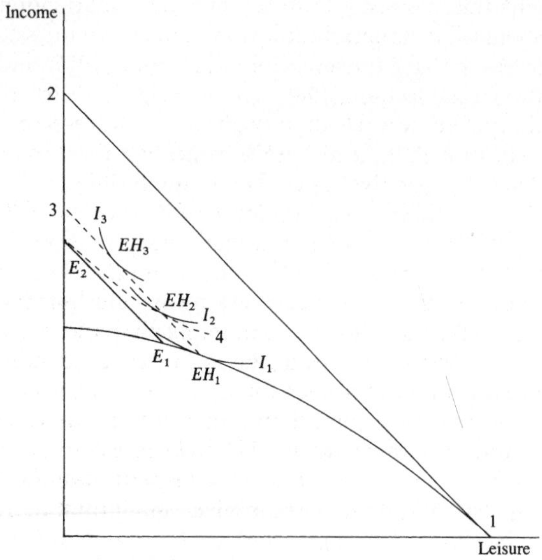

Figure 15.10 Marginal rate of tax from high-income individuals.

Source: based on Brown and Jackson (1986).

Table 15.1 'Optimal' tax assignments

Instruments	Targets	
	Equity	Efficiency
Direct taxation	B1	O1
	D	D
		B2
Indirect taxation	B2	B1

the income of particular individuals over their life-cycle. These considerations aside, optimal tax theory and its prescriptions will always be subject to the administrative and political constraints discussed in the final section of this chapter.

15.5 Optimal design of direct and indirect taxation

Atkinson (1977), in a key article on the design of taxation, first distinguishes between indirect taxation and direct taxation. He concludes that the difference is that direct taxation can be tailored to individual circumstances directly, whereas indirect taxation cannot be so tailored except in a very 'indirect' way through the consumption patterns of different income groups. For our purposes here, commodity tax (differentiated rates) is the indirect tax and income tax (varying marginal rates if required) is the direct tax. Atkinson sets the problem posed in the heading of this section in a targets-and-instruments assignment-type framework which is summarized in Table 15.1. The targets are equity and efficiency, whereas the instruments are indirect and direct taxation. Given the comment already made, it is not surprising that one set of authors has advocated a balance in the use of taxes,

with the assignments (B1–B1) as in the table. The equity case for direct taxes relies on its 'tailoring' characteristics, whereas the efficiency case for indirect taxes relies on the belief that they generate lower welfare costs, perhaps because of lower 'visibility' to the taxpayer.

The other view is the superiority of direct taxation (D) with respect to both targets (hence the D–D assignments in the table). Commodity taxation, on this view, is an unwanted legacy from an earlier 'less developed' stage in economic development when administration and other costs made direct taxes difficult to levy. (Note the large share of indirect taxes in tax revenue raised by today's developing economies.) How can these two views be evaluated? The point Atkinson makes is that the design of taxes is little understood in the absence of optimal tax theory, with the acid test being whether such theory can shed light.

Some of the conclusions the theory offers are as follows:

1. If individual's abilities (and hence wage rates) are identical, equity as a criterion ceases to be relevant and direct taxation (i.e. a poll tax, described as a linear income tax with a zero marginal tax rate) is superior to indirect taxation in minimizing welfare loss (assignment O1 in Table 15.1 with the O standing for the 'optimality' literature insight). This is the 'first best' case that needs modifying when the context changes.

2. If individuals are different, especially in terms of ability (and hence wages rates) as opposed to tastes (as was the case in the section above), then poll taxation should be used to raise revenue (on efficiency grounds) and commodity taxation should be used to achieve equity with higher tax rates on luxuries. This is the reverse assignment of B1–B1 in the table, represented as assignment B2–B2.

3. Consider now the context of a nonlinear environment (varying marginal tax rates). Here the relevant condition is weak separability (defined above) between labour and all goods. If this con-

dition applies, then assignment O1—direct taxation only—applies. However, weak separability may well not obtain, so, for example, leisure-activity goods and labour supply are likely to be connected. If this is so, the 'connected' goods should be taxed at a positive uniform rate. Again, there is a case for both types of tax.

Atkinson argues that these results, which are often counter-intuitive, are not derivable without the formal treatment of tax analysis, especially the weak separability condition. However, he is also quick to note that this optimal tax formulation involves only efficiency and vertical equity as the relevant criteria of optimal taxation and that there are other relevant desiderata if the perspective is widened. Sandmo (1976), for example, notes that the tax administrator might wish to minimize the resource costs to government of assessing and collecting taxes, whereas the man in the street might emphasize the fairness of the tax system at the expense of the economist's notion of efficiency. Although the optimal tax literature is complex, critics argue that it is not complex enough, in that it misses the issues raised below.

15.6 A critique of optimal taxation

Drawing, in particular, on Stiglitz (1988), Ricketts (1981) and Tollison (1987), a number of arguments can be presented as a critique of the underlying approach of optimal taxation.

15.6.1 Ethical problems

The focus of much of welfare economics and of optimal taxation is on equity, in terms of the attainment of particular *ends* (final, utility). However, it is arguable that justice requires us to look at *rules and processes*. A just society may apply as well to one in which individuals are satisfied with property rights as to one in which the focus is about the precise income distribution. Optimal tax regimes might conflict, for example, with the demands of liberals for a constraint of government. Rowley and Peacock (1975, p. 154), for example, are quoted as saying that 'what is required is a recognizable limit on the extent of coercive taxation that might be enshrined in a constitutional rule alterable only by a large majority preference and only then following extensive constitutional debate'. Readers will, by now, recognize that this approach to justice and equity is more in keeping with the *contractarian* approach of the public choice school.

15.6.2 Welfare problems

In optimal tax theory it is assumed that utility is a function of goods consumed and leisure time consumed. Is this a true proxy for the basis of human happiness? As qualifications to this assumption, the following should be noted.

1. Scitovsky (1976) makes the distinction between 'comfort' (depending on a level of consumption) and 'pleasure' (depending on changes in consumption). Might it be better to enjoy successive increases in utility than a constant high level of utility? Considerations of equity in the optimal tax literature may be considered too narrow if income *levels* are an inadequate basis to estimate welfare.

2. Hirsch (1977) and Goodin (1989) have been concerned with 'positional' goods; i.e. the value of goods comes not simply from their consumption, but from the knowledge that they cannot easily be consumed simultaneously by others. This aspect of the analysis of consumer behaviour is missed by the optimal taxation literature.

These arguments, then, are qualifications to the current state of optimal tax theory, and if they were incorporated into the theory they would make the solution of optimal tax rates far more complicated.

15.6.3 General equilibrium problems

Throughout the above analysis of optimal income taxes, it was assumed that there is no shifting of the income tax. Yet there are general equilibrium effects that should be taken into account. Salaries of managers and fees of professionals may be increased as a result of the imposition of high tax rates. For example, in the UK in the 1970s, Bacon and Eltis (1976) argued that increases in taxes (to finance welfare provision) caused wage demand increases.

Over time, there is likely to be adjustment to taxes that, under current arrangements, appear optimal.[5] For example, Stiglitz (1988) argues that, if there is a disincentive effect experienced by skilled labour, it is possible that investment in this sector may be reduced; in the long run, this may reduce the productivity of unskilled labour and reduce their wages.

[5] The follow-on effects of taxation in the long-run choices of workers is considered in chapter 16, where the analysis of Buchanan and Lee (1982) is considered.

15.6.4 Administrative problems

1. In the first instance, optimal tax theory causes difficulties for tax administrators. Calculation of optimal income tax rates requires administrators to have knowledge of utility levels, the distribution of skill levels, and so on. In this way the analysis poses problems as a practical guide to policy.

2. Moreover, if there are costs of administration, 'these should have a bearing on the choice of optimal tax and rate' (Tait 1989, p. 177). Often no allowance is made for the administrative costs of the exercise in optimal tax theory—administrators are assumed to have perfect costless administration in setting rates. Atkinson (1977) notes, with respect to the optimal tax mix question, that relative administrative costs of different tax types need to be incorporated.

While economic theory, in general, is often quite removed from the practical issues of policy, it should be noted that practical problems create some quite specific difficulties for optimal tax theory. Compliance costs have already been referred to in chapter 7. They are, for example, the costs that fall on individual taxpayers in filling in tax returns (see Sandford 1973). Equity considerations are of importance in an analysis of how these compliance costs are (and 'should' be) borne by different taxpayers. Some taxpayers will be able to afford professional accounting assistance, some will not. Access to tax advice and tax avoidance (see chapter 8) is not likely to be the same for all taxpayers, and, arguably, this should be allowed for in any consideration of equity. It is interesting to note, in this respect, that Sandford, Godwin and Hardwick (1989) view 'two-and-a-half' of Smith's four canon's of taxation as being concerned with compliance costs (see section 10.3 above).

15.6.5 Political problems

Following on from this discussion, it can be noted that there is an argument that simplicity of the tax system yields benefits not only in terms of administrative/compliance cost reduction but also in terms of taxpayer-voters being able to make more informed and 'better' choice in the political process. The public choice school stresses the value of tax simplicity (see, in particular, chapter 16). Tax simplicity may well be at variance with the requirements of nonlinear optimal tax theory and could militate against indirect taxation which is generally thought to be less visible.

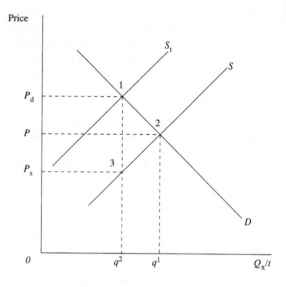

Figure 15.11 Rent-seeking and optimal taxation.

Source: based upon Tollison, R. D. 'Is the theory of rent seeking here to stay?' in C. K. Rowley (ed.), *Democracy and Public Choice*, Basil Blackwell, Oxford, 1987.

15.6.6 Rent-seeking problems

Based to a large extent on Tullock's (1967) paper, a literature on rent-seeking costs was discussed in Chapter 5. This literature disputes the argument that the losses of taxation are adequately captured in the welfare triangle losses described in chapter 7 and used here as the efficiency losses to be minimized in optimal taxation. In Fig. 15.11 an excise tax has been placed on good X. This causes the supply function to shift to the left, from S to S_t. The efficiency loss would be estimated as triangle 123. The area P_d13P_s is tax revenue. This transfer is split between the loss of consumer surplus (PP_d12), which is met by consumers, and the loss of producer surplus (P_sP23), which is met by producers. Public choice analysis argues that consumers are a large group and not easily mobilized; by contrast, producers, as a small group with strong vested interests, are politically mobile (see Olson 1971). It follows that, when producers expect to be successful, they will spend as much as $P23P_s$ to resist this excise tax which reduces producer surplus.[6] In this respect, they will spend resources for the purpose of 'rent protection' (Tollison 1987, p. 149), and this process reflects a real resource loss.

---

[6] For a discussion of the conditions in which rent-seeking costs are equal to the rent to be gained, see chapter 5.

Such additional welfare costs need to be considered when optimal taxation theory attempts to minimize efficiency loss. Tollison notes:

Now the traditional or optimal taxation analysis is in a little trouble. It is a mainstay of optimal taxation that the excess burden imposed by selective excise taxation (123) is minimized, for a given amount of revenue raised, when such taxes are placed on commodities with relatively inelastic demand curves. Unfortunately this optimal taxation rule cannot stand up to the above analysis. It is quite easy to show that, when $P23P_s$ is counted as part of the cost of excise taxation, taxing an industry with a more elastic demand curve, but no organized, rent-protecting opposition to the tax, is socially preferable. (Tollison 1987, p. 150)

The optimal commodity taxation rule, which sought to place higher tax rates on goods with a lower price elasticity of demand, may need modification when rent-seeking costs differ in different product markets.

These criticisms represent a formidable list of problems that confront those working in the field of optimal taxation. It would be a mistake, however, to believe that such researchers are not well aware of the many deficiencies. Results that emerge in optimal taxation literature are often sensitive to the values of elasticities of substitution that are assumed and the nature of the social welfare function that is pursued. Moreover, in practice, the information required is not always easy to extract, and this can introduce a bias by leading 'to the danger of econometrically convenient hypothesis being used' (Tait 1989, p. 174). Stern (1976, p. 162) noted that 'the study of optimum taxation is in its infancy... all our estimates and calculations must be viewed with circumspection and as attempts to understand the best model currently available rather than prescriptions for policy'. The value of this literature may be more in terms of forcing policy-makers to at least think explicitly about the elements (e.g. elasticities of substitution, marginal social utility of income) that affect tax policy. However, even on this score some observers remain sceptical. Tait for example comments:

Indeed, Atkinson (1977) suggests that it is precisely in producing counterintuitive results that the theory is useful (and that the only alternative is intuition). But how useful are striking counterintuitive results if they themselves require limiting and unlikely assumptions? Could it be possible that more intellectual and practical effort put into improving tax administration might do more for revenue security, equity and efficient macroeconomic management, then the more glamorous GEM [general equilibrium model] and optimality work? (Tait 1989, p. 179)

15.7 Summary

In this chapter fiscal theory has generated some conclusions that do not necessarily accord with intuition. To set a lower tax for higher-income individuals would hardly appear 'optimal' to the man in the street. However, there are perfectly good reasons for these results. For example, if the marginal tax rate is reduced for the richest man, we would reduce his disincentive to work. If, as a result, he increases his income, we may increase tax revenue, and the surplus available for redistribution to the poor will have been increased without necessarily making the richest individual any worse off.

While, in this way, it is possible to rationalize the conclusions that spring from optimal tax theory, there can be no question but that the theory has proceeded with little recognition of the informational and administrative problems that beset the implementation of tax policy. Inevitably, this limits both its policy attractiveness and its force, even for those wedded to a social optimality approach.

However, perhaps, as far as the public choice approach is concerned, it exemplifies, *par excellence*, some fundamental aspects of the traditional approach to public finance to which public choice scholars object. Concerned with mathematically solving constrained optimization equations of varying degrees of complexity, it ignores completely the processes through which decisions are made. Solutions are optimal only in the context of mathematical functions that are maximized in academic exercises. The solutions may not, simultaneously, be optimal for the actors involved in the policy-making process. If this is so, what importance can be attributed to optimal tax theory for policy? To explain policy decisions, it is necessary to explain what is in the interests of those who make policy. What is optimal for politicians, for example, and what constraints do they face? This opens the door to a different form of 'optimal tax' literature, and it is to these questions that we turn in chapter 16.

References

Atkinson, A. B. (1977) 'Optimal Taxation and the Direct versus Indirect Taxation Controversy', *Canadian Economic Review*, 10, 4, pp. 590–606.

Atkinson, A. B. and Stiglitz, J. E. (1976) 'The Design of Tax Structure: Direct versus Indirect Taxation', *Journal of Public Economics*, 6, 1, 2, pp. 55–75.

Atkinson, A. B. and Stiglitz, J. E. (1980) *Lectures on Public Economics*. London: McGraw–Hill.

Bacon, R. and Eltis, W. (1976) *Britain's Economic Problem: Too Few Producers*. London: Macmillan.

Brown, C. V. (1983) *Taxation and the Incentive to Work*, 2nd edn. Oxford: Oxford University Press.

Brown, C. V. and Jackson P. M. (1986) *Public Sector Economics*, 3rd edn. Oxford: Basil Blackwell.

Buchanan, J. M. and Lee, D. R. (1982) 'Tax Rates and Tax Revenues in Political Equilibrium', *Economic Inquiry*, 20, 3, pp. 344–54.

Collard, D. (1978) 'A Geometry of Optimal Linear Income Taxation'. Mimeo, University of Bath.

Corlett, W. J. and Hague, D. C. (1953) 'Complementarity and the Excess Burden of Taxation', *Review of Economic Studies*, 21, pp. 21–30.

Diamond, P. A. and Mirrlees, J. A. (1971) 'Optimal Taxation and Public Production: I and II', *American Economic Review*, 61, pp. 8–27 and 261–78.

Deaton, A. and Stern, N. (1986) 'Optimally Uniform Commodity Taxes, Taste Difference and Lump Sum Grants', *Economic Letters*, 20, pp. 263–6.

Ebrahimi, A. and Heady, C. J. (1988) 'Tax Design and Household Composition', *Economic Journal* Conference Papers, 98, 390, pp. 83–96.

Goodin, R. (1989) 'Relative Happiness'. Paper presented to the European Consortium for Political Research, Paris.

Harberger, A. C. (1962) 'The Incidence of the Corporation Income Tax', *Journal of Political Economy*, 70, pp. 215–40.

Harberger, A. C. (1964) 'The Measurement of Waste', *American Economic Review*, 54, 3, pp. 58–76.

Heady, C. (1987) 'A Diagrammatic Approach to Optimal Commodity Taxation', *Public Finance/Finances Publiques*, 42, 2, pp. 250–62.

Heady, C. (1988) 'The Structure of Income and Commodity Taxation', pp. 186–216 in P. G. Hare (ed.), *Surveys in Public Sector Economics*. Oxford: Basil Blackwell.

Heady, C. (1993) 'Optimal Taxation as a Guide to Tax Policy: A Survey', *Fiscal Studies*, 14, 1, pp. 15–41.

Hirsch, F. (1977) *Social Limits to Growth*. London: Routledge & Kegan Paul.

Hyman, D. N. (1987) *Public Finance: A Contemporary Application of Theory to Policy*, 2nd edn. Chicago: Dryden Press.

Kay, J. and King, M. (1986) *The British Tax System*, 4th edn. Oxford: Oxford University Press.

Layard, P. R. G. and Walters, A. A. (1978) *Microeconomic Theory*. New York: McGraw-Hill.

Musgrave, R. A. (1959) *The Theory of Public Finance*. New York: McGraw-Hill.

Musgrave, R. A. (1989) 'The Three Branches Revisited', *Atlantic Economic Journal*, 17, 1, pp. 1–7.

Olson, M. Jr. (1971) *The Logic of Collective Action: Public Goods and the Theory of Groups*. Cambridge, Mass.: Harvard University Press.

Ramsey, F. P. (1927) 'A Contribution to the Theory of Taxation', *Economic Journal*, 37, 145, pp. 47–61.

Ricketts, M. (1981) 'Tax Theory and Tax Policy', pp. 29–48 in A. Peacock and F. Forte, *The Political Economy of Taxation*. Oxford: Basil Blackwell.

Rosen, H. S. (1988) *Public Finance*, 2nd edn. Homewood, Ill.: Irwin.

Rowley, C. and Peacock, A. (1975) *Welfare Economics: A Liberal Restatement*. Oxford: Martin Robertson.

Sandford, C. T. (1973) *The Hidden Costs of Taxation*. London: Institute of Fiscal Studies.

Sandford, C. T., Godwin, M. R. and Hardwick, P. J. W. (1989) *Administration and Compliance Costs*. Bath: Fiscal Publications.

Sandmo, A. (1976) 'Optimal Taxation: An Introduction to the Literature', *Journal of Public Economics*, 6, 1, 2, pp. 37–54.

Scitovsky, T. (1976) *The Joyless Economy*. Oxford: Oxford University Press.

Seade, J. K. (1977) 'The Shape of Optimal Tax Schedules', *Journal of Public Economics*, 7, 2, pp. 203–36.

Stern, N. H. (1976) 'On the Specification of Models of Optimum Income Taxation', *Journal of Public Economics*, 6, 1, 2, pp. 123–62.

Stiglitz, J. E. (1988) *Economics of the Public Sector*, 2nd edn. New York: W. W. Norton.

Tait, A. A. (1989) 'Not So General Equilibrium and Not So Optimal Taxation', *Public Finance/Finances Publiques*, 44, 2, pp. 169–82.

Tollison, R. D. (1987) 'Is the Theory of Rent Seeking Here to Stay?', pp. 143–57 in C. K. Rowley (ed.), *Economics and Democracy: Essays in Honor of Gordon Tullock*. Oxford: Basil Blackwell.

Tullock, G. (1967) 'The Welfare Costs of Tariffs, Monopolies and Theft', *Western Economic Journal*, 5, 3, pp. 224–32.

16 'Positive' optimal taxation

16.1 Introduction

When studying neoclassical microeconomic theory, the assumption or presumption is that individual economic agents will act to maximize their self-interest or, more grandly, their utility. Given that neoclassical economic theory is placed in a market context (reflecting the dominance of markets as the major form of provision of goods and services in Western economies), it is not surprising that economists were rather slow to apply the self-interested viewpoint to public- as opposed to private-sector actors. Indeed, Buchanan (1987, p. 290) says of Musgrave that his 'central and continuing criticism of public choice theory rests squarely on his residual unwillingness to model "public choosers" analogously to the way that we model "private choosers"'. Once this is accepted, a very different perspective is placed on the traditional policy implications of tax (and expenditure) analysis.

As might be deduced from the above quotation, one economist who has consistently exposed the self-interest of individual actors in different institutional settings is the 1986 Nobel laureate Professor James Buchanan,[1] whose approach is elaborated below.

16.2 The context of analysis

In chapters 7 and 15 the traditional approach to taxation economics was presented. That involved at least two elements that will not be central to this chapter. The first is that the tax policy implications are derived separately from the expenditures that require them, so that they are presented essentially as a technical search for a system of taxation that minimizes the welfare costs of taxation. Relatedly, and more importantly, once these technical prescriptions have been derived, it is implicit that selfless politicians and bureaucrats

[1] For a review of Buchanan's contribution to economics, see Sandmo (1990).

will enact them in a neutral, disinterested manner. A second element of the traditional analysis is that a social welfare function that will command wide support can be found to discriminate between alternative tax regimes. Perhaps more accurately, outcomes can be appraised against a number of social welfare functions to offer a menu of possibilities to the policy-maker. At its simplest, the use of an aggregating social welfare function is not anathema to the social optimality analysis as it is to the public choice school.

Congleton (1988) argues that it is the rejection of these two tenets that helps define Buchanan's approach to economics. Selfless enactors of policy are replaced by self-interested utility-maximizers constrained by the institutional context in which they find themselves. The notion of the use of social welfare functions as a measuring rod is replaced at the fundamental level of unanimity or quasi-unanimity so that the test for tax policy alternatives is, in principle at least, the search for tax policy arrangements that would command unanimous consent. Against this background of universal self-interest and actions constrained by institutional settings, we can consider those tax policies that actors in government would choose, as opposed to those that all people would agree to. In particular, the motivating force behind the next section, which offers an account of Brennan and Buchanan (1977, 1980), is a Leviathan government that is seeking to maximize the revenue it can raise—almost any way it can. An omniscient, benevolent government has no role in this play.

16.3 Tax constitution containment of a revenue-maximizing government

The analysis here depends on graphical techniques and is presented as a series of revenue-maximizing

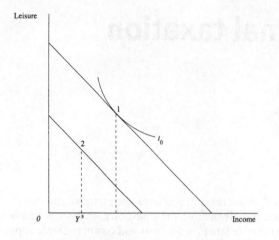

Figure 16.1 Taxation and subsistance income.

challengers from which the appropriate constitutional checks can be deduced. Notice that the assumption is not just that of 'failings in the political process'. It is not just that government 'gets things wrong'; it is that government gets things 'right', but always in terms of maximizing revenue. How can this 'efficient' maximizer of revenue be checked?

Round 1

Challenge (i): A revenue-maximizing (RM) government will use lump-sum taxes to reduce the private income left in the hands of individual to subsistence level OY^s in Fig. 16.1. Position 1 on I_0 is the initial no-tax equilibrium. For example, now treating Y^s as a subsistence utility level I_0, looking back at Fig. 7.2 in

Chapter 7, a RM government would raise 19 in tax, as compared to 17 if it used a lump-sum tax rather than an excise tax.

Constitutional check (i): The tax constitution, paradoxically, would require a less than fully comprehensive tax base. The provision is that tax levels should not be such as to make a utility-maximizing individual choose 'all leisure'. In Fig. 16.2 the individual initially finds his no-tax equilibrium at 1 on I_0. Indifference curve I_* represents utility achievable on the initial budget constraints if all leisure is chosen at point 2. The maximum tax take in leisure units is represented by the indicated vertical distance, which involves a parallel shift of the budget constraint to the point where I_* is only just achievable at point 3. The individual is indifferent between the leisure-income combination at 3 and the all-leisure outcome at 2. Furthermore, achieving the maximum revenue in these circumstances will involve a regressive tax structure.

Round 2

Challenge (ii): A RM government will opt for a regressive tax structure. For the individual to find tangency at point 3 in Fig. 16.3, a tax structure like the one illustrated as $2T$ is required. The convexity of this curve to the origin indicates that, as units of leisure are sacrificed moving from point 2 towards the origin O, successively greater increases in post-tax income are secured; i.e. the tax structure takes less of successive increases in income and is regressive.

Constitutional check (ii): The tax constitution should involve an insistence on proportional taxation or, even more comforting, a progressive tax structure.

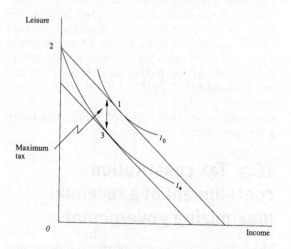

Figure 16.2 Find limits on taxation.

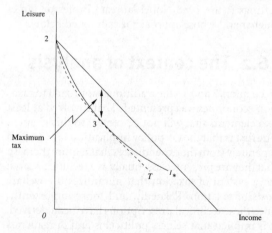

Figure 16.3 Maximizing tax revenue with a regressive tax structure.

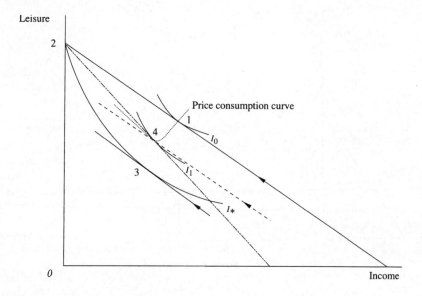

Figure 16.4 Proportional taxation and tax revenue maximization.

Proportional taxation

The line composed of dots in Fig. 16.4 is the individual's price consumption curve, which indicates the equilibrium position that will be found by the individual at different proportional tax rates. The object is to maximize the vertical distance between a point on the price consumption curve and the original budget constraint. This can be done by shifting the budget constraint back in a parallel fashion (dashed lines) towards the origin until the vertical distance is maximized at a point such as 4 on indifference curve I_1. The line composed of both dashes and dots is now the best a RM government can do with a proportional tax, and can be seen to involve less tax revenue than 3 on I_*.

Degressive tax

A degressive tax structure is one in which there is a tax-free 'slice' of income followed by a constant marginal tax rate (so that the average tax rate rises as income rises). In Fig 16.5 the demand for income-generating activity is equated with the marginal cost ($P = £1$) of such activity so that OY is the chosen level of income. The associated marginal revenue curve is labelled MR. A monopoly government would follow the strategy adopted by monopoly firms; it would equate $MC = MR$ and choose tax rate t^*. The insistence on a degressive tax structure moves MR outwards to the right, making the RM optimum tax rate t_d as opposed to the higher level t^*. The greater the tax exempt level, the lower the tax rate becomes.

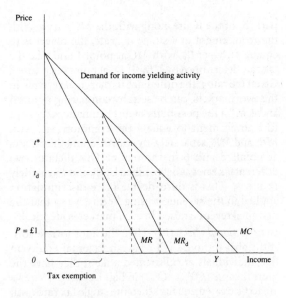

Figure 16.5 Degressive taxation and revenue maximization.

Round 3

Challenge (iii): A RM government would elect to tax-discriminate. In Fig. 16.6(a) the demand curves for income for two different individuals are labelled D_a and D_b. With MC located as illustrated, both choose to earn the same income: $OY_a = OY_b$. The horizontal sum of these two demand curves and their associated marginal revenue curves MR_a and MR_b are shown in

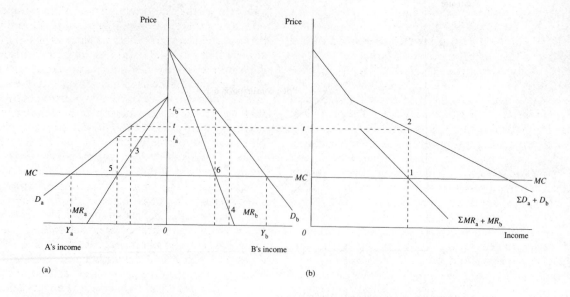

Figure 16.6 RM and tax discrimination.

part (b) of the figure along with the *MC* curve. With the requirement of a single tax rate, the object is to equate $MR_a + MR_b$ with *MC* at point 1 and take the tax rate determined by $\Sigma D_a + D_b$ at point 2, i.e. rate *t*. Given the rate *t*, the difference in marginal revenue in the two 'markets' can be seen by comparing points 3 and 4. With the possibility of discrimination, it pays a RM government to equate the common *MC* with MR_a and MR_b separately. By construction, this occurs at points 5 and 6 in the figure. This dictates two different tax rates as determined by D_a and D_b, namely t_a and t_b. This is third-degree price discrimination applied to the revenue-raising 'industry', so that the marginal revenue raised in each market is identical.

Constitutional check (iii): Here the appropriate constitutional response is to have horizontal equity in that individuals are all treated alike if they have the same income ($OY_a = OY_b$) in Fig. 16.6(a)). If 'equals are to be treated equally', then the single tax rate *t* will emerge.

Round 4

Challenge (iv): A RM government will insist on no evasion and/or avoidance because this would reduce tax revenue. If in Fig. 16.6 there were still only two individuals, both represented by curves labelled b, then the tax rate would be t_b. If by avoidance one individual could adjust his position to that represented by curves labelled a, then a lower tax rate *t* would emerge as desirable.

Constitutional check (iv): In an *ex ante* situation in which individuals do not know their future positions in society (the Rawlsian heuristic), all may accept avoidance as beneficial as a way of decreasing tax rates and checking the actions of a revenue-maximizing government.

In summary, a tax constitution to check a RM government would endorse:

Round 1 Discriminatory taxation
Round 2 Progressive (degressive) tax rates
Round 3 Horizontal equity
Round 4 Avoidance as a not unattractive feature

Note that rounds 2 and 3 in a traditional framework are justified by equity considerations rather than as constraints on a RM government. In this way the public choice school offers a competing and sharply different rationalization of features that are part of many tax systems.

16.4 Taxpayer responses and time horizons

In recent years there has been a lively public debate about the possibility that tax rates and tax revenues are inversely related. The idea can be traced to Adam Smith (1776), but in recent years the Laffer curve has been used to illustrate the relationship. Arthur Laffer's famous curve suggests that an economy might be in such a position that, if tax rates were reduced, tax revenues would be increased (see chapter 11). This proposition has attracted so-called supply-side economists, as well as those who, purely for ideological reasons, would prefer the interference of government to be reduced. But how would such an outcome fit with the assumption that government is a revenue-maximizer? If government is a revenue-maximizer and pursues its task 'efficiently', tax rates could never be pushed above the revenue-maximizing rate. Could tax revenues possibly increase when tax rates are reduced if government were a revenue-maximizer?

Some of the analysis developed by the Leviathan view of government requires a distinction between a short-run and long-run adjustment mechanism. Buchanan and Lee (1982a, 1982b) develop their analysis in the context of supply-side economics widely advocated in the early 1980s. For the government, revenue (expenditures) is a 'good' and the tax rate required to raise the revenue a 'bad'. Importantly, the time horizon is short in that it is less than the time required for taxpayer-voters to fully adjust to any changes in tax rates made. (Note that politicians

unable to sell the capital value of their office consider only their expected tenure as opposed to all future periods, and taxpayers-voters are likely to be rationally ignorant.) In Fig. 16.7(a) D_L is long-run demand curve for the tax base with the long run denoting the period in which all behavioural adjustments to each tax rate can and have been made. Associated with D_L is the long-run Laffer curve LC_L in part (b) of the figure. Beginning from a situation of full adjustment to the tax rate t, it is possible, by taking shorter and shorter periods that allow for less and less adjustment, to derive a family of D and LC_s curves that are period-specific, such as $D_0(\bar{t})$ and $LC_s^0(\bar{t})$. The same process can be repeated for any initial tax rate; for example, the situation for $\bar{\bar{t}}$ is also illustrated. The analysis shows that, for tax rates above the one selected (and for which complete adjustment has taken place), the tax revenue rise in the short run is higher than that in the long run. Political equilibrium is derived in the model by imposing an indifference map between a bad (y axis) and a good (x axis) on the period-specific, initial tax-rate-determined Laffer curves. Equilibria that are consistent with taxpayer-voter actions are to be found on the long-run Laffer curve. For example, in Fig. 16.8 an equilibrium is illustrated on I_0 at e^* with

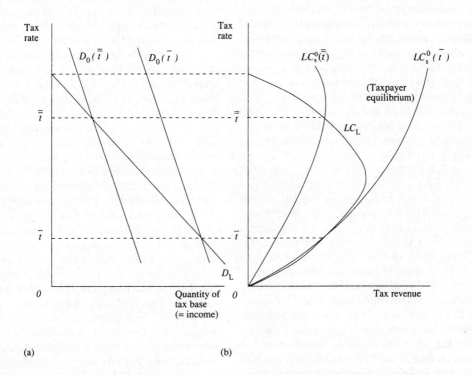

(a)   (b)

Figure 16.7 Derivation of short- and long-run Laffer curves.

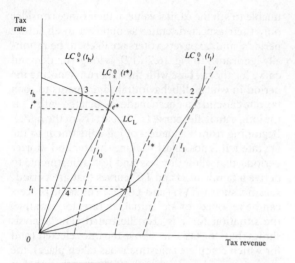

Figure 16.8 Political and taxpayer equilibrium.

the tax rate t^*. In this analysis, equilibrium can be found on the negative sloping section of the long-run Laffer curve. The equilibrium is, however, below the short-term revenue-maximizing position, and this will always be the case where the tax rate is a 'bad'. (A revenue-maximizer would have it as a neutral.)

Adjustment to t^* is also illustrated in the figure. If the starting tax rate were too low (t_1), the government would try to achieve point 2 rather than 1 because this is where an indifference curve tangency on I_1 occurs with the short-run Laffer curve associated with t_1, that is $LC_s^0(t_1)$. A movement therefore occurs from 1 to 2. Such a change is not sustainable except in the short run, because taxpayer adjustment back to the necessary tax rate (t_h) to achieve point 2 results in point 3 on LC_L. Once 3 is reached, a better position can be achieved at e^* and hence t_h will eventually be lowered to t^*, where $LC_s^0(t^*)$, the short-run Laffer curve, coincides with the long run on LC_L and further adjustment is not signalled. It is the tangency of the indifference curve with an LC_s^0 curve on LC_L that determines a final resting place in the comparative statics of this model; hence the important implication is that, as long as there is some element of political myopia, the tax rate will be higher than that achieved by a far-sighted government which would simply seek tangency with LC_L at 1 on I^*. If taxpayers can learn the way in which the government is choosing a tax rate and share the same information, adjustment to a point such as 1 on I^* will be considerably speeded up. The cost of 'slow adjustment' is that a genuine tax-reducing government must initially lose revenue to

move around LC_L. If the government lowered t^* to t_1 in Fig. 16.8, a point like 4 would be achieved in the short run. Leopards trying to change their spots are not believed, at least not in the short term. It is in this context that permanent and binding fiscal constitutions become attractive (a topic further discussed below). Also, this argument acts as a rebuff to critics of the Laffer curve who argue that tax revenues have fallen when tax rates are reduced.

16.5 Rent-seeking and budgetary changes

As noted above in section 10.4.3, Buchanan (1987) makes a related point discussing US tax legislation in 1986. The legislation involved a broadening of the tax base for both corporate and individual taxpayers combined with tax rate reductions. Political agents are seen as rent-maximizers subject to corruption constraints imposed by the law and temporal and survival constraints imposed by the electoral system and institutional context. Because rents are postulated to be positively related to public expenditure size and to shifts in the pattern of expenditures and finance overall, expenditures will be 'too large' and changes in expenditures and taxes made 'too often'.

In Fig. 16.9 the budget changes of rate reductions and base broadening are crudely captured as the movement from 1 to 2. At 1 the tax revenue is raised from an eroded tax base in that good X is excluded. Broadening the tax base in a way that raises the same tax revenue with a lower rate allows taxpayers to adjust to 2 on the higher indifference curve I_2 and can be expected to be popular. As for the rent-seeking political agents, what is in it for them? The broadening alone is clearly attractive, as this allows additional tax revenue while pushing the taxpayer to equilibrium at 3 on I_1. Buchanan argues that the initial pre-reform equilibrium at 1 is likely to be the product of revenue-maximizing political agents, so that further rate increases with the old tax base would serve only to reduce tax revenue. (The individual might find an equilibrium like point 4 on I_0.) In this sense, reform is needed if tax revenue is to be raised.

Hence political agents may be attracted by the rate *and* base reform because, as noted above, rent-seeking opportunities are related to both expenditure and fiscal changes. With the latter, agents may have created the potential for increased rents in the future. Agents gain from the change in that they are now in a position

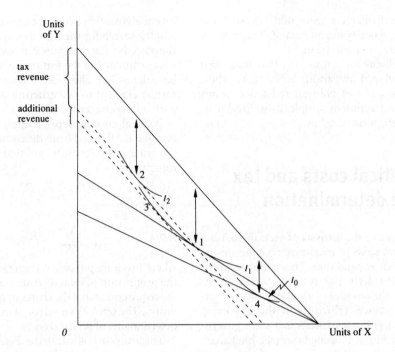

Figure 16.9 The attraction of tax reform.

to gain rents by offering to re-establish tax concessions for those who previously gained most. The lobbyists, whose job it is to facilitate special interests, now find a renewed demand for their talents. In this context Buchanan is arguing that it is the shifts and changes of policy that offer opportunities, so that long-term stability in fiscal and expenditure structures are the way to foil this undesirable aspect of political activity motivated by self-interest.

As far as broadly based taxes are concerned, they should, on this analysis, be ruled out. Any constitutional framework to constrain politicians should include the avoidance of broadly based taxes. By keeping the tax base narrow, excess burden effects help keep the taxpayer 'aware' of the revenue-extracting government. In contrast, chapter 7 (and subsequent chapters) emphasizes excess burdens as a totally negative effect of taxation.

16.6 Tax concessions as 'special interests'

The contributions above have been mainly about tax structure in the form of tax sources, rather than the more detailed specifications of each tax. It is possible, however, to tie up themes discussed elsewhere in this tax structure context. In earlier chapters 'special interests' effects were discussed, and in chapter 8 tax avoidance was introduced. 'Special interests' are pieces of legislation that offer a significant gain to a small number of voters and a small loss to a larger number of voters. Vote-maximizing politicians make such special interests part of their platform if they can win the minority gainers and not lose the majority losers. The higher the marginal rate of taxation, the more attractive it is for individuals to raise post-tax incomes by obtaining tax concessions. Hence in a progressive tax system it is the higher-income groups who often find it easier to organize themselves, because of their command over resources. Sponsoring politicians must seek to obscure the real purpose of the tax concession. With this in mind, the debate over its details should appear to be technical and complex, raising the costs for anyone trying to unravel the purpose of the proposed change in the tax code that will help 'erode' the tax base. Bearing in mind that the loss to any individual from a special interest tax concession is low and the ability of the individual to do anything about it, even if he establishes what is going on, is also low. That is, the costs are high in relation to the potential benefits. The argument is that, if the specifications of a particular tax seem odd, unusual and difficult for the majority to understand, it is probably a 'special interest' tax concession.

This short discussion introduces two ideas that have been developed by various economists. These are the minimization of political resistance to any action and the attraction of complexity in fiscal matters, and they are pursued below.

16.7 Political costs and tax structure determination

The driving force of the analysis of section 16.3 is a government that seeks to maximize revenue-raising to increase public expenditure. This is not to imply that government feels tightly constrained in its expenditure by the amount of taxation. Indeed, one of the 'public choice' criticisms of the Keynesian legacy is that it legitimates deficits that allow governments to spend without raising taxes (see Buchanan, Burton and Wagner 1978). The use of deficits to facilitate increased consumption of 'currently enjoyed services'—a direct gain—is secured at the indirect cost of 'the inflationary impact upon the future' (Buchanan *et al.* 1978, p. 11) and is seen as being politically popular. Hettich and Winer (1984) take a related theme in following Downs's suggestion that maximizing political agents will choose as optimal a tax structure that minimizes the political costs (net loss in voters at the next election) of raising a given tax

revenue. Note that here, expenditure has been decided and the search for the least damaging tax structure is the objective. Tax structure can cover the composition of tax sources and the features of any tax chosen, e.g. base definition, allowable exemptions, etc. It is the former element of tax structure that the authors are particularly concerned with.

Political costs C depend upon the proportion of revenue R_i/R raised from different sources. To set up the issue more formally, politicians may be seen as minimizing

$$(16.1) \qquad C(R_1/R, R_2/R, \ldots, R_n/R, X)$$

subject to

$$(16.2) \qquad \sum_{i=1}^{n} R_i/R = 1$$

where 1 to n are possible revenue sources and R_1/R is the proportion of total revenue from source 1 (hence the requirement that the shares or proportions sum to unity). The term X is a vector of exogenous (outside) determinants of political costs.

The problem is illustrated as Fig. 16.10. In the figure two tax sources labelled 1 and 2 are illustrated, indicating marginal political costs that are rising as more of each source is used. It is assumed that the marginal political cost curves for each source are independent, so that raising more from source 1 does not affect the marginal political costs associated with raising revenue from source 2, and so on. A process of horizontal summation gives the overall marginal political cost of raising taxation. Suppose that OR^* is the decided-upon level of desired revenue and that political agents

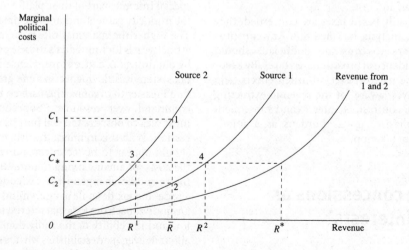

Figure 16.10 Minimizing the political costs of the tax structure.

raise half (OR) from each source: the associated marginal political costs would be OC_1 for source 1 and OC_2 for source 2. Clearly, it would be politically attractive to raise only OR^1 from source 1 and OR^2 from source 2, therefore equalizing marginal political costs from the two sources and reducing the total political cost of raising OR^* to a minimum. In the diagram, the movement away from raising half the revenue ($O\bar{R}$)) from each source can be seen to incur political costs equal to the area $\bar{R}24R^2$ that are swamped by avoided political costs from the use of source 1 equal to $\bar{R}13R^1$.

Hettich and Winer develop their analysis by offering a number of testable hypotheses consistent with their approach:

1. Vote-maximizing politicians will wish to lower the effective tax rates of those taxpayer-voters likely to offer opposition. Such a reduction in the burden of taxation is achieved if 'shifting' is possible (either geographically, or to other layers or tiers of government).

Hirschman (1970) divides opposition into two forms, 'exit' and 'voice'. The argument is that individuals who are initially dissatisfied with the outcome of government or other institutional behaviour will 'exit', i.e. vote with their feet. If 'exit' is impossible, then 'voice' comes into play, i.e. organizing criticisms and pressure for change within the system. The next two hypotheses are built around voice:

2. There is a fixed cost of setting-up opposition. However, the more revenue is raised per pound sterling of a given potential tax base, the greater will be opposition (in total and at the margin), so there is an increased expectation that the fixed cost will be exceeded.
3. Political costs rise at an increasing rate as the revenue raised per pound of potential tax-base rises and, because of economies of scale in voter opposition, organization and information dissemination, the effectiveness of opposition can be expected to grow faster than tax-burden growth.

The next hypotheses deal with exit:

4. Tax structure will be contained by the presence of competing political units; i.e. there is a fear of fiscally induced migration.
5. Greater opposition is engendered by tax sources that are subject to fluctuation. For any mean value of taxation, the higher the variance, the greater the resistance, because variation forces adjustment costs in the form of unanticipated changes in the private sector activities. The lack of certainty

in itself will impose costs on risk-averse individuals.

In brief, if they are to minimize the political costs of taxation, vote-maximising tax-raisers should be aware of: the effective tax price, organization costs, opposition effectiveness, competing fiscal jurisdictions, and the tax-base certainty that their taxpaying voters face.

In chapter 15 literatures on optimal income taxation, optimal commodity taxation and optimal tax combinations were discussed. In this chapter rather fewer contributions to politically optimal income tax and tax combinations have so far been described. There is, however, some recent work on politically optimal commodity taxes. Seiglie (1990) sets out to model a situation where a tax on a commodity X (his example is alcoholic beverages) is both endogenous and determined by political factors. Such a tax has two offsetting political impacts. First, the revenue can finance public expenditures G and secure support from those that gain as a result. Secondly, the incidence of the excise tax T imposes costs on those affected and damages political support from this group. The legal consumption of X depends on T, income level I and regulation details R. Increasing T and R reduces X (i.e. the amount of X consumed), the level of consumers' (CS) and producers' (PS) surplus associated with X, and any negative externalities E related to X. The legislature's political support function S then increases with G, CS and PS and decreases with E. To maximize support, the legislature must set T such that the additional support it receives from increasing G and decreasing E equals the loss of support from decreasing CS and PS. Tax revenue curve TR_0 in Fig. 16.11 allows a maximum level of provision of $G(G')$ with the tax rate (T'). However, the support function is maximized at G^* and T^*, the tax rate being effectively a 'bad' for consumers of X. Given that the deadweight loss of CS and PS will vary directly with the elasticities of demand and supply of X, greater elasticities suggest a lower T and G. With the ending of prohibition in the USA in 1933, each state could choose to become either a 'control' state, being wholesalers and retailers of spirits, wines and sometimes beer as well, or a 'licence' state, using excise taxes and licence fees to raise revenue from private licensed suppliers of alcohol. In control states the absence of wholesalers and retailers with political power to wield has the effect of flattening S_0 so that a higher T and G is optimal at, say, point 2. Lowering the minimum drinking age shifts TR_0 to TR_1 as the revenue from any given T rises. The optimal T and G will tend to

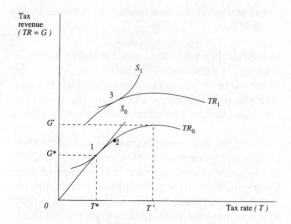

Figure 16.11 The politically optimal commodity tax.

rise as equilibrium is moved from point 1 on S_0 to point 3 on S_1. Lowering the legal drinking age increases PS and CS (for previous non- (illegal) consumers), allowing some gains to be taxed away so as to simultaneously increase G. (The resistance to the increased tax from existing consumers of X is assumed small.) The effect of increasing income on tax revenue varies with the income elasticity of demand for X, essentially rising with positive income elasticities. Using cross-section data for 50 US states, Seiglie found econometric support for these and related propositions suggesting that tax rates are endogenous and are determined by political factors.

16.8 Fiscal illusion and tax structure determination

Taxpayer-voter resistance or opposition is the link to traditional statements about the desirability of different tax options. Least resistance is said to be associated with expenditures that can be financed out of tax revenue raised via 'fiscal drag'; that is, higher income enjoyed by the public combined with the existing tax structure will raise a larger absolute volume of taxation in a passive way. If the tax system is progressive, a larger proportion of total income will automatically flow to the government. Second, it is argued that, if one expenditure is curtailed to free tax revenue for the new expenditure this engenders less opposition than the third, most politically costly, option of a new tax. These generalizations have been lent more precision in recent work on tax visibility.

Taxpayer-voter perception of what is going on is all-important to political agents. (Indeed, the cynical may see the whole of politics as being about deception.) Hence political agents may wish to create or foster so-called 'fiscal illusion'. Puviani (1903) is associated with the development of different notions of illusion[2] which are partly discussed in Goetz (1977).

A number of propositions about fiscal illusion have been explained. First, it is argued that governments operating in the RM (revenue maximizing) tradition will foster income-elastic tax systems. These are systems where real or inflationary changes in income more than proportionately raise tax revenues, i.e. fiscal drag. The argument noted above is that their low visibility results in a low political cost.

Brennan and Buchanan (1980) see a RM government being assisted in a situation where competitive political jurisdictions are absent or sparse, so that 'exit' is impossible or difficult. The hypothesis associated with this is that the extent of fiscal decentralization is important in explaining the level of public expenditure. Since there is more opportunity to exit at lower tiers of government than at higher ones, public expenditure should vary inversely with the level of fiscal decentralization.

Wagner (1976) looks at fiscal illusion, especially in the context of taxpayer-voters' knowledge of the tax prices of public sector goods and services, and he links this to the complexity of the tax revenue structure. Following Kant, he distinguishes between 'noumenon' (things as they are in themselves) and 'phenomenon' (sensible perceptions of the appearance of objects). More complex tax structures involve:

a spatial element (the simplest being one tax);
a temporal aspect (the simplest being levied at one point in time);
a degree of obtrusiveness (less obtrusive taxes would be indirect ones, which might be difficult to distinguish from the price of products; conversely, direct taxation without withholding is obtrusive).

The more complex the tax structure, the higher is the cost of information and the lower the quantity of information that it is rational to collect, other things equal. This observation, combined with the generally small benefit from being informed in terms of being able to influence outcomes in the public sector, sug-

[2] For an interesting article on illusions that extends the discussion of cognitive dissonance in chapter 5, see Akerlof (1989). In the two examples he discusses, individuals wish to feel good about themselves. In the one case fishermen refuse to believe they are depleting the stock of fish by fishing, whereas in the other they choose to defer to experts in such a way as to make themselves 'victims' of expert decisions.

gests that fiscal ignorance will be rife. But will tax-payer-voters be ignorantly optimistic or ignorantly pessimistic? Wagner's answer is the former. His argument is that, in the process of abstraction, individuals ignore some taxes and assign others to subsidiary importance and hence tend to have fairly accurate knowledge of a small subset of all taxes. Given this, individual voter-taxpayers will tend to underestimate tax prices. This process is illustrated in Fig. 16.12. With a simple tax structure, the perceived and actual tax price will coincide at OP_s, resulting in the efficient level of public sector provision Oq^*. However, with a complex tax structure individuals perceive the tax price to be OP_c, resulting in over-provision by the quantity q^*q^c, with the associated welfare cost triangle 123. The implication is that the fiscal constitution should frown on complex tax structures. Note, however, that this position is not universally shared. Downs (1960) argues that individuals will not have adequate knowledge of the benefits of public expenditure, some of which are the results of long-term investment. For example, the benefits of defence expenditure and deterrence are difficult to measure; the benefits of government overseas aid are uncertain; etc. Added to this, Galbraith (1962) argues that individuals are less aware of the benefits of public expenditure because they are not advertised to the extent, or in the same manner, as private goods in the market-place. If benefits of public expenditure are underestimated, taxpayers are ignorantly pessimistic. (The D curve in Fig. 16.12 is biased to the left and Oq^* is 'too small'.) Cullis and Jones (1987) attempt to test whether evidence of taxpayers' perceptions is consist-ent with optimistic ignorance or pessimistic ignorance. They identify ignorance (consistent with Downs's (1957) 'rational voter') but find no reason to suppose that it is always pessimistic or optimistic.

16.9 Empirical evidence

In this section a brief introduction to the empirical work on the theoretical deliberations above is given. As with all empirical work, the data and econometric methods vary between the different contributors; neither aspect of such empirical work is 'ideal', and both are always open to criticism. It must also be remembered that the contributions are from people who take different positions on the significance of a 'political' approach to tax structure determination. The objective here is to outline the extent to which empirical work claims to have identified those characteristics described in section 16.8. (Interested readers should consult the works directly, as in such a short space the authors cited will doubtless feel that their position has been less than fully appreciated.) Oates (1988) notes that fiscal ignorance is necessary but not sufficient for illusion. It is systematic and therefore predictable misperceptions that constitute illusion (fiscal tricks are played on consumer voters). Further he notes there must be limits to illusions or threshold effects such that the illusion is dispelled once it reaches a certain level and that this needs to be borne in mind.

16.9.1 Tax structure to minimize political costs

Recall that Hettich and Winer's (1984) formulation has the politically optimal tax shares dependent on a vector of exogenous determinants of political costs. Political costs do not lend themselves to direct observation. However, the authors do explore how elements in their vector explain the income tax shares of the US states. The factors influencing political costs are grouped under four headings: effective tax price; costs of organizing opposition; tax competition with other states; and tax-base variability. The proxies used gave the authors eight independent variables in their regression equation, of which six proved statistically significant with the correct predicted sign. Hence they claim that their approach 'provides a useful way of modelling tax structures' (p. 82).

16.9.2 Low visibility: revenue elastic tax structures (fiscal drag)

Oates (1975) established some support for the notion that tax revenues and expenditures will be higher in

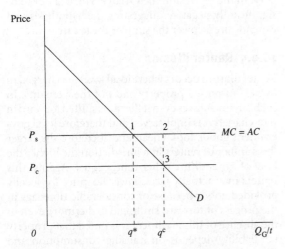

Figure 16.12 Overprovision from 'optimistic' fiscal ignorance.

tax-elastic fiscal jurisdictions (ones where tax-base changes result in a more than proportionate change in tax revenue). However, he doubts that this supports the existence of fiscal illusion in the form of low visibility of tax raising. Di Lorenzo (1982), using county as opposed to state data, found contrary evidence: he establishes a negative relationship between income tax elasticity and the level and growth of local expenditures. Craig and Heins (1980), however, find empirical support for the tax elasticity hypothesis in a test that relies on the levels rather than the growth of expenditure.

Feenberg and Rosen (1987) provide a rationalization of tax-elastic tax structures that is the product of efficiency considerations. If taxpayer-voters have high positive income elasticities for public sector goods and services, the transaction costs of continual budget changes that involve the real resources of the fiscal legislative procedure can be avoided by the introduction of an income-elastic tax structure. The authors, in the substantive part of their paper, exploit a carefully constructed dataset for 49 US states over the period 1978–83. Their finding is that higher rates of public sector growth are not the product of income-elastic tax structure. Given the sophistication of their econometrics and the care taken in the construction of their data set, their final sentence, which reads 'If governments really are out to expand the public sector beyond the size desired by their citizens, they must be using some other mechanisms' (p. 200), has to be treated with respect. But what of the 'other mechanisms'?

16.9.3 Exit: public expenditure and fiscal decentralization

Oates (1975) offers some arguments that suggest that fiscal decentralization and public expenditure may not vary inversely as postulated above.

First, if collective decisions reflect the median voter, it is not clear whether the median voter in a centralized context will demand more or less public sector activity than the median voters in a series of localized political jurisdications. It is a question of preference distribution and population location. Musgrave (1981) notes that, if those who find themselves widely dispersed but on the 'high' public expenditure tail of the distribution of preferences all live in the same community, then very high levels of public expenditure may be approved. Secondly, the production of local publicly provided goods and services tailored to local preferences may be secured only at increased costs because of the loss of economies of scale in

production (but they remain an efficient resource use). Thirdly, taxpayer-voter control is greater at a local than a central level, and therefore it may be rational to 'trust' local governments more than central ones. In short, these arguments imply that it might not be surprising if the inverse relationship did not hold.

Oates used international data for forty-three countries and data for the state–local sectors for the forty-eight contiguous states of the USA to obtain empirical results. His regression results pour cold water on the Brennan–Buchanan hypothesis. The point Oates makes in his conclusion is that the Leviathan school needs to distinguish institutional settings, because not all are equally open to the government as a RM actor. What may be the case for some bureaucratic settings may well not translate to whole fiscal jurisdictions at various tiers of government. Recently, Heil (1991) using two, allegedly superior, international data sets, found no significant relationship between public sector size and fiscal centralization at the national level.

16.9.4 Fiscal illusion: complexity

Wagner (1976) used data on the fifty largest US cities and regressed total current expenditure on eight independent variables, where one of them was the simplicity of the tax structure S measured by

$$(16.3) \qquad S = \sum_{i=1}^{n} R_i^2$$

where n is four major tax categories and R_i is the share of total city revenue generated from a particular category. In the regression the variable S turned out to be significantly negative, suggesting the hypothesis that expenditure is lower the simpler the tax structure.

16.9.5 Renter illusion

Renter illusion occurs where local taxes are charged to owners of rented property and not their tenants. In such circumstances even if the tax is shifted forward in rent charges it is unobserved and therefore local government goods look cheap and therefore the larger the number of renters in a jurisdiction the higher the level of expenditure other things equal. Against this renters may actually face a lower tax price for locally provided goods because of considerable time lags in the process of forward shifting. Furthermore even in the absence of this argument it is noted that property tax liability depends on housing consumption and that renters consume less housing than owners at the same income level and therefore they should be liable to less tax, i.e. a lower tax price is appropriate and there is no illusion.

16.9.6 Debt and illusion

Debt illusion is about individuals failing to realize their income is affected to the tune of the present discounted value of future tax liabilities when debt is issued. A test of this recognizes that other things equal, fiscal jurisdictions adopting debt finance as compared to taxation should exhibit lower property values if the tax commitment associated with the debt is recognised and therefore capitalized. There is some evidence that this is the case, but overall evidence of debt illusion is not great.

Oates (1988) suggests that although illusions are plausible the econometric support is not overwhelming and given tax system endogeneity, competing plausible hypotheses alongside some rather ad hoc theorizing he would take an agnostic position. Not surprisingly the public choice school have embraced the 'fiscal illusion' literature much more firmly.

16.10 Macro-fiscal policy and politics

The macro equivalent of the political cost-minimizing tax structure is the manipulation of fiscal and monetary policy to help win elections. There is now quite an extensive literature on so-called political business cycles which is discussed in section 11.6 above. Pommerehne and Schneider (1983) provide a convenient illustration from that section of a more macro-fiscal study that employs self-interested political agents. They also provide an example of a model in which political ideology matters. In all the approaches above, the ideology of the party in power had no role to play. Pommerehne and Schneider's approach has both supply- and demand-side elements. The supply side arises once a party has been elected and/or is confident of re-election. With a long time to the next election and therefore plenty of time at their disposal, or opinion polls that show their party in the lead, the government is monopolistic and is viewed as maximizing its utility by pursuing ideological goals (typically popular with only a minority of voters). The demand side, Downsian in inspiration, comes into play when there is a short time to re-election or a less than satisfactory opinion poll rating. In order to secure re-election the party must trim its sails towards the median voters' demands irrespective

of ideological beliefs—this popular policy is the authors' so-called 'common fiscal policy'. The empirical work they detail is for Australia which has a short (three-year) election, suggesting relatively little opportunity for the supply side to dominate. However, this is offset by greater discretion, especially over revenue structure, than is typical of many Western democracies.

16.11 Reforms policy

In section 16.3 the desirable characteristics for a constitution to restrain an RM government were (a) discriminatory taxation, (b) progressive tax rates, (c) horizontal equity and (d) the endorsement of opportunities for avoidance. While these kinds of reform could not be ruled out following a traditional approach to public finance, they are in some cases unlikely. Take for example the requirement for progressive taxation and in particular the avoidance of broadly based taxation as features in the tax system. First, Musgrave notes (and here you may refer back to chapter 3):

A progressive distribution of tax burdens may be helpful in approximating a system of Lindahl pricing, given the assumption that income elasticities for demand are in excess of price elasticities, as they may well be. However, this argument applies to general social goods only and not to programs whose benefits are addressed to particular income groups, and it certainly does not hold for transfer programs. (Musgrave 1981, p. 113)

Then later, with reference to avoiding broadly based taxation, he adds:

It has been suggested that the revenue-raising ability of Government should be curtailed by excluding part of the potential base from taxation (*a recommendation in stunning conflict with the widely accepted notion that broad-based taxes are desirable*) and that tax bases should be chosen so as to be complementary to the public service rendered. (Musgrave 1981, p. 113; our emphasis)

The later sections of this chapter have highlighted (possible) sources of inefficiencies and inequities that result from the self-interested behaviour of political agents. The recommendations that followed from the arguments suggested support for:

1. stable tax structures and expenditure patterns;
2. simple and visible (or transparent) tax structures and expenditure patterns;
3. fostering possibilities for 'exit' and (where impossible) 'voice'.

These tax reforms take the form of constraints on a revenue-maximizing government. They are embedded in the constitution; politicians cannot easily ignore them. However, they are only part of a more widespread list of constitutional constraints that may be required. For example, other political restraints suggested to constrain government include the use of two-thirds majority voting for some issues, and greater inter-bureau competition.

Buchanan himself believes that a lot of the problems in the public sector arise because of the division of taxation and expenditure decisions. Following Wicksell, he would support reforms that would unite the two. Tax instruments can be judged only in the context of knowledge of the distribution of public goods and services to be provided and of the institutional framework in which fiscal policies will be decided upon and enacted. At this level fundamental reform would take the form of a fiscal constitution. Brennan and Buchanan (1986), is a contribution to the constitutional perspective (in the context of redistribution—see chapter 9) in which the basic point is that rules will improve the long-run situation and are required to overcome the short-term perspectives of self-interested political agents. Broome (1988) reviews this contribution critically and in doing so offers an insight into the division of opinion to be found within economics on the 'utility' of constitutional economics:

the general point that rules are needed to overcome the instability of politics, for the sake of long-term objectives, is one of their main conclusions. The other is that political processes are unlikely to improve on the free market in distributing income equally, so that there should be rules outlawing or regulating political attempts at redistribution. Of these conclusions, I find the first unremarkable and the second hard to believe. (Broome 1988, p. 282)

16.12 Summary

Although it has historical antecedents, much of the literature reviewed in this chapter is more recent in origin and is unlike the well-worked fields of analysis found in some of the other chapters. The Brennan–Buchanan contributions at the least show an insightful use of monopoly theory. How plausible it is as an account of the main feature of tax systems is difficult to assess. With the majority traditional view of, say, horizontal equity presented as the standard in all texts, it is difficult for those with an existing background in the subject not to view the competing

explanation as, initially at least, an unusual one. However, the logic of the argument is clear and readers must make a judgement. The more empirically based sections of the chapter dealt with the incentives of political actors, who wish to stay in office, and to minimize the political costs of raising the revenue that is necessary for their activities. Using differential visibility as a criterion in tax selection to illude the taxpayer makes perfect sense in the overall revenue 'maximand' explicit in this chapter. The empirical evidence is mixed, and much work remains to be done. It has already been noted that one criticism of the 'normative' optimal tax literature is its failure to include 'transparency' or 'visibility' as one of the relevant features of a tax system described as optimal.

In short, this chapter offers 'positive' predictions about tax structures and appropriate fiscal constitutions that are derived from a view of political agents who seek a political cost-minimizing tax structure with a view to staying in power and/or raising as much tax revenue as is possible within the existing fiscal constitution. A cursory glance to the dates of the references should convince readers that the subject discussed in this chapter is very much a live one. The analysis and discussion pose a stark contrast of approach to the normative prescriptions of the traditional approach to taxation. Reforms[3] in the traditional approach begin with the view that policymakers will make decisions in the best interests of the community. (See Buchanan, Burton and Wagner (1978) for a criticism of Keynes's policy prescriptions along these lines.) They may get things wrong, but there is no presumption that the error is always in terms of expansion of revenue and of the public sector. Decision-makers in government are not infallible, but there is no active conspiracy to maximize revenue. Musgrave sums up the difference between the two approaches:

Constructive reforms are needed to improve the framework of decision-making. There can be no disagreement about this. Indeed, my early distinction between and separation of 'three branches' (allocation, distribution, stabilization) of fiscal action was directed precisely at this purpose. Where I disagree with the Leviathan theorists is on the content of reform. The objective of institutional adjustment, as I see it, should be to induce more efficient decision-making, be it towards expansion or contraction. It should not be to correct for an unproven hypothesis of overexpansion, or to implement value judgements in favour of small budgets. (Musgrave 1981, p. 110)

[3] For a discussion of tax reforms in a positive context see Van Velthoven and Van Winden (1991).

References

Akerlof, G. A. (1989) 'The Economics of Illusion', *Economics and Politics*, **1**, 1, pp. 1–17.

Brennan, G. and Buchanan, J. M. (1977) 'Towards a Tax Constitution for Leviathan', *Journal of Public Economics*, **8**, 3, pp. 255–73.

Brennan, G. and Buchanan, J. M. (1980) *The Power to Tax: Analytical Foundations of A Fiscal Constitution*. Cambridge: Cambridge University Press.

Brennan, G. and Buchanan, J. M. (1986) *The Reason of Rules: Constitutional Political Economy*. Cambridge: Cambridge University Press.

Broome, J. (1988) Review of Brennan and Buchanan (1986), *Economica*, **55**, 218, pp. 282–3.

Buchanan, J. M. (1987) 'Tax Reform as Political Choice', *Economic Perspectives*, **1**, 1, pp. 29–35.

Buchanan, J. M. (1989) 'Richard Musgrave, Public Finance and Public Choice', *Public Choice*, **61**, 3, pp. 289–91.

Buchanan, J. M., Burton, J. and Wagner, R. E. (1978) *The Consequences of Mr Keynes*, Hobart Paper no. 78. London: Institute of Economic Affairs.

Buchanan, J. M. and Lee, D. R. (1982a) 'Tax Rates and Tax Revenues in Political Equilibrium', *Economic Inquiry*, **20**, 3, pp. 344–54.

Buchanan, J. M. and Lee, D. R. (1982b) 'Politics, Time and the Laffer Curve', *Journal of Political Economy*, **90**, 4, pp. 816–19.

Congleton, R. D. (1988) 'An Overview of the Contracterian Public Finance of James Buchanan', *Public Finance Quarterly*, **16**, 2, pp. 131–57.

Craig, E. and Heins, A. (1980) 'The Effect of Tax Elasticity on Public Spending', *Public Choice*, **35**, 3, pp. 267–75.

Cullis, J. G. and Jones, P. R. (1987) *Microeconomics and the Public Economy: A Defence of Leviathan*. Oxford: Basil Blackwell.

Di Lorenzo, T. (1982) 'Tax Elasticity and the Growth of Local Government Expenditure', *Public Finance Quarterly*, **10**, 3, pp. 385–92.

Downs, A. (1957) *An Economic Theory of Democracy*. New York: Harper & Row.

Downs, A. (1960) 'Why the Government is Too Small in a Democracy', *World Politics*, **13**, pp. 451–63.

Feenberg, D. R. and Rosen, H. S. (1987) 'Tax Structure and Public Sector Growth', *Journal of Public Economics*, **32**, 2, pp. 185–202.

Galbraith, J. K. (1962) *The Affluent Society*. Harmondsworth: Penguin.

Goetz, C. J. (1977) 'Fiscal Illusion in State and Local Finance', pp. 176–8 in T. E. Borcherding (ed.), *Budgets and Bureaucrats*. Durham, NC: Duke University Press.

Heil, J. B. (1991) 'The Search for Leviathan Revisited', *Public Finance Quarterly*, **19**, 3, pp. 334–46.

Hettich, W. and Winer, S. (1984) 'A Positive Model of Tax Structure', *Journal of Public Economics*, **24**, 1, pp. 67–88.

Hirschman, A. O. (1970) *'Exit', Voice and Loyalty: Responses to Decline in Firms, Organisations and States*. Cambridge, Mass.: Harvard University Press.

Meade, J. E. Chairman (1978) *The Structure and Reform of Indirect Taxation*. London: Allen & Unwin.

Musgrave, R. A. (1981) 'Leviathan Cometh, or Does He?', pp. 77–120 in H. Ladd and N. Tideman (eds.), *Tax and Expenditure Limitations*, COUPE Papers on Public Economics no. 5. Washington DC: Urban Institute.

Oates, W. E. (1975) 'Searching for Leviathan', *American Economic Review*, **75**, 4, pp. 748–57.

Oates, W. E. (1988) 'On the Nature and Measurement of Fiscal Illusion; A Survey,' pp. 65–82 in G. Brennan, B. S. Grewal and P. Groenewegan (eds.), *Taxation and Fiscal Federalism*. Rushcutters Bay, NSW: Australian National University Press.

Pommerehne, W. W. and Schneider, F. (1983) 'Does Government in a Representative Democracy Follow a Majority of Voters' Preferences? An Empirical Investigation', pp. 61–84 in H. Hanusch (ed.), *Anatomy of Government Deficiencies*. Berlin: Springer-Verlag.

Puviani, A. (1903) *Teoria Illusione Finanziaria*. Palermo: Sandron.

Sandmo, A. (1990) 'Buchanan on Political Economy: A Review Article', *Journal of Economic Literature*, **28**, 1, pp. 50–65.

Seiglie, C. (1990) 'A Theory of the Politically Optimal Commodity Tax', *Economic Inquiry*, **28**, 3, pp. 586–603.

Smith, A. (1776) *An Enquiry into the Nature and Causes of the Wealth of Nations*. London: Nelson, 1873. New York: Random House, 1937.

Van Velthoven, B. and Van Winden, F. (1991) 'A Positive Model of Tax Reform', *Public Choice*, **72**, 1, pp. 61–86.

Wagner, R. E. (1976) 'Revenue Structure, Fiscal Illusion and Budgetary Choice', *Public Choice*, **25**, pp. 45–61.

Author Index

Subject Index